Dynamic, Genetic, and Chaotic Programming

Sixth-Generation Computer Technology Series

Branko Souček, Editor
University of Zagreb

Neural and Massively Parallel Computers: The Sixth Generation
Branko Souček and Marina Souček

Neural and Concurrent Real-Time Systems: The Sixth Generation
Branko Souček

Neural and Intelligent Systems Integration: Fifth and Sixth Generation Integrated Reasoning Information Systems
Branko Souček and the IRIS Group

Fast Learning and Invariant Object Recognition: The Sixth-Generation Breakthrough
Branko Souček and the IRIS Group

Dynamic, Genetic, and Chaotic Programming: The Sixth Generation
Branko Souček and the IRIS Group

Fuzzy, Holographic, and Parallel Intelligence: The Sixth-Generation Breakthrough
Branko Souček and the IRIS Group

Dynamic, Genetic, and Chaotic Programming

The Sixth-Generation

BRANKO SOUČEK
and
The IRIS Group

A Wiley-Interscience Publication

JOHN WILEY & SONS, INC.

New York-Chichester-Brisbane-Toronto-Singapore

In recognition of the importance of preserving what has been written, it is a policy of John Wiley & Sons, Inc., to have books of enduring value published in the United States printed on acid-free paper, and we exert our best efforts to that end.

Library of Congress Cataloging in Publication Data:

Souček, Branko.
Dynamic, genetic, and chaotic programming: the sixth generation / Branko Souček and IRIS Group.
p. cm.—(Sixth-generation computer technology series)
"A Wiley-Interscience publication."
Includes bibliographical references and index.
1. Electronic digital computers—Programming. 2. Neural networks (Computer science) I. IRIS Group. II. Title. III. Series.
QA176.6.S654 1992
005.1—dc20 91-34146
ISBN 0-471-55717-X CIP

Printed in the United States of America

10 9 8 7 6 5 4 3 2 1

CONTRIBUTORS

The IRIS Group presents a forum for international cooperation in research development and applications of intelligent systems. The IRIS International Center is involved in projects, design, measurements, and experiments, as well as in teaching courses and workshops, and consulting. The IRIS invites inquiries and operates under the auspices of the Star Service S.p.A., director V. L. Plantamura. The IRIS research coordinator is Professor B. Souček, IRIS, Star Service—Via Amendola 162/1, 70126—Bari; Italy.

NIRWAN ANSARI
Department of Electrical and Computer Engineering
New Jersey Institute of Technolgy
Newark, New Jersey

IVAN BRATKO
Department of Electrical Engineering and Computer Science
University of Ljubljana
Ljubljana, Slovenia

MING-HWANG CHEN
Department of Electrical and Computer Engineering
New Jersey Institute of Technology
Newark, New Jersey

YUVAL DAVIDOR
Institute of Science
Weizman University
Rehovot, Israel

HUGO DE GARIS
Electrotechnical Laboratory (ETL)
Ibaraki, Japan

IGOR GRABEC
Department of Mechanical Engineering
University of Ljubljana
Ljubljana, Slovenia

VIJAYKUMAR GULLAPALLI
Department of Computer and Information Science
University of Massachusetts
Amherst, Massachusetts

M. C. HAN
Production Engineering Division
Sam Sung Electronics
Suwon, Korea

EDWIN S. H. HOU
Department of Electrical and Computer Engineering
New Jersey Institute of Technology
Newark, New Jersey

YUCHOU HUANG
Department of Electrical and Computer Engineering
New Jersey Institute of Technology
Newark, New Jersey

MARTIN HULIN
SIEMENS
Munchen, Germany

RYOTARO KAMIMURA
Information Science Laboratory
Tokai University
Kanagawa, Japan

JOHN R. KOZA
Department of Computer Science
Stanford University
California

JEAN-HSANG LIN
Department of Electrical Engineering
University of Delaware
Newark, Delaware

REINHARD LOHMANN
Bionik und Evolutionstechnik
Technische Universitat Berlin
Berlin, Germany

BORUT MARIČIČ
Logistic Management Service
Leoben, Austria

VITO LEONARDO PLANTAMURA
Department of Informatics
University of Bari
Bari, Italy

HONG REN
Department of Electrical and Computer Engineering
New Jersey Institute of Technology
Newark, New Jersey

CHARLES SCHELBERG
Flavors Technology Inc.
Amherst, Massachusetts

HANS-PAUL SCHWEFEL
Department of Computer Science
University of Dortmund
Dortmund, Germany

BRANKO SOUČEK
IRIS International Center
Bari, Italy

IVANKA ŠTAJNER
Department of Mathematics
University of Illinois at Urbana-Champaign
Urbana-Champaign, Illinois

TANJA URBANČIČ
Josef Stefan Institute
Ljubljana, Slovenia

CONTENTS

PREFACE

This book deals with dynamic processes, such as natural language, reasoning, decision making, robotics, control, nonstationary environment, complex system design, predictions, time series, and optimization. Five different paradigms are applied to solve the same group of problems: *adaptive learning*, *rule based computing*, *genetic algorithms*, *genetic programming*, and the *software of chaos*. The strengths and weaknesses of one paradigm for solving a given problem are compared to another paradigm and the differences in their performance are presented. The five unique features that make the paradigms suitable for dynamic problems are examined and described. They include:

1. *Adaptive learning:* reinforcement learning and recurrent neural networks,
2. *Rule based computing:* automated knowledge acquisition,
3. *Genetic algorithms:* adaptation of strings of characters or blocks describing dynamic processes,
4. *Genetic programming:* adaptation of hierarchically structured computer programs,
5. *Software of chaos:* nonlinear dynamics in the presence of strange attractors.

The focus is on these unique features, most of which are described here for the first time in book form. In particular, genetic programming has received special attention: it shows a new way for genetically breeding populations of computer programs to solve problems.

This book gives detailed explanations for underlying principles, and then concentrates on concrete examples, and real-world problems and applications. It describes concrete hands-on tools and methods, including: details of computer implementation of software packages on single processor machines, on SIMD, MIMD, and on high-speed accelerator boards; amount of processing required; editing and man-machine interface; simulation runs; results and performance measurements; block diagrams; ready-to-use recipes and solutions. This is a practical, software engineering and application oriented book.

This book presents unified treatment of material that is otherwise scattered over many publications and research reports. Previously unpublished methods and results based on IRIS (Integration of Reasoning, Informing, and Serving) Group are presented. IRIS Group brings together the results from leading American, Asian, and European laboratories and projects. The principles involved imitate the organic evolution processes, parallelism, and collective paradigms of natural populations. Eight important novelties are offered:

- Freedom from the need to specify explicit relations between the input parameters and their effect on performance (genetic programming),
- An adaptive designing machinism unrestricted to explore a very large space of viable structures (optimization),
- Delicate balance between forces of stability and forces of instability, forces on minute scales and forces on grand scales (software of chaos),
- Neural adaptation/rule-based computing hybrids (dynamic control systems),
- Neural adaptation/chaotic hybrids (natural language, time series, predictions),
- Genetic/chaotic hybrids (genetically finding the function that fits a given sample of chaotic data),
- Genetic/neural links (artificial animal, genetic programming in neural network design), and
- Neural/genetic/chaotic hybrids (variability under evolutionary control, context switching, reasoning).

This book is divided into three parts.

Part I *Dynamic Adaptive Learning versus Automated Knowledge Acquistion* introduces and compares various recurrent and temporal neural networks. Dynamic control/robot systems are presented. Reinforcement learning techniques are related to direct adaptive control methods and illustrated on several control tasks. Experiments show that initializing the learning program with an extremely simple partial control rule speeds up the learning process by a factor of 8, and increases reliability. Also, various networks for natural language acquisition and for speech recognition are compared. Experimental results are presented, showing phonema recognition and grammatical competence. Other applications include acoustic emission, tactile sensors, signal processing, and communication.

Part II *Genetic Algorithm and Genetic Programming* introduces evolutionary algorithms: genetic algorithms (GA) and evolution strategies (ES). Underlying principles are explained and computer implementations are described; the taxonomy of algorithms is given; genetic breeding populations of computer programs is presented. The space of possible programmed modules for a most fit individual program is searched. In the search space a computer program that produces some desired output for particular input is discovered. In a number of applications, the search space is the hyperspace of LISP symbolic expressions (called S-expressions) composed of functions and terminals appropriate to the problem domain.

Described applications include: machine learning of functions; solving differential, integral, functional, linear, nonlinear, and quadratic equations; finding a function in symbolic form that fits a given sampling of data points; computer-aided design of robot manipulators; inverse kinematics; adaptive, nonlinear process control; planning of sequence-of-actions based on sensory data; optimization of manufacturing; order dependent processes; scheduling; pattern recognition; self-organization of neural networks and of visual systems; using surface cells to seed and grow new shapes; circuit partitioning; and optimizations in very large and complex domains.

Described experiments and performance measurements show that genetic programming, compared to neural adaptation, can reduce the number of iterations 10 times (multiplex design, nonlinear control).

Part III *The Software of Chaos with Applications* starts with an introduction to the theory of chaos. Interactions in the system cause orbits in the state space to be attracted to a smaller region called strange attractors. Stretching and folding of the state space produce fractal and seemingly random behavior. Adaptive software capable of predicting dynamic phenomena is presented. Here, in the predictor the forthcoming signal is estimated from the prototypes; the operation is demonstrated on a chaotic signal obtained from measurements; and the proper embedding dimension of the chaotic attractor is selected. The application to factory floor scheduling, resource/workload bidding and adaptive control of the dynamic software based on the chaos theory is presented. It is shown that dynamic scheduling works in the complex world of the machine shop regardless of the complexity of the task to be performed. Examples are developed on a powerful Parallel Inference Machine using Paracell language.

This book has been written as a textbook for students, as well as a reference for practicing software designers, engineers, and scientists. An undergraduate-level background is assumed. The treatment is rounded out with a large number of examples, experimental results, details of working systems, illustrations, flowcharts, programs, and a bibliography of over 200 resources. The examples are designed as practical exercises for students, programmers, engineers, and users. The examples also integrate and compare five paradigms on common problems.

Readers interested in other related topics, complementary solutions, and in background material, should combine this book with the other Sixth-Generation Computer Technology Series books listed opposite the title page. These books are independent mutually supporting volumes.

BRANKO SOUČEK

Bari, Italy
February 1992

ACKNOWLEDGMENTS

We acknowledge the encouragement, discussions, and support received from our teachers, collaborators, friends, and colleagues. We are grateful for the grants supporting our research. We thank the institutions where we performed the experiments and research with intelligent systems. The institutions are listed next to the contributors' names. Special thanks to Mrs. Vladimira Zlatić, Mrs. Lisa Van Horn, and John Wiley's editors and reviewers for an outstanding job in preparation, supervising, and copyediting the manuscript.

Dynamic, Genetic, and Chaotic Programming

PART I

Dynamic Neural Networks versus Automated Knowledge Acquisition

CHAPTER 1

Problem/Paradigm Matching

BRANKO SOUČEK

1.1 INTRODUCTION

Real–life, complex, and dynamic domains are characterized by the nonexistence of exact computational models, and, consequently, a traditional computing approach is often inadequate. Some computing methods enable significant progress to be made, yet different studies report that they are successful only when the application is relatively small, simple, well understood, and when experts agree with each other. For more difficult problems, the existing methodology lacks mechanisms for dealing with the nonexistence of

A single compact body of encodable knowledge,
An isolated static body of knowledge, independent of time, related events, and environments,
A perfect, exact, single algorithm for applying the knowledge.

Empirical measurements, simulated computer models, and analogy with humans strongly indicate that better accuracy is obtained when several computing methods, instead of one, are used. This book deals with three competing/cooperating methods: dynamic, genetic, and chaotic programming.

For a long time information processing has faced three major bottlenecks: program development, knowledge acquisition, and analytical analysis/synthesis.

Dynamic, Genetic, and Chaotic Programming, By Branko Souček and the IRIS Group.
ISBN 0-471-55717-X

1.1.1 Program Development

Program development has been a problem for a long time. A hardware designer can confidently rely on many standard building blocks to minimize design time and cost and to improve product's reliability. Yet embedded software is still done the old–fashioned, hard way—by custom crafting. Some new tools have been developed to speed up and automate software development. Moderate progress has been achieved by using computer-aided software engineering (CASE), but new paradigms are needed.

1.1.2 Knowledge Acquisition

In many applications knowledge acquisition cost more money than the hardware. Complex expert systems are based on large rule sets, which are necessary to describe the problem. It is difficult and expensive to collect the facts necessary to extract these rules. Many times the problem's fine structure is unknown, and it is impossible to derive the rules that describe it. The weather forecast for New York depends on meteorological data measured in Tokyo. But in what way? We shall never know the rule set.

Children acquire knowledge of a language by listening to their parents. The child and the parent do not know the mechanism of knowledge acquisition. It is automatic, and it works. Automated knowledge acquisition, or learning, is the ultimate solution for complex information processing tasks.

1.1.3 Analytical Analysis/Synthesis

For small simple problems, analytical methods are the way to proceed. This is not so for complex problems or in dealing with systems whose internal operation is unknown, nonlinear, dynamic, or stochastic. A cat jumps on a tree without using analytical methods to analyze the environment. It energies hundreds of muscles without analytical synthesis of the solution. Imagine a robot capable of jumping on a tree that it has never seen before. It is impossible to design such a robot by using only analytical methods. We must study how Nature did it.

The three bottlenecks are presented in Figure 1.1. Remedies used so far did not remove them, but progress has been achieved in two ways:

1. Software integration based on standardized modules, automated programming, and application generators is successfully used in some application areas, especially in domains of commercial and process control software.
2. Dynamic, genetic, and chaotic programming are the major bypass to the three bottlenecks in many application areas, including complex and dynamic systems, optimization, and decision making. These new paradigms belong to sixth-generation computer technology. For necessary background on the sixth generation, see Souček and IRIS Group [1–4].

1.2 SOFTWARE INTEGRATION, AUTOMATED PROGRAMMING, AND APPLICATION GENERATORS

Ideally, integration is a process of directly attaching modules in a system. Modules must have both integrated and stand-alone capabilities. The system should be expandable to meet the growing integration of information, control, and robotics technologies [3].

Program development, modification, and start-up are considerably simplified by breaking programs into small, clearly defined blocks. Program development costs can be reduced by using standard function blocks for recurrent complex functions. Standard function blocks are off-the-shelf software modules that can be merged into programs written by the user. They can be called many times during program execution and supplied with the required parameters. Good examples are the standard function block libraries for programmable controllers, including the Allen-Bradley Pyramid Integrator family and the Siemens Simatic S5 family, among others. Siemens claims that over 100,000 Simatic installations worldwide are running the same software modules.

The ultimate modules are software components delivered as absolute binary code on electrically programmable read-only memories (EPROMs), disks, or tapes. This eliminates source code manipulations, recompilations, system generation (SYSGEN), and other hazards and labor required to integrate with more traditional, off-the shelf software. Each absolute software component has a private configuration table supplied by the user and containing application- and hardware-related parameters relevant to its operation. Installation involves placing the component (pure code) and its configuration table somewhere in random-access memory (RAM) or read-only memory (ROM) and plugging the address of its configuration table into the software component interconnect bus. This kind of approach is supported, for example, by the Software Components Group Inc.

For further progress in software integration, we must protect software against piracy. Mori and Kawahura [5] define protection levels 0 to 4. The most advanced level is the ABYSS architecture developed by White, Commerford, and Weingart at the IBM Thomas J. Watson Research Center in Yorktown Heights, New York [6,7]. ABYSS is based on the notion of a use-once authorization mechanism called a *token* that provides the "right to execute" a software product. All or part of the software product is executed within a protected processor and is distributed in encrypted form. Physical security for an ABYSS processor is provided by a dense cocoon of wires with resistance constantly monitored by the processor. A change in resistance indicates a likely attempt to penetrate the system.

In 1983, Mori [8,9] invented an approach called *superdistribution*. According to Mori and Kawahara [5], the chief difference between superdistribution and the ABYSS scheme is that superdistribution does not require the physical distribution of tokens or anything else to users of a software product. In other words, ABYSS requires that software be paid for in advance, whereas superdistribution does not. Since 1987, work on superdistribution has been carried out by a committee of the Japan Electronics Industry Development Association (JEIDA), a nonprofit industrywide organization. That committee is now known as the Superdistribution Technology Research Committee.

Superdistribution of software has the following novel combination of desirable properties:

1. Software products are freely distributed without restriction. The user of a software product pays for using that product, not for possessing it.
2. The vendor of a software product can set the terms and conditions of its use and the schedule of fees, if any, to be charged for its use.
3. Software products can be executed by any user having the proper equipment, provided only that the user adheres to the conditions of use set by the vendor and pays the fees charged by the vendor.
4. The proper operation of the superdistribution system, including the enforcement of the conditions set by the vendors, is ensured by tamper-resistant electronic devices, such as digitally protected modules.

Integration of standardized and protected software modules gives the computers a new role—*application receivers*. The integration environment with the necessary utilities is called an *application generator*. Integration supported by the application generators is called *automated programming*.

An application generator can be used to implement a wide range of applications without the need for detailed programming. An application generator can translate relatively high level specifications of application details into a fully operational, functional application system, using many advanced capabilities for application development. Successful and effective use of this generator for application development requires an understanding of available functions, adequate testing, and experience gained through initial applications.

Complex programming within the generator is required to support the application specifications entered on the coding forms or through the Interactive Application Generator facility. Note, however, that the application developer need not know advanced uses of a generator to implement many applications.

Every organization has a backlog of applications to be implemented. With proper planning, the most appropriate applications can be defined and installed, with the following advantages:

- Straightforward definition of displays, and the ability to change them without complex programming,
- Availability of interactive functions, with user-specified codes for terminal operator convenience,

- Variety of files supported, the search capabilities, and other functions to provide adaptability.

After a generator is installed, it is strongly recommended that the user employ the sample problem to (1) ensure that the installation was properly accomplished, (2) gain experience in operating methods, and (3) become familiar with the panel description forms used in the sample problem.

In many areas, this sample problem can be used as a model on which to base applications to be developed. An operational model system can be the vehicle to introduce the use of attribute bytes and different panel types. Recommended changes can be made by modifying the information on the forms and using the generation programs. This encourages a controlled development environment with the involvement of those who will use the results.

Successful application development depends greatly on achieving a feasible, realistic application design that satisfies user requirements and is best adaptable to facilities and capabilities for application execution available within a generator. Extensive facilities are available, and an understanding of these facilities and how they work during application execution is mandatory for the designer to produce feasible application designs.

Application requirements that cannot be accomplished via generator facilities are addressed by coding user-written exit programs in standard procedural languages. These processing routines are linked into the main-line application processing provided by a generator at the appropriate point in the application execution flow.

Human-computer interface is an important factor in the design and application of a generator. The task of the system designer in selecting or designing a suitable interface for a set of users is complicated by the dual function of the interface. The interface has at least two distinct (and sometimes opposing) functions: one to form a link between humans and the computer, and the other to form a barrier.

The most obvious function of the interface is to link the physical (fingers, eyes, etc.) and psychological (decision making, cognitive structure, etc.) aspects of human with the hardware (keyboards, video display unit screens) and software (data base structure, information) of the computer. Thus, the designer tries to produce a "transparent" interface in which the machine characteristics ideally match human attributes; for example, the keyboard layout is suitable for the task and typing skill of the user, the size of the visual display unit (VDU) screen is sufficient for the information absorption rate of the user, the program structure is logical, the commands are easily understood, and so on. The ideal here is a free and unconstrained interaction in which the user can communicate easily and fully with the machine.

However, free and apparently unconstrained interaction requires a link and a barrier between user and computer. The user seldom needs to know exactly the state of the computer core or the current flowing in certain wires.

The most effective interaction occurs when the user is protected by the interface from aspects of the system or computer processing that are either too complex for him or he to understand or are not required for the task. To protect users from unnecessary complexity, for example, of machine code programming, the interface should prevent users from realizing the full potential of the system by protecting them from potentially useful but distracting facilities. In practice, user are often provided with an interface that is unnecessarily sophisticated, to give them access to infrequently used but relevant facilities.

1.3 THE BYPASS: DYNAMIC, GENETIC, AND CHAOTIC PROGRAMMING

Dynamic, genetic, and chaotic programming are new paradigms in information processing. In many application areas they can bypass information processing bottlenecks (Fig. 1.1).

1.3.1 Dynamic Programming

In dynamic programming, classical programming is mixed with learning and adaptation in neural networks. Neural networks are a subclass of massively parallel machines. The basic idea of dynamic programming, as defined in this book, is to create specialized modules for specific types of tasks, with limited adaptation. These modules are mixed with more general adaptive networks to handle new and unusual situation. Adaptive modules are also mixed with programmed modules.

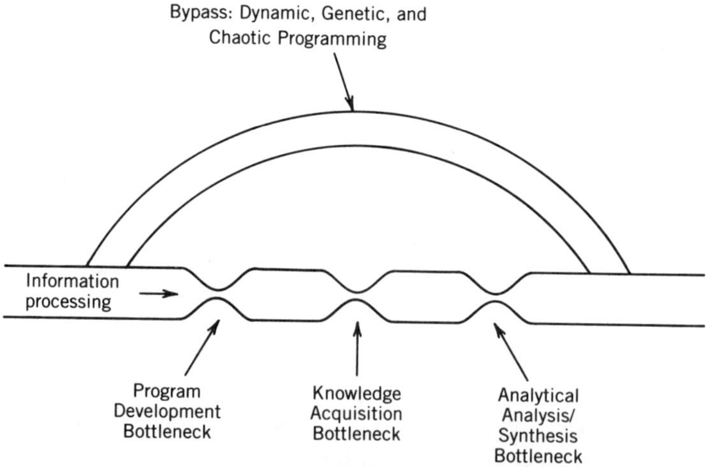

Figure 1.1 *Information processing bottlenecks and the bypass.*

In general, the best way to simplify the design is to introduce modular, hierarchical structures, in which different modules are only loosely coupled. This corresponds to the feature extraction theory and group selection theory of the brain, described by Edelman and Mountcastle [10]. There should be a variety of modules, capable of certain predefined operations inherited from the designer (natural, born with) and able to learn a slightly more difficult set of tasks (nurtured). The problem of nature versus nurture was analyzed by Bergman and Kerszkberg [11], who concluded that

1. Machines with random structures [nonperiodic (NP) arrays] do not perform well. Random start leads nowhere.
2. Machines with identical links between all submodules [totally periodic (P) arrays] never manage. Their architecture is too limited.
3. Machines that are partially, layerwise period (LP arrays) are by far the best. Neither too complicated, like the NP machines, nor too simple, like P's, they are the best learners, because they have the structural features that can adapt to the problem.

According to Bergman and Kerszberg [11], the question of whether intelligent behaviour can be generated efficiently by using a proper balance of nature versus nurture remains open. Biological reality seems to be located somewhere between these two extremes. A good illustration is provided by Marler [12], who studied song learning in birds. Initially, almost random singing patterns fall slowly into the characteristic species song or into some modification thereof, depending on the auditory environment of the young bird. Intelligent information processing also seems to be located between two extremes: fully programmed and fully adaptive. Dynamic programming, described in Part I, shows the way to go for many practical applications.

1.3.2 Genetic Programming

Genetic programming is based on selectionism, as an alternative for programming. Selectionism can arrive at complex intelligent structures through genetic mutation/recombination. Selectionism is a special form of self-organization, which for biological systems is described by Nicolis and Prigogine [13]. Steels [14] has identified examples where selectionist processes could be an alternative for programming:

Recognition To recognize the word, we almost need to know which word we are looking for. Elements of recognition ignite the process of domination. This process, after a while, will feed back to the elements that caused it to happen in the first place.

Context Context is needed to understand the text, but the text provides information on what the context is. Hence, we start with an initial population of many possible contexts. Specific words in the text enforce the domination of a particular context, and, conversely, the context enforces the words in the text.

Goal Selection All potentially executable goals form the initial population. Initial success in execution of the goal will further enforce the goal as more resources and support from the environment are applied to it.

Rule Learning The process starts with a diverse set of rules. When rules are successful, they gain in strength; otherwise they become weaker.

Steels places selectionism above connectionism and symbolic structures. Connectionist models are still too weak to cope with complex representations. Symbolic structures (expert systems) are too rigid in real-world applications, where there are always uncertainties and deviations. Selectionism can arrive at complex structures. Being an open system in a feedback loop with the environment, the selection system provides for uncertainties and deviations.

According to Darwin, the basis of evolution is the occurrence of random hereditary modifications in the organisms of a species. The advantageous modifications are then adopted and disadvantageous ones discarded through natural selection. Selection presents an optimization process for very large complex domains. This optimization is based on the blind and heuristic mechanisms of evolution and population genetics. A genetic algorithm and evolution strategies are simulation procedures based on theoretical models originally proposed by Holland [15], Rechenberg [16], and Schwefel [17]. The model is called an algorithm because it is a computational model, and it is called genetic because its operators are based on simplified concepts of population genetics. In short, genetic algorithms deal with adaptation of strings of characters or blocks, holistically describing dynamic processes.

The concept of genetic programming is derived from genetic algorithms (GA). A definition of genetic programming (GP) is given by Koza in Chapter 10. According to Koza, genetic programming provides a way to search the space of possible computer programs for a highly specialized individual computer program to solve a problem. In the GP paradigm, populations of computer programs are genetically bred using the Darwinian principle of survival of the fittest and a genetic crossover (sexual recombination) operator appropriate for genetically mating computer programs. Koza shows how to reformulate seemingly different problems into a common form (i.e., problem requiring discovery of a computer program) and how the GP paradigm can serve as a single, unified approach for solving problems formulated in this common way.

Genetic algorithms and genetic programming have been applied to a diverse range of domains, more diverse than any other contemporary evolutionary model. Many practical applications are presented in Part II.

1.3.3 Chaotic Programming

Chaotic programming paradigm confronts Monte Carlo and statistically based programming methods with the newly developed theory of chaos. It confronts unpredictable random processes with deterministic chaos, generated by fixed rules that do not themselves involve any element of chance.

The theory of chaos has come out of a striking discovery: Simple deterministic systems with only a few elements can generate seemingly random behavior. Lorenz [18] found chaos in describing the fluid motion: the rising of hot gas or liquid, known as convection. He stated: "We might have trouble forecasting the temperature of the coffee one minute in advance, but we should have little difficulty in forecasting it an hour ahead."

In principle, the future is completely determined by the past; but in practice, small uncertainties are amplified, so behavior is unpredictable in the long term. The determinism inherent in chaos implies that many random phenomena are more predictable than had been thought. Random-looking information gathered in the past and processed by using complicated methods can now be explained in terms of simple laws. Chaos allows order to be found in such diverse systems as the atmosphere, heart beating, fluids, seismology, metallurgy, physiology, or the behavior of a stock market.

The theory of chaos is related to the theory of dynamic systems. A dynamical system consists of two parts: the notion of a state, and a rule that describes the systems dynamics—the way the state evolves with time. Evolution can be visualized in a statespace. Statespace is an abstract construct whose coordinates are the components of the state. For a mechanical system they might be position and velocity. The state space represents behavior in the form of geometrical orbits. It is general phenomenon that internal mechanisms of the system (losses, feedback, friction, cooling) cause orbits to be attracted to a smaller region, called attractors.

Chaotic behavior originates from simple stretching and folding operations, which take place in the statespace, which results in the fractal nature of the chaotic attractor, and reveals more details as the behavior is increasingly magnified. Chaotic systems generate randomness, due to the complex orbits generated by stretching and folding. In this way, chaos provides a mechanism that allows for variability, surprise, or free will within a world governed by deterministic laws. At the same time chaos provides the possibility of putting variability under evolutionary control.

Chaos promises a major breakthrough in information processing. One of the first systems operating on principles similar to chaos was the million-channel, nuclear, real-time, data acquisition system designed by Souček [19, 20]. The data field coming from the cyclotron has been transformed into a new, chaotic field, more suitable for high-speed real-time processing. Data compression of 1000 times has been achieved, resulting in the saving of $1,000,000 in the system design. A transformation box utilized shift registers with exclusive-OR feedback. Its main task was to generate pseudorandom addresses and to scatter deterministic nuclear spectra into seemingly random patterns.

This is the way to design a pseudoassociative processing system, for a fraction of the price of a real associative system. For details, see Souček and Souček [1]. Newly developed applications of chaotic programming are presented in Part III.

1.4 NEURAL COMPUTERS

Neural computers are composed of numerous simple computational elements operating in parallel. The computational element sums N weighted inputs and passes the result through a nonlinearity (sigmoid function). If the result is above a built-in threshold level, the element "fires." In this way a computational element resembles the operation of a biological neuron.

Neural computers are divided into classes based on network topology, computational element characteristics, and training or learning rules. The basic features of neural computers are

- High computational rates due to the massive parallelism,
- Fault tolerance (damage to a few nodes does not significantly impair overall performance),
- Learning or training (the network adapts itself, based on the information received from the environment),
- Goal-seeking (the performance to achieve the goal is measured and used to self-organize the system; programmed rules are not necessary),
- Primitive computational elements (each element resembles one simple logical neuron and cannot do much).

Artificial neural networks are also called *parallel distributed processing* (PDP) systems. In PDP systems, the programs and data patterns are not stored. What is stored is the connection strengths between units that allow these patterns to be recreated. PDP systems could serve as a pattern associator between two sets of units. One set could serve as a visual pattern, the other as an acoustic pattern for the same object. Learning or building the knowledge structure in PDP systems involves modifying the patterns of interconnectivity. Rumelhart et al. [21,22] define the process of learning, using the notation of Figure 1.2.

Output from unit j, o_j, is connected to the input of unit i through the weight w_{ij}. The net input is usually the weighted sum of all inputs to the unit. The state of activation a_i is a function F of the old state a_i and of the net input. The useful, frequently used activation function is a sigmoid function (Fig. 1.3). The output o_i is a function f of the activation state. The useful, frequently used f function is the threshold function.

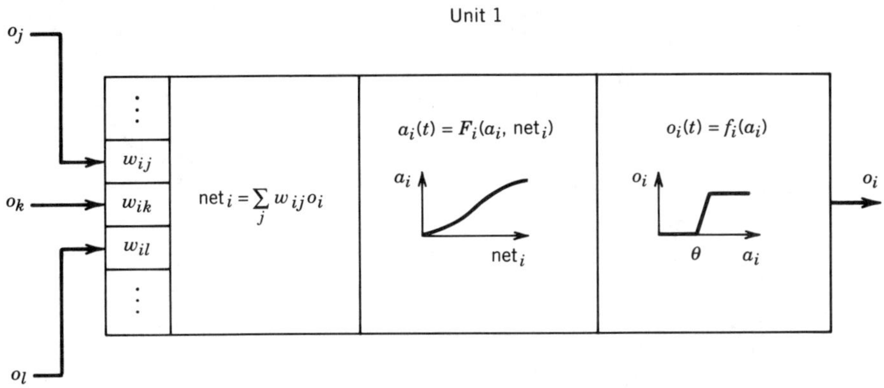

Figure 1.2 *Basic components of a neural network mode.*

Different learning rules to modify the pattern of connectivity as a function of experience have been developed. They include Hebbian learning, the Delta rule, competitive learning, the Hopfield minimum-energy rule, the generalized Delta rule, Sigma-Pi units, and the Boltzmann learning algorithm.

1.5 BACK-PROPAGATION NETWORK

Currently, the most popular mapping neural network is the back-propagation network of Rumelhart et al [21,22]. The back-propagation network has been shown to be capable of implementing approximations to a variety of mappings from R^n to R^m. The approximation achieved has been shown to be optimal in a certain least mean squared error sense. The back propagation is important for multilayered networks with one or more hidden layers. The question for many years was: How does a neuron deeply embedded within a network know what aspect of the outcome of an overall action was its fault? The problem was attached in 1962 by Rosenblatt [23]. The practical solution was given by Rumelhart et al. [21,22] in 1983.

The network is composed of three types of units shown in Figure 1.3: input units; hidden units carrying an internal representation, and output units. The activation of each unit is a sigmoid function f of the weighted sum e: $o = f(e)$:

$$o_j = \frac{1}{1 + \exp(-e_j)} \qquad o_k = \frac{1}{1 + \exp(-e_k)} \tag{1.1}$$

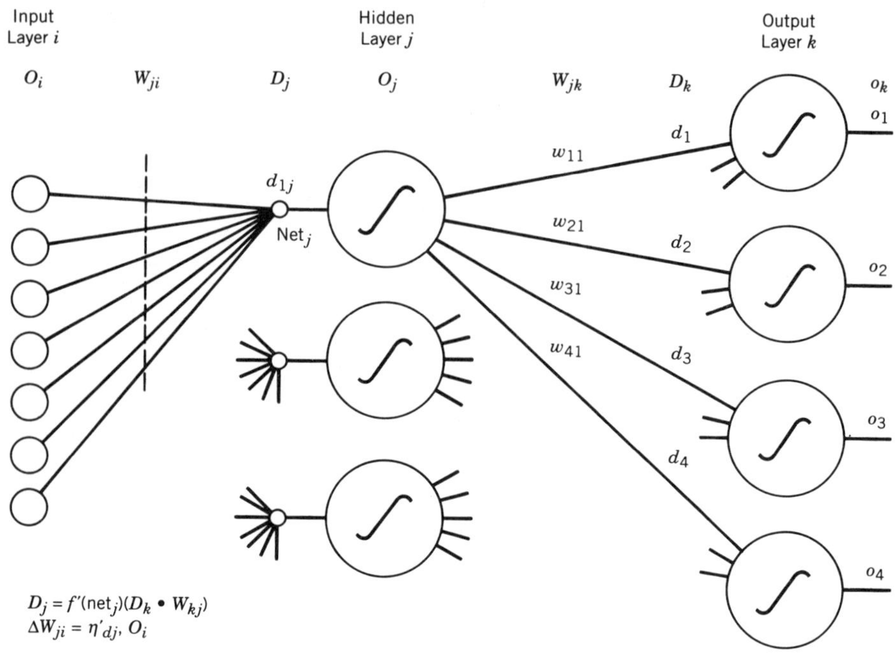

Figure 1.3 *Back-propagation algorithm. Hidden unit layer* j *weight changes.*

$$e_j = \sum_i o_i w_{ji} + \theta_j \qquad e_k = \sum_j o_j w_{kj} + \theta_k \tag{1.2}$$

where θ is a threshold.

A training set of patterns is used to self-organize the network. Typically, one generates a set of sample vectors O_i. The obtained output vector O_k is compared with the target output vector T_k provided by the teacher (Fig. 1.4). Here we concentrate on one unit in layer k. The difference between vector components $t_k - o_k$ defines the error (delta) d_k. In other words, the input to the unit should be corrected by d_k to provide the target output t_k:

$$d_k = (t_k - o_k)f'(e_k) \tag{1.3}$$

Introducing Eq. 1.1 for the activation function f yields the derivative and the delts, d_k:

$$f'(e_k) = \frac{df(e_k)}{de_k} = o_k(1 - o_k) \tag{1.4}$$

$$d_k = (t_k - o_k)o_k(1 - o_k) \tag{1.5}$$

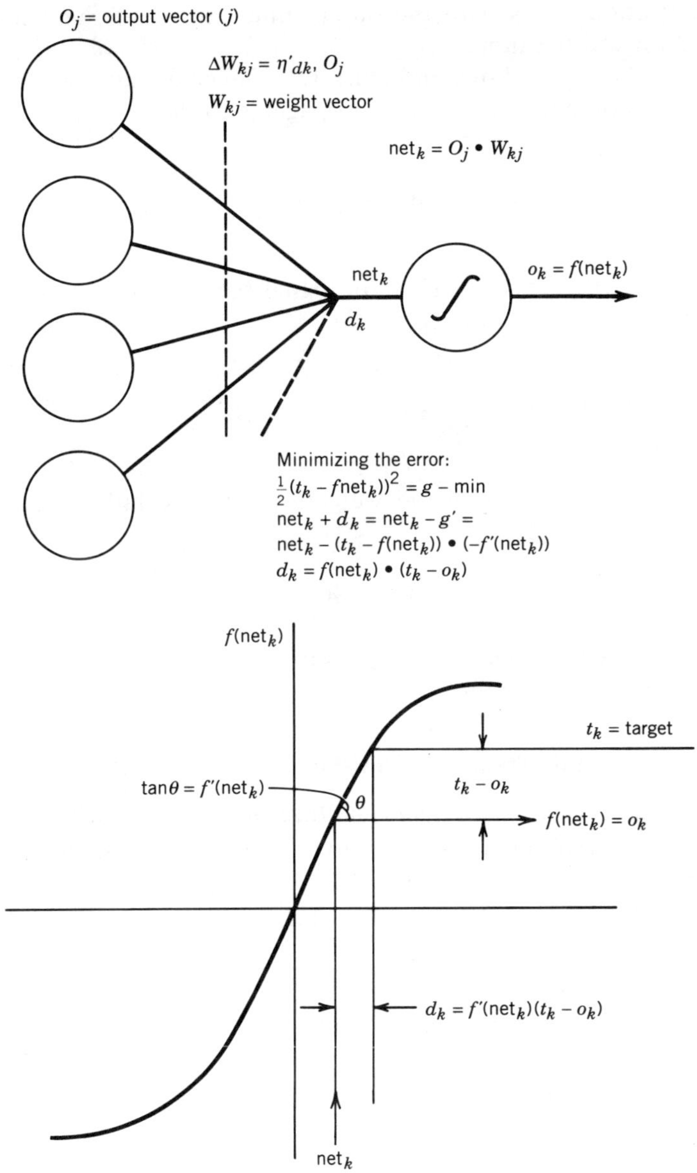

Figure 1.4 *Back-propagation algorithm. Output unit in layer* k *driven from units in layer* j.

This value is used to modify the weights w_{kj} on the output unit k, following the basic Hebbian law of learning. The path is reinforced in proportion to the activations on its ends:

$$\Delta W_{kj} = \eta\, d_k O_j \tag{1.6}$$

Weight correction starts with the output unit (Eq. (1.6)), and it is back-propagated toward the input.

The hidden layer j is shown in Figure 1.3. The error signal d_k on the right side of weight components w_{kj} back-propagates to the left side as

$$D_k W_{kj} = \sum_k d_k w_{kj} \tag{1.7}$$

In analogy to Figure 1.4, this error signal back-propagates through the units in layer j, producing the signal d_j:

$$d_j = f'(e_j) \sum_k d_k w_{kJ} = o_j(1 - o_j) \sum_k d_k w_{kj} \tag{1.8}$$

This value is used to modify the weights w_{ji} on the hidden units, again following the Hebbian law:

$$\Delta W_{ji} = \eta d_j O_i \tag{1.9}$$

The operation of the network involves two phases, as shown in the back-propagation training algorithm.

The Back-Propagation Training Algorithm

Step 1. For all i,j,k, set all weights and thresholds to small random values.

Step 2. Put the input vector into the layer i, and specify the desired target output t_k in layer k.

Step 3. Use the sigmoid nonlinearity (Eq. (1.1)) to calculate outputs of layers j and k.

Step 4. Calculate the error signal $t_k - o_k$.

Step 5. Calculate d_k for the output layer and adjust the weights w_{kj}, using Eqs. (1.5) and (1.6).

Step 6. Working back to the hidden layer, calculate d_j and adjust the weight w_{ji}, using Eqs. (1.8) and (1.9).

Step 7. Repeat by going to step 2.

During the forward phase, the input is presented and propagated toward the output. During the backward phase, the errors are formed at the output and propagated toward the input. The back-propagation algorithm has been tested with different problems and generally performs well. One of the most powerful applications is NETtalk by Sejnowski and Rosenberg [24], a letter-to-phoneme mapping systems.

Although artificial neural networks are inspired by research in neurobiology, there is no evidence that back propagation exists in actual brain mechanisms and that synapses can be used in the reverse direction. Back propagation must be considered only as algorithm for self-organization of artificial learning systems.

Back propagation is a time-consuming algorithm. The learning time is approximately $O(N^3)$ on a serial machine and $O(N^2)$ on a parallel machine that uses a separate processor for each connection, where N is the number of weights in the network. The number of training examples is typically $O(N)$. This means that for large N a great many training examples are needed to provide enough data to estimate the weights.

Rumelhart et al. [21,22] gave the following practical suggestions for using the back-propagation algorithm:

- Start the system with small random weights.
- Extreme values 1 or 0 are difficult to reach, so convert to binary at the values 0.9 or 0.1.
- For every recurrent network, a feedforward network with identical behavior exists.
- In most simulations the entire set of patterns was presented to the system between 1000 and 10,000 times. Investigate what would happen if only a subset of patterns were used for training the system, and watch the system generalize to remaining patterns. More theoretical and experimental research is needed in the domain of generalization.

The goal of learning is to cause the network to achieve a particular global behavior, but the learning should be implemented locally. The back-propagation algorithm with a differentiable activation function (Eq. (1.1)) is a step in this direction. Latest research provides other advanced methods of learning, including the holographic method; see Souček and IRIS Group [3,4].

1.6 ADAPTATION AND LEARNING VERSUS PROGRAMMING

Dynamic processes include natural language, reasoning, decision making, robotics, control, manufacturing, nonstationary environment, system design, prediction, time series, and optimization. In the past, dynamic processes have been analyzed and controlled using rule-based computing. Now adaptation and learning in neural networks are strong competition to programming and computing in many application areas, as shown in Chapters 2 to 8.

In Chapter 2, Gullapalli describes learning and control in dynamic systems via associative reinforcement learning. The chapter gives an overview of reinforcement learning techniques and discusses their role in learning control by relating them to direct adaptive control methods. The power and utility of reinforcement learning techniques are illustrated on several control tasks.

In Chapter 3, Urbančić and Bratko describe automatic knowledge acquisition for dynamic system control. It is shown that a learning control system based on neural networks can be improved by incorporating knowledge into the learning process. The knowledge can be derived automatically. As a case study, the task of inverted pendulum control is discussed. Experiments show that initializing the learning program with a simple incomplete control rule speeds up the learning process by a factor of 8 and increases the reliability.

In Chapter 4, Kamimura and Han describe natural language acquisition based on fully recurrent neural networks. In the fully recurrent neural network, all the units are completely connected. Thus, any kind of restriction can be imposed on the architecture to produce an appropriate structure. Little is known of the performance of the recurrent neural network when the network size is relatively large. The learning process and generalization performance are examined and applied to the problem of natural language acquisition. Well-formedness of sentences, when new sentences had sentence formulae different from the formulae of training sentences, is determined. The results show the possibility that a recurrent neural network could acquire grammatical competence along with creativity.

Recognition and restoration of periodic patterns using fully recurrent neural networks is described by Kamimura in Chapter 5. The network could recognize complex and multiple patterns simultaneously in spite of the existence of noise and degradation in the course of learning.

In Chapter 6, Ansari, Huang, and Lin describe the application of adaptive stack filtering by LMS and perceptron learning. Stack filters possess the weak superposition property and the ordering property known as stacking. They have been demonstrated to be robust in suppressing noise. Two methods are introduced to adaptively configure a stack filter: the least mean square (LMS) algorithm and perceptron learning. Experimental results are presented to demonstrate the effectiveness of the proposed methods to noise suppression.

In Chapter 7, Grabec describes automatic modeling of acoustic emission phenomena by neural networks. Most dynamic phenomena in the environment produce sounds, so the hearing sense has evolved in living beings, by which they can recognize phenomena in their surroundings by merely perceiving sound. An electronic information processing system with a similar ability is determined. General properties of the physical description of acoustic phenomena are related to empirical modeling of natural laws on a special-purpose neural network. The goal is automatic recognition of developing defects in stressed materials, characterization of irregularities in materials on the basis of scattered sound, classification of surfaces by tactic sensing and identification of manufacturing process on the basis of chatter.

Chapter 8, by Ansari, deals with the managing of satellite communication traffic by neural networks, using a new management tool of a dynamic communication network, known as a reconfigurable network. The scheme consists of two levels of management: the pattern recognition task, which selects an exemplar map that best meets the current network requirements, and discrepancy analysis, between the chosen exemplar map and the state of the network. Experimental results are presented to demonstrate that the self-organization model can dynamically configure maps for a satellite communication network.

1.7 SELECTION VERSUS PROGRAMMING

New techniques allow building of computers and systems with an enormous number of components. Such systems cannot be designed, analyzed, or programmed in a classical way. The only way to deal with very complex systems is the way of the nature: evolution and natural selection. Techniques developed in this direction are known as genetic algorithms (GA) and evolution strategies (ES), and are described in Chapters 9 to 16.

In Chapter 9, Davidor and Schwefel introduce GA and ES as methods to solve parameter optimization problems. The basic concepts on which GA and ES are based and the reason why these optimization techniques work better than classical methods are presented. Problem domains suitable for application of GA and ES are discussed.

In Chapter 10, Koza defines genetic programming as a paradigm for genetically breeding populations of computer programs to solve problems. The process of solving problems becomes equivalent to searching a space of possible computer programs for a highly fit individual program. In the GP paradigm, populations of computer programs are genetically bred using the Darwinian principle of survival of the fittest, and using a genetic crossover (sexual recombination) operator appropriate for genetically mating computer programs. Koza presents many concrete applications: Boolean functions, multiplexors, linear, differential, and integral equations, artificial ant, behavior in an ant colony, optimal control of dynamic systems, and time series.

In Chapter 11 Davidor introduces a genetic philosophy to optimization in general and to robotics in particular. By introducing the genetic approach to robot trajectory generation, we can learn much about the adaptive mechanisms of evolution and how these mechanisms can solve real-world problems. It is suggested that deterministic models may sometimes be an obstacle in nonlinear dynamic systems, and we may benefit from natural adaptive models. For example, the dynamic behavior of robot manipulators is so complex that classical optimization methodologies are unable to optimize their performance. Improved manipulator design can be achieved with a GA. He suggests that the use of a GA as a design tool is particularly effective when considering structures that incorporate extensive redundancy.

In Chapter 12, Hou, Ren, and Ansari describe efficient multiprocessor scheduling based on genetic algorithms. The problem can be stated as finding a schedule for a general task graph to be executed on a multiprocessor system so that the schedule length can be minimized. The representation of the search mode is based on the schedule of the task in each individual processor. The proposed genetic operator is based on the precedence relations between the tasks in the task group. Experimental results based on robot inverse dynamics computation task graphs are presented.

In Chapter 13, Ansari, Chen, and Hou introduce a new approach to point pattern recognition: point pattern matching using genetic algorithms. It is necessary to find a subset of points in a pattern that best matches a subset of points in another pattern through a transformation in an optimal sense. The problem is important in computer vision, shape recognition, and motion analysis. A genetic algorithm is developed to search efficiently for the best assignment.

In Chapter 14, de Garis introduces a general concept of genetic programming and its application to the growth of an artificial embryo. Artificial embryology as a new technology is defined. It is likely that similar techniques will be used to grow hypercomplex electronic circuits and to test their functional properties. The principal idea in the experiments described is to use the GA to evolve the so-called neighborhood interaction rules of cellular automata. This allows us to grow arbitrary 2D and 3D shapes (embryos).

In Chapter 15, Lohmann describes structure evolution in neural systems. The algorithm for structure evolution has been established for the purpose of developing a small part of a visual system, a local filter, which is expected to count coherent areas in any binary picture. Structure evolution seems to be an appropriate approach for systematically developing and designing neural systems.

In Chapter 16, Hulin presents evolution strategies for circuit partitioning. He shows that the coding of partitioning is essential for the quality of GA. If the circuit to be partitioned is given on register transfer level, the connectivity structure of the circuit is apparent. Proper coding can express this structure. Hulin describes a two-step coding with this property and its cooperation with the genetic operators. Using this coding the GA can detect the connectivity structure during the optimization process automatically. Two-step coding offers several advantages: shorter computation times, multiple instantiation of components, and reduced number of cut signals.

1.8 CHAOTIC VERSUS RANDOM

The theory of chaos deals with a complex, nonlinear dynamic system. Interactions in the system cause orbits in the state-space to be attracted to a smaller region, called strange attractors. Stretching and folding of the state-space produce fractional and seemingly random behavior. Chaotic software capable of analyzing and predicting dynamic phenomena is presented in Chapters 17 to 20.

In Chapter 17, Plantamura, Souček, and Štajner compare continuous chaos with logical pseudorandom processes. Learning chaotic dynamics in neural networks is discussed. Such networks can approximate a universal class of nonlinear dynamic systems by learning chaotic dynamics.

In Chapter 18, Grabec introduces the theory of chaos. The application is demonstrated on a chaotic signal obtained from measurements. A proper embedding dimension of the chaotic attractor is selected.

In Chapter 19, Maričić compares dynamic, genetic, and chaotic programming. Strengths and weaknesses of one paradigm for solving a problem are compared to another paradigm.

In Chapter 20, Schelberg discusses dynamic scheduling algorithms suitable for high-speed, real-time responses on parallel computers. The subroutines described simulate random and chaotic movements of taxi cabs in a large city and movement of parts through a manufacturing plant. Chaos and parallel processors have opened up a new way of thinking about solving these problems.

1.9 THE PRINCIPLE OF MULTIPLE KNOWLEDGE

In this book several paradigms are applied to solve the same group of problems. Why is this? The principle of multiple knowledge, as defined by Gams and Križman [25], deals with multiple methods, multiple systems, multiple knowledge, and multiple knowledge bases applied to the same domain. According to Gams and Križman [25], it is surprising that the AI literature hardly mentions problems with multiple, contradictory, and redundant knowledge, with the purpose of increasing performance by exploiting these properties. A recent keyword search of 50,000 abstracts from the AI literature over 10 years indicates that only a few refer to this problem. Indeed, computer methods regularly tend to use only a single body of knowledge in the form of one computer procedure.

People usually take quite a different approach in real life. They tend to form expert groups, verify results independently, and cross-check information in order to find the best solution. Experience shows that such an approach generally produces better results than relying on one man or one source of knowledge. In other words, people inherently and successfully use multiple knowledge in most difficult tasks without paying much attention to that phenomenon.

Many well-known AI systems like DENDRAL, MYCIN, PROSPECTOR, and DIPMETER already use multiple knowledge to a degree. It is also present in qualitative modeling, for example, when combining qualitative and quantitative models, and in second-generation expert systems [25–47].

Probably the most relevant work regarding multiple knowledge was reported in empirical learning or learning from examples. Different authors argue that a proper use of multiple knowledge gives better possibilities for analyzing the domain and gives better classification accuracy. Catlet and Jack [41] reported an important increase in classification accuracy in several domains when one knowledge base in the form of a decision tree was constructed for each class instead of classifying all classes with one tree. Similarly, Buntine [40] reported an important increase when 10 decision trees were designed, each time with a different attribute at the root. Another interesting approach was taken by Schlimmer [34], enabling multiple views on the same domain by using different algorithms, each with differently preprocessed input data. Brazdil and Torgo [39] used different algorithms and achieved very significant improvements. A slightly different approach was taken in GINESYS (Gams [26]; Gams, Drobnič and Petkovšek [27], where two methods were applied, one AI and one statistical, on the same data and combined.

In knowledge acquisition, different views of experts sometimes result in construction of multiple knowledge bases (Boose et al. [38]; Clark [45]). Other systems like BLIP [46] are capable of representing several competing hypotheses.

Gams and Križman [25] discuss the principle of multiple knowledge at the level of the basic definition of learning (Charniak and McDermott [44]): Learning can be seen as modifying our knowledge base according to past experience for use in the future. On the basis of modifying the learning schema the principle of multiple knowledge can be defined: In order to achieve better performance, it is generally better to construct and use multiple knowledge bases than one knowledge base as long as they reasonably cooperate.

1.10 INTEGRATED REASONING INFORMATION SYSTEMS (IRIS)

The Japanese Ministry of International Trade (MITI) launched a study of a new information processing technology. The study concludes that the central issue in achieving a computer whose information processing behavior resembles that of the human mind involves constructing a general-purpose optimization machine. Concurrent with a redefinition of a computer's central function is the need for conventional computers and general-purpose optimization machines that are seamlessly integrated. An optimization machine operates with parallel object models. The models present hypotheses about the world. The computer changes these hypotheses when unexpected occurrences contradict these working models. The locking procedures between the unexpected hypotheses and the sensory data stream corresponds with understanding in the brain.

The computer, as well as the brain, is constantly optimizing the models. Optimization involves complex, nonlinear, and dynamic processes. Meth-

TABLE 1.1 Vertical versus Lateral Thinking (following De Bono)

Vertical Thinking	Lateral Thinking
It selects a pathway by excluding alternatives.	It generates as many alternative approaches as possible.
It moves usefully along the pathway.	It investigates several pathways.
It is analytical and concentrates on the most likely.	It is provocative, exploring the least likely.
It is sequential.	It can make jumps.
It has to be correct at every step.	It has to be correct at the end.
It uses fixed categories and classification.	Categories and classification may change as something is looked at now in one way and later in another.

ods and tools include conventional optimization techniques, as well as dynamic, genetic, and chaotic programming.

It is interesting to compare these techniques with thinking. According to De Bono [48], the mind handles information in two ways, called vertical and lateral thinking. Their basic features are outlined in Table 1.1. Vertical thinking develops existing ideas and makes good use of them. Lateral thinking generates new ideas and offers more selections. The two processes are complementary, not antagonistic. Similar processes are present in dynamic, genetic, and chaotic programming.

According to Pittman [49], it seems that the age of thinking computers is here. The U.S. DARPA and others have advanced programs. Why is there not a "Manhattan Project" to make a thinking computer? Are not all the essential software and hardware components for a thinking computer available? How long will it take before there is a thinking computer system that may have self-awareness? The design and adaption of intelligent information systems is a complex problem. The solution asks for international cooperation, a well-structured strategy, and clearly defined goals. IRIS presents a forum for international cooperation in research, development, and application of intelligent systems. IRIS results are reported in the sixth-generation series of books. The long-range international IRIS program coincides with the book topics. IRIS is open for cooperation.

REFERENCES

[1] B. Souček and M. Souček, *Neural and Massively Parallel Computers: The Sixth Generation,* Wiley, New York, 1988.

[2] B. Souček, *Neural and Concurrent Real-Time Systems: The Sixth Generation,* Wiley, New York, 1989.

[3] B. Souček and IRIS Group, *Neural and Intelligent Systems Integration: Fifth and Sixth Generation Integrated Reasoning Information Systems,* Wiley, New York, 1991.

[4] B. Souček and IRIS Group, *Fuzzy, Holographic,and Parallel Intelligence: The Sixth Generation Breakthrough,* Wiley, New York, 1992.

[5] R. Mori and M. Kawahara, Superdistribution: The concept and the architecture, *IEICE Trans.,* E73(7), 1133–1146 (1990).

[6] S. R. White, ABYSS: A trusted architecture for software protection, *Proc. IEEE Symp. on Security and Privacy,* 38–51 (April 1987).

[7] S. H. Weingart, Physical security for the ABYSS system, *Proc. IEEE Symp. on Security and Privacy,* 52–58 (April 1987).

[8] R. Mori and S. Tashiro, The concept of software service system (SSS), *IEICE Trans.,* 170-D(1), 70–81 (January 1987).

[9] S. Tashiro and R. Mori, The implementation of a small scale prototype for Software Service System (SSS), *IEICE Trans.,* J70-D(2), 335–345 (February 1987).

[10] G. M. Edelman and V. B. Mountcastle, *The Mindful Brain,* MIT Press, Cambridge, Mass., 1978.

[11] A. Bergmena and M. Kerszberg, Breeding intelligent automata, *Proc. IEEE 1st Internat. Conf. on Neural Networks,* Vol. II, 63–70 (June 21–24, 1987).

[12] P. Marler, "Song-Learning: innate Species Differences in the Learning Process," in Marler and Terrace, Eds., *The Biology of Learning,* Springer-Verlag, Berlin, 1984.

[13] G. Nicolis and I. Prigogine, *Self-Organization in Nonequilibrium Systems,* Wiley, New York, 1985.

[14] L. Steels, Self-organization through selection, *Proc. IEEE 1st Internat. Conf. on Neural Networks,* Vol. II, 55–62. (June 21–24, 1987).

[15] J. H. Holland, *Adaptation in Natural and Artificial Systems,* University of Michigan Press, Ann Arbor, 1975.

[16] I. Rechenberg, *Evolutionstrategie: Optimierung Technischer Systeme nach Prinzipen der Biologischen Evolution,* Frommann-Holzboog Verlag, Stuttgart, 1973.

[17] H. P. Schwefel, *Numerical Optimization of Computer Models,* Wiley, Chichester, 1981.

[18] E. Lorenz, Deterministic nonperiods flow, *J. Atmos. Sci.* 20, 130–141 (1963).

[19] B. Souček, Direct-recording megachannel analyzer through associative programming of a small computer, *Nuclear Instr. Methods,* 36, 181 (1965).

[20] B. Souček, V. Bonačić, and K. Čuljat, Million Channel Pulse Height Analyzer through Pseudo-Random Digital Transformation, *Nuclear Instr. Methods,* 66(2), 202 (1968).

[21] D. E. Rumelhart and J. L. McClelland, Eds., *Parallel Distributed Processing: Explorations in the Microstructure of Cognition, Vol. I: Foundations,* MIT Press, Cambridge, Mass., 1986.

[22] D. E. Rumelhart, G. E. Hinton, and J. L. McClelland, "A General Framework for Parallel Distributed Processing" in D. E. Rumelhart and J. L. McClelland,

Eds., *Parallel Distributed Processing,* MIT Press, Cambridge, Mass., 1986, pp. 45–76.

[23] F. Rosenblatt, *Principles of Neurodynamics,* Spartan, New York, 1962.

[24] T. J. Sejnovski and C. R. Rosenberg, Parallel networks that learn to pronounce English text, *Complex Syst.* 1, 145–168 (1987).

[25] M. Gams and V. Križman, The principle of multiple knowledge, *Informatica 2 (Ljubljana)* 23–26, (1991).

[26] M. Gams, New measurements highlight the importance of redundant knowledge, *Proc. EWSL 89,* (1989).

[27] M. Gams, M. Drobnič, and M. Petkovšek, Learning from examples: A uniform view, *Internat. J. Man-Machine Studies,* (1991).

[28] R. Jamnik, *Verjetnostni račun,* Mladinska knjiga, Ljubljana, 1978.

[29] J. Keyes, Why export systems fail, *Al Expert,* 4, 11 (1989).

[30] N. Lavrač, S. Džeroski, and M. Grobelnik, Learning Nonrecursive Definitions of Relations with LINUS, Machine Learning—EWSL91, Y. Kodratof, Ed., Springer Verlag, 1991.

[31] I. Mozetić, NEWGEM—Program for learning from examples, Technical documentation, University of Illinois at Urbana-Champaign.

[32] S. S. Murthy, Qualitative reasoning at multiple resolutions, *Proc. Qual. Physics Workshop,* (1988).

[33] J. R. Quinlan, Learning logical definitions from relations, *Machine Learning,* 5(3) (1990).

[34] J. C. Schlimmer, Learning and representation change, *Proc. AAAI 87* (1987).

[35] C. E. Shanon and Weaver, *The Mathematical Theory of Communications,* University of Illinois Press, Urbana, 1964.

[36] P. H. Winston, "Learning Structural Descriptions From Examples," in *The Psychology of Computer Vision,* McGraw-Hill, New York, 1975.

[37] A. Blumer, A. Ehrenfeucht, D. Haussler, and M. K. Warmuth, "Occam's Razor," UCSC-CLR-86-2 (1986).

[38] J. Boose, J. Bradshaw, C. Kitto, and D. Shema, From ETS to Aquinas: Six years of knowledge acquisition tool development, *Proc. EKAW* (1989).

[39] P. B. Brazdil and L. Torgo, Knowledge acquisition via knowledge integration, *Proc. EKAW* (1990).

[40] W. Buntine, Learning classification rules using Bayes, *Proc. Internat. Workshop on Machine Learning,* (1989).

[41] J. Catlett and C. Jack, "Is it Better to Learn Each Class Separately?" Tech. Rep. (1987).

[42] B. Cestnik, I. Kononenko, and I. Bratko, "ASSISTANT 86: a Knowledge-Elicitation Tool for Sophisticated Users," in I. Bratko and N. Lavrač, Eds., *Progress in Machine Learning,* Sigma Press, 1987.

[43] P. Cheesman, "On Finding the Most Probable Model," Tech. Rep. (1989).

[44] E. Charniak and D. McDermott, *Introduction to Artificial Intelligence,* Addison-Wesley, Reading, Mass., 1985.

[45] P. Clark, "Reasoning with Differing Expert Opinions: A Novel Application of Expert System Technology," Tech. Rep. Turing Institute (1990).

[46] W. Emde, "An Inference Engine for Representing Multiple Theories, Knowledge Representation and Organization," in K. Morik, Ed., *Machine Learning*, Springer Verlag, 1989.

[47] M. Gams, "Unifying Principles in Automatic Learning," Ph.D. thesis, Ljubljana (1987).

[48] E. De Bono, *Lateral Thinking*, Pelican Books, Gretna, La., 1970.

[49] T. Pittman, "Thinking Computers," private communication, KLA, Workingham, 1991.

CHAPTER 2

Dynamic Systems Control via Associative Reinforcement Learning

VIJAYKUMAR GULLAPALLI

2.1 INTRODUCTION

The focus of this chapter is the problem of learning control under uncertainty, noise, and the lack of explicit instructional information about how to perform a given control task. Under these circumstances, techniques developed by artificial intelligence researchers for "learning from examples," including the supervised learning techniques studied by neural network researchers, are not directly applicable because these techniques are based on the availability of training information (the "examples") in the form of situation-action training pairs. A useful alternative in such circumstances is a learning technique that can discover appropriate actions in various situations through search guided by evaluative performance feedback. Reinforcement learning methods developed by connectionist researchers are examples of such techniques. This chapter provides an overview of reinforcement learning techniques and discusses their role in learning control by relating them to similar adaptive control methods. Several examples are also presented to illustrate the power and utility of reinforcement learning techniques for learning control.

The chapter is organized as follows. A discussion of the main issues involved in connectionist approaches to learning control is presented in the next section, followed by a section describing associative reinforcement learning methods. Using this overview as the background, three examples of

Dynamic, Genetic, and Chaotic Programming, By Branko Souček and the IRIS Group.
ISBN 0-417-55717-X

learning control via associative reinforcement learning are presented in Section 2.4. The chapter ends with a discussion of the advantages and disadvantages of associative reinforcement learning and a description of some of the directions for further investigation.

2.2 CONNECTIONIST APPROACHES TO LEARNING CONTROL

Connectionist networks are function approximation mechanisms useful for learning to compute a desired function from inputs to outputs. An extensive overview of connectionist learning is provided by the three volumes edited by Rumelhart and McClelland [66,51] or the volume by Hecht-Nielsen [31]. A good brief introduction is provided by Lipmann [48]. Hinton [33] reviews a wide range of connectionist learning methods. Barto [7] provides an overview of various approaches to learning control using connectionist networks. His emphasis is on the relationship between the research in connectionist learning methods and more traditional research in control and signal processing. Additional reviews are provided by Mars [49] and Werbos [77]. The review of connectionist approaches to learning control presented here will be restricted to the main issues and the various approaches taken to resolve them. However, issues pertinent to reinforcement learning applied to control will be discussed in some detail.

In the general problem of learning control, the learning system plays the role of a controller whose actions serve as control inputs to a process as shown in Figure 2.1.* The controller generates control actions based on its inputs, which include the task specification and possible feedback of current and past process outputs and past control actions. The output of the process is an observation of the process state obtained using a set of sensors. Guided by some form of training information, the controller has to learn to generate appropriate control actions for performing the specified task. In general, the training information pertains to the performance of the controller as measured by some predefined *index of performance* (IP).

Three main questions must be answered when designing a learning controller:

1. What kind of training information will be available to the controller?
2. How should the learned control rules be represented?
3. How should the inputs to the controller and its actions (the control signals) be represented?

Answering all of these questions is essential in designing a learning controller. However, this chapter focuses on how the form and content of the

* In all the block diagrams in this chapter, the learning system modules are drawn using white boxes and modules external to the learning system are drawn using shaded boxes.

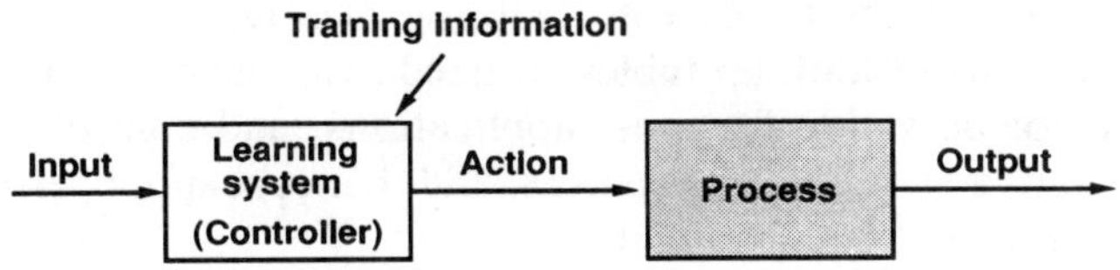

Figure 2.1 *The basic problem setup for learning control. The controller is to learn to control the process through the generation of appropriate actions as control signals. It has to do this using the information supplied to it in the form of the task specification, possible feedback of current and past process outputs and past control actions, and training information.*

training information available in various kinds of control problems affect controller design and performance; questions about the controller's input and output representation and about the details of the learning algorithms are considered here only briefly.

2.2.1 Representation of the Learned Control Rules

Learning appropriate control behaviour involves adjusting the function from inputs to actions computed by the controller in order to satisfy predefined control objectives. When considering this learning process, one can visualize a trade-off between memory and computation that has a direct impact on the learning and performance characteristics of the controller. The following two examples illustrate this trade-off. One method for learning control is to memorize the control signals that must be generated for any given control task. Such rote learning was and still is used in industrial robots that have to repeatedly perform fixed sequences of operations. Clearly, rote learning requires substantial amounts of memory. An alternative method very different from rote learning is to learn a highly constrained parametrized function that can be used to compute appropriate control actions for the process from the given command input. Commonly used in adaptive control schemes [22], this approach to learning typically involves finding the right values of a very small number of parameters.

These two approaches can be contrasted in several ways. To begin with, the main difference between these two approaches is the amount of computation that needs to be performed during learning. Controllers that use rote learning can simply store the control actions corresponding to a control task without having to perform any computation at all, while controllers that learn a parametrized function have to determine how to modify the parameters at each time step. Therefore there can be significant differences in learning speeds, with controllers using rote learning being much faster. Advantages of rote learning also include one-shot learning, good performance on learned tasks, and the ability to handle arbitrarily complex control problems (because all that needs to be done is storage of the appropriate control actions). On the other hand, rote learning clearly suffers from the well-known limitations of look-up tables: it needs vast amounts of memory and hence may not be viable for most applications, and controllers using rote learning cannot generalize across tasks, and, hence, cannot perform tasks on which they have not been trained.

In contrast, controllers implemented as parametrized functions can be much better at generalization across tasks because, at any point of time, whatever function has been learned can be used for computing the control actions for a new task. The validity of such control actions for the task depends on the similarity between the new task and tasks on which the controller has been previously trained. Noisy processes can also be handled by such controllers by adding state information as input to the function. A disadvantage to using controllers that learn parametrized functions is that the control performance improves only gradually with training. These controllers are also restricted by the family of functions they can compute, although this is not a serious limitation in practice.

Although these two extreme examples of methods used by controllers to learn from their experiences illustrate the contrasts between memory-based and computation-based control, we can easily visualize a continuum between these two extremes [7]. Most controllers studied by connectionists lie somewhere along that continuum between the two extremes. Albus's CMAC [2] is an example of a controller that relies more on memory than on computation for learning. So is the approach to robot control described by Atkeson and Reinkensmeyer [5] and by Moore [57]. On the other hand, the architectures of the layered networks used by most connectionists for control (e.g. [11,37,80,45,43]) define a family of functions with the settings of the parameters (the weights) determining the function that is realized. These networks have many more parameters than adaptive learning methods [22], and hence can be regarded as more memory based. But at the same time, the number of parameters is usually far less than that required by the memory-based schemes cited previously. When using connectionist approaches to learning control, we can design the controller to be at any point on the continuum between memory and computation, based on a priori knowledge of the control problem.

2.2.2 Representation of the Controller's Inputs and Actions

The representation selected for the controller's inputs and actions can drastically influence the learning and performance of the controller. Barto [7] discusses the basic issue of choosing a representation and describes various representations used by connectionists. Rather than recounting the discussion here, this section is devoted to a brief description of methods that can be used to select good representations. Two approaches to selecting good representations have been suggested by researchers. The first approach is to use prior knowledge about the function to be learned. This is illustrated by

Kawato, Furukawa, and Suzuki [42], who use a learning component in a robot arm controller to learn to compensate for the effects of unmodeled dynamics. Assuming that the unmodeled dynamics are a function of algebraic terms occurring in the dynamic equations of the robot, they supply the values of these terms to the learning component.

The second and more common approach is to select representations for inputs that best convey some information about than input relative to all possible inputs. For example, a unique representation can be given to each of a finite set of inputs by mapping them onto a set of unit-normal vectors of appropriate length. Alternatively, various coarse coding schemes (Hinton [32]) can be used to capture similarities between the inputs (e.g., [2,56,62]). Linsker [47] and Sanger [67] discuss the benefits of representing inputs by their first few principal components and suggest unsupervised learning mechanisms for performing principal component analysis. Their research is part of the growing interest in input preprocessing methods as mechanisms for speeding up learning.

2.2.3 Training Information

As described in Section 2.2.1, the process of learning control can be viewed as modification of the controller's behavior in order to improve performance as measured by some predefined measure. It is usually assumed that a teacher in the environment supplies the controller information pertinent to its performance.* Several researchers have suggested that learning tasks can be classified based on the quality of the training information provided by the teacher (e.g., [8,40]). One can distinguish two major classes of tasks based on this criterion: *supervised learning tasks* and *reinforcement learning tasks*. In supervised learning tasks, the teacher provides target actions or error gradient vectors that specify how the controller should modify its actions in order to improve performance (Figure 2.2*a*). Thus the teacher can be seen as instructing the controller about the actions to perform in order to improve performance. In contrast, the role of the teacher in reinforcement learning tasks is more evaluative than instructional, and the teacher is sometimes called a *critic* because of this role. As depicted in Figure 2.2*c*, the critic provides evaluations of consequences of the controller's actions, leaving it to the controller to determine how to modify its actions to obtain better evaluations in the future. In other words, the critic in reinforcement learning does not tell the controller *what to do* to improve performance, whereas the teacher in supervised learning does.

An intermediate class of tasks that shares aspects of both supervised and reinforcement learning tasks involves what Jordan and Rumelhart [40] call *learning with a distal teacher*. The teacher in these learning tasks is termed

* Except in the case of *unsupervised learning tasks,* where the necessary information can be considered to be built into the learning system (see [6,8]).

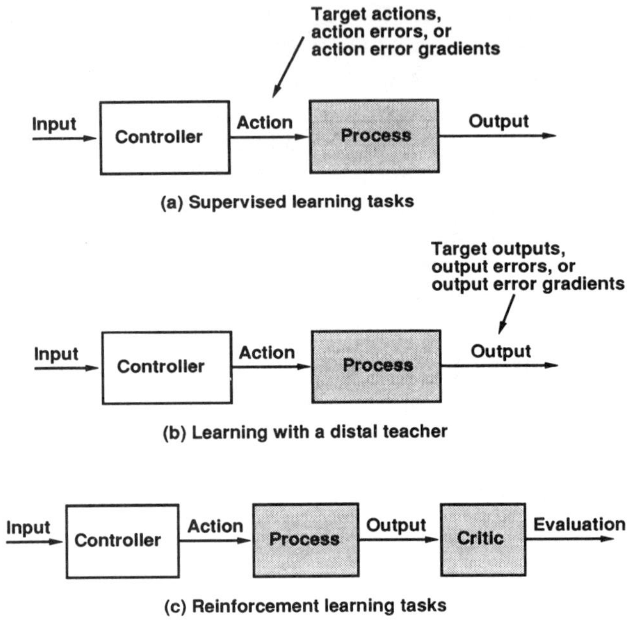

Figure 2.2 *A schematic of the three classes of learning tasks described in the text.* (a) *Supervised learning tasks,* (b) *tasks involving learning with a distal teacher, and* (c) *reinforcement learning tasks.*

"distal," meaning "far from the point of attachment or origin," because the training information it provides pertains to the outputs of the unknown controlled process instead of to the actions of the controller (Figure 2.2*b*). Inasmuch as the teacher provides target outputs or output error gradients, albeit in distal coordinates, these tasks are similar to supervised learning tasks. At the same time, as in reinforcement learning tasks, the controller has to discover the right control actions based on the distal training information. Alternatively, one can view the process and the critic together as a composite "process" whose "output" is the evaluation and thus regard reinforcement learning tasks as special cases of learning with a distal teacher with the objective of extremizing the distal output. In taking this perspective, the distal "error" or the distal "error" gradient in reinforcement learning tasks can be assumed to be any positive value if the evaluation is to be maximized and any negative value if the evaluation is to be minimized.

Learning *methods* used for these three classes of tasks reflect the difference in the content of the training information. Methods for supervised learning are devised primarily to store the situation–action training pairs in a manner that enables good generalization. Several researchers have used supervised learning techniques to train controllers to perform various tasks (e.g., [81,28]). These researchers have used a pre-existing expert as a source for the training data. The (usually human) expert supplies a sufficiently large set of situation–action pairs and the network is trained to produce the corresponding action in each situation. This technique is very easy to implement and is widely used today for training controllers for industrial robots. Widrow and Smith [81] used data provided by a human expert to train a controller to solve a pole-balancing problem. Widrow draws the parallel between this method and knowledge acquisition from an expert when building an expert system. Once trained, the controller can match the expert's performance or even improve upon it. Handelman et al. [28], for example, show how a connectionist controller can use crude training information from a hand-crafted, rule-based controller to learn a generalized control function that has improved performance. However, such generalized control functions may not always lead to improved performance, especially when the teacher provides unreliable training data. Moreover, most complex tasks cannot be performed satisfactorily by any existing controller, and, hence, reliable training data is difficult to obtain. Therefore, most control problems involve reinforcement learning or learning with a distal teacher.

Methods for solving control problems involving reinforcement learning and learning with a distal teacher are more complex than methods appliable to supervised learning tasks. As mentioned earlier, in problems involving reinforcement learning or learning with a distal teacher, appropriate controller actions have to be *inferred* from evaluations or distal training information respectively. In other words, some method for bridging the gap between the form in which training information is available to the controller (evaluations, distal targets, etc.) and the form of information required for successful control (appropriate controller actions) is necessary. Methods devised by researchers for bridging this gap fall into two major categories. *Indirect methods* involve constructing a model of the transformation from the controller's actions to the evaluations or the distal targets and using the model to obtain gradient information for training the controller. *Direct, or model-free, methods* obtain the requisite training information by perturbing the process and observing the effect on the evaluations or the distal process outputs. A more detailed description of these methods follows.

Indirect Methods. An indirect method for obtaining the training information for the controller is described by Jordan [36] (see also Jordan and Rumelhart [40]). Barto [7] calls this method "differentiating a model." The basic idea underlying this method is: in order to determine the appropriate control actions for the controller, it is necessary to determine how to change the control actions so as to effect the desired changes in the distal output of the process or the evaluation. In other words, the gradient of the distal output or evaluation with respect to the controller's action has to be obtained. This can be accomplished easily if we have a model of the process (or the process and the critic) that can be differentiated. Then the model's Jacobian, evaluated at its input, can be used to transform desired changes in

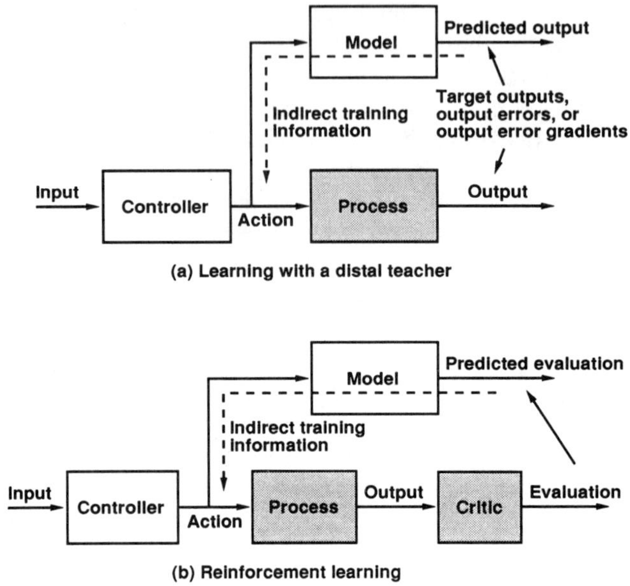

Figure 2.3 *A block diagram of the indirect method for solving control problems involving reinforcement learning or learning with a distal teacher.*

the outputs of the model into changes in the inputs to the model. This is illustrated in Figure 2.3.

Using a task involving learning with a distal teacher, Jordan [36] shows how a back-propagation network [46,63,65,76] can be used to implement this in an elegant manner. Specifically, the network is trained to be a forward model of the process through an operation commonly known as *system identification* in the control literature. Training the network is a supervised learning task with the training data being obtained from the process being modeled; random control signals are fed to the process and the network and the resulting process outputs are used as target network outputs. Once the forward model has been trained to a sufficient degree of accuracy, it is held fixed and the controller's training is begun. In this stage, the forward model is used to predict the process output for each control action generated by the controller, and the difference between the desired process output and the predicted output is back-propagated through the forward model, yielding the error gradient with respect to that control action. Jordan [36] shows that the back-propagation process actually computes a factorization of the transpose of the network Jacobian. Jordan also demonstrates the utility of this technique in a variety of control problems [37,36,40]. Variants of this technique have been applied to control problems by Kawato [41], Miyata [55], Nguyen and Widrow [61], and others. However, as noted by Barto [7] as well as

Jordan and Rumelhart [40], a back-propagation network model is not essential for applying this technique. Any forward model of the process that can be differentiated can be used. In their study of reaching tasks, for example, Massone and Bizzi [50] use a Kinematic Network [34] model of a limb in place of a back-propagation network model.

A similar approach has been proposed for solving reinforcement learning tasks by Jordan and Jacobs [38], Munro [58], Werbos [78], and Williams [85]. As Figure 2.3*b* shows, the idea is to train a connectionist network to model the process together with the critic, instead of the process alone. Training inputs to the network are obtained by generating random control signals and observing the corresponding evaluations returned by the critic. Once the model network has been trained using an appropriate supervised learning method, it can provide the gradient of the evaluation with respect to the controller's actions by, for example, back-propagating through the model. Werbos [77] also suggests how this approach can be used with explicit models for both the process and the critic.

Direct Methods. Instead of resorting to model construction, direct methods use the process itself as a source of training data for training the controller. For learning tasks with a distal teacher, if the command input to the controller is the desired output of the process, direct identification of an inverse model of the process has been proposed as the solution [80]. Such a method has been called *direct inverse modeling* [39] in connectionist literature and *input matching* in adaptive control literature [22]. Training data for the controller is obtained by feeding a variety of control signals to the process and observing the resultant process output. A supervised learning method is used to train the inverse model with the observed process output as input and the control signals as the desired actions. Once trained, the inverse model can be used as a controller that produces an appropriate control action for any desired process output. Widrow et al. [80] used this method to control linear systems. Other researchers have applied this method to the control of nonlinear thermodynamic systems [70], and for learning the inverse kinematics [5,45] and inverse dynamics [43,54] of robots.

Direct inverse modeling appears to be an attractive method for learning control because it is easily implemented and, in most cases, results in good controllers. However, its applicability and usefulness depend on the characteristics of the controlled process. With dynamic processes, for example, the data obtained for training the inverse model depend on the initial state of the process and hence the resultant controller might be ineffective unless the process can be reinitialized to that state. Obviously, this is not always possible. Furthermore, as emphasized by Jordan [36], inverse identification may not yield good results when the process inverse is not unique, i.e., when many different control actions result in the same process output, and hence the training data can include different target actions for the same process

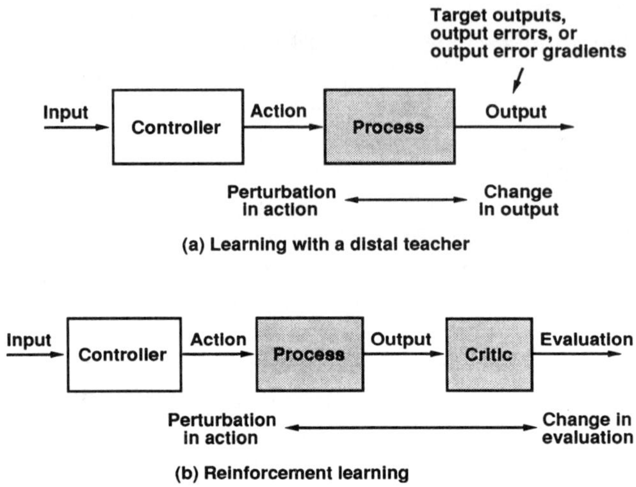

Figure 2.4 *A block diagram of the direct, or model-free, method for solving control problems involving reinforcement learning or learning with a distal teacher by gradient estimation through active perturbation.*

output. In such cases, controllers trained using most supervised learning techniques tend to produce for each process output a control action that is in the convex closure of all the target actions used in training. Therefore, unless the inverse image of a desired process output is a convex set, the control action computed by the controller might not lie in the inverse image.

We do not discuss direct inverse modeling further in this chapter. Instead, we focus on direct methods for determining the gradient of the evaluation or the distal output with respect to the controller's actions without resorting to model construction. Hereinafter, "direct methods" will be used to mean "direct methods for gradient estimation." With direct methods, estimates of the gradient are formed by actively perturbing the controller's actions and observing the consequent change in the evaluation or the distal outputs, as depicted in Figure 2.4. Perturbation of the actions is usually accomplished by adding random noise to the actions of the controller. Hence this process can be regarded as a stochastic search for the best actions, with the gradient estimates being used to determine how to improve the actions. This is a very old idea and examples of its use include the parameter perturbation approach to system identification [15] studied by control theorists, the Kiefer–Wolfowitz process [44] and other related stochastic approximation processes, and various learning algorithms studied by learning automata theorists [59] and mathematical learning theorists [52]. As discussed in Section 2.3, most connectionist reinforcement learning algorithms are also based on this idea. The utility of this approach to learning control has been discussed by Barto, Sutton, and Anderson [11], who used it to control a pole-balancing system.

Other examples of the use of this approach are seen in Barto, Sutton, and Brouwer [12], Franklin [19,20], and Gullapalli [25,26].

Direct versus Indirect Methods: Pros and Cons. Indirect methods are often perceived as having advantages over direct methods when a model of the process, or the process and the critic, is available a priori. With an accurate model, the controller has much more information available regarding the process. Moreover, a model provides means for incorporating domain knowledge that might be useful to the controller. If an adequate model is not available, it can be learned through interactions with the environment. Indeed, connectionist approaches are particularly relevant in such situations because connectionist networks can be trained to model fairly complex processes. Furthermore, once learned, a model can be useful for solving multiple control tasks, and therefore, the costs of model construction can be amortized over several control tasks.

However, uncertainty and noise make constructing an adequate model impractical in many real-world situations, and even if model construction were practical, possession of a model does not necessarily guarantee a solution to the control problem. There is also a relationship between the accuracy of the model and its utility for acquiring control. While the amount of effort needed to form an accurate model can increase dramatically with the complexity of the process, one cannot usually tell beforehand how accurate a model will suffice to quickly learn good control. Unfortunately, using a poor model to train the controller can result in the controller learning inappropriate behavior, which will then have to be corrected by prolonged training. Also since the kinds of control signals that will be used (or even required) for the control problem are not known while constructing the model, the model necessarily must be valid for a wide range of inputs. It is therefore possible that considerable effort is wasted in learning to model the process behavior for control inputs that may never be actually used for control. Moreover, one cannot always wait until an accurate model is constructed before control begins. Some form of control is usually desired while an adequate model is being constructed.

A potential solution to these problems is to localize the model by restricting the range of the inputs to the model and to interleave the modeling and control stages. This approach is often used in adaptive control (see Goodwin and Sin [22]). A second solution, obviously, is to avoid using a model if possible. Because they do not entail the costs of model construction, direct methods have the advantages of computational simplicity, no delay in training a controller, and the ability to perform well even when the process is nonstationary. Furthermore, direct methods are also relatively insensitive to the complexity of the process/process + critic—primarily because they do not have to model the process—and can tolerate uncertainty and noise. The obvious disadvantage of direct methods, however, is that the estimates of the behavior of the process obtained through active perturbation can be of a much poorer quality when compared to those obtained from an accurate process model. Therefore, control acquisition using direct methods can be slow, and direct methods do not scale as well as indirect methods. Moreover, there is no model available for reuse in other control problems.

It is clear that both direct and indirect methods have different advantages and disadvantages and neither method can be regarded as being universally applicable. One observation that can be made is that *direct methods can be useful when the complexity of constructing a model outweighs the complexity of solving the original control problem.* This point will be illustrated later using the results of training controllers for three different processes. The next section presents associative reinforcement learning methods as examples of direct learning methods.

2.3 ASSOCIATIVE REINFORCEMENT LEARNING

Associative reinforcement learning tasks defined by Barto and Anandan [9] combine facets of stochastic learning automata tasks [74,59] and supervised learning pattern classification tasks [16].* In associative reinforcement learning tasks, the learning system interacts in a closed loop with its environment. At each time step, the environment provides the learning system with input $\mathbf{x}$ chosen from a set of input vectors, X. Using this input, the learning system selects a scalar output z from a set of permissible outputs, Z. Based on both $\mathbf{x}$ and z, the environment computes and returns an evaluation or "reinforcement" $r \in R$. Ideally, we would like the system to learn to respond to each input with the output that has the highest expected evaluation. In keeping with the earlier work on learning automata, Barto and Anandan defined associative reinforcement learning tasks as involving selection of one of a finite set of outputs (Z is a finite set), and for which the evaluation is a binary-valued success/failure signal (i.e., $R = \{0,1\}$). Their interest in such tasks led to the development of the $A_{R\text{-}P}$ (associative reward-penalty) algorithm, which they prove has a form of optimal performance in associative reinforcement learning tasks. These conditions on the output and the evaluation, however, are rather restrictive for most applications and one would like to extend the definition of associative reinforcement learning tasks to permit continuous-valued outputs and evaluations. Barto and Jordan [10] present a version of the $A_{R\text{-}P}$ algorithm that can handle the latter case, where the evaluation returned by the environment can take on bounded continuous values (the so-called S-model case [13]). But learning continuous outputs is more difficult, and existing algorithms cannot be easily extended to do so. For example, $A_{R\text{-}P}$ units (as defined in [9]) compute their binary-valued outputs by adding noise to their activations and thresholding the sum. Such units could be easily modified to produce continuous outputs by omitting the

* For a detailed discussion of the relationship, please see the paper by Barto and Anandan [9].

thresholding. Unfortunately, in such units there would be no control over the amount of noise that is added to the activation, and, hence, they would continue to produce random output values regardless of the duration of training. We now present our own efforts towards the development of a suitable algorithm for associative reinforcement learning tasks with continuous outputs and evaluations.

The first step was extending Barto and Anandan's definition of associative reinforcement learning tasks by generalizing their definition to the case when the output z can take on continuous values and the environmental evaluation r lies in the interval [0,1]. Stated formally, associative reinforcement learning tasks involve the following interaction between the environment and the learning system. At time step t the environment provides the learning system with some context vector $\mathbf{x}(t)$ selected from a set of vectors $X \subseteq \Re^n$, where $\Re$ is the set of real numbers. Based on this input, the learning system produces a random output $z(t)$ selected according to some internal probability distribution over some interval $Z \subseteq \Re$. The environment evaluates the output $z(t)$ in the context of the input $\mathbf{x}(t)$ and sends to the learning system an evaluation signal $r(t) \in R = [0,1]$, with $r(t) = 1$ denoting the most favorable evaluation. This evaluation is determined according to some conditional probability distribution $H: R \times X \times Z \rightarrow [0,1]$, where $H(r,\mathbf{x},z) = Pr\{r(t) \leq r \mid \mathbf{x}(t) = \mathbf{x}, z(t) = z\}$. The objective of the learning system is to learn to respond to each input pattern $\mathbf{x} \in X$ with the action $z^{\mathbf{x}} \in Z$ with probability 1, where $z^{\mathbf{x}}$ is such that $E(r \mid \mathbf{x}, z^{\mathbf{x}}) = \max_{z \in Z}\{E(r \mid \mathbf{x}, z)\}$.

The *stochastic real-valued* (SRV) unit algorithm [24,25] incorporates the relevant techniques from various related areas in a learning algorithm that (1) learns the action that yields the highest evaluation in a given context (as a stochastic automaton does), (2) learns to associate different optimal actions with different contexts (as a pattern classifier associates different class labels with different input patterns), and (3) updates a vector of parameters, $\boldsymbol{\theta}$, specifying the optimal actions (as a stochastic approximation procedure does). The SRV algorithm is closely related to stochastic approximation procedures such as the Robbins–Monro [64] and the Kiefer–Wolfowitz [44] procedures and their generalizations [17]. An important feature of the SRV algorithm is that it can be implemented as a *connectionist unit* that can be incorporated into a network. A formal description of the SRV algorithm is presented in the next section.

2.3.1 The Stochastic Real-Valued (SRV) Unit

Designed for associative reinforcement learning tasks defined in the previous section, the SRV unit has the structure shown in Figure 2.5. The interaction between the unit and its stochastic environment takes place as iterations of the following operations. In the sequel, variables are subscripted by the iteration number at which their value is considered. Iteration n begins with the unit receiving an input $\mathbf{x}_n$ chosen randomly from a set of

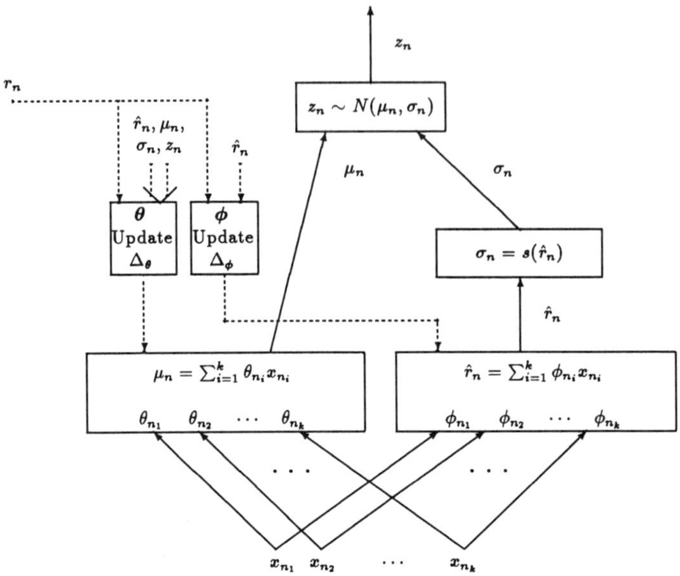

Figure 2.5 *Block diagram of a SRV unit showing the various computations being performed. The flow of signals used to compute the output of the unit is shown with solid lines; the signals used for learning are shown with dashed lines.*

input vectors X. The unit uses $\mathbf{x}_n$ and two internal parameter vectors, $\boldsymbol{\theta}_n$ and $\boldsymbol{\phi}_n$, to compute the two parameters μ_n and σ_n of the Gaussian distribution used to generate the unit's output. The mean μ_n is the inner product $\boldsymbol{\theta}_n^{\mathrm{T}}\mathbf{x}_n$, and the standard deviation, σ_n, is computed in two stages by first computing an expected evaluation $\hat{r}_n$ as the inner product $\boldsymbol{\phi}_n^{\mathrm{T}}\mathbf{x}_n$ and then computing σ_n as a function s of $\hat{r}_n$. The function s is a monotonically decreasing, nonnegative function. Moreover, $s(1.0) = 0.0$, so that when the maximum reinforcement is expected, the standard deviation is zero. The output of the unit, z_n, is generated as a random variable using the Gaussian distribution with parameters μ_n, and σ_n. After the action is emitted, the unit receives evaluative feedback, $r(z_n, \mathbf{x}_n)$, from the environment, which it uses to adjust the parameter vectors $\boldsymbol{\theta}_n$ and $\boldsymbol{\phi}_n$.

The SRV unit uses the following algorithm to update the parameter vector $\boldsymbol{\theta}$, thus generating a sequence of random vectors $\boldsymbol{\theta}_n$:

$$\boldsymbol{\theta}_{n+1} = \boldsymbol{\theta}_n + \sigma_n(r(z_n, \mathbf{x}_n) - \hat{r}_n)(z_n - \mu_n)\,\mathbf{x}_n, \tag{2.1}$$

$$\text{where } \mu_n = \boldsymbol{\theta}_n^{\mathrm{T}}\mathbf{x}_n, \tag{2.2}$$

$$\sigma_n = s(\hat{r}_n), \tag{2.3}$$

$$\hat{r}_n = \boldsymbol{\phi}_n^{\mathrm{T}}\mathbf{x}_n, \text{ and} \tag{2.4}$$

$$z_n \sim N(\mu_n, \sigma_n). \tag{2.5}$$

Equation 2.1 can be written as

$$\boldsymbol{\theta}_{n+1} = \begin{cases} \boldsymbol{\theta}_n + \sigma_n^2\, y_n(\boldsymbol{\theta}_n, \boldsymbol{\phi}_n, \mathbf{x}_n)\, \mathbf{x}_n & \text{if } \sigma_n > 0, \\ \boldsymbol{\theta}_n & \text{if } \sigma_n = 0, \end{cases} \tag{2.6}$$

where

$$y_n(\boldsymbol{\theta}_n, \boldsymbol{\phi}_n, \mathbf{x}_n) = (r(z_n, \mathbf{x}_n) - \hat{r}_n)\left(\frac{z_n - \mu_n}{\sigma_n}\right), \tag{2.7}$$

and μ_n, σ_n, $\hat{r}_n$, and z_n are as defined in (2.2), (2.3), (2.4), and (2.5) respectively. We should note here that faster learning can often be achieved in practice if the term σ_n^2 in (2.6) is replaced by a constant learning rate parameter $\alpha > 0$.

An intuitive explanation for these update equations is the following. We can view the fraction in (2.7) as the *normalized perturbation* that has been added to the mean output of the unit for the given input. If this perturbation has caused the unit to receive an evaluation signal that is *more* than the expected evaluation, then it is desirable for the unit to produce an output closer to the current output z_n. The mean output value should therefore move in the direction of the perturbation. That is, if the perturbation is positive, the unit should update its parameters so that the mean value increases. Conversely, if the perturbation is negative, the parameters should be updated so that the mean value decreases. On the other hand, if the evaluation received is *less* than the expected evaluation, then the unit should adjust its mean in the direction *opposite* to that of the perturbation. Equations (2.6) and (2.7) have this effect on the mean output.

Updating of the parameter vector $\boldsymbol{\phi}$ used for computing the expected evaluation is relatively straightforward. For this, we want to associate with each input vector a corresponding reinforcement value, and because both the input vector and the reinforcement value are supplied to the unit, we can use the LMS rule of Widrow and Hoff to learn this association:

$$\boldsymbol{\phi}_{n+1} = \boldsymbol{\phi}_n + \rho\,(r(z_n, \mathbf{x}_n) - \hat{r}_n)\,\mathbf{x}_n, \tag{2.8}$$

where $\rho > 0$ is a learning rate parameter. This completes the description of the SRV algorithm.

2.3.2 Related Work

Several algorithms related to the SRV algorithm have been described in the literature. Williams [83,84] describes a very similar algorithm involving the use of the Gaussian distribution to generate real-valued outputs. His approach is based on using the derivatives of the logarithm of the Gaussian distribution function to update the mean and standard deviation. Williams shows that, on an average, using these derivatives to update the parameters results in an increase in the expected evaluation from the environment. The SRV algorithm also has components analogous to an earlier algorithm of Sutton [71], which also uses the Gaussian distribution to generate real-valued outputs. However, in his algorithm, the output is controlled by varying the mean alone; the standard deviation is held constant. Harth and Tzanakou [30], in a somewhat similar approach, designed an algorithm, called Alopex, to produce real values that are proportional to a bias with random noise added to it. In the original algorithm, the noise had a fixed distribution, although in more recent versions feedback is used to adjust the noise distribution. Farley and Clark [18] also described a scheme in which the noise level is varied based on changes in performance over previous time steps. More recently, Alspector, Allen, Hu, and Satyanarayana [3] described a reinforcement learning algorithm based on the Boltzmann machine learning algorithm [1], in which the noise in the activation of their stochastic units is controlled so as to keep the units active for a reasonable fraction of the time. In addition to the frequency of activation of the units, they also used measures such as the sum of the magnitudes of weights on links into a unit and the past history of reinforcement to determine the noise amplitude. Algorithms involving stochastic perturbation of the weights of a unit rather than its output have also appeared recently in the literature [29,35]. Although the net effect of perturbing the weights is to perturb the output of the unit, the former is considered easier to implement in hardware realizations of units.

2.3.3 Comparison with Genetic Algorithms

One can draw an analogy between direct reinforcement learning systems and genetic algorithms [21]. The objective of reinforcement learning systems is to learn behaviors that elicit the best possible reinforcement. Genetic algorithms, discussed in greater detail in Part 2 of this book, have the goal of optimizing the *fitness* of the genome. Thus both paradigms are concerned with optimization with respect to an evaluation function. Furthermore, the search process in both paradigms is stochastic, with direct reinforcement learning systems relying on biased random search, while genetic algorithms rely on random mutations and crossovers in the genes of the fittest members of the population. Therefore both rely on active perturbation to obtain training information. However, the two paradigms operate on different time scales: a reinforcement learning system's behavior improves over its lifetime; the fitness of a population of evolving individuals improves over generations. In other words, the ontological improvement of a learning system through direct reinforcement learning of optimal behavior can be considered analogous to phylogenetic evolution of a population of individuals with the highest survival fitness. Of course, major differences exist between the two paradigms, when considered at a more algorithmic or implementational level. Nevertheless, the underlying conceptual similarities are worth noting. These observations indicate that it might be possible to capitalize on the advantages of both paradigms by interleaving ontological improvement of population members with phylogenetic evolution, thus enabling the progeny to inherit behaviors and survival skills learned by their parents over a lifetime. Although not biologically realistic, there is no reason why such a scheme should not be implemented in artificial biosystems.

2.4 LEARNING CONTROL: SOME EXAMPLES

In this section, three control tasks are used to illustrate the utility of direct methods, particularly associative reinforcement learning methods, for learning control. The first of these tasks, a peg-in-hole insertion task, is an example of learning fine-motion control under real-world conditions of uncertainty and noise. The second task is one of learning the inverse kinematics of a simulated underconstrained robot arm. The third and final task involves learning to control an unstable dynamic system, namely a cart-pole system. For all three tasks, the associative reinforcement learning method of choice has been a connectionist network that produces control actions using an output layer of SRV units. In presenting the results of training the networks on these tasks, an attempt has been made to compare and contrast the performance of the direct learning methods with that of indirect learning methods applied to the same task.

2.4.1 Learning Fine-Motion Control: A Peg-in-Hole Insertion Task

As a prototypical example of a task involving interaction between the robot and its environment, the peg-in-hole insertion task has been used by roboticists for testing various approaches to robot control. Peg-in-hole insertion tasks are also very important in industrial robotics because of their prevalence in robot assembly operations. Constituting about 33% of all automated assembly operations, peg-in-hole insertions are the most frequent assembly operations [60]. Both two-dimensional [79] and three-dimensional [27] peg-in-hole tasks have been studied in detail, and a number of solutions to the general problem have been proposed (see [23] for an overview). While the abstract peg-in-hole task can be solved quite easily, real-world conditions of uncertainty and noise can substantially degrade the performance of traditional control methods.

Sources of uncertainty and noise include (1) errors and noise in sensations, (2) errors in execution of motion commands, and (3) uncertainty due to movement of the part grasped by the robot. The first of these is the most common source of uncertainty. Position sensors can be especially unreliable when the robot is interacting with external objects, resulting, for example, in inaccurate knowledge of relative locations of parts of the robot with respect

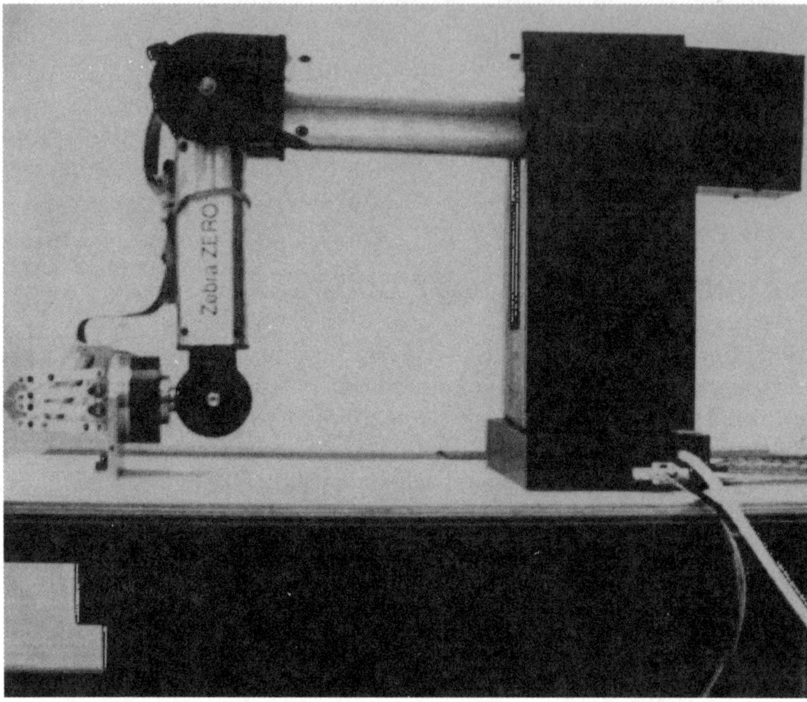

Figure 2.6 *The Zebra Zero robot used for the peg-in-hole insertion task.*

to the external objects. Noisy force sensations further compound the problem of control when the robot is interacting with external objects. The second source of uncertainty is due to the dynamics of the robot itself. Because of friction, gear backlash, and other factors, giving the same command in the same starting configuration can result in different motions of the robot. The third source of uncertainty stems from the possibility of parts moving within the grasp of the gripper. Most grippers have no means of detecting any such motion. Under such conditions, the peg-in-hole problem becomes a good candidate for adaptive solutions [69]. But given these conditions, handcrafting or learning an adequate robot model—a requirement if one is to use indirect methods for training the controller—can be very difficult. It is easier instead to use direct methods to learn a reactive control strategy that enables good performance under uncertainty and noise. This is demonstrated here by using a Zebra Zero robot shown in Figure 2.6 to perform peg-in-hole insertions. This robot is equipped with a force and moment sensor attached to the base of the gripper, and can also sense positions of the links of the arm through position encoders.

As an initial implementation, a two-dimensional version of the peg-in-hole task, depicted in Figure 2.7, was attempted. In this version of the task, there are six inputs provided to the controller at each time step. These are the

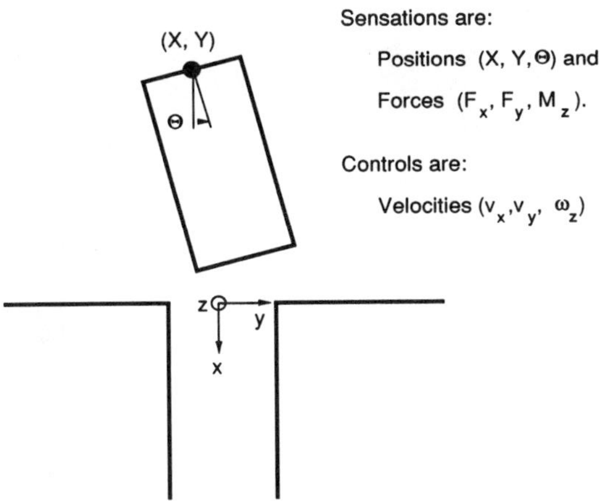

Figure 2.7 *The peg-in-hole task.*

position of the peg (X, Y, Θ), computed from the sensed joint positions of the robot arm, and the force and moment sensations (F_x, F_y, M_z). Using these inputs, the controller has to compute a velocity command for that time step. Because it is acting in a closed loop with the robot, it is possible for the controller to learn a reactive control strategy for performing the insertion task. Figure 2.8 shows the network that was trained using direct reinforcement learning to perform peg insertions. In the experiments reported here,

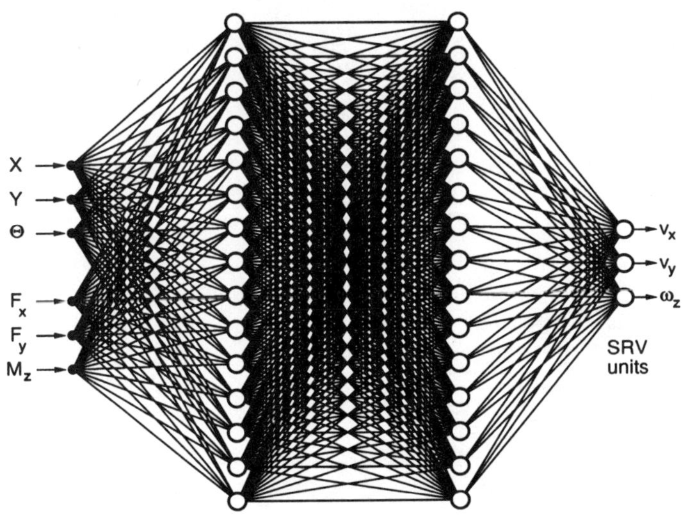

Figure 2.8 *The network used for the peg-in-hole task. The network has an input layer of 6 units, two hidden layers of back-propagation units and an output layer of 3 SRV units. All the units in a layer are connected to all the units in the succeeding layer.*

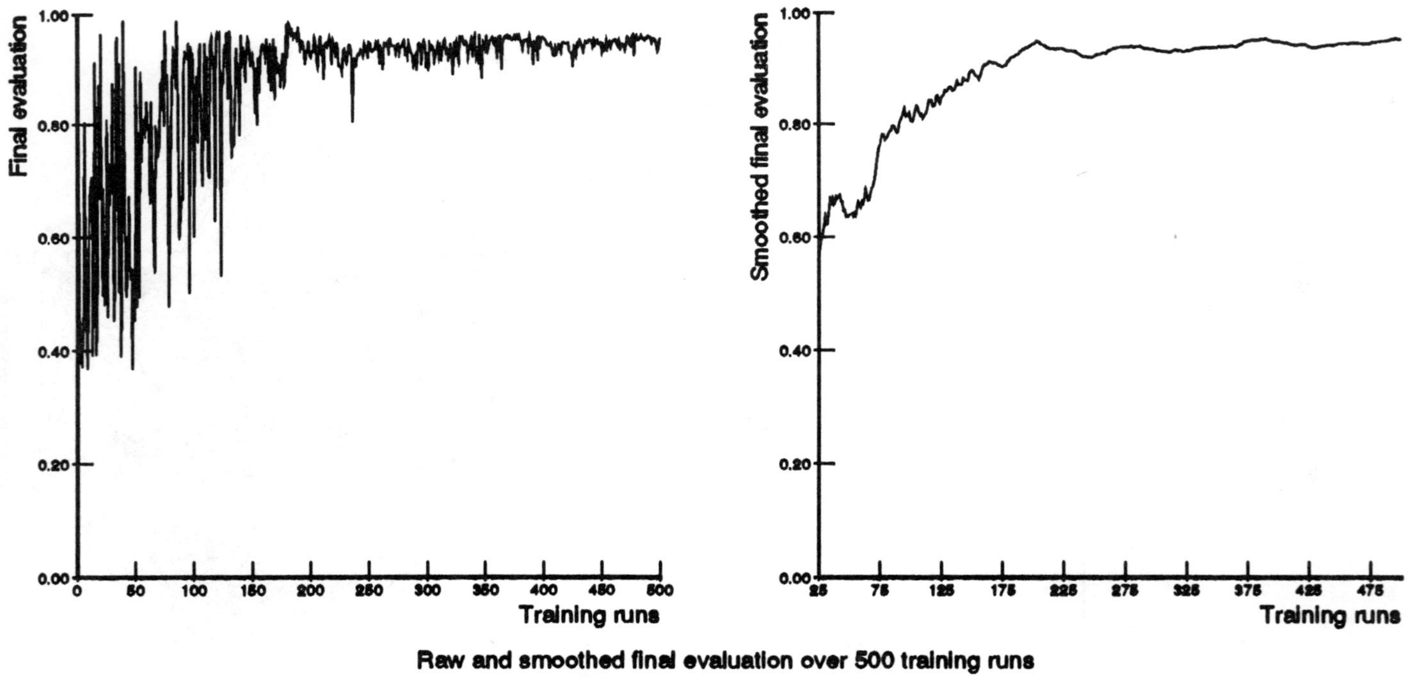

Figure 2.9 *Peg-in-hole task: Final evaluation received over 500 consecutive training runs.*

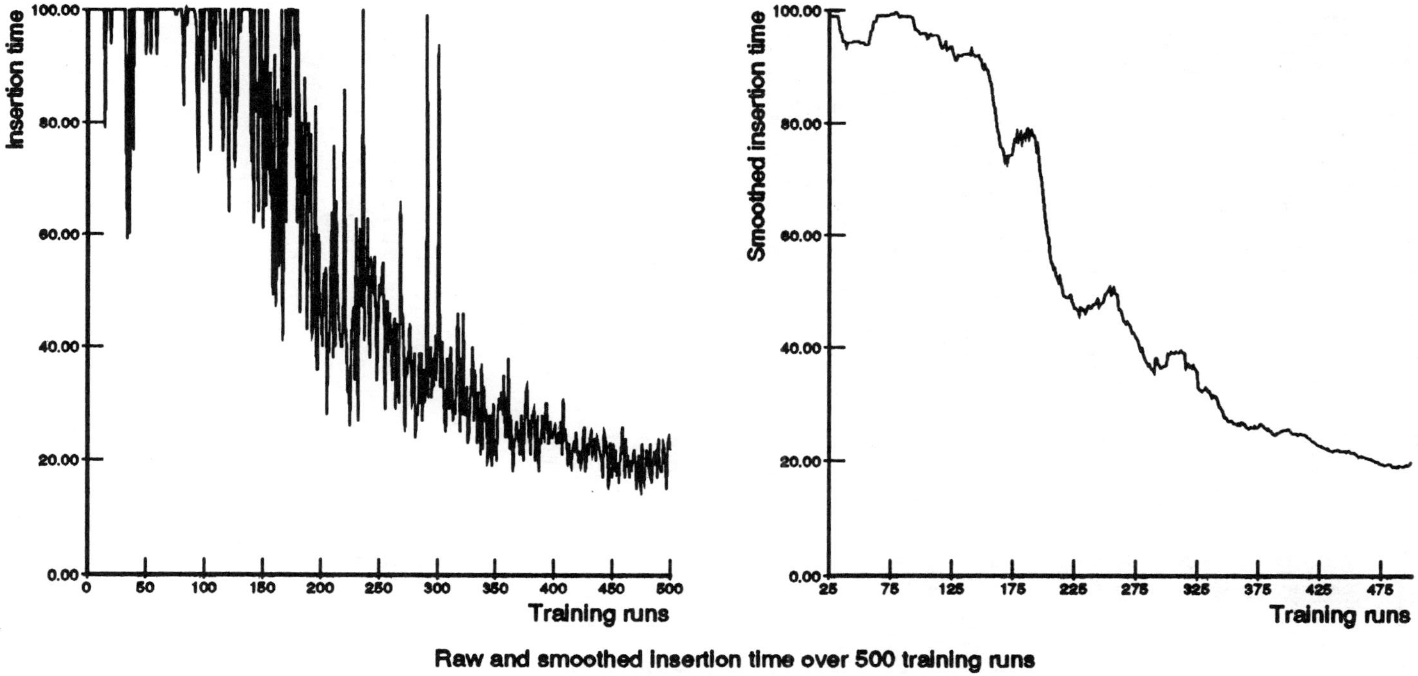

Figure 2.10 *Peg-in-hole task: Insertion time taken on each of 500 consecutive training runs.*

the peg used was 50 mm long and 22.225 mm (0.875 in) wide, while the hole was 23.8125 mm (0.9375 in) wide. Thus the clearance between the peg and the hole was 0.79375 mm (0.03125 in). Training of the controller was carried out as a sequence of training runs. Each training run started with the peg at a random position and orientation with respect to the hole and ended either when the peg was successfully inserted to a depth of 35 mm (1.4 in) into the hole or when 100 time steps had elapsed.

The following interaction took place between the controller and the robot at each time step during training. To begin with, the sensed peg position and forces were input to the controller network, which used them to compute an action command. This command was executed by the robot, resulting in some motion of the peg. The controller's action was then evaluated based on the new peg position and the forces acting on the peg. Two criteria were used in computing this evaluation, which ranged from 0 to 1, with 1 denoting the best evaluation. A base evaluation was computed first, using the discrepancy between the current sensed position of the peg and the desired position with the peg inserted in the hole. A penalty term was then subtracted from this evaluation if any of the sensed forces on the peg exceeded a preset maximum of 0.5 N. Using this evaluation, the controller network updated its weights and the cycle was repeated.

Results. A learning curve showing the final evaluation over 500 consecutive training runs is shown in Figure 2.9. The final evaluation levels off after about 150 training runs because after that amount of training, the controller is consistently able to perform successful insertions. However, performance continues to improve as indicated by the learning curve in Figure 2.10, which shows the time to insertion decreasing continuously over the 500 training runs. These curves indicate that the controller becomes progressively more skillful at the insertion task with training in a manner reminiscent of human skill acquisition through practice. The performance of the controller was tested on nine test cases after 100, 200, 300, 400, and 500 training runs. In the nine test cases, insertion was attempted with the peg at one of nine fixed initial locations and orientations, as listed in Table 2.1 An example of the performance (test case 6) is shown in Figure 2.11.

TABLE 2.1 Test Cases for the Peg-In-Hole Insertion Task

Test case	Initial peg positon (X mm, Y mm, Θ rad)
1	(-20.0, 0.0, 0.0)
2	(-20.0, 25.0, 0.0)
3	(-20.0, -25.0, 0.0)
4	(-20.0, -25.0, 0.15)
5	(-20.0, 25.0, -0.15)
6	(-20.0, -25.0, -0.15)
7	(-20.0, 25.0, 0.15)
8	(-20.0, 0.0, 0.15)
9	(-20.0, 0.0, -0.15)

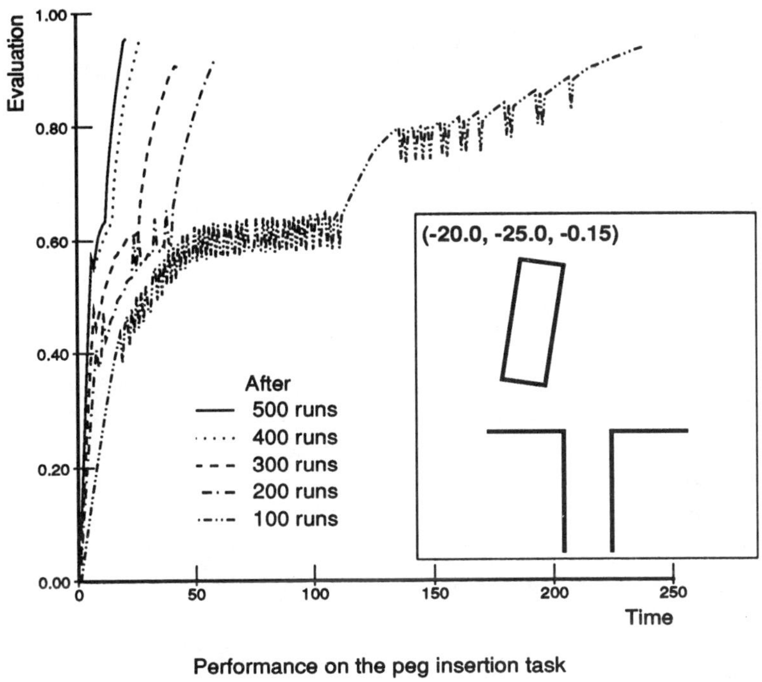

Figure 2.11 *Peg-in-hole task: Performance on a test case 6 after various intervals of training. The inset shows the initial position and orientation of the peg for this test case.*

2.4.2 Learning Inverse Kinematics of an Underconstrained Manipulator

The second task we present involves learning inverse kinematics in underconstrained systems. The task is a robot arm positioning task in which the controller has to move the end-effector of a three-joint planar arm to one of three target locations. To do this, the controller has to solve an inverse kinematics problem, which is to determine appropriate joint angle commands that result in positioning the arm's end-effector at a desired location. The particular version of this task used is illustrated in Figure 2.12. The input to the controller is a command that specifies which of the three square buttons to hit. The actions of the controller are joint angle settings that alter the arm configuration and hence the location of the arm's end-effector. Clearly, this task is an example of learning with distal targets because the targets are desired values of the Cartesian location of the end-effector and the latter is the output of a process (the robot arm) driven by the controller's actions.

A further complication exists here. Due to the presence of excess degrees of freedom in the arm for this task, there are no unique solutions: many different actions of the controller can result in the same end-effector loca-

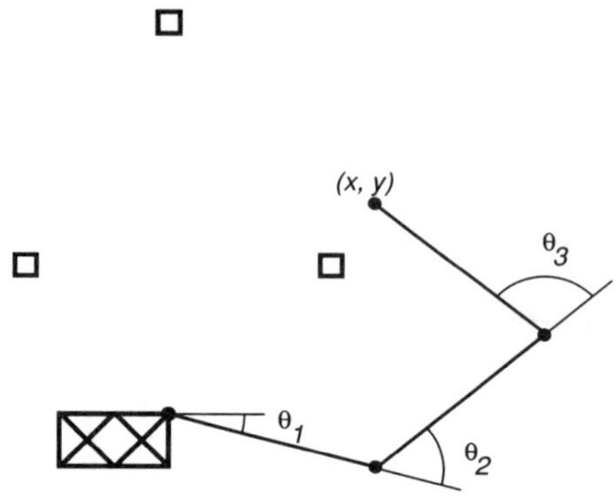

Figure 2.12 *The inverse kinematics task. Based on a command input that specifies which button, the network is to position the end-effector of the robot arm on one of the three buttons.*

tion. This makes it difficult to specify desired actions a priori, and hence training information required for supervised learning cannot be easily obtained. Moreover, as discussed in Section 2.2.3, direct inverse modeling methods are also ineffective under such circumstances. The inverse kinematics problem for underconstrained manipulators is the subject of much robotics research even today. The version of the inverse kinematics problem depicted in Figure 2.12 was studied previously by Jordan and Rumelhart [40], who used an indirect method for solving it. Their solution involved constructing a differentiable forward model of the robot arm and using the forward model to obtain the gradient of an error function in Cartesian space with respect to the control actions.

Jordan and Rumelhart used back-propagation networks for both the controller and the forward model. Their controller had 2 input, 50 hidden and 3 output units and their forward model had 3 input, 50 hidden, and 2 output units. A block diagram of their architecture is shown in Figure 2.13*a*.

A fairly elaborate study of this problem was conducted by Jordan and Rumelhart [40], and one of points they make is that there is a trade-off between the amount of time spent in training the model network and the amount of time required to train the controller using the resulting model (see Figure 16 on page 27 in ref. [40]). They note that in applying indirect methods, often a very crude forward model suffices for solving the control problem. However, as illustrated by their results, using a crude model can also slow down control acquisition. Based on their simulations of the indirect method on this task, two points are worth noting here:

1. Although training the forward model for more than about 500 time steps, or trials, does not result in any significant savings in the amount of training required for the controller on this task, such a limit on the accuracy

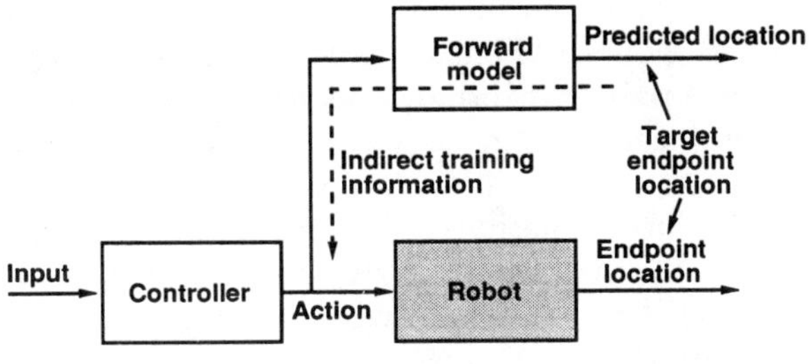

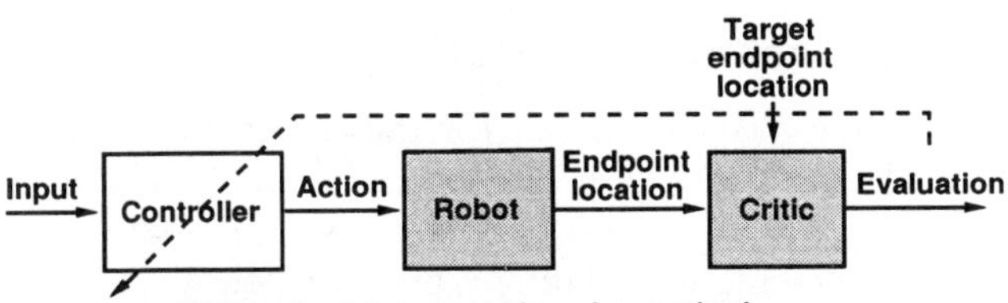

Figure 2.13 *The network architecture used for the inverse kinematics task.* (a) *The architecture used by Jordan and Rumelhart [40];* (b) *the architecture used with the direct learning method.*

of the model is usually not known a priori. This is in fact a significant limitation of indirect approaches. Because the model accuracy needed for any particular task is not known in advance, one cannot minimize the time spent on training the model.

2. It is usually the case that training the controller and the model simultaneously leads to poorer learning performance than training the model first and then training the controller. This is because with simultaneous training the controller starts off by learning incorrect actions based on training information obtained from the initially inaccurate model. This bad initial control knowledge interferes with the subsequent acquisition of good control by the controller. Indeed, in most tasks, it is prudent to construct at least an approximate forward model before commencing training the controller. For the task under consideration, Jordan and Rumelhart [40] find that pretraining the forward model for about 50 trials is essential to ensure stable learning of control.

Results. Simulation results reported by Jordan and Rumelhart indicate that the lowest *total* number of training trials for both the model and the controller is approximately 1250 trials.* We conducted some simulations

* None of the numbers quoted in this section should be taken as definitive because neither Jordan and Rumelhart nor we have attempted to optimize learning speeds through tuning parameters and network structures. The descriptions and results presented here are intended to highlight the qualitative aspects of using direct and indirect methods. We hope that this will motivate rigorous quantitative comparisons of the two methods.

using a direct learning method on this same task. The architecture used in these simulations is shown in Figure 2.13*b*. The controller network used is identical to the one used by Jordan and Rumelhart but with SRV units substituted for the linear units in the output layer. The evaluation function used by the critic was based directly on the error function used in the indirect method. In our simulations, the direct method learned to solve the task in 1269 trials on the average (over 20 runs). This performance is comparable to that of the indirect method and is obtained without the computational overhead of training and using a model.

2.4.3 Learning to Control an Unstable Dynamic System

The unstable dynamic system picked for the experiments reported in this section is the much-studied one-dimensional cart-pole system [4,11,14,38, 53,68,81,82]. The cart-pole learning control task, also known as the pole-balancing or inverted pendulum problem, involves learning to balance a rigid pole mounted on a mobile cart by applying appropriate forces to the cart. As depicted in Figure 2.14, the cart is restricted to move along a one dimensional track of bounded length. The position and velocity of the cart (x, $\dot{x}$) and the pole (θ, $\dot{\theta}$) represent the state of the cart-pole system, and the dynamics of the system are given by the equations

$$\ddot{x} = \frac{F + ml\,[\dot{\theta}^2 \sin\theta - \ddot{\theta}\cos\theta] - \mu_c \operatorname{sgn}(\dot{x})}{M + m}$$

$$\ddot{\theta} = \frac{g \sin\theta - \ddot{x}\cos\theta - \dfrac{\mu_p \dot{\theta}}{ml}}{l\left[\dfrac{4}{3} - \dfrac{m\cos^2\theta}{M + m}\right]}.$$

Here $M = 1.0$ kg and $m = 0.1$ kg are the masses of the cart and the pole respectively, $l = 0.5$ m is *half* the length of the pole, $\mu_p = 0.000002$ is the coefficient of friction of pole on cart, $\mu_c = 0.0005$ is the coefficient of friction of cart on track, $g = -9.8$ m/s^2 is the acceleration due to gravity, and F is the force applied to the cart. Moreover, in these simulations, the track length

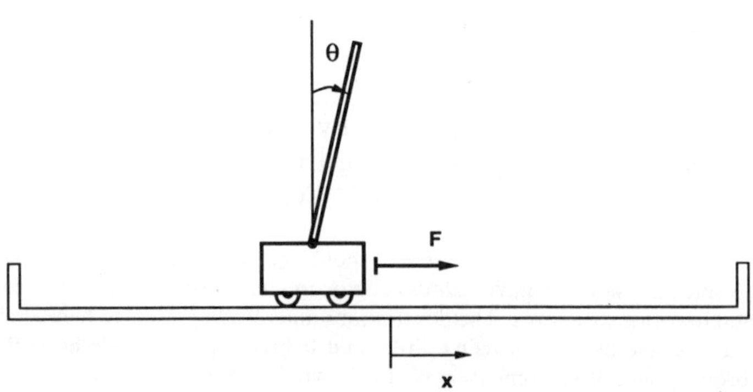

Figure 2.14 *The cart-pole system.*

was 4.8 m. A fourth order Runge–Kutta method with a time step of 0.01 s was used to approximate numerically the solution of these equations.

For this task, training information supplied to the controller is in the form of a failure signal f_{ext} that occurs when the pole falls beyond a critical angle or the cart hits either end of the track. Clearly, the training signal occurs infrequently, creating a difficult *temporal credit assignment problem* [72]. Solutions to this credit assignment problem usually involve training an internal critic network to generate predictions of future evaluations. In the absence of external evaluations, these predictions are used by the learning system as if they were actual evaluations received from the environment. Examples of algorithms used for learning to predict future evaluations include the TD(λ) (temporal difference) family of algorithms developed by Sutton [73] and the related Q-learning algorithm developed by Watkins [75].

As in the previous subsection, the performance of direct and indirect learning methods are compared on this task. The indirect approach, presented by Jordon and Jacobs [38], involves using an internal critic to obtain gradient information for the controller. The direct method is based on reinforcement learning and has been implemented using the Jordan-Jacobs work as a reference, thereby facilitating a direct comparison.

For the cart-pole task, Jordan and Jacobs [38] used the temporal difference algorithm outlined below to train the internal critic. The same algorithm has been used in the simulations reported here. The algorithm was designed to predict z_t, the reciprocal of the time until failure, given the current time step t. Hence z_t should equal 1 on the time step immediately preceding failure, and should also satisfy the relationship

$$\frac{1}{z_t} = \frac{1}{z_{t+1}} + 1.$$

Therefore the error signal used to train the internal critic network to estimate the reciprocal of time until failure is:

$$\varepsilon_{\text{prediction}}(\hat{z}_{t-1}) = \begin{cases} 1/2(1 - \hat{z}_{t-1})^2 & \text{if there is a failure at time } t, \\ 1/2\left(\dfrac{1}{1 + 1/\hat{z}_t} - \hat{z}_{t1}\right)^2 & \text{otherwise,} \end{cases} \tag{2.9}$$

where $\hat{z}_t$ is the estimate produced by the internal critic. Moreover, the evaluation seen by the controller at each time step becomes

$$f_t = \begin{cases} f_{\text{ext}} & \text{if there is a failure at time } t, \\ \hat{z}_t & \text{otherwise.} \end{cases} \tag{2.10}$$

The network architecture used by Jordan and Jacobs [38] is shown in Figure 2.15 (compare with the indirect control architecture shown in Figure 2.3*b*). Although it is very similar to some previously used architectures (e.g., [11,4]), it includes connections (shown as bold lines in Figure 2.15) through

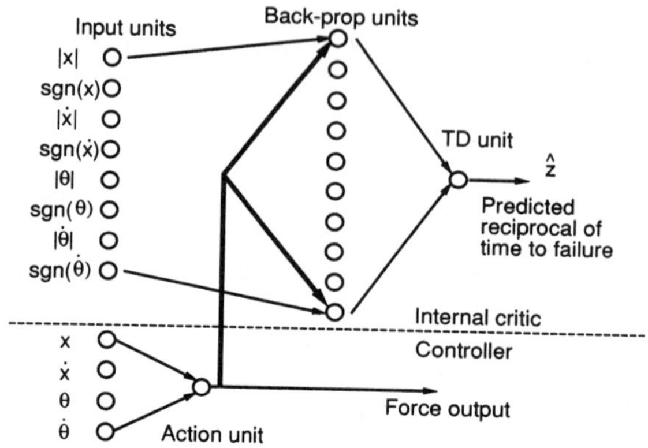

Figure 2.15 *The network architecture used in all the simulations presented in this subsection. The internal critic network has 8 input units, a hidden layer of 10 back-propagation units, and a single temporal difference output unit. The controller has 4 input units and a single-action unit. In simulations of the supervised learning method, a noisy linear unit was used as the action unit, while in simulations of the reinforcement learning method, SRV unit [25] was used.*

which the output of the controller is fed as input to the internal critic.* It is through these connections that error gradients are propagated back to serve as training signals for the controller. The error gradients are computed as follows. Because the goal of the controller is to avoid failure, an appropriate desired evaluation is zero (signifying no failure), and an appropriate distal error function for the controller is

$$\varepsilon_{\text{control}}(f_t) = 1/2(0 - f_t)^2.$$

The corresponding distal error gradient for the controller, f_t, is back-propagated through the internal critic network and through the connections to the controller to provide a proximal error gradient for the controller. The weights of the controller are then adjusted to descend the proximal error gradient, which in turn results in minimizing the distal error and hence driving the evaluation to the desired value of zero. The internal critic network is also trained simultaneously with the controller. In its case, however, back-propagation is used to adjust the weights so as to minimize the prediction error defined in Eq. (2.9).

The architecture of the network used with the direct method was identical to the one used with the indirect method except for one difference (see Figure 2.15). The controller's linear action unit was replaced by a SRV unit [25]. For the direct method, training information for the controller is a reinforcement signal r_t that is computed directly from the evaluation f_t as

* Jordan and Jacobs refer to the internal critic as the *forward model.*

$$r_t = 1.0 - f_t.$$

Maximizing the expected reinforcement therefore results in the desired effect of minimizing the evaluation. The internal critic network is also trained simultaneously, using backpropagation to adjust the weights so as to minimize the prediction error [Eq. (2.9)], as with the indirect method.

Results of the Comparison. Our simulations of the indirect method are replications of those in Jordan and Jacobs [38], and we have tried to keep the differences between simulations of the indirect and direct methods to a minimum. One hundred training runs were performed using both the indirect and direct methods. Each training run represents an attempt to train the network, starting with small random initial weights, to balance the pole. As in [38], a training run lasted until either the pole was balanced for 1000 consecutive time steps or 30,000 failures occurred during the course of the run. Following [38], in all the simulations the controller produced real-valued forces, and we restarted the cart-pole system in a random state after each failure. We also used the input representations in ref. [38] (see Figure 2.15), which take advantage of the symmetries in the cart-pole system dynamics. Furthermore, the learning rate parameters used for the network using the indirect method were also identical to those used in [38].* Instead of optimizing these parameter values for the network using the direct method, the values used with the indirect method were retained.

Additionally, in the simulations using the indirect method, we incorporated Jordan and Jacob's assumption that disturbances in the form of additive noise having a uniform distribution on $[-0.001, 0.001]$ act on the output of the controller. The role of these disturbances is discussed later. In order to evaluate the effect of such disturbances on the direct method, we also ran 100 runs of the direct method with identical noise added to the output of the controller.

When the indirect method was used, 72 out of 100 training runs resulted in success, with the remaining 28 failing to balance the pole on any of 30,000 attempts. The average number of failures before success over all the successful training runs was 11,164.5 and the median was 9244. In the case of the direct method, 93 training runs were successful, with an average number of failures before success of 2385.89, and a median of 1148. When disturbances were added to the output of the reinforcement learning controller, the number of successful runs dropped to 88. The average number of failures before success over all the successful runs was 2689.3 and the median was 1383.5. Histograms of the distribution of the successful training runs in terms of the number of failures before success for each learning method are shown in Figure 2.16.

* These learning rate parameters were 0.05 for the controller and 0.3 for the internal critic network except on the connections from the controller, where the learning rate was 0.9.

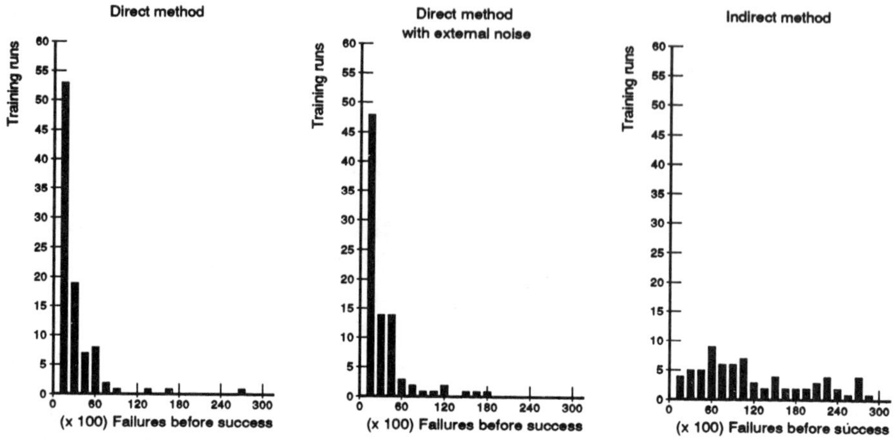

Figure 2.16 *The distributions of the successful training runs in terms of the number of failures before success using each learning method.*

These results indicate a substantial difference between the two learning methods in terms of learning speed and overall learning behavior. Some reasons for these differences are discussed next.

Discussion. One of the reasons that comparison of direct and indirect learning methods on the cart-pole task is particularly meaningful is the necessity of an internal critic for predicting future evaluations in order to solve the temporal credit assignment problem. The internal critic is necessary *regardless* of which of the two learning methods is employed, and has to be built through training experience. Whereas both the direct and indirect methods need the internal critic to obtain evaluations in the absence of the environmental failure signal, the indirect method also uses the *structure* of the internal critic network to translate (via back-propagation) distal errors in evaluations into proximal errors in actions of the controller. Therefore the difference in performance of the two methods essentially arises from differences in the accuracies of the internal critics constructed during training and the manner in which they are used, and *not* from any bias in the task setup or the training information received.*

Let us first consider the problem of building an accurate internal critic. If the internal critic is to produce accurate predictions over all of its input

*If, for example, the environment provided appropriate evaluations at all times, then the direct method would not be required to contruct an internal critic, while the indirect method would still have to do so. Such a situation would be biased in favor of the direct method.

space, it is vital that it sees inputs that are distributed over its entire input space. In other words, exploration of the (state, action) input space is imperative. The two methods under consideration rely on different mechanisms to effect this exploration. In the indirect method, external disturbances in the form of additive white noise are assumed to affect the control output *at all times,* perturbing the actions of the controller and hence introducing variations in the inputs to the internal critic. A potential problem with this approach is the lack of direct control over the noise and hence over the exploration. While higher magnitudes of noise will enable better exploration—leading to a more accurate internal critic and thus to faster acquisition of control—large-magnitude noise is detrimental to the long-term performance of the controller. Conversely, lower noise levels will facilitate stable control after learning but will slow the learning of a useful internal critic and hence the acquisition of control. Unfortunately, because the source of the noise is external to the learning system, its amplitude is clearly beyond the control of the learning system.

In contrast, active exploration of the action space is an integral part of direct methods. In order to discover the best output to produce, direct methods generate actions stochastically and use the resultant evaluations to guide the search for the best output. On the cart-pole task, using reinforcement learning therefore facilitates the desired exploration of the input space of the internal critic. Moreover, direct methods have to directly control the randomness in the output in order to exhibit stable learning behavior. This means that as learning proceeds and performance on the task improves, the exploratory variations in the controller's output decrease, leading to a more stable controller.

The manner in which the internal critic is used to train the controller also has a critical impact on the learning behavior. As discussed earlier, the indirect method is based on the idea of propagating distal errors back along the connections from the controller to the internal critic to serve as training information for the controller. Jordan and Rumelhart [40] show how the back-propagation process computes the gradient of the output of the internal critic with respect to the controller's output. If the controller's training information is to be meaningful, the internal critic has to be reasonably accurate at the current point in (state, action) space, *and* the gradient computed using the internal critic has to have a positive inner product with the true gradient of the output of the internal critic with respect to the controller's actions (see [40], pages 11–13). We have already discussed the factors governing the first condition. The gradient, however, is defined mainly by the weights on the connections from the controller to the internal critic. Therefore the indirect method is critically dependent on the weights on these connections. In other words, the *structure* of the model becomes critical when indirect methods are used.

But because of the redundancy of the information provided to the internal critic via these connections,* the internal critic can make accurate predictions even with arbitrary weights on these connections. While it is true that, in practice, back-propagation tends to drive these weights towards reasonable values, there is reason to believe that the predictions of the internal critic become accurate long before these weights take on meaningful values. This is because accurate predictions are possible independently of these weight values, and once the predictions are accurate, there is no output error to drive the adaptation of these weights. Fully aware of this problem, Jordan and Jacobs [38] sought to mitigate its effect by increasing the learning rate on the connections from the controller to the internal critic. Nonetheless, due to this problem, the provision of meaningful gradient information to the controller is delayed, thereby slowing learning.

In comparison, the direct method relies only on the *output* of the internal critic for its training information. Because the reliability of the predictions of the internal critic is probably higher than that of the gradient estimates obtained using the internal critic's weights, the direct method gets meaningful training information more frequently than the supervised learning method. The drawback of using direct reinforcement learning, however, is that the gradient of the output of the internal critic with respect to the controller's output has to be estimated stochastically. Nevertheless, the results presented indicate that estimation of the gradient by the direct method can be more accurate than estimation of the gradient through the weights of the internal critic.

2.5 CONCLUSIONS

Three control tasks were used in the last section to illustrate how, when the complexity of model construction outweighs the complexity of solving the original control problem, direct reinforcement learning methods can match or surpass the performance of indirect methods. The three tasks were picked to highlight different aspects of the trade-off between direct and indirect methods. For any control problem, the ability to construct an adequate model of the controlled process determines the viability of the indirect approach. With the peg-in-hole insertion task, the main point made was the difficulty of constructing an adequate model under conditions of uncertainty and noise. The inverse kinematics task served to emphasize the trade-off between time spent in acquiring knowledge useful for training the controller (in the form of a model) and using this knowledge to acquire control. The important observation there is that the degree of model accuracy that would ensure fastest acquisition of control is usually not known a priori. Hence,

* Providing the controller's output to the internal critic is redundant because the controller's output is a function of the state of the cart-pole system, which is already provided as input to the internal critic.

optimizing the time spent in model acquisition is very difficult. Finally, the performance comparison on the cart-pole problem underscores the dependence of the indirect method on the appropriateness of the model structure. These results indicate that despite its simplicity, the direct reinforcement learning approach can yield faster, more reliable learning in some control situations. This underscores the importance of considering direct associative reinforcement learning methods as tools for solving control problems.

Acknowledgments

I would like to thank Michael Jordan for providing the simulation package using which some of these simulations were performed and, more importantly, for his advice and many helpful discussions. Andrew Barto and Roderic Grupen provided guidance for which I am grateful. Thanks are also due to Robert Jacobs and Kamal Souccar for their help in conducting the simulations reported here, and to Richard Yee for his comments regarding the presentation. This material is based upon work supported by grants to Andrew Barto from the Air Force Office of Scientific Research, Bolling AFB, (grant AFOSR-89-0526) and by the National Science Foundation (grant ECS-8912623).

REFERENCES

[1] D. H. Ackley, G. E. Hinton, and T. J. Sejnowski, A learning algorithm for Boltzmann machines. *Cognitive Sci.* 9, 147–169 (1985).

[2] J. S. Albus, Mechanisms of planning and problem solving in the brain, *Math. Biosci.* 45, 247–293 (1979).

[3] J. Alspector, R. B. Allen, V. Hu, and S. Satyanarayana, Stochastic learning networks and their electronic implementation, *Proc. IEEE Conf. Neural Information Processing Systems—Natural and Synthetic* (November 1987).

[4] C. W. Anderson, Learning to control an inverted pendulum using neural networks, *IEEE Control Sys. Mag.* 9(3), 31–37 (1989).

[5] C. G. Atkeson and D. J. Reinkensmeyer, Using associative content-addressable memories to control robots, *IEEE Conf. on Decision and Control,* (1988).

[6] H. B. Barlow, Unsupervised learning, *Neural Computation,* 1, 295–311 (1989).

[7] A. G. Barto, "Connectionist Learning for Control: An Overview." Tech. Rep. 89–89, University of Massachusetts, Amherst, Mass. (1989).

[8] A. G. Barto, "Some Learning Tasks from a Control Perspective." COINS Tech. Rep. 91-122, University of Massachusetts, Amherst, Mass. (1991).

[9] A. G. Barto and P. Anandan, Pattern recognizing stochastic learning automata, *IEEE Trans. on Systems, Man, and Cybernetics,* 15, 360–375 (1985).

[10] A. G. Barto and M. I. Jordan, Gradient following without back-propagation in layered networks, *Proc. IEEE 1st Annual Conf. on Neural Networks,* II629–II636, (1987).

[11] A. G. Barto, R. S. Sutton, and C. W. Anderson. Neuronlike elements that can solve difficult learning control problems, *IEEE Trans. on Systems, Man, and Cybernetics,* 13, 835–846 (1983).

[12] A. G. Barto, R. S. Sutton, and P. S. Brouwer, Associative search network: A reinforcement learning associative memory, *IEEE Trans. on Systems, Man, and Cybernetics,* 40, 201–211 (1981).

[13] B. Chandrasekharan and D. W. C. Shen, On expediency and convergence in variable structure automata. *IEEE Trans. on Systems, Man, and Cybernetics,* SSC-4(2), 52–60 (1968).

[14] M. E. Connell and P. E. Utgoff, Learning to control a dynamic physical system. *Comput. Intell.,* 3, 330–337 (1987).

[15] C. S. Draper and Y. J. Li, Principles of optimalizing control systems and an application to an internal combustion engine, *ASME Publications* (September 1951).

[16] R. O. Duda and P. E. Hart, *Pattern Classification and Scene Analysis,* Wiley, New York, 1973.

[17] A. Dvoretzky. On stochastic approximation. *Proc. 3rd Berkeley Symp. on Mathematical Statistics and Probability,* vol. 1, 39–55. University of California Press, Berkeley and Los Angeles, (1956).

[18] B. G. Farley and W. A. Clark, Simulation of self-organizing systems by digital computer. *I.R.E. Trans. Information Theory,* 4, 76–84 (1954).

[19] J. Franklin, "Learning Control of a One Link Robot Arm" ECE Tech. Rep. CCS-87-101, Electrical and Computer Engineering Dept, University of Massachusetts, Amherst, Mass. (February 1987).

[20] J. Franklin, Compliance and Learning: Control Skills for a Robot Operating in an Uncertain World. Ph.D. thesis, University of Massachusetts, Amherst, Mass. (February 1988).

[21] D. E. Goldberg, *Genetic Algorithms in Search, Optimization, and Machine Learning,* Addison-Wesley, Reading, Mass., 1989.

[22] G. C. Goodwin and K. S. Sin, *Adaptive Filtering, Prediction, and Control,* Prentice-Hall, Englewood Cliffs, N.J. 1984.

[23] S. J. Gordon, "Automated assembly using feature localization," Ph.D. thesis Tech. Rep. 932, Massachusetts Institute of Technology, AI Laboratory, MIT, Cambridge, Mass. (1986).

[24] V. Gullapalli, "A Stochastic Algorithm for Learning Real-Valued Functions via Reinforcement Feedback," Tech. Rep. 88-91, University of Massachusetts, Amherst, Mass., (1988).

[25] V. Gullapalli, A stochastic reinforcemnt learning algorithm for learning real-valued functions, *Neural Networks,* 3, 671–692 (1990).

[26] V. Gullapalli, A comparison of supervised and reinforcement learning methods on a reinforcement learning task, *Proc. 1991 IEEE Internat. Symp. on Intelligent Control,* 394–399, (August 1991).

[27] R. E. Gustavson, A theory for the three-dimensional mating of chamfered cylindrical parts, *J. Mechanisms, Transmissions, and Automated Design* (December 1984).

[28] D. A. Handelman, S. H. Lane, and J. J. Gelfand, Goal-directed encoding of task knowledge for robotic skill acquisition, *Proc. 1991 IEEE Internat. Symp. on Intelligent Control,* 388–393 (August 1991).

[29] S. J. Hanson, A stochastic version of the delta rule, *Physica D,* (1989).

[30] E. Harth and E. Tzanakou, Alopex: A stochastic method for determining visual receptive fields, *Vision Research,* 14, 1475–1482 (1974).

[31] R. Hecht-Nielsen, *Neurocomputing,* Addison-Wesley, Reading, Mass., 1989.

[32] G. E. Hinton, "Distributed Representations," Tech. Rep. CMU-CS-84-157, Dept Computer Science, Carnegie-Mellon University, Pittsburgh, Pa. (1984).

[33] G. E. Hinton, Connectionist learning procedures, Tech. Rep. CMU-CS-87-115, Dept Computer Science, Carnegie-Mellon University, Pittsburgh, Pa (1987).

[34] F. A. M. Ivaldi, J. McIntyre, and E. Bizzi, Kinematic networks—A distributed model for representing and regularizing motor redundancy, *Biol. Cybernetics,* 60, 1–16 (1988).

[35] M. Jabri and B. Flower, "Weight Perturbation: An Optimal Architecture and Learning Technique for Analog VLSI feedforward and Recurrent Multi-layer Networks," Tech. Rep. School of Electrical Engineering, University of Sydney, (1991).

[36] M. I. Jordan, "Supervised Learning and Systems with Excess Degrees of Freedom," Tech. Rep. 88-27, University of Massachusetts, Amherst, Mass. (1988).

[37] M. I. Jordan, "Indeterminate motor skill learning problems" in M. Jeannerod, Ed., *Attention and Performance, XIII,* MIT Press, Cambridge, Mass. 1990.

[38] M. I. Jordan and R. A. Jacobs. "Learning to Control an Unstable System with Forward Modeling," in D. S. Touretzky, Ed., *Advances in Neural Information Processing Systems II,* Morgan Kaufman, San Mateo, Calif. 1990.

[39] M. I. Jordan and D. A. Rosenbaum, "Action," in M. I. Posner, Ed., *Foundations of Cognitive Science,* MIT Press, Cambridge, Mass. 1989.

[40] M. I. Jordan and D. E. Rumelhart, "Forward Models: Supervised Learning with a Distal Teacher," Center for Cognitive Science Occasional Paper #40, MIT, Cambridge, Mass., (1990).

[41] M. Kawato, "Computational Schemes and Neural Network Models for Formation and Control of Multijoint Arm Trajectory," in T. Miller, R. S. Sutton, and P. J. Werbos, Ed., *Neural Networks for Control,* MIT Press, Cambridge, Mass. 1990.

[42] M. Kawato, K. Furukawa, and R. Suzuki, A hierarchical neural-network model for control and learning of voluntary movement, *Biol. Cybernetics,* 57, 169–185 (1987).

[43] M. Kawato, Y. Uno, M. Isobe, and R. Suzuki, Hierarchical neural-network model for voluntary movement with application to robotics, *IEEE Control Systems Mag.,* 8, 8–16 (1988).

[44] J. Kiefer and J. Wolfowitz, Stochastic estimation of the maximum of a regression function, *Ann. Math. Stat.,* 23(3) (1952).

[45] M. Kuperstein, Adaptive visual-motor coordination in multijoint robots using parallel architecture, *IEEE Internat. Conf. on Robotics and Automation,* 1595–1602 (1987).

[46] Y. le Cun, Une procedure d'apprentissage pour reseau a sequil assymetrique [A learning procedure for asymmetric threshold network], *Proc. Cognitiva,* 85, 599–604, (1985).

[47] R. Linsker, "An Application of the Principle of Maximum Information Preservation to Linear Systems, in D. S. Touretzky, Ed. *Advances in Neural Information Processing Systems I,* Morgan Kaufman, San Mateo, Calif., 1989.

[48] R. P. Lipmann, An introduction to computing with neural nets, *IEEE ASSP Mag. 4–22 (April 1987).*

[49] P. Mars. "Neural Nets and Robotic Control, Tech. Rep. RIPRREP/1000/33/88, School of Engineering and Applied Science, University of Durham, Durham, UK (1988).

[50] L. Massone and E. Bizzi, "A Neural Network Model of Limb Trajectory Formation," Tech. Report, Department of Brain and Cognitive Sciences, MIT, Cambridge, Mass. 1988.

[51] J. L. McClelland and D. E. Rumelhart, Eds, *Explorations in Parallel Distributed Processing: A Handbook of Models, Programs, and Exercises,* Bradford Books/MIT Press, Cambridge, Mass. 1988.

[52] J. M. Mendel and R. W. McLaren, "Reinforcement Learning Control and Pattern Recognition Systems, J. M. Mendel and K. S. Fu, Eds., *Adaptive, Learning and Pattern Recognition Systems: Theory and Applications,* Academic Press, New York, 1970, 287–318.

[53] D. Michie and R. A. Chambers, "BOXES: An Experiment in Adaptive Control," in E. Dale and D. Michie, Eds., *Machine Intelligence 2,* Oliver and Boyd, White Plains, N.Y., 1968, 137–152.

[54] W. T. Miller, Sensor based control of robotic manipulators using a general learning algorithm, *IEEE J. Robotics and Automation,* 3, 157–165 (1987).

[55] Y. Miyata, "The Learning and Planning of Actions," ICS Rep. 8802, Institute for Cognitive Science, University of California at San Diego, La Jolla, Calif. (1988).

[56] J. Moody and C. Darken, "Learning with Localized Receptive Fields," in D. S. Touretsky, G. E. Hinton, and T. J. Sejnowski, Eds., *Proc. 1988 Connectionist Models Summer School,* Morgan Kaufmann, San Mateo, Calif. (1988).

[57] A. W. Moore, Efficient Memory-based Learning for Robot Control, Ph.D. thesis, Tech. Rep. 209, Computer Laboratory, Cambridge University, (October 1990).

[58] P. Munro, A dual back-propagation scheme for scalar reward learning, *Proc. 9th Annual Conf. Cognitive Science Society,* 165–176, (1987).

[59] K. S. Narendra and M. A. L. Thathachar, *Learning Automata: An Introduction.* Prentice Hall, Englewood Cliffs, N.J. 1989.

[60] J. L. Nevins and D. E. Whitney, Computer controlled assembly, *Science,* 238(2) (February 1978).

[61] D. Nguyen and B. Widrow, "The Truck Backer-upper: An Example of Self-learning in Neural Networks." in T. Miller, R. S. Sutton, and P. J. Werbos, Eds., *Neural Networks for Control.* MIT Press, Cambridge, Mass., 1990.

[62] M. Niranjan and F. Fallside, "Neural Networks and Radial Basis Functions in Classifying Static Speech Patterns," Tech. Rep. CUED/F-INFENG/TR 22, University Engineering Dept., Cambridge University, (1988).

[63] D. B. Parker, "Learning Logic." Tech. Rep. TR-47, MIT Cambridge, Mass., (1985).

[64] H. Robbins and S. Monro, A stochastic approximation method, *Ann. Math. Stat.,* 22(1), 400–407 (1951).

[65] D. E. Rumelhart, G. E. Hinton, and R. J. Williams, "Learning Internal Representations by Error Propagation," in D. E. Rumelhart and J. L. McClelland, Eds., *Parallel Distributed Processing: Explorations in the Microstructure of Cognition, Vol. 1: Foundations.* Bradford Books/MIT Press, Cambridge, Mass., 1986.

[66] D. E. Rumelhart and J. L. McClelland, Ed. *Parallel Distributed Processing: Explorations in the Microstructure of Cognition, Vol. 1: Foundations, Vol. 2: Psychological and Biological models.* Bradford Books/MIT Press, Cambridge, Mass., 1986.

[67] T. D. Sanger, "Optimal Unsupervised Learning in Feedforward Neural Networks," Master's thesis, MIT, Cambridge, Mass., (1988).

[68] O. Selfridge, R. S. Sutton, and A. G. Barto, Training and tracking in robotics, *Proc. 9th Internat. Joint Conf. Artificial Intelligence,* (August 1985).

[69] J. Simons, H. V. Brussel, J. D. Schutter, and J. Verhaert, A self-learning automation with variable resolution for high precision assembly by industrial robots, *IEEE Trans. on Automatic Control,* 27(5), 1109–1113 (October 1982).

[70] V. Srinivasan, A. G. Barto, and B. E. Ydstie, Pattern recognition and feedback via parallel distributed processing, in *Annual Meeting AIChE* (November 1988), (abstract to appear).

[71] R. S. Sutton, Ballistic Bug, (June 1982), (Unpublished working paper).

[72] R. S. Sutton, "Temporal Credit Assignment in Reinforcement Learning," Ph.D. thesis, University of Massachusetts, Amherst, Mass. (1984).

[73] R. S. Sutton. Learning to predict by the methods of temporal differences, *Machine Learning,* 3, 9–44 (1988).

[74] M. L. Tsetlin, *Automaton Theory and Modeling of Biological Systems,* Academic Press, New York, 1973.

[75] C. J. C. H. Watkins, "Learning from Delayed Rewards," Ph.D. thesis, Cambridge University, Cambridge, England (1989).

[76] P. J. Werbos, "Beyond Regression: New Tools for Prediction and Analysis in the Behavioral Sciences," Ph.D. thesis, Harvard University (1974).

[77] P. J. Werbos, Backpropagation and neurocontrol: A review and prospectus, in *Proc. 1989 Internat. Joint Conf. Neural Networks* (June 1989).

[78] P. J. Werbos, "A Menu of Designs for Reinforcement Learning Over Time," in T. Miller, R. S. Sutton, and P. J. Werbos, Eds., *Neural Networks for Control,* chapter 3. The MIT Press, Cambridge, Mass., 1990.

[79] D. E. Whitney, Quasi-static assembly of compliantly supported rigid parts, *J. Dynamic Systems, Measurement, and Control,* 104 (March 1982). Also in *Robot Motion: Planning and Control,* Brady, M., et al. Eds., MIT Press, Cambridge, Mass., 1982.

[80] B. Widrow, J. McCool, and B. Medoff, Adaptive control by inverse modeling, in *Twelfth Asilomar Conf. Circuits, Systems, and Computers*. (1978).

[81] B. Widrow and F. W. Smith, Pattern-recognizing control systems, in *Proc. Computer and Information Sciences (COINS)*. (1964).

[82] A. P. Wieland, Evolving controls for unstable systems, in D. S. Touretsky, J. L. Elman, T. J. Sejnowski, and G. E. Hinton, Eds., *Connectionist Models: Proc. of the 1990 Summer School,* Morgan Kaufmann, San Mateo, Calif. (1991).

[83] R. J. Williams, "Reinforcement Learning in Connectionist Networks: A Mathematical Analysis," Tech. Rep. ICS 8605, Institute for Cognitive Science, University of California at San Diego, La Jolla, Calif., (1986).

[84] R. J. Williams, "Reinforcement-learning Connectionist Systems," Tech. Rep NU-CCS-87-3, College of Computer Science, Northeastern University, Boston, Mass., (1987).

[85] R. J. Williams. On the use of backpropagation in associative reinforcement learning, in *Proc. IEEE Internat. Conf. Neural Networks,* (1988).

CHAPTER 3

Knowledge Acquisition for Dynamic System Control

TANJA URBANČIČ
IVAN BRATKO

3.1 INTRODUCTION

Dynamic system control sometimes has to be achieved in circumstances that are very inconvenient for classical control methods. First, it may be too expensive, or even impossible, to obtain numerical values of the system parameters and variables required for conventional controllers. Second, problems arise when the system to be controlled is highly nonlinear or has time-varying parameters. Finally, sometimes a quantitative, differential equations model is not available. Some alternative artificial intelligence (AI) based approaches promise to overcome these problems. Dealing mostly with qualitative information, these methods potentially provide fast, robust, and understandable control. Control is provided by applying control rules that specify how to react if the system is in a given qualitative state. This chapter describes how *machine learning* [1] and *qualitative modeling* [2] can be used for automatic synthesis of control rules. It shows that the learning approach can be improved by incorporating knowledge into the learning process, and introduces a model-based method by which such knowledge can be derived automatically. As a case study, the task of inverted pendulum control is discussed.

The task of inverted pendulum control has often been chosen to demonstrate and test classical [3,4] and other control techniques [5–9]. The in-

Dynamic, Genetic, and Chaotic Programming, By Branko Souček and the IRIS Group.
ISBN 0-471-55717-X

verted pendulum, usually realized as a pole on a cart, is an example of an inherently unstable, multiple-output system. Besides being an attractive bench-mark problem, the pole-balancing task has much in common with some tasks of greater practical importance, such as two-legged walking and satellite attitude control [10].

The chapter is organized as follows. Section 3.2 describes the inverted pendulum control problem and briefly surveys the existing solutions. In Section 3.3, programs that learn to control the inverted pendulum are outlined. The effects that a simple method of using knowledge has on the learning process are explored. Section 3.4 is devoted to automatic generation of control rules for the inverted pendulum from the probabilistic qualitative model.

3.2 TASK: INVERTED PENDULUM CONTROL

The system to be controlled consists of a rigid pole and a cart. The cart can move left or right on a bounded track. The pole is hinged to the top of the cart so that it can swing in the vertical plane (see Fig. 3.1). A force of fixed magnitude is applied to the cart in the left or right direction to prevent the pole from falling while keeping the cart within the track.

A state of the cart-pole system is determined with the qualitative values of the following variables:

x = position of the cart,
v = velocity of the cart,
fi = inclination angle of the pole,
fiv = angular velocity of the pole.

The allowed range of each variable is divided into a few intervals that correspond to the qualitative values of the variables. Although very important, the question of determining appropriate intervals will not be discussed here.

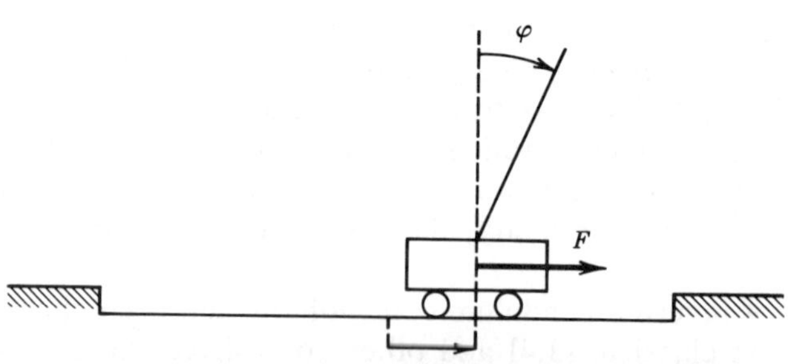

Figure 3.1 *Inverted pendulum.*

Time is measured in steps. At each step we measure qualitative values of *x*, *v*, *fi*, and *fiv* and decide whether to change the force direction. If the values of one or more variables are out of the allowed range, the system is considered to be in a qualitative state "fail."

The system being controlled has the following characteristics:

- It is nonlinear (see the inverted pendulum dynamic equations, Eqs. (3.1) and (3.2)).

$$\ddot{\varphi} = \frac{g \sin \varphi + \cos \varphi \cdot \left[\dfrac{-F - ml\,\dot{\varphi}^2 \sin \varphi}{M + m}\right]}{l\left[\dfrac{4}{3} - \dfrac{m \cos^2 \varphi}{M + m}\right]} \tag{3.1}$$

$$\ddot{x} = \frac{F + ml[\dot{\varphi}^2 \sin \varphi - \ddot{\varphi} \cos \varphi]}{M + m} \tag{3.2}$$

where M = mass of the cart
m = mass of the pole
l = distance from center of mass of pole to the pivot
g = acceleration due to gravity

- It is unstable.
- It is a multiple output system, where more than one variable is to be controlled by only one control force of a limited magnitude.

Classical methods [4,11] can be applied to control the system under several assumptions, including the following:

- Dynamics of the system can be approximated with linear equations (in our case this is true for small values of *fi*).
- System parameters are constant, and their numerical values are known.
- Sufficiently accurate numerical values of the system variables are available.

Michie and Chambers [5] show that an inverted pendulum can be controlled under more relaxed conditions. Their program BOXES uses qualitative instead of numerical values of the variables. Moreover, BOXES learns to control the system without knowing anything about the system dynamics. This approach was further investigated in the context of neural networks [6,8,12] and will be reviewed in Section 3.3.

Another important qualitative solution to the inverted pendulum control problem was found by Makarovič [9]. By reasoning qualitatively about a quantitative, differential equations model, he derived a simple, but surprisingly effective, control rule. As reported, it never failed with a numerical simulator, provided the initial state was within a specified region. Here is the control rule found by Makarovič:

if $fiv > fiv_1$ **then** action RIGHT
else if $fiv < fiv_2$ **then** action LEFT
else if $fi > fi_1$ **then** action RIGHT
else if $fi < fi_2$ **then** action LEFT
else if $v > v_1$ **then** action RIGHT
else if $v < v_2$ **then** action LEFT
else if $x > x_1$ **then** action RIGHT
else if $x < x_2$ **then** action LEFT

Džeroski [11] experimented with rules of the same structure but with the variables ordered in different ways. He found that no less than seven permutations of the variables yielded successful control rules.

Bratko [13] showed how a correct control rule can be formally derived from a very simple QSIM-type qualitative model of the pole-on-cart system. Džeroski [11] observed that this rule is equivalent (up to the values of parameters in the rule) to the "classical" control rule that follows from the application of the calculus of variations to the full differential equations model of pole-on-cart.

3.3 LEARNING CONTROL RULES

3.3.1 Learning To Control a "Black Box"

This section gives basic principles and characteristics of methods used so far to learn control rules. It presents advantages and disadvantages of these methods when solving the inverted pendulum control task. The algorithms BOXES [5], AHC [6,12], and CART [7] are chosen as the most widely known representatives. The survey is based on [5–7,12], on the comparative paper by Sammut [14], and on our experiments with BOXES and AHC.

The starting point, common to all approaches presented here is the assumption that nothing is known about the system being controlled. Programs learn through experiments. Due to the "black box" assumption, initial control decisions are practically random, thus resulting in very short survival times in the first experiments. On the basis of experiments, control decisions are evaluated and possibly changed. Learning takes place until a certain success criterion, usually an experiment with a prescribed period of successful control, is met. The programs are briefly outlined next.

BOXES learns to obtain a reasonable state-action table, or a set of rules that specify action to be applied to the system in a given state. This would not be possible for the original, infinite state-space. The problem becomes tractable by dividing the state-space into "boxes." A box is defined as a

Cartesian product of qualitative values of the system variables, each qualitative value being an interval from a predefined partition. All the ponts within a box are mapped to the same control decision. During one trial, the state-action table is fixed. After a failure detection, meaning the trial is finished, decisions are evaluated with respect to the accumulated numerical information: How many times did the system enter a particular state? How successful was it after particular decisions? and so forth. The following information is accumulated for each qualitative state:

LL = *left life*	Weighted sum of survivals after left decisions taken in this state during previous trials;
RL = *right life*	The same for right decisions;
LU = *left usage*	Weighted sum of the number of left decisions taken in this state during previous trials;
RU = *right usage*	The same for right decisions;
$T_1, T_2, \ldots, T_n$	Times (i.e., steps) at which the system enters this state during the current trial.

After the trial fails, the program updates the figures. For the states in which decision left was taken, the new values are

$$LL_{\text{new}} = LL \cdot DK + \sum_{i=1}^{N} (T_F - T_i)$$

$$LU_{\text{new}} = LU \cdot DK + N$$

$$RL_{\text{new}} = RL \cdot DK$$

$$RU_{\text{new}} = RU \cdot DK$$

where N = number of entries into the state during the run
DK = constant that weights recent experience relative to earlier experience ($DK < 1$)
K = constant that weights global experience relative to local experience
T_F = time when failure occurs

Analogous updates are made for the states with decision right.

For the whole system, GL (global life) and GU (global usage) are computed after each trial:

$$GL_{\text{new}} = GL \cdot DK + T_F$$

$$GU_{\text{new}} = GU \cdot DK + 1$$

These values are used for a numerical evaluation of the success for both actions. The estimates are computed after a trial for each qualitative state:

$$V_{\text{left}} = \frac{LL + K(GL/GU)}{LU + K}$$

and

$$V_{\text{right}} = \frac{RL + K(GL/GU)}{RU + K}$$

The program compares the quality estimates for both actions and chooses the action with the higher estimate to be applied in the state during the next trial.

The AHC (adaptive heuristic control) algorithm follows BOXES in state-space division into qualitative states. It implements learning by two neuronlike elements: ASE (associative search element) and ACE (adaptive critical element). The first learns to choose actions, while the second learns to predict failure and constructs a more informative evaluation function than the failure signal alone can provide. While in BOXES learning takes place only at the end of each trial, AHC also learns during trials.

The CART algorithm decides whether to repeat the last action or to change it at each time step of an experiment. Through heuristic rules, some states are recognized as "desirable," while some others are "undesirable." The estimates for other states are computed by interpolation. Vector analysis in the phase space is carried out for estimating the effect of an action. In the case of a transition toward a more desirable state, the last action is repeated, otherwise it is changed.

We now survey some common advantages and disadvantages of black-box learning as a method for control synthesis. The biggest advantage of black-box learning is its ability to learn without any knowledge about the system being controlled. Next, it is successful in achieving control. More precisely, it has been experimentally verified that a numerical simulator of inverted pendulum can survive 10,000 steps (in our case, this means 200 s) without failure under control obtained by BOXES, AHC, or CART [14,15]. Finally, its amazing *adaptiveness* must be mentioned. Selfridge et al. [12] report on experiments with AHC where the system with standard parameters (Fig. 3.2) was successfully controlled after approximately 70 trials. After that, in less than 20 additional trials, control of a considerably changed system was obtained, no matter whether pole mass, pole length, or track length was changed. According to Connell and Utgoff [7], CART has also mastered all these changes.

However, one can also observe some weaknesses, such as

- Unreliable repeated use of the obtained state-action tables, further explored in Section 3.3.2,

System Parameters

Mass of the cart: $M = 1$ kg
Mass of the pole: $m = 0.1$ kg
Length of the pole: $l = 1$ m
Acceleration due to gravity: $g = 9.8$ m/s^2
Force magnitude: $F = 10$ N

Partition

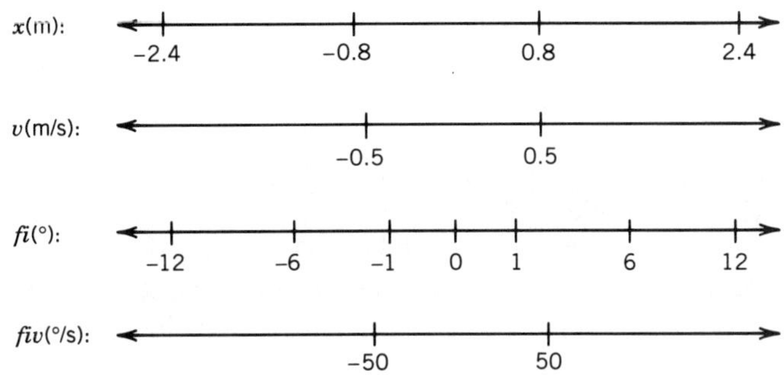

Initial State Constraints $-0.1 \text{ m} < x < 0.1 \text{ m}$
$-6° < fi < 6°$
$v = 0$ m/s
$fiv = 0$°/s

Allowed Region $-2.4 \text{ m} < x < 2.4 \text{ m}$
$-12° < fi < 12°$

Figure 3.2 *Specification of the cart-pole system used in the learning experiments.*

- Important role of ad hoc determined numerical parameters, which make the methods nontransparent and limit their generality,
- Poor explanation capabilities.

Besides, learning is longer than necessary, because the assumption that nothing is known hardly ever corresponds to the real situation.

3.3.2 Adding Knowledge to Learning: Experiments with BOXES

To see how adding domain knowledge affects speed and results of learning, three series of experiments were done. The following variants of learning control rules with program BOXES were explored:

A. Without domain knowledge,
B. With partial domain knowledge, considered as correct and therefore frozen,
C. With partial domain knowledge, allowed to be changed during learning.

The following rule served as partial domain knowledge:

$$\textbf{if } fiv > fiv_1 \textbf{ then } \text{action RIGHT} \qquad (*)$$
$$\textbf{else if } fiv < fiv_2 \textbf{ then } \text{action LEFT}$$

Thresholds $fiv_1 > 0$ and $fiv_2 < 0$ are defined in advance. The rule is *partial* because it specifies action only for some states. The rule is intuitively clear, meaning that too large an angular velocity of the pole requires action RIGHT if the pole is falling to the right, and action LEFT in the opposite case. This is the first part of Makarovič's rule (see Section 3.2).

The differences among the variants A, B, and C are as follows. In case A, learning begins with the table that assigns action LEFT to all the states. In cases B and C, initialization follows the rule (*) for the states covered by the rule, whereas to the others action LEFT is assigned. Further, in cases A and C, all the boxes are subject to learning. On the other hand, in case B only the boxes not covered by the rule (*) learn, while the others retain the action specified by the rule.

Two issues were examined: speed of learning and performances of obtained state-action tables. Therefore, the course of the experiments in each of the three cases was the following. First, the learning process was executed 15 times, resulting in 15 state-action tables. Each time the learning process was completed when a 10,000-step survival (i.e., 200 s) was attained. The number of trials needed for achieving 10,000-step survival was taken as a measure of learning speed. Second, to test the performances of generated knowledge, a numerical simulator of the cart-pole system was controlled 20 times by each obtained state-action table. The reliability of each table was measured as the proportion of successful applications of this table, meaning the proportion of tests ended with 10,000-step survival. Of course, we were interested also in the average survival time achieved by the obtained tables.

In the experiments, all the parameters of the system, discretization of the state-space, initial conditions, and the allowed region were the same as given by Sammut [14] (see Fig. 3.2). The success criterion (i.e., 10,000 steps without failure) and the equations used by the numerical simulator were also the same. For $fiv_{1,2}$ in (*) the values 50° /s were chosen.

The experimental results are collected in Table 3.1.

TABLE 3.1 Comparison of Experimental Results

	Length of Learning Process (aver. no. of trials)	Average Reliability (ratio)	Average Survival (steps)
A	427	3/20	4894
B	50	10/20	7069
C	197	4/20	4679

Comparison of the results for cases A and B shows a great influence of partial knowledge. The learning speed was increased by a factor of 8, reliability by a factor of 3. Rule (*) alone was not effective at all. The system controlled only by rule (*) survived approximately 30 steps (average from 100 experiments). Still, it helped considerably when combined with learning. As expected, the results in case C were between the results of cases A and B. In case C the system's decisions were updated even if the new decision contradicted rule (*). In this respect the system in case C did not show any "awareness" of possessing some knowledge.

Another improvement due to the incorporation of simple control rules is illustrated in Figure 3.3. A characteristic course of learning with the original algorithm (case A) is presented in Figure 3.3*a* and a typical learning in case B is in Figure 3.3*b*. In case A, even after many good trials, extremely bad ones appear frequently. In case B this phenomenon was reduced.

As shown, the learning approach can be improved by incorporating partial knowledge into the learning process. The next section introduces a model-based method by which such knowledge can be derived automatically.

3.4 GENERATING CONTROL RULES FROM A QUALITATIVE MODEL

3.4.1 Probabilistic Qualitative Model of the Inverted Pendulum

In our approach, model *m* is defined as a relation among the current state, the action (i.e., control force), and the next state: *m(CurrentState, Action, NewState)*, meaning that if the system is in *CurrentState,* after a certain time interval it can be in *NewState* if *Action* is performed.

CurrentState and *NewState* are qualitative states. As described in Section 3.2, a qualitative state is determined by qualitative values of the four system variables, where a qualitative value of a variable is one of the predefined intervals. In our model, the partition is very similar to the one introduced by Michie and Chambers [5]. We distinguish five qualitative values of x, v, and *fi* (near_zero, small_positive, large_positive, small_negative, large_negative) and three values for *fiv* (near_zero, positive, negative). Accordingly, the system can be in one of the $375 = 5 \times 5 \times 5 \times 3$ possible qualitative states or in the state "fail."

Although the real value 0 is usually chosen to separate two different qualitative values, this partitioning is different. In this partition, a small positive real value and the corresponding negative value border the interval that represents qualitative value near_zero. This decision is justified because inaccuracy is inherent in every measurement. For example, a small positive value can be measured as negative. Qualitative reasoning based on such a wrong observation would necessarily lead to wrong conclusions, especially when an unstable, rapidly changing system is considered. In such cases it is probably safer to make no conclusion than a wrong one.

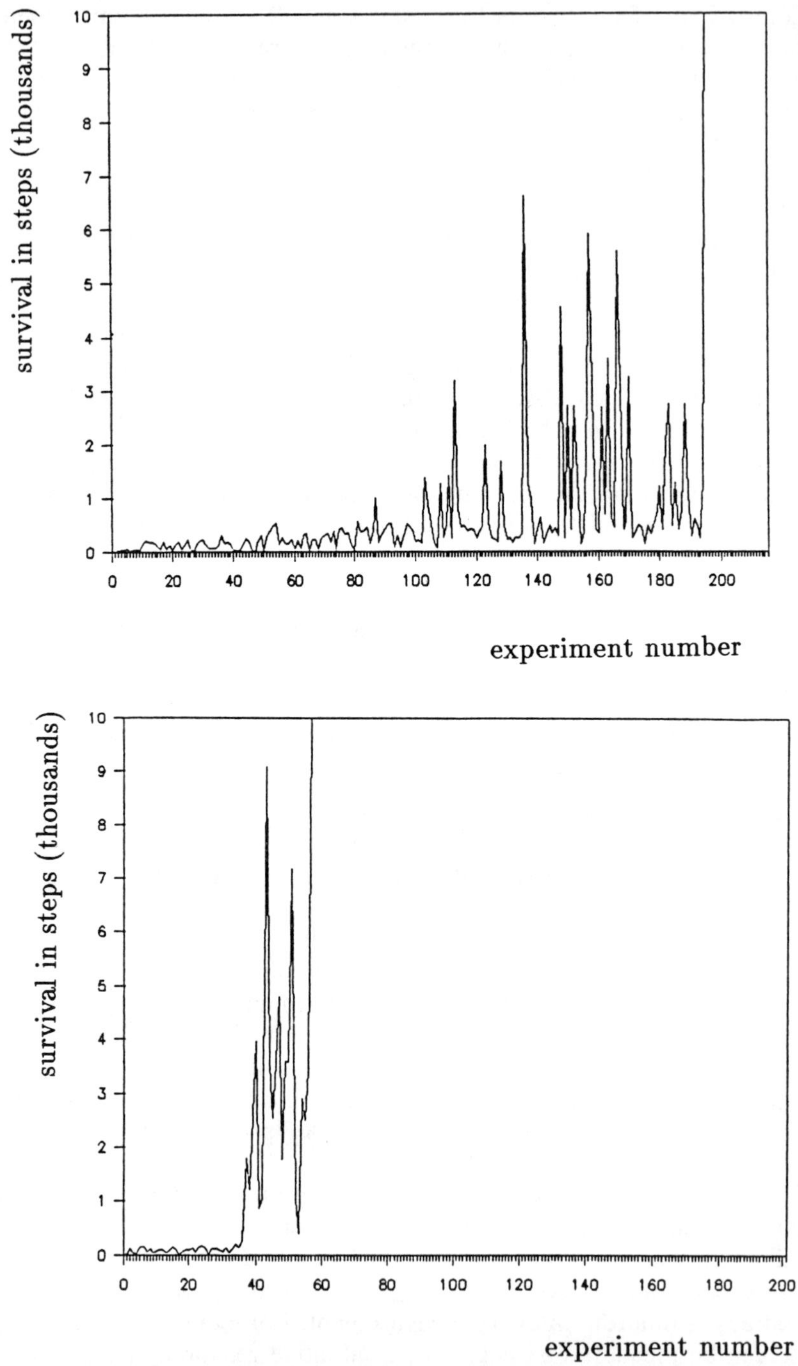

Figure 3.3 *A typical course of learning* (a) *with BOXES without knowledge (variant A),* (b) *with BOXES combined with the rule (*) (variant B).*

State transitions are determined using simplified dynamic equations and interval arithmetic [15]. Each continuous function f: $\mathbf{R} \rightarrow \mathbf{R}$ is replaced by a function F: $\mathbf{R} \times \mathbf{R} \rightarrow \mathbf{R} \times \mathbf{R}$ such that for $I = (x_1, x_2)$, $F(I)$ is defined as

$$F(I) = (\min_{x \in I} f(x), \quad \max_{x \in I} f(x))$$

Similarly, a function f: $\mathbf{R} \times \mathbf{R} \rightarrow \mathbf{R}$ has a corresponding function F such that for intervals I_1 and I_2 the definition of $F(I_1, I_2)$ is

$$F(I_1, I_2) = (\min_{\substack{x \in I_1 \\ y \in I_2}} f(x, y), \quad \max_{\substack{x \in I_1 \\ y \in I_2}} f(x, y))$$

If $F(I_1, I_2)$ is used to get a qualitative value of x, v, fi, or fiv, it must be projected onto the predefined intervals, which represent qualitative values of the corresponding variable. At this step, there is some loss of information. Knowing that $F(I_1, I_2)$ has a nonempty intersection with several qualitative values of the variable, one can only say that the actual numerical value corresponds to one of these qualitative values. Therefore, it is usually impossible to predict exactly in which qualitative state the system will be after a given time interval. The degree of nondeterminism can be reduced by incorporating probabilities into the model. An estimate of probability is assigned to every transition from state S to state S_i. Transition probabilities are also estimated using interval arithmetic. The refined model is now $m(S, A, S_i, p_i)$, where p_i is the estimated probability of the immediate transition from state S to state S_i under control action A, and $A \in \{+, -\}$ denotes the direction of the control force. The probability estimates were computed under the assumption that all the values within intervals were equally likely. It was verified by random simulation that this assumption produced rather accurate estimates of transition probabilities. The model is described in more detail in [16].

By qualitative simulation of the model, all possible transitions together with the respective probabilities can be generated for every qualitative state of the system. Probabilities for transitions to "fail" can also be estimated. This can be done for each qualitative state and for both control actions available (i.e., + or −), resulting in the description of the system's behavior in the form of a probabilistic *state transition graph*.

3.4.2 Building Control Rules

The state transition graph can be used for comparison of the effects of different control decisions, and, consequently, for the construction of *control rules*. The idea is outlined in Figure 3.4.

When controlling an unstable system such as the inverted pendulum, it is important that decisions about actions be made as fast as possible. There-

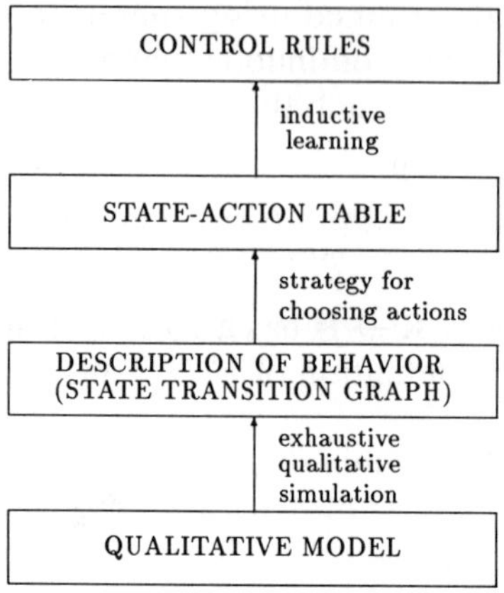

Figure 3.4 *Synthesis of control rules from a qualitative model. The point of inductive learning here is to compress the state-action table.*

fore, we decided to create a state-action table, which is a set of control rules of the form

if *qualitative state S* **then** *action A*

The rules determine which action is to be applied to the system in a qualitative state. A state-action table can be compressed by automatic inductive learning (e.g., Bratko [1]).

The main problem is how to determine appropriate actions for all qualitative states. Each pair (S, A) has to be evaluated with respect to a certain criterion. For each qualitative state S, the action that maximizes the value of (S, A) is chosen. In our approach, the evaluation criterion is the probability of surviving N steps of qualitative simulation without failure (N is a fixed parameter). The qualitative model is used to estimate the probability of surviving N steps of simulation.

Let the system be in qualitative state S. The probability of surviving N steps, assuming the "optimal" action at each step, can be estimated by the recursive function $p_{\text{life}}(S, N)$:

$$p_{\text{life}}(S,0) = \begin{cases} 1 & \text{if } S \neq \textit{fail} \\ 0 & \text{if } S = \textit{fail} \end{cases}$$

$$p_{\text{life}}(S, N) = \begin{cases} \max\limits_{A \in \{+,-\}} \Big(\sum\limits_{m(S,A,S_i,p_i)} p_i p_{\text{life}}(S_i, N-1) \Big), & N \geq 1 \\ 0 \quad \text{if } S = \textit{fail} \end{cases}$$

Since N is fixed, the value $p_{\text{life}}(S,N)$ can be computed for each state S from the exhaustively tabulated relation m. The action that maximizes the value of the expression

$$\sum_{m(S,A,S_i,p_i)} p_i p_{\text{life}}(S_i, N-1)$$

is to be assigned to state S. To avoid unreliable and unconvincing decisions, action remains unspecified if the difference between the compared values is less than ε.

3.4.3 Results

Two groups of state-action tables were built. First, N was fixed at 1, making the decision strategy equivalent to the immediate failure avoiding. For generating a state transition graph, qualitative simulation with a force of fixed magnitude F_{gen} was used. Experimenting with $F_{\text{gen}} = 1, 5, 10, 15$, and 50 N (newtons), we obtained five state transition graphs. From each graph, a state-action table was generated by applying the decision criterion described in the previous section. A second group of state-action tables was built in the same way, with F_{gen} fixed at 1 N while varying N from 1 to 30. The threshold ε was set to 0.01 in all the experiments.

The state-action tables were tested experimentally, and 100 experiments were performed with each state-action table. At the beginning of each experiment, all state variables were set to zero; the time step was 0.02 s. At each time step, a control force of fixed magnitude $F_{\text{con}} = 1$ N was applied in the positive or negative direction, according to the tested state-action table. When the system was in a state with the action unspecified, the force direction was chosen randomly. Survival was measured in time steps. Execution ended when one of the variables fell out of range.

A numerical simulator of the cart-pole system was used in the experiments. The simulator uses the same equations of motion as Anderson [8] to compute accelerations, and the corrected Euler method to obtain the values of v, x, fiv, and fi. All parameters of the system are the same as in Anderson [8]. Results are presented for each group of state-action tables separately.

Group 1:* N = *1, F_{gen} = 1, 5, 10, 15, 20, 50. Test results of the state-action tables from the first group are gathered in Table 3.2. Best results were achieved with the table when a force of 10 N was used for simulation while generating the state transition graph. With this table and $F_{\text{con}} = 1$ N for control, the average survival was 439 steps; the longest experiment (2362 steps) corresponded to 47.24 s of control. This result reveals an interesting phenomenon of *exaggeration:* Reasoning about control with untrue, exaggerated parameters of the system produces better control than reasoning

TABLE 3.2 Control Performance of State-Action Tables, Obtained by the Strategy of Avoiding Immediate Failure

State-action Table	Survival			
F_{gen}	Average	Max.	Min.	Out of Range
1	84	169	71	*fiv, v*
5	85	132	66	*fiv, v*
10	439	2362	156	*v, x*
20	73	120	58	*fiv*
50	42	87	21	*fiv*

with true values of the parameters. This phenomenon is analyzed in detail in Section 3.4.4.

In additional experiments, some extent of *robustness* was noticed. The same table (F_{gen} = 10 N) was successfully applied to the control with F_{con} = 5 N (average from 100 experiments: 408 steps, maximum: 1577 steps) and to the control with F_{con} = 10 N (average: 414 steps, maximum: 1302 steps).

Surprisingly, the rules generated with F_{gen} = 15 N were the same as those with F_{gen} = 10 N. The 15-N force could not be used for control at all since it leads to an immediate failure from the state (0,0,0,0). Still, it generated quite good control rules. Although the estimates for the probability of failure were very high for positive and negative 15-N force, for all the states the same force direction was preferred as with a force of 10 N. This is also why F_{gen} = 15 N is omitted from Table 3.2.

The most successful state-action table was compressed by inductive learning program NEWGEM [17] into a simple control rule:

if ($fiv > 6$) **or**
($v < 0.02$) & ($-6 < fiv < 6$) & ($fi > 1$) or
($v < -0.35$) & ($-6 < fiv < 6$)
then Action = +

An analogous rule was induced for action −.

Group 2:* F_{gen} = *1*, N = *1, 2, 3, 4, 5, . . . , 30. Test results of the state-action tables from the second group are shown in Table 3.3. The results for N = 1, 2, 3, and 4 are approximately at the same level. There is a considerable leap at N = 5, where the average survival increases almost by a factor of 5 and the only variables causing the failure are those related to the cart. Further increasing N does not immediately affect the results. At N = 20, a decrease in the number of survival steps is noticed. At N = 30, the situation is even worse; the angular velocity of the pole is detected to be out of range in 32% of the experiments. The propagation of errors in probability estimates in the model is probably the main reason for this deterioration.

TABLE 3.3 Control Performance of State-Action Tables, Obtained by Maximizing *N*-Step Survival Probability

		Out of Range (%)			
N	Average Survival	*fiv*	*fi*	*v*	*x*
1	84	18		82	
2	88	18		82	
3	90	12		88	
4	87	14		86	
5	374			42	58
6	377			17	83
7	403			15	85
8	441			3	97
9	401				100
10	414				100
11	397				100
12	389				100
13	427				100
14	379				100
15	370				100
16	442				100
20	351				100
30	311	32			68

3.4.4 Analyzing the Effect of Exaggeration

Experimental results of the state-action tables from Group 1 show that, in certain cases, using an exaggerated force in the process of simulation considerably improves the performance of generated control rules. More precisely, if we are supposed to control the system with force $F_{con} = 1$ N, exaggerating the force during the generation of the state transition graph has proved useful. However, not all exaggerated F_{gen} were useful. For $F_{gen} = 10$ N and $F_{gen} = 15$ N survival increased approximately by a factor of 5 if compared with $F_{gen} = 1$ N; however, nothing similar happened in the other cases. On the contrary, exaggerating "too much" ($F_{gen} = 50$) resulted in random control, that is, in no control at all. In the following, we explain these rather unexpected findings.

The state-action tables from Group 1 were generated to minimize the immediate failure probability. By this strategy, it is not useful to generate rules with too weak a force, since in such a case many states are absolutely safe considering one-step look-ahead. Neither positive nor negative action leads directly to a forbidden state. On the other hand, forces with too large a magnitude are not useful since they lead to an immediate failure in both directions. Forces that lead to an immediate failure when oriented in one direction but not in the other are advantageous.

Let us compare the experimental results in Tables 3.2 and 3.3. When moving from $N = 4$ to $N = 5$ in Table 3.3, we notice the same improvement as when $F_{gen} = 10$ N in Table 3.2. To see whether both improvements are due to the same phenomenon, we carried out a mathematical analysis [16]. For each qualitative state of the pole, the following quantities were computed: (a) interval (F_1, F_2) such that for all F from (F_1, F_2), a force of magnitude F detects failure in one direction but not in the other; (b) interval (N_1, N_2) such that for all N from (N_1, N_2), making N steps of simulation with nonexaggerated force ($F = 1$ N) detects failure in one direction but not in the other. The results are shown in Table 3.4 (symmetrical states are omitted). The intersection of the intervals in the third column has property (a) for all qualitative states. Similarly, the intersection of the intervals in the fourth column has property (b) for all qualitative states under consideration.

We now compare the experimental results and the results of the analysis.

1. *Comparison of Tables 3.2 and 3.4* Results were considerably better for $F_{gen} = 10$ N than for $F_{gen} = 1, 5, 20$, and 50 N. For $F_{gen} = 15$ N, the same control rules were synthesized as with $F_{gen} = 10$ N. Both "successful" forces are from the interval (10, 18), while the others are not.
2. *Comparison of Tables 3.3 and 3.4* A leap at $N = 5$ corresponds to the lower bound of the interval (5, 26) in Table 3.4.

To conclude, the analysis confirmed that the effect of using an exaggerated force while generating control rules was the same as the effect of considering longer simulation with a nonexaggerated force. However, on could prefer the first approach for the following reasons:

- Control rules are generated with a simpler, intuitively clearer decision criterion.
- Interval-based, time-driven models are subject to deterioration as the number of simulation steps increases.

TABLE 3.4 Forces That Lead from a Given Qualitative State to an Immediate Failure if Oriented In One direction, but not in the Other (similar for look-aheads that detect failure with the force ($F = 1$ N) oriented in one direction but not the other)

Qualitative State			
fi	*fiv*	(F_1, F_2)	$(N_1\ N_2)$
−1 : 1	6 : 24	(1, 28)	(1, 37)
1 : 6	6 : 24	(1, 28)	(1, 30)
1 : 6	−6 : 6	(10, 18)	(5, 26)
1 : 6	−24 : −6	(1, 27)	(1, 37)
6 : 12	6 : 24	(2, 30)	(1, 26)
6 : 12	−6 : 6	(9, 19)	(4, 30)
6 : 12	−24 : −6	(2, 26)	(2, 56)

On the other hand, it requires finding a suitable degree of exaggeration, that is, one that discriminates well between different control decisions. In general, this is not an easy problem.

3.5 CONCLUSION

This chapter presents different approaches to the automatic synthesis of dynamic systems control using artificial intelligence. It surveys some programs that learn to control the inverted pendulum, emphasizing their successful performance and their adaptability. However, it points out that some improvements could be made to make learning more efficient and to obtain more reliable control rules. Our experiments show that initializing the learning program BOXES [5] with a simple incomplete control rule speeds up the learning process by a factor of 8 and increases the reliability (i.e., the percentage of successful applications of the same set of control rules) from 15% to 50%.

An attempt to synthesize control rules for the inverted pendulum automatically from a qualitative model is described. The lack of quantitative information is tackled by applying interval arithmetic and by incorporating probabilities into the qualitative model. Control rules are generated on the model-based predicted behavior of the system for different control decisions. Under these rules, the program succeeded in controlling the most critical variables of the system, *fi* and *fiv*, but still failed to control all four variables in the long run. For further improvements, the following considerations could be helpful:

- Due to partitioning into small time intervals, important qualitative changes appear only after a certain number of simulation steps, when the propagation of errors may already be critical. A QSIM-like event-driven simulation could be more appropriate.
- The strategies considered here are probably not sufficiently goal-oriented. Instead of avoiding the failure it might be better to determine partial goals by means of backward chaining, and try to achieve them.

Reasoning about physical phenomena can be enhanced using exaggeration, overemphasizing some characteristics of the system under consideration. This technique has already been used for solving the comparative analysis problem [18] and for handling very complex phenomena [19]. Our experiments show that it is also possible to take advantage of exaggeration in the synthesis of control rules. The improvement due to exaggeration is comparable to the one achieved by a deeper look-ahead in the state transition graph. The exaggeration helps to detect some trends of the system's behavior that would have otherwise remained hidden.

The learning approach and the model-based approach can supplement each other: While the former achieves successful control of a system after a number of experiments, the latter can provide partial control without experimentation. Therefore, we intend to combine them in order to take advantage from both.

ACKNOWLEDGMENTS

This research was supported by the Ministry of Science, Research and Technology, Republic of Slovenia.

REFERENCES

[1] I. Bratko, "Machine Learning," in K. J. Gilhooly, Ed., *Human and Machine Problem Solving,* Plenum Press, New York, 1989, pp. 265–287.

[2] D. S. Weld and J. de Kleer, Eds., *Readings in Qualitative Reasoning about Physical Systems,* Morgan Kaufmann, San Mateo, Calif., 1990.

[3] S. Barnett and R. G. Cameron, *Introduction to Mathematical Control Theory,* 2nd ed., Oxford University Press, New York, 1985.

[4] H. Kvakernaak, *Linear Optimal Control Systems,* McGraw-Hill, New York, 1972.

[5] D. Michie and R. A. Chambers, "BOXES: An Experiment in Adaptive Control," in E. Dale and D. Michie, Eds., *Machine Intelligence* 2, Edinburgh University Press, New York, 1968, pp. 137–152.

[6] A. G. Barto, R. S. Sutton, and C. W. Anderson, Neuronlike adaptive elements that can solve difficult learning control problems, *IEEE Trans. Systems, Man and Cybernetics,* SMC-13(5), 834–846 (1983).

[7] M. E. Connel and P. E. Utgoff, Learning to control a dynamic physical system, *Proc. 6th National Conf. on Artificial Intelligence,* Vol. 2, Morgan Kaufmann, San Mateo, Calif., 456–459 (1987).

[8] C. W. Anderson, Strategy learning with multilayer connectionist representations, in P. Langley, Ed., *Proc. 4th Internat. Workshop on Machine Learning,* Morgan Kaufmann, San Mateo, Calif., 103–114 (1987).

[9] A. Makarovič, "A Qualitative Way of Solving the Pole Balancing Problem," Memorandum inf-88-44, University of Twente, The Netherlands (1988). Also published in J. Hayes, D. Michie, and E. Tyugu, Eds., *Machine Intelligence* 12, Oxford University Press, 1991, pp. 241–258.

[10] C. Sammut and D. Michie, "Controlling a 'black box' simulation of a space craft," TIRM-89-039, Turing Institute Press, Glasgow (1989).

[11] S. Džeroski, "Control of Inverted Pendulum," B.Sc. thesis (in Slovene), Faculty of Electr. Eng. and Computer Sci., University of Ljubljana (1989).

[12] O. G. Selfridge, R. S. Sutton, and A. G. Barto, Training and tracking in robotics, *Proc. 9th Internat Conf. on Artificial Intelligence,* Vol. 1, Morgan Kaufmann, San Mateo, Calif., 670–672 (1985).

[13] I. Bratko, Qualitative modelling: Learning and control, *6th Czechoslovak Conf. Artificial Intelligence,* 97–112 (June 1991).

[14] C. Sammut, Experimental results from an evaluation of algorithms that learn to control dynamic systems, *Proc. 5th Internat. Conf. on Machine Learning,* Morgan Kaufmann, San Mateo, Calif., 437–443 (1988).

[15] R. E. Moore, *Interval Analysis,* Prentice-Hall, New York, 1966.

[16] T. Urbančič, "Automatic Synthesis of Knowledge for Dynamic System Control," M. Sc. thesis (in Slovene) Faculty of Electr. Eng. and Computer Sc., University of Ljubljana (1990).

[17] I. Mozetič, "NEWGEM: Program for Learning from Examples," Rep. IJS-DP-4390, Jozef Stefan Institute, Ljubljana (1985).

[18] D. Weld, Exaggeration, *Artificial Intelligence,* 43(3), 311–368 (1990).

[19] O. Raiman, Caricatural reasoning, *Proc. 2nd Workshop on Qualitative Physics,* Paris (1988).

CHAPTER 4

Analysis of Recurrent Back Propagation and Its Application to Language Acquisition

RYOTARO KAMIMURA
M. C. HAN

4.1 INTRODUCTION

This chapter presents the experimental analysis of recurrent neural networks, applied to the problem of natural language acquisition. The knowledge of natural language that native speakers have is referred to as *grammatical competence* [1]. Thus, the problem of language acquisition is reduced to that of acquisition of grammatical competence. The grammatical competence is reflected in the ability to make judgments about the well-formedness of sentences and about the inference of structures in sentences. In this chapter, grammatical competence means the ability to infer the well-formedness of sentences to simplify experiments. Thus, we aim at training the recurrent neural network to attain the level of *"observational adequacy."*

4.1.1 Grammatical Competence

In theoretical linguistics, competence and performance have clearly been distinguished [1,2]. Competence means the native speaker's knowledge of a language. On the other hand, performance is the actual use of a language in concrete situations. Competence can be subdivided into grammatical competence and pragmatic competence. While grammatical competence is concerned with knowledge of the grammar of a language, pragmatic competence is the basis of the ability to use a language effectively and appropriately.

Dynamic, Genetic, and Chaotic Programming, By Branko Souček and the IRIS Group.
ISBN 0-471-55717-X

Grammatical competence is supposed to be reflected in two kinds of intuition: intuition about sentence well-formedness and intuition about sentence structure. In this chapter, we are concerned only with intuition about well-formedness of sentences to simplify the experiments.

4.1.2 Background

Attempts to determine the well-formedness of sentences with neural networks have independently been made by Kamimura [3] and Wyard and Nightingale [4]. Wyard and Nightingale used a single-layer feedforward neural network and showed that the simple network could give good performance with respect to grammatical determination. However, they did not examine the meaning of grammatical determination in the framework of theoretical linguistics. Moreover, their network architecture seems too simple to describe more complex structures of natural language.

4.1.3 Objectives

In this chapter, a fully recurrent neural network is used for the experiments. In the fully recurrent neural network, all units are completely connected. Thus, any kind of restriction can be imposed upon the architecture to produce appropriate architectures for targets. However, little is known of the performance of the recurrent neural network when the network size is relatively large.

In this context, this chapter has three main objectives. First, we analyze the learning process of the recurrent neural network. Specifically, we examine how many propagations or back propagations are needed to obtain approximate values for the recurrent back propagation. Second, the relation between the generalization performance and the number of hidden units is examined. Third, we try to examine whether the recurrent neural network can infer the well-formedness of new sentences. In particular, we attempt to explore the problem of creativity of language.

4.1.4 Creativity of Language

The abilities of grammatical competence must be applied not only to familiar sentences but also to sentences that we have never heard before. This property has been referred to as *creativity* of language. New sentences can be produced and understood that are completely different from familiar sentences with respect to sentence structure. The task of explaining language creativity is certainly too difficult for a network to perform. Thus, to simulate the process of acquisition of grammatical competence with the property of creativity, we simply made training sentences by using a limited number of sentence formulae. Then we tried to evaluate the performance of a recurrent neural network as to the inference of well-formedness of sentences when new sentences had sentence formulae different from the formulae of training sentences. We think that this experiment is certainly related to the property of language creativity, though it is expressed in a very primitive way.

The experimental results showed that the network could correctly infer the well-formedness of new sentences with new sentence formulae. Thus, the results showed the possibility that the recurrent neural network could acquire grammatical competence with the property of creativity.

4.1.5 Recurrent Back Propagation

Let us briefly explain why the recurrent neural network was used for the experiments. The back-propagation learning method has been very popular in the field of neural networks. However, the network architecture is limited to feedforward networks. Recently, the back-propagation learning method has been generalized to the recurrent (feedback) neural network [5,6,7]. Simard [8] pointed out four important properties concerning the advantage of the recurrent neural network over the feedforward network. First, recurrent back propagation can allow arbitrary connections, which make the network more feasible by removing unnecessary constraints on network topology. The network architecture is general enough to take into account the characteristics of the targets. Concerning the structure of language, it is certainly clear that the linguistic structure is extremely complex. Thus, the generality of recurrent back propagation with respect to the network topology is necessary for the study of language. Second, the increased number of connections may diminish noise sensitivity and synchronization problems. Third, the additional connections may enable the network to converge faster. Fourth, the feedback (recurrent) connections can be used to restore or deal with incomplete information. At least, the recurrent neural network is more general and more flexible than the feedforward network. Thus, it is expected to be applied more successfully to complex problems such as natural language processing.

However, little is known of the scaling problem or generalization performance. Thus, we try to examine whether the change in the number of hidden units is related to generalization performance. Experimental results showed that generalization performance did not necessarily depend on the number of hidden units. In particular, it was observed that the network with no hidden units could give the best performance with respect to the generalization performance when new sentences to be estimated had new sentence formulae. The connections among input units may be efficient enough to take into account the characteristics of sequences.

4.1.6 Chapter Outline

In Section 4.2, we briefly explain the network architecture and the recurrent back-propagation procedure used to train the network. In Section 4.3, we present experimental results concerning the inference about the well-formedness of new sentences. After briefly presenting the data and the computational methods used in the experiments in Section 4.3.1, the results about the convergence of the network are shown in Section 4.3.2. In Section 4.3.3, we present experimental results concerning the inference of new sentences with sentence formulae of training sentences. In Section 4.3.4, we present results when new sentences are generated by a phrase structure grammar. Section 4.3.5 is concerned with examination and discussion of results of the inference of new sentences with the new sentence formulae. The chapter concludes in Section 4.4.

4.2 NETWORK ARCHITECTURE AND LEARNING METHOD

We first explain a network architecture used for our experiments. Then the recurrent back-propagation procedure for training the recurrent neural network is briefly presented. The network architecture we used is the fully recurrent network, because we think that network topology should be as general as possible in order to take into account the complex characteristics of natural language.

4.2.1 Network Architecture

A fully recurrent neural network means that all units in the network are completely interconnected. Figure 4.1 shows a fully recurrent network with eight units. Five of the eight units are referred to as *input units*. One unit is called *output unit,* which must produce the solution as to the well-formedness of the sentences. The remaining two units are the *hidden units,* which are neither input nor output units and which are expected to capture the information concerning the structure found in the sentences. In this case, the well-formed sentence, *"the man saw the boy"* is presented. Thus, the network must be trained to produce *"1,"* meaning *"grammatical."* Figure 4.2

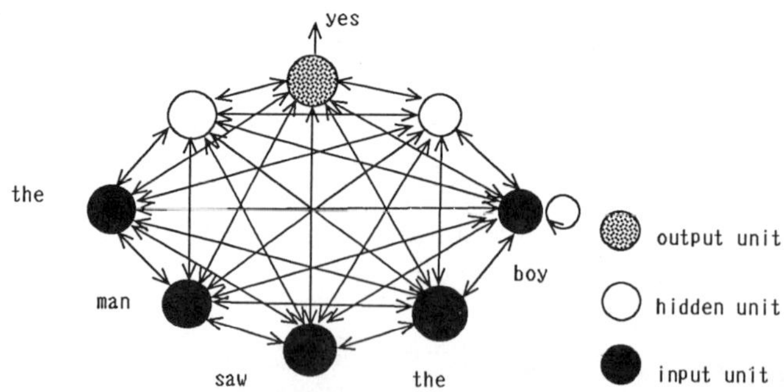

Figure 4.1 *An example of a fully recurrent neural network. A well-formed sentence, "the man saw the boy" is given. The network must generate "1" at an output unit.*

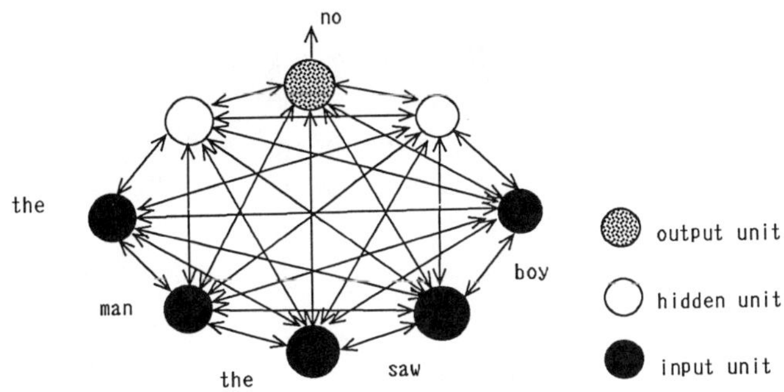

Figure 4.2 *An example of a fully recurrent neural network. An ill-formed sentence, "the man the saw boy" is presented. Thus, the network must produce "0" at an output unit.*

also shows a fully recurrent neural network. In this case, however, an ill-formed sentence is given to the network. Thus, the network must be trained to produce *"0,"* meaning *"ungrammatical."*

4.2.2 Recurrent Back Propagation

Recurrent back propagation is a generalization of the back-propagation learning method in neurodynamical systems, which was developed by Pineda [6,7] and Almeida [5]. In this section, we present the learning algorithm presented by Pineda [6,7] in detail.

Neurodynamical System. Consider a general neurodynamical system defined as

$$\frac{dx_k}{dt} = F_k(\mathbf{x}, \mathbf{w}, \theta) \qquad k = 1, 2, \ldots, N$$

where $\mathbf{x} = (x_1, x_2, \ldots, x_N)^T$ is the state of the system, $\mathbf{w} = (w_{ij})_{N\times N}$ is the internal parameter (the weight matrix), and $\theta = (\theta_1, \theta_2, \ldots, \theta_N)^T$ is the external bias (or control) parameter.

We concentrate on a special case of this general dynamical system, which is appropriate for recurrent networks. Consider a set $\Omega = \{1, 2, \ldots N\}$ of neurons, or units, whose dynamic is given by the following system of coupled differential equations:

$$\frac{dx_k}{dt} = -x_k + f(u_k) + \theta_k \qquad k = 1, 2, \ldots, N \tag{4.1}$$

where x_k represents the activity (mean soma potential) of the kth neuron, and $\mathbf{u} = (u_1, u_2, \ldots, u_N)^T$ is given by

$$u_i = \sum_{j=1}^{N} w_{ij} x_j$$

where w_{ij} denotes the connection strength, or coupling, from the jth to the ith neuron. The function f modulates the neural response, typically taken to be a sigmoidal function given by

$$f(x) = \frac{1}{1 + e^{-x}} \tag{4.2}$$

Let Ω_I, Ω_O, and Ω_H be the input units, the output units, and the hidden units, respectively. Define the external bias θ_k as

$$\theta_k = \begin{cases} \xi_k & \text{if } k \in \Omega_I \\ 0 & \text{if } k \in \Omega_0 \cup \Omega_H \end{cases}$$

The constant θ_k can be taken arbitrary for some specific purposes.

The fixed points (or equilibrium points) of the Eq. (4.1), denoted by $\mathbf{x}^*$, are solutions corresponding to

$$\frac{d\mathbf{x}^*}{dt} = 0$$

that is, solutions of the nonlinear equations

$$x_k^* = f(u_k^*) + \theta_k \tag{4.3}$$

where

$$u_k^* = \sum_{j=1}^{N} w_{kj} x_j^*$$

We assume that at least one such fixed point exists.

Our goal is to find a local algorithm that adjusts $\mathbf{w}$ so that a given fixed initial state $\mathbf{x}^0$ and a given set of input values ξ_k result in a fixed point $\mathbf{x}^*$, whose components along the output units have a desired set of values τ_k, $k \in \Omega_O$. This can be achieved by minimizing a function that measures the error between the desired fixed point and the actual fixed point.

Energy Function. Lyapunov stability requires an energylike function to be monotonically decreasing in time. The most commonly used function is a quadratic error function or a Lyapunov function given by

$$E = \frac{1}{2} \sum_{k=1}^{K} J_k^2 \tag{4.4}$$

where

$$J_k = \begin{cases} \tau_k - x_k^* & \text{if } k \in \Omega_O \\ 0 & \text{otherwise} \end{cases} \tag{4.5}$$

Note that E has a family of minima that exist on the hyperplanes that satisfy $x_k^* = \tau_k$, $k \in \Omega_O$.

Learning Algorithm. A learning algorithm can be described as evolving the fixed point $\mathbf{x}^*$, which is a function of $\mathbf{w}$, toward the hyperplanes $x_k^* = \tau_k$.

A gradient descent algorithm can be used to change Δw to be proportional to the gradient of E. With step size η, we can write the gradient algorithm as

$$\frac{dw_{ij}}{dt} = -\eta \frac{\partial E}{\partial w_{ij}} = \eta \sum_k J_k \frac{\partial x_k^*}{\partial w_{ij}} \tag{4.6}$$

To calculate $\partial x_k^*/\partial w_{ij}$, notice that $\mathbf{x}^*$ is an implicit function of the weight matrix $\mathbf{w}$ and initial state $\mathbf{x}^0$. For $k = 1, \ldots, N$,

$$\begin{aligned} \frac{\partial x_k^*}{\partial w_{ij}} &= f'(u_k^*) \frac{\partial u_k^*}{\partial w_{ij}} \\ &= f'(u_k^*) \frac{\partial(\Sigma_t w_{kt} x_t^*)}{\partial w_{ij}} \\ &= f'(u_k^*) \sum_{t=1}^{N} \left(\frac{\partial w_{kt}}{\partial w_{ij}} x_t^* + w_{kt} \frac{\partial x_t^*}{w_{ij}} \right) \\ &= f'(u_k^*) \cdot \begin{cases} x_j^* + \sum_t w_{kt} \frac{\partial x_t^*}{\partial w_{ij}} & \text{if } k = i \\ \sum_t w_{kt} \frac{\partial x_t^*}{\partial w_{ij}} & \text{if } k \neq i \end{cases} \end{aligned}$$

By gathering the corresponding terms, we have for $k = i$,

$$f'(u_i^*) x_j^* = -w_{i1} f'(u_i^*) \frac{\partial x_1^*}{\partial w_{ij}} - \cdots + (1 - w_{ii} f'(u_i^*)) \frac{\partial x_i^*}{\partial w_{ij}} - \cdots - w_{iN} f'(u_i^*) \frac{\partial x_N^*}{\partial w_{ij}}$$

and, for $k \neq i$,

$$0 = -w_{k1}f'(u_k^*)\frac{\partial x_1^*}{w_{ij}} - \cdots + (1 - w_{kk}f'(u_k^*))\frac{\partial x_k^*}{\partial w_{ij}} - \cdots - w_{kN}f'(u_k^*)\frac{\partial x_N^*}{\partial w_{ij}}$$

This is a system of N linear equations with N unknowns, $\{\partial x_1^*/\partial w_{ij}, \ldots, \partial x_N^*/\partial w_{ij}\}$. We can write this in matrix form. Let

$$\mathbf{p} = \begin{pmatrix} p_1 \\ p_2 \\ \vdots \\ p_N \end{pmatrix} = \begin{pmatrix} \frac{\partial x_1^*}{\partial w_{ij}} \\ \frac{\partial x_2^*}{\partial w_{ij}} \\ \vdots \\ \frac{\partial x_N^*}{\partial w_{ij}} \end{pmatrix}$$

and

$$\mathbf{b} = \begin{pmatrix} b_1 \\ \vdots \\ b_N \end{pmatrix} = \begin{pmatrix} 0 \\ \vdots \\ 0 \\ f'(u_i^*)x_j^* \\ 0 \\ \vdots \\ 0 \end{pmatrix}$$

where $f'(u_i^*)x_j^*$ is at the ith row.

Let $\mathbf{L}$ be the matrix defined by

$$\begin{pmatrix} (1 - w_{11}f'(u_1^*)) & -w_{12}f'(u_1^*) & \cdot & \cdot & -w_{1N}f'(u_1^*) \\ -w_{21}f'(u_2^*) & (1 - w_{22}f'(u_2^*)) & \cdot & \cdot & -w_{2N}f'(u_1^*) \\ \vdots & \cdot & \cdot & \cdot & \cdot \\ -w_{k1}f'(u_k^*) & \cdot & (1 - w_{kk}f'(u_k^*)) & \cdot & -w_{kN}f'(u_k^*) \\ \vdots & \cdot & \cdot & \cdot & \cdot \\ -w_{N1}f'(u_N^*) & \cdot & \cdot & \cdot & (1 - w_{NN}f'(u_N^*)) \end{pmatrix}$$

Note that if we define $\mathbf{F}$ as the diagonal matrix that has $\{f'(u_1^*), \ldots, f'(u_N^*)\}$ as its diagonal elements, then $\mathbf{L}$ can be written as

$$\mathbf{L} = (\mathbf{I} - \mathbf{wF})$$

Then the system of linear equations becomes

$$\mathbf{Lp} = \mathbf{b}$$

If $\mathbf{L}$ is invertible, the system has a unique solution

$$\mathbf{p} = \mathbf{Mb}$$

where

$$\mathbf{M} = \mathbf{L}^{-1}$$

Let

$$\mathbf{J} = (J_1, J_2, \ldots, J_N)^{\mathrm{T}} = (\tau_1 - x_1^*, \ldots, \tau_N - x_N^*) \tag{4.7}$$

Then from (4.6)

$$\begin{aligned}\frac{dw_{ij}}{dt} &= \eta \mathbf{J}^{\mathrm{T}}\mathbf{p} \\ &= \eta \mathbf{J}^{\mathrm{T}}\mathbf{Mb} \\ &= \eta \mathbf{J}^{\mathrm{T}} \begin{pmatrix} M_{1i} \\ M_{2i} \\ \vdots \\ M_{Ni} \end{pmatrix} f'(u_i^*) x_j^* \\ &= \eta f'(u_i^*) \left(\sum_{k=1}^{N} J_k M_{ki} \right) x_j^*\end{aligned}$$

As mentioned in Pineda [6,7], direct matrix inversions are typically nonlocal calculations. However, a local method that is a variant of a relaxation procedure for inverting the matrix $\mathbf{L}$ can be used.

Relaxation Methods. Define $\mathbf{z}^* = (z_1^*, z_2^*, \ldots, z_n^*)^{\mathrm{T}}$ such that

$$\mathbf{z}^{\mathrm{T}} = \mathbf{J}^{\mathrm{T}}\mathbf{M}$$

Then $\mathbf{J}^{\mathrm{T}} = \mathbf{z}^{\mathrm{T}}\mathbf{L}$, which gives

$$J_k = -w_{1k}f'(u_1^*)z_1^* - \cdots + (1 - w_{kk}f'(u_k^*))z_k^* - \cdots - w_{Nk}f'(u_N^*)z_N^*$$

So,

$$z_k^* = J_k + \sum_{j=1}^{N} w_{jk}f'(u_j^*)z_j^* \tag{4.8}$$

This gives a new learning rule

$$\frac{dw_{ij}}{dt} = \eta f'(u_i)z_i^* x_j^* \tag{4.9}$$

where η is a learning rate and z_i^* is a solution of

$$\frac{dz_i}{dt} = -z_i + \sum_{j=1}^{N} (f'(u_j)w_{ji}z_j) + J_i \tag{4.10}$$

So the algorithm consists of the following steps:

1. Find x^* by (4.1).
2. Find the error J_k in (4.5).
3. Find z_k^* from (4.10).
4. Update w_{ij} by (4.9).

4.3 RESULTS AND DISCUSSION

We present experimental results concerning the recurrent neural network applied to the inference of the well-formedness of sentences. We examine the convergence property of a recurrent neural network, changing the number of propagations and back propagations. Then we examine the generalization performance of the recurrent neural network applied to the estimation of the well-formedness of sentences.

4.3.1 Experimental Data

The network was composed of 100 input units, 1 output unit, and several hidden units. The local representation was used to encode the training data. Ten distinct input units were assigned to 10 distinct words. The length of a sentence was limited to 10 words. The learning was considered to be finished when the mean squared error was less than 0.01.

We performed the experiments as follows. First, the data composed of well-formed sentences were generated by using the following sentence formulas [2]:

1. Det Adj N V Det Adj N Prep Det N.
2. Det N V Det Adj N Prep Det N.
3. Det Adj N V Det N Prep Det N.
4. Det N V Det N Prep Det N.
5. Det N V Det Adj N.
6. Det N V Det N.

This word class framework generated 504 well-formed sentences. For example, we had the following well-formed sentences:

1. The small girl pushed the large dog toward the man.
2. The girl pushed the small dog toward the girl.
3. The tall girl pushed the man toward the dog.
4. The girl pushed the dog toward the man.
5. The dog bit the large man.
6. The dog bit the man.

As can be seen in these examples, only 10 distinct words were employed, to simplify the experiments. Then we generated ill-formed sentences by the inversion of the order Adj + N, Subject + Verb + Object, Det + N, and by choosing words randomly. The total number of ill-formed sentences was 3822.

Changing the number of training sentences, we trained the network to minimize the error between the target values and the observed values at the output unit. Half of the training sentences were well-formed, and the remaining were ill-formed. After finishing the learning, we evaluated the performance of the network for new sentences. First, we examined the performance of the network, when it must infer the grammaticality of new sentences which had the same sentence formulae. Second, to the network were given new sentences, which were generated by the following phrase structure grammar:

S → NP VP
VP → V NP
VP → V NP Prep NP
NP → Det Adj N
NP → Det N
Det → the; N → dog; N → man; N → girl; Adj → large; Adj → tall; Adj → small; V → pushed; Prep → toward.

In this case, the sentences that had the sentence formulae of training sentences were completely removed. Thus, the network must estimate the well-formedness of new sentences which had sentence formulae different from those of training sentences. We think that this procedure for the experiments is certainly related to the property of "creativity" of language at least in a very primitive way.

4.3.2 Convergence of the Network

As already mentioned in Section 4.2, the weight update assumes a correct approximation of x^* and z^*. The value of x^* is estimated by recursively propagating the activation value according to Eq. (4.1). The value of z^* is also computed by recursively back-propagating the activation value according to Eq. (4.10). In this section, we examine how many propagations or back propagations are needed to compute the correct approximation of activation values. The experimental results showed that only one or two propagations or back propagations were needed to converge.

First, the network was trained with 20 propagations and back propagations. Figure 4.3 shows mean squared errors as a function of learning cycles (weight updates) with a learning rate ($\eta = 0.6$). As can be seen in the figure, the errors oscillate greatly in the course of learning. However, eventually the network can converge in spite of the violent oscillation. Figure 4.4 also

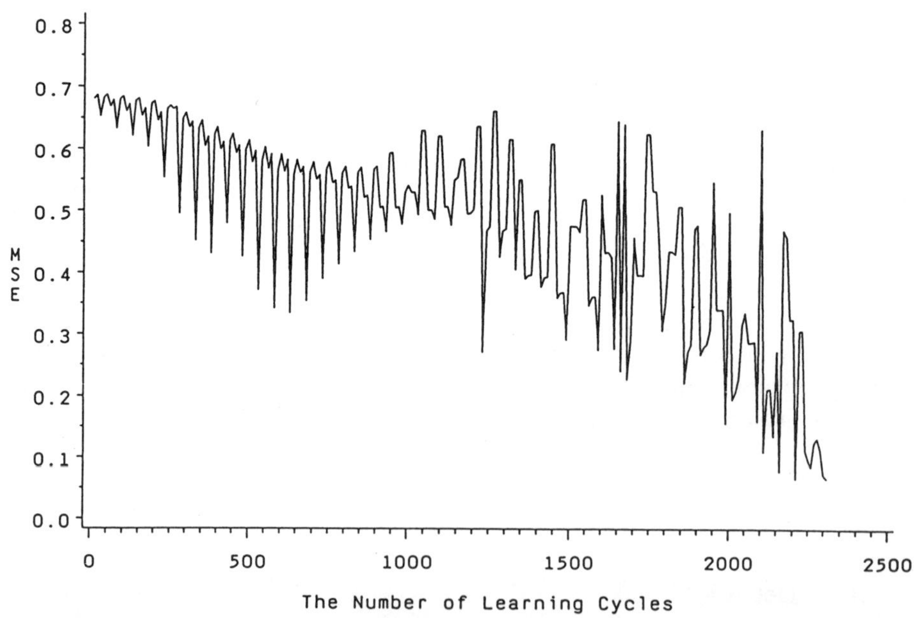

Figure 4.3 *Mean squared errors for a learning rate (η = 0.6). Thirty hidden units were employed. The network was trained with 20 propagations and 20 back propagations.*

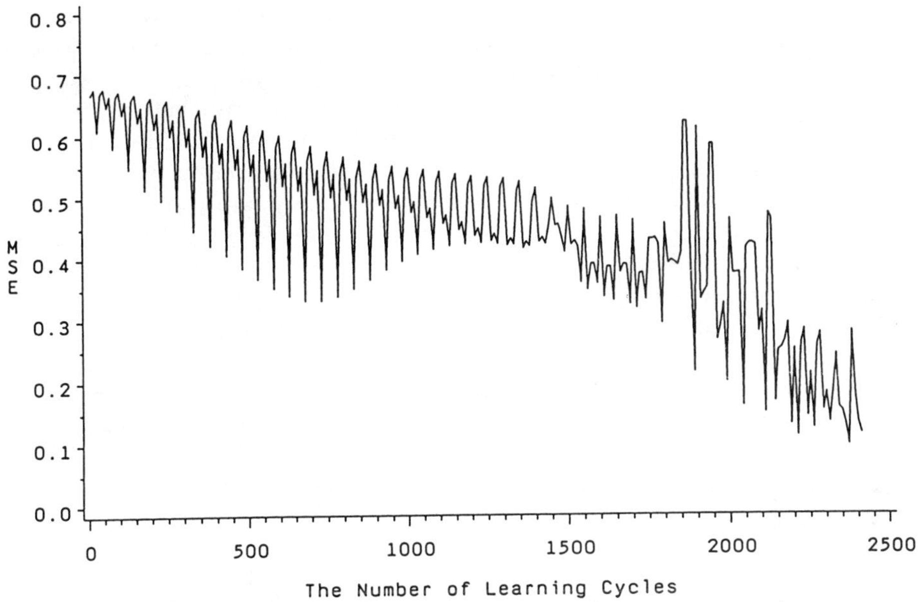

Figure 4.4 *Mean squared errors for a learning rate (η = 0.3). Thirty hidden units were employed. The network was trained with 20 propagations and 20 back propagations.*

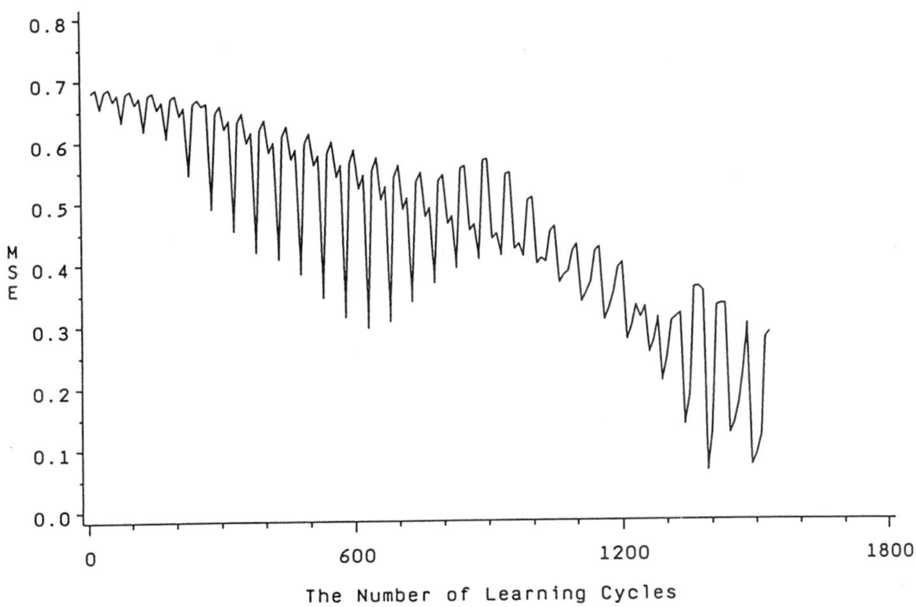

Figure 4.5 *Learning curves for one propagation. Weights were updated immediately after the presentation of the pattern. Twenty back propagations and 30 hidden units were employed.*

shows mean squared errors as a function of learning cycles (weight updates) with a learning rate ($\eta = 0.3$). As expected, the oscillation is slightly moderate due to the small learning rate.

Then the network was trained with a few number of propagations or back propagations. Figure 4.5 shows mean squared errors as a function of learning cycles. In this case, the number of back propagations was 20 and the number of propagations was one. Surprisingly, only one propagation was necessary to converge, as can be seen in this figure. Even if the number of propagations increases to two, we cannot see a big difference between mean squared errors, which is shown in Figure 4.6.

Figure 4.7 shows mean squared errors as a function of learning cycles (weight updates) with only one back propagation. In this case, the number of propagations was fixed for 20 iterations. As can be seen in the figure, only one back propagation is sufficient to converge. When the number of back-propagations increases to two, learning becomes faster (Fig. 4.8). We could not see a big change in convergence when the number of back propagations increased to more than two.

4.3.3 New Sentences with the Same Sentence Formulae

We examine generalization performance for sentences with sentence formulae of training sentences. The relationship between generalization performance of the network and the number of hidden units is also examined.

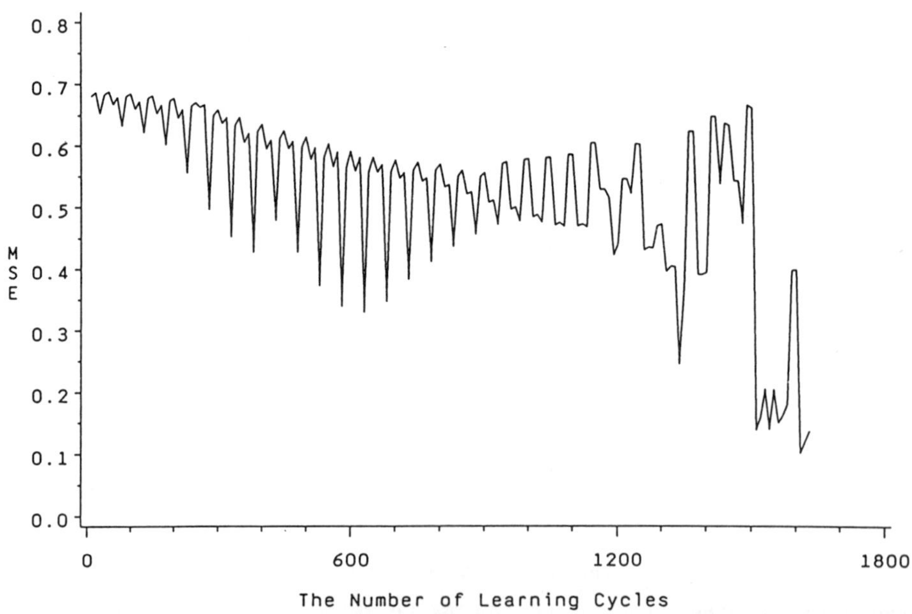

Figure 4.6 *Learning curves for two propagations with 20 back propagations. Thirty hidden units were employed.*

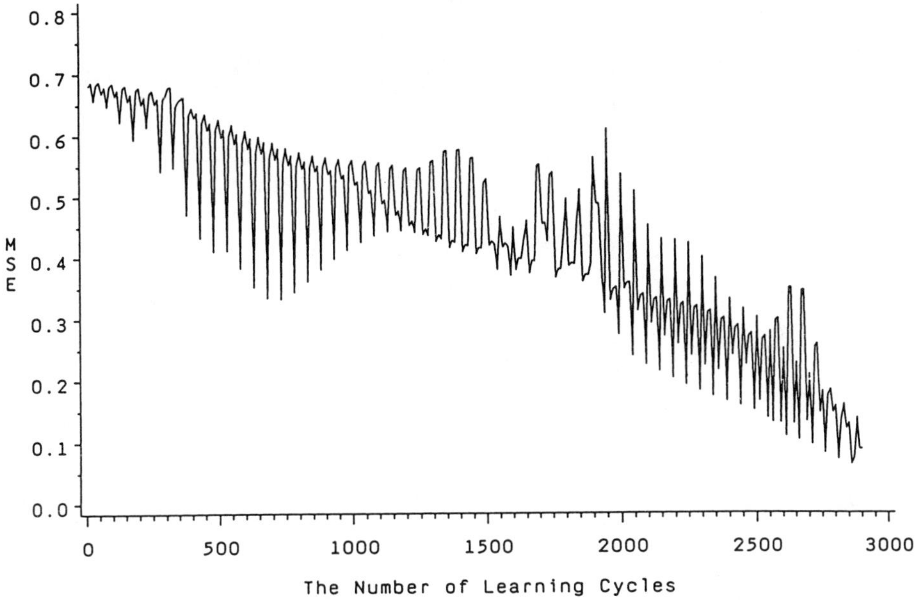

Figure 4.7 *Learning curves for one back propagation with 20 propagations. Thirty hidden units were employed.*

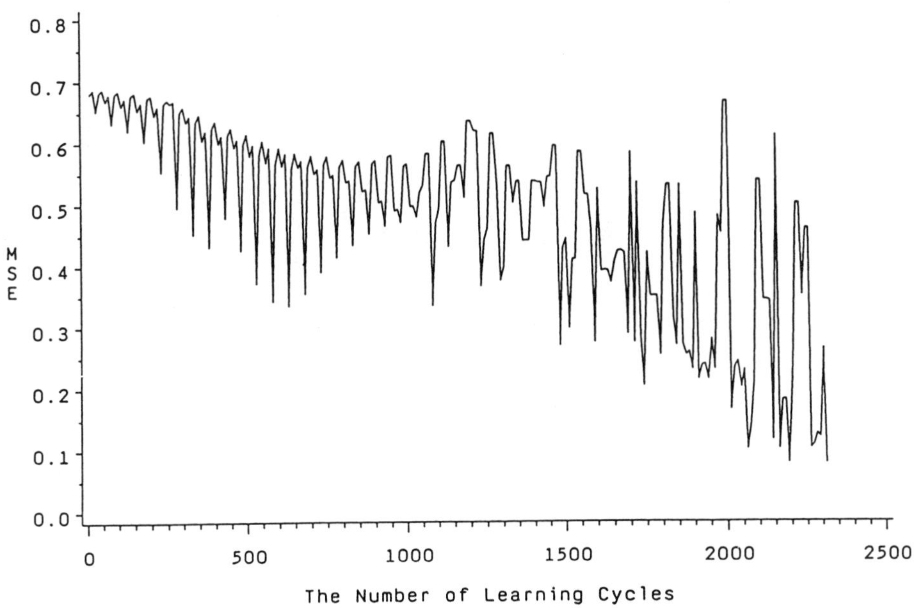

Figure 4.8 *Learning curves for two back propagations with 20 propagations. Thirty hidden units were employed.*

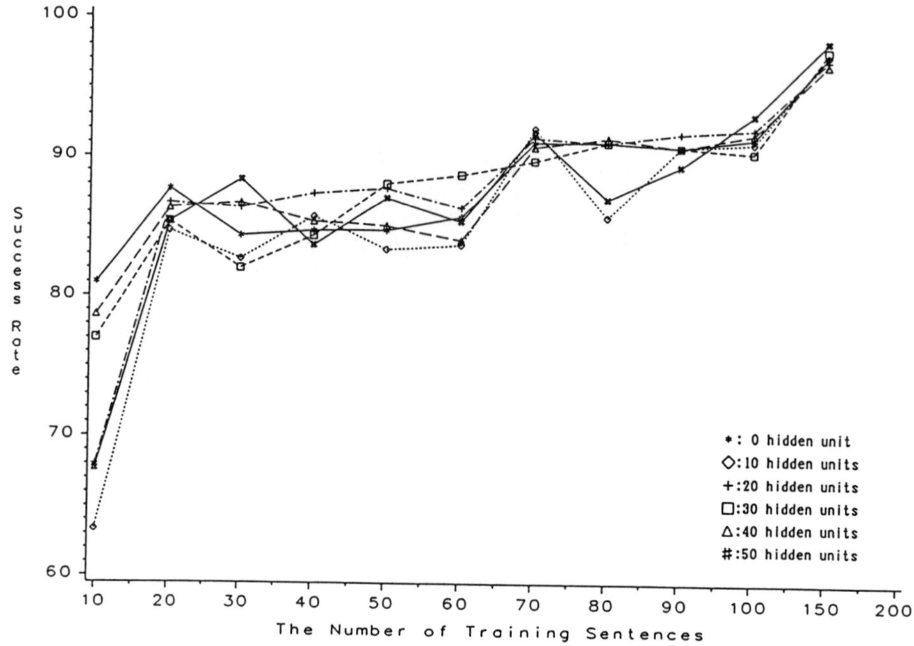

Figure 4.9 *Success rate as a function of the number of training sentences. The success rates were computed by changing the number of hidden units. New sentences were all well-formed sentences and generated by the sentence formulae of training sentences.*

TABLE 4.1 Success Rates for Different Numbers of Hidden Units.

	Number of Hidden Units					
Number of Sentences	0	10	20	30	40	50
10	81.00	63.33	68.00	77.00	78.67	67.67
20	87.67	84.67	86.67	85.33	86.33	85.33
30	84.33	82.67	86.33	82.00	86.67	88.33
40	84.67	85.67	87.33	84.33	85.33	83.67
50	84.67	83.33	87.67	88.00	85.00	87.00
60	85.67	83.67	86.33	88.67	84.00	85.33
70	91.00	92.00	91.33	89.67	90.67	91.67
80	91.00	85.67	91.00	91.00	91.33	87.00
90	90.67	90.67	91.67	90.67	90.67	89.33
100	91.33	91.00	92.00	90.33	91.67	93.00
150	96.67	93.67	95.00	94.00	97.00	96.33
200	97.33	97.33	97.00	97.67	97.67	98.33

The sentences were all well-formed with sentence formulae of training sentences.

Figure 4.9 and Table 4.1 show the success rates as a function of training sentences. The number of new sentences was 300. They were randomly chosen from a set of sentences generated by the training sentence formulae described in Section 4.3.1. Half of the training sentences were well-formed, and the remaining sentences were ill-formed. As can be seen in the figure, the success rates tend to increase in proportion to the number of training sentences. However, the success rates seem to be indifferent to the number of hidden units.

We can also see the same tendency when new sentences are ill-formed with the same sentence formulae. Figure 4.10 and Table 4.2 shows success rates as a function of training sentences. The number of sentences to be estimated was 3200. As can be seen, the success rate increases more or less monotonically in proportion to the number of training sentences. However, the change in the number of hidden units did not make any difference concerning the success rate. These results show that the generalization performance is independent of the number of hidden units and tends to increase monotonically in proportion to the number of training sentences.

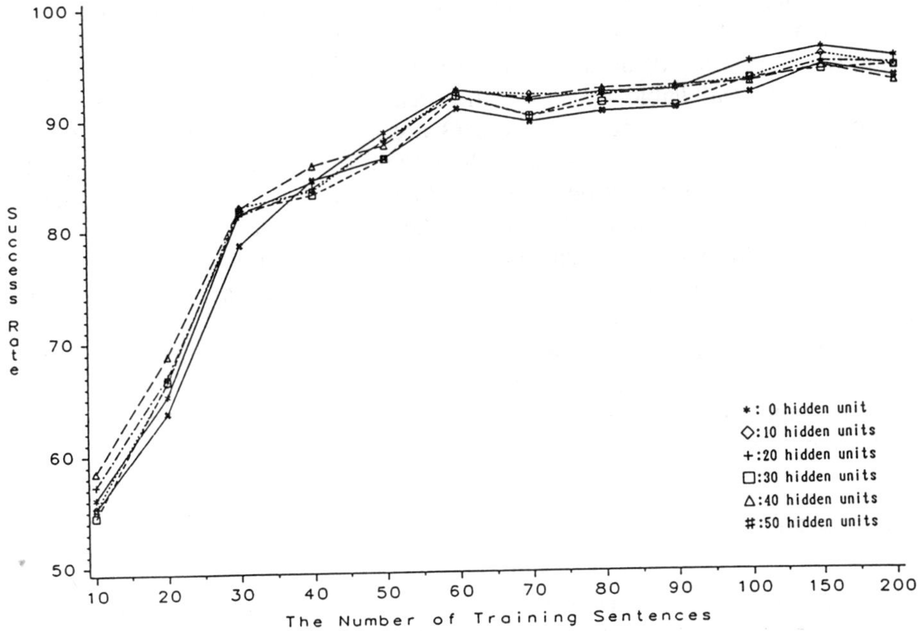

Figure 4.10 *Success rate as a function of training sentences. The success rates were computed by changing the number of hidden units. New sentences were all ill-formed sentences and generated by the training sentence formulae.*

TABLE 4.2 Success Rates for Different Numbers of Hidden Units.

	Number of Hidden Units					
Number of Sentences	0	10	20	30	40	50
10	56.17	55.37	57.30	54.53	58.53	55.27
20	65.30	66.47	67.07	66.60	68.87	63.77
30	81.43	82.10	81.33	81.73	81.97	78.67
40	84.40	83.53	83.80	83.13	85.80	84.50
50	88.70	88.00	87.97	86.33	87.53	86.37
60	92.43	92.33	91.93	91.83	92.43	90.73
70	91.37	91.90	90.00	89.97	91.57	89.47
80	92.07	91.84	91.77	91.13	92.40	90.33
90	92.27	92.47	92.27	90.80	92.63	90.60
100	94.70	93.23	92.97	93.23	92.90	91.93
150	95.93	95.30	94.63	93.93	94.23	94.40
200	95.10	94.20	94.43	94.23	92.90	93.33

The sentences were all ill-formed with sentence formulae of training sentences.

4.3.4 New Sentences from a Phrase Structure Grammar

We evaluate the performance of a recurrent neural network when it is applied to the inference of well-formedness of new sentences generated by a phrase structure grammar described in Section 4.3.1. As mentioned, sentences that had the sentence formulae of training sentences were completely removed from a set of data. The total number of new sentences was 675.

Figure 4.11 and Table 4.3 shows the success rate as a function of training sentences. Generally, the success rates are significantly large at the beginning. The success rate increases gradually and reaches about 100% with 200 training sentences for any number of hidden units except 40. The change in the number of hidden units does not make a big difference in success rate. However, the network performs best with no hidden units. For example, the network with no hidden units shows the highest success rates when the number of training sentences ranges from 10 to 90.

These results shows that the recurrent neural network can correctly infer the well-formedness of new sentences generated by the phrase structure grammar and that the best performance of generalization can be obtained with no hidden units.

4.3.5 Detailed Analysis

We evaluate and discuss in detail the performance of the recurrent neural network applied to the inference of well-formedness of new sentences from the phrase structure grammar.

Figure 4.12 and Table 4.4 show the success rates as a function of the number of training sentences for sentences with new sentence formulae.

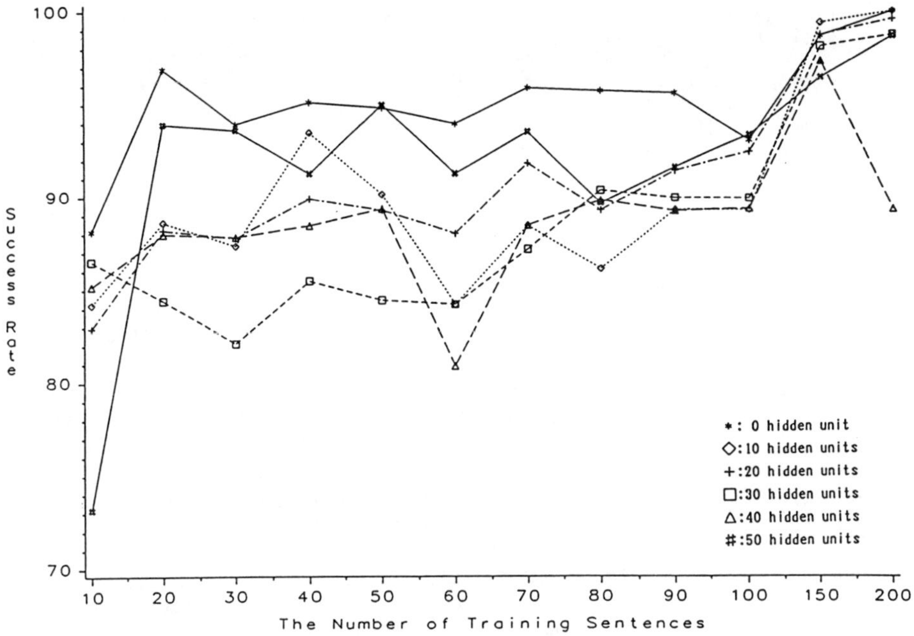

Figure 4.11 *Success rate as a function of training sentences. The sentences were generated by the phrase structure grammar described in Section 4.3.1.*

TABLE 4.3 Success Rates for Different Numbers of Hidden Units.

	Number of Hidden Units					
Number of Sentences	0	10	20	30	40	50
10	88.15	84.21	82.95	86.53	85.19	73.19
20	96.89	88.63	88.21	84.42	88.00	93.93
30	93.93	87.37	87.79	82.11	87.85	93.62
40	95.11	93.47	89.89	85.47	88.44	91.26
50	94.81	90.11	89.26	84.42	89.33	94.96
60	93.93	84.21	88.00	84.21	80.89	91.25
70	95.85	88.42	91.79	87.16	88.44	93.48
80	95.70	86.11	89.26	90.32	89.78	89.63
90	95.56	89.26	91.37	89.90	89.19	91.56
100	93.04	89.26	92.42	89.90	89.33	93.33
150	98.67	99.37	98.73	98.11	97.33	96.44
200	100.00	100.00	99.58	98.74	89.33	98.67

The sentences were all well-formed with new sentence formulae.

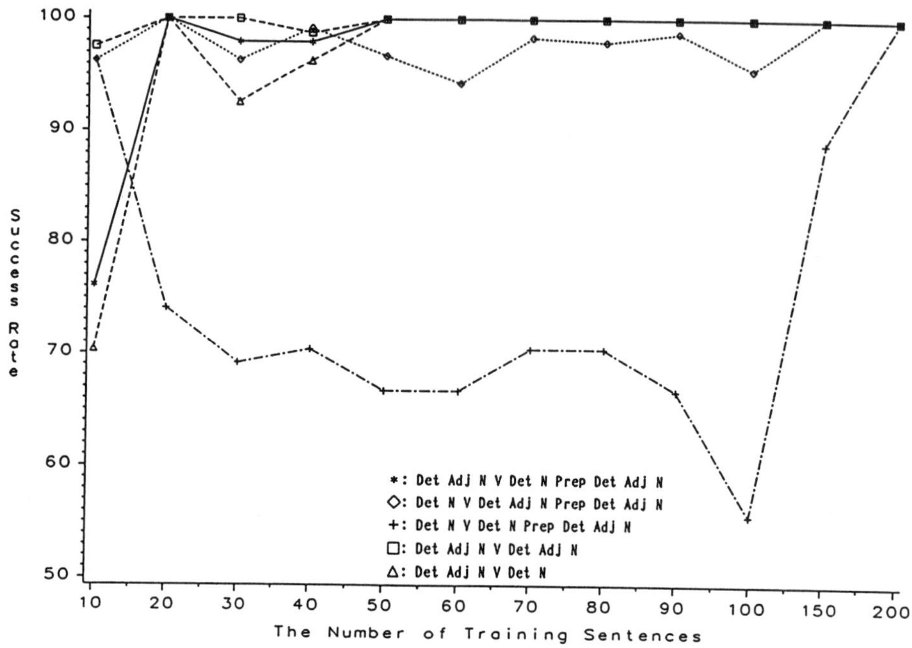

Figure 4.12 *Success rate as a function of training sentences. The sentences were generated by the phrase structure grammar described in Section 4.3.1.*

TABLE 4.4 Success Rates for Sentences with Different Sentence Formulae. No Hidden Units were Employed.

Number of Sentences	Sentence Formulae				
	(1)	(2)	(3)	(4)	(5)
10	76.13	96.29	96.29	97.53	70.37
20	100.00	100.00	74.07	100.00	100.00
30	97.94	96.30	69.14	100.00	92.59
40	97.94	99.18	70.37	98.77	96.29
50	100.00	96.71	66.67	100.00	100.00
60	100.00	94.24	66.67	100.00	100.00
70	100.00	98.35	70.37	100.00	100.00
80	100.00	97.94	70.37	100.00	100.00
90	100.00	98.77	66.67	100.00	100.00
100	100.00	95.47	55.56	100.00	100.00
150	100.00	100.00	88.89	100.00	100.00
200	100.00	100.00	100.00	100.00	100.00

The numbers in the table show sentence formulae: (1)Det Adj NV Det N Prep Det Adj N; (2)Det N V Det Adj N Prep Det Adj N; (3)Det N V Det N Prep Det Adj N; (4)Det Adj N V Det Adj N; (5)Det Adj N V Det N.

When new sentences to be estimated have the sentence formulae (2)Det N V Det Adj N Prep Det Adj N (243 sentences) and (4)Det Adj N V Det Adj N (81 sentences), the success rates are quite large at the beginning (more than 96%). The rate reaches 100% with only 20 training sentences. When the network must infer the well-formedness of new sentences with sentence formulae (1)Det Adj N V Det N Prep Det Adj N (243 sentences) and (5)Det Adj N V Det N (27 sentences), the success rates are more than 70% with 10 training sentences. However, the rates reach 100% immediately with 20 training sentences. Finally, when new sentences with formula (3)Det N V Det N Prep Det Adj N, must be estimated, the success rate shows a strange trajcctory. At the beginning, the rate reaches 96%. Then the rate begins to decrease up to 100 training sentences. Again, the rate begins to increase and reaches 100% with 200 training sentences. Generally speaking, the network can more correctly estimate the well-formedness as the number of grammatical constructions such as Adj N is larger.

These experimental results show that the network can easily estimate the well-formedness of sentences for simpler sentences. For example, sentences 4 and 5 are simple, compared with 1–3. Thus, the success rates for sentences 4 and 5 seem to be higher than those for sentences 1–3. Then sentence 3 has the lowest score with respect to the success rate. In sentence 3, only one construction Adj + N is observed, while sentences 1 and 2 have two constructions Adj + N. The construction Adj + N is a key factor for constructing well-formed and ill-formed training sentences. Thus, the success rate may be in proportion to the number of well-formed constructions.

4.4 CONCLUSION

We have examined the possibility of language acquisition with the recurrent neural network. The knowledge of language that native speakers have is reflected in grammatical competence. Thus, the possibility of acquisition of grammatical competence with a recurrent neural network has been examined. To simplify the experiments, grammatical competence means the ability to make judgments about the well-formedness of sentences. Thus, we only aim to attain the level of observational adequacy. In the experiments, training sentences were made by using a limited number of sentence formulae, and new sentences to be estimated by the network were produced by a phrase structure grammar. All sentences that had the sentence formulae of training sentences were completely omitted from a set of sentences generated by the grammar. Thus, the recurrent network must infer the well-formedness of sentences with new sentence formulae that were not included in the training sentence formulae.

Our experimental results can be summarized by the following three points. First, the number of propagations and back-propagations needed to obtain approximate values for the recurrent back propagation is quite small. This means that only one or two propagations (or back propagations) are needed. Second, the recurrent neural network can correctly infer the well-formedness of new sentences with sentence formulae of training sentences or completely new sentence formulae. The success rate of the inference of well-formedness of sentences with the same sentence formulae increases monotonically in proportion to the number of training sentences. Third, the generalization performance of the recurrent neural network is not necessarily related to the number of hidden units. In some cases, we can obtain the best performance with no hidden units.

These experimental results certainly suggest the possibility of the acquisition of natural language by using a recurrent neural network. Thus, the *"language acquisition device"* [9] can be simulated upon complex interactions of simple units.

REFERENCES

[1] A. Radford, *Transformational Grammar,* Cambridge University Press, Cambridge, England, 1988.

[2] C. L. Baker, *Introduction to Generative-Transformational Syntax,* Prentice-Hall, Englewood Cliffs, N.J. (1978).

[3] R. Kamimura, Recurrent neural network to infer the well-formedness of the sentences, *Proc. COGNITIVA '90,* Vol. 1, 327–334 (1990).

[4] P. J. Wyard and C. Nightingale, A single layer higher order neural net and its application to context free grammar recognition, *Connection Sci.,* 2(4), 347–370 (1990).

[5] L. Almeida, A learning rule for asynchronous perceptrons with feedback in a combinatorial environment, *IEEE 1st Internat. Conf. on Neural Networks,* Vol. 2, 609–618 (1987).

[6] F. J. Pineda, Generalization of back-propagation to recurrent neural networks, *Phys. Rev. Lett.* 59(19), 2229–2232 (1987).

[7] F. J. Pineda, Dynamics and architecture for neural computation, *J. Complexity,* 4, 216–245 (1988).

[8] P. Y. Simard, M. B. Ottaway, and D. H. Ballard, Analysis of recurrent back-propagation, *Proc. 1988 Connectionist Models Summer School,* Carnegie Mellon University, Pittsburgh, Pa., 103–112 (1988).

[9] N. Chomsky, "Generative Grammar: Its Basis, Development and Prospects," *Studies in English Linguistics and Literature,* special issue, Kyoto University of Forcign Studics (1987).

CHAPTER 5

Recognition and Restoration of Periodic Patterns with Time-Dependent Recurrent Neural Networks

RYOTARO KAMIMURA

5.1 INTRODUCTION

This chapter presents some experimental results regarding the recognition and generation of single or multiple periodic patterns. We also show that the network can restore, with appropriate precision original patterns when the patterns are perturbed by noise.

Several attempts to recognize and generate periodic patterns with recurrent neural networks have been made. Some of them were mainly related to the modeling of the central pattern generators in physiological fields [1]. Others were concerned with the examination of performance of recurrent neural network [2,3]. We think that they are concerned with conceptual modeling of our routine behaviors, which are supposed to be performed automatically after receiving initial bias.

However, in former studies, the imperfect reproduction of periodic patterns has been reported. This means that the learning of periodic patterns cannot be explicitly demonstrated, especially where multiple and complex patterns must be learned simultaneously. Moreover, the ideal learning processes have been implicitly supposed in these studies. This means that perfect teacher signals can always be given to the networks. Actually, the teacher signals the networks should receive are far from ideal. They are influenced by uncertain and constantly changing circumstances. Thus, the networks that aim at understanding of human behaviors and the internal

Dynamic, Genetic, and Chaotic Programming, By Branko Souček and the IRIS Group.
ISBN 0-471-55717-X

mechanism of our nervous systems can eliminate the influence of noise and recognize the principal factor hidden beneath the surface.

Using the fully recurrent network with the temporal supervised learning algorithm (TSLA) developed by Williams and Zipser [4,5], we have attempted to recognize and recover the periodic temporal patterns. In the TSLA formulation, the activity of unit at time $t + 1$ is described by the equation $x_i(t + 1) = f(\Sigma_j w_{ij}x_j(t))$, where x_i is a unit activity, w_{ij} is the connection strength, and f is the logistic function. The process of learning consists of the reduction of errors between the target and observed activity at time t. The TSLA has shown great power and generality when applied to simple or complex tasks, such as the simulation of Turing machines. However, few experimental results have been reported regarding the recognition of periodic patterns. Thus, this chapter will be the first to demonstrate the potential and generality of the TSLA regarding the recognition and generation of periodic patterns.

The results of our experiments can be summarized as follows. First, the recurrent network could recognize complex periodic waves, assuming that an appropriate number of hidden units are given. Second, the network could also reproduce the periodic patterns with appropriate precision indefinitely. This means that the network could regenerate the original patterns and estimate correctly the future behaviors of the patterns. Third, the recurrent network could also recognize and generate indefinitely the periodic waves in spite of the existence of much noise. This means that the network was able to regenerate the original periodic waves in the process of learning teacher signals with noise.

In Section 5.2, we briefly present the TSLA. Section 5.3 explains and discusses the experimental results. Section 5.3.1 is concerned with the recognition of single patterns. We deal with the recognition of multiple patterns in Section 5.3.2. Section 5.3.3 presents the results concerning the restoration of single periodic patterns, which are disturbed by the noises. In Section 5.3.4, after summarizing the experimental results, we discuss three problems concerning the recurrent neural network: number of hidden units, learning time, and excessive learning. Section 5.4 summarizes and concludes the chapter.

5.2 THEORY AND COMPUTATIONAL METHODS

We present briefly the formulation of the TSLA developed by Williams and Zipser [4]. Let $x_i(t)$ denote the activity of the ith unit at time t, and let w_{ij} represent the connection strength from the jth unit to the ith unit. Then the activity of the ith unit at time $t + 1$ is

$$x_i(t + 1) = f(s_i(t)) \tag{5.1}$$

where f is the logistic function

$$f(s_i(t)) = \frac{1}{1 + e^{-s_i(t)}} \tag{5.2}$$

and

$$s_i(t) = \sum_j w_{ij} x_j(t) \tag{5.3}$$

Some of the units can be taken as a set of visible units V, which should have their own target values. The network is forced to learn the target values by minimizing the difference between target values and actual values. Consider the difference at time t,

$$e_k(t) = \begin{cases} d_k(t) - x_k(t) & \text{if } \quad k \in V \\ 0 & \text{otherwise} \end{cases} \tag{5.4}$$

where $d_k(t)$ represents a target value. The overall network error at time t is defined as

$$J(t) = \frac{1}{2} \sum_k [e_k(t)]^2 \tag{5.5}$$

The weight change for any weight at time t is

$$\Delta w_{ij}(t) = -\eta \frac{\partial J(t)}{\partial w_{ij}} = \eta \sum_k e_k(t) \frac{\partial x_k(t)}{\partial w_{ij}} \tag{5.6}$$

where η is a learning rate. The derivative $\partial x_k(t)/\partial w_{ij}$ can be computed by the equation

$$\frac{\partial x_k(t+1)}{\partial w_{ij}} = f'(s_k(t)) \left[\sum_l w_{kl} \frac{\partial x_l(t)}{\partial w_{ij}} + \delta_{ik} x_j(t) \right] \tag{5.7}$$

with initial conditions

$$\frac{\partial x_k(t_0)}{\partial w_{ij}} = 0 \tag{5.8}$$

Finally, the overall weight change is simply represented by

$$\Delta w_{ij} = \sum_{t} \Delta w_{ij}(t) \tag{5.9}$$

In the experiments we used a slightly modified version of the TSLA, called *teacher forced learning*. Teacher forced learning consists of replacing actual outputs of visible units by target values. Without teacher forced learning, oscillation cannot be attained. For the teacher forced learning algorithm, see [4] and [5]. For several other minor computational methods we used, see [6] and [7].

5.3 RESULTS AND DISCUSSION

5.3.1 Recognition and Generation of Single Periodic Patterns

We present some results regarding the recognition and automatic generation of single periodic functions. The network we used in the following experiments was composed of one visible unit and nine hidden units. All the computations were performed on SX-1. Four results are discussed. The first three results are those regarding the recognition and generation of single-period functions whose periods range from 10 to 30. The last one is concerned with the recognition of complex functions, which was produced by adding two single periodic functions with different periods.

The regenerated sine wave with period 10 is represented in Figure 5.1. As

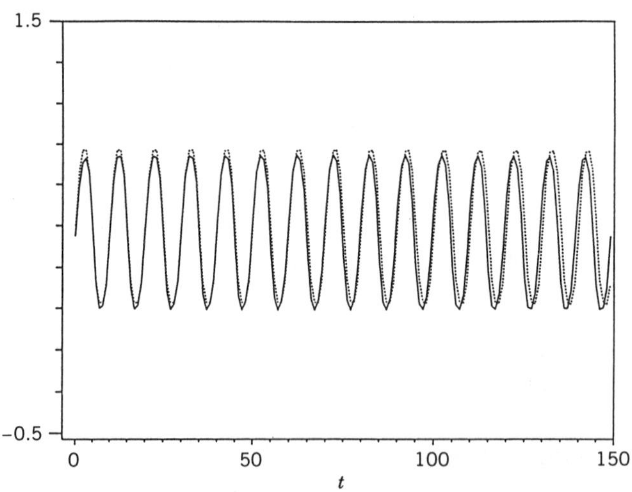

Figure 5.1 *Regenerated since wave (solid line) and original wave (dotted line) with period 10.*

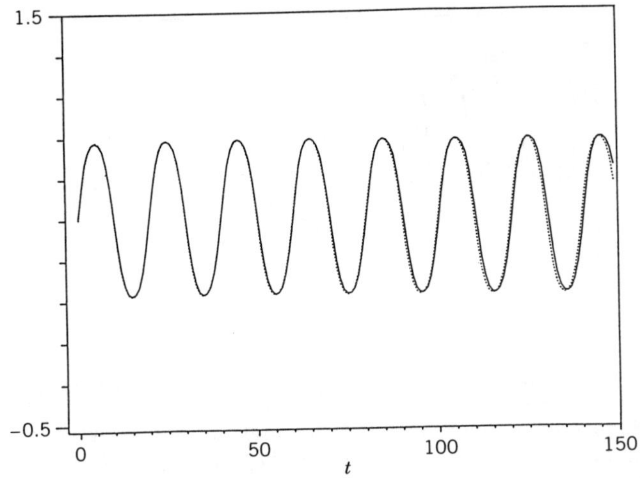

Figure 5.2 *Regenerated sine function (solid line) with period 20 and original pattern (dotted line).*

can be seen, an almost perfect wave was obtained. It took 5264 learning cycles (weight updates or iterations) to reach this point. The period of the regenerated wave tended to be gradually small. We need further learning to reproduce a perfect sine wave.

Figures 5.2 and 5.3 represent regenerated sine waves of periods 20 and 30, respectively. We could also obtain almost perfect target waves. Note that

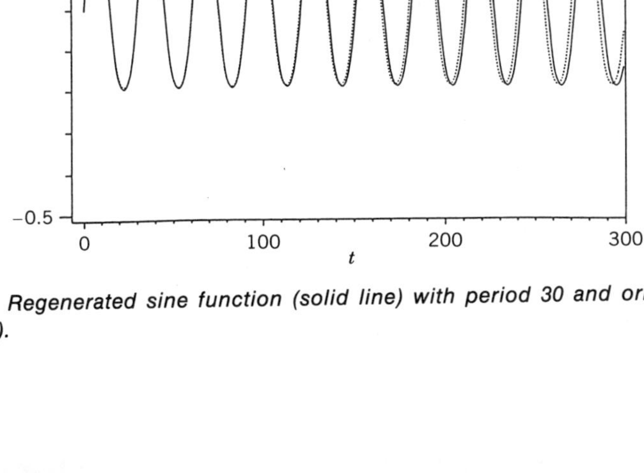

Figure 5.3 *Regenerated sine function (solid line) with period 30 and original pattern (dotted line).*

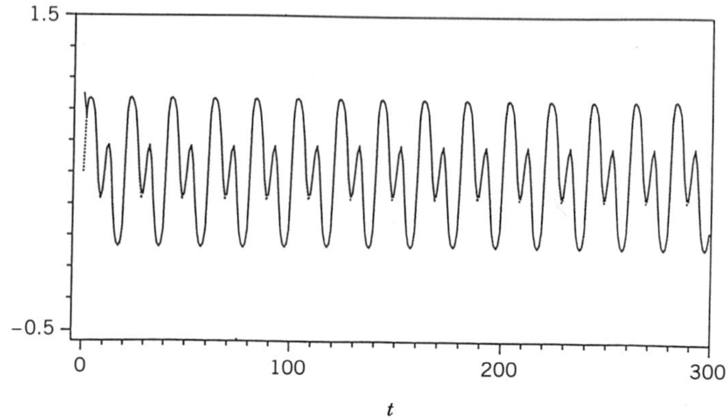

Figure 5.4 *Regenerated complex wave (solid line) and original wave (dotted line). The original one is described by the equation f(2 sin 2πt/20 + 2 sin 2πt/10), where f is a logistic function.*

regenerated sine waves with periods 20 and 30 were obtained after 3439 and 10,606 learning cycles, respectively. The gradual degeneration of perfect periodic waves can also be observed in the figures. This will be overcome only by further training the network.

Finally, Figure 5.4 represents the recognition of a slightly complex function defined by the equation $f(2.0 \sin 2\pi t/20 + 2.0 \sin 2\pi t/10)$. The recurrent network could reproduce this original complex pattern after 53,857 learning cycles. As the figure shows, we cannot find any difference between the original and reproduced patterns except for the first part of the wave.

5.3.2 Recognition and Generation of Multiple Patterns

After finishing the recognition of single patterns, we attempted to recognize multiple patterns simultaneously. It is possible to employ two methods. The first method incorporates multiple patterns into one visible unit, which is possible by taking different initial activity values for different patterns. Second, multiple units can be used to produce different patterns. For example, if we want to recognize two different patterns, two visible units should be prepared. We arbitrarily chose the second method because it is easy to implement.

Figure 5.5 represents the sum of outputs of two visible units. The graph was obtained after 32,493 learning cycles. Two visible units were trained to follow sine functions with slightly different periods, that is, 10 and 12, respectively. The network was composed of two visible units and eight hidden units. As the figure shows, the difference between the original and reproduced patterns is significantly small. This means that the recurrent network can recognize and reproduce multiple periodic patterns simultaneously with

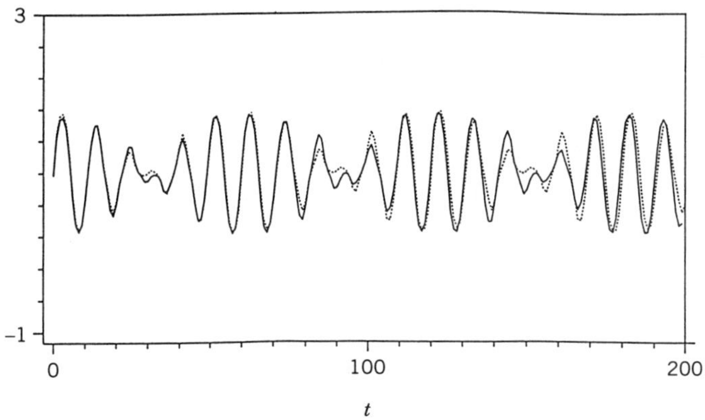

Figure 5.5 *Example of regenerated multiple waves. The wave in the figure was made by taking the sum of the outputs of two visible units, which were trained to follow sine functions with periods 10 and 12, respectively. The network was composed of two visible units and eight hidden units.*

appropriate precision. Moreover, more than two patterns can be simultaneously learned by the network.

5.3.3 Restoration of Periodic Patterns with Noises

We present the results of restoration of the sine function and the computational method that prevents the network from plunging into excessive learning. First, we discuss the method to evade excessive learning, and then we discuss the result of sine function restoration when it is disturbed by noise.

As discussed in the introduction, we want to use teacher signals with noise, hoping that the network can discern the difference between the periodic main part and the peripheral part, that is, noise. The network, in general, has tended to learn the peripheral part, which we call *excessive learning*. To avoid excessive learning, we use a method consisting of a slow learning rate and elimination of extreme variation in error signals. Several methods can be employed for this purpose. For example, in Kamimura [7], Minkowski-r power metrics were used to eliminate the extreme deviation caused by noise. In this chapter, we have used the slow stabilized learning method.

In addition to the slow learning rate, it is desirable for the network to be stable in the learning process. Thus, the method we used is as follows. Equation (5.7) was multiplied by a small constant ε:

$$\frac{\partial x_k(t+1)}{\partial w_{ij}} = \varepsilon f'(s_k(t)) \left[\sum_l w_{kl} \frac{\partial x_l(t)}{\partial w_{ij}} + \delta_{ik} x_j(t) \right] \tag{5.10}$$

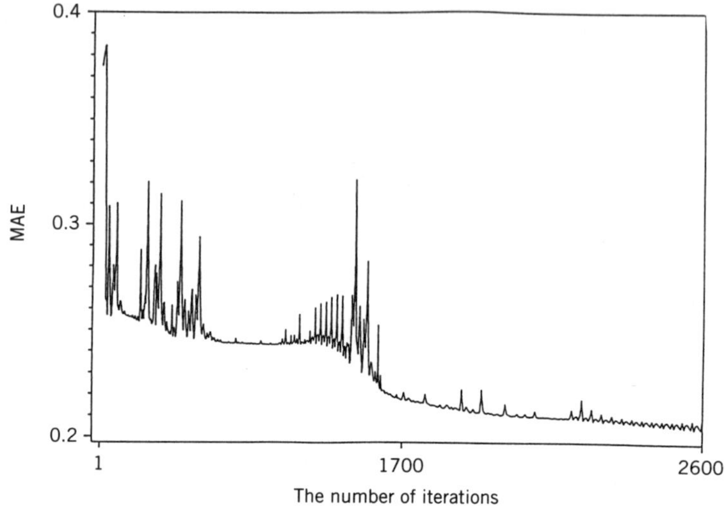

Figure 5.6 *Mean absolute error as a function of learning cycles (iterations).*

where $\varepsilon = 0.7$ in our experiments. This contributed greatly to the stability of the learning process. For further details regarding this stability see Kamimura [7]. The values of Eq. (4.7) are closely related to the error function described in Eq. (4.6). Thus, the reduction of the values of Eq. (4.7) simultaneously reduces the learning rate. In this case, stability is also considered to be ensured as just discussed.

Figure 5.6 represents the mean absolute errors as a function of the learning cycles (iterations) when uniform random noise of size 5 ranging between -2.5 and 2.5 was added to the original periodic function. As can be seen in the figure, the mean absolute errors vary extremely at the beginning of the learning cycles. Then the errors tend to be stable and decrease slowly.

In Figure 5.7, the regenerated wave is reproduced. It has exactly the same period. However the amplitude of the wave is small compared with the original wave. Note that the wave in the figure was obtained after 1910 learning cycles.

The same results were reported by Hanson and Burr [8] regarding the recovery of original spatial static patterns with the back-propagation method. If the size is above the limiting point 5, then the network could not restore the original pattern. The period of the restored patterns tended to be significantly small. Our experimental results suggest a possibility of robust learning of the recurrent network. This means that the network can recognize true temporal patterns even if they are disturbed by random noise. In actual circumstances, the patterns with noise are not exceptional but normal. In these nonideal situations, we can recognize patterns easily. Thus,

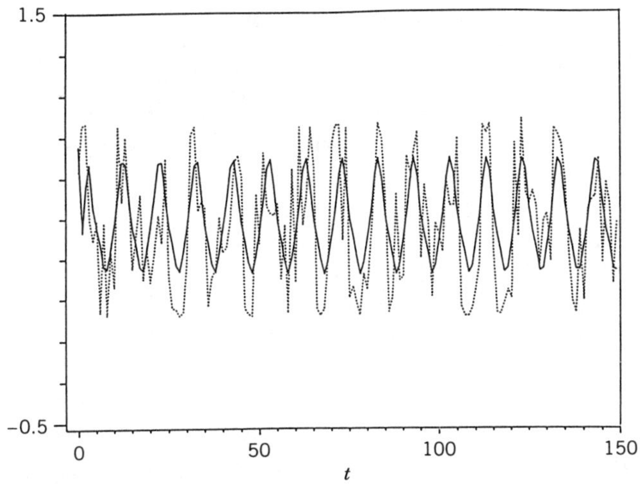

Figure 5.7 *Example of restored sine function with period 10 (solid line) and original pattern (dotted line). The random noise ranged from −2.5 to 2.5.*

the neural network, which aims at imitating the behavior of our brains, should have great potential regarding the reduction of noise. However, as discussed, the recurrent network is not able to positively restore any given pattern, especially in the recognition of temporal patterns.

5.3.4 Discussion

It has been demonstrated that the recurrent neural network with the temporal supervised learning algorithm can recognize and reproduce complex periodic patterns. Current experimental results have shown that the recurrent neural network can recognize and reproduce temporal patterns with more precision than expected from previous studies [1,2,3,5]. We think that the recurrent neural network can be used for many phenomena concerning periodic patterns.

In this section, three problems are discussed: number of hidden units, learning time, and excessive learning of the recurrent neural network. First, we chose the number of hidden units arbitrarily. It has been observed that the pattern of the weight matrix greatly depends on the number of hidden units. Moreover, it sometimes happens that the learning time can be reduced in proportion to the number of hidden units. Thus, we should explore the meaning or role of hidden units within a network mechanism.

Second, memory storage and computational requirements increase on the order of n^3 and n^4, respectively, as can be seen from Eq. (5.7). This problem can be serious when target patterns are very complex and long training sequences are needed. The TSLA may not be competent compared with the same kind of learning methods, for example, Pearlmutter [2,3]. In that method, complete back propagation has been used, which is expected to reduce greatly the computational requirements. However, some attempts to reduce and accelerate the learning process of the TSLA have been made. Zipser [9] has recently proposed a subgrouping technique that seemingly reduces the number of units necessary for computation by dividing the full network into relatively small self-sufficient recurrent networks. Kamimura [7] has also proposed an acceleration method by using Minkowski-r power metrics, which could speed up the learning process significantly. Moreover, the TSLA can be used in real-time mode by slightly changing the weight change described in Eq. (5.9). This real-time mode cannot be shared by other methods.

Third, the recurrent network can learn target patterns excessively, meaning that the noise introduced by outside sources is to be learned by the network. This pertains not only to the recurrent networks but to all types of neural networks. In actual situations, teacher signals cannot be ideal, in that teachers sometimes make mistakes. We learn patterns in the nonideal conditions. Thus, we need to develop methods to eliminate noise in an appropriate way without plunging into excessive learning. Moreover, the behaviors of errors between target and observed values should be considered for the network to be applied practically to noise reduction problems.

5.4 CONCLUSION

We have demonstrated the performance of a recurrent neural network with the temporal supervised learning algorithm when applied to the recognition and restoration of periodic patterns. Three main results can be summarized. First, the recurrent neural network could recognize and reproduce single or multiple periodic patterns with various periods, even if they are complex. We used different visible units for different patterns. It is possible to use one visible unit for different patterns by changing initial state values. The network capacity of the number of patterns is under investigation. Second, the network could recognize and reproduce periodic patterns with appropriate precision. This means that the network could estimate periodic patterns even above the training interval without degeneration. Third, the network could also recognize and regenerate given patterns in spite of the existence of noise.

However, some problems have been pointed out. We have discussed only three of them. First, the performance of recurrent neural networks depends greatly on the number of hidden units. We have no way to determine how many units are necessary and appropriate for given tasks. Since the state of the weight matrix greatly depends on the number of hidden units, which means that the state of connection strength varies according to the number of hidden units, it is necessary to clarify the function and meaning of the hidden units in the network system. Second, the learning of a recurrent network has required an enormous amount of computing time. Some acceleration methods have been developed. However, we need more powerful learning methods if we attempt to apply the recurrent neural network to practical and large-scale problems. The third problem is concerned with excessive learning, which means that the network learns targets excessively. In actual problems, where noise would be frequently introduced, we need new methods to evade excessive learning and to find true targets.

In conclusion, we hope that these experimental results regarding the recognition and restoration of periodic patterns will contribute to the understanding of the internal mechanism of our nervous system concerning central pattern generators or human behavior in general.

REFERENCES

[1] K. Doya and S. Yoshizawa, Adaptive neural oscillator using continuous-time back-propagation learning, *Neural Networks,* 2, 375–385 (1989).

[2] B. A. Pearlmutter, Learning state space trajectories in recurrent neural networks, *Proc. 1988 Connectionist Models Summer School,* Carnegie Mellon University, Pittsburgh, Pa., 113–117 (1988).

[3] B. A. Pearlmutter, Learning state space trajectories in recurrent neural networks, *Neural Computation,* 1(2), 263–269 (1989).

[4] R. J. Williams and D. Zipser, A learning algorithm for continually running fully recurrent neural networks, *Neural Computation,* 1, 270–280 (1989).

[5] R. J. Williams and D. Zipser, Experimental analysis of the real-time recurrent learning algorithm, *Connection Sci.*, 1(1), 87–111 (1989).

[6] S. E. Fahlman, Faster-learning variations on back-propagation: An empirical study, *Proc. 1988 Connectionist Models Summer School*, Carnegie Mellon University, Pittsburgh, Pa., 38–51 (1988).

[7] R. Kamimura, Application of temporal supervised learning algorithm to generation of natural language, *Proc. Internat. Joint Conf. on Neural Networks,* Vol. 1, 201–207 (1990).

[8] S. J. Hanson and D. J. Burr, "Minkowski-*r* Back-Propagation: Learning in Connectionist Models with Non-Euclidian Error Signals," in D. Z. Anderson, Ed., *Neural Information Processing Systems,* American Institute of Physics, New York, 1988, pp. 348–357.

[9] D. Zipser, A subgrouping strategy that reduces complexity and speeds up learning in recurrent networks, *Neural Computation,* 1, 552–558 (1989).

CHAPTER 6

Adaptive Stack Filtering by LMS and Perceptron Learning

NIRWAN ANSARI
YUCHOU HUANG
JEAN-HSANG LIN

6.1 INTRODUCTION

Stack filters are a class of sliding-window nonlinear digital filters that possess the weak superposition property (threshold decomposition) and the ordering property known as the stacking property. They have been demonstrated to be robust in suppressing noise. Two methods are introduced to adaptively configure a stack filter. One is by employing the least mean square (LMS) algorithm, and the other is based on perceptron learning. Experimental results are presented to demonstrate the effectiveness of the proposed methods to noise suppression.

Artificial neural networks or simply neural nets [1] go by many names, such as connectionism, parallel distributed processing, and neuromorphic systems. The goal of neural nets is to achieve good performance via dense interconnection of simple computational elements. These computational elements or nodes used in neural net models are nonlinear. The simplest element sums N weighted inputs and passes the result through a nonlinearity. Neural nets are specified by the net topology, node characteristic, and training or learning rules. These rules specify an initial set of weights and indicate how weights should be adapted during use to improve performance. Both design procedures and training rules are the topic of much current research.

Dynamic, Genetic, and Chaotic Programming, By Branko Souček and the IRIS Group.
ISBN 0-471-55717-X
N. Ansari was partially supported for this work by the New Jersey Department of Higher Education through NJIT Separately Budgeted Research.

The subject of adaptive filters [2,3] has matured to the point where it now constitutes an important part of statistical signal processing. Whenever there is a requirement to process signals that result from operation in an environment of unknown statistics, the use of adaptive filters offers an attractive solution to the problem, as it usually provides a significant improvement in performance over the use of a fixed filter designed by conventional methods. Furthermore, it provides new signal processing capabilities that would not be possible otherwise.

All stack filters [4–10] obey the threshold decomposition property and the stacking property. The difference between two stack filters lies solely in the Boolean operation performed on each level. A necessary and sufficient condition for a Boolean operation to preserve the stacking property was proven by Gilbert [11]. He showed that the operation must be positive, in which case it has a minimum sum of products representation which is free of complements of any of the variables. Thus, only the logical AND and OR operations are permitted. A brief discussion on stack filters is given in Section 6.2.

An adaptive filtering approach [12,13] for stack filters has recently been proposed. In this chapter, two new methods based on LMS and perceptron learning are developed to configure stack filters. Two adaptive algorithms, LMS [14] and Perceptron, along with their properties and differences are discussed in Section 6.3. In Section 6.4, the incorporation of perceptron and LMS learning to configure stack filters is developed. Future research directions are discussed in Section 6.5.

6.2 STACK FILTERS

Median filters [4,5,7,8,15] and other rank-order operators [9] possess two properties called the threshold decomposition property and the stacking property. The first is a limited superposition property; the second is an ordering property that allows an efficient VLSI implementation of the threshold decomposition architecture.

Any filter that possesses the threshold decomposition property and the stacking property is known as a stack filter [10]. Thus, stack filters form a very large class of easily implemented nonlinear filters, which include the rank-order operators as well as all compositions of morphological operators.

6.2.1 Threshold Decomposition and Stacking Properties

Based on the threshold decomposition property and the stacking property, stack filters can be constructed as a "stack" of positive Boolean functions [11]. An entire class of filters that possess the weak superposition property, also called the threshold decomposition, and the stacking property are called stack filters. These properties can be easily illustrated by a rank-order filter such as a median filter with window width 3, as shown in Figure 6.1.

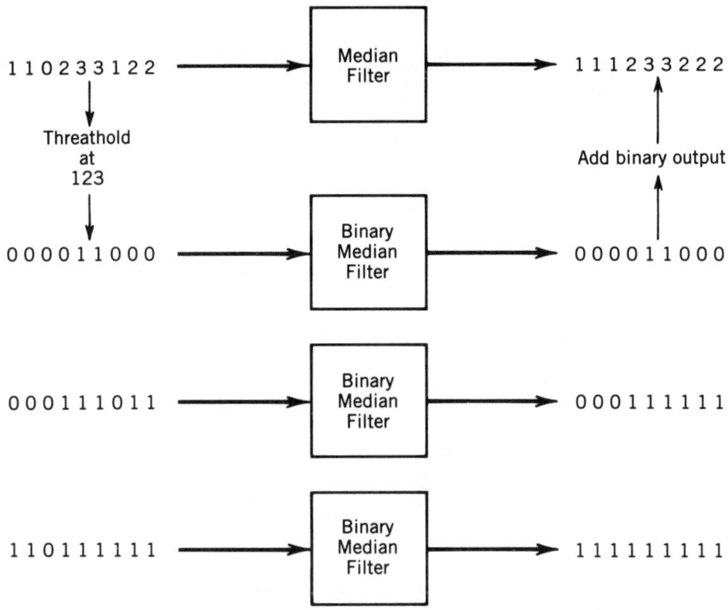

Figure 6.1 *A median filter with a window width of 3.*

Passing an M-valued discrete time signal through a rank-order filter is equivalent to the following procedure:

1. Decomposing the M-valued input signal into a set of $M - 1$ binary signals. The kth binary signal, where $k \in \{1, 2, \ldots, M - 1\}$, is obtained by thresholding the input signal at value k. That is, it takes a value of 1 whenever the input signal is greater than or equal to k, but is 0 otherwise. Note that summing these $M - 1$ binary signals always provides the original input signal, as illustrated in Figure 6.1.
2. Filtering each binary signal independently with its own rank-order filter. Note that each threshold level is performed in parallel. During the process of filtering, each rank-order filter simply adds the number of 1's in the window and compares the result to an integer r, the desired rank of the filter. The output is 1 when the summation is greater than or equal to r, and 0 when the summation is less than r. For example, if the filter's window is $b = 2r + 1$, the filter is a median filter.
3. Adding the output of each binary rank-order filter one sample at a time, as shown in Figure 6.1. It is found that the output of the rank-order filter possesses the stacking property. This means that the binary output signals are piled on top of each other according to their threshold levels. It can be seen that a column of 1's always has a column of 0's on top. The desired output value is simply the value of the threshold level where the transition from 1 to 0 takes place.

6.2.2 Mathematical Model

Consider an M-valued sequence s. The threshold signals $\mathbf{T}^1, \mathbf{T}^2, \cdots \mathbf{T}^{M-1}$ of the sequence are defined by

$$\mathbf{T}^j(i) = \begin{cases} 1 & \text{if } s(i) \geq j \\ 0 & \text{if } s(i) < j \end{cases} \tag{6.1}$$

where i stands for the ith element of the appropriate vector and each element of a threshold vector is binary. Note that these threshold vectors possess the stacking property

$$\mathbf{T}^1 \geq \mathbf{T}^2 \geq \cdots \geq \mathbf{T}^{M-2} \geq \mathbf{T}^{M-1} \tag{6.2}$$

which implies

$$\mathbf{T}^1(i) \geq \mathbf{T}^2(i) \geq \cdots \geq \mathbf{T}^{M-2}(i) \geq \mathbf{T}^{M-1}(i) \tag{6.3}$$

where i is the ith element of the appropriate vector.

Let s_1 and s_2 be two binary sequences. A filter defined by a function $F(\cdot)$ is said to have the *stacking property* if

$$F(s_1) \geq F(s_2) \qquad \text{whenever} \qquad s_1 \geq s_2 \tag{6.4}$$

Based on Eqs. (6.2), (6.3) and (6.4), the output of this filter should have the relationship

$$F(\mathbf{T}^1) \geq F(\mathbf{T}^2) \geq \cdots \geq F(\mathbf{T}^{M-2}) \geq F(\mathbf{T}^{M-1}) \tag{6.5}$$

The function $F(\cdot)$ of a rank-order filter is a Boolean function. This means that if filters with function $F(\cdot)$ have the stacking property, then $F(\cdot)$ must be a positive Boolean function. The operation of these positive Boolean functions is simply the max and min operations. For example, a function $F(\cdot)$ is a positive Boolean function of a stack filter S_F, and $F(x_1, x_2, x_3) = x_1 + x_3$. Thus, the operation of this positive Boolean function is $\max(x_1, x_3)$.

Stack filters are a generalization of median filters. The structure of a median filter root signal [7] is well known, and the structure and analysis of stack filters are similar. Properties and analysis of stack filters have been covered in great detail [10].

6.3 LINEAR DISCRIMINANT FUNCTIONS, LMS AND PERCEPTRON

Linear discriminant functions, the LMS and Perceptron learning rules, which play the major role for configuring the stack filter in this chapter, are briefly discussed.

6.3.1 Discriminant Function and Decision Surface

Linear discriminant functions have a variety of pleasant properties from an analytical point of view and are easy to compute. The problem of finding a linear discriminant function will be formulated as a problem of minimizing a criterion function.

A linear discriminant function [16] is defined by

$$g(\mathbf{x}) = \mathbf{a}^t\mathbf{x} + w_0 \tag{6.6}$$

or

$$g(\mathbf{u}) = w^t u \tag{6.7}$$

where

$$\mathbf{u} = \begin{bmatrix} 1 \\ x \end{bmatrix} \qquad \mathbf{w} = \begin{bmatrix} w_0 \\ \mathbf{a} \end{bmatrix}$$

$\mathbf{x}$ is an input pattern vector, $\mathbf{a}$ is the weight vector, and w_0 is the threshold weight. The linear discriminant function is used to classify the input pattern $\mathbf{x}$ as one of two possible categories, and the decision rule is: Decide class **A** if $g(\mathbf{x}) > 0$, and class **B** if $g(\mathbf{x}) < 0$. Thus, $\mathbf{x}$ is assigned to class **A** if the inner product $\mathbf{a}^t\mathbf{x}$ exceeds the threshold, $-w_0$, and $\mathbf{x}$ is assigned to class **B** if the inner product $\mathbf{a}^t\mathbf{x}$ is less than the threshold, $-w_0$. When $\mathbf{a}^t\mathbf{x} = -w_0$, $\mathbf{x}$ can be assigned to either class **A** or class **B**.

If $g(\mathbf{x}) = 0$, it defines the decision surface that separates points assigned to class **A** from points assigned to class **B**. When $g(\mathbf{x})$ is linear as shown in Eq. (6.6), this decision surface is a *hyperplane*. If $\mathbf{x}_1$ and $\mathbf{x}_2$ are both on the decision surface, then

$$\begin{aligned} \mathbf{a}^t x_1 + w_0 &= \mathbf{a}^t\mathbf{x}_2 + w_0 \\ \mathbf{a}^t(x_1 - \mathbf{x}_2) &= 0 \end{aligned} \tag{6.8}$$

Therefore, $\mathbf{a}$ is normal to the hyperplane. The orientation of the decision surface is decided by $\mathbf{a}$, and the surface location is determined by w_0.

6.3.2 LMS and Perceptron Learning

Consider the structure of an adaptive threshold logical element as shown in Figure 6.2. This structure has two parts: (1) a transversal filter with adjustable tap weights whose values at time n are denoted $w_1(n), w_2(n), \ldots, w_N(n)$, and (2) a mechanism for adjusting these tap weights in an adaptive manner.

During the training process, an additional signal $d(n)$, called the *desired response,* is supplied along with the usual tap input. The desired signal

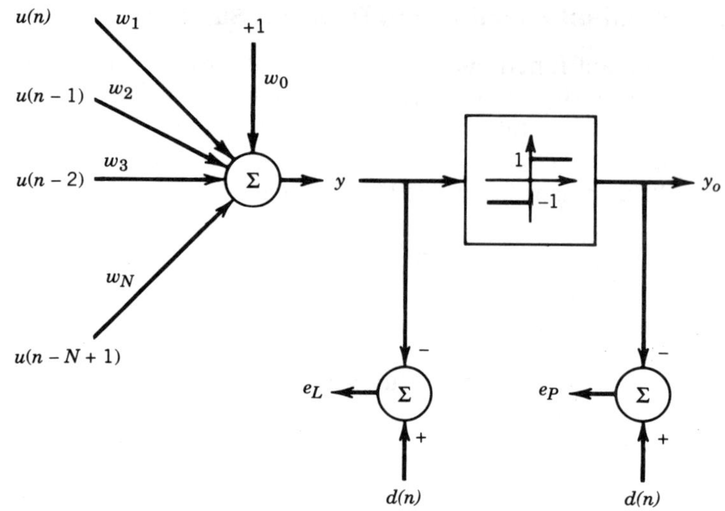

Figure 6.2 *Adaptive threshold logic element—adaptive filter structure by the LMS and Perceptron rules.*

response provides a reference for adjusting the tap weights of the filter. Let $e_L(n)$ and $e_P(n)$ be the estimation errors produced during LMS and perceptron learning, respectively. Thus, as shown in Figure 6.2,

$$e_L(n) = d(n) - \mathbf{w}^t(n)\mathbf{u}(n) \tag{6.9}$$

where $\mathbf{w}^t(n)\mathbf{u}(n)$ is the inner product of the tap weight vector $\mathbf{w}(n)$ and the tap input vector $\mathbf{u}(n)$, and the superscript t stands for vector or matrix transpose. Since there are $N + 1$ inputs that correspond to the N inputs for a filter width of N and a threshold determined by w_0, the weight vector is $\mathbf{w}^t(n) = [w_0(n), w_1(n), w_2(n), \ldots, w_N(n)]$ and the input vector is $\mathbf{u}^t(n) = [1, u(n), u(n-1), \ldots, u(n-N+1)]$.

Here, only real input data, real weights, and real desired output data are considered, and the criterion function is based on the mean squared error

$$J(n) = E[(d(n) - \mathbf{w}^t(n)\mathbf{u}(n))^2] \tag{6.10}$$

If the tap input vector $\mathbf{u}(n)$ and the desired response $d(n)$ are jointly stationary, then the mean squared error $J(n)$ at time n can be written as

$$J(n) = \sigma_d^2 - \mathbf{w}^t(n)\mathbf{p} - \mathbf{p}^t\mathbf{w}(n) + \mathbf{w}^t(n)\mathbf{R}\mathbf{w}(n) \tag{6.11}$$

where σ_d^2 is the variance of the desired response $d(n)$, $\mathbf{p}$ is the cross-correlation vector between the tap input vector $\mathbf{u}(n)$ and the desired response $d(n)$, $\mathbf{R}$ is the autocorrelation matrix of the tap input vector $\mathbf{u}(n)$,

$$\begin{aligned} \mathbf{p} &= E[\mathbf{u}(n)d(n)] \\ \mathbf{R} &= E[\mathbf{u}(n)\mathbf{u}^t(n)] \end{aligned} \tag{6.12}$$

The gradient of the criterion function, ∇, is simply the derivative of the mean squared error J with respect to the tap weight vector $\mathbf{w}$:

$$\nabla = \frac{dJ(n)}{d\mathbf{w}} = -2\mathbf{p} + 2\mathbf{R}\mathbf{w}(n) \tag{6.13}$$

An optimal weight vector such that $J(n)$ is minimized can be obtained by letting $J = 0$.

The simplest choice of estimators $\mathbf{R}$ and $\mathbf{p}$ is to use the instantaneous estimates based on sample values of the tap input and desired response, as defined by

$$\begin{aligned} \mathbf{R} &= \mathbf{u}(n)\mathbf{u}^t(n) \\ \mathbf{p} &= \mathbf{u}(n)d(n) \end{aligned} \tag{6.14}$$

respectively. Correspondingly, the instantaneous estimate of the gradient vector is

$$\nabla(n) = -2\mathbf{u}(n)d(n) + 2\mathbf{u}(n)\mathbf{u}^t(n)\mathbf{w}(n) \tag{6.15}$$

According to the method of steepest descent [3], the updated value of the tap weight vector at time $n + 1$ is computed by using the simple recursive relation

$$\mathbf{w}(n+1) = \mathbf{w}(n) + \tfrac{1}{2}\mu[-\nabla(n)] \tag{6.16}$$

where μ is a positive real-valued constant.

Substituting Eq. (6.13) into Eq. (6.16) gives the following updating rule:

$$\mathbf{w}(n+1) = \mathbf{w}(n) + \mu[\mathbf{p} - \mathbf{R}\mathbf{w}(n)] \tag{6.17}$$

and substituting Eq. (6.14) into Eq. (6.17) gives the following LMS learning rule:

$$\begin{aligned} \mathbf{w}(n+1) &= \mathbf{w}(n) + \mu\mathbf{u}(n)[d(n) - \mathbf{u}^t(n)\mathbf{w}(n)] \\ &= \mathbf{w}(n) + \mu\mathbf{u}(n)e_L(n) \end{aligned} \tag{6.18}$$

where

$$e_L(n) = d(n) - y(n) \qquad y(n) = \mathbf{u}^t(n)\mathbf{w}(n) \tag{6.19}$$

In Figure 6.2, the error $e_P(n)$ is generated after passing the linear output y through the hard-limiting function $f_H(\cdot)$. Thus, the output y_o is

$$y_o(n) = f_H(\mathbf{u}^t(n)\mathbf{w}(n)) \tag{6.20}$$

Replacing y and e_L by y_o and e_P in Eq. (6.18), we obtain the following Perceptron learning rule:

$$\mathbf{w}(n+1) = \mathbf{w}(n) + \mu\mathbf{u}(n)e_P(n) \tag{6.21}$$

where

$$e_P(n) = d(n) - y_o(n)$$

Based on the concept of linear discriminant function, the hard-limiting threshold level should be chosen as follows:

$$y_o = \begin{cases} 1 & \text{if } y > 0 \\ -1 & \text{if } y \le 0 \end{cases} \tag{6.22}$$

The single-layer perceptron can be used with both continuous-valued and binary inputs. This simple net generates much interest when initially developed because of its ability to learn to recognize simple patterns. Rosenblatt [17] proved that if the inputs presented from two classes, **A** and **B**, are separable, then the perceptron procedure converges, and positions the decision hyperplane between these two classes. For a linear separable case, LMS or perceptron learning is good enough to classify the input samples. To classify nonlinearly separable samples, we must use multilayer networks such as multilayer perceptrons [1,18]. Generally speaking, the Perceptron algorithm and LMS algorithm are almost the same. Both perform weight adaptation based on the estimation error by the gradient descent method. However, the estimation errors of the two are different. This difference leads to different behavior. If the samples are not linearly separable, the weight vector adapted by the Perceptron rule may oscillate forever and does not converge to a low-error solution. On the other hand, the weight vector obtained by the LMS rule [18] cannot be unreasonable if the samples are not separable. Both learning rules can be generalized to a more general rule by replacing the hard-limiting function by a sigmoid function [14,19].

6.4 CONFIGURING STACK FILTERS BY LMS AND PERCEPTRON LEARNING

Let $s(n)$ be the original signal sequence, $\eta(n)$ the noise process, and $r(n)$ the resulting sequence. It is assumed that $s(n)$ is corrupted by the additive noise

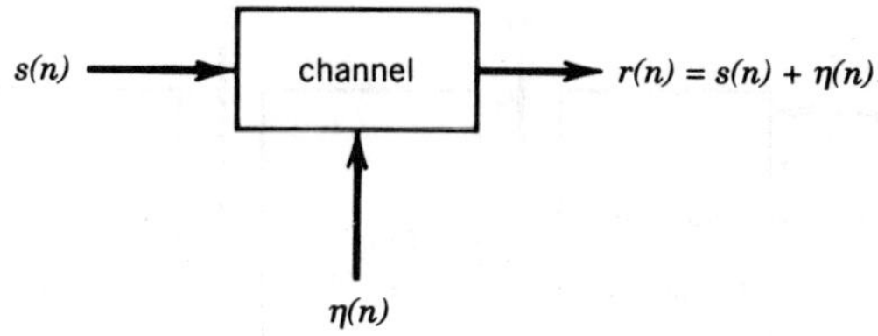

Figure 6.3 *Additive noise channel.*

process $\eta(n)$ and, thus, the resulting sequence $r(n) = s(n) + \eta(n)$, as shown in Figure 6.3.

The problem addressed here is to configure a stack filter S in order to recover the original signal sequence from the corrupted sequence. Since stack filters possess the threshold decomposition and stacking properties, configuring a stack filter is equivalent to first converting the input signal sequence into a sequence of binary signals by threshold decomposition, and then finding the appropriate positive Boolean function used for all levels. Now, the input signal sequence is $r(n)$. Assume $r(n)$ is an M-valued sequence. By threshold decomposition the thresholded binary sequences denoted by $\mathbf{T}^{M-1}, \mathbf{T}^{M-2}, \ldots, \mathbf{T}^2, \mathbf{T}^1$ are obtained, where

$$\mathbf{T}^1 \geq \mathbf{T}^2 \geq \cdots \geq \mathbf{T}^{M-2} \geq \mathbf{T}^{M-1} \tag{6.23}$$

and

$$\mathbf{T}^j(n) = \begin{cases} 1 & \text{if } r(n) \geq j \\ -1 & \text{if } r(n) < j \end{cases} \tag{6.24}$$

Note that 1 and -1 rather than 1 and 0 are adopted here.

Let N be the window width of the stack filter. At each threshold level, the input sequence is a binary sequence, and the output is a binary number. Thus, the input-output relationship can be realized by a Boolean function. Recall from the previous section that some binary Boolean functions can be realized by a linear discriminant function and thus can be trained by the LMS or the Perceptron learning rules. However, the Boolean function obtained by training the single neuron may not be positive. Heuristics, which will be discussed later, are introduced to ensure that the resulting Boolean function is positive.

6.4.1 General Single-Neuron Structure for Configuring Stack Filters

The general single-neuron structure for configuring stack filters is shown in Figure 6.4. The input sequence $r(n)$ is first converted to the thresholded

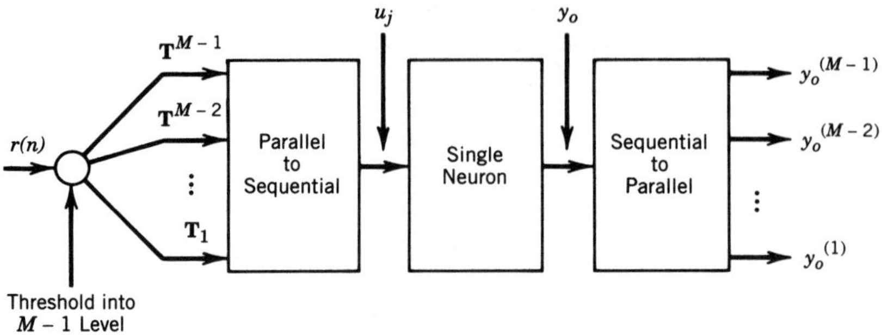

Figure 6.4 *Single-neuron structure to configuring stack filters.*

binary sequence $\mathbf{T}^1, \mathbf{T}^2, \ldots, \mathbf{T}^{M-1}$. For each window sample of width N of $r(n)$, there are $M - 1$ window samples of width N of the thresholded binary sequences; that is, $M - 1$ binary input patterns are presented to the single neuron. Thus, the weights of the neuron are updated by the $M - 1$ binary input patterns $M - 1$ times for each window sample of $r(n)$. The serial binary outputs of the neuron are then stacked back into $M - 1$ levels. Finally, the M-valued filtered output signal is reconstructed, by the stacking property, from the binary outputs by a search for level at which a transition from 1 to -1 occurs.

Let $\mathbf{r}_i$ be the ith window sample of width N of the input sequence $r(n)$, and $\mathbf{T}_i^1, \mathbf{T}_i^2, \ldots, \mathbf{T}_i^{M-1}$ the $M - 1$ thresholded binary input patterns that result from the ith input sample $\mathbf{r}_i$. These parallel $M - 1$ thresholded binary input patterns are transformed into a sequence of binary patterns as follows:

$$\mathbf{u}_j = \mathbf{T}_i^k \qquad \text{where } j = (M-1)(i-1) + k \tag{6.25}$$

The weights of the neurons are then updated by a learning rule. For LMS learning, using Eqs. (6.18) and (6.19), we have

$$\mathbf{w}_{j+1} = \max\left\{\mathbf{w}_j + \frac{\mu \mathbf{u}_j[d_j - \mathbf{w}_j^t \mathbf{u}_j]}{N+1}, 0\right\} \tag{6.26}$$

where

$$j = (M-1)(i-1) + k$$

The max operator is to ensure nonnegative weights. Since the elements of $\mathbf{u}_j$ are either 1 or -1, $\mathbf{u}_j/(N+1) = \mathbf{u}_j/|\mathbf{u}_j|^2$, the normalized input pattern.

Similarly, for perceptron learning, the weights are updated as follows:

$$\mathbf{w}_{j+1} = \max\left\{\mathbf{w}_j + \frac{\mu\mathbf{u}_j[d_j - f_H(\mathbf{w}_j^t\mathbf{u}_j)]}{N+1}, 0\right\} \tag{6.27}$$

where f_H is the hard-limiting function.

Note that during training, negative weights except w_0 are set to zero. These heuristics are introduced in order to preserve the stacking property of a stack filter. After training, the final weight vector is used for the remaining inputs. It is easy to show that the above heuristics preserve the stacking property.

Let $\mathbf{w}^k$ be the weight vector used for the kth thresholded level signal. The kth-level output

$$y_o^k = f_H(y^k)$$

where $y^k = (\mathbf{T}^k)^t\mathbf{w}^k$ and $k = M-1, M-2, \ldots, 1$. Since

$$\mathbf{T}^{M-1} \leq \mathbf{T}^{M-2} \leq \cdots \leq \mathbf{T}^1$$

and

$$\mathbf{w}^{(M-1)} = \mathbf{w}^{(M-2)} = \cdots = \mathbf{w}^{(1)} \geq \mathbf{0}$$

Thus,

$$y_o^{(M-1)} \leq y_o^{(M-2)} \leq \cdots \leq y_o^{(1)}$$

Hence, the stacking property is preserved.

6.4.2 Experimental Results

Two methods to configure stack filters were developed and discussed in detail. The effectiveness of the proposed algorithms for noise suppression is demonstrated by experimental results. Various types of signals and noise have been considered, but only results for two types of signals and the ε-mixture of Gaussian noise are presented.

The ε-mixture of Gaussian noise has the following probability density function:

$$P(y) = (1-\varepsilon)\Phi\left(\frac{y}{\sigma_1}\right) + \varepsilon\Phi\left(\frac{y}{\sigma^2}\right)$$

where $\Phi(y)$ is the probability density function of a Gaussian random variable with zero mean and unit variance. The ε-mixture of Gaussian noise is suitable for representing deviations of sample values from a single distribution.

With probability $1 - \varepsilon$, the added noise for a sample, $\eta(n)$, is a Gaussian random variable with standard deviation σ_1, which represents the background thermal noise; with probability ε, $\eta(n)$ is a Gaussian random variable with standard deviation σ_2, which represents the impulsive noise. In the simulations, the ε-mixture of Gaussian noise is generated with $\varepsilon = 0.8$, $\sigma_1 = 1$, and $\sigma_2 = 10$.

The combination of several sinusoids signal and the ε-mixture of Gaussian noise are shown separately in Figure 6.5. The corrupted signal obtained by adding the signal and noise is shown in Figure 6.6. The filtered output signals obtained by the LMS and the Perceptron rules with various window widths are shown in Figures 6.7–6.10. Figure 6.11 shows the "Mexican hat" signal and the ε-mixture of Gaussian noise. The corrupted "Mexican hat" signal is shown in Figure 6.12. The filtered output signals obtained by the LMS and Perceptron rules with various window widths are shown in Figures 6.13–6.16. In these figures, the first 500 samples are the results obtained during the training, and the remaining samples are the results after having the trained weights fixed. Figures 6.17 and 6.18 show the mean absolute error between the desired output and the filtered output by the LMS and Perceptron rules, using various window widths for the combination of several sinusoids signal and the "Mexican hat" signal, respectively.

From these results, we can draw the following conclusions:

1. The Perceptron rule outperforms the LMS rule in configuring the stack filter.
2. Noise suppression depends on the signal, noise, and filter window width.
3. Filters with larger window widths perform better than those with smaller window widths.

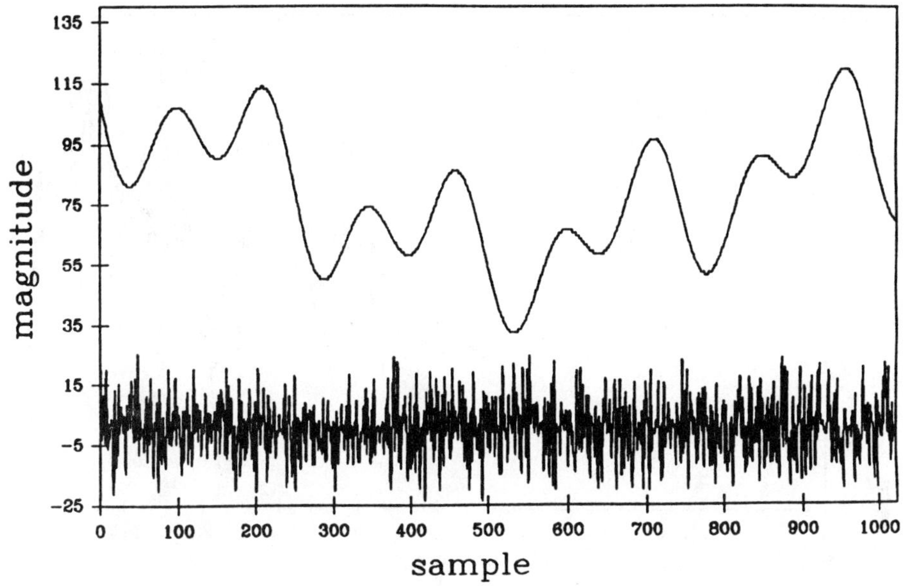

Figure 6.5 *Original signal (a combination of sinusoids) and ε-mixture of Gaussian noise are shown separately.*

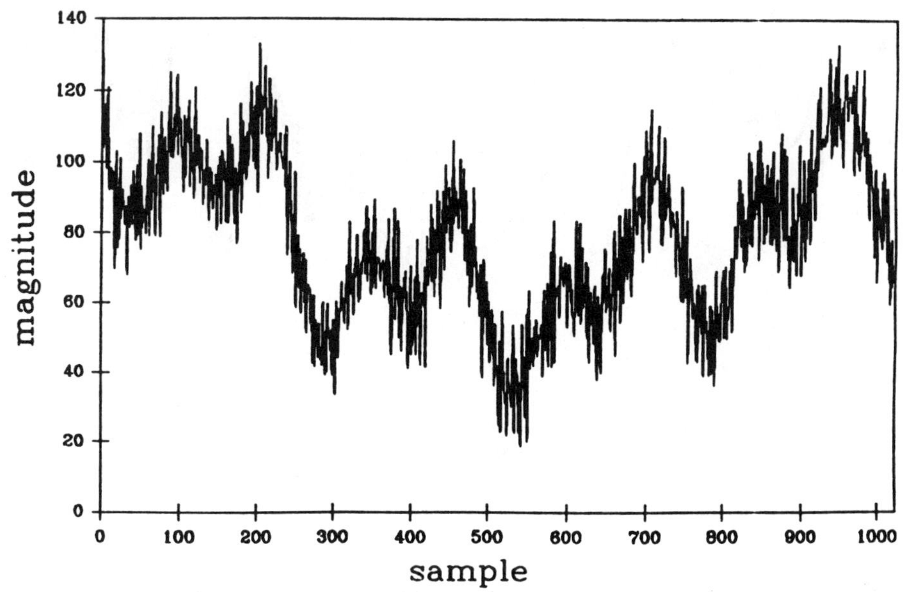

Figure 6.6 *Corrupted signal—a combination of sinusoids + ε-mixture of Gaussian noise.*

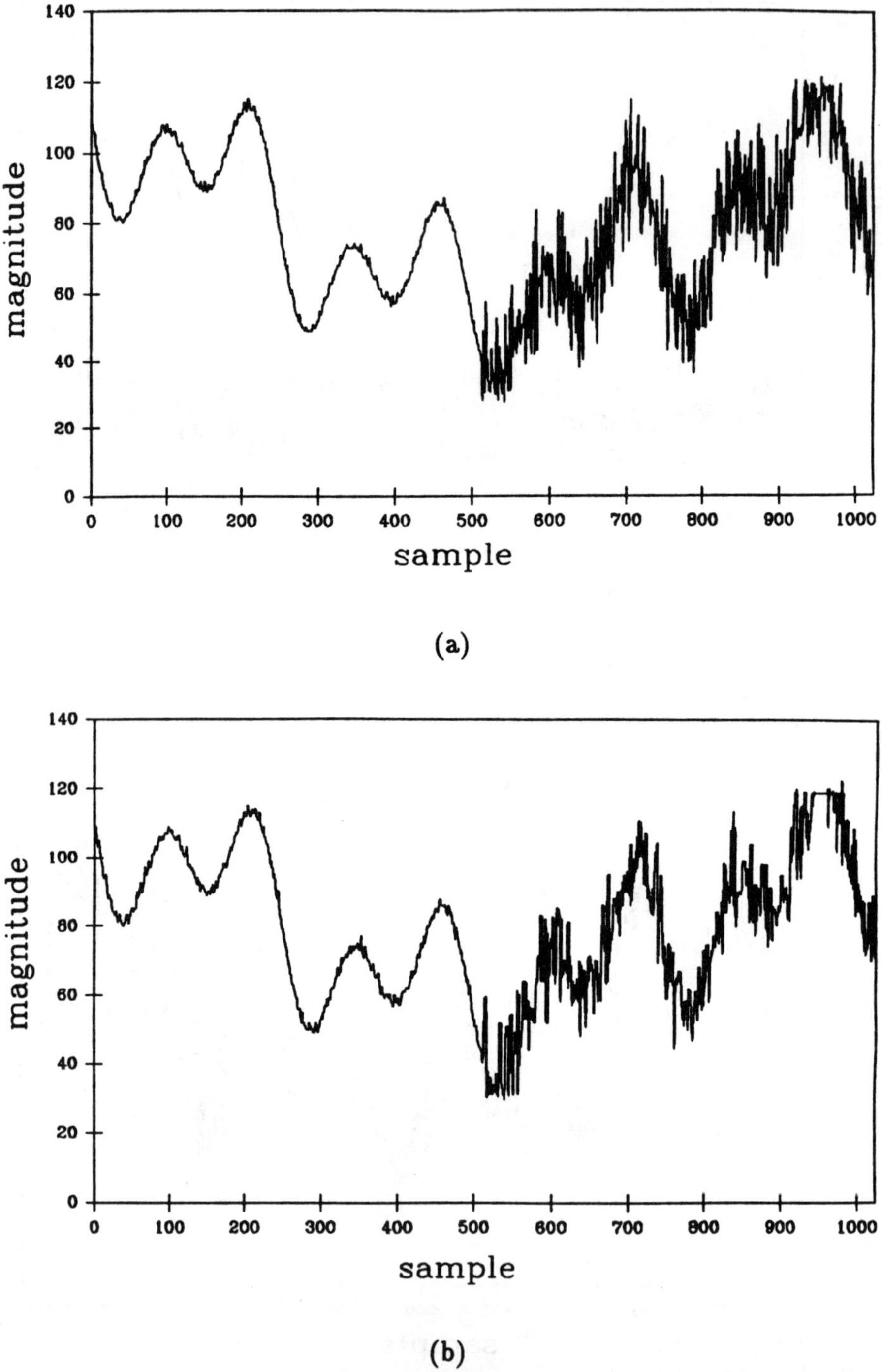

Figure 6.7 *Output signal obtained by filtering the corrupted signal shown in Figure 6.6 by* (a) *the LMS rule,* (b) *the Perceptron rule, using window width = 3.*

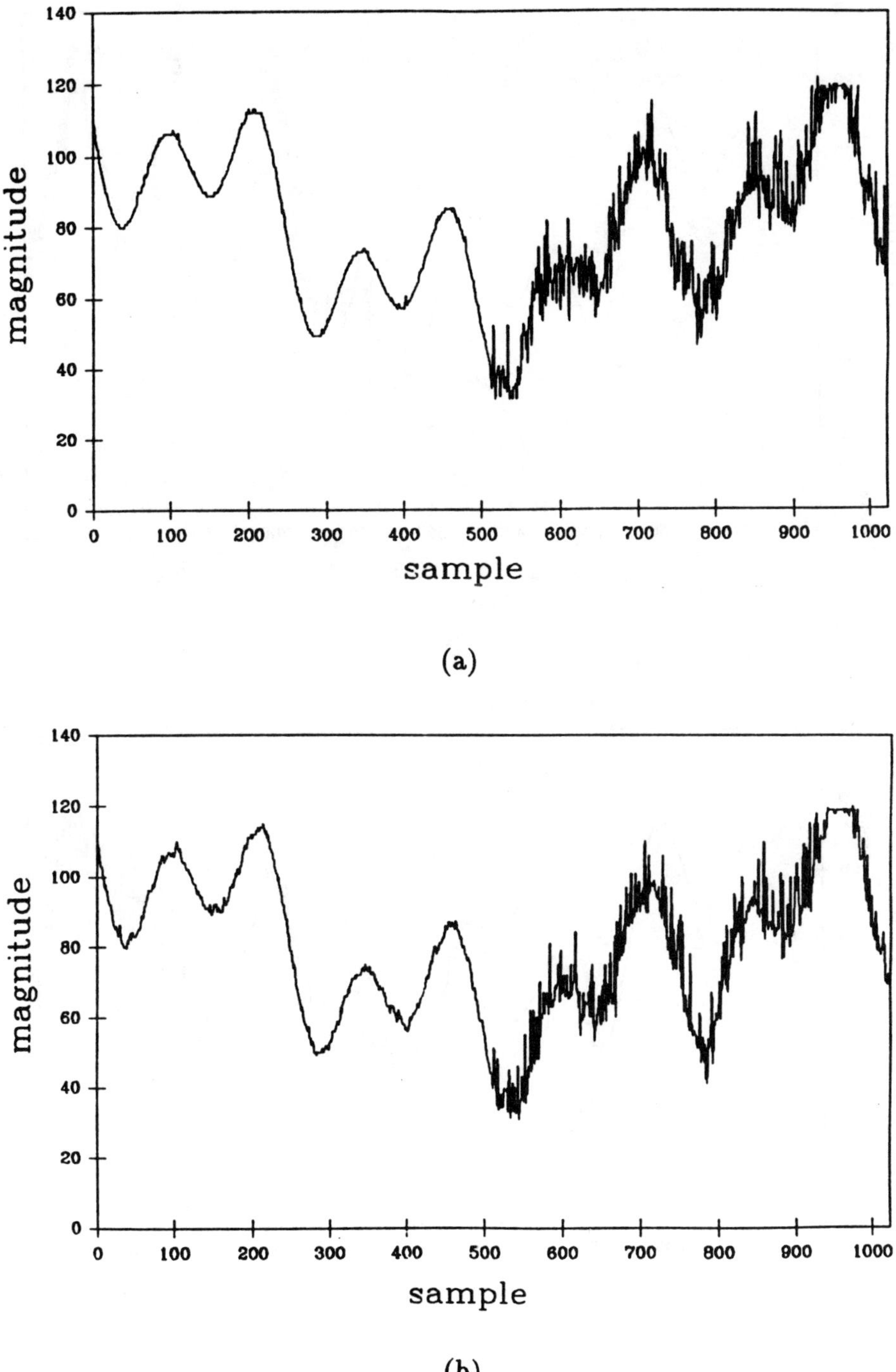

Figure 6.8 *Output signal obtained by filtering the corrupted signal shown in Figure 6.6 by* (a) *the LMS rule,* (b) *the Perceptron rule, using window width = 7.*

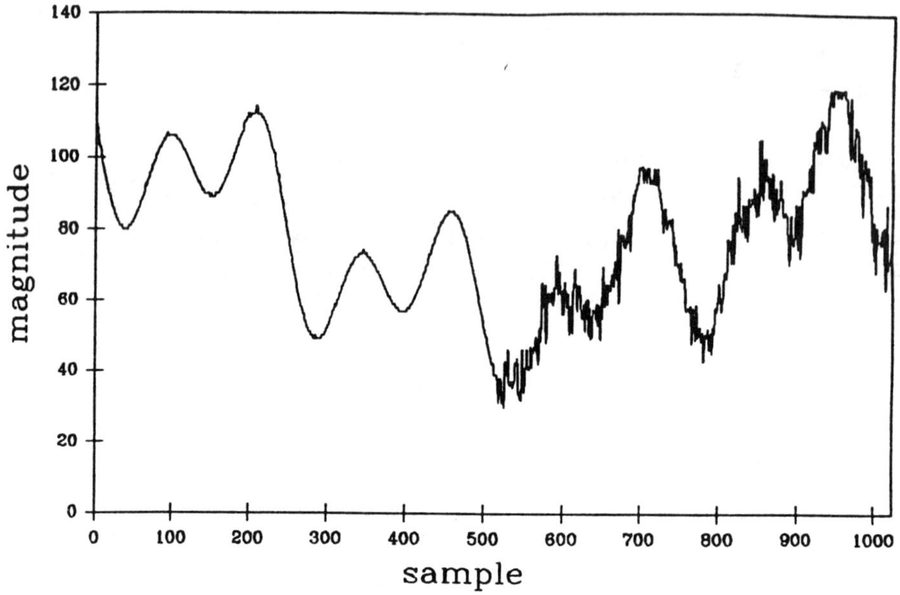

(a)

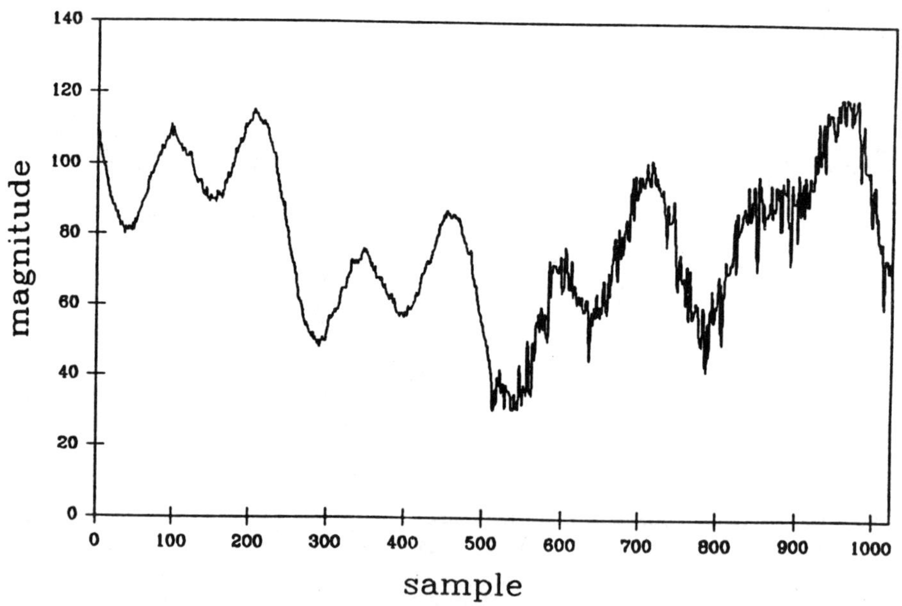

(b)

Figure 6.9 *Output signal obtained by filtering the corrupted signal shown in Figure 6.6 by* (a) *the LMS rule,* (b) *the Perceptron rule, using window width = 11.*

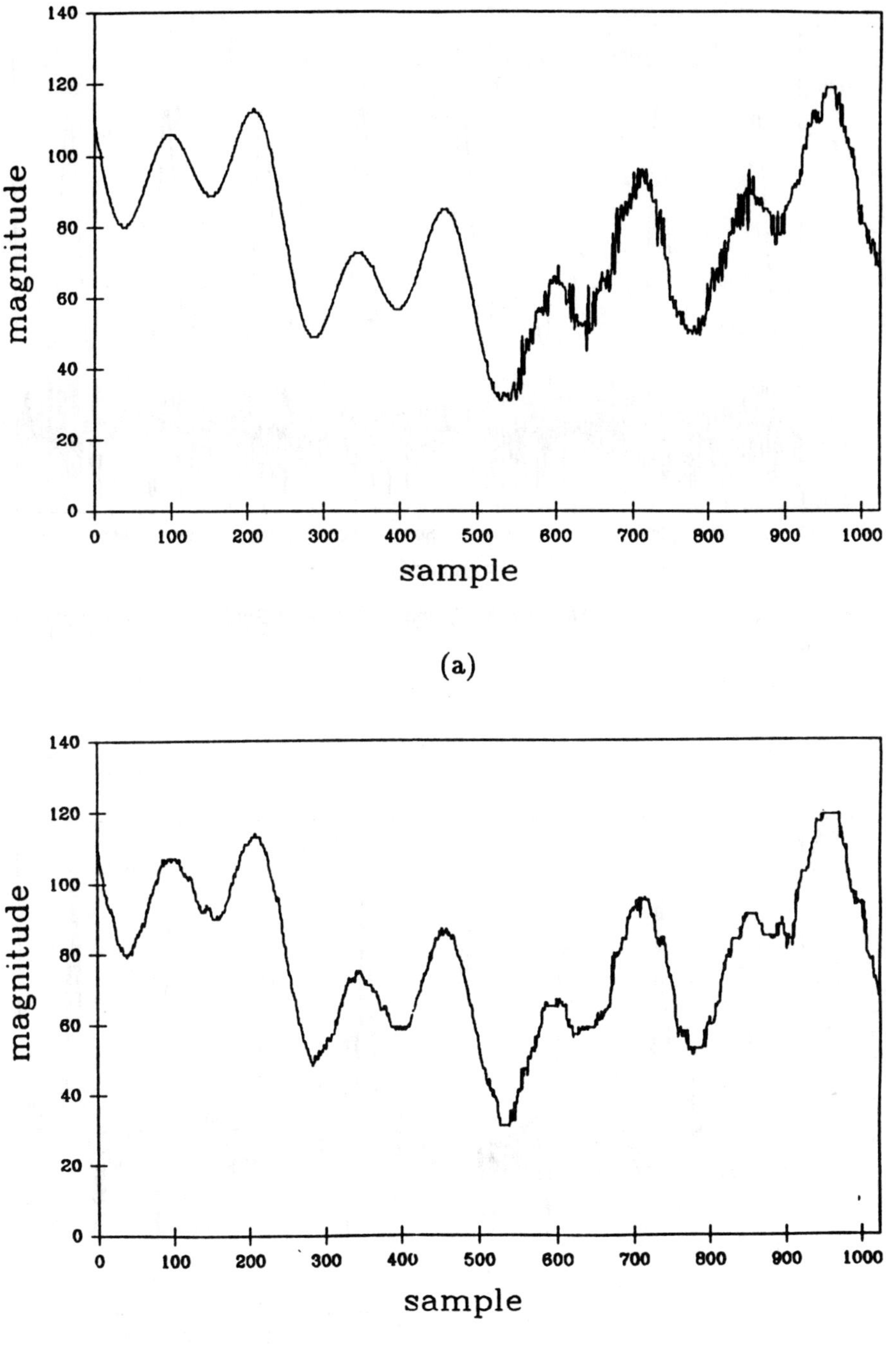

Figure 6.10 *Output signal obtained by filtering the corrupted signal shown in Figure 6.6 by* (a) *the LMS rule,* (b) *the Perceptron rule, using window width = 15.*

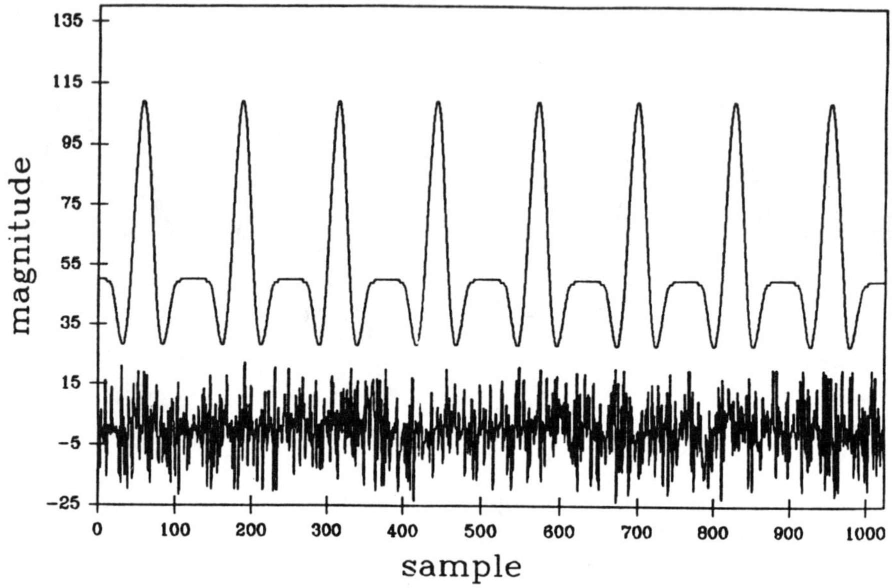

Figure 6.11 *Original signal ("Mexican hat") and ε-mixture of Gaussian noise are shown separately.*

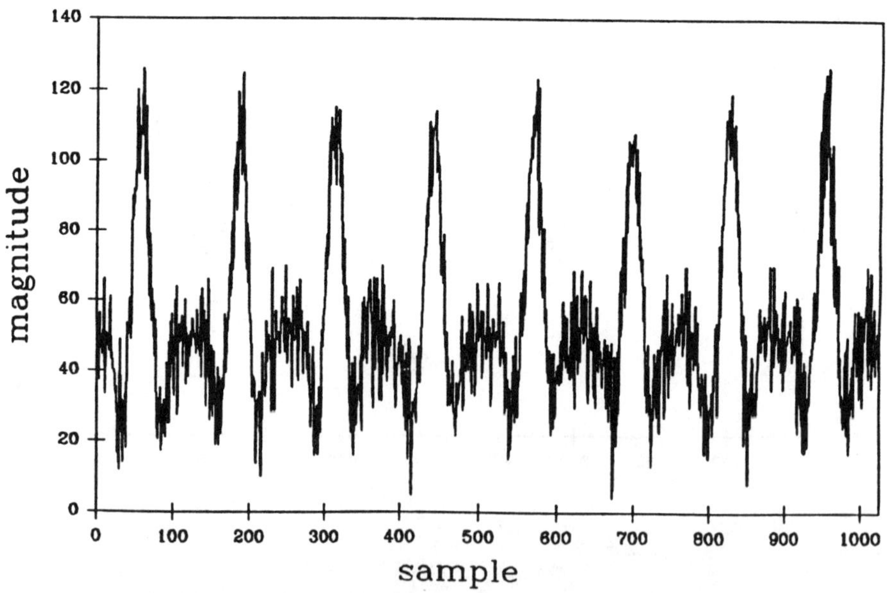

Figure 6.12 *Corrupted signal—"Mexican hat" + ε-mixture of Gaussian nose.*

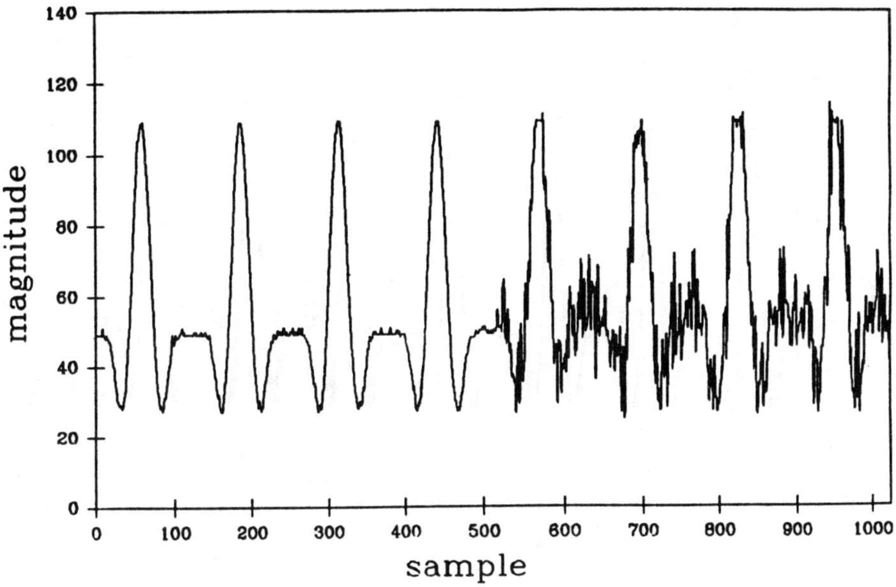

(a)

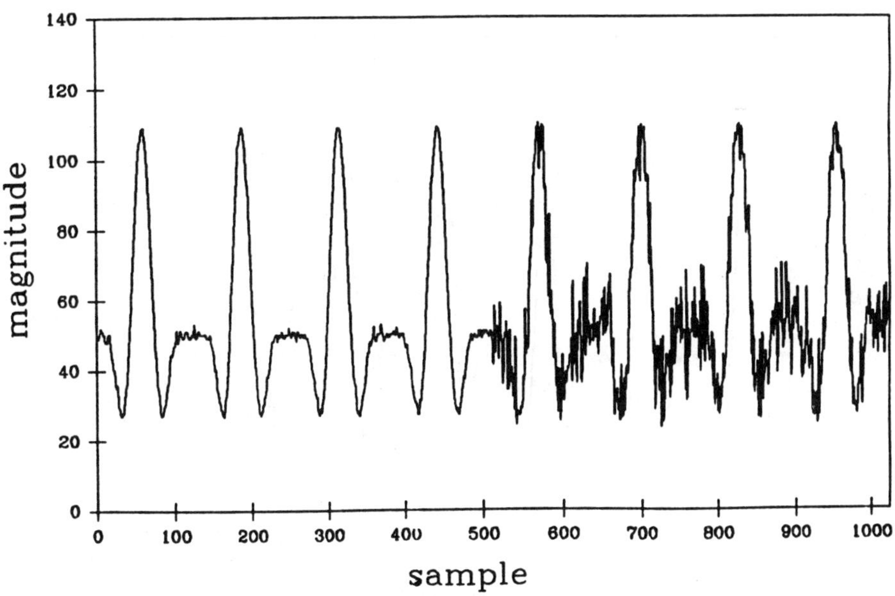

(b)

Figure 6.13 *Output signal obtained by filtering the corrupted signal shown in Figure 6.12 by* (a) *the LMS rule,* (b) *the Perceptron rule, using window width = 3.*

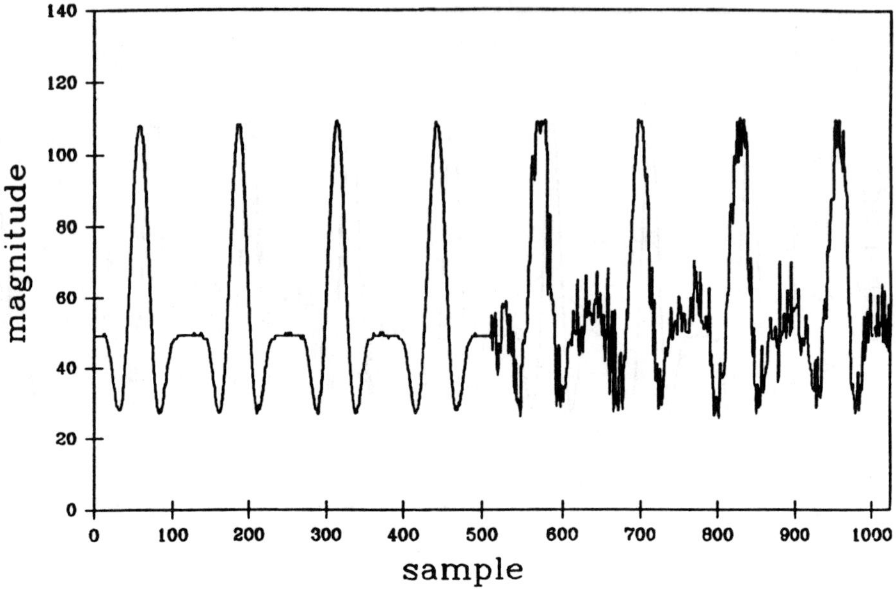

(a)

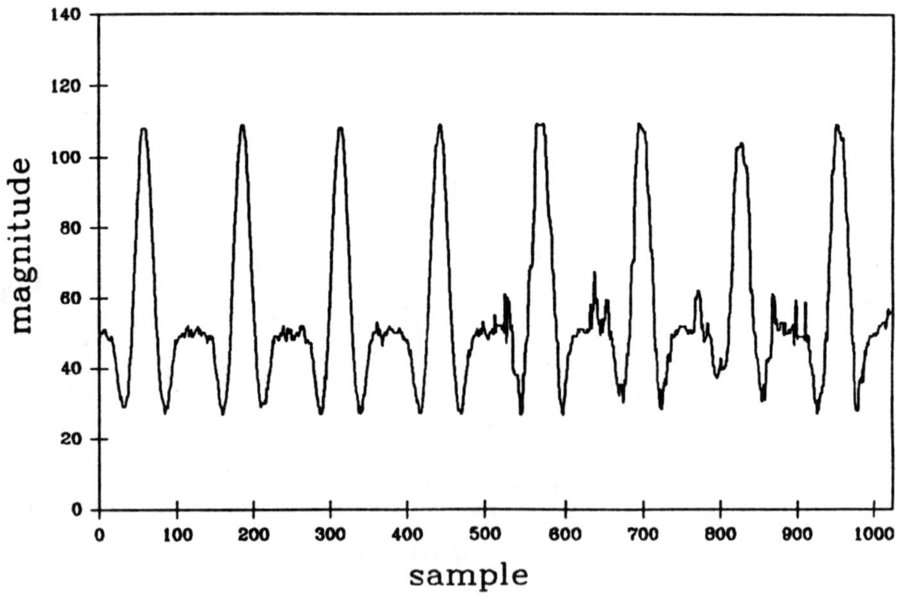

(b)

Figure 6.14 *Output signal obtained by filtering the corrupted signal shown in Figure 6.12 by* (a) *the LMS rule,* (b) *the Perceptron rule, using window width = 7.*

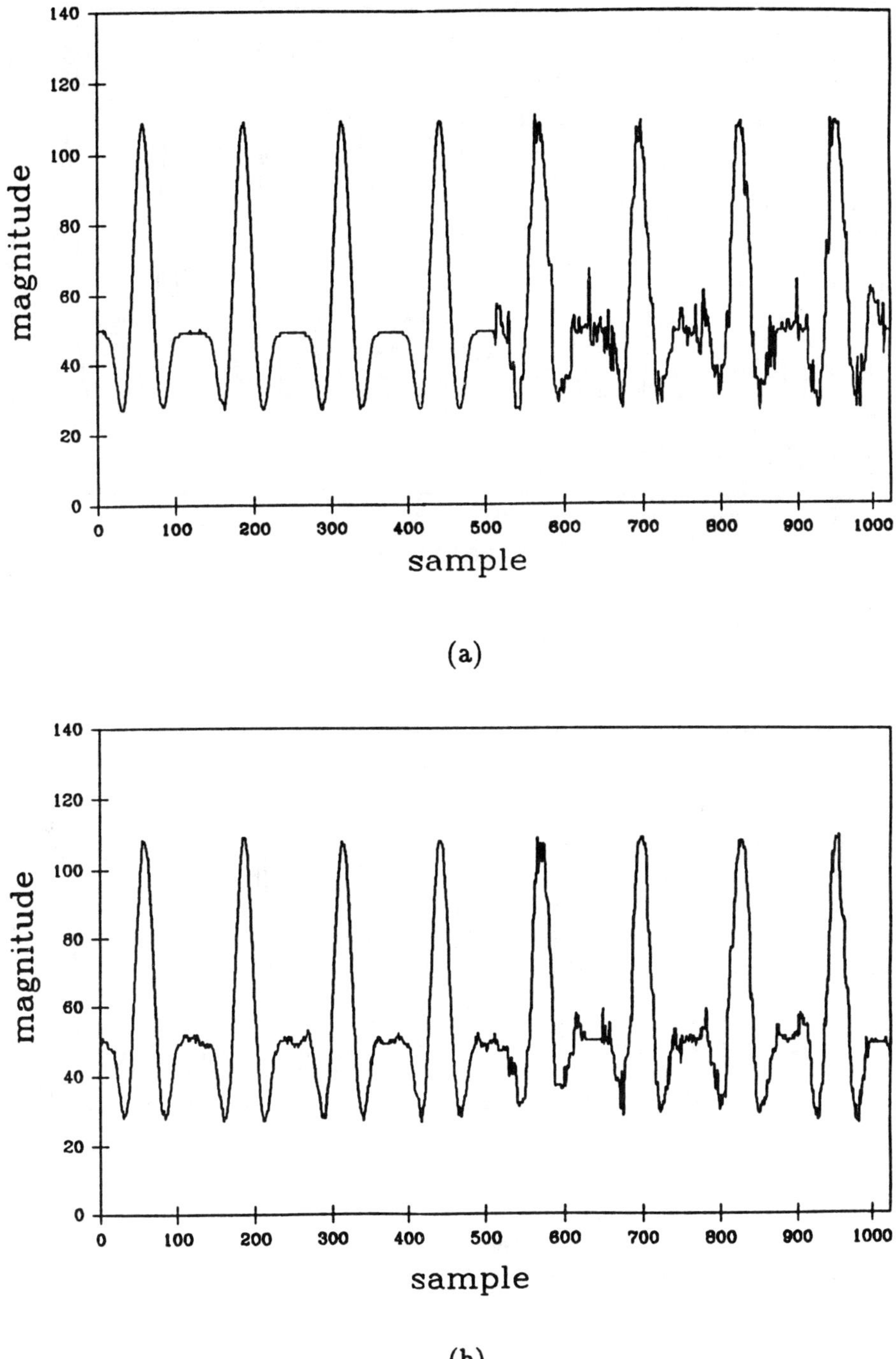

Figure 6.15 *Output signal obtained by filtering the corrupted signal shown in Figure 6.12 by* (a) *the LMS rule,* (b) *the Perceptron rule, using window width = 11.*

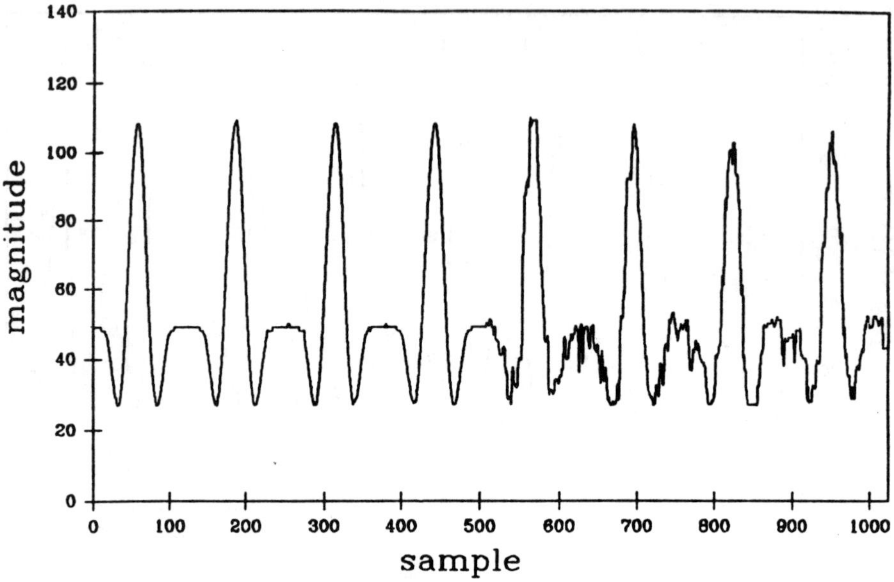

(a)

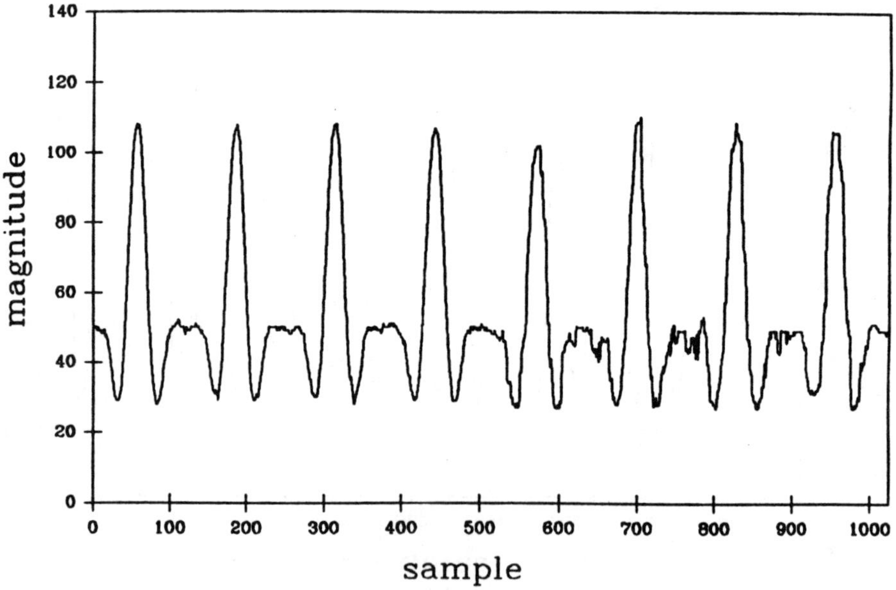

(b)

Figure 6.16 *Output signal obtained by filtering the corrupted signal shown in Figure 6.12 by* (a) *the LMS rule,* (b) *the Perceptron rule, using window width = 15.*

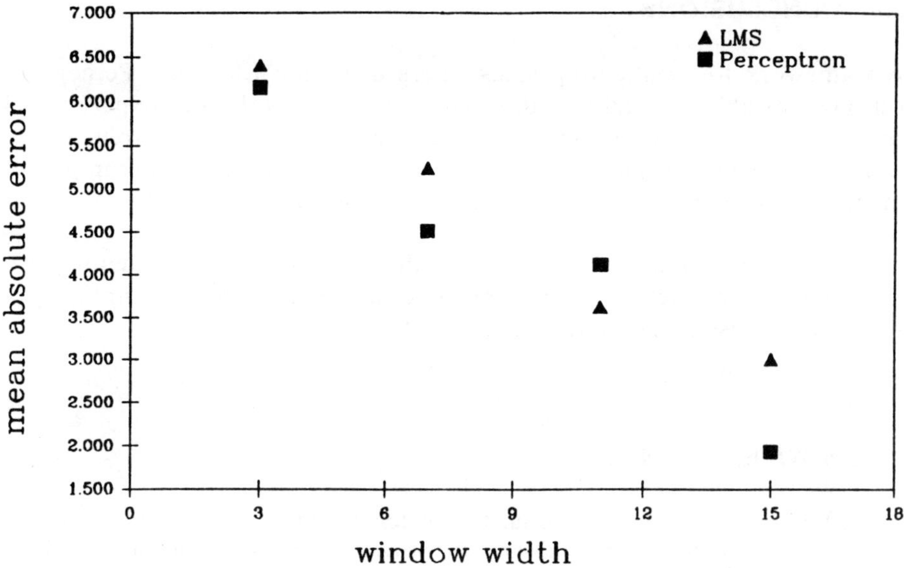

Figure 6.17 *Mean absolute error between the original mixture of sinusoid signal and the recovered signal.*

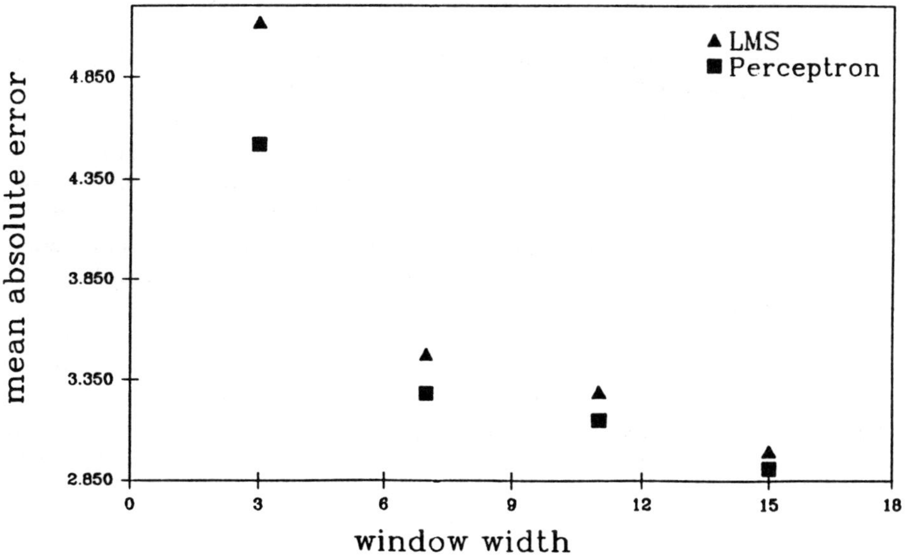

Figure 6.18 *Mean absolute error between the original "Mexican hat" signal and the recovered signal.*

6.5 CONCLUSIONS

A framework for configuring stack filters using the LMS and Perceptron rules was established and tested. It was demonstrated through experimental results that the proposed algorithms perform noise suppression reasonably well. The current design only uses a simple single neuron. Further improvement is expected if a multilayer network (multilayer perceptron) is employed.

Future research efforts include extending a single-neuron structure to a multilayer neural network, and speeding up the training by employing a recently proposed stack filtering architecture [20].

ACKNOWLEDGMENTS

The authors thank Chee-Hung Chu, Center for Advanced Computer Studies, the University of Southwestern Louisiana, for providing the "Mexican hat" signal.

REFERENCES

[1] R. P. Lippmann, An introduction to computing with neural nets, *IEEE Acoust., Speech, Signal Processing Mag.*, 4, 4–22 (April 1987).

[2] S. T. Alexander, *Adaptive signal Processing Theory and Application,* Springer-Verlag, New York, 1986.

[3] S. Haykin, *Adaptive Filter Theory,* Prentice-Hall, Englewood Cliffs, N.J., 1986.

[4] E. Ataman, V. K. Aatre, and K. M. Wong, Some statistical properties of median filters, *IEEE Trans. Acoust., Speech, Signal Processing,* ASSP-29, 1073–1075 (October 1981).

[5] A. C. Bovik, T. S. Huang, and D. C. Munson, A generalization of median filtering using linear combinations of order statistics, *IEEE Trans. Acoust., Speech, Signal Processing,* ASSP-31, 1342–1349 (December 1983).

[6] E. J. Coyle and J. H. Lin, Stack filters and the mean absolute error criterion, *IEEE Trans. Acoust., Speech, Signal Processing,* ASSP-36, 1244–1254 (August 1988).

[7] J. P. Fitch, E. J. Coyle, and N. C. Gallagher, Root properties and convergence rates of median filters, *IEEE Trans. Acoust., Speech, Signal Processing,* ASSP-33, 230–239 (February 1985).

[8] N. C. Gallagher and G. L. Wise, A theoretical analysis of the properties of median filter, *IEEE Trans. Acoust., Speech, Signal Processing,* ASSP-29, 1136–1141 (December 1981).

[9] N. C. Gallagher and G. L. Wide, Threshold decomposition of multidimensional ranked-order operations, *IEEE Trans. Circuits Syst.,* CAS-32, 445–450 (May 1985).

[10] P. D. Wendt, E. J. Coyle, and N. C. Gallagher, Stack filters, *IEEE Trans. Acoust., Speech, Signal Processing,* ASSP-34, 898–911 (August 1986).

[11] E. N. Gilbert, Lattice-theoretic properties of frontal switching functions, *J. Math. Phys.,* 33, 57–67 (April 1954).

[12] C. H. Chu, A genetic algorithm approach to the configuration of stack filters, *Proc. Internat. Conf. on Genetic Algorithms,* 218–224 (June 4–7, 1989).

[13] J. H. Lin, T. M. Selike, and E. J. Coyle, Adaptive stack filtering under the mean absolute error criterion, *IEEE Trans. Acoust., Speech, Signal Processing,* ASSP-38, 938–954 (June 1990).

[14] S. C. Douglas and T. H. Y. Meng, Optimum error nonlinearities for LMS adaptation, *Proc. ICASSP 90,* 1421–1424 (April 3–6, 1990).

[15] J. P. Fitch, E. J. Coyle, and N. C. Gallagher, Median filtering by threshold decomposition, *IEEE Trans. Acoust., Speech, Signal Processing,* ASSP-32, 1183–1188 (December 1984).

[16] R. O. Duda and P. E. Hart, *Pattern Classification and Scene Analysis,* John Wiley & Sons, Menlo Park, Calif., 1973.

[17] R. Rosenblatt, *Principles of Neurodynamics,* Spartan Books, New York, 1959.

[18] B. Widrow, R. G. Winter, and R. A. Baxter, Layered neural nets for pattern recognition, *IEEE Trans. Acoust., Speech, Signal Processing,* ASSP-36, 1109–1118 (July 1988).

[19] S. C. Douglas and T. H. Y. Meng, An adaptive edge detection method using a modified sigmoid-LMS algorithm, *Proc. 23rd Annual Asilomar Conf. on Signal, Syst., Comput.,* 252–256 (November 1989).

[20] J. H. Lin, A new architecture and fast algorithm for stack filters, *Proc. 1991 CISS Conf.,* 335 (March 20, 1991).

CHAPTER 7

Automatic Modeling of Acoustic Emission Phenomena by Neural Networks

IGOR GRABEC

7.1 INTRODUCTION

This chapter deals with automatic modeling of acoustic emission (AE) phenomena by an information processing system composed, like a neural network, out of an array of sensors, a memory, an estimator, and an array of actuators. The focus is on explanation of those properties of the system that enable prediction of data from incomplete measurements. For this purpose a conditional average is estimated from incomplete supplied data and a set of complete prototype data samples. The prototypes are formed during previous experiments by a self-organized adaptive process and are stored in the memory as parameters characterizing formal neurons. The algorithm of self-organization is derived from the principle of maximum preservation of empirical information and leads to similar interaction between formal neurons as observed in biological neural networks. The performance of the system is demonstrated on examples of acoustic emission and touch phenomena. It is demonstrated that forward and inverse acoustic emission problems can be treated by the modeler simulated on a data acquisition system. It is also shown that the same system can be applied for identification of surfaces by touching if a spectrum analyzer is included in it as a preprocessor of time dependent signals from tactile sensors.

In the evolution of living beings, recognition ability has played a decisive role. For this purpose various types of sensory neural networks have

Dynamic, Genetic, and Chaotic Programming, By Branko Souček and the IRIS Group.
ISBN 0-471-55717-X

evolved by natural selection. By them living beings obtain and process information transmitted from the surroundings by various agents like direct contact, heat and mass flow, sound, and light. A common property of various sensory neural networks is that they transform influences from the surroundings into proper actions of living beings. Although natural phenomena are very complex, it is significant that various components of information transmitting agents are often characteristically correlated in a certain environment. Due to this property of Nature, adaptive and associative processing of information in sensory neural networks has evolved. For such a processing it is characteristic that correlated influences from various situations of the environment are memorized. If a similar situation is met later, then only partial excitation of a sensory system can make possible completion of information about the environment by associative recall in the neural network and thus recognition of environmental properties that were not directly sensed [1]. This ability is an advantage in accommodating a living being to a particular environment.

Nature is a dynamic scene. Most dynamic phenomena in our environment produce sounds, so the hearing sense has evolved in living beings by which they can recognize phenomena in their surroundings by merely perceiving sound. The main purpose of this chapter is to show how an electronic information processing system with a similar ability can be constructed. With this aim we first analyze some general properties of the physical description of acoustical phenomena and then relate it to empirical modeling of natural laws and research into artificial neural networks [2–6]. The final goal is to prepare foundations for the construction of an adaptive electronic system applicable in nondestructive testing to automatic recognition of developing defects in stressed materials, characterization of irregularities in materials on the basis of scattered sound, classification of surfaces by tactile sensing, identification of manufacturing processes on the basis of chatter, among others [2–11].

An acoustic phenomenon is physically described by the time-dependent displacement field $\mathbf{u}(\mathbf{r}, t)$. The corresponding waves are emitted from some source field that physically can be best described by the force density $\gamma(\mathbf{r}, t)$. Determination of the displacement filed from the force density is called a forward problem. Its solution can be analytically expressed by the convolution in space and time between force density and response function of the medium transmitting the sound [2,7]. The determination or recognition of the sound source from the detected displacement field corresponds to an inverse problem that is generally ill-posed and requires some method of regularization. Both problems are usually mathematically very involved and most frequently lead to numerical treatment [7,12]. The problem is still more complicated if the source is not characterized directly by the force density but by some other loosely specified quantity or property, such as the roughness of a surface emitting sound due to friction [8]. Similar problems are often encountered in technical practice where various processes are controlled by workers listening to machines [9,10]. If the analytical complexity of such problems is considered [7,12], it is rather surprising that intelligent beings so simply recognize corresponding natural phenomena by perceived sound. This indicates that besides a strict physical description there exists another, maybe more robust, method by which the relation between source and emitted sound can be modeled. Our aim here is to find arguments for its formulation by analyzing the properties of the statistical description of empirical relations between observables, which is more elementary than the analytical physical description of natural phenomena, but still relies on measurements [5,6].

The data obtained by sensing or measurements are generally of random character. The probability distributions must therefore be applied in the treatment and modeling of relations between measured variables corresponding to natural laws. An information processing system can act as an empirical modeler of natural phenomena if it is capable of storing the probability distribution of measured, generally multicomponent variables and of estimating from several measured components the remaining ones in accordance with the stored distribution [5,6]. However, we are interested in a method that could be performed on a digital electronic system. These demands lead to two optimization problems related to the following fundamental questions:

1. How can a continuous multidimensional distribution best be stored in a system composed of a finite number of discrete elements?
2. How can some measured components be applied to associative completion of information about the observed phenomenon from the stored probability density?

In this chapter both problems are treated separately. For the solution of the first problem a maximum entropy principle is applied [13,14]. The derivations are presented in the next section and lead to the formulation of an automatic modeler of natural phenomena. Its structure corresponds to a self-organizing network of formal neurons. How such a network can be applied for the solution of the second problem is explained in the section on optimal recall of empirical information by conditional average. Application of the system composed of the self-organizing neural network and the conditional average estimator to the modeling of acoustic emission and classification of surfaces by touching is demonstrated by the examples.

7.2 EMPIRICAL DESCRIPTION OF NATURAL LAWS

We consider an information processing system including a discrete set of memory units, and we want to establish how an empirical probability distribution function of measured variables can be optimally memorized in it. We also assume that it includes a set of M sensors that provide experimental data $\{x_i; i = 1, \ldots, M\}$ during an observation of the selected phenomenon. Each observation is then described by a sample vector $\mathbf{x} = (x_1, \ldots, x_M)$ representing a point in a M-dimensional space. We suppose that N sequential observations are performed so that a set of vectors $\{\mathbf{x}_1, \ldots, \mathbf{x}_N\}$ represents the empirical information about the phenomenon. We treat these vectors as sample points of a continuous vector random variable $\mathbf{X}$. Its hypothetical probability density function $f(\mathbf{x})$ is not known but can be estimated by the empirical density function [13,14,15]

$$f_e(\mathbf{x}) = \frac{1}{N} \sum_{n=1}^{N} \delta(\mathbf{x} - \mathbf{x}_n) \tag{7.1}$$

Instead of employing the distribution function to describe the properties of the random variable $\mathbf{X}$, we prefer to introduce a finite set of K M-dimensional vectorial prototypes $\{\mathbf{q}_1, \ldots, \mathbf{q}_K\}$ that should optimally represent the typical values of this variable. The reason for this decision is that prototypes can be processed and stored in a discrete system of memory units, whereas a continuously distributed system is needed to represent a distribution function. To make a feasible representation of a random phenomenon, we have to assign to each prototype a probability: $\{P(\mathbf{q}_i): i = 1, \ldots K\}$. By this a mapping $\mathbf{X} \mapsto \mathbf{Q}$ of the continuous random variable $\mathbf{X}$ to a representative discrete random variable $\mathbf{Q}$ is defined. Any mapping from a continuous onto a discrete space causes reduction of information. By an optimal mapping the entropy of information should be least reduced. With respect to preserved information, the optimal map must therefore be related to the maximal possible entropy of information. This happens when the probability distribution of the map corresponds to maximal entropy of information, or when the probability distribution of $\mathbf{Q}$ is uniform: $\{P(\mathbf{q}_i) = 1/K: i = 1, \ldots K\}$. *By assuming uniform distribution, we include the maximum entropy principle in the determination of an optimal mapping.* The corresponding density function,

$$f_r(\mathbf{x}) = \frac{1}{K} \sum_{k=1}^{K} \delta(\mathbf{x} - \mathbf{q}_k) \tag{7.2}$$

is then used to represent the density of the probability distribution of the continuous variable $\mathbf{X}$. However, for this purpose the prototypes must first be determined. With this aim we compare the representative with the empirical density and diminish their discrepancy by adaptation of prototypes. Due to the singularity of the delta function, the functionals are employed for the comparison of both distributions. Therefore, we first introduce an appropriate scalar filter function $w(\mathbf{x}, \mathbf{s})$ or Parzen window [15], in which $\mathbf{s}$ is an M-dimensional vectorial parameter, and then define two filtered functions by the empirical and the representative averages:

$$\langle w \rangle e = \int_{-\infty}^{\infty} w(\mathbf{x}, \mathbf{s}) f_e(\mathbf{x})\, d^M x = \frac{1}{N} \sum_{n=1}^{N} w(\mathbf{x}_n, \mathbf{s}) \tag{7.3}$$

$$\langle w \rangle_r = \int_{-\infty}^{\infty} w(\mathbf{x}, \mathbf{s}) f_r(\mathbf{x})\, d^M x = \frac{1}{K} \sum_{k=1}^{K} w(\mathbf{q}_k, \mathbf{s}) \tag{7.4}$$

As in other optimization problems the mean square of the difference

$$\varepsilon = \varepsilon(\mathbf{q}_1, \ldots, \mathbf{q}_K; N; \mathbf{s}) = \langle w \rangle_r - \langle w \rangle e \tag{7.5}$$

is employed to define the measure of discrepancy between both distributions:

$$\overline{\varepsilon^2} = \int_{-\infty}^{\infty} \varepsilon^2\, d^M s \tag{7.6}$$

By the set $\{\mathbf{q}_1, \ldots, \mathbf{q}_K\}$ *that minimizes the discrepancy* $\overline{\varepsilon^2}$, *we define the optimal mapping* $\mathbf{X} \mapsto \mathbf{Q}$ *of the continuous to the discrete random variable.*

The optimal set of prototypes satisfies the following equations:

$$\frac{\partial \overline{\varepsilon^2}}{\partial q_{lm}} = 0 \quad \text{or} \quad \int_{-\infty}^{\infty} \frac{\partial \varepsilon}{\partial q_{lm}}\, d^M s = 0 \qquad \varepsilon = 1, \ldots, K \quad m = 1, \ldots, M \tag{7.7}$$

The concept of maximal entropy has already been applied by Gibbs [16] to find the probability distribution function that best corresponds to a certain set of measured statistical parameters. In his approach the relative maximum of information entropy is looked for under constraints corresponding to the measured statistical parameters. In order to emphasize this difference, we call the basis of our approach *the second maximum entropy principle* [13,14].

In two trivial cases the optimal mapping corresponding to the absolute minimum $\overline{\varepsilon^2} = 0$ can be guessed by considering the form of both averages:

$$\text{if } N = 1, \quad \text{then } \mathbf{q}_1 = \mathbf{q}_2 = \cdots = \mathbf{q}_k = \mathbf{x}_1 \tag{7.8}$$

$$\text{if } N = K, \quad \text{then } \mathbf{q}_1 = \mathbf{x}_1, \mathbf{q}_2 = \mathbf{x}_2 \cdots \mathbf{q}_k = \mathbf{x}_k \tag{7.9}$$

For $N > K$ the window function $w(\mathbf{x}, \mathbf{s})$ must first be specified, and then the system of equations (7.7) must be solved. Unfortunately a linear filter function $w(\mathbf{x}, \mathbf{s})$ is not adequate to obtain a system of independent equations, and nonlinear functions must be employed. As a consequence, a closed-form solution cannot be found, and we are forced to apply an iterative treatment.

Consider the determination of prototypes at $N \gg K$. Since with increasing N the empirical average $\langle w \rangle_e$ converges to a fixed value, we assume that with increasing N the addition of successive samples causes only minor changes of prototypes, and therefore a linear approximation is applied to express the changes of the difference ε:

$$\varepsilon_1 = \varepsilon(\mathbf{q}_1 + \Delta\mathbf{q}_1, \ldots, \mathbf{q}_K + \Delta\mathbf{q}_K; N + 1) = \varepsilon(\mathbf{q}_1, \ldots, \mathbf{q}_K; N) + \Delta\varepsilon \tag{7.10}$$

where

$$\Delta\varepsilon = \sum_{k=1}^{K}\sum_{i=1}^{M} \frac{\partial\langle w\rangle_r}{\partial q_{ki}} \Delta q_{ki} - \frac{1}{N+1}[w(\mathbf{x}_{N+1}, \mathbf{s}) - \langle w\rangle_e] \tag{7.11}$$

If for $\{\mathbf{q}_1, \ldots, \mathbf{q}_k\}$ the discrepancy $\overline{\varepsilon^2(\mathbf{q}_1, \ldots, \mathbf{q}_K; N)}$ is already minimal, then the minimum of $\overline{\varepsilon_1^2}$ is approximately reached by shifting the prototypes for $\{\Delta\mathbf{q}_1, \ldots, \Delta\mathbf{q}_k\}$ satisfying the conditions

$$\frac{\partial\overline{\varepsilon_1^2}}{\partial(\Delta q_{lm})} = 0 \qquad l = 1, \ldots, K \quad m = 1, \ldots, M \tag{7.12}$$

These conditions yield the following system of linear equations:

$$\sum_{k=1}^{K}\sum_{i=1}^{M} C_{lmki}\,\Delta q_{ki} = B_{lm} \qquad l = 1, \ldots, K \quad m = 1, \ldots, M \tag{7.13}$$

Here the coefficients are determined by the expressions

$$C_{lmki} = \int_{-\infty}^{\infty} \frac{\partial w(\mathbf{q}_k, \mathbf{s})}{\partial q_{ki}} \frac{\partial w(\mathbf{q}_l, \mathbf{s})}{\partial q_{lm}} \, d^M s \tag{7.14}$$

$$B_{lm} = \frac{K}{N+1} \int_{-\infty}^{\infty} [w(\mathbf{x}_{N+1}, \mathbf{s}) - \langle w\rangle_N] \frac{\partial \mathbf{w}(\mathbf{q}_l, \mathbf{s})}{\partial q_{lm}} \, d^M s \tag{7.15}$$

System (7.13) is the foundation for a practical application of the second maximum entropy principle.

For the practical applications it is most convenient if the solution of the linear system (7.13) can be found by iteration. If thc conditions

$$C_{lmki} = 1 \quad \text{for } k = l, m = i \qquad \text{and} \qquad |C_{lmki}| < 1 \quad \text{for } k \neq l, m \neq i \tag{7.16}$$

could be satisfied by a proper selection of the window function $w(\mathbf{x}, \mathbf{s})$, then it is reasonable to represent the system in the form

$$\Delta q_{lm}^{(j+1)} \doteq B_{lm} - \sum_{k \neq l}^{K} \sum_{i \neq m}^{M} C_{lmki} \, \Delta q_{ki}^{(j)} \qquad l = 1, \ldots, K \quad m = 1, \ldots, M \tag{7.17}$$

which is convenient for iteration. It starts with $\Delta \mathbf{q}_l^{(1)} = \mathbf{B}_l$.

The most convenient filter function for comparing the probability densities is the Gaussian:

$$w(\mathbf{x}, \mathbf{s}) = \exp\left[\frac{-(\mathbf{x} - s)^2}{2\sigma^2}\right] \tag{7.18}$$

With this the conditions (7.16) are fulfilled and the integrals in Eqs. (7.14) and (7.15) are analytically expressible as

$$C_{lmki} = \left[\delta_{mi} - \frac{(q_{lm} - q_{km})(q_{li} - q_{ki})}{2\sigma^2}\right] \exp\left[\frac{-(\mathbf{q}_l - \mathbf{q}_k)^2}{4\sigma^2}\right] \tag{7.19}$$

$$B_{lm} = \frac{K}{N+1}\left\{(x_{N+1,m} - q_{lm}) \exp\left[\frac{-(\mathbf{x}_{N+1} - \mathbf{q}_l)^2}{4\sigma^2}\right] - \frac{1}{K}\sum_{k=1}^{K} (q_{km} - q_{lm}) \exp\left[\frac{-(\mathbf{q}_k - \mathbf{q}_l)^2}{4\sigma^2}\right]\right\} \tag{7.20}$$

In the latter expression $\langle w \rangle_e$ has been replaced by $\langle w \rangle_r$ in order to simplify further calculations. The parameter σ in the Gaussian function should approximately correspond to the estimated distance between representative prototypes in multy-dimensional space. If L^M denotes the range of variable $\mathbf{X}$, then it is reasonable to choose $\sigma = L/K^{1/M}$.

For the interpretation of the derived algorithm it is convenient to introduce the following model of an optimal self-organizing system. Let us assume that samples of $\mathbf{X}$ represent a signal transmitted from the environment to the adaptive system consisting of memory cells or formal neurons, characterized by prototypes $\mathbf{q}_l$. The form of the coefficients $\mathbf{B}_l$ indicates that the input signal predominantly influences neurons having prototypes closest to the value of the input sample by attracting them toward this sample value. The interaction between the neurons or self-organization is determined by modified bell-shaped functions consisting of excitation (+) and inhibition (−) parts. Similar properties have also been found in research into self-organization in some biological neural networks and artificial models resembling them [1,17]. The adaptation of the most excited prototypes can be approximately described by accounting for only the influence of the input sample and by assuming that the exponential function in the expression for $\mathbf{B}$ is approximately 1. The prototype change is then described by the formula

$$\Delta \mathbf{q}_l = \frac{K}{N+1}(\mathbf{x}_N - \mathbf{q}_l)$$

corresponding to the well-known self-organization rule of Kohonen [1]. As this rule corresponds only to an approximate, truncated description of the complete equations, the adaptation following it is generally not optimal, although it is quite convenient for numerical treatment.

In order to show performance of the derived self-organization algorithm, we first illustrate an adaptation of five one-dimensional prototypes q_k to a chaotic variable $\mathbf{X}$ generated by the Hénon map. The generated random samples x_N are shown as thin points in Figure 7.1, and the prototypes q_k are shown as thick ones. Starting from the trivial solution (7.9), the prototypes accommodate to the decreasing fluctuation of the empirical distribution of X. The initial fluctuations of prototypes are not due to an incorrect adaptation, but are caused by the description of the chaotic phenomenon by the estimated empirical probability distribution at low N. The empirical and the representative cumulative probability distribution functions of variables X and Q are shown in Figure 7.2. Adaptation of prototypes to the random variable X is evident. In order to demonstrate the adaptation quantitatively, the averages $\langle w \rangle_e$ and $\langle w \rangle_r$ are shown in Figure 7.3. A slight discrepancy of both averages is mainly the consequence of the low chosen number K of representative prototypes. The results were calculated by two iterations, but in this case a similar agreement is obtained even by a single iteration [13,14,18].

As the second example the maximum entropy mapping of a two-dimensional random variable of uniform probability distribution on a circle to eight prototypes is demonstrated. Figure 7.4 shows generated random points on a circle and the five streams of prototype points. The approximately equal distances between limit points indicate the correct adaptation of two-dimensional prototypes $\mathbf{q}_k$ to a uniform circular distribution. This example shows that the method developed is suitable for an optimal representation of chaotic attractors by discrete set of prototypes. Therefore it can be efficiently applied in adaptive systems capable to reproduce and predict chaotic time series [19,20].

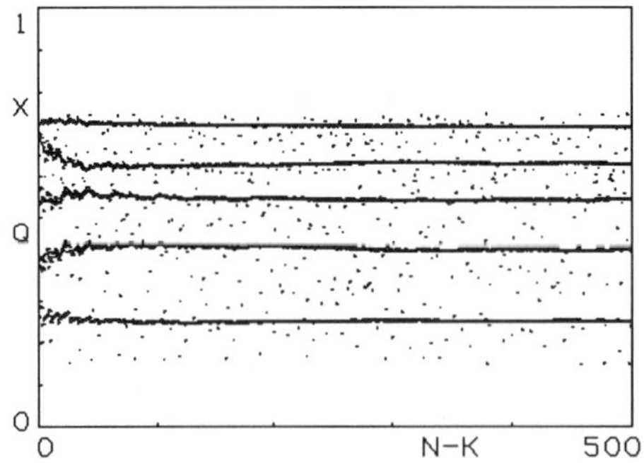

Figure 7.1 *The sample points (thin) and prototypes (bold) versus the number of adaptations $N - K$, $\sigma = 0.07$.*

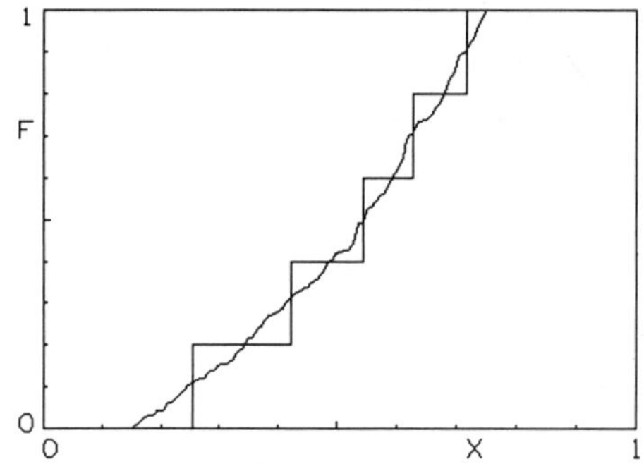

Figure 7.2 *Empirical (line) and representative (staircase) cumulative probability distribution functions, recorded at N = 500.*

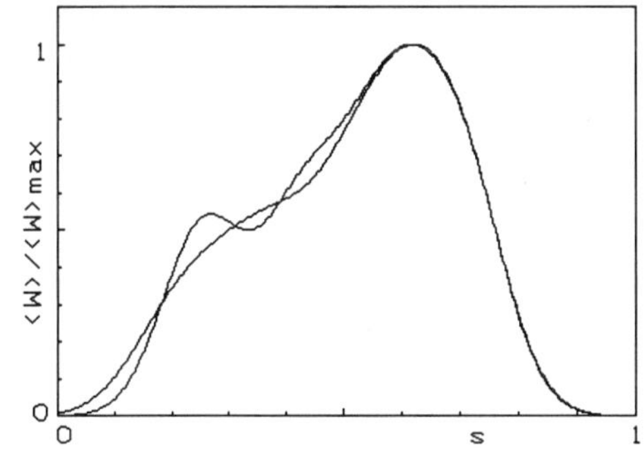

Figure 7.3 *The agreement between empirical and representative averages $\langle w \rangle_e$ and $\langle w \rangle_r$.*

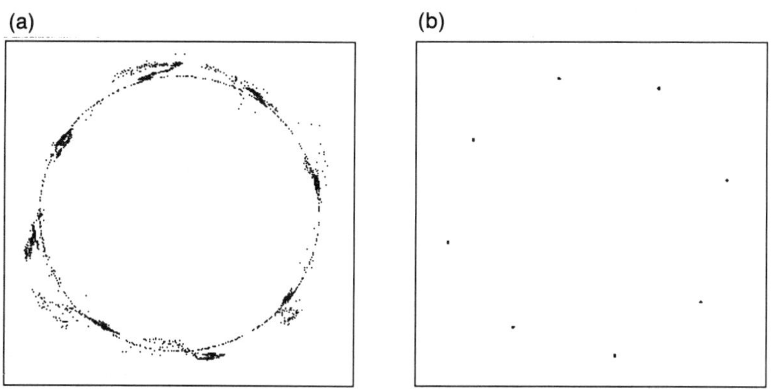

Figure 7.4 (a) *Adaptation of prototypes to a circular distribution. σ = 0.02.* (b) *Final distribution of prototypes.*

7.3 OPTIMAL ASSOCIATIVE RECALL OF STORED INFORMATION

Our task now is to establish how the prototypes obtained by the adaptation process can be applied to estimate the random vector **X** on the grounds of some measured components. Let us consider the sensor array as composed of two subarrays supplying samples of incomplete data represented by the truncated vectors

$$\mathbf{p} = (x_1, \ldots, x_t; \#) \qquad \text{and} \qquad \mathbf{r} = (\#; x_{t+1}, \ldots, x_M) \tag{7.21}$$

in which # denotes the missing part. The complete vector can then be expressed by concatenation:

$$\mathbf{x} = \mathbf{p} \oplus \mathbf{r} = (x_1, \ldots, x_t, x_{t+1}, \ldots, x_M) \tag{7.22}$$

Let us further assume that partial information about the phenomenon is conveyed by the vector **p**, and we want to estimate from it the rest components of the complementary vector **r**. As the optimal solution of this problem, we choose the estimator $\hat{\mathbf{r}} = \hat{\mathbf{r}}(\mathbf{p})$ that minimizes the mean square error:

$$D = \int [\mathbf{r} - \hat{\mathbf{r}}(\mathbf{p})]^2 f(\mathbf{x})\, d^M x \tag{7.23}$$

The calculus of variation yields for the optimal estimator the conditional average

$$\hat{r}_o = \int \mathbf{r} f(\mathbf{r}|\mathbf{p})\, dx_{t+1} \cdots dx_M \tag{7.24}$$

The conditional probability density function can be estimated by using Eq. (7.4):

$$f(\mathbf{r}|\mathbf{p}) = \sum_{k=1}^{K} w(\mathbf{r} - \mathbf{r}_k) w(\mathbf{p} - \mathbf{p}_k) \Big/ \sum_{k=1}^{K} w(\mathbf{p} - \mathbf{p}_k) \tag{7.25}$$

By this function $\hat{\mathbf{r}}_o$ can be expressed in terms of prototypes as

$$\hat{\mathbf{r}}_o = \sum_{k=1}^{K} A_k \mathbf{r}_k \qquad \text{where} \qquad A_k = w(\mathbf{p} - \mathbf{p}_k) \Big/ \sum_{i=1}^{K} w(\mathbf{p} - \mathbf{p}_i) \tag{7.26}$$

This equation shows that the optimal estimator can be approximated by a linear superposition of truncated prototype vectors $\mathbf{r}_k$, where the coefficients A_k are strongly nonlinear functions sensitized to truncated vectors $\mathbf{p}_k$. They represent the measure of similarity between vector **p** and prototypes. By the optimal estimator the completed data vector can be expressed as the concatenation

$$\mathbf{y} = \mathbf{p} \oplus \hat{\mathbf{r}}_o(\mathbf{p}) \tag{7.27}$$

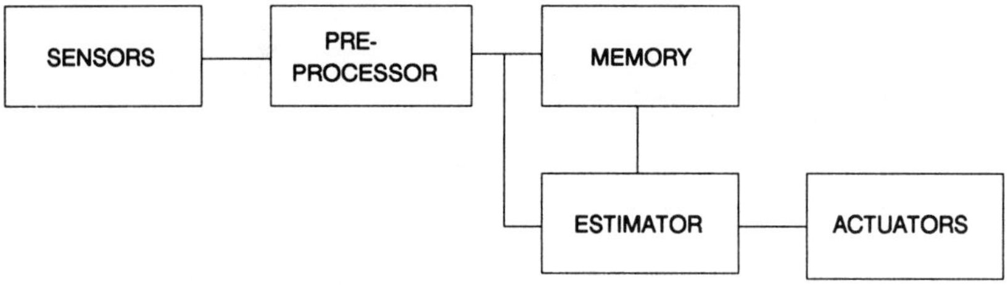

Figure 7.5 *Scheme of the system applicable for automatic modeling of natural phenomena.*

This vector represents the response of the system to excitation by truncated signal **p**. Representation of distribution function by means of prototypes and estimation of missing vector components corresponds to nonparametric multidimensional regression.

In accordance with this presentation, an automatic modeler of natural phenomena must be able to perform two different operations; in the first the prototypes are adapted by self-organized process to the detected samples $\mathbf{x}_n$, while in the second one the input partial data vector is completed by the estimated complementary vector [5,6,18,20]. This corresponds to unsupervised learning and to the recognition or matched analysis of influences from the surroundings. Such a modeler is schematically represented in Figure 7.5. A preprocessor unit can be optionally included into it in order to make feasible transformations of experimental data into a form most appropriate for interpretation or to ensure some invariances in the operation of the system [8,10].

7.4 EXPERIMENTS

The proposed modeler was simulated on a digital computer of a data acquisition system and applied to the modeling of two types of acoustic emission phenomena caused by cracking materials and friction on rough surfaces. The first type is important for the characterization of developing defects in nondestructive testing, while the second one can be applied in the identification of surfaces and manufacturing processes [6,7,8]. In the first type of experiment acoustic emission was caused by breaking a pencil lead on various positions of a steel block of dimensions $50 \times 80 \times 200$ mm^3, as shown in Figure 7.6. Monopole and dipole forces were simulated at each position, and 14 prototypes were applied to characterize the complete experiment. During learning, the data vector was composed of digitized signals from two AE transducers on the sample and encoded descriptors of source position and type of force, while during the analysis, only AE signals were presented to the system simulated on a computer. During experimentation, the complete

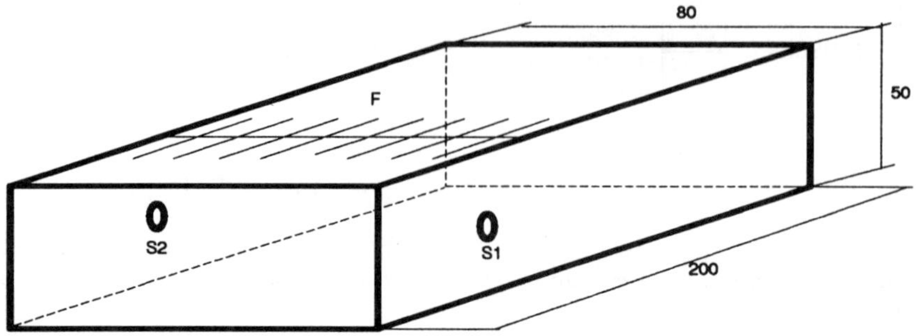

Figure 7.6 *Scheme of the specimen applied for simulation of AE phenomena. F, S_1, and S_2 denote source force and AE sensors.*

data vector comprised 120 components. The set of prototypes is shown by records in Figure 7.7, while the smaller testing series of AE signals is shown in Figure 7.8. The corresponding source descriptors shown in Figure 7.9 were stored separately for the control of system performance. By each of the test AE signals the complementary vector was then estimated by using the standard deviation of all prototypes as parameter σ in the filter function. The set of completed vectors is shown in Figure 7.10. The agreement between original and estimated source descriptors is almost perfect. This example corresponds to the recognition of the AE source on the basis of a detected displacement signal, which is the solution of an elastodynamic inverse prob-

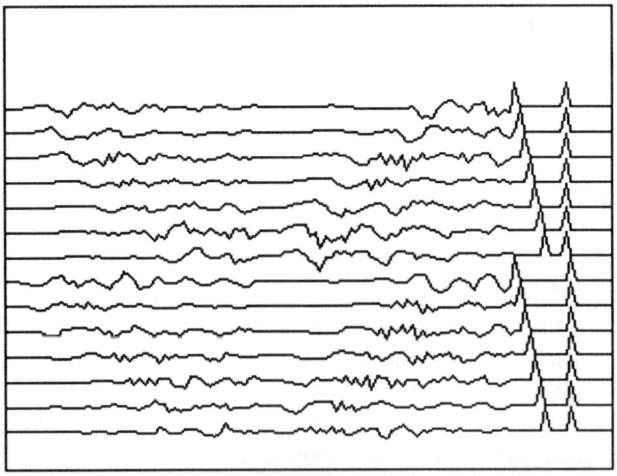

Figure 7.7 *Records of prototype vectors obtained by simulation of acoustic phenomenon on a laboratory specimen. The left side of the record represents AE signals from two sensors, while the two peaks on the right side represent the source descriptors.*

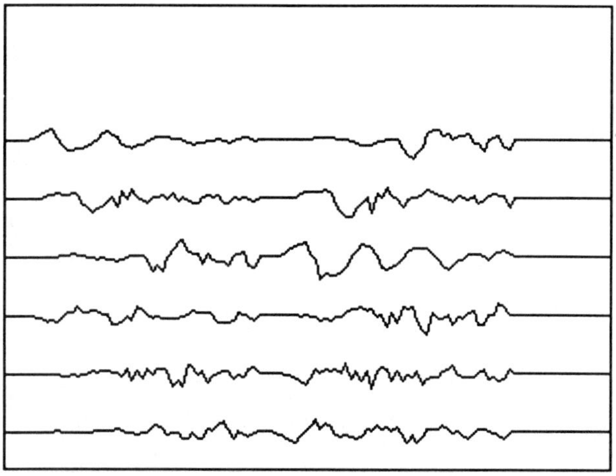

Figure 7.8 *The set of test AE signals applied as partial data about the phenomenon to be recognized.*

lem. When only source descriptors are applied as input vectors, then the AE signals are correctly recalled from the memory, which in this case serves only as a look-up table. The estimation of the signals in this case corresponds to the solution of the forward elastodynamic problem [5,6].

The recognition is quite noiseinsensitive. To show this, the test signals were corrupted by noise reaching the signal-to-noise ratio 1 as shown in Figure 7.11. From them the source descriptors shown in Figure 7.12 were estimated. The maximal peaks in estimated truncated signals correspond to

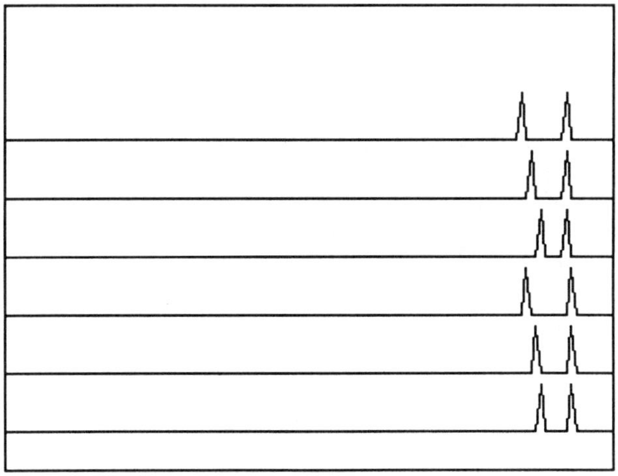

Figure 7.9 *The set of source descriptors corresponding to the signals in Figure 7.7.*

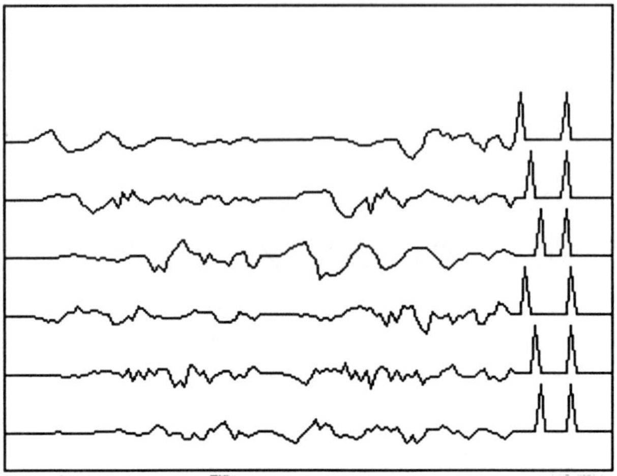

Figure 7.10 *The set of complete records of output signals obtained from the AE signals in Figure 7.7. The source descriptors on the right side of the records were estimated. Agreement with correct descriptions in Figure 7.7 is noticeable.*

the correct source descriptors. If the estimated truncated part is afterwards fed back to the modeler input as a given truncated vector, then the AE signal part estimated from it exhibits reduced noise, as is observable from Figure 7.13. By iteration of alternating estimation process, we obtain a recurrent operation of the modeler. Figure 7.14 shows completed records of vectors obtained after two alternating steps. In the final step the coefficients A_n corresponding to the correct prototypes were to within 10^{-4} equal to 1. This

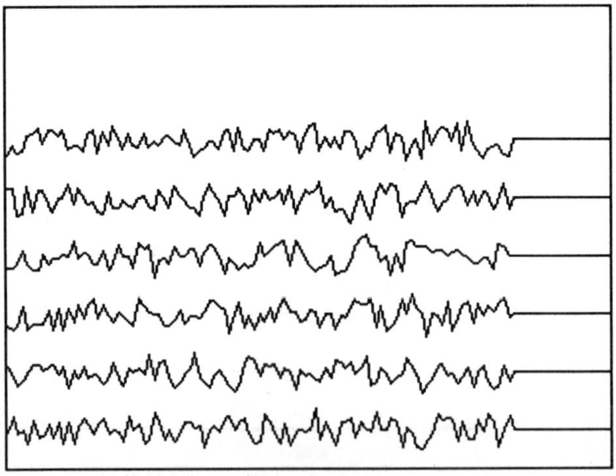

Figure 7.11 *Noise-corrupted AE signals.*

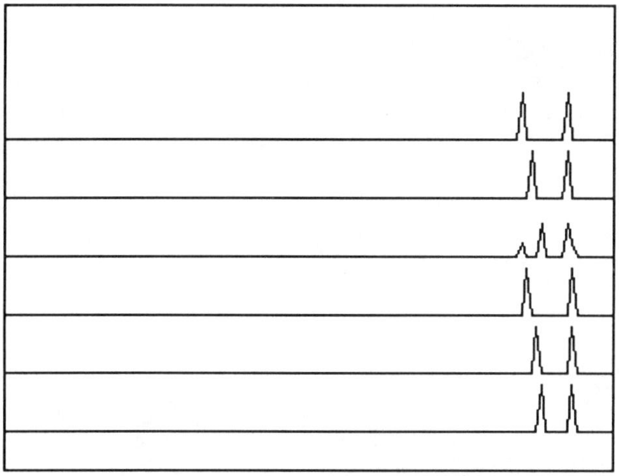

Figure 7.12 *Source descriptors estimated from the noise-corrupted AE signals.*

indicates that the system with incorporated iteration operates as a matched filter with the attractor points determined by prototypes. The developed modeler in this case corresponds to a dynamic system that has attractor points adapted by self-organization to signals from the environment. A similar property has been observed in recurrent neural networks [21]. A more detailed description of the system performance has been given elsewhere together with demonstration of its applicability for the analysis of ultrasonic scattering phenomena [5,6].

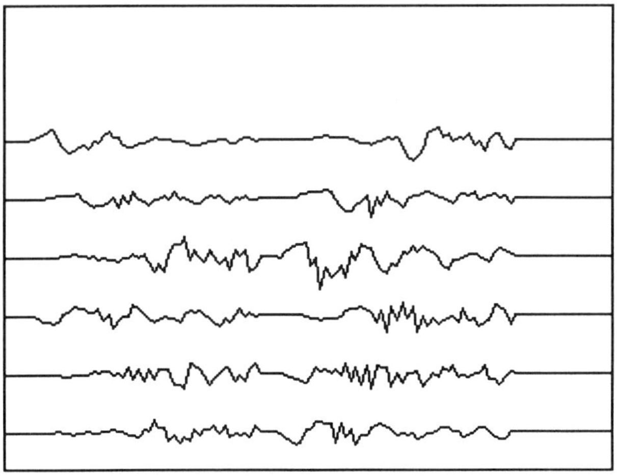

Figure 7.13 *AE signals estimated from the fed-back descriptors shown in Figure 7.11.*

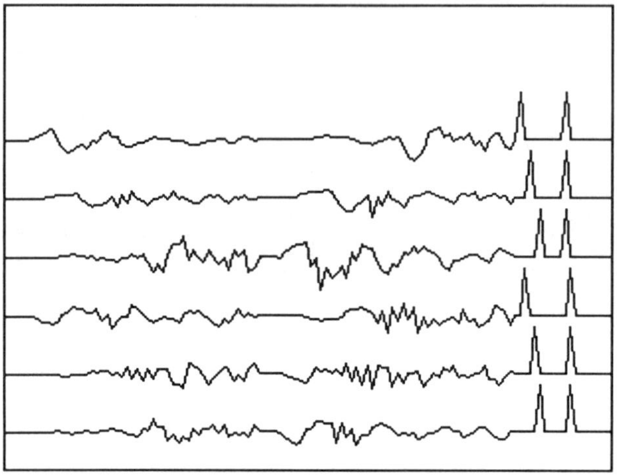

Figure 7.14 *Completed records of output signals obtained from the noise-corrupted signals of Figure 7.10 after two steps of recurrent alternating estimation.*

In our experiments the signal acquisition was triggered by the signal from a small transducer mounted on the pencil tip. When observing nonsimulated phenomena, we must obtain the trigger from the detected AE signal itself. In this case, the form of the AE signal influences the triggering and a time-invariant representation of the signals must be realized by some sort of preprocessing as is, for example, the spectral analysis [8,10]. When pulselike signals are observed, preprocessing can sometimes be avoided [2,3,4] by properly selecting the triggering conditions, but when continuous AE phenomena are observed, it is unavoidable. A typical example is acoustic emission generated by friction on the rough surface, which was treated in the second type of experiment [8]. For experimentation, steel ring samples of inner and outer diameters 110 mm and 130 mm were prepared by various surface finishing. A ring was placed on the top of a plate circulating with a surface speed of 0.1 m/s. As an AE or tactile sensor, a phonograph cartridge with diamond tip was applied as in a plate recorder. The AE signal was led from the cartridge to a spectrum analyzer, where the spectral distribution in the frequency band from 0 to 5 kHZ was determined by fast Fourier transform (FFT). It was represented by 128 spectral components and transfered to the computer, where a 160-dimensional vector was formed by adding 32 components describing the surface properties. The surfaces produced by various manufacturing processes were described by assigning a unit value to one of the descriptor components. In the experiment 20 prototypes were applied to characterize five types of grinding processes. The upper part of Figure 7.15 shows five characteristic prototypes of complete data vectors measured on various surfaces. The descriptor is encoded by the peak of the right of each record. In the bottom record of the same figure a test record of

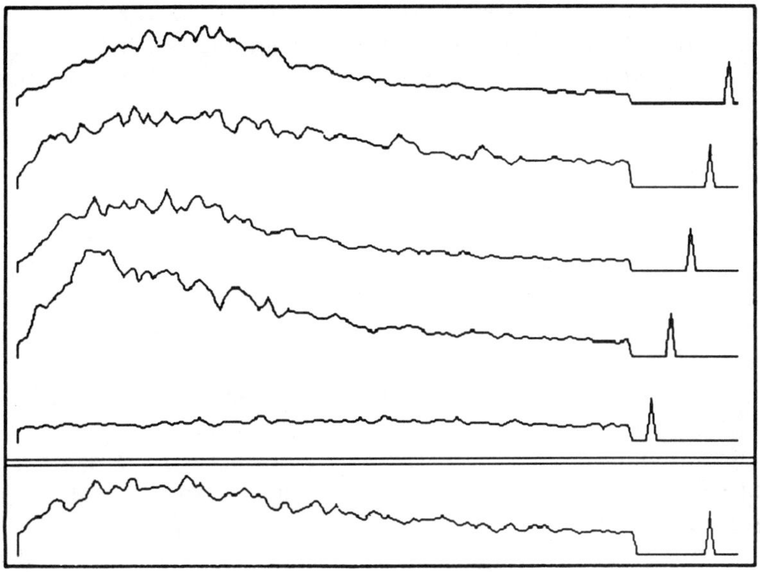

Figure 7.15 *(top) Five prototypes consisting of spectral distribution on the left and descriptor peak on the right. (bottom) Signal composed of measured spectrum and estimated descriptor on the right.*

the surface under examination is completed by the estimated descriptor. At a controlled sliding speed, an almost 100% correct estimation of the surface descriptor was obtained. If the speed was allowed to vary by about 25%, then the recognition ability was decreased by 12% on average. When the recall is not correct, the estimated descriptor pertains to a surface that is most similar to the one analyzed. It has been also found that modest mechanical vibrations and weak pollution of surfaces by fluids applied in manufacturing processes for cooling do not disturb the recognition process significantly, which makes this system quite promising for practical applications in tactile sensing.

7.5 CONCLUSIONS

The examples demonstrated show that the self-organizing algorithm stemming from the second maximum entropy principle is applicable to the construction of a system capable of adapting to multicomponent signals and of predicting their properties on the grounds of partial supplied information. The system is therefore applicable as an automatic empirical modeler of natural phenomena irrespective of their regular or chaotic nature. The discrete structure of the system quite naturally leads to the definition of prototypes. In our description we consider the number of sensors and prototypes to be determined by the construction of the system. The optimization of this number is the object of current research. The emerging properties of the interaction between the prototypes is in surprisingly good agreement with some characteristic properties of real neurons [1,17]. We can therefore conjecture that the maximum entropy principle could also be applied in the explanation of biological evolution.

If the structure of the hearing system in living beings is considered, the inclusion of a spectrum analyzer in the system in order to get time-invariant operation seems to be quite natural. This further suggests that an array of parallel resonant circuits should be applied to accelerate estimation of spectral density of audio signals in the case when self-organization and estimation were also performed in parallel. For the recognition of surfaces only one tactile sensor was mentioned here. Biological tactile systems include spatially distributed sensors operating in parallel. Although such sensory arrays could already have been constructed, we still do not know what a proper neural network layer would be that could ensure spatially invariant representation of tactile signals. Comparison with the processing of visual signals in a retina seems to be instructive.

In our treatment we have not included any prior knowledge about the phenomenon in a modeler structure. Therefore it is applicable for the modeling of various natural phenomena where relations between variables detected by different, specifically selected sensor arrays have to be estimated from empirical observations. However, if some property, for example, a linear dependence between variables, is known in advance, then its general description leads to parametric multidimensional regression. Its application can then ensure invariant operation of the modeler with respect to various transformations of detected signals, such as is scale transformation or shifting in time. Various linear methods of this kind have already been developed on the ground of ad hoc selected learning rules and also lead to adaptive systems with structures of neural networks [2,3,4,22]. But it is still not known how to formulate a general nonparametric regression by which invariances could be automatically discovered and incorporated into the self-organized formation of prototypes.

REFERENCES

[1] T. Kohonen, *Self-Organization and Associative Memory,* Springer-Verlag, Berlin, 1989.

[2] I. Grabec and W. Sachse, Application of an intelligent signal processing system to acoustic emission analysis, *J Acoust. Soc. Am.,* **85,** 1226–1235 (1989).

[3] I. Grabec and W. Sachse, Experimental characterization of ultrasonic phenomena by a learning system, *J. Appl. Phys.,* **66,** 3993–4000 (1989).

[4] I. Grabec, K. Zgonc, and W. Sachse, Application of a neural network to analysis of ultrasonic signals, *Proc. Ultrasonics International '89, Conf.,* Butterworth & Co., Madrid, 796–802 (1989).

[5] I. Grabec and W. Sachse, Automatic modeling of ultrasonic phenomena, *Progress in Acoustic Emission,* V, Japanese Soc. NDI, 196–202 (1990).

[6] I. Grabec and W. Sachse, Automatic Modeling of Physical Phenomena: Application to Ultrasonic Data, *J. Appl. Phys.,* **69,** 6233–6244 (1991).

[7] W. Sachse, B. Castagneda, I. Grabec, K. Y. Kim, and R. Weaver, Recent developments for the quantitative ultrasonic NDE of thick and other composites, *Ultrasonics,* 28, 97–104 (1990).

[8] E. Susič and I. Grabec, Recognition of surfaces from tactile AE signals, *1st Internat. Conf. on AE in Manufacturing,* (1991), Boston, J. Vahaviolos, Ed., ASNT, 141–146.

[9] E. Govekar and I. Grabec, Estimation of drill wear from AE signals using a self-organizing neural network, *1st International Conf. on AE in Manufacturing,* (1991), Boston, J. Vahaviolos, Ed., ASNT, 65–70.

[10] E. Govekar, I. Grabec, and J. Peklenik, Monitoring of a drilling process by a neural network, *Proc. 21st CIRP Seminar on Manufacturing Systems,* Vol. 2 (1989).

[11] R. Šribar, J. Monžina, and I. Grabec, Optoacoustic monitoring of laser manufacturing process by a neural network, *Proc. Ultrasonics Internat. '89, Conf.,* Butterworth & Co., Madrid, 211–218 (1989).

[12] A. Tarantola, *Inverse Problem Theory,* Elsevier, Amsterdam, 1987.

[13] I. Grabec, Self-organization based on the second maximum entropy principle, 1. *IEE Internat. Conf. Artificial Neural Networks, Conf. Pub. 313,* 12–16 (1989).

[14] I. Grabec, Self-organization of neurons described by the maximum entropy principle, *Biol. Cybernetics,* **63,** 403–409 (1990).

[15] R. O. Duda and P. E. Hart, *Pattern Classification and Scene Analysis,* John Wiley & Sons, New York, 1973, Chap. 4.

[16] C. Ray Smith and W. T. Grandy, Jr., Eds., *Maximum Entropy and Bayesian Methods in Inverse Problems,* D. Riedel Dordrecht, 1985.

[17] J. A. Anderson and E. Rosenfeld, Eds., *Neurocomputing, Foundations of Research,* MIT Press, Cambridge, Mass., 1988, pp. 209, 509.

[18] I. Grabec, Empirical modeling of natural phenomena by a self-organizing system, *Internat. Neural Network Conf. 90,* Vol. 2, Kluwer Academic Publishers, Dordrecht, 529–532 (1990).

[19] I. Grabec, "Prediction of a Chaotic Time Series by a Self-Organizing Neural Network," poster, Dynamics Days, Düsseldorf (1990).

[20] I. Grabec, Modeling of natural phenomena by a self-organizing system, *Proc. ECPD Neurocomputing, Summer School and Workshop* (1990), Dubrovnik, Vol. 1, 142–150.

[21] J. Hopfield, Neurons with graded response have collective computational properties like those of two state neurons, *Proc. Nat. Acad. Sci.,* **81,** 3088–3092 (1984).

[22] K. Zgonc and I. Grabec, A multidimensional optimal deconvolution applied to hetero-associative recall of AE signals, *Proc. ECPD Neurocomputing, Summer School and Workshop* (1990), Dubrovnik, Vol. 1.

CHAPTER 8

Managing the Traffic of a Satellite Communication Network by Neural Networks

NIRWAN ANSARI

8.1 INTRODUCTION

There has been an upsurge of interdisciplinary research effort on neural networks in recent years. As a novel application, a neural network model is presented to realize the traffic management task of a satellite communication network. The scheme consists of two levels of management. The front end of the scheme is a derivation of Kohonen's self-organization model to configure maps for the satellite communication network dynamically. The model consists of three stages. The first stage is the pattern recognition task, which selects an exemplar map that best meets the current network requirements. The second stage analyzes the discrepancy between the chosen exemplar map and the state of the network, adaptively modifying the chosen exemplar map to conform closely to the network requirement (input data pattern) by Kohonen's self-organization. Based on certain performance criteria, whether a new map is generated to replace the original chosen map is decided in the third stage. The second level is a routing algorithm that manages the traffic of the network under a fixed configuration. This chapter mainly addresses the first-level management and briefly discusses the conceptual model of the overall scheme. Experimental results are presented to demonstrate that the self-organization model can dynamically configure

Dynamic, Genetic, and Chaotic Programming, By Branko Souček and the IRIS Group.
ISBN 0-471-55717-X

This work has been supported by the NASA Lewis Research Center, Cleveland, OH, contract number NAG3-1244.

maps for a satellite communication network. The incorporation of the two levels represents the continuing effort to maximize the network efficiency and will be reported in the future. The scheme can be incorporated into the onboard central network control of a satellite, thus resulting in a totally autonomous switching satellite.

A new management scheme is developed to automate the traffic management task of a reconfigurable communication network. A communication network that can, depending on the traffic load or owing to partial failure of the network, take on various configurations is known as a *reconfigurable* network. A satellite communication network [1–4] or a survivable network [5,6], for example, is a reconfigurable network. The initial effort is aimed at managing a satellite communication network, and thus the following discussion is directed toward managing the traffic of a satellite communication network.

The objective of traffic management is to best meet the communication requirement of users under the constraint of a fixed network capacity. That is, the probability of having users blocked from accessing the network should be the minimum. Network efficiency is the measure of how few facilities are required to carry the steady busy-hour traffic load of the networks. It is limited by the switching, flexibility, and transmission capacities of the network.

The following reasons are given for the continuing effort and interest to come up with new management schemes to meet the advances of communication systems:

1. Since the invention of the telephone a century ago, the telecommunication network required to interconnect users at different locations on the globe has been growing steadily. With the advent of technological advances such as Broadband Integrated Services Digital Network [7,8,9] (B-ISDN), the network that will meet the demand of high volume data exchange is very complex. Managing the traffic of such a network is an engineering challenge.
2. Due to huge investment in communication facilities, a slight improvement in the operation efficiency would result in considerable saving.
3. The existing network is designed to operate under estimated average busy-hour condition. By its very nature, the system is subject to demands over which it has or no control. The random and noncoincident nature of the telephone or data traffic produces daily deviations in volume and pattern from the average values expected. In addition, unusual conditions can arise due to holidays, component failures, natural disasters, and/or political events. When this occurs, it is essential to utilize the existing facilities efficiently.

8.2 TWO ADOPTED TRAFFIC ROUTING SCHEMES—STATE OF THE ART

Among the many routing schemes that have been suggested or used, one that appears to have a growing appeal is concerned with schemes based on adaptive and learning concepts. Two well-known examples have been adopted in the United States of America and Canada, respectively. Dynamic nonhierarchical routing [10,11,12] (DNHR) is AT&T's version of circuit-switch dynamic routing. It is a time-dependent routing scheme that increases network efficiency by taking advantage of the noncoincidence of busy hours in a large toll network. This increased network efficiency results in lower network costs because fewer trunks and facilities are required compared with usual routing methods. AT&T introduced DNHR into its toll network in 1984 with a network saving of 15%.

The second example is Northern Telecom's dynamically controlled routing [13] (DCR). It is a centralized adaptive routing system. A single network processor sends a set of tandem recommendations for all DCR call destinations to participating DCR exchanges, every 10 s, to update their DCR routing tables. The recommendations are based on an analysis of network status information received by the network processor from the participating exchanges in the 10 s. The recommendations are based primarily on the available outgoing trunk quantity and exchanges utilization level.

8.3 MOTIVATION

Usually, the traditional routing methods and even the dynamic routing methods are used to manage traffic of a network under a fixed configuration [10–13]. A satellite communication network, as opposed to the rigidity of a terrestrial communication network, is flexible and can be configured to various maps. Neural networks can naturally be applied to configure a satellite communication network adaptively. To take advantage of the flexibility of a satellite communication network, we have developed a new scheme to manage traffic of the satellite communication network. The scheme consists of two levels of management. At the first level, a self-organization model is introduced to dynamically configure maps for the network. The second level is a routing algorithm that manages the traffic of the network under a fixed configuration. Preliminary results of the first-level management have been reported in [14] and [15].

Satellite communications [1–4] provide universal coverage, uniform cost, and network flexibility. Recent advances in very small aperture terminal (VSAT) technology [16] has provided a low-cost alternative to more expensive terrestrial links. Satellite communication network traffic management is concerned with maximizing network efficiency when the network is under stress either due to overload or failure. The traffic operator must analyze and monitor the network status constantly, and react promptly to configure the network to meet various network requirements. A typical network consists of thousands of channels. Managing such a network is a very difficult task. In the past, the satellite communication network was usually configured according to a programmed timetable. A new method is developed to adaptively configure maps and route the traffic of the satellite communication network. This method has a potential to make satellite communication network more desirable, especially when emergent services are called for. When terrestrial links are destroyed or damaged by catastrophe, such as hurricane and earthquake, the proposed approach can promptly reconfigure the network to establish communication by deploying VSATs to the disaster areas.

8.4 SATELLITE COMMUNICATION SYSTEMS

Satellite communications are flourishing due to decades of research efforts in the field of radio communications (e.g., microwave, very high frequency (VHF), ultrahigh frequency (UHF)) with the aim of achieving the greatest coverage and capacity at the lowest cost. For example, the dream of television transmission across the oceans was realized via the application of satellite communication at a cost of only 10% to 20% of that of the undersea cable communication.

A satellite communication system [1–3] (see Fig. 8.1) consists of a satellite relay station in space and earth stations containing transmitters and receivers for transmission and reception of signals from satellites.

There are many kinds of satellite communication systems. Among them, the geostationary orbit system is the most popular system used in modern satellite communications. In a geostationary orbit system [3], a satellite at a

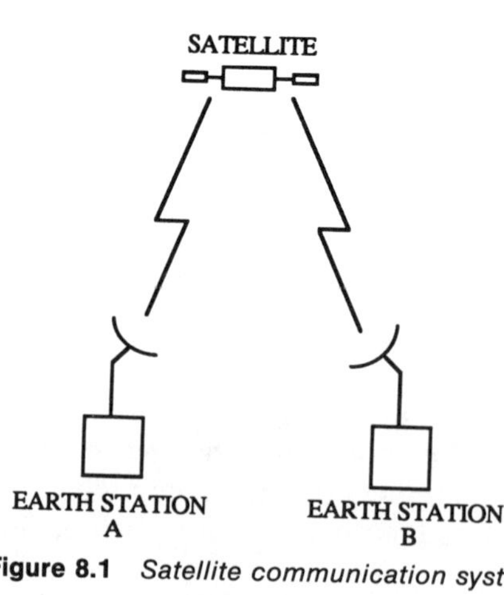

Figure 8.1 *Satellite communication system.*

particular height above the equator moves at a constant speed. It travels around the earth as fast as the earth rotates. Thus, the satellite appears stationary to an observer on the ground. This makes the earth station equipment much simpler, because a complex synchronization mechanism is not needed. On the other hand, additional cost may be incurred to keep the satellites in orbit because geostationary satellites are usually located at higher altitudes.

The main unique properties of satellite communication that distinguish them from terrestrial communication systems are as follows:

1. *The Broadcast Property* A satellite transmission can be received at any point in its coverage area. In principle, three satellites are sufficient to cover the whole earth.
2. *Geographical Flexibility* Unlike terrestrial services, satellite transmission paths or networks built around them are not restricted to any fixed configuration, as they would be by a predefined pattern of underground cables or microwave systems. Within their area of coverage, satellite networks offer an infinite choice of routes. Some underdeveloped countries are so keenly interested in satellite services because the terrestrial services in those countries are either rudimentary or nonexistent. Satellite services may offer the most economic means for providing a sophisticated national telecommunication infrastructure. This high degree of flexibility offers other major benefits, even in regions with well-developed terrestrial services. For example, it enables networks to be rapidly reconfigured and links to be quickly supplied and just as readily terminated, thereby permitting temporary services that previously might have been uneconomical to provide by other means. Finally, access to ship, vehicles, aircraft, and other moving entities is just as easy as fixed locations. Such flexibility is, however, achieved at the expense of requiring higher signal-to-noise ratio and susceptibility to interference.
3. *Distance-Insensitive Costs* The cost of building and maintaining terrestrial transmission facilities is directly proportional to the length of the circuit or transmission route. Because the information travels through a free medium (space), satellite services are not so distance sensitive.

Time-division multiple access (TDMA) is a multiple-access technique used in digital satellite communication. It enables a number of earth stations to share a satellite's capacity by allocating each earth station a time slot to communicate. The network has a mesh topology that allows direct station-to-station communication. The communication established between two stations is known as a *communication link.* The capacity of each link is determined by the number of channels assigned to the link. The total number of channels allocated to each link in the network thus defines the capacity of the network.

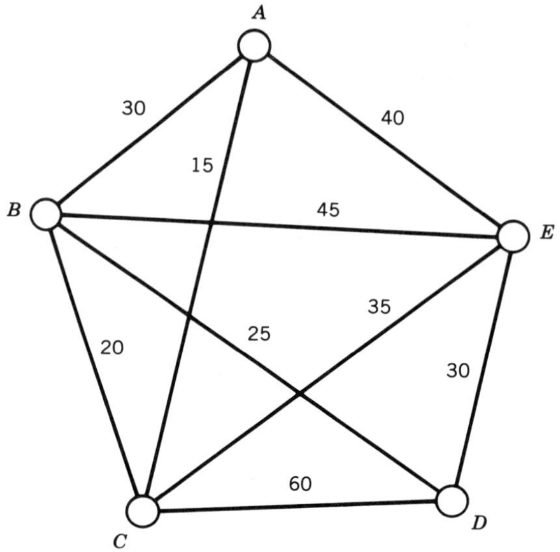

Figure 8.2 *A map of a satellite communication network which has a mesh topology with five nodes and nine links.*

The state of a network is defined by the load and demand of the network. It is quantified by the number of channels demanded for each link of the network. The capacity of the whole network is a constant, but the numbers of channels allocated to each link should vary according to the state of the network. An assignment of channels to links within a network topology is called a *map,* as shown in Figure 8.2. In this figure, the map consists of five nodes and nine links.

8.5 THE NEW MANAGEMENT SCHEME

In the past, digital satellite communication network (without a demand assignment multiple access device) is configured to different maps either according to a programmed time table or via an experienced human operator monitoring the state of the network. Demand assignment multiple access [3] (DAMA) allows the channel assignment of the network to vary slightly according to the change of the traffic in the satellite communication network. There are two kinds of DAMA schemes. One is the centralized control demand assignment where the requests for the channels are sent over a control channel to the central controller, which arbitrates requests and returns order information to the requesting earth station. The whole network thus depends on the well-being of the central controller. When the central controller malfunctions, the whole network will be out of service. The second one is the distributed control demand assignment. Each earth station

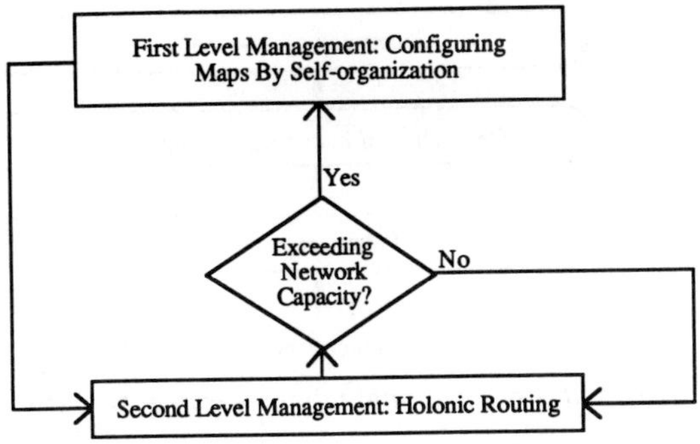

Figure 8.3 *The proposed two-level management scheme.*

keeps a data base of the status of the channels and selects, if available, a channel as needs arise. Thus, equipment for maintaining a network data base is complex and more expensive than in the first scheme.

The DAMA schemes both search for idle channels from the network randomly and return the channels to the network after communication services have been completed. They are not concerned with the whole network efficiency and traffic loss. In order to achieve high network efficiency, a management scheme consisting of two levels, as shown in Figure 8.3, is developed. The first level will adaptively configure maps for the satellite communication network, and the second level will route the traffic under the fixed configuration. When the load is less than the capacity of the network, the network control center can simply use the second level to route the traffic. Holonic routing [17] is proposed for the second-level management. When the average waiting time for each call or package is high enough, the network control center should use the first-level management to reassign the number of channels allocated to each link.

8.5.1 First-Level Management

The channel assignment problem of the satellite communication network is posed as a pattern recognition and generation problem. During the network operation, the state of the network fluctuates constantly. A total of N exemplar maps to which the network can configure are initially selected. Each exemplar map can accommodate a typical demand of the network for a certain time during network operation. Exemplar maps are assumed to be provided by an experienced operator of the network or derived from the network statistics. As mentioned, if the network does not exceed its capacity, the second-level management to route the traffic is sufficient, and thus the first-level management to configure maps for the network is not necessary. Throughout the discussion of the first-level management, it is assumed that the network exceeds its capacity, and the state of the network is con-

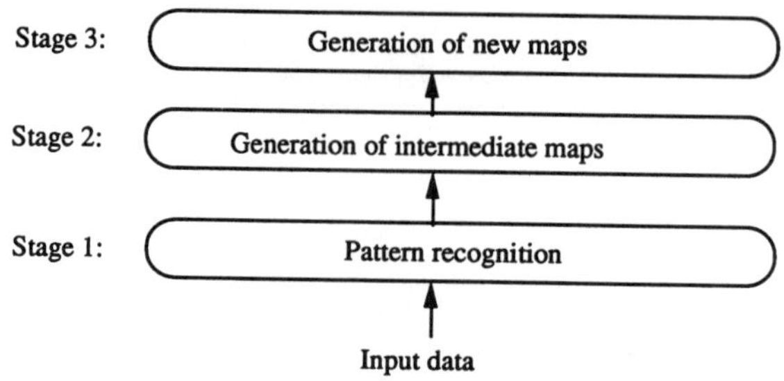

Figure 8.4 *The self-organizational model—first-level management.*

stantly compared to each of the exemplar maps. This defines the pattern recognition task (see Fig. 8.4). In this sense, it is a supervised learning. The chosen exemplar map can be adaptively changed according to certain performance criteria. That is, depending on how close the state of the network is matched to each of the exemplar maps, one of the following three actions will be taken:

1. The original exemplar map, which resembles the state of the network, is retained.
2. A different exemplar map, which resembles the state of the network, is selected.
3. A new map is generated to replace one of the existing maps if the state of the network is remotely different from any of the existing exemplar maps for a long time.

The Self-Organization Model for Configuring a Network. The self-organization model (SO model) consists of three stages as shown in Figure 8.4. The first stage performs the pattern recognition task. In this stage, the SO model determines the exemplar pattern (map) that resembles most closely the input data. The input data represent the state of the network. The second stage analyzes the discrepancy between the chosen exemplar map and the state of the network and generates intermediate maps that gradually deviate from the exemplar map and converge closely to the input data pattern. A new map is finally generated by the third stage. Let

L = total number of links in a network,

T = total number of channels in the network,

$R_i(t)$ = number of channels in link i required by users at time t,

$C_{ij}(t)$ = total number of channels assigned to link i of the jth exemplar map at time t. Here, the parameter t indicates that exemplar map j is time varying.

The original N exemplar maps are assumed given. The state of the network is also assumed updated constantly from the common signaling channel [3] (CSC) of the satellite communication system, and converted to numerical values denoted by $R_i(t)$. To perform the recognition task, the state of the network, $R_i(t)$, is updated as input data to the first stage of the SO model. The SO model computes the distance (metric) between the input data, $R_i(t)$, and each of the exemplar maps as follows:

$$D_j(t) = \sum_{i=1}^{L} |D_{ij}(t)| \qquad (j = 1, 2, \ldots, N) \tag{8.1}$$

where

$$D_{ij}(t) = R_i(t) - C_{ij}(t) \qquad (i = 1, 2, \ldots, L \quad j = 1, 2, \ldots, N)$$

indicates the busyness of link i in the network if exemplar map j is used. If $D_{ij}(t) > 0$, it implies that link i of the network is overloaded when map j is used; that is, channels allocated to link i of map j do not meet those demanded by the users in link i. If $D_{ij}(t) < 0$, it means that link i of map j provides more than enough channels required by the users in link i. Thus, $D_j(t)$ indicates the resemblance between the input data $R_i(t)$ and exemplar map j.

Furthermore, instead of using $D_j(t)$, the following normalized distance, $\overline{D}_j(t)$, is adopted as the metric:

$$\overline{D}_j(t) = \sum_{i=1}^{L} \frac{|D_{ij}(t)|}{R_i(t)} \qquad (j = 1, 2, \ldots, N) \tag{8.2}$$

The normalized distance is used so that the pattern recognition task will select the exemplar map that distributes the load of the network *most evenly*. The exemplar map that best meets the requirement of the network is the one that yields the smallest normalized distance, $\overline{D}_j(t)$. This metric is only used in the pattern recognition task to select an exemplar map that resembles the state of the network most closely. The second stage will self-adaptively change the chosen exemplar map to conform to the trend of the input data (the fluctuating state of the network).

The exemplar map selected by the first stage of the SO model may not satisfy the requirement of the network. If the chosen exemplar map meets the network requirement, that is, $\overline{D}_j(t)$ is small, the map remains unchanged. If the chosen map does not satisfy the network requirement, the algorithm proceeds to the second stage. The second stage modifies the exemplar map to better meet the requirement of the network. Note that only the exemplar map selected by the first stage is modified. The resulting modified map produced by the second stage is known as an *intermediate* map. This process is governed by the following equation, similar to Kohonen's self-organization [18]:

$$C'_{ij}(t+1) = C'_{ij}(t) + \beta(n(j))D'_{ij}(t)$$
$$(i = 1, 2, \ldots L \quad j = 1, 2, \ldots, N) \tag{8.3}$$

where $D'_{ij}(t) = R_i(t) - C'_{ij}(t)$.

Here, $C'_{ij}(t)$ is the number of channels of link i of map j being modified, and $\beta(n(j))$, $0 < \beta(n(j)) < 1$, is a gain factor. Here, the prime is used to distinguish the map being modified in the second stage from the original exemplar map chosen in the first stage. The modified map generated in the second stage may or may not replace the original exemplar map—this is determined by the third stage. As map j is being modified, $D'_{ij}(t)$ indicates the busyness of link i of the modified map j. Now, $D'_{ij}(t) > 0$ and $D'_{ij}(t) < 0$ have been defined, and $n(j)$ is the number of occurrences of exemplar map j being selected. When a new exemplar map j is generated by the third stage, this number is reset to 0. The function $\beta(n(j))$ is monotonically decreasing:

$$\beta(n(j)) = k_1^{-(n(j)+k_2)} \tag{8.4}$$

The gain factor $\beta(n(j))$ has three effects. It affects the drift of map j being modified to converge to the input pattern. It also determines whether a new map j will be generated in the third stage, which will be discussed shortly. Finally, it affects how fast a new map is generated.

In the third stage of the SO model, the convergence factor $E(j)$ is computed to decide whether a new map should be generated to replace the exemplar map:

$$E(j) = \operatorname*{Max}_i \{|\beta(n(j))D'_{ij}(t)|\} \qquad (i = 1, 2, \ldots, L) \tag{8.5}$$

From Eqs. (8.4) and (8.5), $E(j)$ is getting smaller when the jth map has been selected more often, indicating that the modified (intermediate) map j is attaining more closely to the network requirement; $E(j)$ indicates how close the modified map j is to the required load. A new map is thus generated based on the following conditions:

If $E \geq r$,

$$C_{ij}(t+1) = C_{ij}(t) \qquad (i = 1, 2, \ldots, L) \tag{8.6}$$

Else,

$$C_{ij}(t+1) = C'_{ij}(t) \qquad \text{for } B \leq T \tag{8.7}$$

or

$$c_{ij}(t+1) = \frac{T}{B} C'_{ij}(t) \qquad \text{for } B \geq T \tag{8.8}$$

where

$$B = \sum_{i=1}^{L} C'_{ij}(t)$$

is the total number of channels assigned to the modified map j at time (iteration) t, r is the threshold set to define whether a new channel assignment is made, T, as defined earlier, is the capacity of the whole network.

From Eqs. (8.4), (8.7), and (8.8), if the jth map has been selected often enough (i.e., $\beta(n(j))$ is small enough to make E less than r), the SO model generates a new map j to replace the original chosen exemplar map. If the capacity of the modified map exceeds the capacity of the network, the modified map is normalized as shown in Eq. (8.8).

Experimental Results. Various satellite communication networks with different number of links and capacity have been simulated. All results are similar. As an example, a simulation of a satellite communication network with 10 links and a capacity of 1000 channels is presented. Ten original exemplar maps are given and shown in Table 8.1. Figure 8.5 shows the simulation results. It shows the number of channels required by users and the channels assigned by the algorithm as a function of time for each link of the network. The network requirement fluctuates slightly (random data), from $t = 1$ to $t = 199$, and changes drastically at transition $t = 200$, and then varies slowly until $t = 500$. The jagged line in each graph indicates the requirement for the link as a function of time t, and the lower smoother line is the number of channels that the SO model suggests providing for that link.

TABLE 8.1 Ten Exemplar Maps, Each with 10 Links and a Capacity of 1000 Channels

Map	Link									
No.	1	2	3	4	5	6	7	8	9	10
Map 1	100	100	100	100	100	100	100	100	100	100
Map 2	120	80	120	80	120	80	120	80	120	80
Map 3	130	70	130	70	130	70	130	70	130	70
Map 4	150	50	150	50	150	50	150	50	150	50
Map 5	120	110	100	120	110	100	80	90	100	70
Map 6	80	90	100	80	90	100	120	110	100	130
Map 7	70	85	135	70	85	135	110	100	90	120
Map 8	60	140	100	60	140	70	110	110	120	90
Map 9	40	60	200	40	60	100	100	100	200	100
Map 10	140	60	140	60	140	60	200	0	200	0

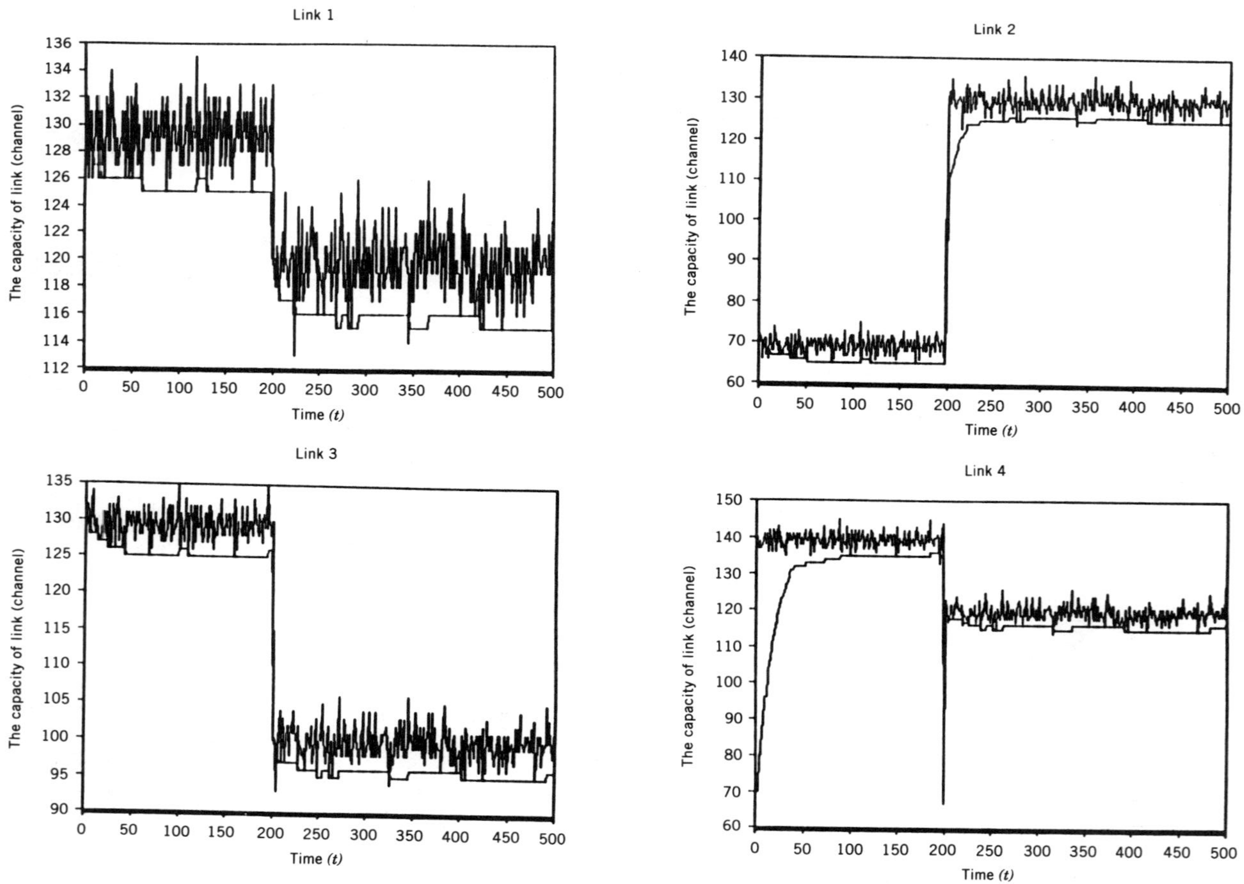

Link 1
Link 2
Link 3
Link 4
The capacity of link (channel)
Time (t)

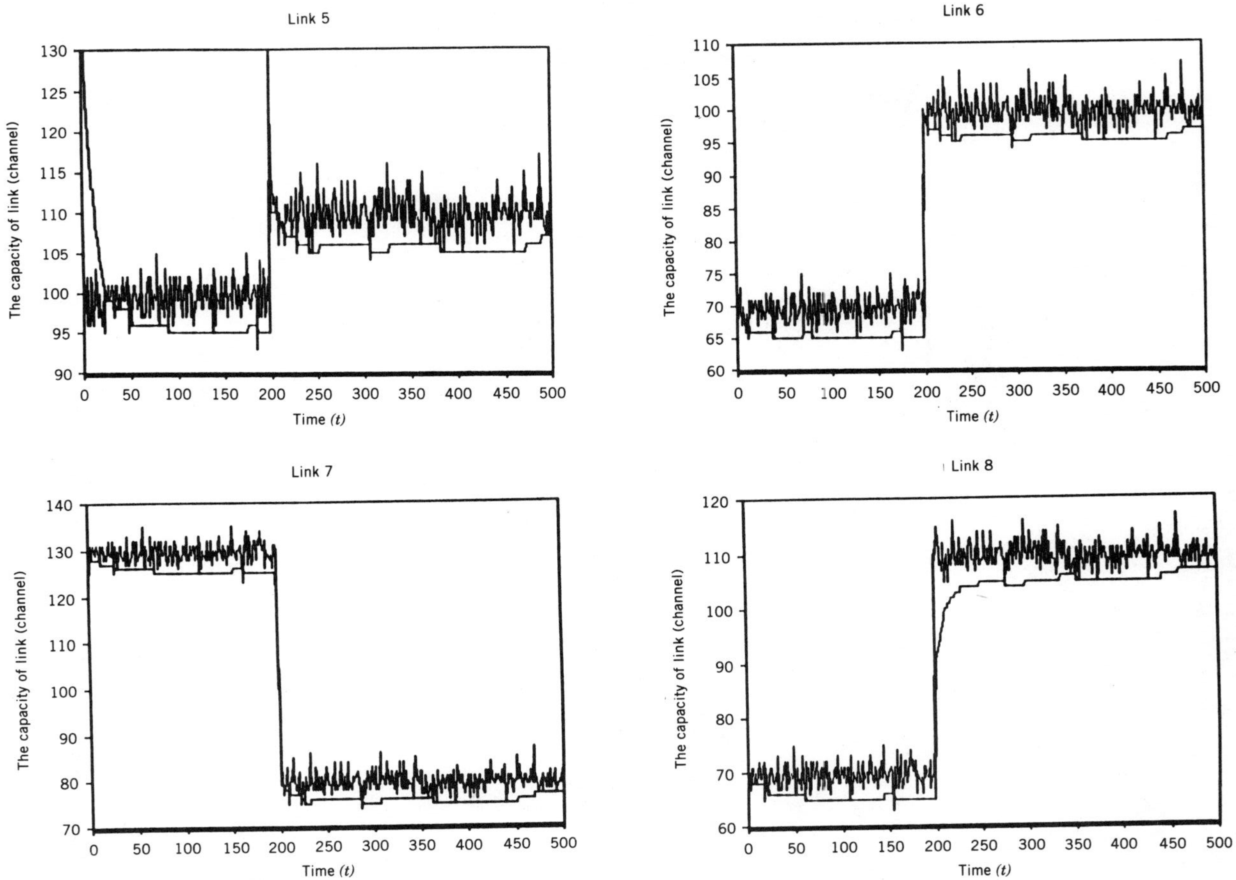

Figure 8.5 *The results of applying the self-organization model to the simulated network with 10 links and a capacity of 1000 channels. The jagged line in each graph indicates the requirement for the link, and the lower smoother line is the number of channels that the model suggests providing for that link, both versus time. (Continues on page 178.)*

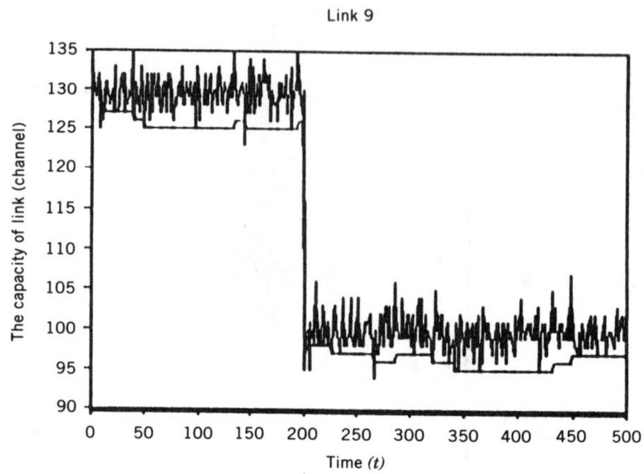

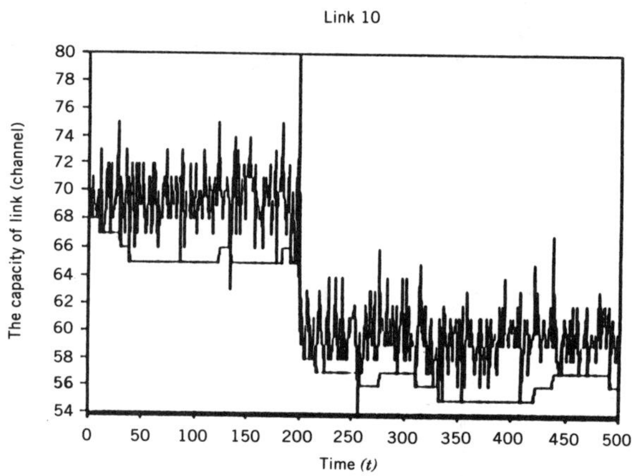

Figure 8.5 (*Continued*)

In the simulation, the demand of the network is larger than the capacity. The channels assigned by the algorithm, under the constraint of a fixed capacity and overloaded network, follow the trend of the demand closely.

8.5.2 Second-Level Management

The second-level management is a routing algorithm. After a map has been chosen by the first-level management, traffic is routed under the chosen fixed configuration. Various routing algorithms are being considered, including the neural-network-based algorithm known as holonic routing [17]. The incorporation of the two levels represents the continuing effort to maximize the network efficiency, and experimental results will be reported in the future.

8.6 DISCUSSION AND FURTHER WORK

The overall conceptual model of the new management scheme has been presented. The first-level management along with experimental results have also been discussed in detail. The remaining major task is the incorporation of the two levels of management. As mentioned earlier, when the load is less than the capacity of the network, traffic of the network can be managed by a routing algorithm (second-level management). Thus, when the network exceeds its capacity, a criterion function that indicates the extent of overload of the network is required to determine whether the network should be reconfigured by the self-organization model (first-level management). The implementation of the new scheme into the onboard central network control of a satellite will also be investigated and explored.

REFERENCES

[1] G. B. Bleazard, *Introducing Satellite Communications,* Halsted Press, New York, 1985.

[2] Kamilo Feher, *Satellite/Earth Station Engineering,* Prentice-Hall, Englewood Cliffs, N.J., 1983.

[3] T. Pratt and C. W. Bostian, *Satellite Communication,* Wiley, New York, 1986.

[4] D. W. E. Rees, *Satellite Communications: The First Quarter Century of Service,* Wiley, New York, 1990.

[5] J. P. Labourdette and A. S. Acampora, Partially reconfigurable multihop lightwave networks, *Proc. IEEE GLOBECOM'90,* 34–40 (December 2–5, 1990).

[6] E. I. Tsai, B. A. Coan, M. Kerner, and M. P. Vecchi, A comparison of strategies for survivable network design: Reconfigurable and conventional approaches, *Proc. IEEE GLOBECOM'90,* 49–55 (December 2–5, 1990).

[7] H. Yamaguchi, Views on future telecommunications services and technologies, *NTT Review,* 1(10), 6–15 (May 1990).

[8] K. Murano, K. Murakami, E. Iwabuchi, T. Katsuki, and H. Ogasawara, Technologies towards broadband ISDN, *IEEE Communications Mag.,* 28(4), 66–70 (1990).

[9] M. Frame, Broadband service needs, *IEEE Communications Mag.,* 28(4), 59–62 (1990).

[10] G. R. Ash and V. S. Mummert, AT&T carves new routes in its nationwide network, *AT&T Bell Lab. Rec.* 10, 102–106 (August, 1984).

[11] G. R. Ash, Use of a trunk status map for real-time DNHR, *Proc. Internat. Teletraffic Conf.* 11, 56–72 (1985).

[12] G. R. Ash, Building a dynamic routing architecture, *Telephony,* 5(6), 42–51 (June 27, 1983).

[13] B. R. Hurley, C. J. R. Seidl, and W. F. Sewell, A survey of dynamic routing methods for circuit-switched traffic, *IEEE Communications Mag.,* 25(9), 13–21 (1987).

[14] N. Ansari and Y. Chen, A neural network model to configure maps for a satellite communication network, *Proc. IEEE GLOBECOM'90,* 1042–1046 (December 2–5, 1990).

[15] N. Ansari and Y. Chen, Configuring maps for a satellite communication network by self-organization, *J. Neural Network Computing,* 2(4), 11–17 (Spring 1991).

[16] D. Chakraborty, VSAT communications: An overview, *IEEE Communications Mag.,* 26(5), 10–24 (1988).

[17] A. Chugo, W. Sotelo, and I. Iida, Holonic routing scheme based on neural computations, *Proc. IEEE GLOBECOM'90,* 1366–1370 (December 2–5, 1990).

[18] T. Kohonen, *Self-Organization and Associative Memory,* Springer-Verlag, Berlin, 1984.

PART II

Genetic Algorithms and Genetic Programming

CHAPTER 9

An Introduction to Adaptive Optimization Algorithms Based on Principles of Natural Evolution

YUVAL DAVIDOR
HANS-PAUL SCHWEFEL

9.1 INTRODUCTION

Genetic algorithms (GA) and *evolution strategies* (ES) are algorithms that imitate the principles of natural evolution as a method to solve parameter optimization problems. Though these two methodologies have emerged at more or less the same time and have many features in common, they have evolved in a totally different way. In this chapter on the optimization powers of these techniques, we present the basic concepts on which GA and ES are based on and provide a rationale as to why these optimization techniques work, and work better than other, classical methods in certain problem domains.

The idea to use the principles of organic evolution processes as rules for optimum-seeking procedures emerged independently on both sides of the Atlantic more than two decades ago. Both approaches mimic operators and information processing paradigms, such as reproduction and selection of natural populations to achieve efficient and robust optimization algorithms. These algorithms can be viewed as a mathematical or an algorithmic presentation of Darwin's observations and the, later, new synthesis theory of evolution.

In the United States, Holland, in his 1975 book *Adaptation in Natural and Artifical Systems* [1], set the framework for GA as part of a general framework of adaptation. Holland's book is a projection of separate ideas on which he worked for many years before the book's publication. He mentions in his book the applicability of GA to parameter optimization, which was

Dynamic, Genetic, and Chaotic Programming, By Branko Souček and the IRIS Group.
ISBN 0-471-55717-X

first realized experimentally by De Jong [2]. To date, many have used GA to solve a diverse range of engineering problems together with a continued effort to advance the theory concerned with these algorithms.

On the other side of the Atlantic, the German school of thought developed a different version, called *evolution strategies*. They were first introduced by Rechenberg in the 1960s [3], and further developed by Schwefel [4].

We present the two optimization methodologies used in later chapters as the basis for solving a diverse range of hard problems.

9.2 GENETIC ALGORITHMS

It is a popular statement that species, as the result of evolution, are well adapted to their environmental niche. Another common statement about the natural world is that organisms are well equipped to observe and respond to repetitive events but are usually helpless against the unexpected. The rationale is almost self-explanatory. It is too costly for an organism to develop specialized response mechanisms to sporadic events, because they occur so infrequently. The cost of responding to the unusual is simply too high compared with the rare gains such capabilities reward. Therefore, the natural world, as living organisms perceive it, is composed from cyclic events that may or may not interact in a complex fashion. This leads to the fundamental aspect of establishing a problem solver mechanism based on the theory that evolution is an efficient process that implicitly locates optimal solutions to aspects of the events exhibited by the environment.

The problem is not as simple as finding the best trait for each event present, because it is difficult to decompose the environment into independent events, and it is even harder to find an optimal trait for each event, because traits interact in a highly nonlinear way. This is also the fundamental feature of GA—the efficient exploration of multiparametric and complex spaces to locate optimal sets of parameter values that represent optimal solutions. The Darwin and modern theories of evolution suggest a biological, partly philosophical, explanation of why the combination of selection and heredity reproduction results in a robust adaptive search process that continuously finds organisms with better, more highly fit traits. Holland, in the early 1960s, suggested an "evolutionary" algorithm, based on a simplified mechanism of evolution, and a partly theoretical, partly experimental explanation of why it is such an efficient and robust optimization mechanism. Holland's algorithmic model is called a genetic algorithm, and its central theorem is called the *schema theorem* [1]. Although much work has been done in extending the schema theorem to be more accurate and applicable to a broader class of GA models, we present it in its original form because it presents the fundamental processes that occur in a GA in a clear and demonstrative way. Inquisitive readers may refer to advance analysis of the schema theorem [5,6,7].

The game Mastermind is a good example for demonstrating the essence of an evolutionary search and the operation of GA. In Mastermind there are two four-digit integers, one for each of the two players. Each player chooses a four-digit number and keeps it hidden from the other player, whose aim is to discover that number before the other player discovers his or hers. The only restriction is that the numbers must not contain repeating digits. Because the order of the digits is important, the set of different four-digit numbers contains 5040 elements ($5040 = 10 \times 9 \times 8 \times 7$).

Each player in turn constructs a four-digit number, which he or she guesses to be the number his or her opponent chose. The opponent responds to the guess by indicating how many digits of the guessed number are correct, and how many of the correct digits are also in their right position. For example, if the chosen number is 4710 and the first guessed number is 5018, then the response should indicate that there are two correct digits and that one of them is in its right position (Table 9.1). The players try to find the correct four digits and place them in their correct positions by trial and error. If the second guessed number is 7921 and therefore has two correct digits, but the third guess 2583 has none, then 1 is a correct digit and its place is not at the far right (Table 9.1). Experience has shown that it takes about six attempts for good players to guess the opponent's number correctly.

The information elimination process, such as 2 does not appear in the opponent's combination, leads to substantial reductions in the search space. This reduction in the amount of information requiring processing is called, in machine learning a *subgoal reward,* as it is a milestone on the road of reaching the end goal, and, hence, the complete solution to a given problem. The information elimination process described for the Mastermind game can also be described in a more compact way with a schema—an information similarity template. For example, a Mastermind schema $*, *, 2, *$, where "$*$" designates a wild card, discusses all number combinations that have a 2 in the third position. We shall come back to schemata in the next section. For now we note the implicit/explicit use of schemata in Mastermind and how progress in this game is based on establishing as many schemata as possible and on identifying those schemata that are highly rewarding (instantiate number combinations that receive high scores).

However, if we were to modify the representation of the four-digit numbers so that players used an enumerative table when each four-digit number had a running entry code and the entry code rather than the number combination was used, then the game would degenerate into a random search and become painfully boring. Though we have neither destroyed the variety of

TABLE 9.1 The Mastermind Game for Number 4710

Guess No.	The Guess	Score	
		Correct Digits	Correct Position
1	5018	1	1
2	7921	2	0
3	2583	0	0

the domain nor changed any of the rules (the number of correct digits and correct positions is still available to the players), the game loses its essence because the players cannot observe correlations between their guessed numbers and the value of these guesses. In other words, the players have no way of identifying subgoals. Again, the similarity templates used by the player and the similarity among four-digit numbers enables experienced players to determine the correct number with only a few guesses out of the large number of possible combinations (5040!).

In the following section we show how the Mastermind paradigm of locating the correct value of four-integer parameters can be generalized as an optimizing technique.

9.2.1 The Genetic Algorithm Machinery

In a GA, the solution space of a problem is represented as a set of values corresponding to a set of parameters defining a point in the solution space. A GA is a general procedure to solve optimization problems of the following form: Given a function f: $D \rightarrow R$ (f: $R \rightarrow R$), find an element $d \in D$ that optimizes f. The function f is called the *objective function*. Each element d is represented in the form $d = g(x_1, x_2, \ldots, x_l)$ (g: $R^l \rightarrow R$). Each element x_i of the l-tuple $\mathbf{x}$ is defined over a finite alphabet of cardinality k. Therefore, there are k^l different tuples in the parametric space, and those k^l tuples represent k^l solutions.

The algorithm proceeds as follows:

Step 0: A sample, $\mathcal{P}$, the *parent population,* of size n l-tuples is selected at random without replacement from the k^l solution space. The value of these random solutions is evaluated with the objective function $f(g(\mathbf{x}))$.

Step 1: A second sample, $\mathcal{O}$, the *offspring population,* of size n is created from $\mathcal{P}$ by selecting tuples probabilistically relative to their function value, with replacement.

Step 2: With probability P_m per tuple element, the value of an element x_i in $\mathcal{O}$ (the offspring population) is changed at random. This operator is called a *mutation* operator.

Step 3: With a probability P_c per tuple, each two tuples of $\mathcal{O}$ undergo a *crossover* operation. Crossover means a random selection of an index point along the tuple and the exchange of trailing subtuples between the two tuples involved. If the tuple position selected as a cross point is denoted by j, the first tuple denoted by **A**, and the second by **B**,

$$A_1, A_2, \ldots, A_{j-1}, A_j, A_{j+1}, \ldots, A_l$$

$$B_1, B_2, \ldots, B_{j-1}, B_j, B_{j+1}, \ldots, B_l$$

then this crossover operation produces the two new tuples

$$A_1, A_2, \ldots, A_{j-1}, A_j, B_{j+1}, \ldots, B_l$$

$$B_1, B_2, \ldots, B_{j-1}, B_j, A_{j+1}, \ldots, A_l$$

Step 4: Evaluate the value of the tuples in $\mathbb{C}$ with the objective function $f(g(\mathbf{x}))$.
Step 5: Replace $\mathcal{P}$ by $\mathbb{C}$ and repeat steps 1–4 until all tuples in the parent population are identical (or until some other stopping criterion is met).

It is common practice to choose values for the crossover probability and mutation probability such that $P_c \gg P_m$. The reason is that mutations have the effect of increasing the tuples diversity and thus slowing down the convergence (it is, after all, a random noise over the x_i values). Crossover, on the other hand, has the effect of trying different combinations of tuples that already proved to be relatively good. Because one assumes that one can say something about the whole tuple by knowing its x_i elements, making more copies of good tuples and recombining them is just like trying to extract the partial set of x_i's that gave the tuple its high function value and combining them with other good partial sets. The reason for maintaining mutations at all is that practical implementations are often restricted to a relatively small sample size and, therefore, are subject to sampling errors. A low level of mutations introduces a background noise that helps to prevent premature convergence to a local optimum. Furthermore, mutations have the effect of a local optimizer (such as a hill climbing, and will be shown in Section 9.5 when we discuss evolutionary stategies).

9.2.2 The Schema Theorem

The schema theorem has been constructed by Holland to demonstrate the information processing and convergence powers of a GA, and has come to serve as the central theorem of GAs for almost a decade. However, the schema theorem is incomplete. It is a mathematical description of a particular GA and assumes certain conditions, which are hard to fulfil in practical implementations. The importance of the schema theorem is therefore primarily demonstrative, in explaining the effect the genetic operators (reproduction, mutation, crossover, and selection) have on adaptation and optimization. It is beyond the scope of this chapter to present a more accurate schema theorem, and it is also of marginal importance for the basic understanding of how GAs work.

The most important aspect of an optimization algorithm, especially when dealing with heuristic algorithms in huge and complex domains, is that there be a balance between the exploration of new regions in the solution space and exploitation of those good regions that were already discovered. The schema theorem explains how such a balance is realized by a GA implicitly through the use of the operators introduced in the previous section (steps 1 through 5).

We introduce the notion of a schema H with the addition of a # symbol, a "don't care" symbol, to the alphabet used thus far by the x_i parameters. A kth-order hyperplane of D is defined to be the $(l - k)$-dimensional subspace of D, specified by fixing exactly k of the l positions in the tuple and leaving the remaining positions as "don't cares" (Fig. 9.1). A member of such a

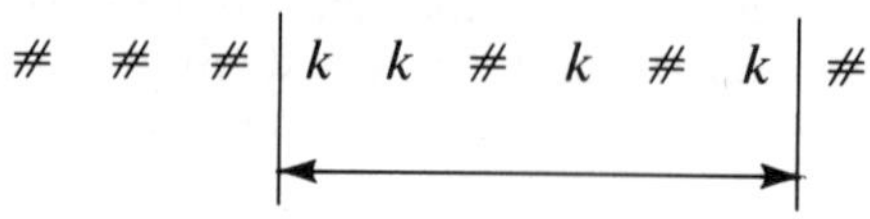

Figure 9.1 *A four-dimensional schema (the* k*'s denote the specific positions of the schema with defining length* δ(H) = *5 and order* o(H) = *4.*

hyperplane is called a *schema,* and a schema defines a hypercube that contains all tuples that match the schema in its k specific positions.

For example, let $l = 3$ and x_i take the Boolean values {0,1} plus the "don't care" symbol {#}, so $x_i = \{0, 1, \#\}$. The schema $H = 0\#\#$ belongs to the first-order hyperplane {0##, 1##} and instantiates a hypercube whose elements are the tuples {000, 001, 010, 011}.

Again, one may recognize the meaning and importance of a schema structure by returning to the Mastermind game. Knowing that the number 3 is correct and its correct position is in the second place loosely translates to the schema #3##, which is an important statement about the problem. We will show that similar statements emerge implicitly in a GA as the result of proliferation and decay of schemata.

A schema represents a subspace of the solution space. Since we want to optimally allocate search efforts to those regions in the solution space that seem to be promising, schemata are a good tool for designating such regions and for analyzing the allocation of trails taking place in a GA.

When discussing the allocation of trails in GA, Holland used an analogous problem borrowed from *decision theory,* called the *K-armed bandit problem,* which presents the optimal allocation of trails as a policy that minimizes the expected losses in the next set of trials. In heuristic probabilistic algorithms such as GA, this means that the choice of next trials should be the best possible with regard to the probability of getting closer to the goal based on previous trials. Therefore, the optimal allocation of trials is that policy that allocates an exponentially increasing (or decreasing) number of trials to regions of the search space based on the observed value of that region in previous trials. In schema terms, the number of instances of every schema present in $\mathcal{P}$ should grow (or decay) in $\mathcal{O}$ at an exponential rate proportional to the schema average observed function value. Based on the analysis of the K-armed bandit problem, Holland suggested that this rate is achieved by a proportional replication of tuples as in steps 1 and 4 of the simple GA presented in the previous section. A GA was said to use a proportional replication of tuples (step 1) and uniform elimination of tuples (step 4). The combined effect of these processes creates a biased frequency of x_i values in $\mathcal{O}$ and, consequently, of the distribution of schemata frequencies in successive offspring populations.

For example, if the average function value of tuples in $\mathcal{P}$ that begin with a 0 (those tuples that are instantiated by the schema $0\#\# \cdots \#$) is higher than that of those beginning with a 1, then, on average, tuples beginning with a 0 will be replicated more frequently than those beginning with 1. This leads to the increased frequency of tuples beginning with a 0 in $\mathcal{O}$ and to the frequency of the schema $0\#\# \cdots \#$).

Resulting from the proportional replication and uniform elimination of tuples is the following implicit replication of schemata. If we denote the number of tuples present in $\mathcal{P}$ at time t that belong to the schema H by $M(H, t)$, then the number of schema H instances in $\mathcal{O}$, $M(H, t + 1)$, is

$$M(H, t + 1) = M(H, t)\ (f_H(t)/(\bar{f}(t)) \qquad \text{where } f_H(t) = \frac{\sum_{tuples \in H} f(g(\mathbf{x}))}{\sum_{tuples \in H^1}}$$

is the average schema value calculated from the sample $\mathcal{P}$ and $\bar{f}(t)$ is the average function value over all tuples (schemata) in $\mathcal{P}$. To obtain a qualitative notion of the growth rate of such an allocation policy, let us assume that a particular schema remains above average by a fixed amount $c\bar{f}(t)$ (c being a constant) for t number of cycles. This leads to the following exponential growth:

$$M(H, t) = M(H, 0)\left[\frac{\bar{f}(t) + c\bar{f}(t)}{\bar{f}(t)}\right]^t = M(H, 0)(1 + c)^t$$

The same holds for all schemata, whether below or above average value.

Thus far, we have only discussed the optimal allocation of trails, not how such trials materialize. The replication part of the algorithm does not introduce new solution points since it replicates points that already exist (tuples in $\mathcal{P}$). New search points are formed by the mutation (step 2) and crossover (step 3) processes. It is clear that the creation of new tuples based on tuples in $\mathcal{O}$ after step 1 will distort the exponential growth discussed earlier. To estimate the disruption effect of these two processes on schemata growth, we present two new characteristics of schemata: the defining length of a schema, $\delta(H)$, and the order of a schema, $o(H)$.

The defining length of a schema is defined as the distance between the two farthest positions in the tuple that are fixed (Fig. 9.1). Consequently, the probability that a crossover operation will destroy a given schema H is the probability that the cross point falls at any of the positions within the specific region of the schema (ignoring the low probability that the crossover involves two identical schemata) and equals $P_c\ \delta(H)/(l - 1)$. The order of a schema denotes the number of specific positions in the schema (k positions). The probability of destroying a schema due to a mutation event is therefore $o(H)^{P_m} \approx P_m o(H); P_m \ll 1$. This leads to the a lower bound approximation of the schemata growth due to mutation, crossover, and selection, called by Holland the schema theorem, given by

$$M(H, t + 1) = M(H, t)\frac{f_H(t)}{\bar{f}(t)}\left[1 - P_c\frac{\delta(H)}{l - 1} - P_m o(H)\right]$$

We now turn back to our illustrative example of the Mastermind game, and restate the benefits of using a parametric representation. The schema theorem tells us that at each sampling of a tuple a big ensemble of information statements are made implicitly about the solution space through the growth or decay of schemata. Since each solution point is represented by a tuple, and a tuple instantiates 2^l different schemata (irrespective to the cardinality of the alphabet used), the more detailed a representation is more schemata are being processed and the implicit parallelism is increased. This leads to a faster convergence.

Each schema represented in the sample $\mathcal{P}$ increases or decreases according to Eq. 1 on page 189 independently of what is happening to other schemata in $\mathcal{P}$. The crossover continually introduces new schemata while testing still existing schemata in new contexts without much interference to the ranking process of above and below average schemata. This is the implicit parallelism which is so fundamental in GAs. Since there is a finite (and limited) number of different schemata present in $\mathcal{P}$ and further, that not all schemata are being processed at the same rate, the implicit parallelism is an idealized situation which is not realized in a simple GA. Holland derived a more practical bound of the amount of schemata being processed efficiently (meaning being processed with an error rate less than some specified value) in a simple GA and came up with a figure of merit of $\mathcal{O}(n^3)$ where n is the size of the sample $\mathcal{P}$. This cubic implicit parallelism exited many practitioners who took this result out of its original context and selected ever larger population sizes. Goldberg has rederived Holland's bound and showed the fallacy of such reasoning in basing the selection of population size on Holland's $\mathcal{O}(n^3)$ figure of merit [Goldberg (25), Goldberg (26)]. In his work, Goldberg provides a figure of merit of the expected number of unique schemata in a population of size n and of strings of specified length l which seem to work well on serial machines. Consequently, Goldberg derives an estimate of the number of schemata $\mathcal{S}$ being processed optimally as a function of the population size n and the number of parameters l in the l-tuple as

$$\mathcal{S}(n, l) = \sum_{i=0}^{l} \binom{l}{i} 2^i \left\{1 - \left[1 - \left(\frac{1}{2}\right)^i\right]^n\right\}$$

Other advances in fields of GAs were made during the last few years. We shall emphasize those that are most relevant and fundamental to this introduction chapter. Comparative studies of the effect of different recombination operators, representation format and population size indicate that the three are strongly linked. Linked at the heart of the operation of a GA so that theoretically any representation with a given recombination operator may be mapped into a different representation which is GA-easy [Vose and Liepins (27)]. Though the number of transformation matrices is larger than the size of the original solution space and that there is no efficient algorithm at present which is capable of locating the appropriate matrix, it indicates that there is for any given function optimization problem a combination of representation and recombination which result in a GA-easy domain. A similar argument can be applied to the type of a recombination operator which raises the question of the use of the traditional recombination operators and their restrictive adaptability. This leads also to early proposals of adapting the GA operators on-line to optimize the performance of the algorithm.

9.2.3 Summary

Much progress in GA research was made from the early 1970s, when GAs were tried, used and tested by graduate students, to the present, where hundreds and possibly thousands of scientists and engineers use GAs to solve an extremely diverse range of difficult problems. A lot of good research was conducted in this field to reach the stage where it can be used as a convenient tool to solve optimization problems. Side by side to applications, the theory of GAs is continuing to mature. A lot of research effort is invested in deepening our understanding issues of representation, adaptation and information processing associated with GAs and their application.

This effort involves the study of the effect of different operators, such as crossover (and others which were not mentioned in this introductory chapter), and the interaction between the various operators. At the moment, we experience an abundance of successful GA applications some of which are presented in this book and elsewhere [Davis (8), Davidor (9)], and in the proceedings of the international conferences on genetic algorithms held biannually.

9.3 EVOLUTION STRATEGIES

Similar to GA, ES are algorithms that imitate the principles of natural evolution as a method of solving parameter optimization problems. This section focuses on the ES introduced by Rechenberg at Berlin [3], and further developed by Schwefel [4]. Evolution strategies were first applied to experimental optimization problems with more or less continuously changeable parameters. Numerical applications, however, followed soon after.

The overall goal of a parameter optimization problem $f\colon M \subseteq \mathbf{R}^n \rightarrow \mathbf{R}$, $M \neq \emptyset$, where f is the *objective function,* is to find a vector $x^* \in M$ such that

$$\forall x \in M\colon f(x) \geq f(x^*) = f^* \tag{9.1}$$

where f^* is called a *global minimum,* x^* is the *minimum location* (*point* or *set*), and

$$M = \{x \in \mathbf{R}^n | g_j(x) \geq 0 \; \forall j \in \{1, \ldots, q\}\} \tag{9.2}$$

is the set of feasible solutions for a problem with inequality constraints $g_j\colon \mathbf{R}^n \rightarrow \mathbf{R}$. For an unconstrained problem $M = \mathbf{R}^n$.

Since $\max\{f(x)\} = -\min\{-f(x)\}$, the restriction to minimization is without loss of generality. In the following a minimization problem is assumed. A similar argument holds for the opposite sign within the formation of the inequality constraints. In general, the optimization task is complicated by the possibility of nonlinear objective functions with multiple local optima. A *local minimum* $\hat{f} = f(\hat{x})$ is defined by the following condition:

$$\exists \varepsilon > 0 \ \forall x \in M: \|x - \hat{x}\| < \varepsilon \Rightarrow \hat{f} \leq f(x) \tag{9.3}$$

Even if there is only one local optimum, it may be difficult to find a path toward it if the objecive function or its derivatives has discontinuities, if noise is present or if an optimum is moving over time.

9.3.1 Survival of the Fittest: (1 + 1)-ES

The following two-member ES, conceived by Rechenberg [3] in the 1960s, is based on a population consisting of one parent individual (a real-valued vector) and one descendent, created by adding normally distributed random numbers to every component of the vector. The better of both individuals then serves as the ancestor of the following iteration/generation. Such a (1 + 1)-ES can be described as the 8-tuple

$$(1 + 1) - \text{ES} = (P^0, m, s, c_d, c_i, f, g, t) \tag{9.4}$$

where

$P^0 = (x^0, \sigma^0) \in I; I = \mathbf{R}^n \times \mathbf{R}$	population
$m: I \rightarrow I$	mutation operator
$s: I \times I \rightarrow I$	selection operator
$c_d, c_i \in \mathbf{R}$	step-size control
$f: \mathbf{R}^n \rightarrow \mathbf{R}$	objective function
$g_j: \mathbf{R}^n \rightarrow \mathbf{R}; j \in \{1, \ldots, q\}$	constraint functions
$t: I \times I \rightarrow \{0, 1\}$	termination criterion

Here, P^0 denotes the initial population consisting of a single parent that produces, by mutation, a single offspring, resulting in

$$\begin{aligned} P'^t &= (a_1'^t, a_2'^t) \in I \times I \\ a_1'^t &= P^t = (x^t, \sigma^t) \\ a_2'^t &= m(P^t) = (x'^t, \sigma^t) \end{aligned} \tag{9.5}$$

The mutation operator is applied to all components of the object parameter vector x^t. According to the biological observation that offspring are somehow similar to their parents and that smaller changes occur more often than larger ones, the mutations are realized by normally distributed random numbers:

$$x'^t = x^t + \mathbf{N}_0(\sigma^t) \tag{9.6}$$

where $\mathbf{N}_0$ denotes a vector of independent Gaussian random numbers with zero mean and standard deviation (scalar) σ^t. The selection operator then determines the fitter individual, whether the ancestor or descendent, to become the parent of the next generation:

$$P^{t+1} = s(P'^t) = \begin{cases} a_2'^t & \text{if } f(x'^t) \leq f(x^t) \wedge g_j(x'^t) \geq 0 \ \forall j \in \{1, \ldots, q\} \\ a_1'^t = P^t & \text{else} \end{cases} \tag{9.7}$$

The iteration process $P^t \to P^{t+1}$ stops when the termination criterion $t(P^t, P^{t+1}) = 1$ occurs. The function t depends on the implementation, and elapsed CPU time, elapsed number of generations, and absolute or relative progress per generation might also be considered.

In our description so far, the standard deviation σ^t remains constant over time. Born has shown that for a (1 + 1)-ES and a "regular" optimization problem, global convergence can be achieved with probability 1 as long as $\sigma^t > 0$ holds [10]. As is well known concerning similar theorems for *simulated annealing* [11] and GA [12], such results are not of much practical value due to the unlimited time condition. In fact, we are interested more in the expectation of the *convergence rate* φ, given by the distance covered per trial toward the optimum.

Rechenberg calculated the convergence rates for the model functions

$$f_1(x) = F(x_1) = c_0 + c_1 x_1, \ \forall i \in \{2, \ldots, n\}: \quad \frac{-b}{2} \leq x_i \leq \frac{b}{2}$$

$$f_2(x) = \sum_{i=1}^{n} x_i^2 \tag{9.8}$$

where $x = (x_1, \ldots, x_n)^{\mathrm{T}} \in \mathbf{R}^n$, and f_1 is the *corridor model* and f_2 is the *sphere model*. For these simple model functions the expectations of the rates of convergence are [4]:

$$\varphi_1 = \frac{\sigma}{\sqrt{2\pi}} \left(1 - \sqrt{\frac{2}{\pi}} \frac{\sigma}{b}\right)^{n-1} \quad \text{for } n \gg 1 \tag{9.9}$$

$$\varphi_2 = \frac{\sigma}{\sqrt{2\pi}} \left(\exp\left(-\left(\frac{n\sigma}{\sqrt{8}r}\right)^2\right) - \sqrt{\pi}\,\frac{n\sigma}{\sqrt{8}r}\left(1 - \operatorname{erf}\left(\frac{n\sigma}{\sqrt{8}r}\right)\right)\right) \quad \text{for } n \gg 1$$

where $\operatorname{erf}(x)$ is the well-known error function. The rate of convergence for the sphere model depends on the current location within the search space, where r denotes the Euclidean distance from the optimum. For the corridor model the width b acts like a topological parameter. From (9.9) it is possible to determine the optimal standard deviations σ_k^{opt} and the corresponding maximum convergence rates $\varphi_k^{\max}$ $(k = 1, 2)$ according to $d\varphi_k/d\sigma_k|_{\sigma_k^{\mathrm{opt}};\varphi_k^{\max}} = 0$:

$$\sigma_1^{\text{opt}} = \sqrt{\frac{\pi}{2}}\frac{b}{n} \qquad \varphi_1^{\max} = \frac{1}{2e}\frac{b}{n} \tag{9.10}$$

$$\sigma_2^{\text{opt}} \approx 1.224\,\frac{r}{n} \qquad \varphi_2^{\max} \approx 0.2025\,\frac{r}{n}$$

In both cases the optimal "mean step size" σ^{opt} and the maximum rate of convergence are inversely proportional to the number of object variables n.

The probabilities for a successful mutation are

$$p_1 = \frac{1}{2}\left(1 - \sqrt{\frac{2}{\pi}}\frac{\sigma}{b}\right)^{n-1} \qquad \text{for } n \gg 1 \tag{9.11}$$

$$p_2 = \frac{1}{2}\left(1 - \operatorname{erf}\left(\frac{n\sigma}{\sqrt{8r}}\right)\right) \qquad \text{for } n \gg 1$$

which become $p_1^{\text{opt}} = 1/2e \approx 0.184$ and $p_2^{\text{opt}} \approx 0.270$ for $\sigma = \sigma^{\text{opt}}$. From these findings Rechenberg postulated his 1/5 *success rule: The ratio of successful mutations to all mutations should be 1/5. If it is greater than 1/5, increase the mutation variance; if it is less, decrease* σ^2.

Though, in general, problems of interest may have characteristics different from those of the model functions used above, the following heuristic often helps to dynamically adjust σ^t—not individually, however, for the n different decision variables x_i. Hence, the mutation operator is extended by the following equation [4,13]:

$$\sigma^{t+n} = \begin{cases} c_d\sigma^t & \text{if } p_m > 1/5 \\ c_i\sigma^t & \text{if } p_m > 1/5 \\ \sigma^t & \text{if } p_m = 1/5 \end{cases} \tag{9.12}$$

where p_m is the measured frequency of successful mutations, averaged, say, over intervals of $10n$ trials. There are good reasons to use the factors $c_d = 0.82$ and $c_i = 1/0.82$ for the adjustment, which should take place every n mutations. Note that with (9.6) and (9.12) the operator m now consists of a random component and a deterministic component.

The 1/5 success rule is a measure to increase the efficiency at the cost of effectiveness or robustness. It may lead the (1 + 1)-ES to premature termination even in the case of unimodal functions if there are discontinuities or active restrictions.

9.3.2 Elimination of the Worst: (μ + 1) − ES

So far the population principle has not really been used. The (1 + 1)-ES can be designated as some kind of a probabilistic gradient search technique—not, however, as a pure random or Monte Carlo method. To introduce the population concept into the algorithm, Rechenberg proposed a first *multi-membered* ES, where $\mu > 1$ parents can participate in the generation of one offspring. Schwefel labeled it $(\mu + 1)$-ES, and it can be formalized as

$$(\mu + 1)\text{-ES} = (P^0, \mu, r, m, s, c_d, c_i, f, g, t) \tag{9.13}$$

where m, c_d, c_i, f, and g_j are as defined above and

$P^0 = (a_1^0, \ldots, a_\mu^0) \in I^\mu \quad I = \mathbf{R}^n \times \mathbf{R}$	population
$\mu > 1$	number of parents
$r\colon I^\mu \rightarrow I$	recombination operator
$s\colon I^{\mu+1} \rightarrow I^\mu$	selection operator
$t\colon I^\mu \rightarrow \{0, 1\}$	termination criterion

With the introduction of μ parents instead of only one, imitation of sexual reproduction is possible. Consequently, realized with the additional recombination operator r:

$$\begin{aligned}
r(P^t) &= a' = (x', \sigma') \in I \qquad x' \in \mathbf{R}^n, \quad \sigma' \in \mathbf{R} \\
x_i' &= \begin{cases} x_{a,i}, & \mathscr{X} \leq 1/2 \\ x_{b,i}, & \mathscr{X} > 1/2 \end{cases} \qquad \forall_i \in \{1, \ldots, n\} \\
\sigma' &= \begin{cases} \sigma_a, & \mathscr{X} \leq 1/2 \\ \sigma_b, & \mathscr{X} > 1/2 \end{cases}
\end{aligned} \tag{9.14}$$

where $a = (x_a, \sigma_a)$, $b = (x_b, \sigma_b) \in I$ are two parents internally chosen by r. By convention, all parents in a population have the same mating probabilities; that is, parents a and b are determined by uniform random numbers $\mathscr{X}$ on the interval [0, 1] taken anew for each single decision. The symbol r is called a *discrete* recombination operator, since component values are chosen from one parent or the other.

The new selection operator s removes the least-fit individual (the offspring or a parent) from the population before the next generation starts, producing one new descendent. This kind of "selection" has been used by the well-known polytope strategies of Nelder and Mead [14] as well as Box [15] (so-called simplex and complex strategies):

$$\begin{aligned}
P'^t &= (a_1'^t, \ldots, a_{\mu+1}'^t) = (a_1^t, \ldots, a_\mu^t, m(r(P^t))) \\
P^{t+1} &= s(P'^t) \text{ such that } \forall a_i^{t+1} = (x, \sigma) \, \exists \, a_j'^t = (x', \sigma')\colon f(x') < f(x)
\end{aligned} \tag{9.15}$$

The mutation operator m and the adjustment of σ^t is realized in the same manner as for a $(1 + 1) - \text{ES}$ ((9.4), (9.5), (9.12)). Self-adaptation of the step size has not been possible within the $(\mu + 1) - \text{ES}$ scheme, since offspring with reduced mutation variance are always preferred and thus would lead to premature termination.

9.3.3 $(\mu + \lambda)$-ES and (μ, λ)-ES

The motivation to extend the (1 + 1)-ES and $(\mu + 1)$-ES to a $(\mu + \lambda)$-ES and a (μ, λ)-ES has been twofold [4,13]: to use parallel computers, and to enable self-adaptation of strategic parameters like the standard deviations of the mutations. Instead of changing σ^t (now an n-vector) by an exogenous heuristic in a deterministic manner, we consider σ^t as part of the genetic information of an individual. Consequently, it is subject to recombination and mutation. Those individuals with better adjusted strategy parameters are expected to perform better. Thus, selection should favor them accordingly, and sooner or later those individuals are expected to dominate the population; that is, a better parameter setting will emerge by self-adaptation without a deterministic metarule or hierarchical concept.

As the nomenclature $(\mu + \lambda)$-ES suggests, μ parents produce λ offspring and the whole population is reduced again to the μ parents of the next generation; in other words, the selection operates on the joined set of parents and offspring. Thus, parents survive until they are superseded by better offspring. It might even be possible for very well adapted individuals to survive forever. This feature gives rise to some shortcomings of the $(\mu + \lambda)$-ES:

1. In problems with an optimum moving over time, a $(\mu + \lambda)$-ES gets stuck at an outdated good location if the internal parameter setting becomes unsuitable to jump to the new field of possible improvements.
2. The same happens if the measurement of the fitness (objective) or the adjustment of the object variables are subject to noise, say, in experimental settings.
3. For a $(\mu + \lambda)$-ES with $\mu/\lambda \geq p_{f(x)}^{opt}$ (probability for a successful mutation) there is a deterministic selection advantage for those offspring that reduce some of their σ_i (9.9).

In order to avoid these effects, one should switch to a (μ, λ)-ES where only the offspring undergo selection, whereas the ancestors are forgotton; hence, $\lambda > \mu$ must be valid. The limited life span (here one generation/iteration) allows getting rid of inappropriate internal parameter settings. This may result in short phases of recession, but it avoids long stagnation phases due to misadapted stragegy parameters, which may be viewed as some kind of "internal model" of the environment. The $(\mu + \lambda)$-ES and (μ, λ)-ES fit into the same formal framework, the only difference being the limited lifetime of individuals in (μ, λ)-ES. Thus, only a formal description of a (μ, λ)-ES is presented here:

$$(\mu, \lambda)\text{-ES} = (P^0, \mu, \lambda; r, m, s; \Delta\sigma; f, g, t) \tag{9.16}$$

where r, m, f, g_j, and t are as above, and

$P^0 = (a_1^0, \ldots, a_\mu^0) \in I^\mu; I = \mathbf{R}^n \times \mathbf{R}^n$	population
$\mu \in \mathbf{N}$	number of parents
$\lambda \in \mathbf{N}; \lambda > \mu$	number of offspring
$s: \quad I^\lambda \rightarrow I^\mu$	selection operator
$\Delta\sigma \in \mathbf{R}$	step-size metacontrol

For a $(\mu + \lambda)$-ES the selection operator s is modified to $s: I^{\mu+\lambda} \rightarrow I^\mu$. The major difference in the ES variants given before result from the handling of the internal strategy vector σ^t, which now is incorporated into the genetic information of an individual $a_i^t = (x^t, \sigma^t) \in I$ and is no longer controlled by some subsidiary algorithm like the 1/5 success rule. As a result, the mutation operator is different:

$$\begin{aligned} a_i'^t &= r(P^t) & \sigma''^t &= \sigma'^t \exp \mathbf{N}_0(\Delta\sigma) \\ m(a_i'^t) &= a_i''^t = (x''^t, \sigma''^t) & x''^t &= x'^t + \mathbf{N}_0(\sigma''^t) \end{aligned} \tag{9.17}$$

Mutation not only works on x^t but also on σ^t. The adjustment of σ^t by the 1/5 success rule has been replaced by a random modification, where unsuitable σ''^t are removed by selection. It has to be emphasized here that no other selection criterion than before is used, the fitness of σ''^t is evaluated only indirectly by the change of the x^t that they provoke. The operators r and s work as in (9.13).

A $(1, \lambda)$-ES could be investigated as was done with respect to the $(1 + 1)$-ES. In particular, severe analytical problems arise as soon as one has to look for the stationary distribution of a population when $\mu > 1$. Details omitted here may be found in [4,13]. For the corridor model and sphere model (9.8) and for $\mu = 1$, the maximum rates of convergence at optimum σ^t could be deduced in a similar way as for the simplest ES version. The corresponding best values for λ, the number of offspring per generation, within a $(1, \lambda)$-ES running on a SISD* computer are

$$\lambda_1 = 6 \qquad \lambda_2 = 5 \tag{9.18}$$

On average, at least one out of λ_1 (λ_2) offspring represents an improvement of the objective function; that is, the probability for a successful offspring is approximately $1/\lambda_1$ $(1/\lambda_2)$. These values are pretty close to Rechenberg's 1/5 success rule. On a MIMD computer, a multimembered ES easily outperforms the simple $(1 + 1)$-ES by far, and it has the additional advantage of being able to escape from local optima as soon as μ is increased beyond 1. As for the $(1 + 1)$-ES, the maximum rate of convergence is inversely proportional to n, the number of object variables [4,13].

Evolution strategies that are operated with a small value of μ and an optimal ratio of μ/λ for a maximum rate of convergence are, however, still biased toward local search. As a result, such ES tend to reduce their genetic

SISD = single instruction, single datum; MIMD = multiple instruction, multiple data.

variety (i.e., the number of different alleles (specific parameter settings) in a population) as soon as they are attracted by some local optimum.

9.3.4 Sexual Propagation

When a population moves uphill along a ridge or downhill along a narrow valley, the individuals will have positions either on one side or the other of the ridge/ravine. In this case intermediate recombination of parents on different sides of the collective pathway (which is close to the gradient if $n \gg 1$) may yield extraordinary success:

$$\begin{aligned} r(P^t) &= a' = (x', \sigma') \in I \\ x_i' &= \tfrac{1}{2}(x_{a,i} + x_{b,i}) \qquad i = 1, \ldots, n \\ \sigma_i' &= \tfrac{1}{2}(\sigma_{a,i} + \sigma_{b,i}) \end{aligned} \tag{9.19}$$

Again, $a = (x_a, \sigma_a)$ and $b = (x_b, \sigma_b)$ are two parents chosen by r. Unfortunately, this type of recombination tends to reduce the genetic diversity of the population, but, on the other hand, it is a measure to avoid overadaptation, especially with respect to the strategy parameters. In ES the model functions suggest that the achievable rate of progress is inversely proportional to the number of object variables; hence, individuals moving in a subspace of the object variables can exhibit a temporarily larger convergence rate than those moving in the full space. These individuals will reach a relative optimum only, and the whole evolution process may stagnate there for a while.

By intermediate recombination, a random but unsuitable extinction of a mutation step size σ_i is always reverted (increased again) as long as there is no mate with a similar step-size adaptation. Actually, the commonly used implementation of $(\mu + \lambda)$-ES and (μ, λ)-ES contains five types of recombination [13]:

$$r(P^t) = a' = (x', \sigma') \in I$$

$$x_i' = \begin{cases} x_{a,i} & \text{(A) no recombination} \\ x_{a,i} \text{ or } x_{b,i} & \text{(B) discrete} \\ \tfrac{1}{2}(x_{a,i} + x_{b,i}) & \text{(C) intermediate} \\ x_{a,i} \text{ or } x_{b_i,i} & \text{(D) global, discrete} \\ \tfrac{1}{2}(x_{a,i} + x_{b_i,i}) & \text{(E) global, intermediate} \end{cases} \tag{9.20}$$

where $a, b, b_i \in P^t$ are parents chosen by r. Note that with global recombination the mating partners for the recombination of a *single* component x_i' are chosen anew from the population resulting in a higher mixing of the genetic information than in the standard case (B). An experimental comparison of most traditional, commonly used, direct optimization strategies to ES on a set of 50 test functions, including multimodal as well as unimodal ones, restricted as well as unrestricted ones, has shown rather good results for ES. Their convergence rate is comparable to other direct optimum-seeking algorithms, but their reliability as well as their chance to find a low-dimensional global optimum has been found to be remarkably better than for the other strategies compared [13]. Best results were obtained with different recombination types for the object variables (discrete) and the strategy parameters (intermediate).

9.3.5 Polygeny and Pleiotropy

In ES mutation realizes a kind of hill-climbing search procedure (9.12), when it is considered in combination with selection. With dedicated σ_i for each object variable x_i preferred directions of search may be established only along the axes of the coordinate system. In general, the best search direction is *not* aligned on those axes. Thus, an optimal rate of progress is achieved only by chance when suitable mutations coincide—when they are correlated. Otherwise, the trajectory of the population through the search space is zigzagging along the gradient. In order to avoid this reduction of the rate of progress, the mutation operator can be extended again to handle *correlated mutations,* which require an additional strategy vector θ.

$$\begin{aligned} m(a_i'^t) &= a_i''^t = (x'', \sigma'', \theta'') \in I \qquad I = \mathbf{R}^n \times \mathbf{R}^n \times \mathbf{R}^w \\ \sigma'' &= \sigma'^t \exp \mathbf{N}_0\,(\Delta\sigma) \\ \theta'' &= \theta'^t + \mathbf{N}_0(\Delta\theta) \\ x'' &= x'^t + \mathbf{C}_0(\sigma'', \theta'') \end{aligned} \tag{9.21}$$

where $\mathbf{N}_0$ denotes a vector of independent Gaussian random numbers with expectation zero and standard deviations $\Delta\sigma$ and $\Delta\theta$, respectively (for more details see [13]), and $\mathbf{C}_0(.,\,.)$ refers to a normally distributed random vector with expectation zero and probability density

$$p(\mathbf{C}_0(.,\,.)) = \sqrt{\frac{\det \mathbf{A}}{(2\pi)^n}} \exp\left(-\frac{1}{2}\,\mathbf{N}_0(\sigma'')^{\mathrm{T}}\,\mathbf{A}\,\mathbf{N}_0(\sigma'')\right) \tag{9.22}$$

The diagonal elements of the covariance matrix $\mathbf{A}^{-1}$ are the independent variances $\sigma_i''^2$ (squares of the mutation step sizes) of the object variables x_i^t, while the off-diagonal elements represent the covariances $c_{i,j}$ of the mutations. It may be useful to restrict the space of equal probability density to the surface of n-dimensional rotating hyperellipsoids, which are realized by a set of inclination angles $\theta'' \in \mathbf{R}^w$ of the main axes of the hyperellipsoid, $w = n(n-1)/2$. This helps to keep the covariance matrix positive definite. The standard deviations σ_i'' serve as a kind of mean step size along those axes.

Like the strategy parameter σ^t, θ^t is also incorporated into the genetic representation of an individual and modified in a similar way; that is, the recombination operator is extended to work on the inclination angles θ^t, as with the mutation step size σ^t (9.12). This way the ES may adapt to any preferred direction of search by means of self-learning. Due to the additional metaparameter $\Delta\theta$, the signature of an ES with correlated mutations is defined as

$$(\mu, \lambda)\text{-ES} = (P^0, \mu, \lambda; r, m, s; \Delta\sigma, \Delta\theta; f, g, t) \tag{9.23}$$

The step sizes σ_i of an individual make up an ellipsoid of equal probability density to place an offspring if these step sizes are applied to x^t of the individual itself. In long, narrow valleys the step sizes with simple mutations must be smaller than those with correlated mutations, where a single step size may reach far into the valley if it is oriented appropriately. In such situations the resulting rate of convergence is much higher.

Introducing the possibility of correlated mutations allows for collective learning of dependencies between the object variables. Self-adaptation of the covariances or inclination angles within the (μ, λ)-ES thus may be seen as learning of the "natural laws" acting in the "environment" given by the topology of the objective function.

The biological phenomena of polygeny (i.e., one phenotypic feature of an individual is influenced by several genes) and pleiotropy (i.e., one gene influences several phenotypic features) as well as allometry show that this kind of epigenetic transformation is by no means a merely artificial construct within evolutionary processes. Under appropriate conditions (limited lifetime of the individuals, recombination, and medium selection pressure) the adaptation of the internal model of the environment, as represented by the set of strategy parameters, leads to a sometimes considerable speedup of the optimum-seeking algorithm [16]. If unsuitably set up, the (μ, λ)-ES exhibits punctuated equilibrium behavior, as it has been called by biologists. In this case, long stagnation phases are irregularly interrupted by sudden changes of the gene pool, which are not due to the environmental conditions, but are intrinsic to the evolution process itself.

9.4 SUMMARY

Evolution strategies went through a long period of stepwise development since the formulation of the basic ideas in the middle of the 1960s. Some important milestones in their development were the

- Analytical convergence rate calculations, which led to the development of the 1/5 success rule;
- Introduction of a population instead of an individual, which also allowed for the sexual recombination process;
- Self-learning process of strategy parameters by means of incorporating them into the set of genetically inherited variables;

- (μ, λ)-ES, which introduces a forgetting principle and is important in changing environments as well as a measure against overadaptation, especially of the strategy parameters;
- Introduction of additional strategy parameters to allow for correlated mutations and thus self-learning of simple natural laws in the topological environment.

The third and fifth points establish a two-level learning process, since not only the object-variable population adapts according to the response surface, but the strategy parameters are changed with respect to the actual topological requirements. There are, however, difficulties as well as opportunities of the two-level collective learning in [16]. The strategy parameters make up an internal model of the objective function, which is learned on-line during the optimum seeking without any exogenous controlling instance or additional measure of fitness.

Besides the different levels of genotypic/phenotypic information representation and different selection mechanisms, the two-level learning in ES is the most striking difference between ES and GA [17].

Current research concerning ES deals with applications like the traveling salesman problem [18,19] girder-bridge optimization [20], neural networks [21], vector optimization [22], and parameter optimization in general [10,23,24].

ACKNOWLEDGMENTS

This work was supported in part by the Center for Absorption in Science, The Ministry of Immigrant Absorption, The State of Israel. Y. Davidor is a recipient of a Sir Charles Clore Fellowship.

REFERENCES

[1] J. H. Holland, *Adaptation in Natural and Artificial Systems,* University of Michigan Press, Ann Arbor, 1975.

[2] K. A. De Jong, "*An Analysis of the Behavior of a Class of Genetic Adaptive Systems,*" Ph. D. dissertation, University of Michigan; *Dissertation Abstracts International,* 36(10), 5140B (1975).

[3] I. Rechenberg, *Evolutionsstrategie: Optimierung Technischer Systeme nach Prinzipien der biologischen Evolution,* Frommann-Holzboog Verlag, Stuttgart, 1973.

[4] H.-P. Schwefel, "*Evolutionsstrategie und numerische Optimierung,*" dissertation, Technische Universität Berline (1975).

[5] W. S. Spears and K. A. De Jong, An analysis of multi-point crossover, *Proc. Foundations of Genetic Algorithms Workshop,* Indiana University, Bloomington, Morgan Kaufmann, San Mateo, Calif. (in press).

[6] K. A. De Jong and W. S. Spears, An analysis of the interacting roles of population size and crossover in genetic algorithms, *Proc. 1st Internat. Conf. on Parallel Problem Solving from Nature,* Springer-Verlag (in press).

[7] D. E. Goldberg, (1987) "Simple Genetic Algorithms and the Minimal, Deceptive Problem," in L. Davis, Ed., *Genetic Algorithms and Simulated Annealing,* Pitman, London, 1987, pp. 74–88.

[8] L. D. Davis, *Genetic Algorithms Handbook,* Van Nostrand Reinhold, New York, 1991.

[9] Y. Davidor, *Genetic Algorithms and Robotics: A Heuristic Strategy for Optimization,* World Scientific, 1991.

[10] J. Born, "Evolutionsstrategien zur numerischen Lösung von Adaptationsaufgaben," dissertation A, Humboldt-Universität, Berlin (1978).

[11] Emile H. L. Aarts and Jan Korst, *Simulated Annealing and Boltzmann Machines,* Wiley, Chichester, 1989.

[12] A. E. Eiben, E. H. L. Aarts, and K. M. Van Hee, "Global Convergence of Genetic Algorithms: An Infinite Markov Chain Analysis," in H.-P. Schwefel and R. Männer, Eds., *Parallel Problem Solving from Nature,* Springer-Verlag, Berlin, 1991, pp. 4–12.

[13] H.-P. Schwefel, *Numerical Optimization of Computer Models,* Wiley, Chichester, 1981.

[14] J. A. Nelder and R. Mead, A simplex method for function minimization, *Computer J.* 7, 308–313 (1965).

[15] M. J. Box, A new method of constrained optimization and a comparison with other methods, *Computer J.,* 8, 42–52 (1965).

[16] H.-P. Schwefel, Collective phenomena in evolutionary systems, in *31st Annual Meeting Internat. Soc. for General System Research,* Vol. 2, 1025–1033 (1987).

[17] F. Hoffmeister and T. Bäck, "Genetic Algorithms and Evolution Strategies: Similarities and Differences," Tech. Rep. "Grüne Reihe" No. 365, Dept. Computer Science, University of Dortmund (November 1990).

[18] M. Herdy, "Application of the 'Evolutionsstrategie' to Discrete Optimization Problems," in H.-P. Schwefel and R. Männer, Eds., *Parallel Problem Solving from Nature,* Springer-Verlag, Berlin, 1991, pp. 188–192.

[19] G. Rudolph, Global optimization by means of evolution strategies, in H.-P. Schwefel and R. Männer, Ed., *Parallel Problem Solving from Nature,* Springer-Verlag, Berlin, 1991, pp. 209–213.

[20] R. Lohmann, "Application of Evolution Strategy in Parallel Populations," in H.-P. Schwefel and R. Männer, Eds., *Parallel Problem Solving from Nature,* Springer-Verlag, Berlin, 1991, pp. 198–208.

[21] R. Salomon, "Improved Convergence Rate of Back-Propagation with Dynamic Adaptation of the Learning Rate," in H.-P. Schwefel and R. Männer, Eds., *Parallel Problem Solving from Nature,* Springer-Verlag, Berlin, 1991, pp. 269–273.

[22] F. Kursawe, "A Variant of Evolution Strategies for Vector Optimization," in H.-P. Schwefel and R. Männer, Eds. *Parallel Problem Solving from Nature,* Springer-Verlag, Berlin, 1991, pp. 193–197.

[23] U. Bernutat-Buchmann and J. Krieger, "Evolution Strategies in Numerical Optimization on Vector Computers," in Feilmeier, Joubert, and Schendel, Eds., *Parallel Computing 83,* Elsevier, Amsterdam, 1984, pp. 99–105.

[24] J. Born and K. Bellmann, *"Numerische Parameteroptimierung in Mathematischen Modellen Mittels einer Evolutionsstrategie," in Lecture Notes in Control and Information Sciences,* Vol. 18 Springer, Berlin, 1979, pp. 157–167.

[25] D. E. Goldberg, "Optimal Initial Population Size for Binary-coded Genetic Algorithms," TCGA Report No. 85001, University of Alabama, Tuscaloosa (1985).

[26] D. E. Goldberg, Sizing populations for serial and parallel genetic algorithms, *Proc. 3rd Internat. Conf. on Genetic Algorithms,* George Mason University, Morgan Kaufmann, San Mateo, Calif. (1989e).

[27] M. D. Vose and G. E. Liepins, Schema disruption, *Proc. 4th Internat. Conf. on Genetic Algorithms,* University of California, Morgan Kaufmann, San Mateo, Calif. (1991).

CHAPTER 10

The Genetic Programming Paradigm: Genetically Breeding Populations of Computer Programs to Solve Problems

JOHN R. KOZA

10.1 INTRODUCTION

Many seemingly different problems in machine learning, artificial intelligence, and symbolic processing can be viewed as requiring the discovery of a computer program that produces some desired output for particular inputs. When viewed in this way, the process of solving these problems becomes equivalent to searching a space of possible computer programs for a highly fit individual computer program. The recently developed genetic programming paradigm described here provides a way to search the space of possible computer programs for a highly fit individual computer program to solve (or approximately solve) a surprising variety of different problems from different fields. In the genetic programming paradigm, populations of computer programs are genetically bred using the Darwinian principle of survival of the fittest and a genetic crossover (sexual recombination) operator appropriate for genetically mating computer programs. This chapter shows how to reformulate seemingly different problems into a common form (i.e., a problem requiring discovery of a computer program) and how the genetic programming paradigm can serve as a single, unified approach for solving problems formulated in this common way.

A central question in computer science is "How can computers learn to program themselves to solve problems?" Existing paradigms for machine learning all involve searching a space of specialized structures for a good or

Dynamic, Genetic, and Chaotic Programming, By Branko Souček and the IRIS Group.
ISBN 0-471-55717-X

best structure to solve a problem. In each paradigm, the structures involved are distinctly different from computer programs.

- Connectionists envision the solution to a given problem as being a set of real-valued weights. The weights are used to amplify or diminish signals passing along the connecting lines of a neural network. One of several neural network paradigms is used to search for a best set of weights. The neural network using this best set of weights is then used to solve the problem.
- Selectionists envision the solution to a problem as being a fixed-length character string (i.e., chromosome). Each chromosome represents a possible approach to solving the problem. The conventional genetic algorithm is used to search for a good or best chromosome. The best chromosome specifies the approach to be used to solve the problem.
- Inductionists envision the solution to a given problem as being a decision tree. Each decision tree classifies each instance of a given problem into a class representing a possible solution to the problem. An inductive method, such as ID3, is used to search for a good or best decision tree. The best decision tree is then used to solve the problem.

Searching for a specialized structure, such as a weight vector, chromosome, or decision tree, can be an efficient way to solve certain classes of problems. Moreover, such specialized structures often facilitate mathematical analysis that might otherwise not be possible. However, these specialized structures are often an unnatural and difficult way of viewing the problem and expressing a solution. In many cases, the flexibility that is really wanted and needed is provided by computer programs. Computer programs offer the flexibility to

- Perform computations on variables of many different types,
- Perform alternative computations conditioned on the outcome of intermediate calculations,
- Perform iterations and recursions,
- Define computed values and subprograms so that they can be subsequently reused,
- Arrange groups of operations into hierarchies.

Producing solutions in hierarchical form is especially important because hierarchies are efficient, easy to understand, and lend themselves to scaling up.

The flexibility we want and need also includes flexibility as to the size, shape, and structural complexity of the solution. The user should not be required to specify the size, shape, and structural complexity of the solution in advance. Instead, the size, shape, and structural complexity of the solution should emerge during the problem-solving process. In other words, the size, shape, and structural complexity should be part of the answer produced by a problem-solving technique—not part of the question.

Once we realize that what we really want and need is the flexibility offered by computer programs, we start to view searches for specialized structures such as weight vectors, chromosomes, or decision trees as flanking actions against the overall problem of getting computers to learn to program themselves. This chapter is a direct frontal assault on the problem of getting computers to learn to program themselves. Our goal is to find a computer program to solve a problem by searching the space of possible computer programs. The recently developed genetic programming paradigm described here offers a way to genetically breed a computer program to solve (or approximately solve) the problem.

This chapter offers no mathematical proof that the genetic programming paradigm can always be successfully used to solve all problems of every conceivable type. It does, however, provide much empirical evidence that this new paradigm can be used to solve a surprising variety of seemingly different problems from many fields. This chapter makes two main points.

1. A wide variety of seemingly different problems from many fields can be reformulated as requiring the discovery of a computer program that produces some desired output when presented with particular inputs. That is, these seemingly different problems can be reformulated as problems of program induction.
2. The new genetic programming paradigm provides an efficient and effective way to search the space of possible computer programs for a highly fit individual computer program to solve (or approximately solve) the problem of program induction.

We deal with point 1 in Section 10.2, where we show that many seemingly different problems, such as automatic programming, optimal control, planning, finding game-playing strategies, symbolic regression, and programming emergent behavior, can all be viewed as problems of program induction. Of course, there is no reason to do this unless there is some good way to do program induction. Accordingly, the remainder of this chapter deals with point 2. We describe a single, unified approach to solving the problem of program induction, namely, the genetic programming paradigm. We demonstrate that this new paradigm is effective by presenting numerous examples from many fields. Existing paradigms for machine learning or artificial intelligence would probably find it impossible to successfully solve all of these problems. Nonetheless, we use a single, unified approach regardless of whether the example involves automatic programming, optimal, control, planning, finding game-playing strategies, symbolic regression, or programming emergent behavior.

The goal of this chapter is to establish point 2 with empirical evidence. At some point the reader may begin to feel that the examples being presented have merely become repetitions of the same thing. Indeed, they are. When the reader starts viewing genetic solutions to the aforementioned problems as the same thing, this chapter will have succeeded in communicating its main point.

10.2 THE PERVASIVENESS OF PROGRAM INDUCTION

Program induction involves the inductive discovery of a computer program, from the space of possible computer programs, that produces some desired output when presented with some input. As an example of program induction, consider the pair of linear equations

$$a_{11}x_1 + a_{12}x_2 = b_1$$

$$a_{21}x_1 + a_{22}x_2 = b_2$$

in two unknowns x_1 and x_2. The mathematical formula for solving these equations starts with six given values (i.e., a_{11}, a_{12}, a_{21}, a_{22}, b_1, and b_2) as input and produces, as output, the values of the unknowns that satisfy the equations. Program induction involves finding the computer program that implements this formula. The process uses a finite sampling of combinations of the inputs and correct outputs to induce a computer program. The induced computer program should produce the correct output for any case form the original finite sampling and should also generalize so as to produce the "correct" output for a previously unseen case.

A wide variety of seemingly different problems can be reformulated as a problem of program induction. This fact is obscured by the different terminology used in different fields to describe the concept of program induction. Depending on the terminology of the field involved, the computer program may be called a formula, plan, control strategy, computational procedure, model, decision tree, game-playing strategy, transfer function, mathematical expression, or composition of functions. Similarly, the inputs to the computer program may be called sensor values, state variables, independent variables, attributes, information to be processed, input signals, input values, known variables, or arguments of a function. The output from the program may be called a dependent variable, a control variable, category, class, move, decision, action, effector, result, output signal, output values, unknown variables, or the value returned by a function.

10.2.1 Symbolic Regression

Symbolic regression (symbolic function identification) involves finding a mathematical expression, in symbolic form, that provides a good, best, or perfect fit between a given finite sampling of values of the independent variables and the associated values of the dependent variables. That is, symbolic regression involves finding a model that fits a given sample of data.

When the variables are real-valued, symbolic regression involves finding the functional form and the numerical coefficients for the model. Symbolic regression differs from conventional linear, quadratic, or polynomial regression, which involve finding the coefficients for a function whose form (linear, quadratic, or polynomial) has been prespecified.

In any case, the mathematical expression being sought in symbolic regression can be viewed as a computer program that takes the values of the independent variables as input and produces the values of the dependent variables as output.

Symbolic regression of real-valued variables is discussed in Section 10.11. It is later discussed with constant creation in Section 10.12. If the data are noisy data from the real world, this problem of finding the model from the data is often called *empirical discovery* (see Sec. 10.13). If the independent variable consists of nonnegative integers, symbolic regression may be called sequence induction (see Sec. 10.10). Machine learning of the Boolean 11-multiplexer function is symbolic regression applied to a function with a Boolean range and domain (Sec. 10.6).

10.2.2 Planning

Planning in artificial intelligence and robotics requires finding a plan that receives information from detectors or sensors about the state of various objects in a system and then uses that information to select effector actions that change the state of the objects in the system.

An example of a planning problem involves discovering a robotic action plan to navigate an artificial ant along an irregular trail to find the food lying along the trail (Sec. 10.7). Another example involves discovering a plan for stacking blocks in the correct order (Sec. 10.16).

The desired plan in a planning problem can be viewed as a computer program. The computer program takes the information from the sensors or detectors as its input and produces effector actions as its output. The effector actions, in turn, cause a change in the state of the objects of the system.

10.2.3 Optimal Control

Optimal control involves finding a control strategy that uses the state variables of a system to choose the control variables that will change the state of the system to the desired target state with minimal cost. An example of a time-optimal control problem involves discovering a bang-bang control strategy for balancing a broom on a moving cart in minimal time. The state variables of the system are the position of the cart, velocity of the cart, angle of the broom, and angular velocity of the broom. The control variable is the bang-bang force that may be applied to the system.

The desired control strategy in an optimal control problem can be viewed as a computer program. The computer program takes the state variables of the system as its input and produces values of the control variable as its output. The control variables, in turn, cause a change in the state of the system (Sec. 10.17).

10.2.4 Automatic Programming

Randomizers (e.g., computer programs that convert a sequence of consecutive integers into a high-entropy sequence of random digits) are considered difficult to write. Automatic programming of a randomizer is another example of program induction. The desired computer program takes a sequence of consecutive integers as its input and produces a sequence of bits with high entropy as its output (Sec. 10.9).

10.2.5 Minimax Strategy for Playing a Game

Game playing requires finding a strategy that specifies what move a player is to make at each point in the game, given the known information about the game. This information may be an explicit history of the previous moves by the players or an implicit history of previous moves in the form of a current "state" of the game (e.g., in chess, the position of each piece on the board).

The game-playing strategy can be viewed as a computer program that takes the known information about the game as its input and produces a move as its output (Sec. 10.18).

10.2.6 Emergent Behavior

Emergent behavior involves the repetitive application of seemingly simple rules that lead to complex overall behavior. The evolution of the sets of rules that produce emergent behavior is a problem in program induction. An example is finding a set of rules for controlling the behavior of an individual ant that, when simultaneously executed in parallel by all the ants in the colony, causes the ants to work together to locate and transport available food to the nest. The computer program (i.e., set of rules) takes the sensory input of each ant as input and produces actions by the ants as output (Sec. 10.19).

10.3 THE CONVENTIONAL GENETIC ALGORITHM

Before discussing the genetic program paradigm, we first describe the conventional genetic algorithm. In nature, the evolutionary process occurs when the following conditions are satisfied:

- An entity must have the ability to reproduce (or approximately reproduce) itself.

- There must be a population of such self-reproducing entities.
- There must be some variety among the entities in the population.
- There must be some difference in ability to survive in the environment associated with the variety.

Variety is manifested as variation in the chromosomes of the entities, which, in turn, is reflected in variation in the structure and behavior of the entities. This variation is reflected as differences in the rate of survival. The existence of some variability that has some differential effect on the rate of survivability is almost inevitable. Thus, the presence of the first condition (i.e., self-reproducibility) typically is sufficient to start the evolutionary process.

Thus, in nature, entities with the ability to reproduce themselves become better able to perform tasks in their environment because the more-fit entities survive at a differentially higher rate. Over a period of time and many generations, the population becomes more fit in performing its tasks in its environment. That is, the population evolves to higher levels of fitness. The structure of individuals in the population changes over time because of the relentless effects of natural selection.

John Holland's pioneering book *Adaptation in Natural and Artificial Systems* [1] described how the evolutionary process in nature can be applied to artificial systems. In particular, Holland's genetic algorithm is a highly parallel mathematical algorithm that transforms a population of individual mathematical objects (typically fixed-length character strings patterned after chromosome strings) into a new population using

- The operation of Darwinian fitness proportionate reproduction (survival of the fittest),
- The naturally occurring genetic operation of sexual recombination (crossover), and,
- A small amount of occasional random mutation.

Many problems can be solved by using the conventional genetic algorithm operating on fixed-length character strings. An overview of genetic algorithms can be found in Goldberg [2]. Recent research work in the field is reported in Davis [3,4], Schaffer [5], Rawlins [6], and Belew and Booker [7].

The use of fixed-length character strings has permitted Holland and others to construct a significant body of theory as to why genetic algorithms work. Much of this theoretical analysis depends on the mathematical tractability of the fixed-length character strings as compared with mathematical structures that are more complex and comparatively less susceptible to theoretical analysis. Nonetheless, the use of fixed-length character strings as the representational scheme leaves many problems unsettled.

Representation is a key issue in genetic algorithm work because genetic algorithms directly manipulate the coded representation of the problem and because the representation scheme can severely limit the window by which the system observes its world.

As Davis and Steenstrup [8] point out, "In all of Holland's work, and in the work of many of his students, chromosomes are bit strings."

For many problems in machine learning and artificial intelligence, the most natural known representation for a solution is a hierarchical computer program of indeterminate size and shape, as opposed to character strings whose size has been determined in advance. It is sometimes difficult, unnatural, and overly restrictive to represent hierarchies of dynamically varying size and shape with fixed-length character strings.

String-based representation schemes do not provide the hierarchical structure central to the organization of computer programs (into programs and subroutines) and the organization of behavior (into tasks and subtasks). They provide no convenient way of representing arbitrary computational procedures or of incorporating iteration or recursion when these capabilities are inherently necessary to solve the problem. Moreover, these schemes do not have dynamic variability. The initial selection of string length limits in advance the number of internal states of the system and the computational complexity of what the system can learn.

The predetermination of the size and shape of solutions and the preidentification of the components of solutions have been a bane of machine learning systems from earliest times as well as in later efforts in automatic programming. The need for more powerful representations in the genetic algorithm field has been recognized for some time [9].

The structure of the individual mathematical objects manipulated by a genetic algorithm can be more complex than fixed-length character strings. Smith [10] departed from Holland's emphasis on fixed-length character strings by introducing variable-length strings (including strings whose elements were if-then rules rather than single characters).

The introduction of the genetic classifier system [11,12] continued the trend toward increasing the complexity of the structures undergoing adaptation using the genetic algorithm. The genetic classifier system is a highly parallel cognitive architecture in which the genetic algorithm adaptively modifies a population of if-then rules (whose condition and action parts are fixed-length binary strings). Examples of applications of genetic classifier systems include Wilson's [13,14] learning of Boolean functions and Forrest's [15] work on parallelization of classifier systems.

Wilson [16] extended Holland's bucket brigade algorithm for credit allocation in genetic classifier systems by introducing hierarchical credit allocation. Wilson's hierarchical credit allocation encourages the creation of hierarchies of rules in lieu of the exceedingly long sequences of rules that are otherwise characteristic of classifier systems. Wilson's efforts recognize the central importance of hierarchies in representing the tasks and subtasks (that is, programs and subroutines) that are needed to solve complex problems.

Goldberg et al. [17] introduced the messy genetic algorithm that processes populations of variable-length character strings. Messy genetic algorithms solve problems by combining relatively short, well-tested substrings that deal with part of a problem to form longer, more complex strings that deal with all aspects of the problem.

As will be seen, the genetic programming paradigm is a further continuation of the trend toward increasing the complexity of the structures undergoing adaptation using the genetic algorithm. The genetic programming paradigm provides a way to genetically breed a population of hierarchical computer programs to solve problems.

In the genetic algorithm field, Cramer [18] used the genetic algorithm operating on fixed-length character strings to generate computer programs with a fixed structure (consisting of an operation and two operands in a hypothetical assembly language) and reported on the highly epistatic nature of the problem.

Fujiki and Dickinson [19] implemented analogs of the genetic operations in the conventional genetic algorithm operating on strings to manipulate the individual clauses of a LISP computer program consisting of a single conditional (COND) statement. The individual if-then clauses of Fujiki and Dickinson's COND statement were parts of a strategy for playing the iterated prisoner's dilemma game.

10.4 OVERVIEW OF THE GENETIC PROGRAMMING PARADIGM

In Section 10.2, we showed that it was possible to reformulate a wide variety of seemingly different problems from many fields of problems of program induction. In this section, we describe the recently developed genetic programming (GP) paradigm, which provides a way to do program induction. In the paradigm, populations of computer programs are genetically bred using the Darwinian principle of survival of the fittest and a genetic crossover (recombination) operator appropriate for genetically mating computer programs. The structures undergoing adaptation in the GP paradigm are hierarchical computer programs of dynamically varying size and shape.

The process of solving many problems can be reformulated as a search for a most fit individual computer program in the space of possible computer programs. This simulated evolutionary process starts with an initial population of randomly generated computer programs composed of functions and terminals appropriate to the problem domain. The functions may be standard arithmetic operations, programming operations, or mathematical functions; logical functions; and domain-specific functions. Depending on the problem, the computer program may be Boolean-valued, integer-valued, real-valued, complex-valued, vector-valued, symbolic-valued, or multiple-valued.

Each computer program in the population is measured in terms of how well it performs in the problem environment. We call this measure *fitness*.

Typically the computer program is run over many fitness cases so that fitness is averaged over a variety of representative situations.

Unless the problem is so small and simple that it can be solved by blind random search, the computer programs in the initial random generation will have exceedingly poor fitness. Nonetheless, some individuals in the population will turn out to be fitter than others. Then the Darwinian principle of reproduction and survival of the fittest and the genetic operation of sexual recombination (crossover) are used to create a new offspring population of individual computer programs from the current population of programs. In particular, a genetic process of sexual reproduction between two parent computer programs is used to create offspring computer programs. The parent computer programs are selected in proportion to fitness. The resulting offspring programs are composed of subexpressions (subtrees, subprograms, subroutines, "building blocks") from their parents. Then the new population of offspring (i.e., the new generation) replaces the old population of parents (i.e., the old generation). Each new individual in the new population of computer programs is then measured for fitness, and the process is repeated.

At each stage of this highly parallel, locally controlled, and decentralized process, the state of the process consists only of the current population of individuals. Moreover, the driving force of this process is the observed fitness of the individuals in the current population in grappling with their problem environment.

As will be seen, this algorithm will produce populations of computer programs that, over a period of generations, tend to exhibit increasing average fitness in dealing with their environment. In addition, these populations of computer programs tend to robustly (i.e., rapidly and effectively) adapt to changes in the environment.

Typically, the single best individual in the population at the time of termination of a run is designated as the result produced by the genetic programming paradigm.

The inherent hierarchical character of the computer programs produced by the GP paradigm is an important feature. In many cases, the results contain default hierarchies that solve the problem in a relatively understandable and parsimonious way.

The dynamic variability of the computer programs developed along the way to a solution is also an important feature of the GP paradigm. In each case, it would be difficult and unnatural to try to restrict the size and shape of the eventual solution in advance. It would also narrow the window by which the system views the world and might well preclude finding the problem solution.

Another important feature of the GP paradigm is the absence, or relatively minor role, of preprocessing of inputs and postprocessing of outputs. The inputs, intermediate results, and outputs are typically expressed directly in terms of the natural functions and arguments from the problem domain. The output of the GP paradigm comes in the form of a computer program that takes the inputs appropriate to the problem and produces the outputs required by the problem. This means that the results are expressed in terms of the problem domain.

The GP paradigm is a domain-independent ("weak") method that provides a single, unified approach to finding a computer program to solve a problem. In this chapter, we show how to reformulate these seemingly different problems into a common form (i.e., a problem of induction of a computer program), and we then describe the use of the GP paradigm.

In summary, the GP paradigm genetically breeds computer programs to solve problems by executing the following three steps:

1. Generate an initial population of random compositions of the functions and terminals of the problem (computer programs).
2. Iteratively perform the following substeps until the termination criterion has been satisfied:
   a. Execute each program in the population and assign it a fitness value according to how well it solves the problem.
   b. Create a new population of computer programs by applying the following two primary operations. The operations are applied to computer program(s) in the population chosen with a probability based on Darwinian fitness.
      (i) Copy existing computer programs to the new population.
      (ii) Create new computer programs by genetically recombining randomly chosen parts of two existing programs.
3. The single best computer program in the population at the time of termination is designated as the result of the GP paradigm. This result may be a solution (or approximate solution) to the problem.

Figure 10.1 is a flowchart of the steps of the GP paradigm.

10.4.1 Choice of Programming Language

Virtually any programming language (e.g., PASCAL, FORTRAN, C, FORTH, LISP) can express and evaluate the compositions of functions and terminals necessary to implement the GP paradigm. Any programming language that can manipulate computer programs as data and compile, link, and execute the new programs (or support an interpreter to execute the new programs created) can be used.

We have chosen the LISP (LISt Processing) programming language for the work with the GP paradigm for several reasons, which we discuss in detail. LISP is the most widely known and used example of a functional programming language. All examples in this chapter use the Common LISP dialect of LISP.

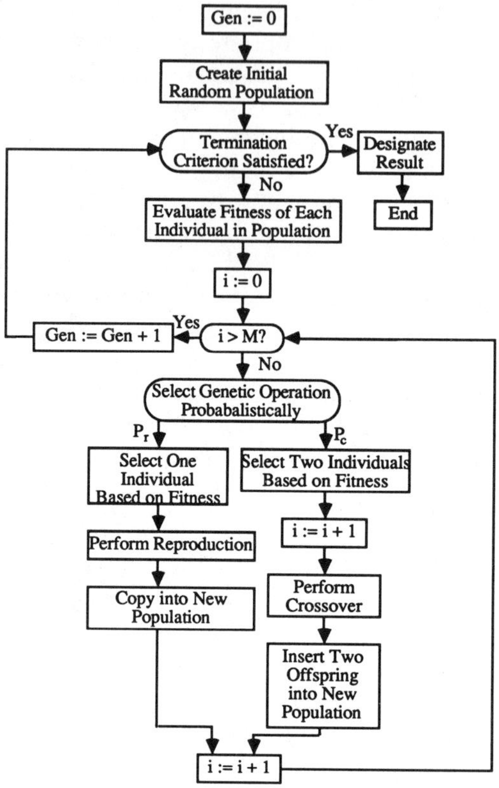

Figure 10.1 *Flowchart for the GP paradigm.*

LISP has, for our purposes here, only two types of entities, namely atoms and lists. The constant 7 and the variable TIME are examples of atoms in LISP. Lists in LISP consist of an ordered set of items inside a pair of parentheses, such as (+ 1 2) and (A B C).

The LISP system works so as to evaluate whatever it sees. Constant atoms evaluate to themselves when seen by LISP, while variable atoms evaluate to their current value. When a list is seen by LISP, the list is evaluated by treating whatever is just inside the opening parenthesis as a function and then applying the function to the rest of the list (which is treated as arguments to the function).

We use the name *symbolic expression* (S-expression) for a list or atom in LISP. S-expressions are the programs of LISP. In fact, they are the only syntactic form in LISP. For example, (+ 1 2) is a LISP S-expression. The addition function (+) appears just inside the opening parenthesis. The S-expression calls for the application of the addition function + to two arguments (the atoms 1 and 2). The value returned as a result of the evaluation of the S-expression (+ 1 2) is 3.

If any of the arguments are themselves lists (rather than atoms that can be immediately evaluated), Common LISP first evaluates these unevaluated lists (in a recursive, depth-first way, starting from the left) before proceeding.

The LISP S-expression (+ (* 2 3) 4) illustrates the way that computer programs in LISP can be viewed as compositions of functions. This S-expression calls for the application of the addition function (+) to two arguments, namely, the sub-S-expression (* 2 3) and the constant atom 4. To complete the evaluation of (+ (* 2 3) 4), LISP first evaluates (* 2 3), which calls for application of the multiplication function (*) to the constant atoms 2 and 3. The entire S-expression (+ (* 2 3) 4) illustrates the composition of functions.

Now consider the LISP S-expression

```
(+ 1 2 (IF (> TIME 10) 3 4))
```

which illustrates how functional languages enable us to view computer programs (with their conditional actions) as compositions of functions and arguments. In the subexpression (> TIME 10), the function > is applied to the variable atom TIME and the constant atom 10. It then evaluates to either T (true) or NIL (false), depending on the current value of TIME.

The logical value returned by (> TIME 10) becomes the first argument of the function IF, which takes three arguments. It returns the result of evaluating its second argument (constant atom 3) if its first argument evaluates to T, and it returns the result of evaluating its third argument (constant atom 4) if its first argument is NIL. Thus, this S-expression evaluates to either 6 or 7, depending on whether the current value of TIME is greater than 10.

Any LISP S-expression can be graphically depicted as a rooted, point-labeled tree with ordered branches. The tree corresponding to the preceding S-expression is shown in Figure 10.2. The three internal points of the tree are labeled with functions (e.g., +, IF, and >). The six external points (leaves) of the tree are labeled with terminals (e.g., TIME 1, 2, 10, 3, and 4).

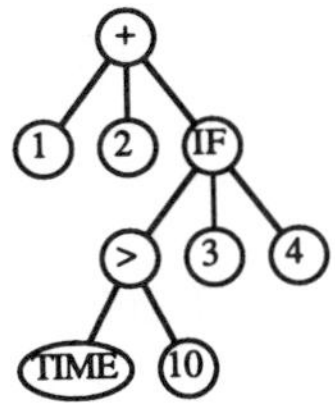

Figure 10.2 *Rooted, point-labeled tree with ordered branches corresponding to the LISP S-expression (+ 1 2 (IF (> TIME 10) 3 4)).*

The root of the tree is labeled with the function (i.e., +) appearing just inside the opening parenthesis of the S-expression. Note that this tree form of a LISP S-expression is equivalent to the parse tree that many compilers construct internally to represent a computer program.

We chose LISP for the work with the GP paradigm for six reasons.

1. In LISP, programs and data have the same form (i.e., S-expressions). Thus, it is possible and convenient to treat a computer program in the genetic population as *data* so that it can first be genetically manipulated. Then it is possible and convenient to immediately execute the result of the manipulation as a *program*.
2. The S-expression is equivalent to the parse tree for the computer program. In spite of their outwardly different appearance and syntax, most compiled programming languages internally convert, at the time of compilation, a program into a prase tree representing the underlying composition of functions and terminals of that program. This parse tree is usually not accessible (at least not conveniently) to the programmer. If it were accessible, it would have a different appearance and syntax than the programming language itself. We need access to the parse tree because we want to genetically manipulate the parts of computer programs (i.e., subtrees of the parse tree). LISP gives us the ultimate in convenient access to this parse tree because a LISP program is its own parse tree.
3. The EVAL function of LISP provides an almost effortless way of executing a computer program that was just created or genetically manipulated.
4. LISP facilitates the programming of structures whose size and shape change dynamically (rather than being predetermined in advance). Moreover, LISP's dynamic storage allocation and garbage collection provide administrative support for programming of dynamically changing structures. The underlying philosophy of all aspects of LISP is to impose no limitation on programs beyond the limitation inherently imposed by the physical and virtual memory limitations of the computer on which the program is run. While it is possible to handle structures whose size and shape change dynamically in many programming languages, LISP is especially well suited for it.
5. LISP facilitates convenient handling of hierarchical structures.
6. Software environments offering an unusually rich collection of programming tools are commercially available for LISP.

Note that we did not choose LISP because we intended to make special use of its list data structure or list manipulation functions (such as CAR or CDR).

10.5 DETAILED DESCRIPTION OF THE GENETIC PROGRAMMING PARADIGM

Adaptation involves the progressive modification of some structure so that it performs better in its environment. Learning is a form of adaptation for which performance consists of solving a problem. Holland's *Adaptation in Natural and Artificial Systems* [1] provides a general perspective on adaptation and identifies the key features common to every adaptive (or learning) system. In the remainder of this section, we use this perspective to describe the GP paradigm in terms of the

- Structures that undergo adaptation,
- Initial structures,
- Fitness measure that evaluates the structures,
- Operations performed to modify the structures,
- State (memory) of the system at each stage,
- Method for designating a result,
- Method for terminating the process, and
- Parameters that control the process.

10.5.1 Structures Undergoing Adaptation

In every adaptive system or learning system, some structure or structures are undergoing adaptation. For nongenetic adaptive algorithms, it is typically a *single* point in the search space of the problem. For conventional genetic algorithms and the GP paradigm, such structures are the individual points, in a *population* of points, from the search space of the problem. That is, the genetic approach involves a parallel search. The structures undergoing adaptation are hierarchically structured computer programs, of which the size, shape, and complexity can dynamically change during the process.

The set of possible structures in the GP paradigm is the set of all possible compositions of functions that can be composed recursively from the available set of N_{func} functions from the function set $F = \{f_1, f_2, \ldots, f_{N_{\text{func}}}\}$ and the available set of N_{term} terminals from the terminal set $T = \{a_1, a_2, \ldots, a_{N_{\text{term}}}\}$. Each function f in F takes a specified number $z(f)$ of arguments $b_1, b_2, \ldots, b_{z(f)}$. The functions in the function set may be

- Arithmetic operations (+, −, etc.)
- Mathematical functions (Sin, Cos, Exp, etc.)
- Boolean operations (such as AND, OR, NOT)
- Logical operators (such as If-Then-Else)
- Iterative operators (such as Do-Until)

- Functions permitting recursion
- Domain-specific functions

The terminals are typically either constant atoms (such as the number 3) or variable atoms (representing, perhaps, the inputs, sensors, or state variables of some system).

Consider the function set

$$F = \{\text{AND, OR, NOT}\}$$

and the terminal set

$$T = \{\text{D0, D1}\}$$

where D0 and D1 are Boolean variable atoms that serve as arguments for the functions. We can combine the set of functions and terminals into a set C as follows:

$$C = F \cup T = \{\text{AND, OR, NOT, D0, D1}\}$$

Now consider an even-parity function with two arguments. This function returns T if an even number (0 or 2) of its arguments (D0 and D1) are T; otherwise, it returns NIL. This Boolean function can be expressed in disjunctive normal form (DNF) and represented by the S-expression

```
(OR (AND (NOT D0) (NOT D1)) (AND D0 D1))
```

The rooted, point-labeled tree with ordered branches corresponding to this S-expression is shown in Figure 10.3. The five internal points of the tree are labeled with functions (OR, AND, NOT, NOT, and AND). The four external points (leaves) of the tree are labeled with terminals (D0, D1, D0, and D1, respectively). The root of the tree is labeled with the function appearing just inside the outermost left parenthesis of the S-expression (OR).

The search space for the GP paradigm is the hyperspace of valid LISP S-expressions that can be recursively created by compositions of the avail-

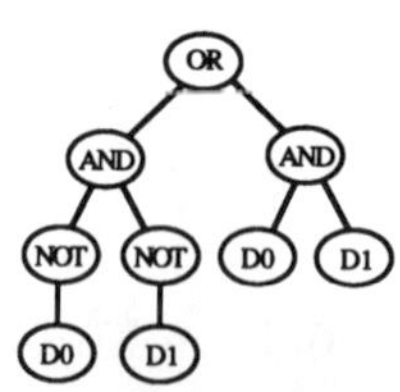

Figure 10.3 *Rooted, point-labeled tree corresponding to the LISP S-expression for the even-parity function (OR (AND (NOT D0)(NOT D1))(AND D0 D1)).*

able functions and available terminals for the problem. This search space can, equally be viewed as the hyperspace of rooted point-labeled trees with ordered branches having internal points labeled with the available functions and external points (leaves) labeled with the available terminals.

The structures that undergo adaptation in the GP paradigm differ from the structures that undergo adaptation in the conventional genetic algorithm operating on strings in that they are hierarchical structures rather than one-dimensional linear strings.

In the GP paradigm, the terminal set and function set should be selected to satisfy the requirements of closure and sufficiency.

Closure. Each function in the function set should be well defined for any combination of arguments that may be encountered. These argument values may arise from a terminal or a function. For example, if the function set consists of the Boolean functions AND and OR and the terminal set consists of Boolean variables that can only assume the value T or NIL, then the closure property is satisfied. On the other hand, if the arithmetic operation of division is in a function set along with terminals that can assume the value of zero, the closure property is not satisfied unless some arrangement is made to deal with the situation when division by zero is attempted. One approach is to use the protected division function %. This function returns a 1 when division by zero is attempted and the normal quotient otherwise. Similar arrangements may be required when the square root or logarithm function may be applied to a zero-valued variable.

If the closure property does not prevail, we must then address alternatives such as (1) discarding individuals that do not evaluate to a result within the desired domain, or (2) assigning some penalty to the fitness of such individuals and then proceeding somehow.

Sufficiency. The set of functions and terminals used should be capable of solving the problem. For example, one would not be able to induce Kepler's third law for planetary motion if the terminal set contained only the diameter of each planet (as opposed to its distance from the sun) or if the function set contained only addition and subtraction (instead of the functions needed to state the third law).

The user of the GP paradigm should know or believe that some composition of the functions and terminals he or she supplies can yield a solution to the problem. In some domains (e.g., Boolean functions), the requirements are well known. For example, removing the function NOT from the function set F = (AND, OR, NOT} creates a function set that is no longer sufficient for expressing many Boolean functions, including the even-parity function.

The choice of the set of available functions and terminals directly affects the character of the solutions that can be attained, and form the basis for generating potential solutions. For example, if one does symbolic regression on the absolute value function with a function set containing the If-Then-

Else function and subtraction, one obtains a solution in the familiar form of a conditional test on x that returns either x or $-x$, depending on whether x is greater than or less than zero, respectively. On the other hand, if one does symbolic regression on the absolute value function with a function set containing only the cosines of odd harmonics and the ordinary arithmetic operations, one instead gets the first few terms of the Fourier series approximation to the absolute value function.

10.5.2 Initial Structures

Initial structures in the GP paradigm consist of the individuals in the initial population of individual S-expressions for the problem. Generating each S-expression in the initial population is done by randomly generating a rooted, point-labeled tree with ordered branches representing the S-expression. We begin by selecting one of the functions from the set F at random (using a uniform distribution) to be the label for the root of the tree. We restrict selection of this label to F because we want to generate a hierarchical structure, not a degenerate structure consisting of only a single terminal. For example, in Figure 10.4 the function + (taking two arguments) was selected from a function set F as the label for the root of the tree.

Whenever a point of the tree is labeled with a function f from F, then $z(f)$ lines, where $z(f)$ is the number of arguments taken by the function f, are created to radiate from that point. Then for each radiating line an element is randomly selected to be the label for the end point of that line. If a function is chosen to be the label for any such end point, the generating process then continues recursively as just described. For example, in Figure 10.5 the function $*$ from the set $C = F \cup T$ of functions and terminals was selected as the label of the internal nonroot point at the end of the first (leftmost) radiating line from the point with the function +. This function $*$ takes two arguments, so we show two lines radiating from the point with function $*$.

On the other hand, if a terminal is chosen to be the label for any point, that point becomes an end point of the tree and the generating process is terminated for that point. For example, in Figure 10.6 the terminal A from the terminal set T was selected to be the label of the first line radiating from the point labeled with the function $*$.

This generative process can be implemented in several ways, resulting in initial random trees of different sizes and shapes.

The generative method we believe does best over a broad range of prob-

Figure 10.4 *Generation of a random tree might begin with labeling the root of the tree with the + function.*

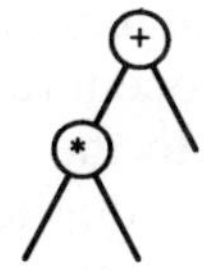

Figure 10.5 *Generation of a random tree might continue with labeling of an internal nonroot point with the $*$ function.*

lems is one we call *half-ramping*. It produces a mixture of trees of various sizes and shapes. This method is used on all problems presented here. It involves creating an equal number of trees of each depth between 2 and some maximum depth (which is 6 for all problems in this chapter). The depth of a tree is the length of the longest path from the root to an end point.

Then for each value of depth, 50% of the trees of that depth are created in each of two ways:

1. Of the trees of the specified depth, 50% are "full" in that the path lengths between every end point and the root are equal to the maximum. This is accomplished by restricting the random selection of the label for points of the tree at depths smaller than the maximum to the set F and restricting the random selection of the label for points at depths equal to the maximum to the terminal set T.
2. Of the trees of the specified depth, 50% are variably shaped in that the path lengths between an end point and the root are no greater than the specified maximum. This is accomplished by making the random selection of the label for points of the tree at depths smaller than the maximum from the set $C = F \cup T$ while restricting the random selection of the label for points at depths equal to the maximum to T. We use a uniform random probability distribution to make these selections from the sets.

Duplicate individuals are unproductive deadwood that waste computational resources and undesirably reduces the genetic diversity of the population. In the GP paradigm, duplicate random individuals are created relatively often when the tree size is small or when the size of the terminal set happens

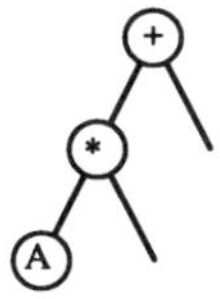

Figure 10.6 *Generation of a random tree might continue with labeling of an external point with the terminal* A.

to be large relative to the size of the function set. Thus, after an S-expression is created from the generative procedure, but before it is inserted into the initial population, it is compared to the S-expressions already in the initial population. If the S-expression is a duplicate, it is rejected. The generating process continues until the desired number of unique S-expressions is created.

The variety of a population is the percentage of individuals for which no exact duplicate exists in the population. The variety of the initial random population is 100%.

10.5.3 Fitness

Each individual in a population is assigned a numerical fitness value as a result of its interaction with its environment. Fitness is the driving force of Darwinian selection in nature. It is, likewise, the driving force for genetic algorithms and the GP paradigm. In this section we describe four measures of fitness: raw fitness, standardized fitness, adjusted fitness, and normalized fitness.

Raw fitness is the measure of fitness stated in the natural terminology of the problem itself. It is usually, but not always, evaluated over a set of fitness cases. These fitness cases provide a basis for evaluating the fitness of the S-expressions in the population over representative situations so that a range of numerical raw fitness values can be obtained. The fitness cases are typically a small finite sample of the domain space (which is usually very large or infinite). Therefore, the fitness cases must be representative of the domain space as a whole because they form the basis for generalizing the obtained results to the entire domain space.

The definition of raw fitness depends on the problem. For many problems, raw fitness can be defined as the sum of the distances (i.e., errors), taken over all fitness cases, between the point in the range space returned by the S-expression for the set of arguments for the fitness case and the correct point in the range space for the fitness case. The S-expression may be, for example, Boolean-valued, integer-valued, real-valued, complex-valued, or symbolic-valued. If the S-expression is integer-valued or real-valued, the sum of distances is the sum of absolute values of the differences (or, if desired, the sum of the squares of the differences) between the numbers involved.

When raw fitness represents error, the raw fitness $r(i, t)$ of an S-expression i in the population of size M at any generational time step t is

$$r(i, t) = \sum_{j=1}^{N_e} |S(i, j) - C(j)|$$

where $S(i, j)$ is the value returned by S-expression i for fitness case j (of N_e

cases), and $C(j)$ is the correct value for j. If the S-expression is Boolean-valued or symbolic-valued, the sum of distances is equivalent to the number of mismatches.

Raw fitness may be something other than error. For example, in optimal control problems, raw fitness may be the cost of an individual control strategy (as measured in time, distance, dollars, etc.). In some problems, raw fitness is a score of some kind (e.g., amount of points scored, benefit achieved, food eaten, subgoals satisfied, etc.). Note that because raw fitness is stated in the natural terminology of the problem, the better value may be lower (as when raw fitness represents error) or higher (as when raw fitness represents food eaten, benefit achieved, etc.).

Standardized fitness $s(i, t)$ restates the raw fitness so that a lower numerical value is better. If a lower value of raw fitness is better, then

$$s(i, t) = r(i, t)$$

If a higher value is better, then

$$s(i, t) = r_{\max} - r(i, t)$$

where $r_{\max}$ is the maximum possible value of raw fitness.

Adjusted fitness $a(i, t)$ is computed from standardized fitness $s(i, t)$:

$$a(i, t) = \frac{1}{1 + s(i, t)}$$

The adjusted fitness lies between 0 and 1. Unlike standardized fitness, the adjusted fitness is bigger for better individuals in the population.

It is not necessary to use adjusted fitness in the GP paradigm. We believe this adjustment is generally helpful, so we use it consistently on all problems in this chapter. Adjusted fitness has the benefit of exaggerating the importance of small differences in the value of standardized fitness as these values start approaching zero in later generations of a run. Adjusted fitness is especially beneficial if the standardized fitness actually reaches zero when a perfect solution to the problem is found (e.g., as in symbolic regression problems when an error of zero denotes a perfect fit).

Normalized fitness $n(i, t)$ $n(i, t)$ is

$$n(i, t) = \frac{a(i, t)}{\sum_{k=1}^{M} a(k, t)}$$

It has three desirable characteristics.

1. It ranges between 0 and 1.
2. It is larger for better individuals in the population.
3. The sum of the normalized fitness values is unity.

When we use the phrases *proportional to fitness* or *fitness proportionate* in this chapter, we are referring to normalized fitness.

As will be seen, it is also possible for the fitness function to give some weight to secondary factors, such as the efficiency of the S-expression (Sec. 10.16.2) and compliance with the initial conditions of a differential equation (Sec. 10.15.1).

10.5.4 Operations for Modifying Structures

The two primary operations for modifying structures undergoing adaptation in the GP paradigm are (1) Darwinian fitness proportionate reproduction and (2) crossover (sexual recombination).

Reproduction. The operation of reproduction for the GP paradigm is the basic engine of Darwinian reproduction and survival of the fittest. Each time this operation is performed, it operates on only one parental S-expression and produces only one offspring S-expression. In other words, it is an asexual operation.

The operation of reproduction consists of two steps. First, a single S-expression is selected from the population according to some selection rule based on fitness. Second, the individual is copied from the current population into the new population (i.e., the new generation).

There are many selection rules based on fitness. The most popular selection rule (and the one used here) is fitness proportionate selection. If $f(s_i(t))$ is the fitness of individual s_i in the population at generation t, then each time the reproduction operation is performed each individual in the population has a probability of $f(s_i(t))/\Sigma_{j=1}^{M} f(s_j(t))$ of being copied into the next generation. The reproduction operation in this case is called *fitness proportionate reproduction*.

Note that the parent remains in the population while selection is performed during the current generation. That is, the selection is done with replacement (i.e, reselection) allowed. Parents can be selected, and, in general, are selected, more than once for reproduction during the current generation. Indeed, the differential rate of survival and reproduction for more fit individuals is an essential part of genetic algorithms.

Crossover (Recombination). The crossover (sexual recombination) operation for the GP paradigm creates variation in the population by producing new offspring that consist of parts taken from each parent. The crossover operation starts with two parental S-expressions and produces two offspring S-expressions. In other words, it is a sexual operation. In general, at least one parent is chosen from the population with a probability equal to their respective normalized fitness values. In this chapter, both parents are so chosen.

The operation begins by independently selecting, using a uniform probability distribution, one random point in each parent to be the crossover point for that parent. Note that the numbers of points in the two parents typically are not equal because the S-expressions in the population are of various shapes and sizes.

The crossover fragment for a parent is the rooted subtree whose root is the crossover point for that parent and where the subtree consists of the entire subtree lying below the crossover point (i.e., more distant from the root of the original tree). Viewed in terms of lists in a LISP S-expression, the crossover fragment is the sublist starting at the crossover point.

The first offspring S-expression is produced by deleting the crossover fragment of the first parent from the first parent and then inserting the crossover fragment of the second parent at the crossover point of the first parent. The second offspring is produced in a symmetric manner.

As will be seen, the crossover operation is well defined and syntactically legal for any two S-expressions and any two crossover points. For example, consider the parental S-expressions in Figure 10.7. The functions in these S-expressions are the Boolean AND, OR, and NOT. The terminals are the Boolean arguments D0 and D1. Each point of the two S-expressions has been numbered in a depth-first, left-to-right way.

Equivalently, in terms of LISP S-expressions, the two parents are

```
(OR (NOT D1) (AND D0 D1))
```

and

```
(OR (OR D1 (NOT D0)) (AND (NOT D0) (NOT D1))
```

Assume that the points of both trees are numbered in a depth-first way starting at the left. Suppose that the second point (out of the six points of the

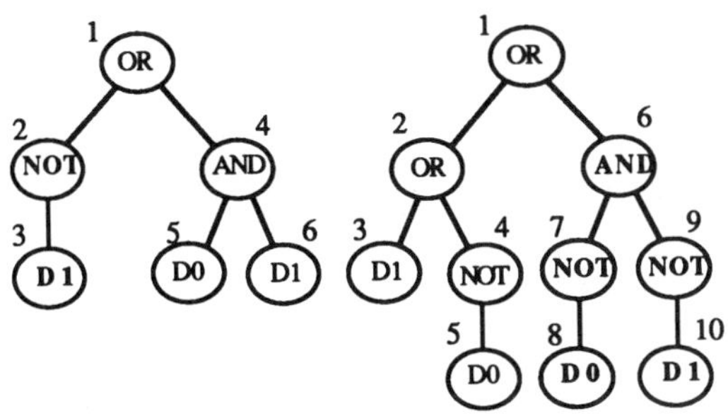

Figure 10.7 *Two parental LISP S-expressions.*

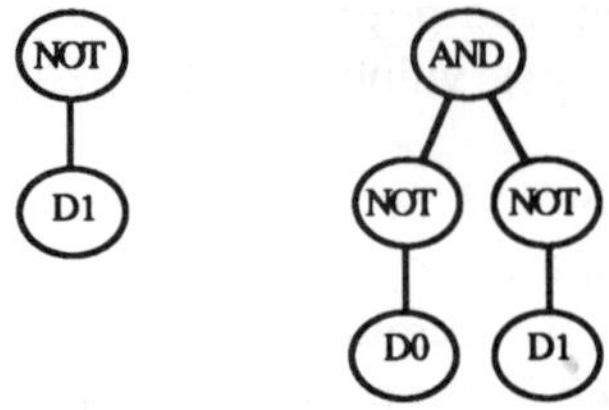

Figure 10.8 *Two crossover fragments selected from the parents from Figure 10.7.*

first parent) is randomly selected as the crossover point for the first parent. The crossover point of the first parent is therefore the NOT function. Suppose also that the sixth point (out of the 10 points of the second parent) is selected as the crossover point of the second parent. The crossover point of the second parent is therefore the AND function. The underscored boldface portions of the two parental S-expressions are the crossover fragments. Figure 10.8 shows these fragments, and Figure 10.9 shows the two offspring resulting from crossover.

Note that the first offspring happens to be a perfect solution for the even-parity function, namely

(OR **AND (NOT D0) (NOT D1))** (AND D0 D1))

The second offspring is

(OR (OR D1 (NOT D0)) **(NOT D1))**

Note that because entire subtrees are swapped and because of the closure property of the functions themselves, this genetic crossover (recombination) operation produces syntactically legal LISP S-expressions as offspring in all situations.

If the root of one parental S-expression happens to be selected as the crossover point, the crossover operation will insert the entire first parent

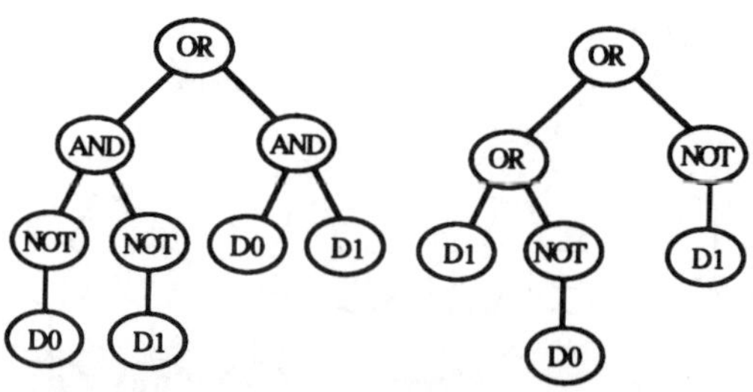

Figure 10.9 *Two offspring produced by the crossover operation using the parents from Figure 10.7 and the crossover fragments from Figure 10.8.*

into the second parent at the crossover point of the second parent. That is, in this event, the entire first parent will become a subtree within the second parent. In addition, in this event, the crossover fragment of the second parent will become the second offspring.

If the roots of two parents both happen to be chosen as crossover points, the crossover operation simply degenerates to an instance of reproduction on those two parents.

Note that if an individual mates with itself or two identical individuals mate, the two resulting offspring will generally be different (because the crossover points selected are, in general, different for the two parents). This contrasts with conventional genetic algorithms that operate on fixed-length character strings where the one selected crossover point applies to both parents.

If a terminal is located at the crossover point in precisely one parent, then the subtree from the second parent is inserted at the location of the terminal in the first parent, and the terminal from the first parent is inserted at the location of the subtree in the second parent. In this event, the crossover operation often has the effect of increasing the depth of one tree and decreasing the depth of the second tree.

If terminals are located at both crossover points selected, the crossover operation merely swaps these terminals from tree to tree. The effect of crossover, in this event, is akin to a point mutation. Thus, occasional point mutation is an inherent part of the crossover operation.

A maximum permissible size (measured via the depth of the tree) is established for offspring created by the crossover operation. This limit prevents large amounts of computer time being expended on a few extremely large individual S-expressions. Of course, if we could execute all the S-expressions in the population in parallel (as nature does) in a manner such that the infeasibility of one individual in the population would not disproportionately jeopardize the resources needed by the population as a whole, we would not need such a size limitation. If a crossover between two parents would create an offspring of impermissible size, the contemplated crossover operation is aborted for that offspring, and the first of its parents is arbitrarily chosen to be reproduced into the new population.

10.5.5 The State of the System

The state of the GP paradigm at any point during the process consists only of the current population of individuals in the population. There is no additional memory or centralized bookkeeping necessary.

10.5.6 Result Designation

The single best individual in the population at the time of termination of the GP paradigm is typically designated as the result produced by the paradigm.

This method of results designation is sometimes called *winner takes all* and is used herein.

Note that the very best individual is not guaranteed to be present in the population at the time of termination unless some specific effort is made to preserve this individual (the elitist strategy).

Alternatively, the entire population at the time of termination of the GP paradigm can be designated as the result produced by the paradigm.

10.5.7 Termination

As for termination, as Yogi Berra once said, "It ain't over until it's over, and even then, it's not over." The GP paradigm parallels nature in that it is a continuing process. As a practical matter, the GP paradigm is terminated when either a prespecified maximum number N_{gen} of generations have been run or when some termination criterion is satisfied. One possible termination criterion is that the standardized fitness of some individual in the population either equals zero or is within a preestablished neighborhood of zero.

10.5.8 Control Parameters

The GP paradigm is controlled by various parameters, including two major parameters and five minor parameters. The major parameters are the population size M and the number of generations N_{gen} to be run. Unless otherwise indicated, the population size is 500 for all problems in this chapter, and the number of generations is 51 (i.e., an initial random generation plus 50 subsequent generations). Note, if termination is under control of a problem-specific termination criterion, this parameter merely provides an overall maximum number of generations.

Two minor parameters control the frequency of performing the genetic operations; one parameter controls the percentage of internal (function) points chosen as crossover points; and two parameters help conserve computer time. The values of the five minor parameters are the same for all problems presented here.

1. Crossover was performed on 90% of the population for each generation. That is, if the population size is 500, then 450 individuals (225 pairs) from each generation were selected with a probability equal to their normalized fitness (with reselection allowed) to participate in crossover.
2. Fitness proportionate reproduction was performed on 10% of the population on each generation. That is, if the population size is 500, 50 individuals from each generation were selected with a probability equal to their normalized fitness (with reselection allowed).
3. In selecting crossover points, we used a probability distribution that allocates 90% of the crossover points equally among the internal (func-

tion) points of each tree and allocates the remaining (10% equally among the external (terminal) points of each tree. We believe this distribution promotes the recombining of larger structures. In contrast, a uniform distribution over all points might do an inordinate amount of mere swapping of terminals from tree to tree in a manner more akin to point mutation than the desired recombining of ''building block'' substructures.

4. A maximum depth of 17 was established for S-expressions created by the crossover operation.
5. A maximum depth of 6 was established for the random individuals generated for the initial population.

10.6 LEARNING OF A BOOLEAN FUNCTION

In previous sections, we discussed the background and details of the GP paradigm. The rest of this chapter illustrates its use. In each section we show how we approached the problem so that it could be solved with the GP paradigm.

The examples were selected to illustrate a variety of problems from many areas. They involve integer-valued, real-valued, Boolean-valued, and symbolic-valued functions. Some problems require iteration for their solution, and some involve functions whose real functionality is the side effects they cause on the state of the system involved rather than the actual value returned by the function. Many are bench-mark problems that have been the subject of previous study in machine learning, artificial intelligence, induction, neural nets, decision trees, and classifier systems.

Since the GP paradigm is probabilistic, we almost never get precisely the same result twice. Moreover, we almost never get the solution to the problem in the form we contemplated (although these solutions may be equivalent to what we contemplated). For each problem, we show the result from a particular run to illustrate the representation scheme and the type of results one gets. No one run and no result is truly typical or representative of all runs. In choosing the result for each problem, we avoided showing the ''prettiest'' or most convoluted result.

We show the amount of computer processing required to produce a solution with 99% probability over a series of runs for selected problems. All of the problems presented have been repeatedly solved on dozens or hundreds of occasions. For each problem the author believes that sufficient information is provided here or via references to allow the experiment to be independently replicated to produce substantially similar results (within the limits inherent in any process involving stochastic operations).

We present the first problem in great detail.

10.6.1 Boolean 11-Multiplexer

The problem of machine learning of a Boolean function requires developing a composition of functions that can return the correct value of the function after seeing examples of combinations of arguments associated with the correct value of the function. This problem is a special case of the general problem of symbolic function identification (symbolic regression) discussed later in connection with real-valued functions.

Boolean functions provide an especially useful test bed for machine learning for several reasons.

1. It is intuitively easy to see how the *structural* components of the S-expression for a Boolean function contribute to the overall *performance* of the Boolean expression. This direct connection between structure and performance is much harder to comprehend for many of the other problems.
2. There are fewer practical computer implementation obstacles for Boolean functions than for other problems. For example, we need not be concerned with error conditions (such as floating-point overflows and underflows) arising from randomly generated computer programs and genetically recombined computer programs.
3. Boolean problems have an easily quantifiable search space.

Let us first consider the problem of learning the Boolean 11-multiplexer function. The solution of this problem using the GP paradigm will serve to show the interplay of

- The genetic variation inevitably created in the initial random generation
- The small improvements for some individuals in the population via localized hill climbing from generation to generation
- The way individuals become specialized and able to correctly handle certain subcases of the problem (case splitting)
- The creative role of crossover in recombining valuable parts of more fit parents
- How the nurturing of a large population of alternative solutions to the problem (rather than a single point in the solution space) helps avoid false peaks in the search for the problem solution

This problem also illustrates the importance of hierarchies in solving problems and making the ultimate solution understandable. Moreover, the progressively changing size and shape of the various individuals in the population in various generations show the importance of not determining in advance the size and shape of the ultimate solution or the intermediate results that may contribute to the solution.

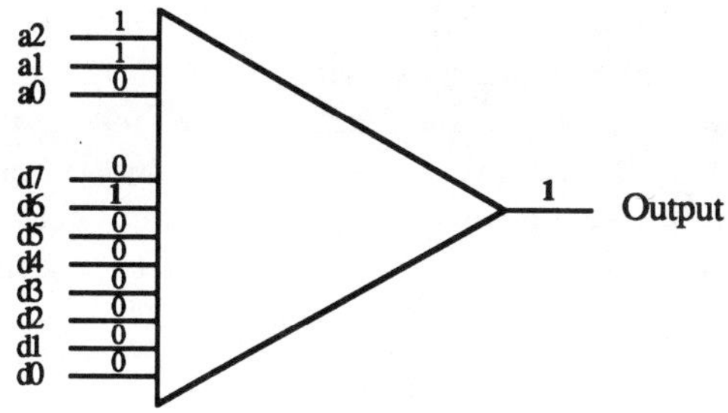

Figure 10.10 *Boolean 11-multiplexer.*

The input to the Boolean N-multiplexer function consists of k address bits a_i and 2^k data bits d_i, where $N = k + 2^k$. That is, the input to the Boolean multiplexer function consists of the $k + 2^k$ bits $a_{k-1}, \ldots, a_1, a_0, d_2k_{-1}, \ldots, d_1, d_0$. The value of the Boolean multiplexer function is the Boolean value (0 or 1) of the data bit singled out by the k address bits of the multiplexer. For example, for the Boolean 11-multiplexer (where $k = 3$), if the three address bits $a_2a_1a_0$ are 110, the multiplexer singles out data bit 6 (d_6) to be the output of the multiplexer. Figure 10.10 shows a Boolean 11-multiplexer with an input of 11001000000 and corresponding output of **1.**

Five major steps are involved in using the GP paradigm:

1. Select the set of terminals that will be available for constructing S-expressions.
2. Select the set of functions that will be available for constructing S-expressions.
3. Identify the fitness function for the problem.
4. Select the parameters for running the algorithm.
5. Select the criterion for designating a result and terminating a run.

Select the Set of Terminals. This choice is especially straightforward for this problem. The terminal set has 11 elements that correspond to the 11 inputs to the Boolean 11-multiplexer:

$$T = \{A0, A1, A2, D0, D1, \ldots, D7\}$$

None of these 11 terminals are distinguished as address lines or data lines.

Select the Set of Functions. The set of available functions is

$$F = \{AND, OR, NOT, IF\}$$

having two, two, one, and three arguments, respectively. The IF function is the Common LISP function that performs the IF-THEN-ELSE operation. That is, the IF function returns the results of evaluating its third argument (the "else" clause) if its first argument is NIL, and otherwise returns the results of evaluating its second argument (the "then" clause).

This step (performed by the user) is equivalent to a similar required step in other machine-learning paradigms. For example:

- In the induction of decision trees using ID3 (and its variants), the user selects the set of attribute-testing functions that can appear at the internal points of the decision tree.
- In neural net problems, the user selects the external functions to be activated by the output of a neural network.
- In conventional genetic algorithms operating on strings, the user determines how certain external functions are to be activated by a chromosome in the user's chosen representation scheme.
- In genetic classifier systems, the user selects the external functions to be activated by the output interface of the classifier system.

This determination is often not explicitly identified as a necessary step by researchers using other paradigms because the researcher often considers the choice of functions to be inherent in the statement of the problem (a view that is especially understandable if the researcher is focusing on only one specific problem in one specific area).

The function set F of basic logical functions satisfies the closure property and is known to be sufficient to realize any Boolean function. For this problem and most of the problems herein, the function set is not only minimally sufficient to solve the problem at hand, but contains additional functions.

The search space is the set of all LISP S-expressions that can be recursively composed of functions from the function set and terminals from the terminal set. Another way to look at the search space is that the Boolean multiplexer function with $k + 2^k$ arguments is a particular one of 2^{k+2^k} possible Boolean functions of $k + 2^k$ arguments. For example, when $k = 3$, then $k + 2^k = 11$, and this search space is of size $2^{2^{11}} = 2^{2048} \approx 10^{616}$. Every possible Boolean function of $k + 2^k$ arguments can be realized by at least one LISP S-expression composed from the functions and terminals stated (for example, disjunctive normal form).

Identify the Fitness Function. Fitness is usually evaluated over many fitness cases. The set of fitness cases must be representative of the problem as a whole. The reader may find it helpful to think of these fitness cases as the environment in which the genetic population of computer programs must adapt. There are $2^{11} = 2048$ possible combinations of the 11 arguments $a_0a_1a_2d_0d_1d_2d_3d_4d_5d_6d_7$. With each combination, there is an associated correct value of the 11-multiplexer function. For this problem, we use the entire set of 2048 combinations of arguments as the fitness cases for evaluating fitness. That is, we do not use sampling.

We begin by defining raw fitness in the simplest way that comes to mind, using the natural terminology of the problem. The raw fitness of a LISP S-expression is simply the number of fitness cases (taken over all 2048 fitness cases) where the Boolean value returned by the S-expression for a combination of arguments is the correct Boolean value. Thus, the raw fitness of an S-expression can range over 2049 different values between 0 and 2048. A raw fitness of 2048 denotes a correct individual S-expression. Throughout this chapter, we find it convenient to define a problem-specific performance measure called "hits". We define the auxiliary hits measure for this problem to be equal to the raw fitness.

After defining raw fitness, we define standardized fitness. Since a bigger value of raw fitness is better, standardized fitness is different from raw fitness for this problem. In particular, it equals r_{max} (i.e., 2048) minus the observed raw fitness. Standardized fitness can also be viewed as the sum, taken over all 2048 fitness cases, of the Hamming distances between the Boolean value returned by the S-expression for a combination of arguments and the correct Boolean value. The Hamming distance is zero if the Boolean value returned by the S-expression agrees with the correct Boolean value, and is unity if it disagrees. Thus, the sum of the Hamming distances is equivalent to the number of mismatches.

Select the Values of Parameters. A population of size 4000 was chosen.

Select the Criterion for Designating a Result and Terminating a Run. In this problem we have a way to recognize a solution when we find it. When the raw fitness is 2048 (i.e., the standardized fitness is zero), we have a correct solution. Thus, we terminate a run after a specified maximum number of generations N_{gen} (e.g., 51) or earlier if we find an individual with a raw fitness of 2048. For all problems in this chapter, we terminate a run after 51 generations, and we designate the best single individual in the population at the time of termination as the result of the GP.

We now illustrate the GP paradigm by discussing one run of the Boolean 11-multiplexer in detail. The process begins with the generation of the initial random population (i.e., generation 0). Predictably, the initial random population includes a variety of highly unfit individuals. Many individual S-expressions in this population are merely constants, such as the contradictory (AND A0 (NOT A0)). Other individuals are passive and merely pass an input through as the output, such as (NOT (NOT A1)). Other individuals are inefficient, such as (OR D7 D7). Some of these initial random individuals base their decision on precisely the wrong arguments, such as (IF D0 A0 A2). This individual uses the data bit D0 to decide what output to take. Many of the initial random individuals are partially blind in that they do not incorporate all 11 arguments known to be necessary to solve the problem. Some S-expressions are just nonsense, such as

```
(IF (IF (IF D2 D2 D2) D2 D2) D2 D2)
```

Nonetheless, even in this highly unfit initial random population, some individuals are somewhat fitter than others. In the valley of the blind, the one-eyed man is king. For this run, the individuals in the initial random population had values of standardized fitness ranging from 768 mismatches (i.e., 1280 matches or hits) to 1280 mismatches (i.e., 768 matches). The worst individual in the population for the initial random generation was

```
(OR (NOT A1) (NOT (IF (AND A2 A0) D7 D3)))
```

This individual had a standardized fitness of 1280 (i.e., raw fitness of only 768).

As it happens, a total of 23 individuals out of the 4000 in this initial random population tied with the highest score of 1280 matches (i.e., hits) on generation 0. One of these 23 high-scoring individuals was the S-expression

```
(IF A0 D1 D2)
```

This individual scores 1280 matches by scoring 512 matches for the one quarter (i.e., 512) of the 2048 fitness cases for which A2 and A1 are both NIL, and by scoring an additional 768 matches on 50% of the remaining three quarters (i.e., 1536) of the fitness cases.

This individual has obvious shortcomings. Notably, it is partially blind in that it uses only 3 of the 11 necessary terminals of the problem. Hence, this individual cannot possibly be a correct solution to the problem. Nonetheless, it does some things right. For example, this individual uses one of the 3 address bits (A0) as the basis for its action. It could easily have done this wrong and used 1 of the 8 data bits. In addition, this individual uses only data bits (D1 and D2) as its output. It could have done this wrong and used address bits. Moreover, if A0 (which is the low-order binary bit of the 3-bit address) is T, this individual selects 1 of the 4 odd-numbered data bits (D1) as it output. Moreover, if A0 is NIL, this individual selects 1 of the 4 even-numbered data bits (D2) as its output. In other words, this individual correctly links the parity of the low-order address bit A0 with the parity of the data bit it selects as its output. This individual is far from perfect, but it is far from being without merit. It is more fit than 3977 of the 4000 individuals in the population.

The average standardized fitness for all 4000 individuals in the population for generation 0 is 985.4. This value forms the baseline and serves as a useful bench mark for monitoring later improvements in the average standardized fitness of the population as a whole.

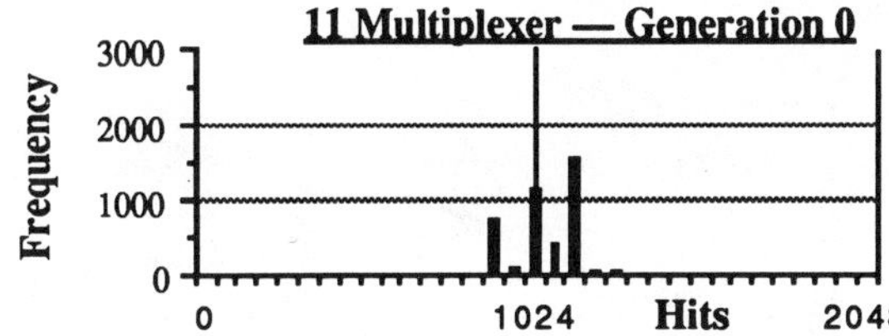

Figure 10.11 *Hits histogram for generation 0.*

The hits histogram is a useful monitoring tool based on the auxiliary hits measure. The histogram is a way of viewing the population as a whole for a particular generation. The horizontal axis is the number of hits (i.e., matches for this problem), and the vertical axis is the number of individuals in the population scoring that number of hits. Fifty different levels of fitness are represented for the population at generation 0. To make this histogram legible, we divided the horizontal axis into buckets of size 64. For example, 1553 individuals out of 4000 (i.e., about 39%) had between 1152 and 1215 matches (hits). This well-populated range includes the mode of the distribution, which occurs at 1152 matches (hits). There are 1490 individuals with 1152 matches (hits). Figure 10.11 shows the hits histogram of the population for generation 0 of this run.

The Darwinian reproduction operation and the genetic crossover operation are then applied to parents selected from the current population with probabilities proportionate to fitness to breed a new population. When these operations are completed, the new population (i.e., the new generation) replaces the old population.

In going from the initial random generation (generation 0) to generation 1, the GP paradigm works with the inevitable genetic variation existing in an initial random population. The initial random generation is an exercise in blind random search. The search is a parallel search of the search space because there are 4000 individual points involved.

Although the vast majority of the new offspring are again highly unfit, some of them tend to be somewhat fitter than others. Moreover, over a period of time and many generations, some of them tend to be slightly fitter than those in the earlier generation. The average standardized fitness of the population immediately begins improving (i.e., decreasing) from the baseline value of 985.4 for generation 0 to about 891.9 for generation 1. We typically see this kind of generally improving trend in average standardized fitness from generation to generation. In this run the average standardized fitness improves monotonically between generations 2 and 9 and assumes the values 845, 823, 763, 731, 651, 558, 459, and 382, respectively. We usually see a generally improving trend in average standardized fitness from generation to generation, but not necessarily a monotonic improvement.

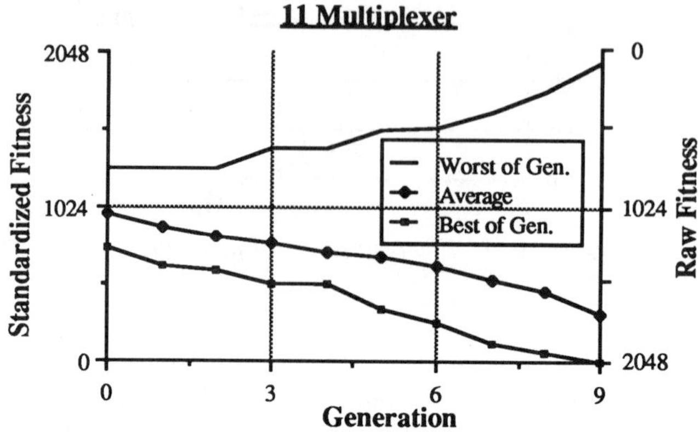

Figure 10.12 *Standardized fitness of worst-of-generation individual, average standardized fitness of population, and standardized fitness of best-of-generation individual for generations 0 through 9.*

In addition, we similarly usually see a generally improving trend in the standardized fitness of the best single individual in the population from generation to generation. In this run the standardized fitness of the best single individual in the population improves monotonically between generations 2 and 9. It assumes the values 640, 576, 384, 384, 256, 256, 128, and 0 (i.e., a perfect score), respectively.

On the other hand, the standardized fitness of the worst single individual in the population fluctuates considerably. For this run, the standardized fitness of the worst individual starts at 1280, fluctuates considerably between generations 1 and 9, and then deteriorates (increases) to 1792 by generation 9.

Figure 10.12 shows the standardized fitness (i.e., mismatches) for generations 0 through 9 of this run for the

- Best single individual in the population,
- Worst single individual in the population, and
- Average for the population.

In generation 1, the raw fitness for the best single individual in the population rises to 1408 matches (i.e., standardized fitness of 640). The only individual in the population that attained this high score was

```
(IF A0 (IF A2 D7 D3) D0)
```

Note that this individual performs better than the best individual from generation 0 for two reasons. First, it considers 2 of the 3 address bits (A0 and A2)

in deciding which data bit to choose as output, whereas the best individual in generation 0 considered only 1 of the 3 address bits (A0). Second this individual incorporates 3 of the 8 data bits as its output, whereas the best individual in generation 0 incorporated only 2 of the 8 potential data bits as output. Although still far from perfect, the best individual from generation 1 is less blind and more complex than the best individual of the previous generation. This best-of-generation individual consists of 7 points, whereas the best-of-generation individual from generation 0 consisted of only 4 points.

In generation 2, the best raw fitness remained at 1408; however, the number of individuals in the population sharing this high score rose from 1 to 21. The high point of the hits histogram advanced from 1152 for generation 0 to 1280 for generation 2. There are 1620 individuals with 1280 hits.

In generation 3, one individual in the population attained a new high score of 1472 matches (i.e., standardized fitness of 576). This individual has 16 points and is

```
(IF A2 (IF A0 D7 D4)
       (AND (IF (IF A2 (NOT D5) A0) D3 D2) D2))
```

Generation 3 shows further advances in fitness for the population as a whole. The number of individuals with 1280 hits (the high point for generation 2) has risen to 2158. Moreover, the center of gravity of the fitness histogram has shifted significantly from left to right. In particular, the number of individuals with 1280 hits or better has risen from 1679 to 2719.

In generations 4 and 5, the best single individual has 1664 hits. This score is attained by only one individual in generation 4, but by 13 individuals in generation 5, of which one is

```
(IF A0 (IF A2 D7 D3)
       (IF A2 D4 (IF A1 D2 (IF A2 D7 D0))))
```

Note that this individual uses all 3 address bits (A2, A1, and A0) in deciding on the output. It also uses 5 of the 8 data bits. By generation 4, the high point of the histogram has moved to 1408 with 1559 individuals.

In generation 6, four individuals attain a score of 1792 hits. The high point of the histogram has moved to 1536 hits.

In generation 7, 70 individuals attain this score of 1792 hits.

In generation 8 there are four best-of-generation individuals that attain a score of 1920 hits. The mode (high point) of the histogram has moved to 1664, and 1672 individuals share this value. Moreover, an additional 887 individuals score 1792.

In generation 9, the individual that emerged with a perfect score of 2048 hits is

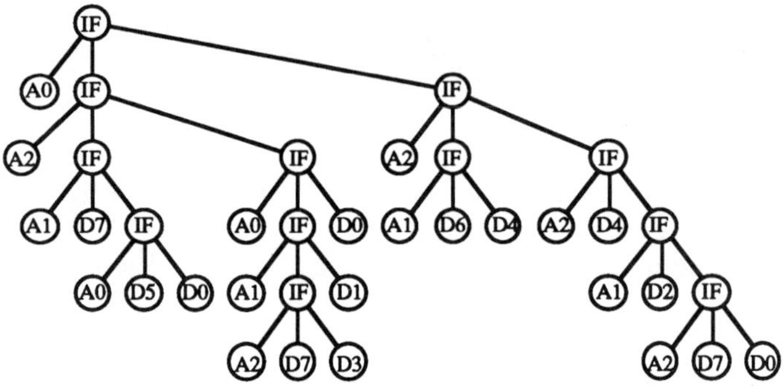

Figure 10.13 *100% correct individual from generation 9.*

```
(IF A0  (IF A2  (IF A1 D7  (IF A0 D5 D0))
                (IF A0  (IF A1  (IF A2 D7 D3)  D1)  D0))
        (IF A2  (IF A1 D6 D4)
                (IF A2 D4  (IF A1 D2  (IF A2 D7 D0)))))
```

Figure 10.13 shows this individual. It is a hierarchical structure of 37 points (i.e., 12 functions and 25 terminals).

Note that the size and shape of this solution emerged from the GP paradigm. It was not specified in advance, but evolved as a result of reproduction, crossover, and the relentless pressure of fitness. In generation 0, the best single individual in the population had 4 points. The number of points in the best single individual in the population varied from generation to generation. It was 37 for generation 9.

The correct individual can be simplified to

```
(IF A0  (IF A2  (IF A1 D7 D5)  (IF A1 D3 D1))
        (IF A2  (IF A1 D6 D4)  (IF A1 D2 D0)))
```

Thus, it can be seen that this individual correctly performs the 11-multiplexer function by first examining address bits A0, A2, and A1 and then making appropriate choice of the 8 possible data bits.

Figure 10.14 shows, side by side, the hits histograms for generations 3, 5, 7, and 9 of this run. As one progresses from generation to generation, note the left-to-right "slinky" undulating movement of the center of mass of the histogram and the high point of the histogram. This movement reflects the improvement of the population as a whole as well as the best single individual in the population. There is a single correct individual with 2048 hits at generation 9; however, because of the scale of the vertical axis of this histogram, it is not visible in a population of size 4000.

Further insight can be gained by studying the genealogical audit trail of

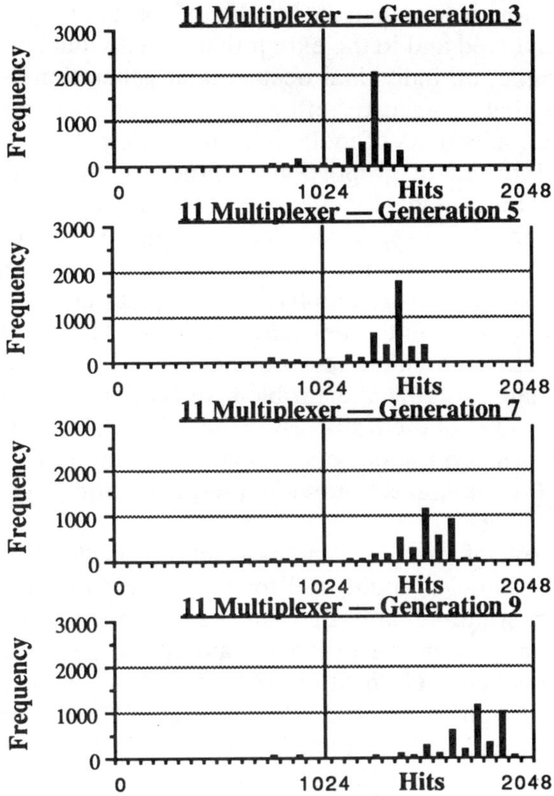

Figure 10.14 *Hits histogram for generations 3, 5, 7, and 9 for the Boolean 11-multiplexer problem.*

the process. This audit trail consists of a complete record of the details of each genetic operation performed. For the operations of fitness proportionate reproduction and crossover, the details consist of the individual(s) chosen for the operation and, for crossover, the points chosen within both participating individuals.

Construction of the audit trail starts with the individuals of the initial random generation (generation 0). Certain additional information, such as the individual's rank location in the population (found by sorting by normalized fitness) and its standardized fitness, is also carried along as a convenience in interpreting the genealogy. Then, as each operation is performed to create a new individual for the next generation, a list is recursively formed consisting of the type of operation performed, participating individual(s), its details (e.g., crossover point selected), and a pointer to the audit trail previously assembled for the individual(s) participating in that operation.

An individual occurring at generation h has up to 2^{h+1} ancestors. The number of ancestors is less than 2^{h+1} to the extent that operations other than crossover are involved and to the extent that an individual crosses over with itself. For example, an individual occurring at generation 9 has up to 1024 ancestors. Note that an ancestor often appears more than once in this genealogy because all selections of individuals to participate in the basic genetic operations are skewed in proportion to fitness with reselection allowed. Moreover, even for a modest value of h, 2^{h+1} will typically be greater than the population size. This repetition does nothing to reduce the size of the genealogical tree. Even with the use of pointers from descendents back to ancestors, construction of a complete genealogical audit trail is exponentially expensive in computer time and memory. The audit trail must be constructed for each individual of each generation because the correct individual(s) eventually solving the problem is (are) not known in advance. Thus, there are 4000 audit trails. By generation 9, each trail recursively incorporates information about operations involving up to 1024 ancestors. The audit trail for the correct individual in generation 9 occupies about 27 densely printed pages.

The creative role of crossover and case splitting is illustrated by an examination of the genealogical audit trail for the correct individual emerging at generation 9. This individual is the child resulting from the most common genetic operation used in the process, namely crossover. The first parent from generation 8 had rank location 58 (out of 4000, with rank 0 being the best) in the population and scored 1792 hits (out of 2048). The second parent from generation 8 had rank location 1 and scored 1920 hits. It is typical that the individuals selected to participate in crossover have relatively high rank locations in the population, since crossover is performed among individuals in a mating pool created proportional to fitness.

The first parent from generation 8 (scoring 1792) was

```
(IF A0  (IF A2 D7 D3)
        (IF A2 (IF A1 D6 D4)
               (IF A2 D4 (IF A1 D2 (IF A2 D7 D0)))))
```

Figure 10.15 shows this first parent. Note that this first parent starts by examining address bit A0. If A0 is T, the boldface underscored portion then examines address bit A2. It then, partially blindly, makes the output equal D7 or D3 without even considering address bit A1. Moreover, this portion does not even contain data bits D1 and D5.

On the other hand, when A0 is NIL, this first parent is correct. In that event, it examines A2; if A2 is T, it then examines A1 and makes the output equal to D6 or D4, according to whether A1 is T or NIL. Moreover, if A2 is NIL, it twice retests A2 (unnecessarily, but harmlessly) and then correctly makes the output equal to (IF A1 D2 D0). Note that the correct portion of this first parent, namely, the subexpression

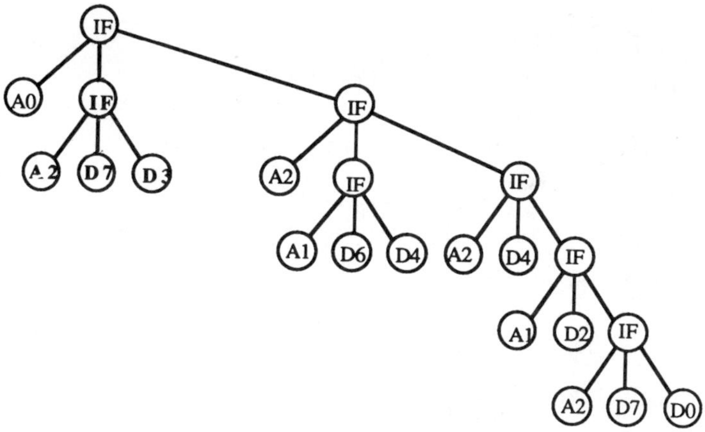

Figure 10.15 *First parent (scoring 1792 hits) from generation 8 for 100% correct individual in generation 9.*

```
(IF A2 (IF A1 D6 D4)
       (IF A2 D4 (IF A1 D2 (IF A2 D7 D0))))
```

is itself a 6-multiplexer.

The embedded 6-multiplexer tests A2 and A1 and correctly selects among D6, D4, D2, and D0. This fact becomes clearer if we simplify this subexpression by removing the two extraneous tests and D7 (which is unreachable). We get

```
(IF A2 (IF A1 D6 D4)
       (IF A1 D2 D0))
```

In other words, this imperfect first parent handles part of its environment (the even-numbered data bits) correctly and part incorrectly (the odd-numbered data bits).

The tree representing this first parent has 22 points. The crossover point chosen at random at the end of generation 8 was point 3 and corresponds to the second occurrence of IF function. That is, the crossover fragment consists of the incorrect subexpression

```
(IF A2 D7 D3)
```

The second parent from generation 8 (scoring 1920 hits) was

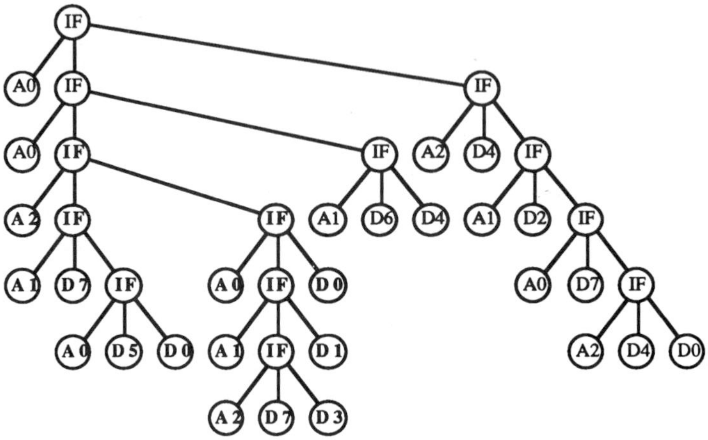

Figure 10.16 *Second parent (scoring 1920 hits) from generation 8 for 100% correct individual in generation 9.*

```
(IF A0 (IF A0 (IF A2 (IF A1 D7 (IF A0 D5 D0))
                        (IF A0 (IF A1 (IF A2 D7
                                             D3)
                                      D1)
                               D0))
               (IF A1 D6 D4))
       (IF A2 D4
               (IF A1 D2 (IF A0 D7 (IF A2 D4 D0)))))
```

See Figure 10.16. The tree representing this second parent has 40 points. The crossover point chosen at random was point 5, which corresponds to the third occurrence of the IF function. That is, the crossover fragment consists of the boldface underscored subexpression of this second parent.

This subexpression correctly handles the case when A0 is T (i.e., the odd-numbered addresses). It makes the output equal to D7 when the address bits are 111; it makes the output equal to D5 when the address bits are 101; it makes the output equal to D3 when the address bits are 011; and it makes the output equal to D1 when the address bits are 001.

Note that the correct portion of this second parent, namely, the subexpression

```
(IF A2 (IF A1 D7 (IF A0 D5 D0))
       (IF A0 (IF A1 (IF A2 D7 D3) D1) D0))
```

is itself a 6-multiplexer. This embedded 6-multiplexer tests A2 and A1 and

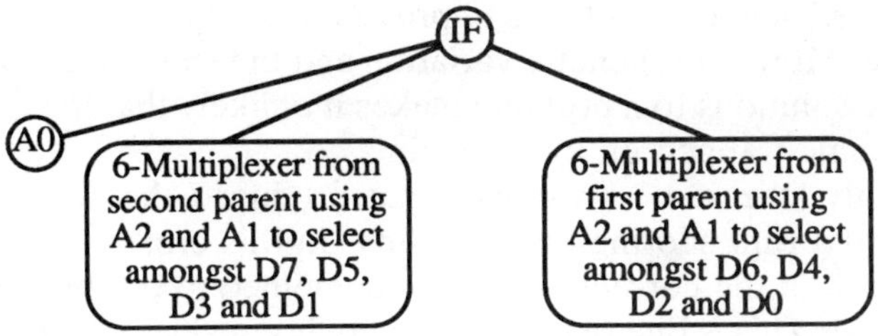

Figure 10.17 *Simplified 100% correct individual from generation 9 shown as a hierarchy of two 6-multiplexers.*

correctly selects among D7, D5, D3, and D1. This fact becomes clearer if we simplify this subexpression as

```
(IF A2 (IF A1 D7 D5)
       (IF A1 D3 D1))
```

In other words, this imperfect second parent handles part of its environment correctly (odd-numbered data bits) and part of its environment incorrectly (even-numbered data bits).

Even though neither parent is perfect, they contain complementary, coadapted portions that, when mated, produce a correct offspring individual. In effect, the creative effect of the crossover operation blends the two cases of the implicitly "case-split" environment into a single correct solution.

Figure 10.17 shows this case splitting by showing the correct offspring from generation 9 as two 6-multiplexers. Figure 10.18 also shows this simplified version of the correct individual from generation 9.

Not all crossovers between individuals are useful and productive. A large fraction of the individuals produced by genetic operations are useless. But the existence of a population of alternative solutions to a problem provides the ingredients with which genetic recombination (crossover) can produce some improved individuals. The relentless pressure of natural selection

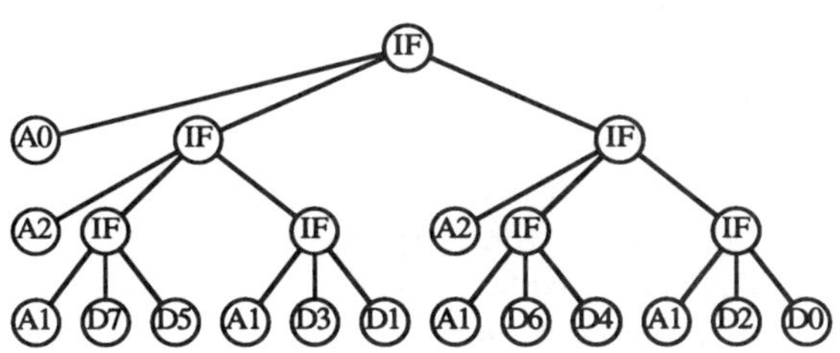

Figure 10.18 *Simplified 100% correct individual from generation 9 shown as a hierarchy of two 6-multiplexers.*

based on fitness then causes these improved individuals to be preserved and to proliferate. Moreover, genetic variation and the existence of a population of alternative solutions to a problem makes it unlikely that the entire population will become trapped on local maxima.

Interestingly, the same crossover that produced the correct individual also produced a runt scoring only 256 hits. In this crossover, the two fragments not used in the correct individual combined to produce an unusually unfit individual. This is one reason why there is considerable variability from generation to generation in the worst single individual in the population.

As one traces the ancestry of the correct individual created in generation 9 into the genealogical audit tree (i.e., toward earlier generations), one encounters parents scoring generally fewer and fewer hits. That is, one encounters more S-expressions that perform irrelevant, counterproductive, partially blind, and incorrect work. But if we look at the sequence of hits in the forward direction, we see localized hill climbing in the search space occurring in parallel throughout the population as the creative operation of crossover recombines complementary, coadapted portions of parents to produce improved offspring.

10.6.2 Hierarchies and Default Hierarchies

Note that the result of the GP paradigm is always hierarchical. As we saw, the solution to the 11-multiplexer problem was a hierarchy consisting of two 6-multiplexers. In one run where we applied the GP paradigm to the simpler Boolean 6-multiplexer, we obtained the correct solution

```
(IF (AND A0 A1) D3 (IF A0 D1 (IF A1 D2 D0)))
```

which is also a hierarchy. It correctly handles the fitness cases where (AND A0 A1) is true and the remaining fitness cases where it is false.

Default hierarchies often emerge from the GP paradigm. A default hierarchy incorporates partially correct subrules into a perfect overall procedure by allowing the partially correct (default) subrules to handle the majority of the environment and then dealing in a different way with specific exceptional cases in the environment. The previous S-expression is a default hierarchy in which the output defaults to

```
(IF A0 D1 (IF A1 D2 D0))
```

three quarters of the time. However, in the specific exceptional fitness case where A0 and A1 are both T, the output is D3.

Default hierarchies are considered desirable in induction problems [11,12] because they are often parsimonious and are a humanlike way of dealing with situations. Wilson's [13] noteworthy BOOLE experiments originally found a set of eight If-Then classifier system rules for the Boolean 6-multiplexer that correctly (but tediously) handled each subcase of the problem. Subsequently, Wilson [14] modified the credit allocation scheme and successfully produced a default hierarchy.

10.6.3 Results over a Series of Runs

In the previous section we described a run of the GP paradigm in which we obtained a solution to the Boolean 11-multiplexer problem.

A basic statistic associated with runs of the GP paradigm (and the genetic algorithm) is the probability of success p_s that a run produces a desired result within a specified number of generations N_{gen} with a population of size M. We obtain p_s by making a substantial number of runs.

The value of p_s depends strongly on the choices of

- Population size M
- Maximum number of generations N_{gen} to be run,
- Secondary parameters of the genetic algorithm,
- All the fixed minor details of our implementation of the algorithm.

Figure 10.19 shows the probability of success p_s over 200 generations for 309 runs of the Boolean 6-multiplexer problem. This graph rises monotonically, since the probability is cumulative from generation 0, and approaches 100% asymptotically as the number of generations grows. There is a point after which additional generations produce only small increases in the probability of success p_s. For example, at generation 50, p_s is about 67%. At generation 100, p_s is 83%. At generation 150, p_s is 87%. At generation 200, p_s is 89%.

Neither conventional genetic algorithms (GA) operating on fixed-length

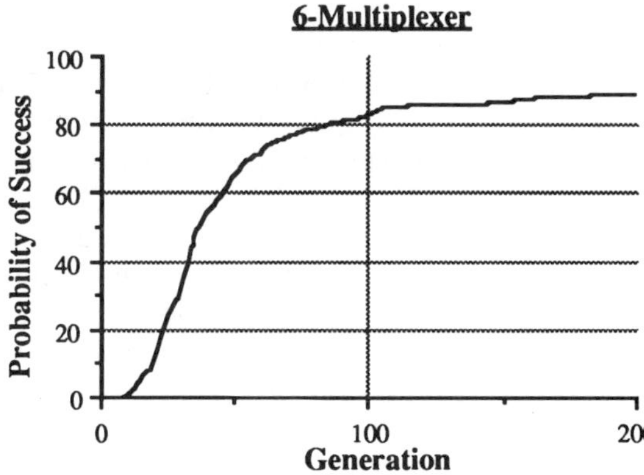

Figure 10.19 *Probability of success for runs of Boolean 6-multiplexer for 200 generations.*

character strings nor the GP paradigm always produce the desired results on a run of the algorithm. For one thing, GA inherently involve probabilistic steps. Thus, anything can happen on a run and nothing is guaranteed. Some runs simply do not produce the desired results within a particular amount of time. For example, GA may prematurely converge (i.e., converge to a sub-optimal result). The exponentially increasing allocation of future trials on the basis of the current estimates of the fitness of the population is both the strength and weakness of GA. It is a strength because it is the fundamental reason why GA work in the first place. It is a weakness because it may result in premature convergence.

The effects of randomness, premature convergence, unfortuitous initial conditions, and other chaotic effects on GA can be minimized by making entirely separate multiple independent runs, which lend themselves to parallel computer architectures and yield virtually linear speedup, but that is not the point here. The best single individual from all of these runs is then designated as the problem solution.

One way to measure the amount of computational resources required by the GP paradigm (or the GA in general) is to determine the likely number of independent runs needed to produce a desired result with a certain probability, say $z = 99\%$. Once we determine the likely number of independent runs required, we can then multiply this number by the amount of processing required for each run.

Once we have obtained the probability of success p_s by measurement, we can say that the probability of achieving the desired result at least once within K runs is $1 - (1 - p_s)^K$. If we are seeking to achieve the desired result with a probability of, say, $z = 1 - \varepsilon = 99\%$, then the number K of independent runs (niches) required is

$$\frac{\log(1 - z)}{\log(1 - p_s)} = \frac{\log \varepsilon}{\log(1 - p_s)} \qquad \text{where } \varepsilon = 1 - z$$

rounded up to the next highest integer. For example, if p_s is 90%, then K is 2.

We can measure the number of individuals that need to be processed by a GA to solve a problem. For example, we ran 54 runs of the Boolean 11-multiplexer problem with $M = 4000$ and $N_{\text{gen}} = 201$ (i.e., generation 0 plus 200 additional generations).

Figure 10.20 shows the probability of success p_s of a run for various numbers of generations for $M = 4000$. By generation 10, for example, only about 28% of the runs produced at least one individual with a perfect score of 2048 matches. By generation 15, 78% of the runs produced a perfect solution. By generation 20, 90% of the runs produced a perfect solution.

With $p_s = 90\%$ by generation 20, the previous formula indicates that $K = 2$ independent runs are required to ensure a 99% probability of solving the problem. Therefore, the number of individuals that need to be processed to ensure the 99% probability is no more than 160,000 (i.e., $2 \times 20 \times 4000$).

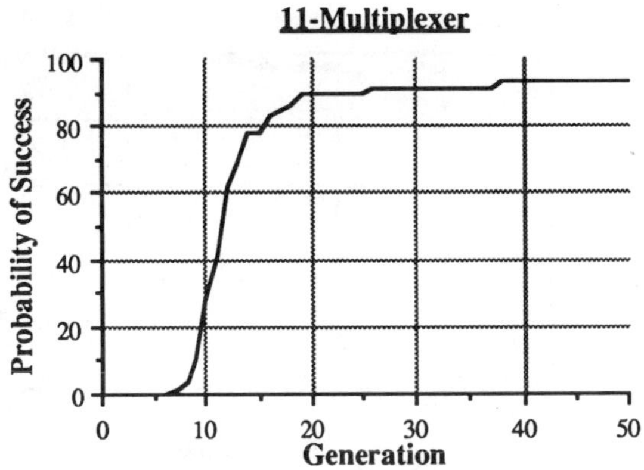

Figure 10.20 *Probability of success for runs of 11-multiplexer problem with population size* M = *4000.*

This number does not reflect the fact that some successful runs would, in practice, be terminated without executing all 20 generations. The size of the search space (2^{2048}) for the 11-multiplexer is very large in relation to the number of individuals that need to be processed (no more than 160,000).

In the Boolean 11-multiplexer problem described, we chose an unusually large and probably nonoptimal population size (i.e., 4000) so as to produce a solution in a sufficiently small number of generations (i.e., 9) to allow us to economically run a genealogical audit trail.

In general, the selection of the optimal population size is a difficult problem for both the GP paradigm and the conventional GA operating on strings. The number of individuals that must be processed to give a 99% probability of finding a solution is a complex function of all the factors that influence p_s. These factors include M, N_{gen}, various secondary parameters, and all other choices (e.g., method of creating the initial population) involved in the run.

Figure 10.21, for example, shows p_s of a run of the 6-multiplexer problem for various numbers of generations $M = 500$, $M = 1000$, and $M = 2000$. Clearly, the optimal population size is not 500, but some larger number in the neighborhood of 1000 to 2000.

10.6.4 Nonrandomness of Results

The number of possible compositions using the sets of available functions and available terminals is very large. In particular, the number of possible trees representing such compositions increases rapidly as a function of the number of points in the tree. This is true because of the large number of ways of labeling the points of a tree with functions and terminals. The number of possible compositions of functions is very large in relation to the 40,000

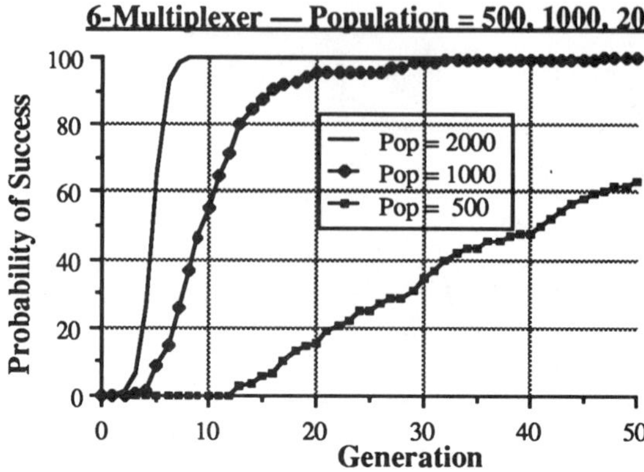

Figure 10.21 *Probability of success for runs of the 6-multiplexer problem with population size* M = *500, 1000, and 2000.*

individuals processed in generations 0 through 9 in the run of the GP paradigm previously described or the 160,000 previously mentioned.

There is a theoretical possibility that the probability of a solution to a problem may be low in the original search space of the Boolean 11-multiplexer problem (i.e., all Boolean functions of 11 arguments), but that the probability of randomly generating a composition of functions that solves the problem might be significantly higher in the space of randomly generated compositions of functions. The Boolean 11-multiplexer function is a unique function out of the $2^{2^{11}} = 2^{2048}$ possible Boolean functions of 11 arguments and 1 output. The probability of randomly choosing zeros and ones for the 2^{11} lines of a truth table so as to create this Boolean function is only 1 in $2^{2^{11}}$. However, there is a theoretical possibility that the probability of randomly generating a composition of the functions AND, OR, NOT, and IF that performs the 11-multiplexer function might be better than 1 in 2^{2048}. There is no a priori reason to believe that this is so—that is, that compositions of functions that solve the Boolean multiplexer problem are denser in the space of randomly generated compositions of functions than solutions in the original search space.

To test this possibility, we performed the following control experiment for the Boolean 11-multiplexer problem. We generated 5,000,000 random S-expression to see if we could randomly generate a composition of functions that solved the problem. We used the same algorithm and parameters used to generate the initial random population in the normal runs of the problem. No correct individual was found in this blind search. In addition, on the first 1,000,000 random S-expressions, we computed an entire hits histogram of raw fitness values. The high score in this histogram was only 1408 hits (out of a possible 2048), and the low score was 704 hits. Moreover, only 10 individuals achieved 1408. The high point of the hits histogram distribution came at 1152 hits, the second highest at 896 hits, and the third highest at 1024 hits. The size of the search space (2^{2048}) for the 11-multiplexer is very large in relation to the number of individuals processed in a typical run solving the 11-multiplexer.

A similar control experiment was conducted for the Boolean 6-multiplexer problem (with a search space of $2^{2^6} = 2^{64}$) involving 10,000,000 individuals. As before, no correct individual was found in this blind random search. In fact, no individual had more than 52 (of 64 possible) hits. As with the 11-multiplexer, the size of the search space is very large in relation to the number of individuals processed in a typical run solving the 6-multiplexer.

We conclude that solutions to these problems in the space of randomly generated compositions of functions are not denser than solutions in the original search space of the problem. Therefore, we conclude that the results described here are not the fruits of random search.

We have evidence suggesting that the solutions to many functions are appreciably *sparser* in the space of randomly generated compositions of functions than solutions in the original search space of the problem. Consider, for example, the odd-2-parity function with two Boolean arguments (i.e., exclusive-OR (XOR) function). The odd-k-parity function of k Boolean arguments returns T if the number of arguments equal to T is odd, and returns NIL otherwise. There are only $2^{2^2} = 2^4 = 16$ possible Boolean functions with two Boolean arguments and one output. Thus, in the search space of truth tables for Boolean functions, the probability of randomly choosing T's and NILs for the 16 lines of a truth table that realizes this Boolean function is only 1 in 16.

First, we generated 100,000 random individuals using the function set F = {AND, OR, NOT}. If randomly generated compositions of the basic Boolean functions that realize the XOR function were as dense as solutions are in the original search space of the problem (i.e., the space of truth tables for Boolean functions of two arguments), we would expect about 6250 in 100,000 (i.e., 1 in 16) random compositions of functions to realize XOR. Instead, we found that only 110 out of 100,000 randomly generated compositions realized the XOR, a frequency of only 1 in 909. In other words, randomly generated compositions of functions realizing the XOR are about 57 times sparser than solutions in the original search space of truth tables for Boolean functions.

Second, we generated an additional 100,000 random individuals, using the function set F = {AND, OR, NOT, IF}. We found that only 116 out of 100,000 randomly generated compositions realized the XOR (a frequency of 1 in 862). That is, with this second function set, randomly generated compositions of functions realizing the XOR are about 54 times sparser than solutions in the original search space of truth tables for Boolean functions.

Third, we generated 100,000 random individuals using the function set F = {AND, OR, NAND, NOR}. We found that only 118 out of 100,000 randomly generated compositions realized the XOR (a frequency of 1 in 846). That is, randomly generated compositions of functions realizing XOR are about 53 times sparser than solutions in the original search space of truth tables for Boolean functions.

In other words, solutions to the odd-parity (XOR) function with two arguments appear to be 53 to 57 times sparser in the space of randomly generated compositions of functions than solutions in the original search space of the problem.

We then performed similar experiments on two Boolean functions with three Boolean arguments and one output, namely, the odd-3-parity function and the 3-multiplexer function (i.e., the IF-THEN-ELSE function). There are only $2^{2^3} = 2^8 = 256$ Boolean functions with three Boolean arguments and one output. The probability of randomly choosing a particular combination of T's and NILs for the 256 lines of a truth table is 1 in 256, so we should expect about 39,063 random compositions per 10,000,000 to realize a particular Boolean function. However, after randomly generating 10,000,000 compositions of AND, OR, and NOT, we found only 730 3-multiplexers and no odd-3-parity functions. That is, our randomly generated compositions of functions realizing the 3-multiplexer function are about 54 times sparser than solutions in the original search space of Boolean functions. We cannot make the comparison for the odd-3-parity function, but it is presumably tens of thousands of times scarcer than the one in 256.

These three results concerning the odd-3-parity function, the 3-multiplexer function, and the odd-2-parity (XOR) function should not be too surprising, since the parity and multiplexer functions have long been identified by researchers as functions that often pose difficulties for paradigms for machine learning, artificial intelligence, neural nets, and classifier systems [13,14,20,21].

In summary, as to these bench-mark Boolean functions, compositions of functions solving the problem are substantially *less dense* than solutions in the search space of the original problem.

The reader would do well to remember the origin of the concern that compositions of functions solving a problem might be denser than solutions to the problem in the search space of the original problem. In Lenat's work on discovering mathematical laws via heuristic search [22] and related areas [23], the mathematical laws being sought were stated, in many cases, directly in terms of the list (the primitive data type of LISP). In addition, the lists in Lenat's artificial mathematician (AM) laws were manipulated by list manipulation functions that are unique or peculiar to LISP. Specifically, in many experiments in Lenat [22], the mathematical laws sought were stated directly in terms of lists and list manipulation functions such as CAR (which returns the first element of a list), CDR (which returns the tail of a list), and so on. In his *mea culpa* article "Why AM and EURISKO appear to work" [24], Lenat recognized that LISP syntax may have overly facilitated discovery of his previously reported results, namely, mathematical laws stated in terms of LISP's list manipulation functions and LISP's primitive object (i.e., the list).

In contrast, the problems here are neither stated nor solved in terms of objects or operators unique to LISP. The solution to the Boolean multiplexer function is expressed in terms of ordinary Boolean functions. The solutions to the numerical problems (such as symbolic regression, broom balancing) are expressed in terms of ordinary arithmetic operations. The solutions to the planning problems (such as block stacking) are expressed in terms of ordinary iteration operations and various domain-specific robotic actions (move a block from one place to another).

Virtually any programming language could be used to express these solutions. LISP was chosen primarily because of its many convenient features (most importantly, that data and programs have the same form, which corresponds to the parse tree of a computer program). LISP was not chosen because of the list as a primitive data type or because of its functions for manipulating lists (e.g., CAR and CDR). Neither lists nor list manipulation functions are involved in any of the problems described here (except in the irrelevant and indirect sense that LISP uses lists to do things, unseen by the user, that other programming languages do in different ways).

In summary, there is no a priori reason (nor any reason we have since discovered) to think that there is anything about the syntax of the programs generated by the GP paradigm, nor the syntax of LISP that makes it easier to discover solutions to problems involving ordinary (i.e., nonlist) objects and functions. In addition, the control experiments verify that the results obtained are not the fruits of a random search.

10.7 ARTIFICIAL ANT PROBLEM

As a second illustration of the GP paradigm, we consider a task devised by Jefferson et al. [25] for an artificial ant attempting to find the food lying along an irregular trail. The setting for the problem is a 32×32 toroidal grid in the plane. The John Muir trail (and the somewhat more difficult Sante Fe trail designed by Christopher Langton) is an irregular winding trail with food in 89 of the 1024 cells. The Santa Fe rail has single gaps, double gaps, single gaps at corners, double gaps (knight moves) at corners, and triple gaps (long knight moves) at corners. The artificial ant begins in the cell identified by the coordinates (0, 0) and is facing East.

The Santa Fe trail is shown in Figure 10.22. Food is represented by solid black squares, gaps in the trail by gray squares. The numbers identify key features of the trail in terms of the number of pieces of food occurring up to that feature. For example, the number 3 highlights the first corner. It appears after three pieces of food. Similarly, the number 11 highlights the first gap in the tail. The number 38 highlights the first knight's move.

The goal of this problem is to find a computer program for performing the task of following the trail and eating all of the food with a reasonable number of time steps.

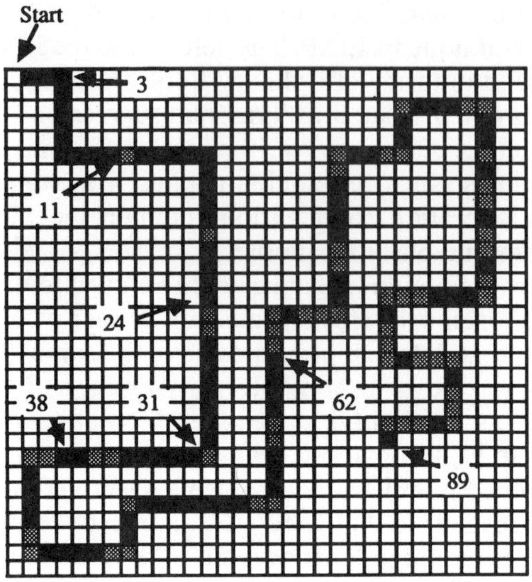

Figure 10.22 *Santa Fe trail for the artificial ant problem with 89 pieces of food shown in black.*

The artificial ant has a very narrow and limited view of the world. In particular, the ant has a sensor that can see only the single immediately adjacent cell in the direction the ant is currently facing. Specifically, the ant can execute one of four functions:

1. RIGHT turns the ant right (and does not move the ant).
2. LEFT turns the ant left (and does not move the ant).
3. MOVE moves the ant forward in the direction it is facing. When an ant moves into a square, it eats the food, if any, in that square.
4. IF-FOOD-HERE senses the contents of the single immediately adjacent cell in the direction the ant is facing and allows one of two alternative actions to be taken based on whether food is present.

When Jefferson et al. used the conventional GA operating on strings to find the finite-state automaton to solve this problem, they had to develop a representation scheme to convert the state transition table of the potential automaton into binary strings of length 453. In the GP paradigm, the problem can be approached and solved in a more natural and direct way.

Recall that in the first two steps we identify the sets of terminals and functions. We adopt Jefferson's four operators, as previously listed.

We are not primarily concerned with the three overt state variables of the ant (vertical and horizontal positions of the ant on the grid and the direction the ant is facing), but with finding food. So we must use the information that the ant's very limited sensor provides about food in the outside world. Thus, one natural approach to this problem using the GP paradigm is to put the sensing function IF-FOOD-HERE into the function set. This function has two arguments: It executes the first argument if the ant's sensor senses food; otherwise, it executes the second argument.

If the function set contains the operation that processes information, the terminal set should contain the actions that the ant should take given the outcomes of this information processing. Thus,

$$T = \text{(MOVE), (RIGHT), (LEFT)}$$

These three terminals are actually functions with no arguments that operate via their side effects on the ant's state. They take one time step each.

Although the IF-FOOD-HERE function is the only essential function for this problem, it is often useful to include some connective glue in the function set to facilitate the formation of sequences of operations. PROGN is the Common LISP connective function that sequentially executes its arguments from left to right as individual steps in a program. For example,

```
(PROGN (RIGHT) (LEFT))
```

turns the ant to the right and then to the left. It is often useful to include the PROGN function in the function set with both two and three arguments. Thus, the function set is

$$F = \{\text{IF-FOOD-HERE, PROGN, PROGN}\}$$

taking two, two, and three arguments, respectively.

The third major step is to identify the fitness function. The natural measure of fitness of a computer program in this problem is the amount of food found by an ant executing the program. We allowed the ant 400 time steps for the program. Thus, the raw fitness of the computer program is the amount of food (ranging from 0 to 89) that the ant has found within the maximum allowed amount of time.

For this problem, a bigger value of raw fitness (i.e., amount of food eaten) is better. Thus, standardized fitness is the maximum value of raw fitness (i.e., 89) minus raw fitness.

Note that there are no explicit fitness cases. The implicit fitness cases are the various states of the ant that arise along its actual trajectory. These states sufficiently represent this problem to allow the ant to learn to solve it.

The GP paradigm starts with the generation of 500 random computer programs recursively composed from the available functions and terminals.

Predictably, this initial population includes a wide variety of highly unfit programs. The most common type of individual in the initial random population fails to move at all. For example, (PROGN (RIGHT) (LEFT)) unconditionally turns the ant right and left while not moving the ant anywhere. Similarly, the program (IF-FOOD-HERE (RIGHT) (LEFT)) senses some information from the outside world and then conditionally turns the ant various ways, though still not moving it. Both of these highly unfit individuals get 0 of the 89 pieces of food when they are mercifully terminated by the expiration of the allotted time.

Some randomly generated computer programs move without turning. For example, (PROGN (MOVE) (MOVE)) shoots across the grid from West to East without looking or turning. This highly active, albeit undirected, behavior finds 3 of the 89 pieces of food.

Another highly unfit random computer program (which we call the "quilter" because it traces a quiltlike pattern across the toroidal grid) moves and turns without looking:

```
(PROGN (RIGHT)
       (PROGN (MOVE) (MOVE) (MOVE))
       (PROGN (LEFT) (MOVE)))
```

Yet another program (the "looper") finds the first 11 pieces of food on the trail and then goes into an infinite loop when it encounters the first single gap in the trail. One program (the "avoider") correctly observes some of the food along the trail until the first gap in the trail. Then it actively avoids this food by carefully moving around it until it eventually returns to its starting point. The S-expression for the avoider is

```
(IF-FOOD-HERE (RIGHT)
              (IF-FOOD-HERE (RIGHT)
                            (PROGN (MOVE) (LEFT))))
```

The avoider's path is marked by X's in Figure 10.23.

In one run, the best single individual in the initial random population was able to find 32 of the 89 pieces of food, whereas the worst single individual in the population found none of the food. The average amount of food found was about 3.5 pieces.

The Darwinian reproduction operation and the genetic crossover operation were then applied to parents selected from the current population with probabilities proportionate to fitness to breed a new population of offspring computer programs.

Figure 10.24 shows the standardized fitness of the worst single individual, the standardized fitness of the best single individual, and the average standardized fitness of the population between generations 0 and 21 of one run of the artificial ant. The standardized fitness of the best single individual gener-

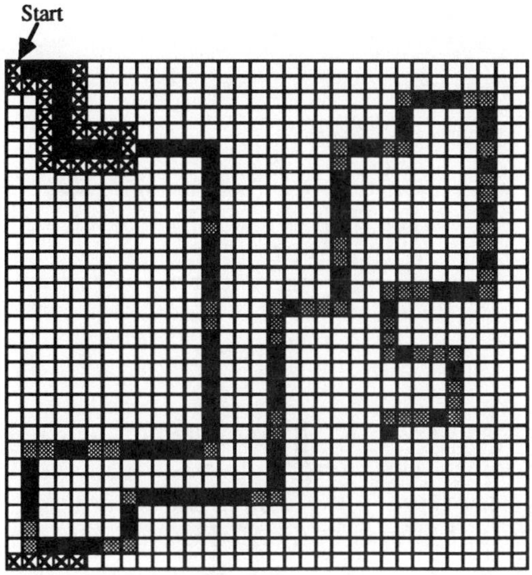

Figure 10.23 *Avoider's path along Santa Fe trail.*

ally improves (i.e., trends toward zero) from generation to generation, although this improvement is not monotonic. The average value of standardized fitness value starts at about 85.5 (i.e., 3.5 pieces of food found) and then generally improves from generation to generation. Note that there is at least one individual in the population at every generation that finds no food at all, so the worst-of-generation plot runs horizontally across the top of the graph with a fitness value of 89 (i.e., zero pieces of food).

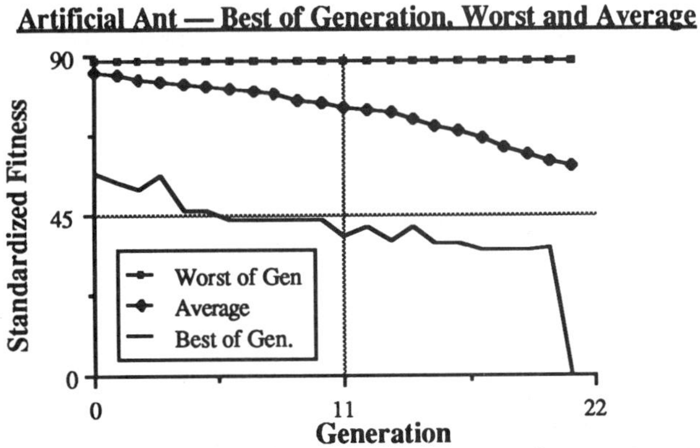

Figure 10.24 *Standardized fitness of worst-of-generation individual, average standardized fitness of population, and standardized fitness of best-of-generation individual for the artificial ant problem.*

The individual computer program scoring 89 out of 89 that emerged on generation 21 is

```
(IF-FOOD-HERE (MOVE)
              (PROGN (LEFT)
                     (PROGN (IF-FOOD-HERE (MOVE)
                                          (RIGHT))
                     (PROGN (RIGHT)
                            (PROGN (LEFT)
                                   (RIGHT))))
                     (PROGN (IF-FOOD–HERE (MOVE)
                                          (LEFT))
                            (MOVE))))
```

This S-expression has 18 points and is graphed in Figure 10.25. It is a correct solution to this problem. The interpretation is as follows: The test IF-FOOD-HERE senses whether there is any food in the square that the ant is facing. If food is present, the left branch of the IF-FOOD-HERE test is executed and the ant MOVES forward. When the ant moves onto a place on the grid with food, the food is eaten and the ant receives credit for the food.

If the IF-FOOD-HERE test at the beginning of the S-expression sense no food, the ant enters the three-step PROGN sequence immediately below the IF-FOOD-HERE test. The ant first turns LEFT. Then a two-step PROGN sequence begins with the test IF-FOOD-HERE. If food is present, the ant MOVES forward. If not, the ant turns RIGHT. Then the ant turns RIGHT again. Then the ant pointlessly turns LEFT and RIGHT in another two-step PROGN sequence. The net effect is that the ant is now facing right relative to its initial facing direction. The ant next executes the final two-step PROGN subtree at the far right of the figure. If the ant now sense food via the IF-FOOD-HERE test, the ant MOVES forward. Otherwise, the ant turns LEFT. The ant has now returned to its initial facing direction. The ant now unconditionally MOVES. Note that there is no testing of the backwards directions. The repeated application of this control program allows the ant to

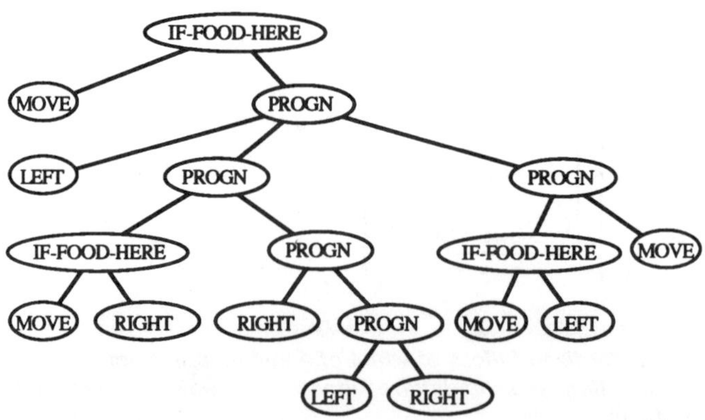

Figure 10.25 *Solution to artificial ant problem from generation 21.*

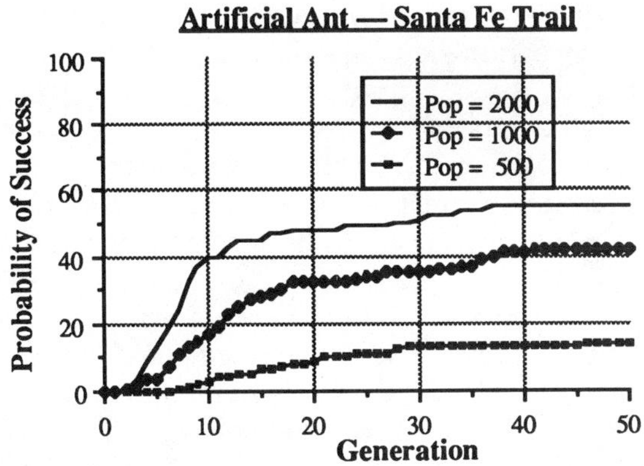

Figure 10.26 *Probability of success for the artificial ant problem for* M = *500, 1000, and 2000.*

negotiate all of the gaps and irregularities of the trail and to collect all of the food in the allotted time.

In summary, we have shown how to use the GP paradigm to genetically breed a computer program that successfully navigates the artificial ant to find 100% of the food along the Santa Fe trail.

Note that in the GP paradigm, we made no assumption in advance about the size, shape, or complexity of the eventual solution. The solution found in generation 21 had 18 points. We did not specify that the solution would have 21 points nor did we specify the shape or content of the S-expression. The size, shape, and content of the S-expression that solves this problem evolved in response to the selective pressure provided by the fitness measure (i.e., amount of foot eaten).

Figure 10.26 shows the probability of success p_s (computed from 55 runs) that at least one S-expression causes the artificial ant to traverse the entire trail and collect all 89 pieces of food (before timing out) as a function of the number of generations for population sizes of 500, 1000, and 2000. In particular, the probability of success p_s by generation 10 with a population size of 2000 is 40%. With $p_s = 40\%$, K is 9, and no more than 180,000 individuals (i.e., 9 times 2000 times 10) need to be processed to ensure a 99% probability of solving the problem.

10.8 SOLVING A PAIR OF LINEAR EQUATIONS

Suppose we want to solve a pair of consistent, nonindeterminate linear equations

$$a_{11}x_1 + a_{12}x_2 = b_1$$

$$a_{21}x_1 + a_{22}x_2 = b_2$$

for the first of its two real-valued variables (x_1). In other words, we are seeking a computer program that takes a_{11}, a_{12}, a_{21}, a_{22}, b_1, and b_2 as its inputs and produces x_1 as its output. Without loss of generality, we can assume that the coefficients of the equations were prenormalized so the determinant is 1. The solution can be viewed as a search for a mathematical expression (S-expression) from the hyperspace of possible mathematical expressions that can be composed from a set of available functions and arguments.

First we identify the set of terminals. In previous problems, the terminal set consisted of the information that the mathematical expression must process to solve the problem. Here the information that must be processed by a computer program to find x_1 are the values of a_{11}, a_{12}, a_{21}, a_{22}, b_1, and b_2. Thus, the terminal set is

$$T = \{\text{A11, A12, A21, A22, B1, B2}\}$$

Next, we identify the set of functions used to generate expressions that attempt to fit the finite sample of data. The function set might consist of addition (+), subtraction (−), multiplication (*), and the protected division function (%) (Sec. 10.5.1):

$$F = \{+, -, *, \%\}$$

Each function takes two arguments.

Third, we identify the fitness function. The fitness cases used to evaluate the fitness of any proposed S-expression are 10 randomly generated pairs of consistent, nonindeterminate linear equations (i.e., set of values of a_{11}, a_{12}, a_{21}, a_{22}, b_1, and b_2 and the associated correct values of x_1 and x_2). In this problem, the raw fitness is measured by the erroneousness of the S-expression. Each genetically produced S-expression is evaluated for fitness in the following way: First, the value of x_1 produced by the S-expression as the solution to equation pair i (i.e., x^g_{1i}) is substituted into one equation of pair i to find the corresponding value of x_2 (i.e., x^g_{2i}). Next, we determine the Euclidean distance in the plane between the genetically produced solution point (x^g_{1i}, x^g_{2i}) for equation pair i and the actual solution point (x^s_{1i}, x^s_{2i}) for equation pair i. Then these distances are summed over all 10 pairs of equations. This sum is the raw fitness of the S-expression. If the S-expression were a correct general formula for solving a pair of linear equations, this sum would be zero. Thus, standardized fitness equals raw fitness for this problem.

The auxiliary hits measure is defined such that we score one hit if the distance between the genetically produced solution point and the actual solution point for a pair of equations is less than 0.01. Figure 10.27 shows, for i of 1 and 2 only, the distance (error) between (x^g_{1i}, x^g_{2i}) and (x^s_{1i}, x^s_{2i}). The lines connect the two points that apply to an equation pair. Thus, they

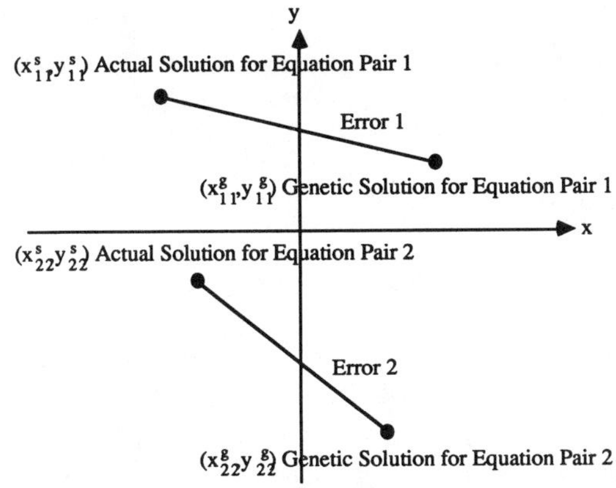

Figure 10.27 *The line in the top half of this figure connects the actual solution point for equation pair 1 with the genetically produced solution point for equation pair 1. This line represents the error associated with equation pair 1. The line in the bottom half of this figure represents the error for equation pair 2.*

graphically represent the error. If the S-expression were the correct general formula for solving a pair of linear equations, the two points would overlap and there would be no line (i.e., the error would be zero).

Predictably, this initial population of random S-expressions includes a wide variety of highly unfit S-expressions. The worst individual from the initial random population (i.e., generation 0) has a raw fitness value of 119,051. The average raw fitness for generation 0 (the initial random generation) is 2622. This value serves as a baseline by which to measure future (nonrandom) performance. The average raw fitness of the population immediately begins improving from the baseline value for generation 0 of 2622 to 632, 341, 342, 309, and so on. In addition, the worst individual in the population also begins improving from 119,051 for generation 0 to 68,129, 2094, and so on.

The single best individual S-expression from generation 0 had a raw fitness value of 125.8 and is

```
(+ (- A12 (* A12 B2)) (+ (* A12 B1) B2))
```

This S-expression is equivalent to

$$a_{12}b_1 + b_2 + a_{12} - a_{12}b_2$$

The best individual begins improving and has a fitness value of 106 for generations 1 and 2, 103 for generation 3 through 5, 102 for generations 6 through 20.

The best single S-expression in generations 21 and 22 had a fitness value of 62 and is

```
(+ (- A12 (* A12 B2)) (* A22 B1))
```

which is equivalent to

$$a_{22}b_1 + a_{12} - a_{12}b_2$$

This individual differed from the known correct solution by only one term, +A12.

The best single S-expression in generations 23 through 26 had a raw fitness value of 58 and is

```
(+ (- A22 (* A12 B2)) (* A22 B1))
```

which is equivalent to

$$a_{22}b_1 + a_{22} - a_{12}b_2$$

This individual differed from the known correct solution by only one term, +A22.

Starting with generation 27, a perfect solution for x_1 emerges:

```
(- (* A22 B1) (* A12 B2))
```

which is equivalent to $a_{22}b_1 - a_{12}b_2$.

Figure 10.28 shows the probability of success p_s (based on 122 runs) that at least one S-expression scores 10 hits (i.e., the error is less than 0.01 for all 10 pairs of equations) as a function of the number of generations for a

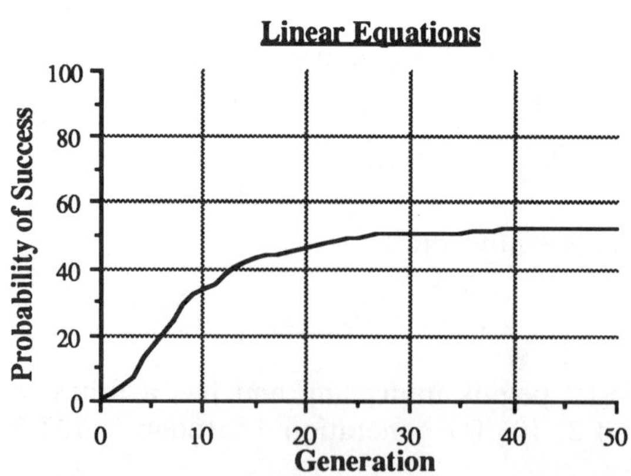

Figure 10.28 *Probability of success for the linear equations problem for* M = *500.*

population size $M = 500$. Since by generation 15 p_s is 44%, K is 8. Therefore, no more than 60,000 individuals (i.e., 8 times 500 times 15) need be processed to ensure a 99% probability of solving the problem.

10.9 RANDOMIZER

Another way to measure fitness is to write a computer program that generates a stream of pseudorandom numbers. Numbers "chosen at random" are useful in a variety of scientific, mathematical, engineering, and industrial applications, including Monte Carlo simulations, sampling, decision theory, game theory, instant lottery ticket production, and others. However, random numbers are difficult to create.

Our goal is to genetically breed a computer program to convert a sequence of consecutive integers into a sequence of random binary digits. The input to our randomizer will merely be an argument J running consecutively from 1 to 16,384 (2^{14}). In other words, each random binary digit as output will be a function of a consecutive integer J as input.

The set of terminals (and the set of functions are the ingredients from which the S-expressions are composed. The only variable in each S-expression for a randomizer is the argument J. The terminal set for this problem also contains several small integers, so

$$T = \{J, 0, 1, 2, 3\}$$

Since we anticipate creation of a randomizer consisting of steps similar to those used in congruential randomizers, the function set is

$$F = \{+, -, *, \text{QUOT\%}, \text{MOD\%}\}$$

taking two arguments each. The protected modulus function MOD% uses the protected division function % (Sec. 10.5.1) to compute the modulus, and the protected integer quotient function QUOT% uses % to compute the integer quotient.

An S-expression composed of these functions and terminals will always produce a numerical value. Since we want binary digits as output, we wrap the S-expression in an output interface (which we call the "wrapper"), which specifies that any positive numerical output will be interpreted as a binary 1 and any other output will be interpreted as a binary 0.

This problem has 16,384 fitness cases, namely, the values of J between 0 and 16,383. The fitness measure is a number computed from the entire sequence of 16,384 binary digits. There are numerous possible approaches to measuring the randomness of sequences [27]. Our goal is to have statistical independence among the sequence of binary digits. In particular, we desire that, for any integer N (where $N = 1, \ldots, \infty$), the probabilities of each of the 2^N possible subsequences of length N should all be equal to $1/2^N$ (within an acceptably small error $\varepsilon \geq 0$). No finite sequence can satisfy these test.

However, if the window size N is limited to some finite fixed integer N_{max}, then "only" $2^{N_{max}}$ probabilities must be estimated when $N = N_{max}$.

More importantly, these $2^{N_{max}}$ separate probabilities can be conveniently summarized into a scalar quantity by using the concept of entropy for this set of events and probabilities. Entropy (which is measured in bits) is a maximum when the probabilities of all possible events are equal. The entropy E_h for the set of 2^h probabilities for the 2^h possible subsequences of length h is

$$E_h = -\sum_j P_{hj} \log_2 P_{hj}$$

The index j ranges over the 2^h possible subsequences. By convention, $\log_2 0 = 0$ when computing entropy. This sum attains its maximum value of h precisely when the probabilities of all 2^h possible subsequences are equal to $1/2^h$.

As h runs from 1 to N_{max}, it is convenient to further summarize the N_{max} separate scalar values of entropy into a single scalar value by summing them to obtain E_{total} as follows:

$$E_{total} = \sum_{h=1}^{N_{max}} \left[-\sum_j P_{hj} \log_2 P_{hj} \right]$$

When

$$E_{total} = \sum_{h=1}^{N_{max}} h = \frac{N_{max}(N_{max} - 1)}{2}$$

then the sequence may be viewed as being random (in this sense).

If we choose $N_{max} = 7$, then the maximum raw fitness associated with the best result will be 28 bits. Standardized fitness is 28 minus raw fitness.

In one run, the best single S-expression of the 500 individuals in the initial random generation scored 20.920 bits and had 63 points. When simplified, it is equivalent to

```
(+ J (* (* (MOD% J 3) 3) (QUOT% (+ J 1) 4)))
```

This best-of-generation individual does a credible job of randomizing bits when the window is narrow. In particular, it gets a perfect 1.000 bit out of a possible 1.000 bit for subsequences of length 1, and it gets 1.918 bits out of a possible 2.000 bits for subsequences of length 2.

In contrast, this best-of-generation individual gets only 4.002 bits out of a possible 6.000 for subsequences of length 6 (i.e., only 67% of the possible score) and only 4.252 bits out of a possible 7.000 for subsequences of length 7 (i.e., only 61% of the possible score).

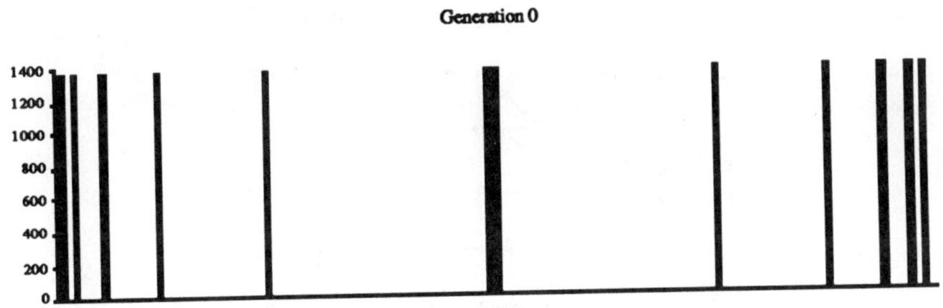

Figure 10.29 *Best-of-generation randomizer for generation 0 showing the frequencies of the 128 different 7-bit patterns.*

In Figure 10.29, the horizontal axis ranges over the $2^7 = 128$ possible subsequences of length 7. The vertical axis is the number of occurrences of each of the 128 possible subsequences for the best-of-generation individual for generation 0 for 16,384 values of J. A maximal entropy randomizer would have 16,384/128 = 128 occurrences of each of the 128 possible subsequences for 16,384 values of J. As can be seen, the best-of-generation individual from the initial random generation has about 1365 occurrences each for 12 of the 128 possible subsequences of length 7.

After two generations of this run, the entropy of the best-of-generation individual improved to 22.126 bits. After four generations, it improved to 26.474 bits. Figure 10.30 shows the best-of-generation individual for generation 4. As shown, after only four generations many more of the 128 possible subsequences of length 7 are now represented.

Figure 10.31 shows the progress, from generation to generation, of each of the seven components (i.e., for $h = 1$ through 7) of E_{total} for the best-of-generation individual for generations 0 through 14. Entropy for short subsequence lengths reaches its maximum level after just a few generations, while entropy for the longer subsequence lengths requires additional generations.

Between generations 5 and 13, entropy attained and slowly improved within the 27.800 to 27.900 area.

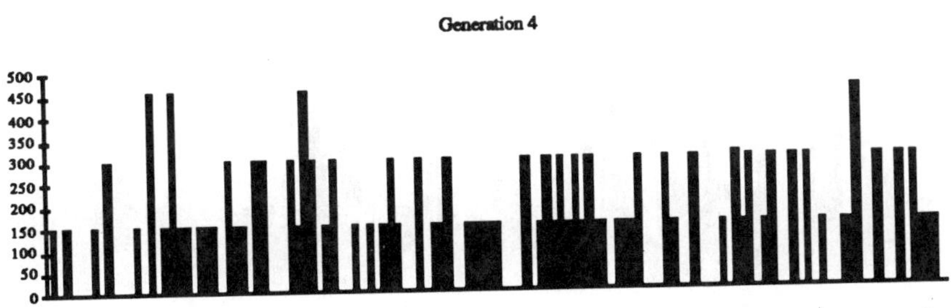

Figure 10.30 *Best-of-generation randomizer for generation 4 showing the frequencies of the 128 different 7-bit patterns.*

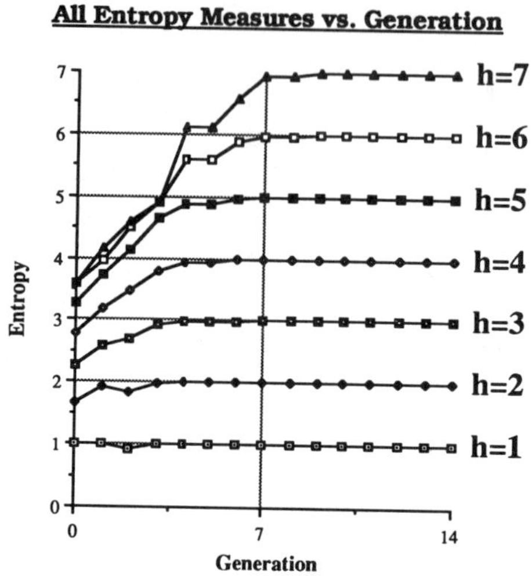

Figure 10.31 *The seven components of total entropy E_{total} for the best-of-generation individual for generations 0 through 14.*

Figure 10.32 shows that by generation 7 all 128 subsequences of length 7 are generated by the best-of-generation randomizer. The number of occurrences are, however, far from equal at this stage.

On generation 14, we obtained an individual S-expression that attained a nearly maximal entropy of 27.996. This S-expression has 153 points, Figure 10.33 shows the simplified version (with 41 points) of this individual. In scoring 27,996, this randomizer achieved a maximal value of entropy of 1.000, 2.000, 3.000, 4.000, 5.000, and 6.000 bits for sequences of lengths 1, 2, 3, 4, 5, and 6, respectively, and a near-maximal value of 6.996 for the 128 (2^7) possible sequences of length 7. Figure 10.34 shows that each of the 128 possible subsequences of length 7 are generated by the best-of-generation individual from generation 14. The number of occurrences of each subsequence is in the neighborhood of 128.

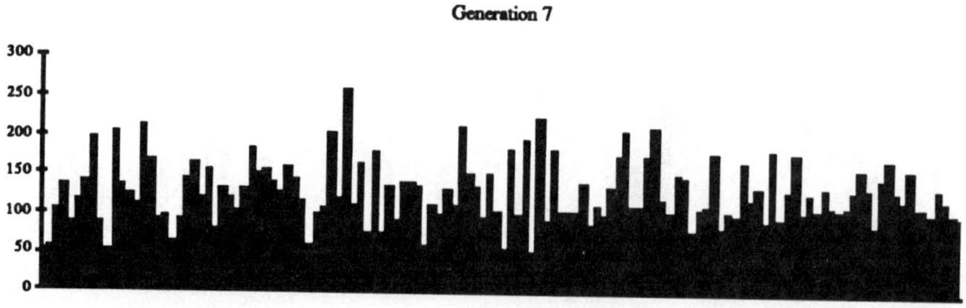

Figure 10.32 *Best-of-generation randomizer for generation 7 showing the frequencies of the 128 different 7-bit patterns.*

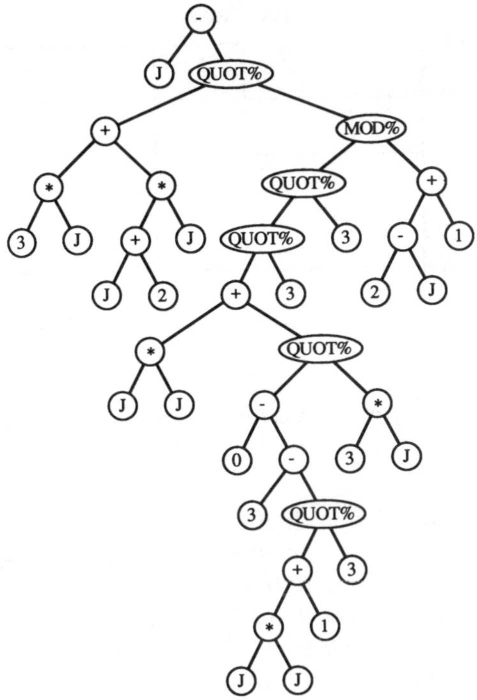

Figure 10.33 *Simplified version of best-of-generation individual from generation 14 of randomizer problem (with entropy of 27.996).*

Note that the progressive change in size and shape of the individuals in the population is a characteristic of the GP paradigm. The size (153 points) and shape of the best-scoring individual from generation 14 differs from the size (63 points) and shape of the best-scoring individual from generation 0. The size and particular hierarchical structure of the best-scoring individual from generation 14 was not specified in advance. Instead, the entire struc-

Figure 10.34 *Best-of-generation randomizer for generation 14 showing the frequencies of the 128 different 7-bit patterns.*

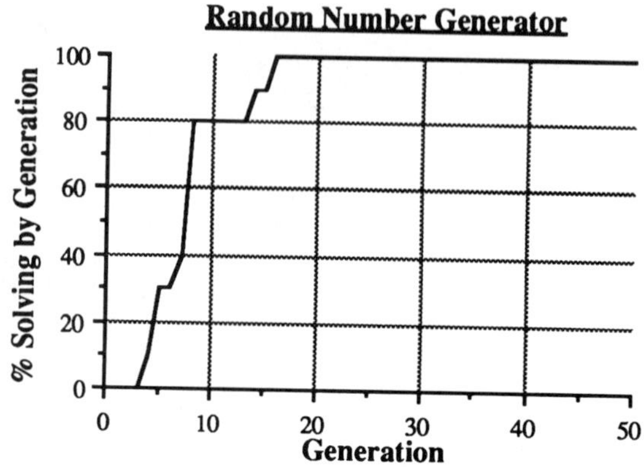

Figure 10.35 *Probability of success for the randomizer problem with* M = *500.*

ture evolved as a result of reproduction, crossover, and the relentless pressure of the fitness measure (i.e., entropy). Note that achieving better entropy requires a more complex computation.

Figure 10.35 shows p_s (based on 10 runs) for $M = 500$, with success defined as attaining an entropy of 27.990 or better. By generation 15, $p_s = 0.90$. Thus, to ensure a 99% probability of solving the problem, we need $K = 2$ independent runs with a population of 500 for 15 generations. That is, no more than 15,000 individuals need be processed.

We now compare the genetically produced randomizer with the following five randomizers [26]:

1. The Park-Miller congruential randomizer described in Anderson [26]:

$$x_i = 7^5 x_{i-1} \mod[2^{31} - 1]$$

2. IBM's URN08 (RANDU) congruential randomizer:

$$x_i = 65{,}539 x_{i-1} \mod 2^{31}$$

3. The SR[3,28,31] shift-register randomizer starting with a seed value x_0 and then producing subsequent elements of the random sequence recursively in a shift register (end off, with zero fill) in a 31-bit shift register:

```
temp =(XOR xi-1 (SHIFT-RIGHT xi 3))
xi =(XOR temp (SHIFT-LEFT temp 28))
```

where XOR is the exclusive-OR operation.

4. The two-sequence shuffling randomizer SHUFFLE using the Park-Miller multiplicative congruential randomizer to produce an initial set of uniformly distributed random numbers between 0.0 and 1.0 and then using the shift-register randomizer SR[3,28,31] to call out numbers from this set of numbers and additional calls on the Park-Miller randomizer to replace the numbers called out.
5. The RANDOM randomizer from Texas Instruments.

The following list compares the shortfall in entropy from the maximal 28.000 bits for the genetically bred randomizer and the five commercial randomizers. We used the same 16,384 points and look-back of $h = 7$.

Randomizer	Entropy Shortfall
Park-Miller	0.009
IBM RANDU	0.010
Shift register	0.010
SHUFFLE	0.015
TI RANDOM	0.009
Genetic	0.004

As can be seen, the genetically bred randomizer has precisely the characteristic for which it was bred (i.e., high entropy). With respect to that measure of randomness, it exceeded the performance of the other five randomizers.

Additional discussion of tests for randomizers can be found in Knuth [27].

10.10 SEQUENCE INDUCTION

Sequence induction involves discovering a mathematical expression (computer program, LISP S-expression) that can generate any arbitrary element in an infinite sequence $S = S_0, S_1, \ldots, S_j, \ldots$ after seeing only a relatively small number of specific examples of the values of the sequence. For example, suppose one is given $S = 1, 2, 5, 10, 17, 26, 37, 50, 65, \ldots$ as the first nine values of an unknown sequence. If the index j starts at zero, one would easily induce the computational procedure $j^2 + 1$ as the way to compute the sequence element S_j for any specified index j.

Of course, there is no one correct answer to an induction problem. An infinite number of sequences agree with the finite number of specific examples in the given sequence. Nonetheless, induction is at the heart of learning, and the ability to correctly perform induction is widely viewed as an important component of human intelligence.

Consider the following example of sequence induction. Suppose one is given the first 20 values of the simple nonrecursive sequence of integers

$$S = 1, 15, 129, 547, 1593, 3711, 7465, 13539, 22737,$$
$$35983, 54321, 78915, 111049, 152127, 203673,$$
$$267331, 344865, 438159, 549217, 680163, \ldots$$

The goal is to identify a mathematical expression that produces this sequence of integers.

Sequence induction is symbolic regression (symbolic function identification) where the domain (i.e., independent variable) ranges over the integers 0, 1, 2, and 3 . . . . The terminal set consists of the index J (i.e., the independent variable) and small integers such as 0, 1, 2, and 3:

$$T = \{J, 0, 1, 2, 3\}$$

The function set is

$$F = \{+, -, *\}$$

The fitness cases for this problem consist of the first 20 elements of the given sequence. Raw fitness is the sum, taken over the 20 fitness cases, of the absolute value of the difference between the value produced by the S-expression for sequence position J and the actual value of the sequence for J. Standardized fitness equals raw fitness for this problem. The auxiliary hits measure is defined so as to count as exact match as a hit. Thus, the number of hits can range between 0 and 20.

Note that the values of this sequence range over more than five orders of magnitude.

In the initial random generation of one run, the raw fitness of the worst single individual in the population was about 3×10^{13}; the average raw fitness of the initial random generation was about 6×10^{10}; and the raw fitness of the best single individual was 143,566.

By generation 38, the raw fitness of the best-of-generation individual had improved to 2740. For generation 42, the raw fitness (i.e., error) of the best-of-generation individual had improved to 20. In a sequence whose largest element is 680,163, an error of only 20 is nearly perfect. This S-expression was

```
(+ (+ (- (* (* 0 1) (- (* 3 J) (+ (* 0 1) J))) 2) (*
(* (* 2 J) (+ 1 J)) (* (+ J J) (- J 2))))
(- (- (+ 2 0) (* (* 1 J) (- (- (- (+ (- (* 2 J) (+ 2
0)) (- J 3)) (- J 1)) (* (* 3 J) (+ J 1))) (- (- (+ J
J) (* (- (- (+ J (+ 0 J)) (- J 2)) (* (* 3 J) (+ J
1))) 3)) (* (- J 2) (- 2 J)))))) (* (- (+ 2 J) (* J
2)) (* (* J J) (- J 3)))))).
```

which is equivalent to

$$5j^4 + 4j^3 + 3j^2 + 2j\underline{\mathbf{+0}}$$

The following correct individual S-expression emerged on generation 43:

```
(+ (+ (- (* (* 0 1) (- (* 3 J) (+ (* 0 1) J))) 2) (*
(* (* 2 J) (+ 1 J)) (* (+ J J) (- J 2))))
(- (- (+ 3 0) (* (* 1 J) (- (- (- (+ (- (* 2 J) (+ 2
0)) (- J 3)) (- J 1)) (* (* 3 J) (+ J 1))) (- (- (+ J
J) (* (- (- (+ J (+ 0 J)) (- J 2)) (* (* 3 J) (+ J
1))) 3)) (* (- J 2) (- 2 J)))))) (* (- (+ 2 J) (* J
2)) (* (* J J) (- J 3)))))
```

which is equivalent to

$$5j^4 + 4j^3 + 3j^2 + 2j\underline{\mathbf{+1}}$$

This is the desired mathematical expression.

Note that there is only one difference between the S-expressions in generations 42 and 43: The boldface underscored (+ 2 0) subexpression in generation 42 becomes (+ 3 0) in generation 43. This difference corresponds to a numerical difference of 1, which, over the 20 fitness cases, accounts for the difference of 20 in raw fitness (i.e., sum or errors).

Induction of recursive sequences, such as the Fibonacci sequence and Hofstadter sequence, using the GP paradigm is discussed in Koza [28].

10.11 SIMPLE SYMBOLIC REGRESSION

The learning of the Boolean multiplexer function (Sec. 10.5) and the induction of sequences (Sec. 10.9) are examples of the general problem of symbolic function identification (symbolic regression). In this section, we discuss symbolic regression as applied to real-valued functions over real-valued domains.

In ordinary linear regression, one is given a set of values of various independent variable(s) and the corresponding values for the dependent variable(s). The goal is to discover a set of numerical coefficients for a linear combination of the independent variable(s) that minimizes some measure of error (such as the square root of the sum of the squares of the differences) between the given values and computed values of the dependent variable(s). Similarly, in quadratic regression, the goal is to discover a set of numerical coefficients for a quadratic expression that similarly minimizes error. In

Fourier "regression" the goal is to discover a set of numerical coefficients for sine and cosine functions of various periodicities that similarly minimizes error.

It is left to the researcher to decide whether to do a linear regression, quadratic regression, a higher order polynomial regression, or whether to try to fit the data points to some nonpolynomial family of functions (e.g., sines and cosines of various periodicities). But often the issue is deciding what type of function most appropriately fits the data, not merely computing the numerical coefficients after the type of function for the model has already been chosen. In other words, the real problem is often both the discovery of the correct functional form that fits the data and the discovery of the appropriate coefficients that go with that functional form. We call the problem of finding a function, in symbolic form, that fits a given finite sample of data *symbolic regression*. It is "data to function" regression.

For example, suppose we are given a sampling of the numerical values from an unknown curve over 20 points in some domain, such as the real interval $[-1.0, +1.0]$. That is, we are given a sample of data in the form of 20 pairs (x_i, y_i), where x_i is a value of the independent variable in $[-1.0, +1.0]$ and y_i is the associated value of the dependent variable. For example, these 20 pairs (x_i, y_i) might include

$$\begin{array}{ll} (-0.40, & -0.2784) \\ (+0.25, & 0.3320) \\ \dots\dots & \dots\dots \\ (+0.50, & 0.9375) \end{array}$$

The (x_i, y_i) pairs are the fitness cases that will be used to evaluate the fitness of any proposed S-expression.

The goal is to find a function, in symbolic form, that is a good or perfect fit to the 20 pairs of numerical data points. The solution can be viewed as a search for a mathematical expression (S-expression) from a hyperspace of possible S-expressions that can be composed from a set of available functions and arguments. The terminal set is $T = \{X\}$. The function set might consist of +, −, *, %, the sine function SIN, the cosine function COS, the exponential function EXP, and the protected logarithm function RLOG. The RLOG function returns 0 for an argument of 0 and the logarithm of the absolute value of the argument otherwise. Thus,

$$F = \{+, -, *, \%, \text{SIN}, \text{COS}, \text{EXP}, \text{RLOG}\}$$

taking two, two, two, two, one, one, one, and one argument, respectively.

The raw fitness for this problem is the sum, taken over the 20 fitness cases, of the absolute value of the difference (distance, error) between the value in the real-valued range space produced by the S-expression for a value of x_i and the correct y_i in the range space. In other words, fitness is the sum of the errors. This method of measuring fitness is the single most common method used here.

The closer this sum is to zero, the better is the computer program. Standardized fitness is, therefore, equal to raw fitness.

The GP paradigm starts with the generation of 500 random S-expressions recursively composed from the available functions and terminals. Predictably, this initial population of random S-expressions include a wide variety of highly unfit S-expressions.

In one run, the worst single individual in the initial random population (generation 0) was

```
(EXP (- (% X (- X (SIN X))) (RLOG (RLOG (* X X)))))
```

The sum of the absolute values of the differences between this worst single individual and the 20 data points was as big as Avogadro's number (about 10^{23}). That is, the raw fitness of this worst individual was about 10^{23}.

The median individual in the initial random population was

```
(COS (COS (+ (- (* X X) (% X X)) X)))
```

which is equivalent to

$$\text{Cos}[\text{Cos}(x^2 + x - 1)]$$

The sum of the absolute values of the differences between this median individual and the 20 data points was merely 23.67. That is, its raw fitness was 23.67. In other words, the distance between the curve for this median individual and the unknown curve (actually the quartic function $x^4 + x^3 + x^2 + x$) averaged 1.2 for each of the 20 data points. Figure 10.36 shows that the curve for the median individual and the correct quartic curve are somewhat close.

The second best individual in the initial random population, when simplified, was

$$x + [\text{RLog } 2x + x] * [\text{Sin } 2x + \text{Sin } x^2]$$

The sum of the absolute values of the differences between this second best individual and the 20 data points was 6.05. That is, its raw fitness was 6.05. The average distance between the curve for this second best individual and the unknown curve $x^4 + x^3 + x^2 + x$ for the 20 points was about 0.3 per data point. Figure 10.37 shows that the curve for the second best individual

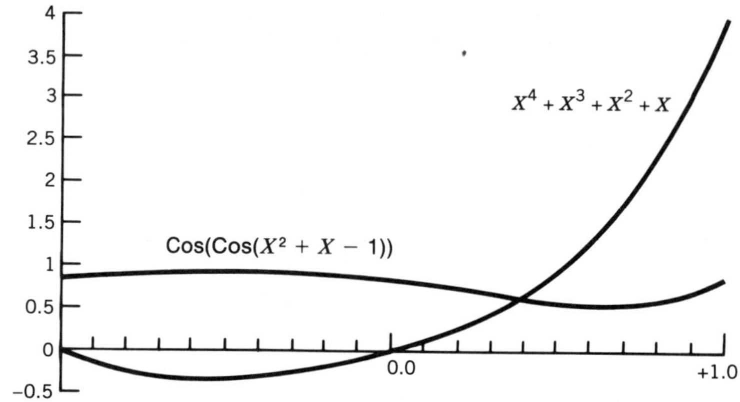

Figure 10.36 *Comparison of the median individual from generation 0 and the correct quartic curve for the symbolic regression problem.*

is considerably closer to the target curve than is the median individual.

The best single individual in the population at generation 0 was the S-expression containing 19 points:

```
(* X (+ (+ (- (% X X) (% X X)) (SIN (- X X)))
        (RLOG (EXP (EXP X)))))
```

which is equivalent to xe^x. The sum of the absolute value of the differences between this best-of-generation individual and the unknown curve $x^4 + x^3 + x^2 + x$ for the 20 data points was 4.47. That is, its raw fitness was 4.47. The

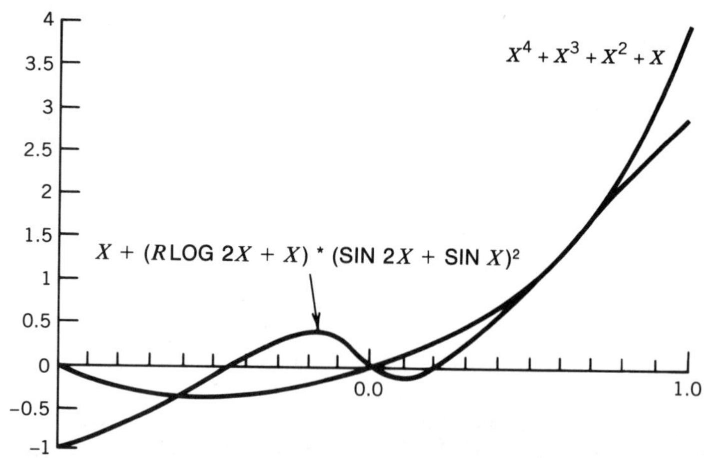

Figure 10.37 *Comparison of the second best individual from generation 0 and the correct quartic curve for the symbolic regression problem.*

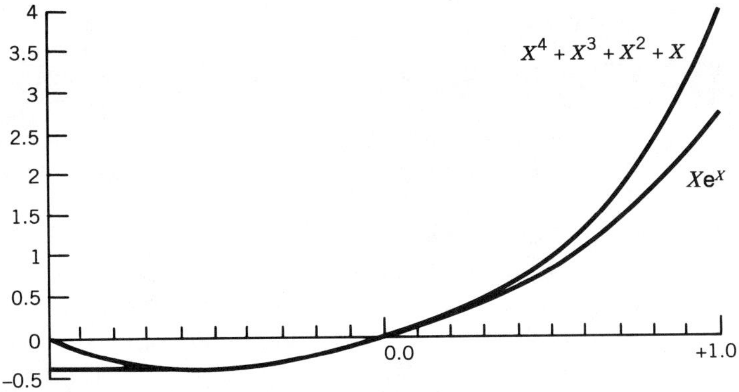

Figure 10.38 *Comparison of the best-of-generation individual from generation 0 and the correct quartic curve for the symbolic regression problem.*

average distance between the curve for this best individual and the unknown curve $x^4 + x^3 + x^2 + x$ for the 20 points is about 0.22 per data point. Figure 10.38 shows that this best-of-generation individual is considerably closer to the target curve than is the second best individual above.

We define a hit to be a fitness case for which the absolute error between the S-expression and the correct curve is ≤ 0.01. The best-of-generation individual from the initial random population (namely xe^x) came within this hits criterion for 2 of the 20 fitness cases. That is, it scored two hits. All the other individual in the population scored only one hit or zero hits.

Although xe^x is not a particularly good fit (much less a perfect fit) to the unknown curve $x^4 + x^3 + x^2 + x$, this individual is nonetheless better than the worst individual in the initial random population, the median individual, and the second best individual. When graphed, xe^x bears some similarity to $x^4 + x^3 + x^2 + x$. First, xe^x and $x^4 + x^3 + x^2 + x$ are zero when x is zero. The exact agreement of the two curves at the origin accounts for one of the two hits scored by xe^x, and the closeness of the two curves for another value of **x** near zero accounts for the second hit. Second, when $x \rightarrow +1.0$, $xe^x \rightarrow 2.7$ and $x^4 + x^3 + x^2 + x \rightarrow 4.0$ (somewhat nearby). Also, when x is between 0.0 and about -0.7, xe^x and $x^4 + x^3 + x^2 + x$ are very close.

By generation 2, the best single individual in the population was

```
(+ (* (* (+ X (* X (* X (% (% X X) (+ X X)))))
         (+ X (* X X)))
      X)
   X)
```

which has 23 points and is equivalent to

$$x^4 + 1.5x^3 + 0.5x^2 + x$$

The sum of the absolute value of the differences between this individual and $x^4 + x^3 + x^2 + x$ for the 20 data points was 2.57. That is, the raw fitness of this best-of-generation individual improved to 2.57 for generation 2 as compared to 4.47 from generation 0. This is an average of about 0.13 per data point. This best-of-generation individual from generation 2 scored five hits as compared to only two hits for the best-of-generation individual from generation 0.

This best-of-generation individual from generation 2 bears much greater similarity to the target function than any of the predecessors discussed. It is, for example, a polynomial, and a polynomial of the correct order (i.e., 4). Moreover, the coefficients of two of its four terms are correct (the coefficients of x^4 and x). In addition, the incorrect coefficients (1.5 for the cubic term and 0.5 for the quadratic term) are not too different from the correct coefficients (1.0 and 1.0).

Notice that even though no numerical coefficients were explicitly provided in the terminal set, the rational coefficients 0.5 for x^2 was created by GP by first creating $1/2X$ (by dividing $X/X = 1$ by $X + X = 2X$) and then multiplying by X. Similarly, the fractional rational coefficient 1.5 for the cubic term x^3 was created.

By generation 34, the sum of the absolute values of the differences between the best single individual and $x^4 + x^3 + x^2 + x$ for the 20 data points was 0.0. That is, the raw fitness of the best single individual in the population for generation 34 attained the perfect value 0.0. This individual, of course, also scored 20 hits.

This best-of-generation individual for generation 34 was the S-expression

```
(+ X (* (+ X (* (* (+ X (- (COS (- X X)) (- X X))) X)
                X))
        X))
```

Note that (COS (− X X)) evaluates to 1.0. This S-expression is equivalent to $x^4 + x^3 + x^2 + x$, the unknown curve. This individual is graphically depicted in Figure 10.39.

Note that the best-of-generation individual from generation 0 is not only not the correct solution, but it is not even of the correct functional form. Nonetheless, the GP paradigm did not get trapped in this local optimum (nor any subsequent local optima). Instead, it was able to break out from suboptimal areas of the search space and discover the correct solution to the problem.

The best-of-generation S-expression from generation 34 has 20 points. Note that there were varying numbers of points in the best-of-generation S-expression from the various intermediate generations. We did not specify that the solution would have 20 points, nor did we specify the shape or content of the S-expression. The size, shape, and content of the S-expression that solves this problem evolved in response to the selective pressure provided by the fitness (error) measure.

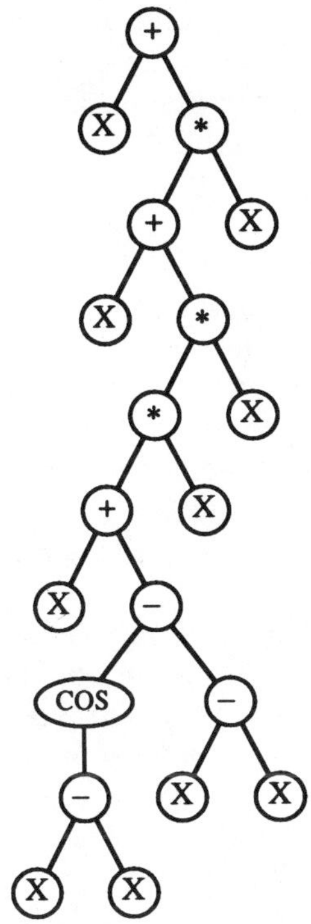

Figure 10.39 *Solution from generation 34 of the symbolic regression problem.*

In summary, we have shown how to use the GP paradigm to find a quartic function, in symbolic form, that perfectly fits this finite sample of data. This was achieved in spite of the fact that the function set contained numerous extraneous functions (e.g., −, %, RLOG, EXP, SIN, and COS).

10.12 SYMBOLIC REGRESSION WITH CONSTANT CREATION

Symbolic regression is one form of symbolic function identification. Problems in this area require finding a function in symbolic form that fits a given finite sampling of data points.

In the previous example of symbolic regression where the unknown curve was $x^4 + x^3 + x^2 + x$, the terminal set T consisted only of the independent variable X. There was no explicit facility for creating a numerical constant. Nonetheless, the constant 1.0 was created indirectly on two occasions via the expressions (% X X) and (COS (− X X)), and constants such as 0.5, 1.5, and other small rational constants were created with similar expressions. However, the process of symbolic regressions requires a general method for discovering the appropriate numerical coefficients.

The problem of constant creation can be solved by expanding the terminal set by one terminal (called the *ephemeral random constant* $\Re$). Thus, the terminal set for a symbolic regression problem with one independent variable becomes

$$T = \{X, \Re\}$$

During the creation of the initial random population (i.e., generation 0), whenever $\Re$ is chosen for any point of the tree, a random number of a specified type in a specified range is generated and attached to the tree at that point. For example, in the real-valued symbolic regression problem at hand, the ephemeral random constants are floating-point type with range between −1.0 and +1.0. In a problem involving integers (e.g., induction of a sequence of integers), random integers over a specified range (such as −5 to +5) are created for $\Re$.

This random generation is done anew each time when an $\Re$ terminal is encountered so that the initial random population contains a variety of different random constants of the specified type. Once generated and inserted into the S-expressions of the initial random population, these constants are fixed thereafter.

After the initial random generation, the numerous random constants arising from the $\Re$ terminals will then be moved around from tree to tree by the crossover operation. These random constants will become embedded in various subtrees that carry out various operations on them.

This moving around of the random constants is not haphazard, but is driven by the overall goal of achieving ever better levels of fitness. For example, a symbolic expression that is a reasonably good fit to a target function may become a better fit if a constant is, say, decreased slightly. A slight decrease can be achieved in several different ways. For example, there may be a multiplication by 0.90, a division by 1.10, a subtraction of 0.08, or an addition of −0.004. If a decrease of precisely 0.09 in a constant would produce a perfect fit, a decrease of 0.07 is usually more fit than a decrease of only 0.05. Thus, the relentless pressure of the fitness function in the natural selection process determines the direction and magnitude of the adjustments in numerical constants.

Constant creation is illustrated in the next section.

10.13 EMPIRICAL DISCOVERY

An important problem area in virtually every area of science is finding the relationship underlying empirically observed values of the variables measuring a system. In practice, the observed data may be noisy, and there may be no known way to express the relationships involved in a precise way.

The problem of discovering empirical relationships from actual observed data is illustrated by the well-known nonlinear econometric exchange equation

$$P = \frac{MV}{Q}$$

This equation states the relationship between the gross national product Q of an economy, the price level P, the money supply M, and the velocity of money V.

Suppose that our goal is to find the econometric model expressing the relationship between quarterly values of P and the three other quantities. That is, our goal is to rediscover that $P = MV/Q$ from the actual observed noisy time series data. Many economists believe that inflation (which is the change in the price level) can be controlled by the central bank via adjustments in the money supply M.

In particular, suppose we are given the 120 actual quarterly values (from 1959:1 to 1988:4) of four econometric time series:

- The annual rate for the United States Gross National Product in billions of 1982 dollars (conventionally called GNP82),
- The Gross National Product Deflator (normalized to 1.0 for 1982) (called GD),
- The monthly values of the seasonally adjusted money stock M2 in billions of dollars, averaged for each quarter (called M2), and
- The monthly interest rate yields of three-month Treasury bills, averaged for each quarter (called FYGM3).

The four time series were obtained from the CITIBASE data base of machine-readable econometric time series [29].

The actual long-term historic postwar value of the M2 velocity of money in the United States is 1.6527 [30]. Thus, the correct exchange equation for the United States in the postwar period is the multiplicative (nonlinear) relationship

$$\text{GD} = \frac{1.6527 * \text{M2}}{\text{GNP82}}$$

The sum of the squared errors between the actual GD from 1959:1 to 1988:4 (120 quarters) and the fitted GD series calculated from the foregoing model was 0.077193. The correlation R^2 was 0.993320.

We first divided the 30-year, 120-quarter period into a 20-year, 80-quarter in-sample period running from 1959:1 to 1978:4 and a 10-year, 40-quarter out-of-sample period running from 1979:1 to 1988:4. This allows us to use the first two thirds of the data to create the model and to use the last third of the data to test the model.

The terminal set is

$$T = \{\text{GNP82, FM2, FYGM3, } \Re\}$$

Terminals GNP82, FM2, and FYGM3 correspond to the independent variables of the model and provide access to the values of the time series. The $\Re$ is the ephemeral random constant terminal allowing various random floating-point constants to be inserted at random among the initial random LISP S-expressions. In effect, the terminals are functions of the unstated, implicit time variable that ranges over the various quarters.

The set of functions chosen is

$$F = \{+, -, *, \%, \text{EXP, RLOG}\}$$

taking two, two, two, two, one, and one arguments, respectively.

Notice that we are not told a priori whether the unknown functional relationship between the given observed data (the three independent variables) and the target function (the dependent variable GD) is linear, multiplicative, polynomial, exponential, logarithmic, or otherwise. The unknown functional relationship could be any combination of these types of functions. We are also not given the known constant value V for the velocity of money. We are not told that the addition, subtraction, exponential, and logarithm functions contained in the function set and the three-month Treasury bill yields (FYGM3) contained in the terminal set are all irrelevant to finding the econometric model for the dependent variable GD.

The fitness of an S-expression is the sum, taken over the 80 in-sample quarters, of squares of differences between the value of the price level produced by the S-expression and the target value of the price level given by the GD time series.

The initial random population (generation 0) was, predictably, highly unfit. In one run, the sum of squared errors between the single best S-expression in the population and the actual GD time series was 1.55. The correlation R^2 was 0.49.

As before, after the initial random population was created, each successive new generation in the population was created by applying the operations of fitness proportionate reproduction and genetic recombination (crossover). In generation 1, the sum of the squared errors for the new best single individual in the population improved to 0.50. In generation 3, the sum of the squared errors for the new best single individual in the population improved to 0.05. This is approximately a 31 : 1 improvement over the initial random generation. The value of R^2 improved to 0.98. In addition, by generation 3, the best single individual in the population came within 1% of the actual GD time series for 44 of the 80 in-sample points.

In generation 6, the sum of the squared errors for the new best single individual in the population improved to 0.027. This is approximately a 2 : 1 improvement over generation 3. The value of R^2 improved to 0.99. In gener-

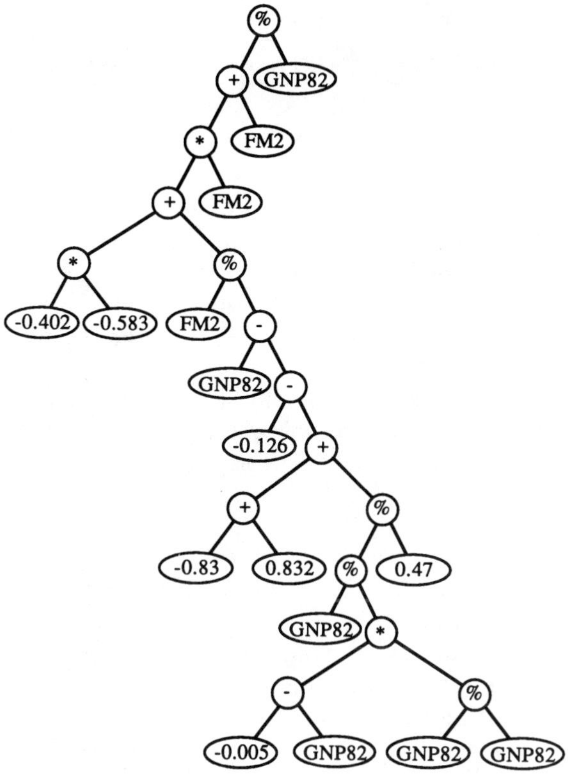

Figure 10.40 *Best result for exchange equation.*

ation 7, the sum of the squared errors for the new best single individual in the population improved to 0.013. This is approximately a 2:1 improvement over generation 6.

In generation 15 the sum of the squared errors for the new best single individual in the population improved to 0.011. This is an additional improvement over generation 7 and represents approximately a 141:1 improvement over generation 0. The correlation R^2 was 0.99.

In one run, the best single individual had a sum of squared errors of 0.009272 over the in-sample period. Figure 10.40 graphically depicts the best-of-generation individual, which is equivalent to

$$\text{GD} = \frac{1.634 * \text{M2}}{\text{GNP82}}$$

Table 10.1 shows the sum of the squared errors and R^2 for the entire 120-quarter period, the 80-quarter in-sample period, and the 40-quarter out-of-sample period:

TABLE 10.1 Squared Errors and Correlations

Data Range	1–120	1–80	81–120
R^2	0.993480	0.997949	0.990614
Sum of squared error	0.075388	0.009272	0.066116

Figure 10.41 shows GD from 1959:1 to 1988:4 and the fitted GD series calculated from the genetically produced model for 1959:1 to 1988:4. The actual GD series is shown as a line with dotted points. The fitted GD series is a simple line. Figure 10.42 shows the residuals from the fitted GD series for 1959:1 to 1988:4.

In Koza [31], we divided the 30-year, 120-quarter period into a 10-year, 40-quarter out-of-sample period running from 1959:1 to 1968:4 and a 20-year, 80-quarter in-sample period running from 1969:1 to 1988:4 and obtained a virtually identical model.

10.14 SYMBOLIC INTEGRATION AND DIFFERENTIATION

Symbolic integration (and differentiation) involves finding the mathematical expression that is the integral (or derivative) in symbolic form of a curve. Symbolic integration and differentiation are direct extensions of the symbolic regression process. The curve may be presented as a mathematical expression in symbolic form or a discrete sampling of data points (i.e., the symbolic form of the curve is not explicitly specified). If the curve is presented as a mathematical expression, we first convert it to a finite sample of data points by taking a random sample of values $\{x_i\}$ of the independent variable in the expression over some appropriate domain. We then pair each value of x_i with the result y_i of evaluating the expression for x_i.

Thus, regardless of the form in which the curve is presented, we can begin the process of symbolic integration with a finite sampling of pairs of numeri-

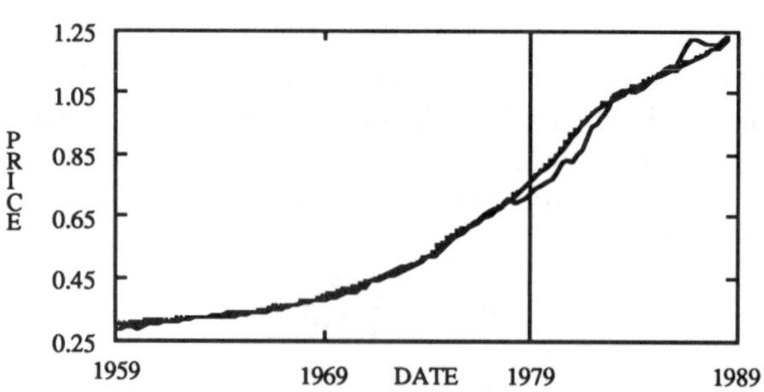

Figure 10.41 *Gross National Product Deflator and fitted series computed from genetically produced model.*

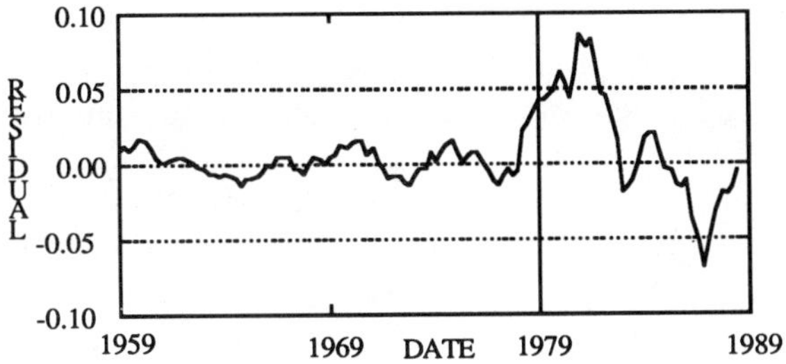

Figure 10.42 *Residuals between the Gross National Product Deflator and fitted series computed from genetically produced model.*

cal values (x_i, y_i). If there are, say, 50 (x_i, y_i) pairs (for i between 0 and 49), then, for convenience, we assume that the values of x_i have been sorted so that $x_i < x_{i+1}$ for i between 0 and 48. The domain values x_i lie in some appropriate interval.

The goal is to find in symbolic form a mathematical expression that is a perfect fit (or good fit) to the *integral* of the curve by using only the given 50 pairs of numerical points. For example, if the curve is

$$\text{Cos } x + 2x + 1$$

the goal would be to find its integral in symbolic form,

$$\text{Sin } x + x^2 + x$$

given the 50 pairs (x_i, y_i). The domain appropriate to this example might be the interval $[0, 2\pi]$.

Symbolic integration is merely symbolic regression with an additional preliminary numerical integration step. Specifically, we numerically integrate the curve defined by the given set of 50 points (x_i, y_i) over the interval starting at x_0 and running to x_{49}. The integral $I(x_i)$ is a function of x_i. The value of $I(x_0)$ for the first point x_0 is zero. For any other point x_i, $1 < i < 49$, we perform a numerical integration by adding the areas of the i trapezoids lying between x_0 and x_i. We thereby obtain an approximation to the value for $I(x_i)$ of the curve for each point x_i, and thus obtain 50 new pairs $(x_i, I(x_i))$ for $0 < i < 49$. These 50 pairs are the fitness cases for this problem.

We then perform symbolic regression in the same manner as described in Section 10.11 to find the mathematical expression for the curve defined by the 50 new pairs $(x_i, I(x_i))$. This expression is the integral in symbolic form of the curve defined by the original 50 points (x_i, y_i).

When applying the GP paradigm, we define the terminal $T = \{X\}$. Second, we define the function set

$$F = \{+,\ -,\ *,\ \%,\ \text{SIN},\ \text{COS},\ \text{EXP},\ \text{RLOG}\}$$

taking two, two, two, two, one, one, one, and one arguments, respectively.

As each individual genetically produced function f_j is generated, we evaluate $f_j(x_i)$ to obtain 50 pairs $(x_i, f_j(x_i))$. The raw fitness of an individual genetically produced function is the sum of the absolute value of the difference between the value $f_j(x_i)$ of the individual genetically produced function f_j at domain point x_i and the value of the numerical integral $I(x_i)$. Standardized fitness equals raw fitness for this problem. A hit occurs when $f_j(x_i)$ comes within 1% of the target value $I(x_i)$.

In one run, the best single S-expression in generation 4 was

```
(+ (+ (- (SIN X) (- X X)) X) (* X X))
```

This S-expression scored 50 hits and had standardized fitness of virtually zero. The standardized fitness (error) does not reach zero exactly because the integral is merely a numerical approximation and because of the small errors inherent in floating point calculations. This S-expression is equivalent to

$$\text{Sin } x + x^2 + x$$

which is the symbolic integral of

$$\text{Cos } x + 2x + 1$$

One could, of course, add a constant of integration, if desired.

In another run, $x^4 + x^3 + x^2 + x$ was obtained as the symbolic integral of $4x^3 + 3x^2 + 2x + 1$.

Symbolic differentiation involves finding the mathematical expression that is the derivative in symbolic form of a given curve. The approach is similar to that of symbolic integration. It is desirable to have a larger number of points for numerical differentiation (e.g., 200 points) than for numerical integration (e.g., 50 points) because of its relative inaccuracy. Specifically, we numerically differentiate the curve defined by the given set of 200 points (x_i, y_i) over the interval starting at x_0 and running to x_{199}. The derivative $D(x_i)$ is a function of x_i. For any point x_i other than the end points x_0 and x_{199}, we take the derivative to be the average of the slope of the curve between x_{i-1} and x_i and the slope of the curve between x_i and x_{i+1}. For x_0 and x_{199} the derivative is the unaveraged slope of the curve. We thereby obtain a value for $D(x_i)$ for each point x_i, and obtain 200 new pairs $(x_i, D(x_i))$ for i between 0 and 199. These 200 pairs are the fitness cases for this problem.

10.15 SOLVING EQUATIONS

The GP paradigm can be used to solve equations where the solution is in the form of a function that satisfies the given equation, such as differential equations (with given initial conditions), integral equations, general functional equations, and inverse problems. Without loss of generality, we will assume that all equations have been transformed so that the right-hand side is zero.

10.15.1 Differential Equations

For some differential equations, it is possible, using exact analytic methods, to find the exact function that solves the equation. However, for most differential equations, only numerical approximation methods are available. The problem of solving a differential equation may be viewed as the search in a hyperspace of compositions of functions and arguments for a particular composition (i.e., LISP S-expression, computer program) that satisfies the equation and its initial conditions.

Example 1. Consider the simple differential equation

$$\frac{dy}{dx} + y \operatorname{Cos} x = 0$$

having an initial value $\hat{y} = 1.0$ for an initial value $\hat{x} = 0.0$. The goal is to find a function that satisfies this equation and its initial condition. The function that does this is $e^{-\operatorname{Sin} x}$.

We start by generating 200 random values of the independent variable x_i over some appropriate domain, such as the unit interval [0, 1]. We sort the 200 x_i into ascending order. We are seeking a function $f(x)$ such that, for every one of the 200 values x_i of the variable x, we get zero when we perform the following computation: Add the derivative $f'(x_i)$ at the point x_i (i.e., dy/dx) to the product of $f(x_i)$ at point x_i (i.e., y) and the cosine of x_i. This rewording of the problem immediately suggests an orderly general procedure for genetically finding the function $f(x)$ that satisfies the differential equation.

Given the set of 200 ascending values of x_i, we define a curve resulting from applying the function g to be the 200 pairs $(x_i, g(x_i))$, where g is some operation.

When the jth individual genetically produced function f_j in the population (i.e., S-expression) is generated by the GP paradigm, we apply f_j to generate a curve. Specifically, we obtain 200 values of $f_j(x_i)$ corresponding to the 200 values of x_i. We call these 200 pairs $(x_i, f_j(x_i))$ the curve resulting from applying the genetically produced function f_i, or the f_i or y curve.

We then numerically differentiate this curve $(x_i, f_i(x_i))$ with respect to x_i. We obtain a new set of 200 pairs $(x_i, f_j'(x_i))$ that we call the curve resulting from applying the differentiation function, or the derivative curve.

We then apply the cosine function to obtain yet another curve. We take the cosine of the 200 random values of x_i to obtain a new set of 200 pairs $(x_i, \text{Cos } x_i)$, which we may call the curve resulting from applying the cosine function, or the cosine curve.

We then apply the multiplication function to the cosine curve and the y curve to obtain still another curve. We multiply the curve consisting of the set of 200 pairs $(x_i, \text{Cos } x_i)$ by $f_j(x_i)$ to obtain a new curve consisting of the set of 200 pairs $(x_i, f_j(x_i) * \text{Cos } x_i)$.

We then apply the addition function to this new curve and the derivative curve to obtain a new curve consisting of the set of 200 pairs $(x_i, f_j'(x_i) + f_j(x_i) * \text{Cos } x_i)$.

To the extent that all 200 values of $f_j'(x_i) + f_j(x_i) * \text{Cos } x_i$ are close to the right side of the given differential equation (i.e., the zero curve) for the 200 values of x_i, the genetically produced function f_j is a good approximation to the solution of the equation. Equivalently, to the extent that the curve consisting of the 200 pairs $(x_i, f_j'(x_i) + f_j(x_i) * \text{Cos } x_i)$ is close to the zero curve (i.e., the curve consisting of the 200 pairs (0, 0)), f_j is a good approximation to the solution of the equation.

The problem of solving the differential equation is now equivalent to a symbolic regression problem over the set of points $(x_i, f_j'(x_i) + f_j(x_i) * \text{Cos } x_i)$.

In the solution of differential equations, the fitness of an individual genetically produced function is expressed in terms of two components. The first component tells how well the function satisfies the differential equation as just described. The second tells how well the function satisfies the initial condition of the differential equation. The first component should receive the majority of the weight in calculating fitness. We arbitrarily assign it 75% of the weight in the examples to follow. The second component receives the rest of the weight.

The first component in computing the raw fitness of a genetically produced function f_j is the sum of the absolute values of the differences between the zero function (i.e., the right side of the equation) and $f_j'(x_i) + f_j(x_i) * \text{Cos } x_i$ for i between 0 and 199:

$$\sum_{i=0}^{199} f_j'(x_i) + f_j(x_i) * \text{Cos } x_i$$

The closer this sum of differences is to zero, the better.

Computation of the second component in the raw fitness of a function f_j starts with the absolute value of the difference between the value of $f_j(\hat{x})$ for the initial condition point $\hat{x}$ and the value $\hat{y}$ for the initial condition. Since this difference is constant over all 200 points, we multiply it by 200 to obtain this second component. The closer this value is to zero, the better.

For differential equations, the raw fitness of a genetically produced function f_j is 75% of the first component plus 25% of the second component. The closer this overall sum is to zero, the better. Thus, standardized fitness equals raw fitness for this problem.

We now apply the method to solving the given differential equation. The terminal set is $T = \{X\}$. The function set is

$$F = \{+, -, *, \%, \text{SIN}, \text{COS}, \text{EXP}, \text{RLOG}\}$$

taking two, two, two, two, one, one, one, and one argument, respectively.

In one run, the best individual S-expression in the initial random population (generation 0) was, when simplified, equivalent to e^{1-e^x}. Its raw fitness was 58.09. Only 3 of the 200 points were hits. This individual satisfies the initial condition (i.e., $\hat{y} = 1.0$ when $\hat{x} = 0.0$). This nonzero raw fitness of 58.09 (averaging 0.29 for each of the 200 points) comes entirely from the 75% component of raw fitness representing nonsatisfaction of the differential equation.

By generation 2, the best-of-generation individual in the population was, when simplified, equivalent to $e^{1-e^{\text{Sin}\,x}}$. Its raw fitness was 44.23. Only 6 of the 200 points were hits. Since this individual also happens to satisfy the initial condition perfectly, the raw fitness of 44.23 (i.e., 0.221 for each of the 200 points) comes entirely from nonsatisfaction of the equation.

Although not a solution to the differential equation, this individual is a better approximation to the solution than the best-of-generation individual from generation 0.

By generation 6, the best single individual S-expression in the population was, when simplified, equivalent to $e^{-\text{Sin}\,x}$. The raw fitness of this best-of-generation individual is down to a mere 0.057. Moreover, 199 of the 200 points are hits. Note that we do not necessarily get exactly 200 hits because of errors associated with numerical differentiation (particularly at the end points of the interval). Since this individual happens to satisfy the initial condition perfectly, this raw fitness of 0.057 (i.e., approximately 0.0003 for each of the 200 points) comes entirely from nonsatisfaction of the equation. This function is the exact solution to the differential equation and its initial conditions.

Tables 10.2 to 10.4 of intermediate values for the best-of-generation individuals from generation 0, 2, and 6 further clarify the process. In each simplified calculation, we use only five equally spaced x_i points in the interval [0, 1], instead of 200 randomly generated points. These five values of x_i are shown in line 1.

Table 10.2 applies to the best-of-generation individual from generation 0, namely e^{1-e^x}.

TABLE 10.2 Simplified Calculation for the Best-of-Generation Individual from Generation 0

1	x_i	0.0	0.25	0.50	0.75	1.0
2	$y = e^{1-e^x}$	1.00	0.753	0.523	0.327	0.179
3	Cos x_i	1.00	0.969	0.876	0.732	0.540
4	$y *$ Cos x_i	1.00	0.729	0.459	0.239	0.097
5	dy/dx	−0.989	−0.955	−0.851	−0.687	−0.592
6	$dy/dx + y *$ Cos x	0.011	−0.225	−0.392	−0.447	−0.495

Line 2 of Table 10.2 shows the value of this best-of-generation individual from generation 0 for the five values of x_i. Line 3 shows the cosine of each value of x_i. Line 4 is the product of line 2 and line 3 and equals $y *$ Cos x_i for each value of x_i.

Line 5 shows the numerical approximation to the derivative dy/dx for each value of x_i. For the three x_i points that are not end points of [0, 1], this numerical approximation to the derivative is the average of the slopes to the left and right of x_i. For the two end points of [0, 1], the derivative is the slope at the nearest point.

Line 6 is the sum of line 4 and line 5 and is an approximation to the value of the left side of the differential equation for the five values of x_i. Recall that if the S-expression were a solution to the differential equation, line 6 would be all zero or approximately zero (to match the right side of the equation). This best-of-generation individual from generation 0 is not a solution to the differential equation. We did not expect the values of line 6 to be zero.

Table 10.3 applies to the best-of-generation individual from generation 2, namely $e^{1-e^{\text{Sin}\,x}}$.

Lines 1 through 5 are calculated for this best-of-generation individual from generation 2 in the same manner as before. Again, line 6 is an approximation to the value of the left side of the differential equation for the five values of x_i. The sum of the absolute value of the three non-end-point values of line 6 is 0.74. Their average magnitude is 0.247. If we multiply this number by 200, we get 49.4. This value is close to the more accurate raw fitness of 44.23 obtained before with 200 points, even though we are using only five x_i points (instead of 200) and the Δx is 0.25 (instead of an average of only 0.005). This best-of-generation individual from generation 2 is not a solution to the differential equation. We did not expect the values on line 6 to be zero.

TABLE 10.3 Simplified Calculation for the Best-of-Generation Individual from Generation 2

1	x_i	0.0	0.25	0.50	0.75	1.0
2	$y = e^{1-e^{\text{Sin}\,x}}$	1.00	0.755	0.541	0.376	0.267
3	Cos x_i	1.00	0.969	0.878	0.732	0.540
4	$y *$ Cos x_i	1.00	0.732	0.474	0.275	0.144
5	dy/dx	−0.979	−0.919	−0.758	−0.547	−0.437
6	$dy/dx + y *$ Cos x	0.021	−0.187	−0.283	−0.271	−0.292

TABLE 10.4 Simplified Calculation for the Best-of-Generation Individual from Generation 6

1	x_i	0.0	0.25	0.50	0.75	1.0
2	$y = e^{-e^{\text{Sin}\,x}}$	1.0	0.781	0.619	0.506	0.431
3	$\text{Cos}\,x_i$	1.0	0.969	0.878	0.732	0.540
4	$y * \text{Cos}\,x_i$	1.0	0.757	0.543	0.370	0.233
5	dy/dx	−0.877	−0.762	−0.550	−0.376	−0.299
6	$dy/dx + y * \text{Cos}\,x$	0.123	−0.005	−0.007	−0.006	−0.067

The third calculation, Table 10.4, applies to the best-of-generation individual from generation 6, namely $e^{-\text{Sin}\,x}$.

Line 6 of Table 10.4 is an approximation to the value of the left side of the differential equation for the five values of x_i. Note that the three non-endpoint values in line 6 are −0.005, −0.007, −0.006, all very close to zero. These near-zero numbers indicate that we have at least a good approximation to a solution of the differential equation. As mentioned, when we use 200 points (instead of just five), the values on line 6 approximately average a mere 0.0003 for generation 6.

In summary, we solved the given differential equation for a function that satisfied the differential equation and its initial conditions.

Example 2

$$\frac{dy}{dx} - 2y + 4x = 0$$

with initial condition such that $\hat{y} = 4$ when $\hat{x} = 1$.

In one run, the best single individual S-expression in generation 28 was

```
(+ (* (EXP (- X 1)) (EXP (- X 1))) (+ (+ (+ X X) 1))
```

which is equivalent to $e^{-2}e^{2x} + 2x + 1$, the exact solution to the differential equation.

10.15.2 Integral Equations

Integral equations involve the integral of the unknown function. They can be solved by the GP paradigm by using the same general approach as before. At some point, however, we take the integral of the genetically produced function, instead of a derivative.

An example of an integral equation is

$$y(t) - 1 + 2\int_{r=0}^{r=t} \text{Cos}(t - r)y(r)\,dr = 0$$

In one run, we found the solution

$$y(t) = 1 - 2te^{-t}$$

to the equation.

10.15.3 Inverse Problems

The problem of finding the inverse function is simply a problem of symbolic regression with the values of the original independent variable interchanged with the values of the original dependent variable.

10.15.4 General Functional Equations

General functional equations can be solved by the GP paradigm using the same general approach as for differential equations.

10.16 PLANNING—BLOCK STACKING

Planning in artificial intelligence and robotics requires finding a plan that receives information from sensors about the state of the various objects in a system and then uses that information to select a sequence of actions to change the state of the objects in that system. We have previously seen planning in the artificial ant problem. The planning problem in this section involves an explicit iterative operation.

The block-stacking problem is a robotic planning problem involving rearranging uniquely labeled blocks into a specified order on a single target tower. In the version of the problem involving nine blocks, the blocks are labeled with the nine letters of FRUITCAKE or UNIVERSAL. The goal is to automatically generate a plan [32] that solves this problem. This problem illustrates the use of an iterative operator DU (Do Until).

The *stack* is the ordered set of blocks that are currently in the target tower (where the order is important). The *table* is the set of blocks that are currently not in the target tower (where the order is not important). The initial configuration consists of certain blocks in the stack and the remaining blocks on the table (see Fig. 10.43). The desired final configuration consists of all the blocks in the stack in the desired order (i.e., UNIVERSAL) and no blocks remaining on the table.

Three sensors dynamically track the system. Sensor CS dynamically specifies the top block of the stack. Sensor TB (Top correct Block) dynamically specifies the top block on the stack such that it and all blocks below it are in the correct order. Sensor NN (Next Needed) dynamically specifies the block immediately after TB in the goal UNIVERSAL (regardless of whether there are incorrect blocks in the stack).

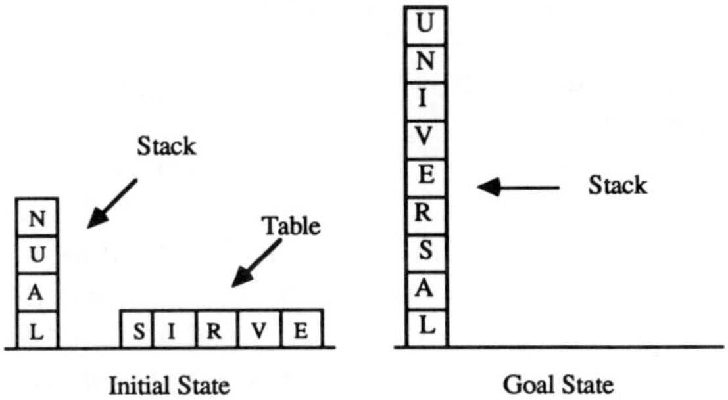

Figure 10.43 *A possible initial state and the goal state for the block-stacking problem.*

Figure 10.44 shows the stack consisting of URSAL, the sensor CS is U, while the sensor TB is R since RSAL are in the correct order. The sensor NN (next needed) is E, since E is the block that belongs on top of RSAL.

The terminal set T for this block-stacking problem is

$$T = \{\text{TB, NN, CS}\}$$

Each terminal is a variable atom that may assume, as its value, one of the nine block labels or NIL.

The function set F is

$$F = \{\text{MS, MT, DU, NOT, EQ}\}$$

having one, one, two, one, and two arguments, respectively.

The function MS (Move to the Stack) has one argument. The S-expression (MS x) moves block x to the top of the stack if x is on the table. MS does nothing if x is already on the stack, if the table is empty, or if x is NIL. MS and MT, described later, return NIL if they do nothing and T if they do something; however, their real functionality is their side effects on the stack and table, not their return values.

The function MT (Move to the Table) has one argument. The S-expression (MT x) moves the top item of the stack to the table if x is anywhere in

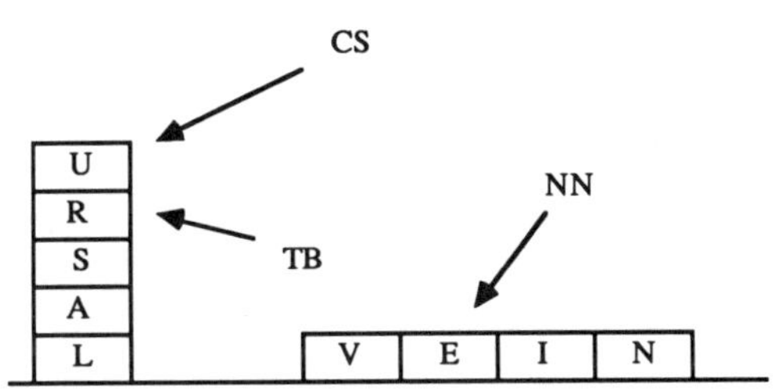

Figure 10.44 *The initial values for the sensor variables NN, TB, and CS.*

the stack. MT does nothing if x is on the table, if the stack is empty, or if x is NIL.

The iterative operator DU has two arguments. The S-expression (DU *work predicate*) iteratively does the work until the *predicate* becomes satisfied (i.e., becomes non-NIL). The DU operator is similar to the REPEAT loop found in many programming languages. Note that DU differs from the typical LISP S-expression in that the *work* and *predicate* arguments are not evaluated outside DU and then passed to DU when they have been evaluated. Instead, these arguments are evaluated dynamically inside DU on each iteration. First, the *work* is evaluated, then the *predicate*. These two evaluations are performed, in sequence, as if the LISP function EVAL were operating inside the DU operator. Note that in an iterative construction, the execution of the *work* will often change some variable that will then be tested by *predicate*. Indeed, that is usually the purpose of the loop. Thus, it is important to suppress premature evaluation of the *work* and *predicate* arguments of the DU operator.

The GP paradigm involves executing randomly generated computer programs and genetically manipulated computer programs. As a result, individual S-expressions in this problem can contain an unsatisfiable termination predicate. Thus, it is a practical necessity (when working on a serial computer) to place a limit on the number of iterations allowed by any one execution of DU. Moreover, since the individual S-expressions in the genetic population often contain complicated and deep nestings of numerous DU operators, a similar limit must be placed on the total number of iterations allowed for all DU functions that may be evaluated in the process of evaluating any individual S-expression for any case. In particular, the DU operator times out if there have been more than 25 iterations for an evaluation of a single DU operator or if there have been more than 100 iterations for all DU operators that are evaluated for an individual S-expression for some fitness case. If we could execute all the individual LISP S-expressions in parallel (as Nature does) so that the infeasibility of one individual in the population does not bring the entire process to a halt, we would not need these limits.

Note that even when a DU operator times out, it nevertheless returns a value. This explicit return value resulting from the evaluation of DU is in addition to the side effects that may have already been performed by the arguments to the DU function on the state variables of the system. The return value is a Boolean value that indicates whether the *predicate* was satisfied or whether the DU operator timed out. If the predicate of a DU operator is satisfied when the operator is first called, then the DU operator does not work at all and simply returns T.

Note that each function returns some value under all conditions (in addition to whatever side effects it has on the stack and table). This guarantees closure of the function set so that every possible S-expression that might be created can be executed.

The raw fitness of an individual plan (i.e., computer program) for the block-stacking problem is the number of initial conditions (i.e., fitness cases) for which the plan produces the desired final configuration of blocks after it is executed. For this problem, there are millions of different fitness cases of N blocks distributed between the stack and the table. Sampling of the fitness cases is required to evaluate the fitness of a plan in a reasonable amount of time.

Thus, we construct a structured sampling of fitness cases for measuring fitness. If there are N blocks, there are $N + 1$ fitness cases in which the blocks, if any, in the initial stack are all in the correct order and in which there are no out-of-order blocks on top of the correctly ordered blocks in the initial stack. There are also $N - 1$ additional fitness cases where there is precisely one out-of-order block in the initial stack on top of whatever number of correctly ordered blocks, if any, happen to be in the initial stack. There are additional fitness cases with more than one out-of-order block in the initial stack on top of various numbers of correctly ordered blocks in the initial stack. In lieu of the millions of possible fitness cases, we construct a structured sampling of 166 fitness cases for measuring fitness:

- The 10 cases where the 0–9 blocks in the stack are already in correct order,
- The eight cases where there is precisely one out-of-order block in the initial stack on top of whatever number of correctly ordered blocks, if any, happen to be in the initial stack, and
- A structured random sampling of 148 additional cases with between zero and eight correctly ordered blocks in the initial stack and a random number (between 2 and 8) of out-of-order blocks on top of the correctly ordered blocks.

Raw fitness is the number of fitness cases (out of 166) that the plan (computer program) correctly handles. A plan correctly handles a fitness case if the stack contains nine blocks spelling UNIVERSAL when it is finished.

Raw fitness ranges between 0 and 166. Standardized fitness, in turn, equals 166 minus raw fitness. A standardized fitness of zero corresponds to 166 correctly handled cases.

Obviously, the construction of a sampling such as this must be done so that the process is not misled into producing solutions that correctly handle some unrepresentative subset of the entire problem but cannot correctly handle the entire problem.

10.16.1 Correctly Stacking Blocks

The first version of the block-stacking problem involves finding a plan that can correctly stack the nine blocks onto the stack in the desired order after starting with any of the 166 fitness cases. Each plan is executed (evaluated) once for each fitness case.

The initial random population of plans contains a variety of complicated, inefficient, pointless, and counterproductive plans. For example, the initial random plan (EQ (MT CS) NN) unconditionally moves the top of the stack to the table and then performs the useless Boolean comparison between the sensor value NN and the return value of the MT function.

The initial random plan (MS TB) futilely attempts to move the block TB (which already is in the stack) from the table to the stack.

Many initial random plans are so ill-formed that they perform no action at all on the stack and the table. These plans score a raw fitness of 1 (out of a maximum of 166) because they leave the stack untouched in the one fitness case consisting of an already perfectly arranged stack. Other initial random plans are even more unfit and even disrupt a perfectly arranged initial stack.

Some idiosyncratic initial random plans achieve modest fitness levels, but have no utility in general. They contain action sequences that happen to work on two, three, or four of the fitness cases. For example, the plan

```
(EQ (MS NN) (EQ (MS NN) (MS NN)))
```

moves the next needed block (NN) from the table to the stack three times. This plan works in the four specific fitness cases where the initial stack consists of six, seven, eight, or nine correct blocks and no out-of-order blocks.

In one run, an individual plan emerged in generation 5 that correctly handled 10 of the 166 fitness cases. This plan correctly handles the 10 fitness cases in the first group itemized, where the blocks, if any, initially on the stack happen to already be in the correct order and where there are no out-of-order blocks on top of these correctly ordered blocks. This plan was

```
(DU (MS NN) (NOT NN))
```

which uses the iterative operator DU to do the work (MS NN) of moving the needed block onto the stack from the table until the predicate (NOT NN) is satisfied. This predicate is satisfied when there are no more blocks needed to finish the stack (i.e., sensor NN is NIL).

Figure 10.45 shows this partially correct plan moving five needed blocks (E, V, N, I, and U) to a stack containing four blocks (R, S, A, and L) that are already in the correct order.

This plan does not produce a correct final stack if any block initially on the stack was incorrect. Thus, it performs incorrectly in 156 of the 166 fitness cases. Nonetheless, it will prove to be a useful "building block" in the final correct plan.

As additional generations are run, the performance of the best single individual plan in the population typically increases somewhat from genera-

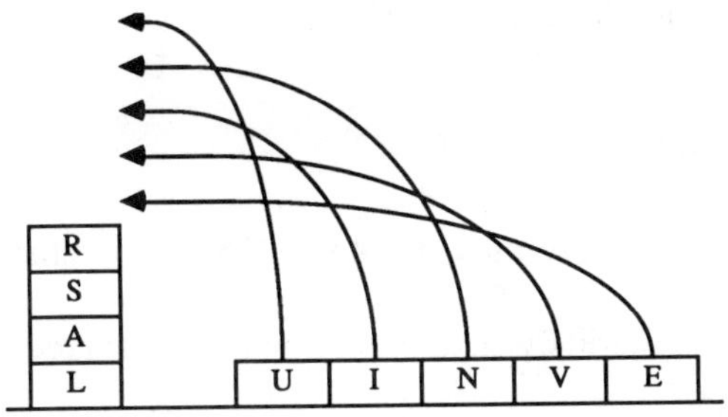

Figure 10.45 *Five blocks to go on top of RSAL being moved from table to stack.*

tion to generation. These progressively improving plans each deal correctly with a few more additional cases. At the same time, the overall average fitness of the population also tends to increase somewhat from generation to generation as the population begins to contain additional higher scoring plans.

In generation 10 of one run, the best single individual plan in the population achieved a perfect score (that is, the plan produced the desired final configuration of blocks in the stack for 100% of the fitness cases). This correct plan was

```
(EQ (DU (MT CS) (NOT CS)) (DU MS NN) (NOT NN)))
```

shown in Figure 10.46. The plan has two subplans connected via the function EQ (merely serving as a connective). The first subplan is

```
(DU (MT CS) (NOT CS))
```

which does the work of first moving CS (i.e., the top of the stack) to the table. This continues until the predicate (NOT CS) becomes T, which occurs

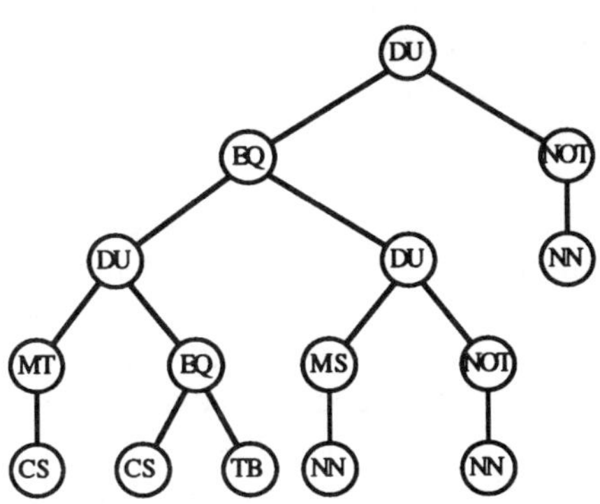

Figure 10.46 *100% correct, but inefficient, plan for stacking blocks from generation 10.*

when the top of the stack becomes NIL (i.e., the stack becomes empty). The second subplan

```
(DU (MS NN) (NOT NN))
```

does the work of iteratively moving block NN to the stack until there is no remaining block NN.

Notice that the previously discovered partially correct plan

```
(DU (MS NN) (NOT NN))
```

was incorporated as a subplan into the correct final hierarchy as a result of the crossover operation. It participated in the critical crossover operation because its relatively high fitness (i.e., a raw fitness of 10 out of a possible 166) allowed it to be selected as a parent to participate in the crossover operation that produced the correct final plan.

10.16.2 Efficiently Stacking Blocks

The correct solution found in the basic version of the block-stacking problem is highly inefficient in that it removes all the blocks, one by one, from the stack to the table (even if they are already in the correct order in the stack). This plan then moves the blocks, one by one, from the table to the stack. As a result, it uses 2319 block movements to handle the 166 cases. We should not be surprised by this, since the concept of efficiency was not involved in any way in the basic version of the problem.

The most efficient way to solve this version of the block-stacking problem, in terms of minimizing total block movements, is to remove only the out-of-order blocks from the stack and to move the next needed blocks to the stack from the table. This approach uses only 1641 block movements to handle the 166 fitness cases.

Note, however, that nothing in the fitness function defined for the basic version of the block-stacking problem gave any consideration whatsoever to efficiency as measured by the total number of block movements involved. The only consideration in the fitness function that we defined was whether the plan correctly handled each of the 166 fitness cases (either at its natural time of termination or when it timed out).

We can, however, simultaneously breed a population of plans (computer programs) for two attributes at one time. We can specifically breed a population of plans for correctness and efficiency by using a combined fitness measure that assigns a majority of the weight (say 75%) to correctness and a minority of weight (say 25%) to a secondary attribute (i.e., efficiency).

Specifically, if a plan correctly handles all 166 fitness cases, it would receive 75 points toward the combined fitness measure. If a plan correctly handles zero cases out of 166, it would receive zero points toward the combined fitness measure. If a plan correctly handles 40% of the 166 cases (i.e., 67 cases), it would receive 30 points (40% of 75) toward the combined fitness measure. Then, if that plan took 1641 block movements, it would receive 25 additional points toward the combined fitness measure. If the plan took between 0 and 1640 block movements to perform its work, the 25 points available for efficiency would be scaled linearly upward so that a plan making zero block movements would receive no points. If the plan made between 1642 and 2319 block movements, the 25 points available for efficiency would be scaled linearly downward so that a plan making 2319 block movements would receive no points. If a plan made more than 2319 block movements, it would also receive no points.

In one run, the best single individual from the initial random population performed correctly in only 1 of the 166 cases and made 6590 block movements. This plan was incorrect and inefficient.

However, by generation 11, the best individual in the population was

```
(DU (EQ (DU (MT CS) (EQ CS TB))
        (DU (MS NN) (NOT NN)))
    (NOT NN))
```

This plan is both correct and efficient in terms of total block movements. It uses the minimum number (1641) of block movements to correctly handle all 166 fitness cases. See Figure 10.47.

In this plan, the subplan

```
(DU (MT CS) (EQ CS TB))
```

iteratively moves CS (the top block) of the stack to the table until the predicate (EQ CS TB) becomes satisfied.

Figure 10.48 shows the out-of-order blocks (I and V) being moved to the table from the stack until R becomes the top of the stack. Then CS equals TB.

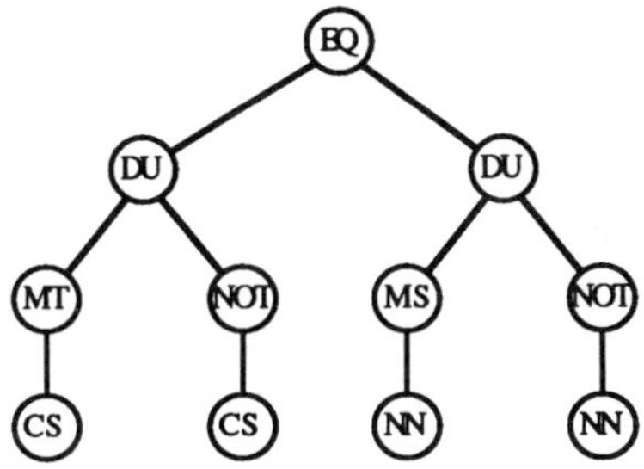

Figure 10.47 *Correct and efficient solution to the block-stacking problem.*

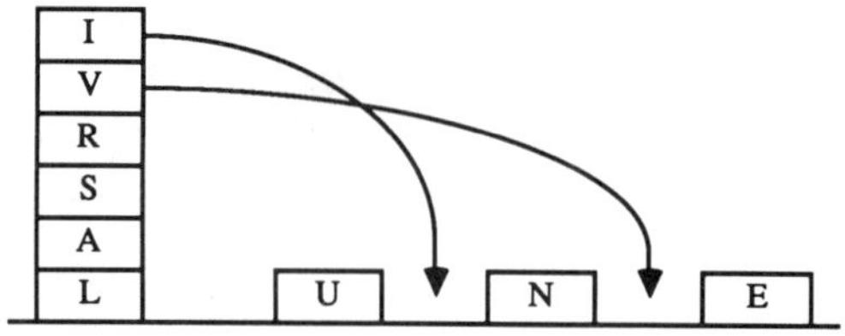

Figure 10.48 *Out-of-order blocks I and V being moved from stack to table.*

Next the previously discovered second subplan

```
(DU (MS NN) (NOT NN))
```

iteratively moves the next needed blocks to the stack until there is no longer any next needed block.

Notice that the function EQ serves only as a connective between the two subplans. Notice also that the outermost DU function performs no function (but does no harm), since the predicate (NOT NN) is satisfied at the same time as the identical predicate of the second subplan. In that regard, these functionless elements are similar to the approximately 99% of nucleotide bases (out of approximately 2.87 billion) in the human genome that never get expressed into protein.

10.17 OPTIMAL CONTROL

Optimal control problems involve a system described by state variables. The future state of the system is determined by the choice of certain control variables. The objective in optimal control is to choose the control variables so as to cause the system to go to a specified target state with an optimal (typically minimal) cost.

The problem of balancing a broom in minimal time by applying a bang-bang force from either direction is a well-known optimal control problem [33]. The broom-balancing problem involves a push cart with mass m_c moving on a one-dimensional frictionless track and a broom (inverted pendulum) of mass m_b pivoting on the top of the cart. The broom has an angle θ (measured from the vertical) and an angular velocity ω. The distance from the center of mass of the broom to the pivot is λ.

This system has one control variable, a bang-bang force F of fixed magnitude that can be applied to the center of mass of the cart at each time step so as to accelerate the cart toward the positive or negative direction along the track. The four state variables of this system are position x, velocity v, angle θ, and angular velocity ω.

Figure 10.49 shows the cart at time t with position $x(t)$, velocity $v(t)$, angle

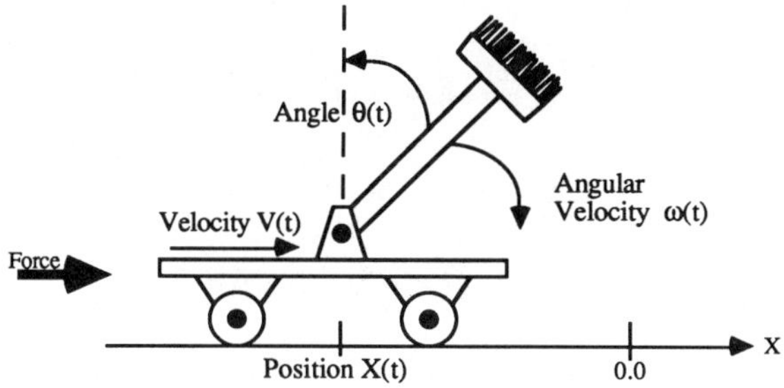

Figure 10.49 *Moving cart with pivoting broom.*

$\theta(t)$ between the broom and the vertical, and angular velocity $\omega(t)$. The bang-bang force is applied so as to accelerate the cart toward the positive direction.

At each time step, the choice of value of the control variable (i.e., the quantity u equal to a multiplier of either $+1$ or -1 to the magnitude $|F|$ of the force F) at time step t causes a change in the state variables of the system at time step $t + 1$.

The state transitions of this system are expressed by nonlinear differential equations. At each discrete time step τ, the current state of the system and the force being applied at that time step are used to compute the state of the system at the next time step.

In particular, the angular acceleration of the broom $\Phi(t)$ at time t is given by Anderson [34] as

$$\Phi(t) = \frac{g \text{ Sin } \theta + \text{Cos } \theta \dfrac{-F - m_p \lambda \omega \theta^2 \text{ Sin } \theta}{m_c + m_p}}{\lambda\left[\dfrac{4}{3} - \dfrac{m_p \text{ Cos}^2 \theta}{m_c + m_p}\right]}$$

The angular velocity $\omega(t + 1)$ of the broom at time $t + 1$ is therefore

$$\omega(t + 1) = \omega(t) + \tau\Phi(t)$$

Then, as a result of this angular acceleration $\Phi(t)$, the angle $\theta(t + 1)$ at time $t + 1$ is, from Euler approximate integration,

$$\theta(t + 1) = \theta(t) + \tau\omega(t)$$

The acceleration $a(t)$ of the cart on the track is

$$a(t) = \frac{F + m_p\lambda[\theta^2 \text{ Sin } \theta - \omega \text{ Cos } \theta]}{m_c + m_p}$$

The velocity $v(t + 1)$ of the cart on the track at time $t + 1$ is therefore

$$v(t + 1) = v(t) + \tau a(t)$$

The position $x(t + 1)$ of the cart on the track at time $t + 1$ is

$$x(t + 1) = x(t) + \tau v(t)$$

The problem is to find a time-optimal control strategy (i.e., a computer program) for balancing the broom that satisfies the following three conditions:

1. The control strategy (computer program) specifies how to apply the bang-bang force at each time step for any combination of the state variables.
2. The system comes to rest with the broom balanced (i.e., reaches a target state with approximate speed 0.0, approximate angle θ of 0.0, and approximate angular velocity ω of 0.0).
3. The time required is minimal.

The constants here are $m_c = 0.9$ kg, $m_b = 0.1$ kg, gravity $g = 1.0$ m/s^2, time step $\tau = 0.02$ s, and length $\lambda = 0.8106$ m.

In this section, we consider only the version of the broom-balancing problem that controls the three state variables v (VEL), θ (ANG), and ω (AVL). Thus, the terminal set is

$$T = \{v, \theta, \omega, \mathcal{R}\}$$

where $\mathcal{R}$ is the ephemeral random constant for floating-point random numbers.

The function set consists of addition, subtraction, multiplication, division, the sign function (SIG), the absolute value function (ABS), the square root of the absolute value function (SRT), the square function (SQ), the cube function (CUB), and the greater-than function (GT). GT is a function of two arguments, which returns +1 if its first argument is greater than its second argument and returns −1 otherwise.

$$F = \{+, -, *, \%, \text{SIG}, \text{ABS}, \text{SRT}, \text{SQ}, \text{CUB}, \text{GT}\}$$

taking two, two, two, two, one, one, one, one, one, and two arguments, respectively.

The use of the protected division function (%), the square root of absolute value function (SRT), and the greater-than function (GT) together guarantee closure of the function set.

Since we do not know the exact mathematical solution to this problem, we have no guarantee of the sufficiency of the function set.

We included the SIG, ABS, SQ, and CUB because they might prove useful. Each additional function in the function set of the GP paradigm usually slightly reduces the efficiency of the run. On the other hand, the solution produced by the paradigm rarely comes in the precise form we anticipate. Moreover, the large benefits produced by having one additional function in facilitating a rapid and relatively parsimonious solution often far outweighs the slight cost of having one extraneous function in the function set. For example, the artificial ant problem (Sec. 10.7) can be solved without having both the LEFT and RIGHT functions. We believe that, when in doubt, it is often better to include potentially extraneous functions.

Each control strategy is executed (evaluated) on every time step of each fitness case. This problem requires an output interface (wrapper) to guarantee that every value returned as a result of the execution of a control strategy is translated into some appropriate bang-bang force. For this problem, the wrapper specifies that any positive numerical output will be interpreted so as to apply the bang-bang force F to accelerate the system toward the positive direction. Any other output (of whatever type) will be interpreted so as to apply F to accelerate the system toward the negative direction.

If an wrapper is needed by a problem, the type is determined by the choice of terminal set and function set. Most problems require no wrapper in the GP paradigm because we are free to choose the functions and terminals in terms that are very natural for the problem. This problem requires a wrapper because we want a binary result (i.e., the bang-bang force), whereas the state variables (terminals) and functions applied to the state variables are real-valued. The randomizer problem (Sec. 10.9) required a similar wrapper to create a binary result.

Figure 10.50 shows a control surface partitioning the three-dimensional $v\theta\omega$ state space. When the system is at a point (v, θ, ω) in the state-space above the control surface, the force F is applied to accelerate the cart toward the positive direction. Otherwise, the force is applied to accelerate the cart toward the negative direction.

The fitness cases for this problem consist of 10 initial condition cases. Position is chosen randomly between -0.2 and $+0.2$ m. Velocity v is chosen randomly between -0.2 and $+0.2$ m/s. Angle θ is chosen randomly between -0.2 rad (about 11.5°) and $+0.2$ rad. Angular velocity ω is chosen randomly between -0.2 and $+0.2$ rad/s. The force F is 1.0 N.

Time was discretized into 300 time steps of 0.02 s. The total time available before the system times out for a given control strategy is thus 6 s. If the square root of the sum of the squares of the velocity v, angle θ, and angular velocity ω is less than 0.07 (the hit criterion), the system is considered to have arrived at its target state (i.e., with the broom balanced and the cart at rest). If a control strategy brings the system to the target state for an fitness

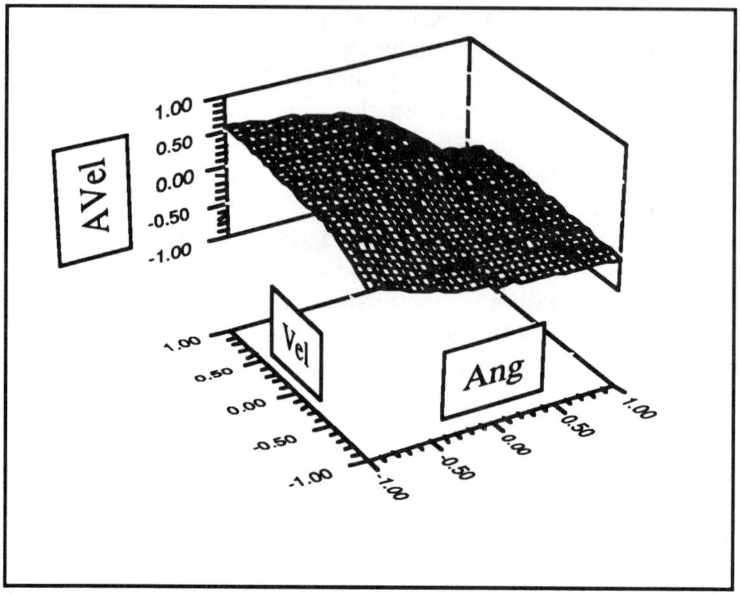

Figure 10.50 *Illustrative control surface partitioning the three-dimensional space for the broom-balancing problem.*

case, its fitness for that case is the time required (in seconds). If a control strategy fails to bring the system to the target state before it times out for an initial condition case, its fitness for that case is set to 6 s (i.e., the maximum). The fitness of a control strategy is the average time for the strategy over all 10 fitness cases.

The initial population of random control strategies in generation 0 includes many highly unfit control strategies, including totally blind strategies that ignore all the state variables, partially blind strategies that ignore some of the state variables, strategies that repetitively apply the force from only one direction, strategies that are correct only for a few specific fitness cases, strategies that are totally counterproductive, and strategies that cause wild oscillations and meaningless gyrations.

In one run, the average time consumed by the initial random strategies in generation 0 averaged 5.3 s. A majority of these 300 random individuals timed out at 6 s (and very likely would have timed out even if more time had been available). However, even in this highly unfit initial random population, some control strategies are better than others.

The best single control strategy in generation 0 was the nonlinear control strategy $v^2 + \theta$, which averaged 3.77 s. Note that this strategy is partially blind in that it does not even consider the state variable ω in specifying how to apply the bang-bang force.

The average population fitness improved to 5.27, 5.23, 5.15, 5.11, 5.04, and 4.97 s per fitness case in generations 1 through 6, respectively.

The best single individual of generation 4 was the simple linear control strategy (+ (+ ANG AVL) AVL), equivalent to $\theta + 2\,\omega$. The corresponding control surface is a plane.

In generation 6, the best individual was the nonlinear control strategy $\theta + \sqrt{|\omega| - \omega^2}$. This individual performed in an average of 2.66 s. Moreover, it succeeded in bringing in 7 out of the 10 fitness cases to the target state. This compares to only four such hits for the best single individual of generation 0 (where about two thirds of the individuals in the population scored only one hit).

By generation 10, the average population fitness had improved to 4.8 s and scored eight hits. The best single individual was $\theta + 2\,\omega - v^2$. Note that this individual is not partially blind and considers all three state variables.

By generation 14, the average fitness had improved to 4.6 s, and, for the first time, the mode of the hits histogram moved from 1 (where it started at generation 0) to 4. In generation 14, 96 of the 300 individuals scored four hits.

The best single individual of generation 16 is

```
(+ (* (SQ (+ ANG AVL)) (SRT AVL))
   (+ (- ANG (SQ VEL)) AVL))
```

which is equivalent to $\sqrt{\omega}\,(\theta + \omega)^2 + \omega + \theta - v^2$.

Figure 10.51 shows the highly nonlinear control surface corresponding to this S-expression.

In generation 24, we attained one individual that scored 10 hits. When simplified, the nonlinear control strategy is $v + \theta + 2\omega + \theta^3$. This individual had a raw fitness of 2.63 s. By generation 24, the population average fitness improved to 4.2 s.

Generation 27 is the last time we see a linear control strategy as the best individual in the population. The best single individual in the population at generation 27 was $v + 2\theta + 3\omega$. This individual scored 10 hits and had fitness of 2.16 s. Note that the computer program or control strategy can be viewed as defining the optimal control surface that partitions the state-space. For this generation, the control surface is a plane.

In generation 33, the best single individual is $8\omega^3 + v + \theta + \omega$, which resembles the ultimate solution we attain in generation 46. This individual had fitness of 1.57 s. Moreover, 15% of the individuals in the population in generation 33 scored 10 hits.

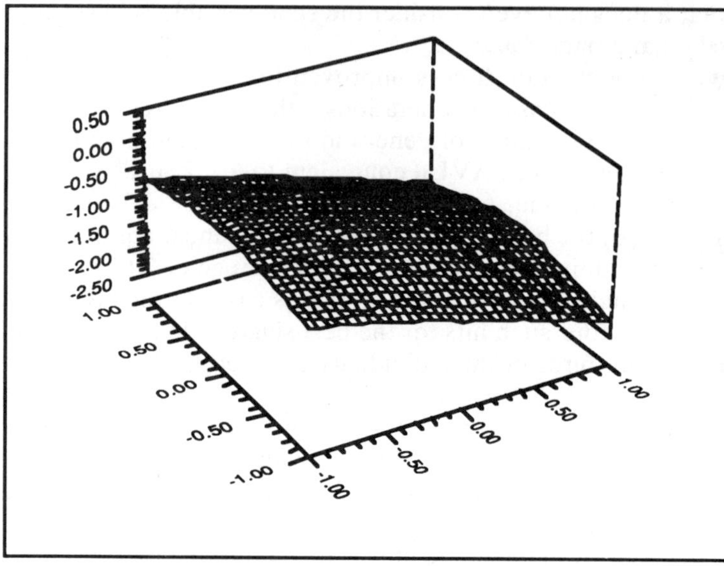

Figure 10.51 *Control surface for the best-of-generation individual for generation 16 of the broom-balancing problem.*

The best single individual for generation 34 was

```
(+ (+ (+ (CUB (+ AVL AVL)) (+ VEL AVL)) ANG)
   (ABS (ABS (SQ (* (* (SRT 0.24000001)
                       (+ (SRT ANG) AVL))
                    (ABS VEL))))))
```

which is equivalent to

$$(2\omega)^3 + v + \omega + \theta + |\,[\sqrt{0.24}(\sqrt{\theta} + \omega)|v|]^2|$$

Figure 10.52 shows the nonlinear control surface corresponding to this S-expression.

By generation 35, the high point of the hits histogram of the population moved from 4 to 10. In particular, 30% of the individuals in the population scored 10 hits. The best single individual was

```
(+ (+ (+ (CUB (+ AVL AVL)) (+ VEL AVL)) ANG)
   (ABS (ABS (SQ ANG))))
```

which is equivalent to $(2\omega)^3 + v + \omega + \theta + \theta^2$.

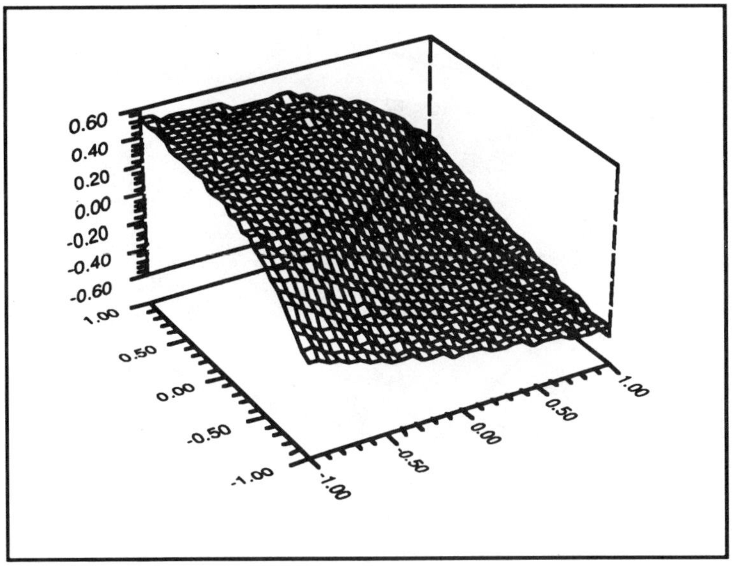

Figure 10.52 *Control surface for the best-of-generation individual for generation 34 of the broom-balancing problem.*

The best single individual for generation 40 was

```
(+ (+ (+ (CUB (+ AVL AVL)) (+ VEL AVL)) ANG)
   (+ (+ (CUB (+ (+ VEL AVL) ANG)) (+ VEL AVL)) ANG))
```

which is equivalent to

$$(2\omega)^3 + 2(v + \omega + \theta) + (v + \omega + \theta)^3$$

The best single individual for generation 44 was

```
(+ (+ ANG AVL) (+ (+ (+ (CUB (+ AVL AVL))
                        (+ VEL AVL)) ANG) VEL))
```

which is equivalent to $2(v + \omega + \theta) + (2\omega)^3$.

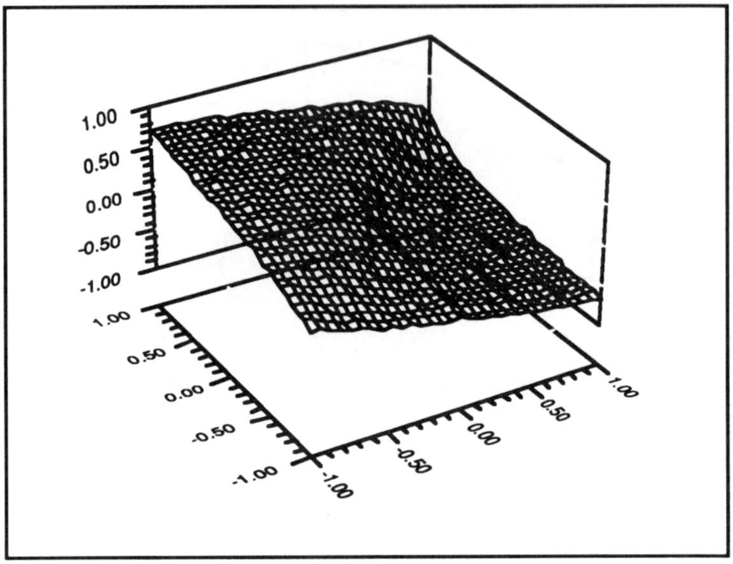

Figure 10.53 *Control surface for the best-of-generation individual for generation 46 of the broom-balancing problem.*

Finally, in generation 46, the best single individual was

```
(+ (+ (+ (CUB (+ AVL AVL)) (+ VEL AVL)) ANG)
   (+ (* (+ VEL AVL) (+ (SRT ANG) AVL)) ANG))
```

which corresponds to the eight-term nonlinear control strategy

$$v + 2\theta + \omega + 8\omega^3 + \omega^2 + v\omega + v\sqrt{\theta} + \omega\sqrt{\theta}$$

Figure 10.53 shows the nonlinear control surface corresponding to this S-expression.

Figure 10.54 shows the progressive improvement (decrease) during this run of the average raw fitness of the population and the best-of-generation individual. The raw fitness of the worst single individual in the population is at the top of the graph for almost every generation, indicating the presence of at least one individual that timed out for all 10 fitness cases.

There is no known solution for this problem, nor is there any specific test we can perform on an apparent solution that we obtain to verify that it is the optimum.

The decision as to when to terminate a run presents some difficulty in optimization problems in general, since we are seeking both the unknown optimal time and the computer program that achieves it.

After its discovery, this single best control strategy found in generation 46

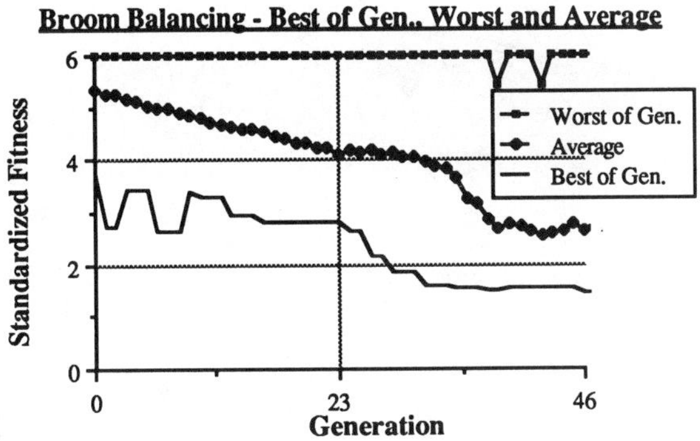

Figure 10.54 *Standardized fitness for worst-of-generation individual, average standardized fitness for population, and standardized fitness for best-of-generation individual for the broom-balancing problem.*

was retested on 1000 additional random initial condition points. It performed in an average of 1.51 s.

In another test, this control strategy from generation 46 averaged 2.65 s when the initial conditions consisted of the eight corners of the $v\theta\omega$ cube. In another test, it took 4.24 s when the initial conditions consisted of the hardest two corners of the cube (i.e., where the velocity, angle, and angular velocity have the same sign). This control strategy never timed out for any internal point or any corner point of the cube.

A pseudo-optimal strategy developed by Keane [35,36] served as an approximate guide for verifying the attainment of the optimal value for time. This pseudo-optimal strategy is an approximate solution to a linear simplification of the problem. It averaged 1.85 s over the 1000 random fitness cases in the retest, and 2.96 s for the eight corners of the cube. Moreover, it was unable to handle the two hardest corners of the cube. These results (in average seconds per fitness case) are summarized in Table 10.5.

We know of no control strategy for this formulation of the broom-balancing problem as good as

$$v + 2\theta + \omega + 8\omega^3 + \omega^2 + v\omega + v\sqrt{\theta} + \omega\sqrt{\theta}$$

TABLE 10.5 Performance for 3-Dimensional Broom-Balancing Problem

Control Strategy	1000 Points	Eight Corners	Worst Two Corners
Benchmark pseudo-optimum	1.85	2.96	Infinite
$v + 2\theta + \omega + 8\omega^3 + \omega^2 + v\omega + v\sqrt{\theta} + \omega\sqrt{\theta}$	1.51	2.65	4.24

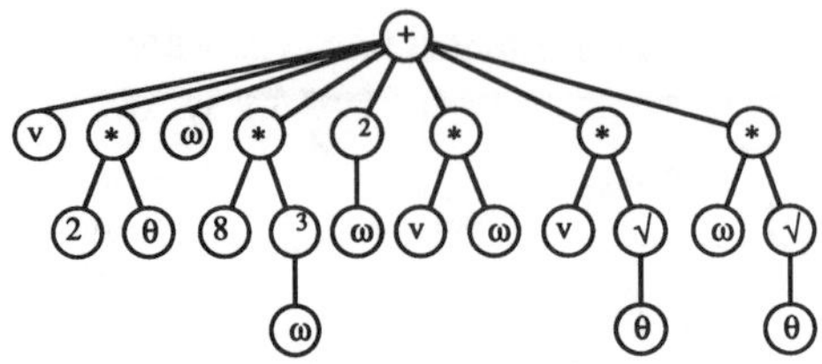

Figure 10.55 *Best-of-generation individual from generation 46 of the broom-balancing problem.*

from generation 46 of the run described earlier. We do know that this control strategy had the best time of the many similar control strategies that we discovered, that there were numerous other control strategies that were only slightly worse (thereby suggesting possible convergence), and that this control strategy is slightly better than the bench-mark pseudo-optimal strategy developed by Keane.

Figure 10.55 graphically depicts the control strategy from generation 46.

10.18 MINIMAX STRATEGY FOR A GAME

The problem of discovering a strategy for playing a game is an important problem in game theory. In a game, there are two or more independently acting players who make choices (moves) and receive a payoff based on the choices they make. A strategy for a player in a game is a way of specifying what choice the player is to make at some point in the game from all of the allowable choices at that time, given all the information available to the player at that time.

The problem of discovering a strategy for playing a game can be viewed as requiring the discovery of a computer program. Depending on the game, the desired program takes as its input either the entire history of past moves in the game or the current state of the game. The program then produces the next move as its output.

Consider the discrete 32-outcome game whose game tree is presented in extensive form in Figure 10.56. This game is a two-person, competitive, zero-sum game in which the players make alternating moves. On each move, a player can choose to go L (left) or R (right). Each internal point of this tree is labeled with the player who must move. Each line is labeled with the choice (either L or R) made by the moving player. Each end point of the tree is labeled with the payoff (to player X). After player X has made three moves and player O has made two moves, player X receives (and player O pays out) the payoff shown at the end point of the game tree.

Since this is a game of complete information, each player has access to complete information about an opponent's previous moves (and his or her

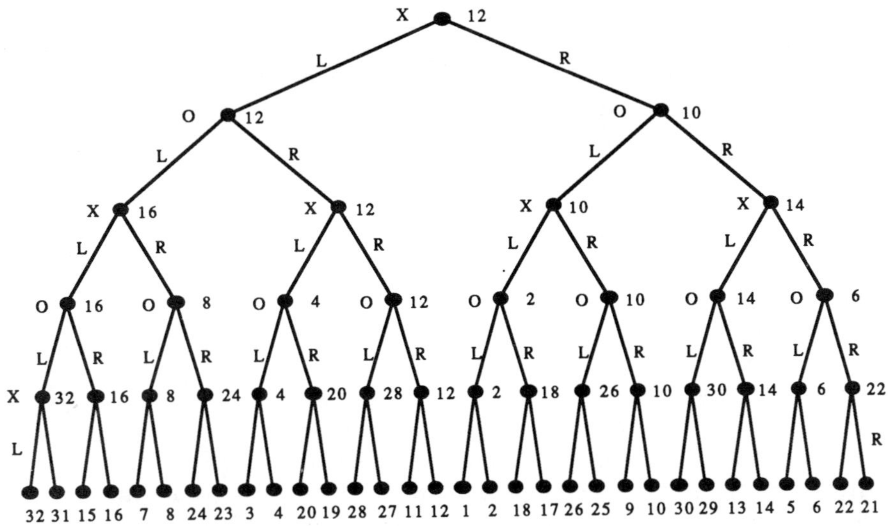

Figure 10.56 *Thirty-two-outcome game tree with payoffs.*

own previous moves). This historical information is contained in five variables: XM1 (X's move 1), OM1 (O's move 1), XM2 (X's move 2), OM2 (O's move 2), and XM3. These variables each assume one of three possible values: L (left), R (right), or U (undefined). A variable is undefined prior to the time when the move to which it refers has been made. Thus, at the beginning of the game, all five variables are undefined. The variables defined and undefined indicate the point to which play has progressed during the game. For example, if both players have moved once, XM1 and OM1 are defined (each as either L or R), but XM2, OM2, and XM3 are undefined (i.e., have the value U).

A strategy for a player in a game specifies which choice that player is to make for every possible situation that may arise. In this game, a strategy for player X must specify his or her first move if it happens to be at the beginning of the game. Second, a strategy for player X must also specify his or her second move if player O has already made one move. Third, a strategy for player X must also specify his or her third move if player O has already made two moves.

Since player X moves first, that move is not conditioned on any previous one. But, player X's second move depends on player O's first move and, in general, on his or her own first move. Similarly, player X's third move depends on player O's first two moves and, in general, his or her own first two moves.

Similarly, a strategy for player O must specify what choice player O is to make for every possible situation that may arise for player O.

A strategy here is a computer program whose inputs are the relevant historical variables (XM1, OM1, XM2, and OM2) and whose output is a move (L or R) for the player involved. Note that there is no reference to XM3, since the game ends as soon as X makes his or her third move.

The four testing functions CXM1, COM1, CXM2, and COM2 provide the facility to test each historical variable that is relevant to deciding upon a player's move. Each of these functions is a specialized form of the CASE function in LISP. For example, CXM1 has three arguments and evaluates its first argument if XM1 is undefined, evaluates its second argument if XM1 is L, and evaluates its third argument if XM1 is R. Functions CXM2, COM1, and COM2 are similarly defined.

The terminal set is T = {L, R}. The function set is F = {CXM1, COM1, CXM2, COM2}. Each function takes three arguments.

The fitness of a strategy for a player in a game is the average payoff received when that strategy is played against all possible sequences of combinations of moves by the opposing player. Thus, when we compute the fitness of an X strategy, we must test the X strategy against all four possible combinations of O moves—that is, O's choice of L or R for moves 1 and 2. When we compute the fitness of an O strategy, we must test it against all eight possible combinations of X moves—that is, X's choice of L or R for moves 1, 2, and 3. Note that it is not sufficient, in general, for player X to play only against an opponent who plays the minimax strategy, because X must also learn to take advantage of mistakes (nonminimax play by the opponent).

When two minimax strategies are played against each other, the payoff is 12, which is the value of this game. A minimax strategy typically takes advantage of nonminimax play by the other player.

A hit for this problem (which we also sometimes call a minimax hit in problems involving games) is the number of fitness cases (out of four for player X or eight for player O) where the strategy being tested achieves a payoff at least as good as the minimax strategy.

We now proceed to evolve a game-playing strategy for player X for this game.

In one run, the best single individual game-playing strategy for player X in generation 6 was

```
(COM2 (COM1 (COM1 L (CXM2 R (COM2 L L L)
                            (CXM1 L R L))
                     (CXM1 L L R)) L R)
      L (COM1 L R R))
```

Note that this strategy for player X is a composition of functions CXM1, COM1, CXM2, COM2 and terminals L and R, and that it returns a value of L or R.

This strategy for player X simplifies to

```
(COM2 (COM1 L L R) L R)
```

The interpretation is as follows. If both OM2 and OM1 are U, it must be player X's first move. That is, we are at the beginning of the game (i.e., the root of the game tree). In this situation, the first argument of the COM1 function embedded inside the COM2 function of this strategy specifies that player X is to move L. The left move by player X at the beginning of the game is player X's minimax move because it takes the game to a point with minimax value 12 (to player X) as opposed to a point with minimax value 10.

If OM2 is undefined but OM1 is defined, it must be player X's second move. In this situation, this strategy specifies that player X moves L if OM1 was L and player X moves R if OM1 was R. If OM1 was L, player O has moved to a point with minimax value 16. Player X should then move L (rather than R) because that move will take the game to a point with minimax value 16 (rather than 8). If OM1 was R, player O has moved to a point with minimax value 12. This move is better for O than moving L. Player X should then move R (rather than L), because that move will take the game to a point with minimax value 12 (rather than 4).

If OM1 and OM2 are defined, it must be player X's third move. If OM2 was L, player X can choose between a payoff of 32 or 31 or between a payoff of 28 or 27. In either case, player X moves L. If OM2 was R, player X can choose between a payoff of 15 or 16 or between a payoff of 11 or 12. In either case, player X moves R. In this situation, this S-expression specifies that player X moves L if OM2 was L, and player X moves R if OM2 was R.

If player O has been playing his or her minimax strategy, this S-expression will cause the game to finish at the end point with the payoff of 12 to player X. However, if player O was not playing his or her minimax strategy, this strategy will cause the game to finish with a payoff of 32, 16, or 28 for player X. The total of 12, 32, 16, and 28 is 88. The attainment of these four values for player X (each greater than or equal to 12) constitutes four hits for player X.

Note that we needed the minimax strategy for player O to serve as the environment for evolving this game-playing strategy for player X.

We now proceed to evolve a game-playing strategy for player O.

In one run of the GP paradigm, the best single individual strategy for player O in generation 9 had a fitness of 52 and scored eight hits. This minimax O strategy was

```
(CXM2 (CXM1 L (COM1 R L L) L) (COM1 R L (CXM2 L L R))
      (COM1 L R (CXM2 R (COM1 L L R) (COM1 R L R)))).
```

which simplifies to

```
(CXM2 (CXM1 # R L) L R)
```

Note that, in simplifying this strategy, we inserted the filler symbol # to indicate a situation that can never arise.

10.19 EMERGENT BEHAVIOR FOR AN ANT COLONY

The repetitive application of seemingly simple rules can lead to complex overall "emergent behavior" [37]. Examples of complex overall behavior that emerges from relatively simple rules occur in the study of cellular automata, Lindenmayer systems, fractals, and chaos, as well as in Nature.

Emergent functionality, according to Steels [38], means that an overall function is not achieved in the familiar way by a hierarchical system of components, but indirectly by the interaction of more primitive components with the world and among themselves. Emergent functionality is one of the main themes of research in artificial life [39,40].

One avenue of work in emergent behavior involves researchers writing sets of rules that produce the desired complex overall behavior. In this section, we use the GP paradigm to evolve the sets of rules.

In this section, we genetically breed a computer program controlling the behavior of an individual ant that, when simultaneously executed in parallel by all the ants in an ant colony, causes the emergence of interesting higher level collective behavior for the colony as a whole.

In particular, the goal is to genetically evolve a common computer program governing the behavior of the individual ants such that the collective behavior of the ants consists of efficient transportation of food to the colony. In Nature, when an ant discovers food, it deposits a trail of chemicals (called pheromones) as it returns to the nest with the food. The pheromonal cloud (which dissipates over time) aids other ants in efficiently locating and exploiting the food source [41,42]. An equivalent problem involves robots on the moon bringing rock samples back to the space ship [38].

In this problem, 144 pellets of food are piled eight deep in two 3×3 piles located in a 32×32 toroidal area. There are 20 ants. The state of each ant consists of its position and the direction it is facing (out of eight possible directions). Each ant initially starts at the nest and faces in a random direction. Each ant in the colony is governed by a common computer program associated with the colony.

The following nine operations are available:

1. MOVE-RANDOM randomly changes the direction in which an ant is facing and then moves the ant two steps in the new direction.
2. MOVE-TO-NEST moves the ant one step in the direction of the nest. This implements the gyroscopic ability of ants to navigate back to their nest.

3. PICK-UP picks up food (if any) at the current position of the ant if the ant is not already carrying food.
4. DROP-PHEROMONE drops pheromones at the current position of the ant (if the ant is carrying food). The pheromones immediately form a 3 × 3 cloud around the drop point. The cloud decays over time.
5. IF-FOOD-HERE is a two-argument function that executes its first argument if there is food at the ant's current position; otherwise it executes the second (else) argument.
6. IF-CARRYING-FOOD is a similar two-argument function that tests whether the ant is currently carrying food.
7. MOVE-TO-ADJACENT-FOOD-ELSE is a one-argument function that allows the ant to test for immediately adjacent food and then move one step toward it. If food is present in more than one adjacent position, the ant moves to the position requiring the least change of direction. If no food is adjacent, the "else" clause of this function is executed.
8. MOVE-TO-ADJACENT-PHEROMONE-ELSE is a function similar to function No. 7 based on adjacency of pheromones.
9. PROGN is the LISP connective function that executes its arguments in sequence.

Each of the 20 ants in a colony executes the colony's common computer program at each time step. The execution of the program is done serially for each ant for a given time step. Thus, the action of one ant can alter the state of the system for other ants (e.g., by picking up food or dropping pheromones). Since the ants initially face in random directions, make random moves, and encounter a changing pattern of food and pheromones created by the activities of other ants, the 20 ants almost always have different states and pursue different trajectories.

The terminal set is

T = {MOVE-RANDOM, MOVE-TO-NEST, PICK-UP, DROP-PHEROMONE}

The function set is

F = {IF-FOOD-HERE, IF-CARRYING-FOOD, MOVE-TO-ADJACENT-FOOD-ELSE, MOVE-TO-ADJACENT-PHEROMONE-ELSE, PROGN}

The raw fitness of a computer program is measured by how many of the 144 food pellets are transported to the nest within the allotted time (which limits the total number of time steps and the total number of operations that any one ant can execute) when all the ants execute the program.

Mere random motion by the 20 ants in a colony will, on average, only bring the ants into contact with about 56 of the 144 food pellets within the allotted time. The task is substantially more complicated than merely coming in contact with food at random. After coming into contact with food, the ants must pick up the food and move toward the nest. Moreover, even this sequence of behavior is not sufficient to efficiently solve the problem in any reasonable amount of time. When ants come in contact with food, they must do something that makes the task easier than mere random search thereafter; they must establish a pheromonal trail as they carry the food back to the nest. This trail allows other ants to locate the food. In addition, all ants must always be on the lookout for such pheromonal trails and must, if they are not already carrying food, follow such trails to the food when they encounter them.

In a typical run, 93% of the random computer programs in the initial random generation did not transport even one of the 144 food pellets to the nest within the allotted time. About 3% of these programs transported only one of the 144 pellets. Even the best single computer program of those created in the initial generation successfully transported only 41 pellets (i.e., only about 2 per ant).

As the GP paradigm is run, the population as a whole and its best single individual both generally improve from generation to generation. In one run, the best single individual in the population in generation 10 scored 54; the best-of-generation individual in generation 20 scored 72; the best-of-generation individual in generation 30 scored 110; the best-of-generation individual in generation 35 scored 129; the best-of-generation individual in generation 37 scored 142; and the best-of-generation individual in generation 38 scored 144 (i.e., 100%).

Figure 10.57 shows the progressive improvement during that run of the worst single individual in the population, the average standardized fitness of the population, and the best-of-generation individual.

In generation 38, a program emerged that allowed the 20 ants to successfully transport all 144 food pellets to the nest within the allotted time. The program is

```
(PROGN (PICK-UP) (IF-CARRYING-FOOD (PROGN (MOVE-TO-
ADJACENT-PHEROMONE-ELSE (MOVE-TO-ADJACENT-FOOD-ELSE
(MOVE-TO-ADJACENT-FOOD-ELSE (MOVE-TO-ADJACENT-FOOD-
ELSE (PICK-UP))))) (PROGN (PROGN (PROGN (PROGN (MOVE-
TO-ADJACENT-FOOD-ELSE (PICK-UP)) (PICK-UP)) (PROGN
(MOVE-TO-NEST) (DROP-PHEROMONE))) (PICK-UP)) (PROGN
(MOVE-TO-NEST) (DROP-PHEROMONE)))) (MOVE-TO-ADJACENT-
FOOD-ELSE (IF-CARRYING-FOOD (PROGN (PROGN (DROP-
PHEROMONE) (MOVE-TO-ADJACENT-PHEROMONE-ELSE (IF-
CARRYING-FOOD (MOVE-TO-ADJACENT-FOOD-ELSE (PICK-UP))
(MOVE-TO-ADJACENT-FOOD-ELSE (PICK-UP))))) (MOVE-TO-
```

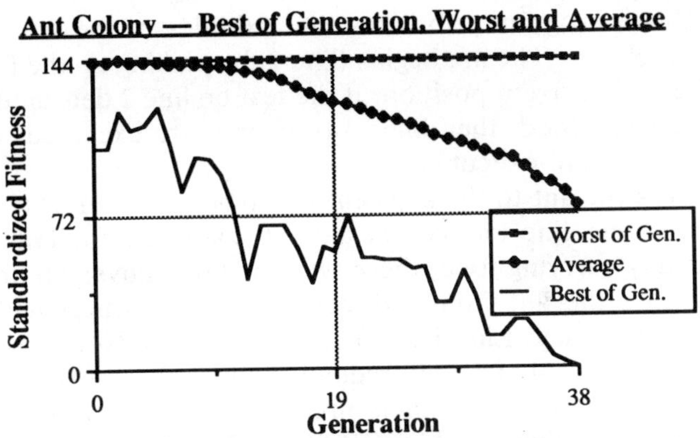

Figure 10.57 *Standardized fitness for worst-of-generation individual, average standardized fitness for population, and standardized fitness for best-of-generation individual for emergent behavior in the ant colony.*

```
NEST)) (IF-FOOD-HERE (PICK-UP) (IF-CARRYING-FOOD
(PROGN (IF-FOOD-HERE (MOVE-RANDOM) (IF-CARRYING-FOOD
(MOVE-RANDOM) (PICK-UP))) (DROP-PHEROMONE)) (MOVE-TO-
ADJACENT-PHEROMONE-ELSE (MOVE-RANDOM)))))))
```

which is essentially equivalent to the simplified program

```
(PROGN (PICK-UP)
      (IF-CARRYING-FOOD
         (PROGN (MOVE-TO-ADJACENT-PHEROMONE-ELSE
                   (MOVE-TO-ADJACENT-FOOD-ELSE (PICK-UP)))
                 (MOVE-TO-ADJACENT-FOOD-ELSE (PICK-UP))
                  (MOVE-TO-NEST)
                  (DROP-PHEROMONE)
                  (MOVE-TO-NEST)
                  (DROP-PHEROMONE))
          (MOVE-TO-ADJACENT-FOOD-ELSE
               (IF-FOOD-HERE
                  (PICK-UP)
                  (MOVE-TO-ADJACENT-PHEROMONE-ELSE
                     (MOVE-RANDOM))))))
```

This program is a prioritized sequence of conditional behaviors that work together to solve the problem. First, the program causes the ant to pick up any food it may encounter. Failing that, the second priority established by this conditional sequence causes the ant to follow a previously established pheromonal trail. And, failing that, the third priority of this conditional sequence causes the ant to move at random.

This simplified program prioritizes the activities of the ant and can be interpreted as follows: The ant begins (line 1) by picking up the food (if any) located at the ant's current position. If the test on line 2 determines that the ant is now carrying food, then lines 3 through 9 are executed. Otherwise, lines 10 through 14 are executed.

Line 3 moves the ant to the adjacent pheromones (if any). If there is no adjacent pheromone, line 4 moves the ant to the adjacent food (if any). Since the ant is already carrying food, these two potential moves on lines 3 and 4 generally distract the ant from a direct return to the nest and therefore merely reduce efficiency. Line 5 is a similar distraction. Note that the PICK-UP operations on lines 4 and 5 are redundant since the ant is already carrying a food pellet. Given that the ant is already carrying food, the sequence of MOVE-TO-NEST on line 6 and DROP-PHEROMONE on line 7 is the winning combination that establishes the pheromone trail as the ant moves toward the nest with food. This move sequence is repeated redundantly in lines 8 and 9. The establishment of the pheromone trail between the pile of food and the nest is an essential part of efficient collective behavior for exploiting the food source.

Lines 10 through 13 apply when line 2 determines that the ant is not carrying food. Line 10 moves the ant to adjacent food (if any). If there is no adjacent food but there is food at the ant's current position (line 11), the ant picks up the food (line 12). On the other hand, if there is no food at the ant's current position (line 13), the ant moves toward any adjacent pheromones (if any). If there are no adjacent pheromones, the ant moves randomly (line 14).

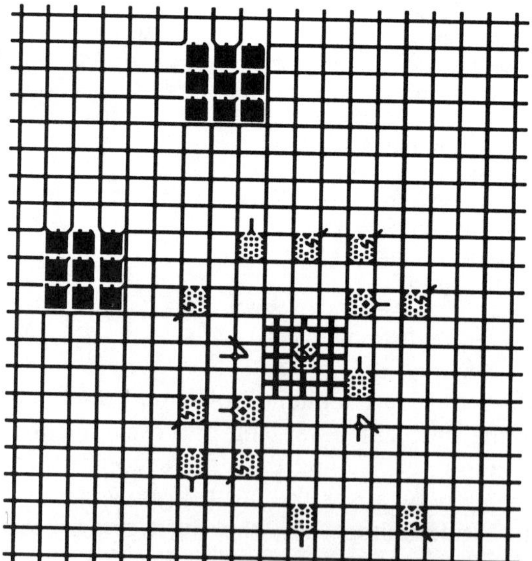

Figure 10.58 *The first phase of the emergent behavior in an ant colony.*

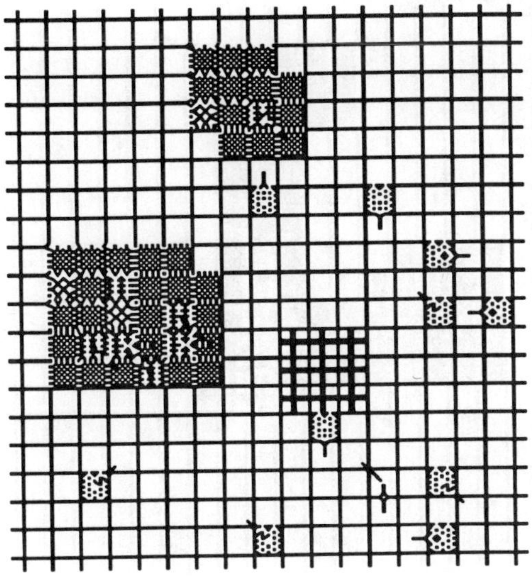

Figure 10.59 *The second phase of the emergent behavior in an ant colony.*

The collective behavior of the ant colony governed by the 100% fit program can be visualized as a series of major phases. The first phase occurs when the ants have just emerged from the nest and are randomly searching for food.

Figure 10.58 represents time step 3 of the execution of the 100% fit program. The two 3 × 3 piles of food are shown in black in the western and northern parts of the part of the grid shown. The nest is indicated by nine + signs slightly southeast of the center of the grid. The ants are shown in gray with their facing direction indicated.

The second phase occurs when some ants have discovered some food, have picked up the food, and have started back toward the nest, dropping pheromones as they go. The beginnings of the pheromonal clouds around both the western and northern piles of food are shown in Figure 10.59 (representing time step 12).

The third phase occurs when pheromonal trails have been established linking both piles of food with the colony. The first 2 (of the 144) food pellets have just reached the nest in Figure 10.60 (representing time step 15).

This third phase persists for some time as the ants transport the bulk of the food from the piles to the nest.

Figure 10.61 shows the premature (and temporary) disintegration of the pheromonal trail connecting the northern pile of food with the nest while food still remains in the northern pile. The pheromonal trail connecting the western pile of food with the nest is still intact. At this point (time step 129), 118 of the 144 food pellets have been transported to the nest.

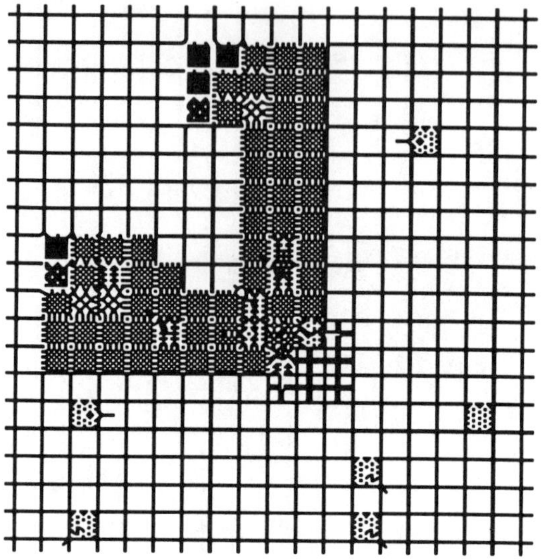

Figure 10.60 *The third phase of the emergent behavior in an ant colony.*

Figure 10.62 (representing time step 152) shows the western pile has been entirely cleared by the ants, and the pheromonal trail connecting it to the nest has already dissipated. The former location of the western pile is shown as a blank area. Of the 144 food pellets, 136 have been transported to the nest. The pheromonal trail connecting the nest to the northern pile (with eight remaining food pellets) has been reestablished.

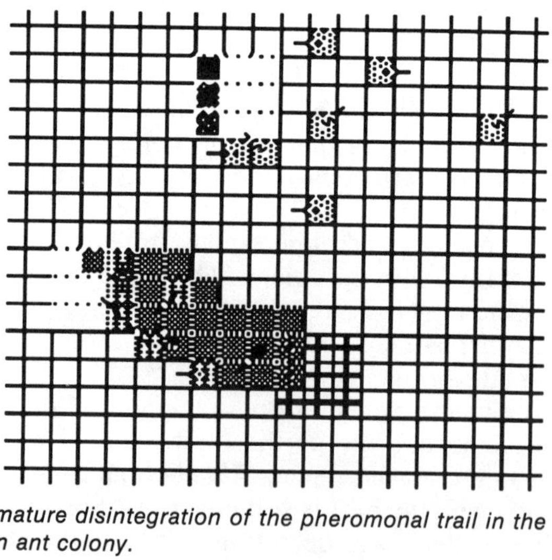

Figure 10.61 *Premature disintegration of the pheromonal trail in the problem of emergent behavior in an ant colony.*

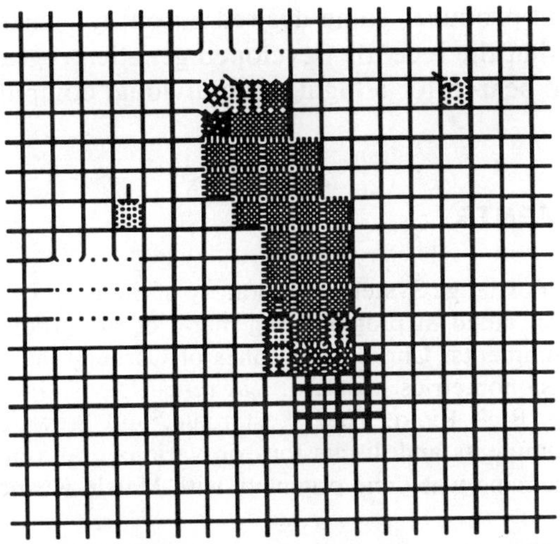

Figure 10.62 *Exhaustion of the western pile of food in the problem of emergent behavior in an ant colony.*

Shortly thereafter, the run ends with all 144 food pellets in the nest.

A visualization of the application of the GP paradigm to this problem (as well as to planning, empirical discovery, inverse kinematics, game playing, and the Boolean 11-multiplexer problems) can be viewed in the *Artificial Life II Video Proceedings* videotape [43].

10.20 ADDITIONAL EXAMPLES

The GP paradigm has been applied in many additional problem domains. For example, induction of decision trees and concept formation can be done [44]. In addition, when the LISP S-expressions return more than one value, even more complex structures can be evolved with the GP paradigm. One example is the simultaneous discovery of the architecture and weights for a neural network [45].

Also, more than one population can be evolved at the same time to solve problems such as simultaneously evolving minimax strategies for both players in a game [46,47].

Additional information and examples can be found in Koza [28,48].

10.21 CONCLUSIONS

We have shown that many seemingly different problems in machine learning and artificial intelligence can be viewed as requiring the discovery of a computer program that produces some desired output for particular inputs. We have also shown that the recently developed genetic programming paradigm provides a way to search for a highly fit individual computer program.

ACKNOWLEDGMENTS

James Rice of the Knowledge Systems Laboratory of Stanford University created all of the graphics here, aided in programming many of the problems, and provided numerous useful comments. Christopher Jones of Cornerstone Research analyzed the results of the econometrics problem. Lawrence Davis, John Holland, Martin Keane, John Perry, Rick Riolo, Tom Westerdale, and Stewart Wilson provided numerous useful comments and discussions on various drafts of this chapter. The work on broom balancing was done originally with Martin Keane [35,36].

REFERENCES

[1] J. H. Holland, *Adaptation in Natural and Artificial Systems,* University of Michigan Press, Ann Arbor, 1975.

[2] D. E. Goldberg, *Genetic Algorithms in Search, Optimization, and Machine Learning,* Addison-Wesley, Reading, Mass., 1989.

[3] L. Davis, Ed., *Genetic Algorithms and Simulated Annealing,* Pittman, London, 1987.

[4] L. Davis, *Handbook of Genetic Algorithms,* Van Nostrand Reinhold, New York, 1991.

[5] J. D. Schaffer, Ed., *Proc. 3rd Internat. Conf. on Genetic Algorithms,* Morgan Kaufmann, San Mateo, Calif. (1989).

[6] G. Rawlins, Ed., *Proc. Workshop on the Foundations of Genetic Algorithms and Classifier Systems, July 15–18, 1990,* Morgan Kaufmann, San Mateo, Calif. (1991).

[7] R. Belew and L. Booker, Eds., *Proc. 4th Internat. Conf. on Genetic Algorithms.* Morgan Kaufmann, San Mateo, Calif. (1991).

[8] L. Davis and M. Steenstrup, "Genetic Algorithms and Simulated Annealing: An Overview," in L. Davis, Ed., *Genetic Algorithms and Simulated Annealing,* Pittman, London, (1987).

[9] K. A. De Jong, Learning with genetic algorithms: An overview, *Machine Learning,* 3(2), 121–138 (1988).

[10] S. F. Smith, "A Learning System Based on Genetic Adaptive Algorithims," Ph.D. dissertation, University of Pittsburgh, Pittsburgh, Pa., (1980).

[11] J. H. Holland, "Escaping Brittleness: The Possibilities of General-Purpose Learning Algorithms Applied to Parallel Rule-Based Systems," in R. S. Michalski, J. G. Carbonell, and T. M. Mitchell, Eds., *Machine Learning: An Artificial Intelligence Approach,* Vol. II, Morgan Kaufmann, Los Altos, Calif., 1986, pp. 593–623.

[12] J. H. Holland, K. J. Holyoak, R. E. Nisbett, and P. A. Thagard, *Induction: Processes of Inference, Learning, and Discovery,* MIT Press, Cambridge, Mass., (1986).

[13] S. W. Wilson, Classifier systems and the animat problem, *Machine Learning,* 3(2), 199–228 (1987).

[14] S. W. Wilson, Bid competition and specificity reconsidered, *J. Complex Systems,* 2(6), 705–723 (1988).

[15] S. Forrest, *Parallelism and Programming in Classifier Systems,* Pittman, London, (1991).

[16] S. W. Wilson, Hierarchical credit allocation in a classifier system, *Proc. 10th Internat. Joint Conf. on Artificial Intelligence,* Vol. I, Morgan Kaufmann, San Mateo, Calif., 217–220 (1987).

[17] D. E. Goldberg, B. Korb, and K. Deb, Messy genetic algorithms: Motivation, analysis, and first results, *Complex Systems,* 3(5), 493–530 (October 1989).

[18] N. L. Cramer, A representation for the adaptive generation of simple sequential programs, *Proc. Internat. Conf. on Genetic Algorithms and Their Applications,* Grefenstette, J. J., Ed., Lawrence Erlbaum, Hillsdale, N.J., 1985, pp 183–187.

[19] C. Fujiki and J. Dickinson, Using the genetic algorithm to generate LISP source code to solve the prisoner's dilemma, *Genetic Algorithms and Their Applications: Proc. 2nd Internat. Conf. on Genetic Algorithms,* Grefenstette, J. J., Ed., Lawrence Erlbaum, Hillsdale, N.J., 1987, pp. 236–240.

[20] J. R. Quinlan, An empirical comparison of genetic and decision-tree classifiers, *Proc. 5th Internat. Conf. on Machine Learning,* Morgan Kaufmann, San Mateo, Calif., 1988, pp. 135–141.

[21] A. G. Barto, P. Anandan, and C. W. Anderson, "Cooperativity in Networks of Pattern Recognizing Stochastic Learning Automata," in K. S. Narendra, Ed., *Adaptive and Learning Systems,* Plenum, New York, 1985, pp. 235–246.

[22] D. B. Lenat, "AM: An Artificial Intelligence Approach to Discovery in Mathematics as Heuristic Search," Ph.D. dissertation, Computer Science Dept., Stanford University (1976).

[23] D. B. Lenat, "The Role of Heuristics in Learning by Discovery: Three Case Studies," in R. S. Michalski, J. G. Carbonell, and T. M. Mitchell, Eds. *Machine Learning: An Artificial Intelligence Approach,* Vol. I, Morgan Kaufman, Los Altos, Calif., 1983, pp. 243–306.

[24] D. B. Lenat and J. S. Brown, Why AM and EURISKO appear to work, *Artificial Intelligence,* 23, 269–294 (1984).

[25] D. Jefferson, R. Collins, C. Cooper, M. Dyer, M. Flowers, R. Korf, C. Taylor, and A. Wang, "The Genesys System: Evolution as a Theme in Artificial Life," in D. Farmer, C. Langton, S. Rasmussen, and C. Taylor Eds., *Artificial Life II, Santa Fe Institute Studies in the Sciences of Complexity,* Vol. XI, Addison-Wesley, Redwood City, Calif., 1991, pp. 549–578.

[26] S. L. Anderson, Random number generators on vector supercomputers and other advanced architectures, *SIAM Rev.,* 32(2), 221–251 (June 1990).

[27] D. E. Knuth, *The Art of Computer Programming,* Vol. 2, Addison-Wesley, Reading, Mass., (1981).

[28] J. R. Koza, *Genetic Programming,* MIT Press, Cambridge, Mass., 1992.

[29] Citibank *CITIBASE: Citibank Economic Database (Machine Readable Magnetic Data File), 1946-Present,* Citibank New York, 1989.

[30] J. J. Hallman, R. D. Porter, D. H. Small, "M2 per Unit of Potential GNP as an Anchor for the Price Level," Staff Study 157, Board of Governors of the Federal Reserve System, Washington, D.C. (April 1989).

[31] J. R. Koza, A genetic approach to econometric modeling, *Proc. 2nd Internat. Conf. on Economics and Artificial Intelligence,* P. Bourgine and B. Walliser, Eds. Pergamon Press, Elmsford, N.Y. (1991).

[32] M. R. Genesereth and N. J. Nilsson, *Logical Foundations of Artificial Intelligence,* Morgan Kaufmann, Los Altos, Calif., 1987.

[33] B. Widrow, The original adaptive neural net broom balancer, *IEEE Internat. Symp. on Circuits and Systems,* Vol. 2 (1987).

[34] C. W. Anderson, Learning to control an inverted pendulum using neural networks, *IEEE Control Systems Mag.* 9(3), 31–37 (April 1989).

[35] J. R. Koza and M. A. Keane, Cart centering and broom balancing by genetically breeding populations of control strategy programs, in *Proc. Internat. Joint Conf. on Neural Networks,* Vol. I, Lawrence Erlbaum, Hillsdale, N.J. (1990).

[36] J. R. Koza and M. A. Keane, Genetic breeding of nonlinear optimal control strategies for broom balancing, *Proc. 9th Internat. Conf. on Analysis and Optimization of Systems,* 47–56, Springer-Verlag, Berlin (1990).

[37] S. Forrest, Ed., *Emergent Computation: Self-Organizing, Collective, and Cooperative Computing Networks,* MIT Press, Cambridge, Mass. (1990). Also in *Physica D 1990.*

[38] L. Steels, Towards a theory of emergent functionality. *From Animals to Animats: Proc. 1st Internat. Conf. Simulation of Adaptive Behavior,* J.-A. Meyer, and S. W. Wilson, MIT Press, Cambridge, Mass., 1991.

[39] C. G. Langton, *Artificial Life II, Santa Fe Institute Studies in the Sciences of Complexity,* Vol. VI, Addison-Wesley, Redwood City, Calif. 1989.

[40] D. Farmer, C. Langton, S. Rasmussen, and C. Taylor, Eds., *Artificial Life II, Santa Fe Institute Studies in the Sciences of Complexity,* Vol. XI, Addison-Wesley, Redwood City, Calif., 1991.

[41] M. Travers and M. Resnick, "Behavioral Dynamics of an Ant Colony: Views from Three Levels," *Proc. Artificial Life II Video,* C. G. Langton, Ed. Addison-Wesley, Redwood City, Calif., 1991.

[42] M. Resnick, Animal simulations with *Logo: massive parallelism for the masses, *From Animals to Animats: Proc. 1st Internat. Conf. on Simulation of Adaptive Behavior,* J.-A. Meyer and S. W. Wilson, Eds. MIT Press, Cambridge, Mass., 1991.

[43] J. R. Koza and J. P. Rice, A genetic approach to artificial intelligence, *Proc. Artificial Life II Video,* C. G. Langton, Ed. Addison-Wesley, Redwood City, Calif., 1991.

[44] J. R. Koza, "Concept Formation and Decision Tree Induction Using the Genetic Programming Paradigm," in H.-P. Schwefel and R. Maenner, Eds., *Parallel Problem Solving from Nature,* Springer-Verlag, Berlin, 1991, pp. 124–128.

[45] J. R. Koza and J. P. Rice, Genetic generation of both the weights and architecture for a neural network, *Proc. Internat. Joint Conf. Neural Networks,* Vol. II, IEEE Press, New York, 397–404 (July 1991).

[46] J. R. Koza, "Evolution and Co-Evolution of Computer Programs to Control Independent-Acting Agents," *From Animals to Animats: Proc. 1st Internat. Conf. on Simulation of Adaptive Behavior,* J.-A. Meyer and S. W. Wilson, Eds. MIT Press, Cambridge, Mass., 1991, pp. 366–375.

[47] J. R. Koza, "Genetic Evolution and Co-Evolution of Computer Programs," in D. Farmer, C. Langton, S. Rasmussen, and C. Taylor, Eds., *Artificial Life II, Santa Fe Institute Studies in the Sciences of Complexity,* Vol. X, Addison-Wesley, Redwood City, Calif., 1991, pp. 603–629.

[48] J. R. Koza, Hierarchical genetic algorithms operating on populations of computer programs, *Proc. 11th Internat. Joint Conf. on Artificial Intelligence (IJCAI),* Vol. I, Morgan Kaufman, San Mateo, Calif., 1989, pp. 768–774.

CHAPTER 11

Genetic Algorithms in Robotics

YUVAL DAVIDOR

11.1 INTRODUCTION

This chapter reviews genetic algorithm models applied in the complex domain of robotics and presents solutions to some of its difficult problems. The problems discussed are inverse kinematics, path planning, and system design and integration.

Robotic applications have thrived in the last two decades and have revolutionized the approach to manufacturing. The main impetus resulted from the realization that robotics technology provides flexibility in the form of reprogrammability (serving industry as a jack-of-all-trades). However, to produce such a flexible yet economical machine, the system's components (mechanical structure, motion actuators, control, and programming language) must be relatively sophisticated. This results in a system that is highly complex, nonlinear, and tightly coupled.

Mechanically, a robot arm is an open kinematic chain composed of relatively stiff joints with a link between adjacent joints (Fig. 11.1). Since a robot arm performs its task through the motion of its *end-effector* attached to the last joint, the last joint is the primary component of the whole structure. Each joint represents one degree of freedom, and is held in position by actuators (such as an electric motor or a hydraulic cylinder). The actuators drive all joints independently. Obviously, the individual joint motions must be synchronized so that the whole structure will move in a controlled fashion. The actuators are connected to a processor called the motion controller.

Dynamic, Genetic, and Chaotic Programming, By Branko Souček and the IRIS Group.
ISBN 0-471-55717-X

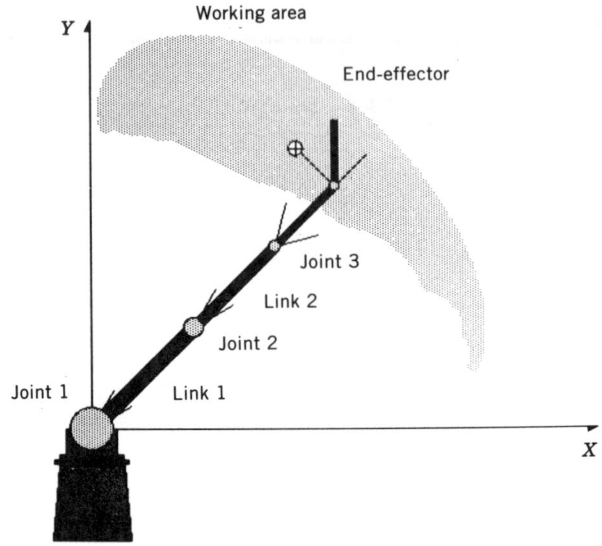

Figure 11.1 *A four-link robotic arm, the allowed movement for each link designated by the black lines extending from the respective joints, and the resulting working area (shaded area).*

Attempting to encapsulate the essence of a robot system in a model for the purpose of developing an autonomous optimization procedure presents the "black box uncertainty" syndrome, which describes a situation where an uncertainty exists as to whether all relevant data is known and whether the available data are relevant. Therefore, it is not surprising that it is very difficult to optimize robotic systems.

11.2 PREVIOUS APPLICATIONS OF GENETIC ALGORITHMS TO SOLVE DIFFICULT PROBLEMS IN ROBOTICS

This section deals with two applications of genetic algorithms (GAs) in order to solve two important problems in robotics: the inverse kinematics problem for both determined and redundant systems, and the achieving of autonomous path/trajectory planning for the robot arm.

11.2.1 Inverse Kinematics for Redundant Manipulators

Most robot applications are based on a motion trajectory composed of a sequence of spatial displacements of the end-effector. An *arm configuration* is a unique arm structure defined by a set of joint positions. Given the positions, the end-effector's position is computationally trivial and uniquely determined. The calculation of the end-effector's position when the joint positions are known is called *direct kinematics,* and is given in the form of a matrix—a coordinate transformation matrix from joint positions to end-effector positions and orientation in a world coordinate system. However, programming a robot to move along a given path usually requires the specifications of spatial positions and orientations for the end-effector and not arm-configurations. This requires the calculation of *inverse kinematics*—the set of joint positions that bring the end-effector to the desired spatial location. Inverse kinematics involves the inversion of the direct kinematics matrix and is not easy to compute. Furthermore, it is not always possible to obtain the inverse kinematics for nonredundant arms due to computational reasons. Clearly, it is impossible (without additional constraints) to compute the inverse matrix for a redundant robot, since the mapping from the world coordinates of the end-effector to joint coordinates is not 1-1.

In order to solve the inverse kinematics problem for redundant manipulators, additional constraints should be introduced by which the determinant of the inverse matrix becomes nonzero. Considerable effort has been invested in solving this problem optimally. Research in this field focuses on finding those additional constraints that optimally restrict the solutions of the inverse kinematics in a practical sense. These attempts suffered from some or all of the following problems:

1. Restricted flexibility and impaired optimality due to externally imposed fixed constraints intended to make the determinant nonzero,
2. Applicability to only one degree of freedom redundancy,
3. The need for good initial guesses of solution values from which classical numerical methods can optimize the solution.

In 1989, Khoogar et al. suggested a heuristic model for finding optimal solutions to the inverse kinematics problem by using a GA [1]. This work is summarized here. The model is based on a simple GA that searches for an optimal arm configuration for a given end-effector position. Therefore, instead of solving the inverse kinematics, the GA searches for an arm configuration that solves the problem optimally. The solution space is the set of joint positions in angle notation. Each continuous angle is represented by a 10-bit unsigned floating-point binary number. For example, when considering a 4-degrees-of-freedom 3D robot arm (meaning one joint redundancy) a 40-bit-long string is required.

The optimization criterion involved two terms. The first gave high scores to end-effector positions close to the desired position, thus working toward accurate solutions (Fig. 11.2). The second gave high scores to a minimal total joint displacement change relative to the current arm configuration (Fig. 11.3), thus working toward optimal solutions. The reasons for applying GA to this problem are as follows:

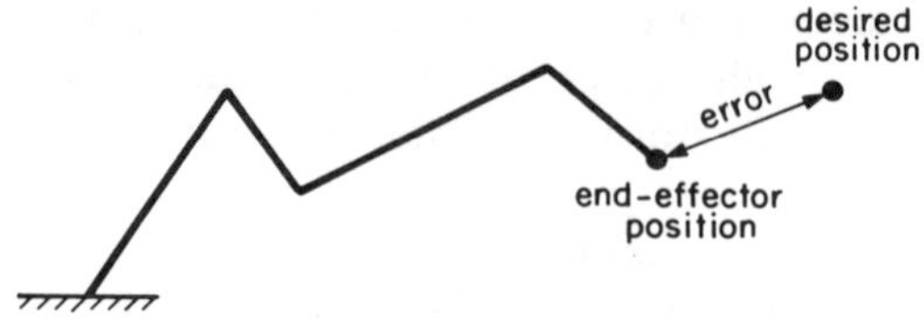

Figure 11.2 *The first term in the optimization criterion for solving the inverse kinematics problem. The smaller the error, the greater the fitness becomes.*

1. The cost function of the algorithm does not make any assumptions about the solution space, such as continuity, differentiability, and so forth.
2. There is no need to compute the Jacobian matrix, which relates incremental joint motions to incremental Cartesian motions of the end-effector.
3. No artificial constraints are needed since the GA uses direct kinematics only.
4. The mechanical limits of the robot joints are considered directly, so the solutions are physically realizable.
5. The GA represent the continuous angles as finite-resolution discrete values. This makes the solution more natural in final implementation.

The performance of this model is quite impressive (Figs. 11.4 and 11.5). Within a few hundred evaluations, a near-optimal arm configuration is identified. Though for on-line trajectory generation this procedure is too slow, it offers a good method for off-line programming.

The foregoing work was inconclusive in three respects. First, it lacked a detailed comparison of different methods with that of the GA. Second, it is not clear how the GA will perform when dealing with bigger problems (additional redundant joints and more degrees of freedom in the arm). Third, the mechanical limitations of the arm were not included, so an important feature of the problem was not considered. There is a possibility that during motion among arm configurations, one or more links will be blocked due to a mechanical limit. This problem is addressed and solved in another GA model designed to solve the general optimal path-planning problem, and is presented in the next section.

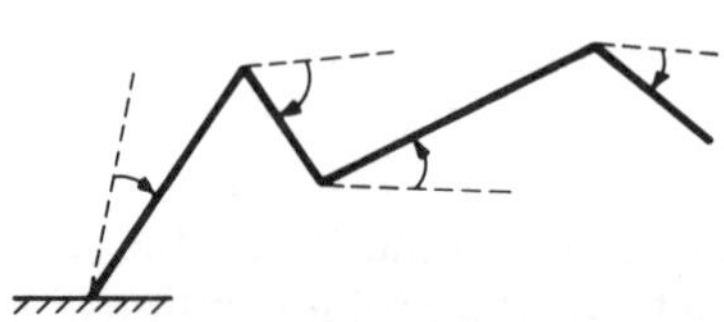

Figure 11.3 *The second term in the optimization criterion. The smaller the net joints displacement, the greater the fitness becomes.*

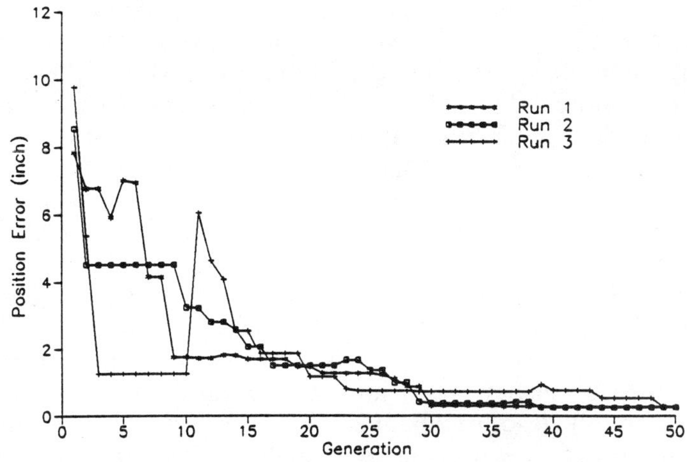

Figure 11.4 *Positioning error for three runs. Reprinted with permission from J. K. Parker, A. R. Khoogar, and D. E. Goldberg, "Inverse kinematics of redundant robots using genetic algorithms,"* 1989 IEEE International Conference on Robotics and Automation, *271–276.*

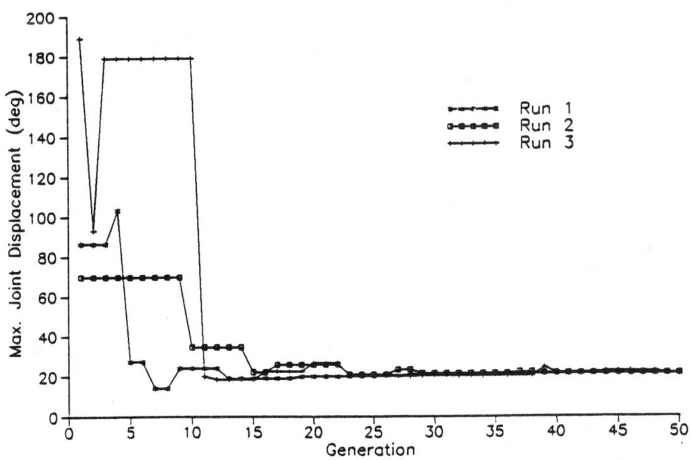

Figure 11.5 *Maximum joint displacement for three runs. Reprinted with permission from J. K. Parker, A. R. Khoogar, and D. E. Goldberg, "Inverse kinematics of redundant robots using genetic algorithms,"* 1989 IEEE International Conference on Robotics and Automation, *271–276.*

11.2.2 Robot Path Planning*

An end-effector trajectory is created by programming a sequence of arm configurations for the arm to follow. Optimization means the identification of the optimal number of intermediate end-effector positions and their spatial location.

* The work summarized in this section appears in full in Y. Davidor, *Genetic Algorithms and Robotics: A Heuristic Strategy for Optimization,* World Scientific, 1991.

The complexity of programming a trajectory can be appreciated by means of an example. Let us examine the vertical plane in which the end-effector is required to follow the straight line connecting points A and B (Fig. 11.6*a*). One robot program can list sites 1 and 2 for the end-effector to visit (Fig. 11.6*b*), while another program might consider sites 3, 4, 5, and 6 (Fig. 11.6*c*). Yet another possible trajectory, which also accounts for the effect of gravity, is composed of sites 7, 8, 9, and 10 (Fig. 11.6*d*). A typical industrial application involves trajectories with hundreds of discrete intermediate visiting points, resulting in an astronomical number of possible trajectories.

The quality of the resulting end-effector path of each of the alternative programs is quite different, though all trajectories aim at taking the arm from A to B as close as possible to the straight line connecting the two points. Making the decision of how many intermediate positions are necessary or needed to accurately describe a path is the fact that most intermediate end-effector positions can be realized by a multitude of arm configurations. Though only a minimal number of descriptions and arguments concerning the system were touched upon, it is possible to see that mechanical inaccuracies, mechanical coupling, and dynamic effects turn path planning into a complex problem to optimize.

The set of joint positions that defines an arm configuration is the basic gene in this model. Now that the genes are defined, it is possible to construct the full genotype. A string of l n-joint positions forms a genotype of length l of an n-joint structure. More formally, the general description of a trajectory is

$$\{\alpha_{1,1}, \alpha_{1,2}, \ldots, \alpha_{1,k}, \alpha_{2,1}, \ldots, \alpha_{2,k}, \alpha_{1,k}, \ldots, \alpha_{1,k}\}$$

where $\alpha_{i,j}$ is the position of the ith joint of the jth arm configuration. The purpose of the optimization is now clear: to find a sequence of α's that results in optimal dynamic behavior of the arm. The following section proposes a technique to optimize arbitrary robot trajectories.

The varying-length, order-dependent strings use a different crossover mechanism for matching cross sites than the traditional one historically suggested by Holland. After an arm configuration is chosen as a cross site in one parent string, the corresponding arm configuration in the second parent is determined according to its proximity to the end-effector's position.

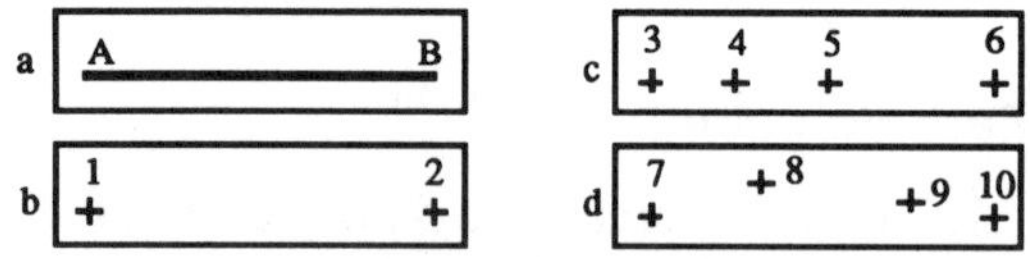

Figure 11.6 *Illustrating the complexity in generating a trajectory.* (a) *The desired straight-line path between the starting end* A *and the terminating end* B. (b) *One possible trajectory specified by two arm configurations that correspond to the end-effector being at the two ends of the desired path.* (c) *Another alternative trajectory with four end-effector positions along the desired path.* (d) *Another possible trajectory specification for the straight-line path.*

The concept of the foregoing crossover mechanism can be illustrated by the road system. Driving between two arbitrary points *A* and *B*, one can devise several alternative routes, while some routes may even have shared journeys. The logical and economical way of combining different routes is to switch over at either shared stretches of road or at intersections of routes. However, the cavalier driver may switch routes when he or she is not close to a shared stretch (or to a route that has no shared stretches with his or her current route at all) and thus endure the additional distance. For that reason, switching routes is more likely to occur at route positions where the two routes are close to each other.

Some Path-Planning Trails. The size of the trajectory space considered for this application is $\approx 10^{40}$. The results presented are typical convergence results (the detailed material is considered to be beyond the scope of this chapter but can be found in [2–5].

It is important to compare the performance of the GA with that of a random search and a greedy algorithm. Figure 11.7 plots the convergence rates for the three search algorithms: GA (hollow squares), hill climbing (hollow triangles), and random search (solid triangles).

11.3 OPTIMAL DESIGN OF ROBOT MANIPULATORS

The dynamic behavior of robot manipulators is complex, so complex that classical optimization methodologies are unable to optimize their perfor-

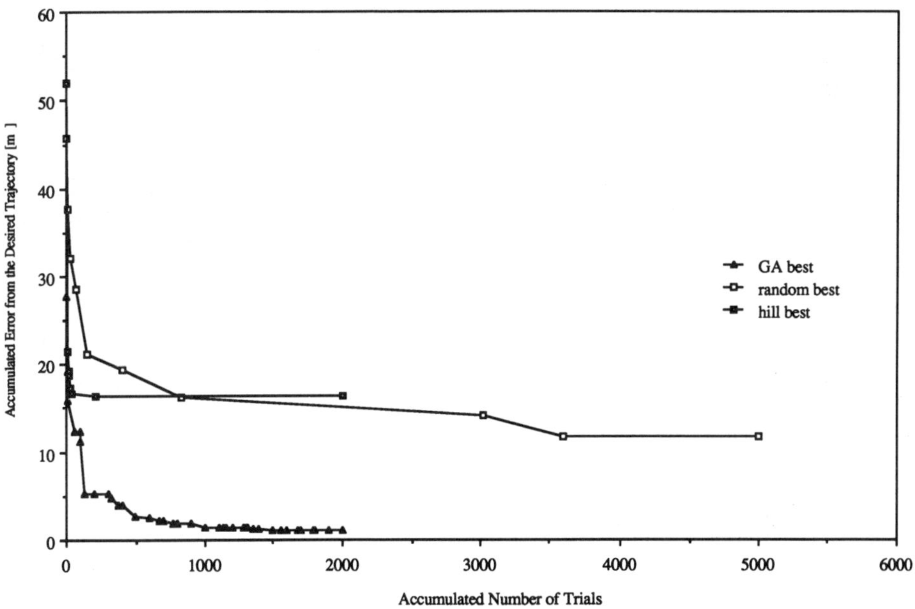

Figure 11.7 *Best trial results of a random search, analogous crossover GA, and a hill-climbing algorithm.*

mance. Thus, though improved performance would yield high financial rewards, industrial robots exhibit suboptimal performance. It is generally accepted that the mechanical design of manipulators—the morphology of the articulate arm—is the element impairing robot utility. This is because design methodologies are too rigid and inflexible to offer novel design concepts. Furthermore, in spite of their supremacy, highly redundant structures are not being utilized because they are even more complex to design and control by current technology.

In this section the design of a robotic manipulator is done by a GA. Initially, the GA is applied to the morphology optimization of a three-joint, revolute planar robot manipulator, but the model is not restricted to the amount of redundancy it considers.

11.3.1 Why Optimize the Morphology of Robot Manipulators?

Robotics research has advanced considerably during the last decade and has resulted in a totally new approach to manufacturing and design. The main reason for the intensive work has been the realization that robotics technology provides a mechanical structure whose operation can be controlled in a flexible fashion. However, robot systems are complex; they are composed of a medley of subsystems and feedback loops where hundreds of variables may affect their operation.

The mechanical design of the arm has hindered the further improving of performance, and the core problem in optimizing the mechanical design is that there is no straightforward algorithm to discover optimal kinematic parameters for an arbitrary structure [6]. Robotics research attempted to improve performance by restricting the mechanical design and improving the motion-planning algorithms. Thus, control circuitry becomes inundated with sophisticated routines while static and dynamic performances have not improved substantially.

The approach of compensating with software what hardware was unable to deliver suffers from two fundamental drawbacks. First, it attempts to mend too late and often too little (clearly, the morphological specifications set bounds on what can be achieved by control). Second, and equally important, the design methodology which relies on control to provide high performance, directs robotics research to consider structures that lend themselves to analytical study (such as the use of a serial design) but are kinematically less attractive [7,8].

Several novel works attempt to improve the mechanical design either by introducing new structures or algorithms for improving existing structures [9,10,11]. However, improvements have been limited, and, most important of all, no general design methodology capable of optimizing arbitrary structures with minimal restrictions on the style of design, amount of redundancy, and type of structure has been introduced.

11.3.2 Why Use a GA To Optimize Robot Manipulators?

A GA analyzes systems as a whole, and this holistic aspect of the algorithm enables it to tackle complex problems successfully. Optimization through a GA offers two important novelties:

1. Freedom from the need to specify explicit relations between the input parameters and their effect on performance,
2. An adaptive designing mechanism unrestricted in the exploration of a very large space of viable structures.

In attempting to find improved manipulator structures, one cannot ignore the need for new design methodologies and a greater variety of structures. Traditionally, engineering design had an equivocal attitude toward adopting structural ideas from Nature. Robot manipulators are a good example of this dualism. Manipulators incorporate, in a superficial way, design concepts from Nature (such as the serial limb structure) that, paradoxically, do not lend themselves to improved performance. It was recently suggested that different types of structures, structures typically found in nature, are more suitable for the current and future use of manipulators. As Hayward comments: "The organic quality of biological systems, which any person engaged in engineering research can easily appreciate, is far from being achieved by any technological systems" [8]. However, no existing design methodology is pliant enough to produce such structural solutions because they are too dependent on *ad hoc* and rigid constraints. In other words, design methodologies to date lack flexibility.

The motivation to use a GA as a design environment is based on the following dogma: In Nature, species are well adapted to their environmental niche in spite of the organisms' great complexity. The complexity of manipulators is analogous to that found in natural systems. Thus, in the attempt to overcome prohibitive complexity, one may draw analogies from natural structures and nurturing mechanisms that can produce such structures. It follows that if the essence of natural selection and evolution can be brought to the design table, then it might be possible to obtain both the high adaptability and diversity in design that is so characteristic of the natural world.

11.3.3 Overall Approach

The proposed model of GA is capable of optimizing redundant robot manipulators by considering the optimal length of joints and joint movements. The model is flexible in the sense that it can optimize any type of a manipulator structure with no theoretical limits on the degree of redundancy a given structure may incorporate. Furthermore, the optimization criterion, being external to the GA, is a modular component that can be tailored to describe any performance specifications based on kinematic parameters. This work demonstrates the principle of kinematic and morphological optimization of general mechanisms in the context of redundant robot manipulators. In Section 11.4, preliminary proof-of-principle results are presented for a few typical robot structures.

The *working area* (enclosed by the *working envelope*) designates the spatial space reachable by the end-effector. It is clear that redundant structures can reach several end-effector positions through a multitude of different arm configurations. This flexibility is an important property of redundant manipulators and for robot applications, such as collusion avoidance. The average number of multiple end-effector positions is termed *kinematic redundancy,* K_r. Recall that any mechanical structure has a finite positioning accuracy; thus, K_r is calculated as

$$K_r = \frac{|\text{all possible arm configurations}|}{|\text{all possible end-effector positions}|} \geq 1$$

The Genetic Algorithm Model. The GA environment requires a manipulator to be represented as a string of parameters that define the structure. The following representation has been adopted. A manipulator is defined by a set of binary n-tuples, one for each joint. The set of l n-tuples constitutes the string representing a manipulator of l joints. Each tuple consists of a link specification (type, minimum angle, and maximum angle) in Euler notation, and a joint specification (type and size). In the general case, each tuple contains parameters specifying the relevant joint structure.

The initial population (size 100) is generated at random. The performance of the corresponding manipulators (defined by the strings in the population) is evaluated according to a given performance criterion. The performance is translated into a fitness measure according to a predefined fitness function.

Only a simplified version of this model is considered for the initial tests. The manipulator is a specific type—a three-joint revolute planar arm. There are 128 possible discrete lengths for the first two joints (the length of the third is set automatically due to the requirement that the arm be of unit length), and the movement sector limits are represented with nine binary digits. This setting is translated into a 68-bit string structure, and a manipulator space of about 10^{20} ($128^2 \times 512^6$).

The evaluation process used a 120×120 grid system, having its center overlapping the origin of the axes located at the center of the first link (Fig. 11.1). The manipulator is moved systematically through all its joint positions in 5° intervals from the minimal position to the maximum (the interval size is a compromise between accuracy and consumption time). The position of the resulting end-effector is recorded on the grid and produces the working area and the topology of the repeated visits.

11.3.4 Kinematic Synthesis for a Complete Morphological Design

To better understand the interaction between a performance criterion and the corresponding optimal kinematical parameters, the proposed model for the optimization of manipulator morphology is first tested in a constraint environment. The manipulator is restricted to a three-joint planar manipulator (one degree of freedom is redundant).* The parameters of the manipulator subject to optimization are the lengths of the three joints and the movement sector of their corresponding joints. The total length of the three joints is a unit length, while the movement sector of each joint may take any value between zero and 2π. Thus, an optimization of a manipulator aims at locating the optimal division of a unit length among the three joints, and the optimal allocation of movement for each joint for a given performance criterion.

First Criterion—Maximum Size and Compactness of the Working Area. The fitness function in this first criterion is designed in such a way so that manipulators with a larger (and centered around the origin of the primary axes) working area have a higher fitness, or

$$\text{Fitness} = \frac{A^2}{\sqrt{I_x I_y}} \tag{11.1}$$

where A is the working area (in area units), and I_x and I_y are the second moments with respect to the horizontal and vertical axes X and Y, respectively. Theoretically, the maximum working area is a circle of unit length radius whose origin overlaps that of the primary axes (see Fig. 11.8 for the best manipulator among the random population). Applying the GA based on this criterion produced the maximum working area possible (a full circle) within 2000 evaluations. This manipulator has a $K_r \approx 3$ and a total of 1040° joint movement (out of 360 + 360 + 360 = 1080° maximum).

It is clear that such an optimization task is very simple to achieve with a redundant structure, because there are many manipulators that produce the maximum working area and the manipulator space is of very low modality. To make the problem more complex, constraints are introduced to the first performance criterion in the form of a cost on the movement of each joint angle α_i. Thus,

$$\text{Fitness} = \frac{A^2}{\sqrt{I_x I_y}} \frac{1}{3} \sum_{i=1}^{3} f(\alpha_i) \qquad f(\alpha_i) = \begin{cases} 1 & 0 \le \alpha < 40 \\ \left(1 - \dfrac{\alpha}{2\pi}\right)^2 & 40 \le \alpha < 60 \\ \left(1.1 - \dfrac{\alpha}{2\pi}\right)^3 & 60 \le \alpha \le 360 \end{cases} \tag{11.2}$$

* Human perception and intuition work well with structures incorporating up to 3 degrees of freedom. Because of this trait and the requirement to consider a redundant structure, a three-link planar manipulator is used.

Figure 11.8 *The best three-joint manipulator among the initial sample of 100 manipulators evaluated with criterion (11.1).*

Operating with the second performance criterion, the GA optimized a manipulator that provided 80% of the maximum working area, but economized substantially the redundancy in the joints movement (sum joint movement was reduced to only 620°). Consequently, K_r was reduced below 2.

To investigate the utility of the model in finding optimal design solutions, the model was tested with two additional performance criteria.

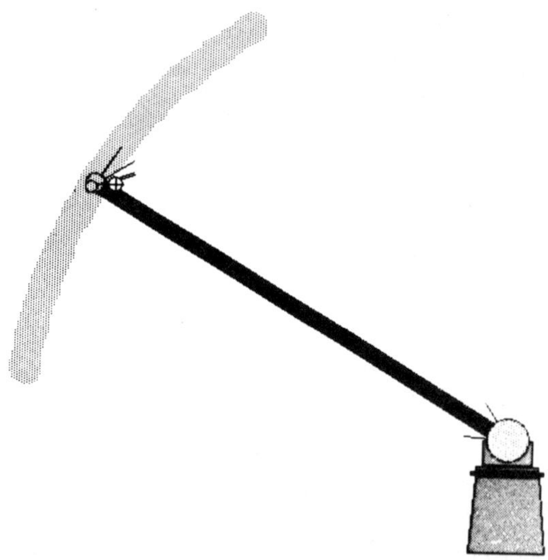

Figure 11.9 *Adaptation toward criterion (11.3). Best manipulator found within 2000 evaluations.*

Second Criterion—Maximum Flexibility in Placing the End Effector. The second criterion investigates the optimal morphology of a manipulator that is required to maximize its kinematic redundancy, or

$$\text{Fitness} = \frac{K_r^2}{\sqrt{I_x I_y}} \frac{1}{3} \sum_{i=1}^{3} f(\alpha_i) \tag{11.3}$$

The optimal manipulator for this criterion among the initial population exhibited $K_r \approx 43$ and $A = 638$. Figure 11.9 shows the adapted manipulator found within 2000 elevations. This optimal manipulator exhibited a $K_r \approx 505$ at the cost of pronounced shrinkage of the working area ($A = 76$). When the cost of joint movement was removed, the optimal manipulator adapted itself accordingly and increased the movement sector of the first joint, thus resulting in a working area shaped like a closed ring.

Third Criterion—A Rectangular Working Envelope. A counterintuitive problem is selected as the third performance criterion. The aim is to find the manipulator that will produce the most rectangular working area (noting that all joints are revolute). The fitness function used to represent this criterion is

$$\text{Fitness} = \frac{1}{1 + (V - A)} \leq 1 \tag{11.4}$$

where V is the area of the rectangle enclosing the working area A. When the working area is a perfect rectangle, the working area and the enclosing rectangle overlap. The optimal manipulator found within 2000 evaluations is shown in Figure 11.10.

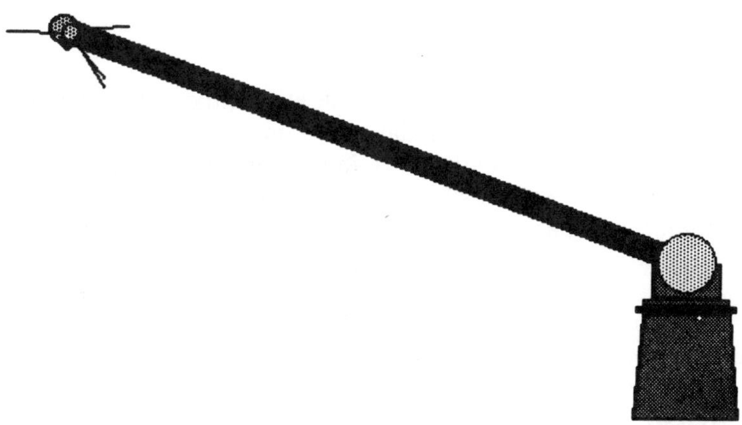

Figure 11.10 *Adaptation toward criterion (11.4). Best manipulator found within 2000 evaluations.*

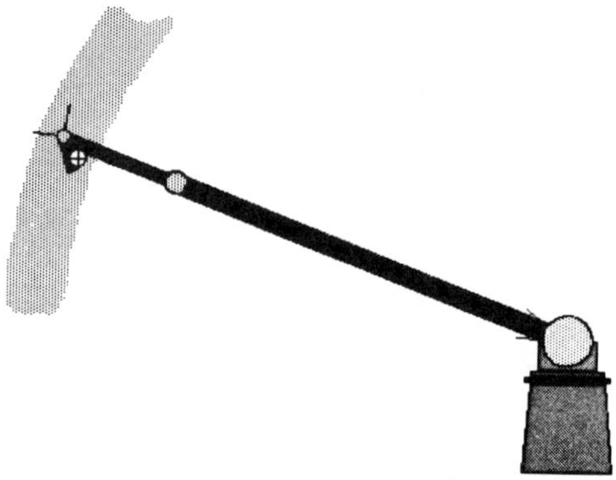

Figure 11.11 *Adaptation toward criterion (11.5). Best manipulator found within 2000 evaluations.*

Certainly the manipulator the GA found is indeed the optimal design for criterion (11.4). The further away the working area is from the origin, the straighter and more parallel is its working envelope; and the smaller it is, the smaller the difference between the working area and its enclosing rectangle. However, a manipulator is expected to move and perform tasks. Therefore, criterion (11.4) is modified to exhibit a balance between as large a working area as possible while keeping it as rectangular as possible (Fig. 11.11). The fitness function for this application then becomes

$$\text{Fitness} = \frac{A}{1 + (V - A)} \tag{11.5}$$

and the corresponding manipulator is shown in Figure 11.11.

11.3.5 Conclusions

This chapter discussed the concept of adopting biological metaphors to improve mechanical design of redundant robot manipulators. A model of a GA was introduced, and a simplified version of this model was applied to few simple design tasks. Before summarizing the model and its applicability to this domain, we remark on the scale-up and universality of the proposed model.

For clarity, the present proof-of-principle examples avoided two important issues: the availability of formal performance criterion for arbitrary optimal manipulators, and the mechanics of the performance evaluation aspect of the simulation. These issues are at the heart of this work and are recognized by the author to be the stumbling block in implementing problem-solving metaphors such as GA to real-world problems.

Defining a performance criterion is an elusive task, both theoretically and empirically, because one often cannot tell whether a given criterion encompasses the desired performance. The problem lies in the difficulty of explicitly formalizing abstract goals as required in a GA application. For example, it is not at all clear which is the best (or even correct) definition of squareness for the purpose of producing a square working area (as criterion (11.4) shows).

The second issue, the availability of performance evaluation mechanisms, is again an artifact of the mechanisms of a GA. In nature, performance evaluation is readily available and is provided freely in the form of relative proliferation. However, in the artificial environment, performance has to be evaluated explicitly, sometimes requiring prohibitive computation resources (even in massively parallel architectures).

These difficulties, are external to GA. A new concept of morphological design of manipulators was introduced. It was shown in a few simplified examples that a model of natural selection and reproduction can optimize manipulator morphology and that this design environment is highly adaptive and robust. Even at the simplified level of the present model, which was deliberately chosen as such to serve as an intuitive proof-of-principle, the GA performed surprisingly well. Not only did it find the correct optimal solutions, but it did so more efficiently than a greedy algorithm. It is recognized that the utility of this model, and similar models, applied to other design domains, greatly depends on further research. The main moral of this work lies in accepting that engineers should uninhibitedly look into natural mechanisms and nurturing environments in order to develop new design methodologies and design concepts. Furthermore, the problematic issues of optimizing manipulators, discussed in Section 11.1 may greatly benefit from this natural design style.

11.4 SUMMARY

Applications of GA to solve difficult real-world problems in robotics were presented. They were applied to three issues identified in contemporary robotics technology as the bottlenecks to improving and expanding performance. The solutions offered to these problems represent a new approach to solving complex problems where good models of the system do not exist. This approach is the GA approach.

In particular, this chapter summarizes attempts to overcome a complexity that prevents further development of sophisticated robotics systems, systems that can perform more complicated tasks, more accurately, more reliably, and more efficiently. It is of great interest to follow these inchoate attempts using GA in robotics and to witness how Nature-motivated optimization algorithms can improve the standard and quality of our achievements in manufacturing and engineering.

ACKNOWLEDGMENTS

This work was supported in part by the Centre for Absorption in Science, The Ministry of Immigrant Absorption, The State of Israel. The author wishes to thank Loen Zlajpa for allowing the free use of his simulation of robot dynamics used in the work reported in Section 11.2.2, Yaron Goldberg for his valuable work in programing and debugging the algorithm used in Section 11.3, and Alistair Dunlop for developing the 2D graphic display of the robot manipulator used in Section 11.3. Y. Davidor is a recipient of a Sir Charles Clore Fellowship.

REFERENCES

[1] J. K. Parker, A. R. Khoogar, and D. E. Goldberg, Inverse kinematics of redundant robots using genetic algorithms, *IEEE Internat. Conf. on Robotics and Automation,* 271–276 (1989).

[2] Y. Davidor, Lamarckian sub-goal reward in genetic algorithm, *European Conf. on Artificial Intelligence,* 189–194 (1990).

[3] Y. Davidor, Robot programming with a genetic algorithm, *IEEE Internat. Conf. on Computer Systems and Software Engineering,* 186–191 (1990).

[4] Y. Davidor, "A Genetic Algorithm Applied to Robot Path-Planning," in L. Davis, Ed., *The Genetic Algorithm Handbook,* Van Nostrand Reinhold, New York, 1991.

[5] Y. Davidor, *Genetic Algorithms and Robotics: A Heuristic Strategy for Optimization,* World Scientific Publishing, Singapore, 1991.

[6] J. Lenarcic, U. Stanic, and P. Oblak, Some kinematic considerations for the design of robot manipulators. *1st Internat. Conf. on Robotics,* (1987).

[7] V. Hayward, "An Analysis of Redundant Manipulators from Several View-Points, in A. K. Bejczy, Ed., *NATO Advanced Research Workshop on Robot With Redundancy: Design, Sensing and Control,* Springer Verlag, XXX, 1988.

[8] V. Hayward, "Borrowing Some Design Ideas from Biological Manipulators to Design an Artificial One," in P. Pario et al. Eds., *NATO Advance Research Workshop, Robots and Biological Systems,* Springer Verlag, XXX, 1989.

[9] R. L. Fox and K. C. Gupta, Optimization technology as applied to mechanism design, *ASME J. Eng. Industry,* 657–663 (1973).

[10] J. M. Hollerbach, Optimum kinematic design for a seven degrees of freedom manipulator, *2nd Internat. Symp. on Robotics Research,* 215–222 (1984).

[11] D. C. H. Yang and T. W. Lee, Heuristic combinatorial optimization in the design of manipulator workspace, *IEEE Trans. on Systems, Man and Cybernetics,* **SMC-14**(4), 571–580 (1984).

CHAPTER 12

Efficient Multiprocessor Scheduling Based on Genetic Algorithms

EDWIN S. H. HOU
HONG REN
NIRWAN ANSARI

12.1 INTRODUCTION

The problem of multiprocessor scheduling can be stated as finding a schedule for a general task graph to be executed on a multiprocessor system so that the schedule length can be minimized. This scheduling problem is known to be NP-complete, and methods based on heuristic search have been proposed to obtain optimal and suboptimal solutions to the problem. Genetic algorithms have recently received much attention as robust stochastic searching algorithms for various optimization problems. In this chapter, an efficient method based on genetic algorithms is developed to solve the multiprocessor scheduling problem. The representation of the search node is based on the schedule of the tasks in each processor. The genetic operator proposed is based on the precedence relations between the tasks in the task graph. Experimental results based on robot inverse dynamics computation task graphs are presented.

Multiprocessor scheduling has been a source of challenging problems for researchers in computer engineering. The general problem of multiprocessor scheduling can be stated as scheduling a set of partially ordered computation tasks onto a multiprocessor system so that an objective function will be optimized. The difficulty of the problem depends heavily on the topology of the task graph representing the precedence relations among the computation tasks, the topology of the multiprocessor system, the number of parallel

Dynamic, Genetic, and Chaotic Programming, By Branko Souček and the IRIS Group.
ISBN 0-471-55717-X

processors, the uniformity of the task processing time, and the objective function chosen. In general, finding an optimal algorithm for multiprocessor scheduling is computationally intractable even under simplified assumptions [1]. Due to this computational complexity issue, heuristic algorithms have been proposed to obtain optimal and suboptimal solutions to various scheduling problems.

Various approaches to the general multiprocessor scheduling problem have been proposed [2–5]. Due to the intractability of the problem, heuristic approaches have been developed to solve the problem. Kashara and Narita [4,5] proposed a heuristic algorithm (critical path/most immediate successors first) and an optimization/approximation algorithm (depth first/implicit heuristic search). Chen et al. [6] developed a state-space search algorithm (A^*) coupled with a heuristic derived from the Fernandez and Bussell bound to solve the multiprocessor scheduling problem.

The task scheduling problem considered in this chapter is based on the deterministic model; that is, the execution time and the relationship between the computation tasks is known. The precedence relationship among the tasks is represented by an acyclic directed graph, and the task completion time can be nonuniform. We assume that the multiprocessor system is uniform and nonpreemptive (that is, the processors are identical) and that a processor completes the current task before executing a new one. This chapter presents an efficient method based on genetic algorithms to solve the multiprocessor scheduling problem. Genetic algorithms have recently received much attention as robust stochastic searching algorithms for various optimization problems [7,8,9]. This class of methods is based on the mechanics of natural selection and natural genetics that combines the notion of survival of the fittest, random and yet structured search, and parallel evaluation of the nodes in the search space. This chapter is organized as follows. First, a brief introduction to genetic algorithms is given. The representation of the task graph and the search nodes are presented next, followed by how the initial population of the search nodes are generated. Next, the fitness function, the construction of three genetic operators, crossover, reproduction, and mutation, are discussed. Finally, we present experimental results based on the problem of scheduling the robot inverse dynamics computations.

12.2 GENETIC ALGORITHMS

Genetic algorithms have been successfully applied to various optimization problems, such as the traveling salesman problem as gas pipeline optimization. Their success can be attributed to the following principles [10]:

1. They use a coding of the parameter set rather than the parameters themselves.

2. They search from a population of search nodes instead of a single one.
3. They use probabilistic transition rules.

A genetic algorithm consists of a string representation ("genes") of the nodes in the search space, a set of genetic operators for generating new search nodes, a fitness function to evaluate the search nodes, and a stochastic assignment to control the genetic operators.

Typically, a genetic algorithm consists of the following steps:

1. *Initialization* An initial population of the search nodes are randomly generated.
2. *Evaluation of Fitness Function* The fitness value of each node is calculated according to the fitness function (objective function).
3. *Genetic Operations* New search nodes are generated randomly by examining the fitness value of the search nodes and applying the genetic operators to the search nodes.
4. Repeat steps 2 and 3 until convergent.

We can thus see that genetic algorithms utilize the notion of survival of the fittest—passing "good" genes to the next generation of strings, and combining different strings to explore new search points.

The construction of a genetic algorithm for any problem can be separated into four distinct yet related tasks:

1. Choice of the representation of the strings,
2. Design of the genetic operators,
3. Determination of the fitness function,
4. Determination of the probabilities controlling the genetic operators.

Each task greatly affects the solution obtained and the performance of the genetic algorithm. In the following sections we briefly examine each of them for the problem of multiprocessor scheduling.

12.3 MULTIPROCESSOR SCHEDULING WITH GENETIC ALGORITHMS

A task system can be represented by a directed acyclic task graph, TG = (V, E), consisting of a finite nonempty set of vertices V and a set of finite directed edges E connecting the vertices. The collection of vertices $V = \{T_1, T_2, \ldots, T_m\}$ represents a set of computation tasks to be executed, and the directed edges $E = \{e_{ij}\}$ (e_{ij} represents a directed edge from vertex T_i to T_j) implies that a partial ordering or precedence relation $\gg$ exists between the

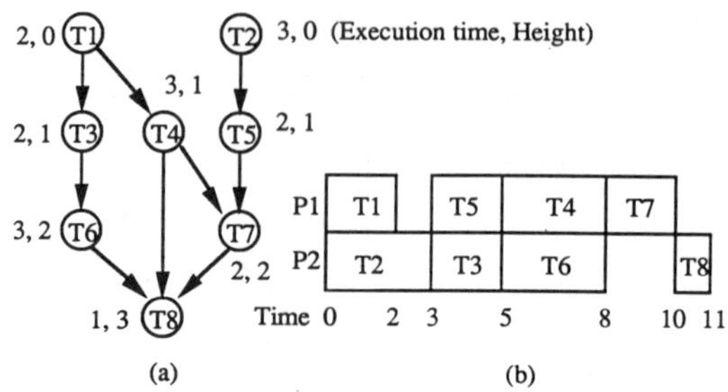

Figure 12.1 (a) *Task graph TG.* (b) *A schedule for two processors.*

tasks. That is, if $T_i \gg T_j$, then T_i must be completed before T_j can be initiated. A simple task graph with eight tasks is illustrated in Figure 12.1*a*.

The problem of optimal scheduling of a task graph and a multiprocessor system with p processors is to assign the computation tasks to the processors in such a way that the precedence relations are maintained and that all tasks are completed in the shortest possible time. The time that the last task is completed is called the *finishing time* (FT) of the schedule. Figure 12.1*b* illustrates a schedule for the example task graph TG for two processors. We will also adopt the following notation when discussing task graphs:

$$\begin{aligned} \text{PRED}(T_i) &= \text{set of predecessors of } T_i, \\ \text{SUCC}(T_i) &= \text{set of successors of } T_i, \\ \text{et}(T_i) &= \text{execution time of } T_i. \end{aligned}$$

12.3.1 String Representation

Davis [11] considered the problem of finding a representation for genetic algorithms in the problem of job shop scheduling. An intermediary, encoded representation of the schedules and a decoder was used that would always yield legal solutions to the problem. The representation is somewhat complicated and is for a different problem.

An important factor in deciding the string representation for the search nodes is that all the search nodes are represented and the representation is unique. It is also desirable, but not necessary, that each string correspond to a legal search node (see Fig. 12.2). The design of the genetic operator will be greatly simplified if the string representation space and the search space are in 1-1 correspondence (see Sec. 12.3.4).

For the multiprocessor scheduling problem, a legal search node (a schedule) is one that satisfies (1) the precedence relations among the tasks and (2) every task is present and appears only once in the schedule (completeness and uniqueness). The string representation used in this chapter is based on

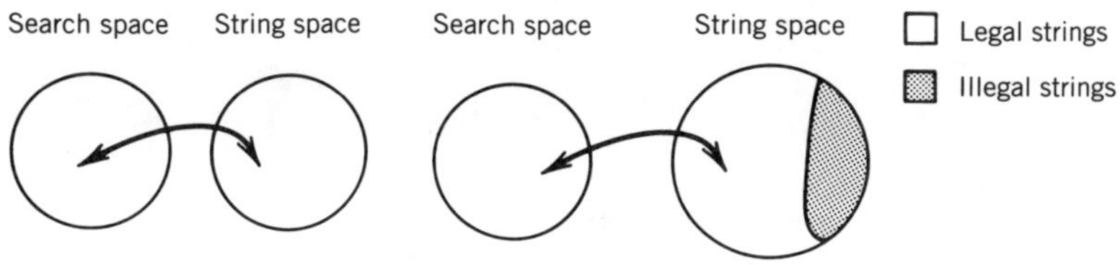

Figure 12.2 *Mapping between string representation space and search space.*

the schedule of the tasks in each processor. This representation eliminates the need to consider the precedence relations between the tasks scheduled to different processors. However, the precedence relations within the processor must still be maintained.

The representation of the schedule for genetic algorithms must accommodate the precedence relations between the computational tasks. This is resolved by representing the schedule as several lists of computation tasks. Each list represents the computational tasks executed on a processor, and the order of the tasks in the list indicates the order of execution (see Fig. 12.3). This ordering allows us to maintain the precedence relations for the tasks executed in a processor (intraprocessor precedence relation) and ignore the precedence relations between tasks executed in different processors (interprocessor precedence relation). This is because the interprocessor precedence relation does not come into play until we actually calculate the finishing time of the schedule. This list representation of a schedule for the N tasks can be further viewed as a permutation of N numbers (see Fig. 12.4). Thus, a legitimate schedule for N tasks and m processors is a permutation of N numbers with m cycles. The permutation representation of schedules is useful when we actually implement the genetic algorithm.

12.3.2 Initial Population

One of the merits of the genetic algorithm is that it searches many nodes in the search space in parallel. This requires us to generate an initial population of the search nodes randomly. The population size is typically problem dependent and has to be determined experimentally. To facilitate the generation of the schedule and the construction of the genetic operator, we define the height of each task in the task graph as

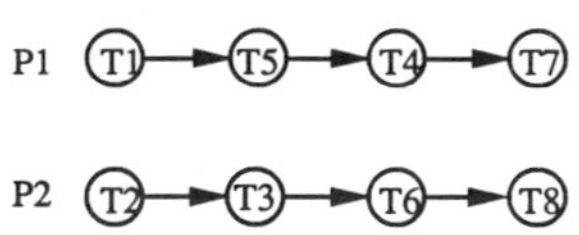

Figure 12.3 *List representation of schedule.*

$$\begin{pmatrix}1&2&3&4&5&6&7&8\\5&3&6&7&4&8&1&2\end{pmatrix} = \begin{pmatrix}1&5&4&7\\5&4&7&1\end{pmatrix}\begin{pmatrix}2&3&6&8\\3&6&8&2\end{pmatrix}$$

i corresponds to Ti

Figure 12.4 *Permutation.*

$$\text{height}(T_i) = \begin{cases} 0 & \text{if PRED}(T_i) = \emptyset \\ 1 + \max\limits_{T_j \in \text{PRED}(T_i)} \text{height}(T_j) & \text{otherwise} \end{cases}$$

This height function in a way conveys the precedence relations between the tasks. In fact, if there is a path from T_i to T_j (that is, there exists a series of directed edges leading from T_i to T_j), then T_i must be executed before T_j and height(T_i) < height(T_j). However, if there is no path between the two tasks, then the order of execution between them can be arbitrary.

In order to simplify the construction of the genetic operator (see Sec. 12.3.4), we imposed the following condition on the schedules were generated: The list of tasks within each processor of the schedule is ordered in ascending order of their height. For example, in processor P_1 of Figure 12.2, we have

$$\text{height}(T_1) < \text{height}(T_5) \leq \text{height}(T_4) < \text{height}(T_7)$$

One major drawback of having this condition is that the optimal schedule may not satisfy it. To reduce the likelihood of this happening, we can modify the definition of height as follows. We can define the new height (height′) of a task T_j to be a random integer between max height(T_i) + 1 and min height(T_k) − 1 over all $T_i \in$ PRED(T_j) and $T_k \in$ SUCC(T_j). We can then use the following algorithm to generate the initial population of schedules.

Algorithm Generate-Schedule

This algorithm randomly generates a schedule of the task graph TG for a multiprocessor system with p processors.

GS1. [Initialize.] Compute height′ for every task in TG.

GS2. [Separate the tasks according to their height.] Partition the tasks in TG into different sets $G(h)$ (the set of tasks with height h) according to the value of height′.

GS3. [Loop p-1 times.] For the first p-1 processors, do step GS4.

GS4. [Loop for each set of tasks.] For each set $G(h)$, $NG(h) \leftarrow$ number of tasks in $G(h)$ and do step GS5.

GS5. [Form the schedule for a processor.] Randomly generate a number r between 0 and $NG(h)$. Pick r tasks from $G(h)$ and assign them to the current processor.

GS6. [Last processor.] Assign the remaining tasks in the set $G(h)$ to the last processor.

By repeatedly applying this algorithm, we can generate the initial population of search nodes needed.

12.3.3 Fitness Function

The fitness function is essentially the objective function for the problem. It provides a means of evaluating the search nodes, and it also controls the reproduction process. For the multiprocessor scheduling problem, we can consider factors such as throughput, finishing time, and processor utilization for the fitness function. The fitness function used for our algorithm is based on the finishing time of the schedule. To compute the finishing time of a schedule using our representation, we need to calculate the two sets of values

$\text{ftt}(i)$ = finishing time of task T_i

$\text{ftp}(j)$ = finishing time for processor P_j

The finishing time of a schedule is then

$$FT = \max_{P_j} \text{ftp}(j)$$

To calculate the finishing time of each processor, we can apply the following algorithm.

Algorithm Finishing-Time

This algorithm calculates the finishing time of a schedule represented as several lists of tasks.

FT1. [Initialize.]
For each processor P_j, $\text{ftp}(j) \leftarrow 0$.

FT2. [Loop for every task T_i.]
For each task T_i in processor P_j, do steps FT3, FT4, and FT5.

FT3. [Task T_i has no predecessor.]
If $\text{PRED}(T_i) = \emptyset$, $\text{ftt}(i) \leftarrow \text{et}(i) + \text{ftp}(j)$.

FT4. [Task T_i has predecessors.]
Otherwise, $\text{ftt}(i) \leftarrow \text{et}(i) + \max\{\text{ftt}(k), \text{ftp}(j)\}$, where $T_k \in \text{PRED}(T_i)$.

FT5. [Update the finishing time of processor P_j.]
ftp(j) ← ftt(i).

FT6. [Calculate the finishing time of the schedule.]
FT ← max ftp(j) over all P_j.

The fitness function is then 1/FT.

12.3.4 Genetic Operators

The function of the genetic operators is to create new search nodes based on the current population of search nodes. New search nodes are typically constructed by combining or rearranging parts of the old search nodes. The idea (as in genetics) is that with a properly chosen string representation of the search nodes, certain structures in the representation would represent the "goodness" of that search node. Thus, by combining the good structures of two search nodes, we may obtain an even better one. Relating this idea to multiprocessing scheduling, we see that certain portions of a schedule may belong to the optimal schedule. By combining several of these "optimal" parts, we can find the optimal schedule efficiently.

If the string representation space and the search space are not in 1-1 correspondence, then we must design the genetic operator carefully. If the number of strings that correspond to illegal search nodes is relatively small, then it may be acceptable to allow the genetic operator to generate illegal strings (see Fig. 12.5*a*) and discard them later with a legality test. However, if the number of strings that correspond to illegal search nodes is comparable to those representing legal search nodes, then too much computation time will be wasted in generating the illegal strings and checking the new strings. In this case, a "good" genetic operator is one that would always generate a string representing a legal search node (see Fig. 12.5*b*). However, this may not be achievable due to factors such as the high computational cost of the operator.

For the multiprocessor scheduling problem, the genetic operators used must enforce the intraprocessor precedence relations and the completeness

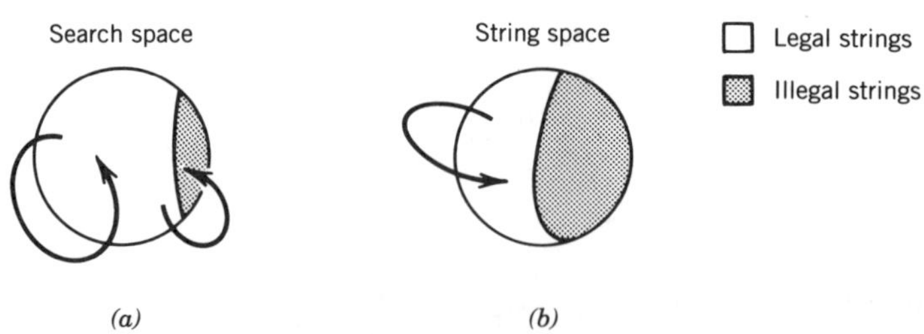

Figure 12.5 *Genetic operator that generates both* (a) *legal and illegal strings,* (b) *legal strings.*

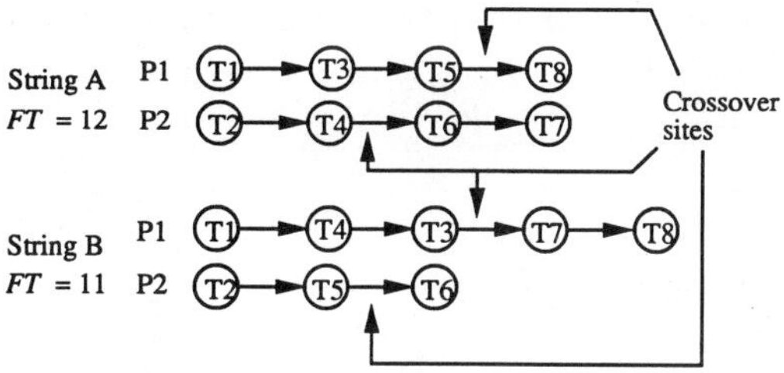

Figure 12.6 *Two different strings.*

and uniqueness of the tasks in the schedule as discussed in Section 12.3.1. This would ensure that the new strings generated always represent legal search nodes. We will develop a genetic operator for the scheduling problem based on the notion of crossover [10].

Crossover. Consider the two strings (schedules) in Figure 12.6. We can create new strings by exchanging portions of the two strings with the following method:

1. Select sites (crossover sites) where we can cut the lists into halves (see Fig. 12.6).
2. Exchange the bottom halves of P_1 in string A and string B.
3. Exchange the bottom halves of P_2 in string A and string B.

The new strings created are shown in Figure 12.7. Notice that one of the new strings has a smaller finishing time than the previous two strings. This is the optimal finishing time for the task graph TG using two processors. The operation described can be easily extended to m processors and appears to be quite effective. However, we still have to find a method to select the crossover sites and show that the new strings generated are legal.

Notice that the crossover sites used in our example always lie between tasks with two different heights (height(T_5) $\neq$ height(T_8), height(T_4) $\neq$ height(T_6), etc.), and the result is two legal strings. It appears that the selection of the crossover sites is strong related to the legality of the strings generated. It can be easily shown that if the crossover sites are chosen in such a way that (1) the heights of the tasks next to the crossover sites are

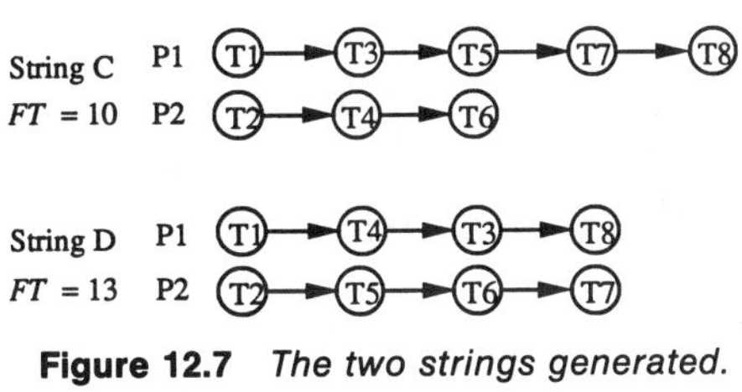

Figure 12.7 *The two strings generated.*

different and (2) the heights of all the tasks in front of the crossover sites are the same, then the new strings generated will always be legal. The crossover operation is summarized in the algorithm Crossover.

Algorithm Crossover

This algorithm performs the crossover operation on two strings (A and B) and generates two new strings.

C1. [Select crossover sites.] Randomly generate a number c between 0 and the maximum height of the task graph.

C2. [Loop for every processor.] For each processor P_i in string A and string B, do step C3.

C3. [Find the crossover sites.] Find consecutive tasks T_{ji} and T_{ki} in processor P_i such that $c = \text{height}'(T_{ji}) < \text{height}'(T_{ki})$, $\text{height}'(T_{ji})$ are the same for all i.

C4. [Loop for every processor.] For each processor P_i in string A and string B, do step C5.

C5. [Crossover.] Exchange the bottom halves of the tasks in string A and string B for each processor P_i.

Although the crossover operation is powerful, it may not be desirable to perform it all the time. This is because the crossover operation is random in nature and may possibly eliminate the optimal solution. Typically, its operation is controlled by a crossover probability. The value of this crossover probability is usually determined experimentally.

Reproduction. A commonly used genetic operator is reproduction. The reproduction process is typically based on the fitness values of the strings. The principle is that strings with higher fitness value will have a higher chance of surviving to the next generation. The rationale here is that "good" strings have high fitness value, and they should be preserved into the next generation. Typically, a biased roulette wheel is used to implement reproduction. Each string in the population occupies a slot size proportional to its fitness value. random numbers are generated and used as an index into the roulette wheel to determine which string will be passed to the next generation. Because the strings with higher fitness will have larger slots, they are more likely to be selected and passed onto the next generation.

We can make a slight modification to the basic reproduction operation by always passing the best string in the current generation to the next generation. This modification will increase the performance of the genetic algorithm. The reproduction operation is summarized in the following algorithm.

Algorithm Reproduction

This algorithm performs the reproduction operation on a population of strings *POP* and generates a new population of strings *NEWPOP*.

R1. [Initialize.] Let *NPOP* ← number of strings in *POP*.
R2. [Construct the roulette wheel.] *NSUM* ← sum of all the fitness value of the strings in *POP;* form *NSUM* slots and assign string to the slots according to the fitness value of the string.
R3. [Loop *NPOP* − 1 times.] Do step R4 *NPOP* − 1 times.
R4. [Pick a string.] Generate a random number between 1 and *NSUM* and use it to index into the slots to find the corresponding string; add this string to *NEWPOP*.
R5. [Add the best string.] Add the string with the highest fitness value in *POP* to *NEWPOP*.

Mutation. Mutation can be considered as an occasional (with small probability) random alternation of the value of a string. One can think of mutation as an escape mechanism for premature convergence. For the multiprocessor scheduling problem, mutation is applied by randomly exchanging two tasks with the same height. The mutation operation is summarized in the following algorithm.

Algorithm Mutation

This algorithm performs the mutation operation on a string and generates a new string.

M1. [Pick a task.] Randomly pick a task T_i.
M2. [Match height.] Search the string for a task T_j with the same height.
M3. [Exchange tasks.] Form a new string by exchanging the two tasks, T_i and T_j, in the schedule.

12.3.5 Complete Algorithm

We can now combine all the algorithms discussed to form the genetic algorithm for multiprocessor scheduling.

Algorithm Find-Schedule

This algorithm attempts to solve the multiprocessor scheduling problem.

FS1. [Initialize.] Call Generate-Schedule *N* times and store the strings created in *POP*.

FS2. [Repeat until convergent.] Do steps FS3–FS7 until convergent.

FS3. [Compute fitness values.] Compute the fitness value of each string in *POP*.

FS4. [Perform reproduction.] Call the algorithm Reproduction.

FS5. [Perform crossover.] Do step FS6 *NPOP*/2 times.

FS6. [Crossover.] Pick two strings from *NEWPOP* and call the algorithm Crossover with a probability *PROB-CROSSOVER*. If Crossover is performed, put the new strings in *TEMP-POP;* otherwise put the two strings picked in *TEMP-POP*.

FS7. [Mutation.] For each string in *TEMP-POP,* call the algorithm Mutation with a probability *PROB-MUTATION*. If mutation is performed, put the new string in *POP;* otherwise put the string picked in *POP*.

12.4 SIMULATION RESULTS

The genetic algorithm we discussed was applied to task graphs for Newton-Euler inverse dynamic equations for the Stanford manipulator and elbow manipulator [5]. The Stanford manipulator task graph consists of 88 tasks and task processing times ranging from 1 to 111 μs. The genetic algorithm was run with a population size of 20, crossover probability 0.5, and mutation

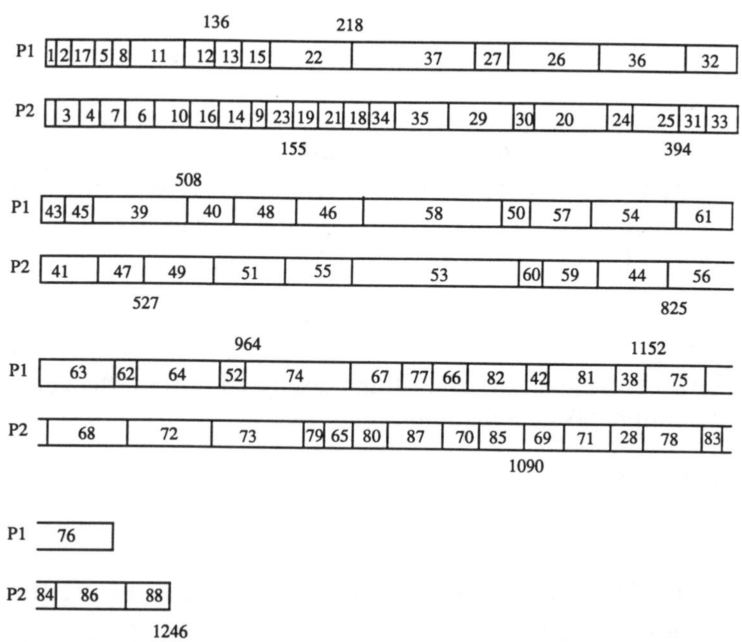

Figure 12.8 *Best schedule for two processors found by genetic algorithm.*

TABLE 12.1 Comparison of Genetic Algorithm Solution and Optimal Solution for Stanford Manipulator Task Graph

	Processing Time (μs)	
Number of Processors	Genetic Algorithm Solution	Optimal Solution
2	1246	1242
3	938	843
4	774	659
5	679	586
6	527	573
10	590	570

probability 0.003. Table 12.1 summarizes the solution obtained from the genetic algorithm and the optimal solution for the task graph. Figure 12.8 illustrates the solution found by the genetic algorithm with two processors. The algorithm converges to a solution in 2000 generations, which is extremely fast. The elbow manipulator has 103 tasks and task processing times ranging from 10 to 570 μs. Table 12.2 summarizes the solution found by the genetic algorithm for the task graph of the elbow manipulator.

12.5 CONCLUSIONS

We considered the problem of scheduling a task graph onto a microprocessor system so that the schedule length is minimized. A stochastic search method based on genetic algorithms was proposed. The representation of the search nodes (schedules) used are in the form of lists of computation tasks. This eliminates the need to consider the precedence relations between tasks in different processors and allows us to construct a crossover genetic opera-

TABLE 12.2 Genetic Algorithm Solution for the Elbow Manipulator Task Graph

Number of Processors	Processing Time (μs) Genetic Algorithm Solution
2	12,340
3	8,940
4	7,260
5	6,980
6	6,630
10	6,630

tor. The genetic operator developed takes into account the precedence relations of the tasks and guarantees that the new strings generated are legal. The proposed genetic algorithm was tested with the Newton-Euler inverse dynamic equations task graphs for the Stanford manipulator and elbow manipulator.

REFERENCES

[1] M. R. Garey and D. S. Johnson, *Computer and Intractability, A Guide to the Theory of NP-Completeness,* W. H. Freeman and Co., New York, 1979.

[2] C. V. Ramamoorthy, K. M. Chandy, and M. J. Gonzalez, Optimal scheduling strategies in a multiprocessor system, *IEEE Trans. Computers,* C-21, 137–146 (February 1972).

[3] T. L. Adams, K. M. Chandy, and J. R. Dickson, A comparison of list schedules for parallel processing systems, *Comm. Assoc. Computing Machinery,* 17, 685–690 (December 1974).

[4] H. Kasahara and S. Narita, "Practical multiprocessing scheduling algorithms for efficient parallel processing," *IEEE Trans. Computers,* C-33(11), 1023–1029 (November 1984).

[5] H. Kasahara and S. Narita, Parallel processing of robot-arm control computation on a multimicroprocessor system, *IEEE J. Robotics and Automation,* RA-1(2), 104–113 (June 1985).

[6] C. L. Chen, C. S. G. Lee, and E. S. H. Hou, Efficient scheduling algorithms for robot inverse dynamics computation on a multiprocessor system, *IEEE Trans. on Systems, Man, and Cybernetics,* 18(5), 729–743 (December 1988).

[7] John J. Grefenstette, Ed., *Proc. 1st Internat. Conf. on Genetic Algorithms and Their Applications* (July 24–26, 1985).

[8] John J. Grefenstette, Ed., *Proc. 2nd Internat. Conf. on Genetic Algorithms and Their Applications* (July 28–31, 1987).

[9] J. David Schaffer, Ed., *Proc. 3rd Intern. Conf. on Genetic Algorithms* (June 4–7, 1989).

[10] D. E. Goldberg, *Genetic Algorithms in Search, Optimization, and Machine Learning,* Addison Wesley, Reading, Mass., 1989.

[11] L. Davis, Job shop scheduling with genetic algorithms, *Proc. 1st Internat. Conf. on Genetic Algorithms and Their Applications,* John J. Grefenstette, Ed., 136–140 (July 24–26, 1985).

CHAPTER 13

A Genetic Algorithm for Point Pattern Matching

NIRWAN ANSARI
MING-HWANG CHEN
EDWIN S. H. HOU

13.1 INTRODUCTION

The problem considered in this chapter is to find a subset of points in a pattern that best match to a subset of points in another pattern through a transformation in an optimal sense. An exhaustive search to find the best assignment mapping one set of points to another set is, if the number of ponts that are to be matched is large, computationally expensive. A genetic algorithm is developed to search for the best (''almost the best'') assignment efficiently. To map the point pattern matching into the framework of a genetic algorithm, a fitness function inversely proportional to the match error, a scheme to encode an assignment between two sets of ponts into a string, and a new genetic operator known as mixed-type partial matching crossover are developed. Experimental results have demonstrated the robustness and the fast convergence of the algorithm. The proposed algorithm can be applied to n-dimensional point patterns and any transformation, but only results for two-dimensional point patterns and a similarity transformation are presented.

Point pattern matching is an important task in computer vision that is applicable to shape recognition [1–6] and motion analysis [7,8]. The problem addressed in this chapter is that of recognizing and locating objects that are represented by a set of points. That is, each object is represented by a set of

Dynamic, Genetic, and Chaotic Programming, By Branko Souček and the IRIS Group.
ISBN 0-471-55717-X
This work was partially supported by the New Jersey Department of Higher Education through NJIT Separately Budgeted Research.

dominant points (shape features). Information about the order of these points is not known or provided. The problem is to find a subset of points in a point pattern that match to a subset of points in another point pattern through a transformation in a certain optimal sense with the constraint that the mapping is single. In a general setting, the points are arranged in n-dimensional space, and the transformation is specified according to the geometric and environmental constraints of the problem. Only two-dimensional (2D) point patterns and the similarity transformation are considered, even though the algorithm itself is not restricted to them.

After formulating the problem in the next section, genetic algorithms are reviewed in Section 13.3. The proposed method is discussed in detail in Section 13.4, and experimental results are presented in Section 13.5.

13.2 PROBLEM FORMULATION

The point pattern matching problem can be formulated as follows: Given two sets of point patterns, $P = \{p_i: p_i \in R^N, i = 1, 2, 3, \ldots, m\}$ and $O = \{o_j: o_j \in R^N, j = 1, 2, 3, \ldots, n\}$, the problem is to find an assignment $P' \rightarrow O'$, $P \supseteq P'$, and $O \supseteq O'$ such that the error between $T\{P'\}$ and O' is minimized, where T is a predefined transformation. In this chapter, only 2D point patterns, $N = 2$, are considered, and T is a similarity transformation: $T =$ {rotation, translation, scaling}.

In contrast to conventional search techniques that evaluate the fitness of a function to be optimized sample by sample sequentially, a genetic algorithm evaluates a set of samples in parallel. A genetic algorithm consists of a string representation ("genes") of the node in the search space, a set of genetic operators for generating new search nodes, a fitness function to evaluate the search nodes, and a stochastic assignment to control the genetic operators. The success of genetic algorithms can be attributed to

1. Survival of the fittest,
2. Passing "good" genes to the next generation of strings,
3. Combining different strings to explore new search points.

To map the matching problem into a genetic algorithm framework, we must define a fitness function, a coding scheme, a set of genetic operators, and the rules to control operators suitable to the matching problem. To search for the "best" assignment, we use a fitness function to provide the payoff information indicating how good the assignment is. A fitness value inversely proportional to the match error is used. The better the assignment, the smaller is the error or the larger is the fitness value. Each assignment is coded into a string; that is, each string indicates which of the model points is assigned to the observed points, and vice versa. The genetic operators consist of reproduction, crossover, and mutation. A new genetic operator known as *mixed-type partial matching crossover (MPMX)*, discussed in Section 13.4, is introduced. The initial population is a set of strings generated by a random number generator. The initial population contains good and bad strings (assignments). Depending on the fitness value of each string in the initial population, a new population is reproduced by the reproduction operator. The reproduction operator, acting like natural selection, passes strings that yield higher fitness values to the new population. Strings in the population are then crossovered in pairs to produce new strings. A new string contains partial information from its parents. The purpose for the mutation operator is to perturb or change the string. The mutation operation is performed like an insurance policy. A detailed description of the operators is given in Sections 13.3 and 13.4.

13.3 GENETIC ALGORITHMS

Genetic algorithms [9] were first introduced by John Holland, his colleagues, and his students at the University of Michigan. Genetic algorithms have recently received much attention as robust stochastic searching methods for various applications. This class of methods is based on the mechanics of natural selection and natural genetics that combines the notion of survival of the fittest, random and yet structured search, and parallel evaluation of nodes in the search space.

A genetic algorithm consists of a string representation ("genes") of the node in the search space, a fitness function to evaluate the search nodes, a set of genetic operators for generating new search nodes, and a stochastic assignment to control the genetic operators. The construction of a genetic algorithm for any problem can be separated into four distinct and yet related tasks:

1. Choice of the representation of the string,
2. Design of the genetic operators,
3. Determination of the fitness function,
4. Determination of the probabilities controlling the genetic operators.

13.3.1 String Representation

To solve any optimization problem using a genetic algorithm, we need a coding scheme to encode the parameters of the problem into a string. In general, it is desirable to have a coding scheme that

1. Is simple,
2. Spans the range of the parameter to avoid illegal codes (an illegal code is one that cannot be represented),
3. Can be easily manipulated by genetic operators.

13.3.2 Fitness Function

A fitness function (objective function, cost function) must be relevant to the problem being optimized. A well-defined fitness function is necessary to ensure success. The fitness value of each string is computed from the fitness function. A good string (gene) is one that scores a high fitness value.

13.3.3 Population Size

A genetic algorithm evaluates a set of nodes after genetic operators. A larger set of nodes increases the searching speed, but the required computation is more intense. A population size N no greater than 300 is recommended.

13.3.4 Basic Genetic Operators

Reproduction. The reproduction operation is performed as follows:

1. Normalize the fitness value of each string such that the sum of the fitness values of all the strings in the current population is equal to 1.
2. Partition a unit-length scale into N (the population size) slots, where each slot size is in proportion to the normalized fitness value of a string in the current population.
3. Generate N random numbers from 0 to 1 and see where the number falls on the scale. The string corresponding to the division where a random number falls is selected to be a member for the new population.

Note that strings that have higher fitness values are more likely to be reproduced in the new population.

Crossover. The crossover operator is the most important operator in genetic algorithms. It is the "mating" operator that allows production of new strings through a combination of parts of strings. One simple way of performing the crossover operator is as follows:

1. Pairs of members of the newly reproduced strings are randomly selected for mating.
2. For each pair of selected strings, parts of the strings are swapped to form a pair of new strings. The position of a string to which the swapping takes place is randomly selected.

Each new string produced contains partial information from its parents. The mechanics of reproduction and crossover are surprisingly simple, involving random number generation and string copies. After the reproduction and crossover operations, the strings in the population may have to go through the mutation operation, discussed next.

Mutation. If the reproduction according to fitness values in combination with the crossover operator gives genetic algorithms the bulk of their processing power, what then is the role of mutation in a genetic algorithm? Mutation is needed because, even though reproduction and crossover effectively search and recombine extant notions, occasionally they may become overzealous and lose some potentially useful genetic materials (1's or 0's at particular locations). In an artificial genetic system, the mutation operator protects against such irrecoverable loss. In the simple genetic algorithm [9], mutation is the occasional (with small probability) random alteration of the value of a string position. In the binary coding of the earlier example, this simply means changing a 1 to a 0, and vice versa. By itself, mutation is a random walk through the string space. When used sparingly with reproduction and crossover, it is an insurance policy against premature loss of important notions [9].

Mutation plays a decidedly secondary role in the operation of genetic algorithms. Mutation rate is similarly small in natural populations, thus implying that mutation is appropriately considered as a secondary mechanism of genetic algorithm adaptation. The mutation operator may be implemented in a number of ways. The binary coding of strings is the easiest way to execute.

13.3.5 Other Genetic Operators: Inversion and Reordering Operators

To solve more complex problems, we modify some basic genetic operators. The inversion and reordering operators are derived from the basic operators, but they are more complicated. Three operators fall into the category of inversion and reordering operators [9]: PMX (partial match crossover), OX (order crossover), and CX (cycle crossover). These operators have been applied to many complex problems.

PMX. Consider the strings $A1$ and $A2$:

$$A1\text{: } 1\ 2\ 3\ 4\ 5\ 6\ 7\ 8 \qquad A2\text{: } 2\ 5\ 7\ 8\ 1\ 4\ 3\ 6$$

Using simple crossover at cross site 4, yields the two new strings

$$A1'\text{: } 1\ 2\ 3\ 4 \mid 1\ 4\ 3\ 6 \qquad A2'\text{: } 2\ 5\ 7\ 8 \mid 5\ 6\ 7\ 8$$

In certain optimization problems, such as the traveling salesman problem, a string cannot have repeated genes. In this case, the simple crossover operator may yield illegal strings (strings with repeated genes), as shown here.

Under PMX, two strings are aligned, and two crossing sites are picked uniformly at random along the strings. These two points define a matching section that is used to affect a cross through position-by-position exchange operations. Consider strings $A1$ and $A2$ again:

$A1$: 1 2 | 3 4 5 | 6 7 8 $A2$: 2 5 | 7 8 1 | 4 3 6

The two offspring strings are obtained as follows:

$A1'$: 5 2 | 7 8 1 | 6 3 4 $A2'$: 2 1 | 3 4 5 | 8 7 6

PMX proceeds by positionwise exchange. First, mapping string $A1$ to string $A2$, the 7 and the 3, the 8 and the 4, and the 1 and the 5 exchange places. Similarly mapping string $A2$ to string $A1$, the 3 and the 7, the 4 and the 8, and the 5 and the 1 exchange places. Each string contains ordering information partially determined by each of its parents. Operators OX and CX are similar to PMX. See [9] for a detailed description of them.

Typically, a genetic algorithm consists of the following steps:

1. *Initialization* An initial population of the search nodes is randomly generated.
2. *Evaluation of Fitness Values of Strings in Population* The fitness function must be relevant to the problem being optimized.
3. *Reproduction* Based on the fitness values of strings in the population, a new pool of population of strings is produced for the subsequent genetic operations such as crossover and mutation. Strings having larger fitness values are more likely reproduced.
4. *Crossover* The crossover operator is the mating operator that allows production of new strings through combination of parts of strings. A simple crossover operation is done by swapping parts of a pair of strings to form a new pair of strings. Pairs of strings are randomly selected for mating, and the position of a string to which the swapping takes place is also randomly selected.
5. *Mutation* Mutation is the occasional (with small probability) random alteration of the value of a string. For a binary code, mutation can be performed by inverting a bit in the code. The position of the bit being inverted is randomly selected.
6. Repeat steps 2–5 until convergence or a predefined number of generations has been reached.

From the preceding description, it is seen that the notion of survival of the fittest, passing good genes to the next generation of strings, and combining different strings to explore new search nodes are present in a genetic algorithm.

13.4 THE POINT PATTERN MATCHING PROCEDURE USING A GENETIC ALGORITHM

13.4.1 Match Error

The point pattern matching problem, as defined earlier, is formulated as follows: Given two sets of point patterns, $P = \{p_i : p_i \in R^N, i = 1, 2, \ldots, m\}$ and $O = \{o_j : o_j \in R^N, j = 1, 2, 3, \ldots, n\}$, find an assignment $P' \to O'$, where $P \supseteq P'$ and $O \supseteq O'$, such that the match error between $T\{P'\}$ and O' is minimized; the match error is a predefined quantity that indicates the quality of match, and T is a predefined transformation. In this chapter, only 2D point patterns, $N = 2$, and a similarity transformation T = {rotation, scaling, translation} are used. Let O be an observed 2D point pattern, and P a model 2D point pattern. The 2D similarity transformation is defined by the mapping $x \to u$, $x, u \in R^2$, such that

$$\begin{bmatrix} u \\ v \end{bmatrix} = \begin{bmatrix} a & b \\ -b & a \end{bmatrix} \begin{bmatrix} x \\ y \end{bmatrix} + \begin{bmatrix} e \\ f \end{bmatrix}$$

The similarity transformation can be written as

$$\begin{bmatrix} u \\ v \end{bmatrix} = S \begin{bmatrix} \cos\theta & \sin\theta \\ -\sin\theta & \cos\theta \end{bmatrix} \begin{bmatrix} x \\ y \end{bmatrix} + \begin{bmatrix} e \\ f \end{bmatrix}$$

where S = scale factor
θ = angle of rotation
e = translation in x axis
and f = translation in y axis

Let $P' = \{(x_i, y_i) : (x_i, y_i) \in R^2, i = 1, 2, 3, \ldots, k\}$ be a subset of model points. To find how well P' is assigned to O' under a similarity transformation, we must find the parameters of the similarity transformation that maps P' to O' in an optimal sense, in this case, in the minimum least squared error sense. Let (u'_i, v'_i) be the result obtained by transforming (x_i, y_i) under T; that is, $T\{(x_i, y_i)\} = \{(u'_i, v'_i)\}$. Mapping P' by this transformation, we obtain

$$\begin{bmatrix} u' \\ v' \end{bmatrix} = S \begin{bmatrix} \cos\theta & \sin\theta \\ -\sin\theta & \cos\theta \end{bmatrix} \begin{bmatrix} x \\ y \end{bmatrix} + \begin{bmatrix} e \\ f \end{bmatrix}$$

The squared error between the two sets of points $T\{P'\}$ and O' is defined as

$$\varepsilon = \sum_{i=1}^{k} ((u_i - u'_i)^2 + (v_i - v'_i)^2)$$

$$= \sum_{i=1}^{k} ((u_i - ax_i - by_i - e)^2 + (v_i + bx_i - ay_i - f)^2)$$

To find the parameters of the transformation that will achieve the minimum least squared error, simply take the derivatives of the error ε with respect to each parameter and set them to zero:

$$\frac{\partial \varepsilon}{\partial a} = \sum (u - ax - by - e)(-x) + (v + bx - ay - f)(-y) = 0$$

$$\frac{\partial \varepsilon}{\partial b} = \sum (u - ax - by - e)(-y) + (v + bx - ay - f)(x) = 0$$

$$\frac{\partial \varepsilon}{\partial e} = \sum (u - ax - by - e)(-1) = 0$$

$$\frac{\partial \varepsilon}{\partial f} = \sum (v - bx - ay - f)(-1) = 0$$

Rewriting this in matrix form, we obtain

$$A \begin{bmatrix} a \\ b \\ e \\ f \end{bmatrix} = C,$$

where

$$A = \begin{bmatrix} \sum_1^k (x_i^2 + y_i^2) & 0 & \sum_1^k x_i & \sum_1^k y_i \\ 0 & \sum_1^k (x_i^2 + y_i^2) & \sum_1^k y_i & \sum_1^k x_i \\ \sum_1^k x_i & \sum_1^k y_i & \sum_1^k 1 & 0 \\ \sum_1^k y_i & \sum_1^k x_i & 0 & \sum_1^k 1 \end{bmatrix}$$

$$C = \begin{bmatrix} \sum_1^k (u_j x_i + v_j y_i) \\ \sum_1^k (u_j y_i - v_j x_i) \\ \sum_1^k u_j \\ \sum_1^k v_j \end{bmatrix}$$

The least squared error derived from the similarity transformation quantifies how well P' is mapped to O'. That is, it only quantifies how well a portion of the model point pattern P matches to the corresponding portion of the observed point pattern O. A small error indicates that the portion of the model points match well to the corresponding observed points. It does not, however, account for the overall goodness of match between point pattern P and point pattern O. To account for this goodness, we use the following heuristic measure [1,2], which penalizes incomplete matching of the model point pattern:

$$\varepsilon' = \begin{cases} \dfrac{\varepsilon}{S}\left(1 + \left(\dfrac{m-2}{k-2}\right)\log_2\left(\dfrac{m-2}{k-2}\right)\right) & k > 3 \\ \infty & k = 0, 1, 2 \end{cases}$$

where k is the number of model points that match the observed points, m is the number of model points, and S is the scale factor.

The heuristic measure, which can be regarded as an error measure for the overall goodness of match between the model and the observed point pattern, is referred to as the match error. If only one or two model points match those in the observed points, the least squared error is always zero because there always exists a similarity transformation that perfectly maps a set of one or two points to another set. Such cases where two or less model points match to those in the scene are considered as undetermined cases; that is, these cases have insufficient evidence of match between the model and the observed point pattern. The logarithmic term of the match error serves as a penalty factor for incomplete matching of the model points. When all model points match those in the observed points ($k = m$), the match error equals the normalized least squared error. The penalty is larger when fewer model points match those in the observed point pattern. The smaller the error, the larger is the fitness value. The reciprocal value of the match error is used as the fitness function in the algorithm. That is, the fitness function is

$$f = \begin{cases} \dfrac{1}{\varepsilon'} & \text{for } \varepsilon' > 0 \\ \infty & \text{elsewhere} \end{cases}$$

13.4.2 String Representation

As discussed in Section 13.3, encoding of the parameters of an optimization problem into genetic strings are problem-dependent and not unique. In the point pattern matching problem, there are m model points and n observed points. The objective is to find the "best" assignment (labeling) between subsets of model and observed point patterns. The parameters to be encoded is the assignment between the two subsets of points. Different assignments yield different fitness values. Each genetic code consists of m cells (genes), where each cell represents a model point. Each cell takes on an integer between 0 and n. The value of each cell indicates an assignment of match from the model point (that corresponds to this cell) to an observed point. A value of 0 indicates that the model point corresponding to this cell does not match any of the observed points. A value of i indicates that this model point matches the ith observed point. Note that the cell value, except 0, in each string must be distinct because the mapping from the model points to the observed points is single. A string can, however, have several 0's, because it is possible that some model points do not match those of the observed points.

Consider the following code with 12 cells: 2 5 7 0 9 1 3 4 6 11 10 12. The cell position from the left indicates the label of a model point. For example, the sixth cell corresponds to the sixth model point. In this code, the first model point is assigned to the second observed point, the second to the fifth, the third to the seventh, the fourth is not assigned, the fifth to the ninth, and so on. The strings in the initial population are generated as follows:

1. Check the number of model points and observed points. If the number of model points is greater than the number of observed points, $m - n$ model points must not be assigned; that is, each code must have at least $m - n$ cells with 0 value. Randomly pick $m - n$ cells of the code, and assign these cells a 0 value. The rest of the cell values are also randomly picked, provided that the cell values (except 0) are not repeated.
2. If the number of observed points is greater than or equal to the number of model points, simply randomly assign n values to the m cells. Again, cell values (except 0) are not allowed to repeat.

13.4.3 Population Size

There is no fixed rule to select the size of the population. It is usually determined by trial and error. In general, the larger the population size, the faster is the convergence. However, the computation for each population is more intense. Here, the population size is 30.

13.4.4 Genetic Operators: Reproduction

This operator is similar to the one discussed in Section 13.3. The purpose of reproduction is to pass good strings for genetic operators such as crossover and mutation. For the point pattern matching problem, the reproduction operation is performed as follows:

1. Normalize the fitness value of each string such that the sum of the fitness values of all the strings in the current population is equal to 1.

2. Partition a unit-length scale into 30 slots, where each slot size is in proportion to the normalized fitness value of a string in the current population.
3. A new population of strings is reproduced by picking 29 random numbers (which are uniformly distributed on [0, 1]) and noting where the numbers fall on the scale. The string corresponding to the division where a random number falls is selected to be a member for the new population. Twenty-nine random numbers are picked because the best string in the current generation is always passed to the new population. Then 30 strings, including the best string passed to the new population, form a reproduction pool.

Reordering (Crossover Operator). Consider an observed point pattern consisting of n points and a model pattern consisting of m points. Each string thus consists of m cells because there are m model points. The cell value ranges from 0 to n. As mentioned, the value of each cell indicates an assignment of a match from the model point that corresponds to this cell to an observed point indicated by the cell value.

For the point pattern matching problem, the assignment (labeling) between a set of model points and a set of observed points must satisfy the following two constraints:

1. A model point cannot be assigned to more than one observed point.
2. An observed point cannot be assigned to more than one model point.

The simple crossover operator discussed in Section 13.3 thus cannot be applied directly to this problem. The reason is that the crossover operator may result in a string with repeated cell values, thus violating the constraints. The crossover operator should thus be modified with some type of reordering. A new operator known as mixed-type partial matching crossover (*MPMX*) is introduced.

The MPMX operator is illustrated by an example. Let $m = 12$ and $n = 15$. Thus, each string consists of 12 cells, and each cell takes on an integer value between 0 and 15. Consider the strings

$A1$: 1 2 7 6 9 13 8 0 4 11 12 5

$A2$: 0 15 2 4 5 6 7 1 3 8 9 0

Before using the MPMX operator, we define the following operators:

1. $\{X\} \cap \{Y\}$ = find the set of cell values common to string X and string Y, where $\{X\}$ = the set of cell values in string X. For example, $\{A1\} \cap \{A2\} = \{0,1,2,4,5,6,7,8,9\}$

2. $\{X\}\backslash\{Y\}$ = find the set of cell values in string X different (not common) from those in string Y. For example, $\{A1\}\backslash\{A2\} = \{11,12,13\}$, and $\{A2\}\backslash\{A1\} = \{15,3\}$. Note that $\{A1\} = (\{A1\} \cap \{A2\}) \cup (\{A1\}\backslash\{A2\})$, and $\{A2\} = (\{A1\} \cap \{A2\}) \cup (\{A2\}\backslash\{A1\})$, where $\{A1\}$ = set of cell values of string $A1$, and $\cup$ is the union operator.
3. $C(\{X\})$ = number of cell values in string X. For example, $C(\{A1\}) = 12$.

The MPMX operation on two strings, MPMX($A1$, $A2$), is summarized by the following procedure:

1. Determine $\{A1\} \cap \{A2\}$, $\{A1\}\backslash\{A2\}$, and $\{A2\}\backslash\{A1\}$.
2. Compute $C(\{A1\} \cap \{A2\})$, $C(\{A1\}\backslash\{A2\})$, and $C(\{A2\}\backslash\{A1\})$.
3. Form two matching sections as follows:
   a. Generate a random integer number N_1 between 0 and $C(\{A1\} \cap \{A2\})$.
   b. Generate a random integer number N_2 between 0 and min-$\{C(\{A1\}\backslash\{A2\}), C(\{A2\}\backslash\{A1\})\}$.
   c. Randomly select N_1 cell values from $\{A1\} \cap \{A2\}$.
   d. Randomly select N_2 cell values from $\{A1\}\backslash\{A2\}$.
   e. Randomly select N_2 cell values from $\{A2\}\backslash\{A1\}$.
   f. The first matching section is formed by the union (union operator) of those cell values obtained by steps c and d.
   g. The second matching section is formed by the union (union operator) of those cell values obtained by steps c and e.
4. Rotate the cell position of the first matching section.
5. Cell values in string $A1$ and string $A2$ are then swapped (exchanged) according to the mapping of cell values between the rotated first section and the second matching section.

Returning to the example mentioned earlier and following this procedure, we find the MPMX operator yields

1. $\{A1\} \cap \{A2\} = \{0,1,2,4,5,6,7,8,9\}$, $\{A1\}\backslash\{A2\} = \{11,12,13\}$, and $\{A2\}\backslash\{A1\} = \{15,3\}$.
2. $C(\{A1\} \cap \{A2\}) = 9$, $C(\{A1\}\backslash\{A2\}) = 3$, and $C(\{A2\}\backslash\{A1\}) = 2$.
3. a. Say $N_1 = 4$.
   b. $N_2 = 1$.
   c. $\{1,5,6,7\}$ are four randomly selected cell values from $\{A1\} \cap \{A2\}$.
   d. $\{12\}$ is randomly selected from $\{A1\}\backslash\{A2\}$.
   e. $\{3\}$ is randomly selected from $\{A2\}\backslash\{A1\}$.
   f. The first matching section becomes M_1 = 1 5 6 7 12.
   g. The second matching section becomes M_2 = 1 5 6 7 3.
4. Rotating M_1 yields M_1' = 5 6 7 12 1.

5. According to the positionwise mapping between the first rotated matching section and the second matching section M_2 (e.g., cell value of 5 in string $A1$ becomes 1, cell value of 6 in string $A1$ becomes 5, and so on; likewise, cell value of 1 in string $A2$ becomes 5, and so on), two new strings are generated:

$A1$: 3 2 6 5 9 13 8 0 4 11 7 1

$A2$: 0 15 2 4 6 7 12 5 1 8 9 0

Note that cell value 0 is not selected for the matching section because each string may have more than one cell having value 0, thus violating the matching constraints. The MPMX operator satisfies the constraints that each resulting cell has a unique cell value in a string except cell value 0.

Mutation. Since the string used for the point pattern matching problem is not binary, the bit inversion described in Section 13.3 cannot be applied directly. In addition, each cell value (except 0) in a string cannot be repeated. Thus, the following mutation procedure is adopted:

1. Check the cell value of the string. If some cell values (out of all possible cell values) are not assigned in the string, randomly pick a cell in the string and replace this cell with a cell value randomly picked from those unassigned cell values.
2. If the string contains all the possible cell values, randomly swap the values between two cells in a string.

Note that, as in natural selection, mutation rarely occurs, and thus an artificial mutation operation is not always carried out. That is, mutation occurs with a small probability in each generation.

Inversion. Inversion simply means taking the "complement" of each cell value of a string. For example, if a cell value ranges from 0 to n, the complement of a cell value, x, is $(n + 1 - x)$; that is, it is an "$n + 1$ complement." The complement of the string 3 2 6 5 9 13 8 14 4 11 7 1 is 13 14 10 11 7 3 6 2 12 5 9 15. Note that the inversion operation induces a drastic change in the string. Thus, the probability of carrying the inversion operation is even much smaller than that of mutation.

13.4.5 The Point Pattern Matching Procedure

The point pattern matching procedure can be summarized as follows:

1. Select a fixed population size of strings, and randomly select an initial population. Let N be the size. In the experiments in the next section, $N = 30$ is used.

2. Assign probabilities for the reordering operation, the mutation operation, and the inversion operation. Usually the probabilities for mutation and inversion operation are very small.
3. *Reproduction* Evaluate the fitness value for each string. The fitness value defined earlier is inversely proportional to the least squared error. Normalized the sum of the fitness values of the population to 1, and divide a scale of 1 into N divisions where the width of each division corresponds to the normalized fitness value of a string. A new generation of strings is reproduced by picking $N - 1$ random numbers (which are uniformly distributed on [0,1]) and noting where this number falls on the scale. The string corresponding to the division where a random number falls is selected to be a member of the next generation. Note that good strings have a good chance of being duplicated in the next generation. We select $N - 1$ random numbers because the best string in the current generation is always passed to the new reproduction pool. Thus, a total of N strings form a reproduction pool.
4. *Reordering* Pick every pair of strings except the best string in the population. For each pair of strings, generate a random number distributed on [0,1]. If the number is less than the assigned crossover probability, perform the MPMX operation on the present pair of strings.
5. *Mutation* For each string in the population, generate a random number distributed on [0,1]. If the value is less than the assigned mutation probability, perform the mutation operation on the current string.
6. *Inversion* For each string in the population, generate a random number distributed on [0,1]. If the value is less than the assigned inversion probability, perform the inversion operation on the current string.
7. Repeat steps 3–6 until convergence or a predefined number of generations has been reached.

13.5 EXPERIMENTAL RESULTS

In this section, experimental results are presented to demonstrate the robustness of the proposed approach for point pattern matching. Numerous simulations that can be categorized into several cases have been performed. In the following set of simulations, a library of four model point patterns, each consisting of 12 points, are created as shown in Figure 13.1. The observed point patterns are made up of points belonging to one or more model objects that have undergone a similarity transformation. In addition, compared to the model point patterns, extraneous points or missing points may be introduced in the observed point patterns. Cases where the observed point pattern is derived from one or more model point patterns with noise added on the points are also considered. Note: T is a similarity transformation, T = {rotation, translation, scaling}.

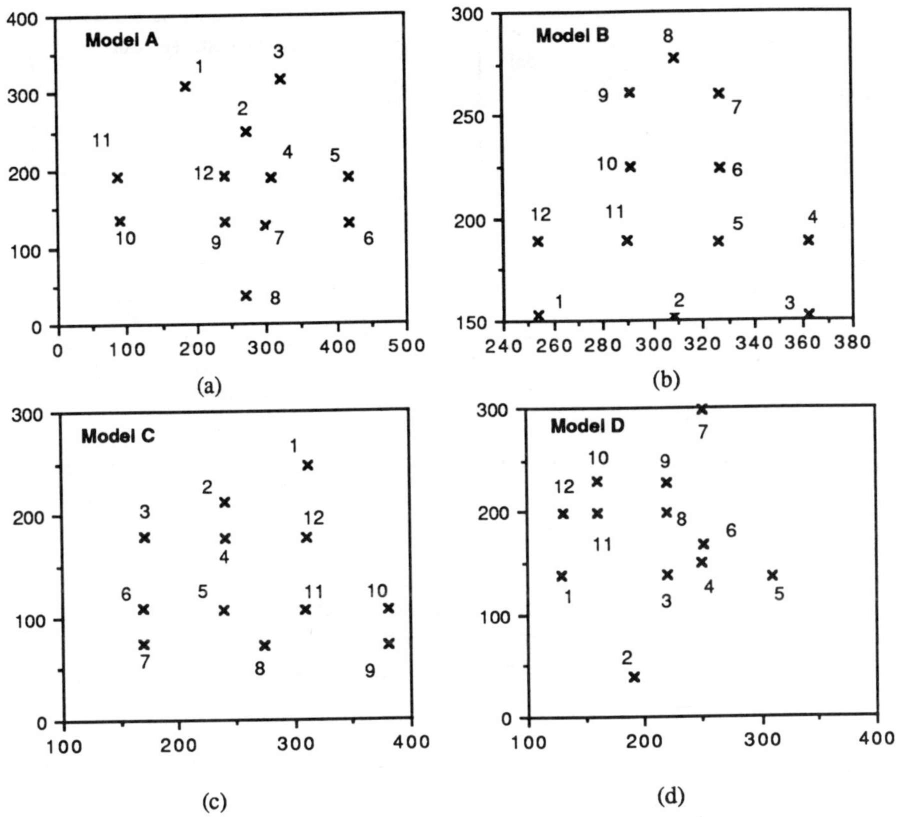

Figure 13.1 *Four model point patterns:* (a) *model A,* (b) *model B,* (c) *model C, and* (d) *model D.*

Case 1. Observed Pattern = Model Pattern. In this case, the observed point pattern is obtained from model A by just randomly changing the labels of the model points. Figure 13.2*a* shows the mapping from model A to the observed point pattern. Figure 13.2*b* shows that it takes nine generations to reach the best match between model A and the observed pattern. The match error is 0 in this case.

Case 2. Observed Pattern = T{Model Pattern}. The observed point pattern is obtained by transforming model A through a similarity transformation. Figure 13.3*a* shows the mapping from model A to the observed point pattern. Figure 13.3*b* shows that it takes nine generations to converge to the best match with match error = 0.

Case 3. Observed Pattern = T{Model Pattern} + Extraneous Points. The observed point pattern is obtained by transforming model A through a

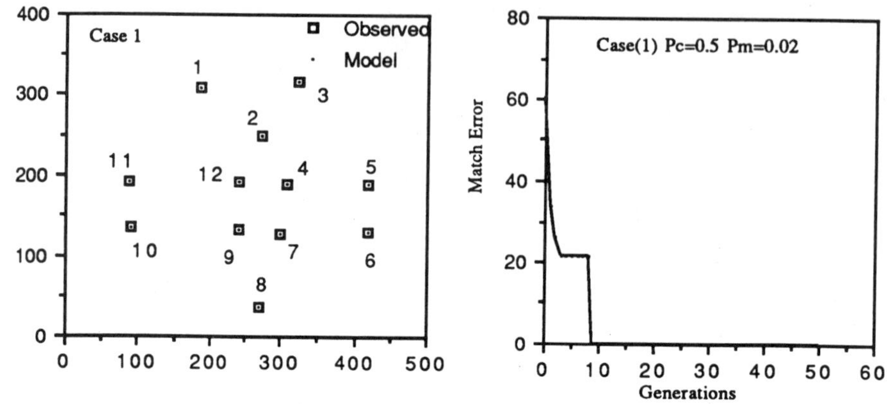

(a) (b)

Figure 13.2 *Experiment case 1:* (a) *Mapping model A to the observed pattern;* (b) *the convergence plot.*

similarity transformation plus three extraneous points. Figure 13.4*a* shows the mapping from model A to the observed point pattern. In this case, as shown in Figure 13.4*b*, it takes over 350 generations to converge to the best match with zero match error.

Case 4. Observed Pattern = *T*{*Model Pattern*} + *Extraneous Points* {*Close to Observed Points*}. The observed point pattern is obtained by transforming model A through a similarity transformation plus three extraneous points that are close to some observed points. The match error is 0 in this case. Figure 13.5*a* shows the mapping from model A pattern to the

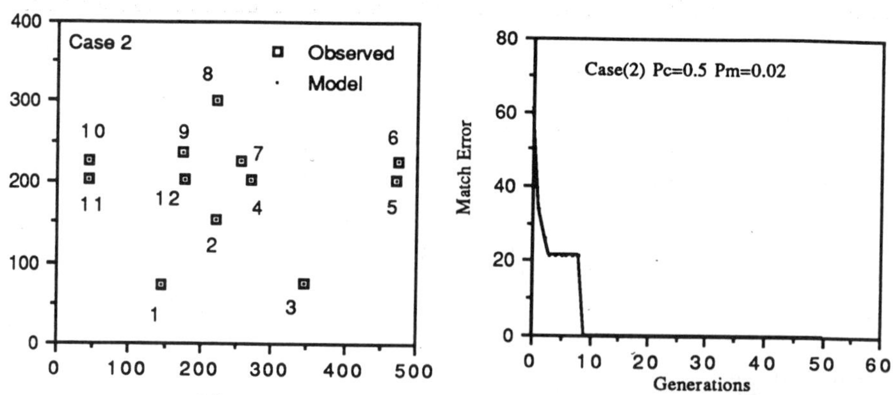

(a) (b)

Figure 13.3 *Experiment case 2:* (a) *Mapping model A to the observed pattern;* (b) *the convergence plot.*

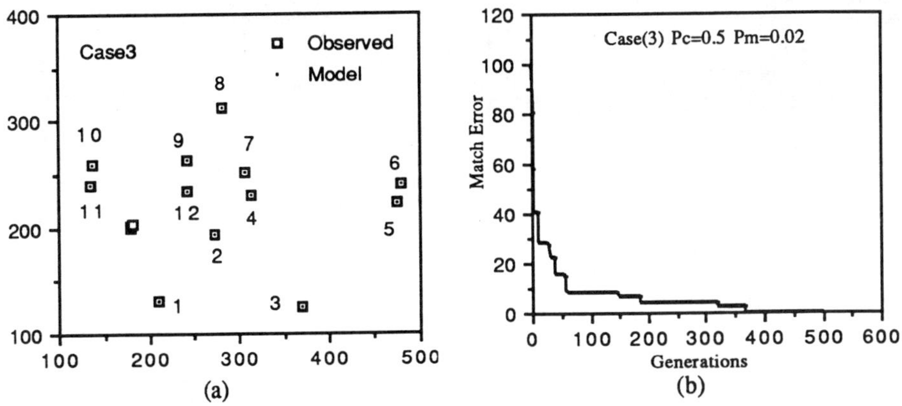

Figure 13.4 *Experiment case 3:* (a) *Mapping model A to the observed pattern;* (b) *the convergence plot.*

observed point pattern. Figure 13.5*b* shows that it takes less than 50 generations to converge to the best match.

Case 5. Observed Pattern = *T*{*Model Pattern* − *Some Points*}. The observed point pattern is obtained by transforming a portion of model A through a similarity transformation. That is, two points from the original point pattern are missing. Figure 13.6*a* shows the mapping from model A to the observed point pattern. Figure 13.6*b* shows that it takes less than 50 generations to converge to the best match. The match error is 0.

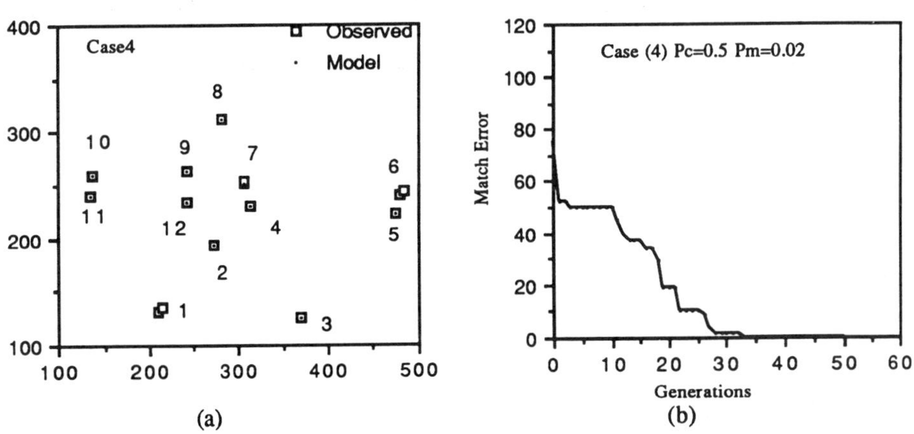

Figure 13.5 *Experiment case 4:* (a) *Mapping model A to the observed pattern;* (b) *the convergence plot.*

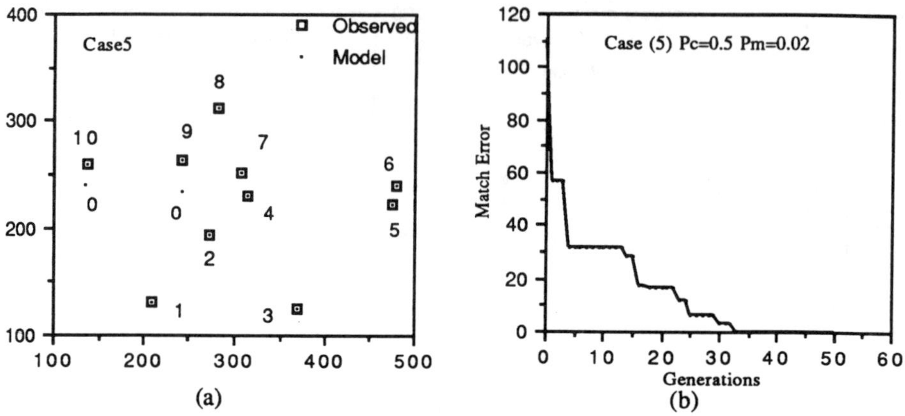

Figure 13.6 *Experiment case 5:* (a) *Mapping model A to the observed pattern;* (b) *the convergence plot.*

Case 6. Observed Pattern = *T{Model Pattern}* + *Noise.* The observed point pattern is obtained by transforming model A through a similarity transformation. In addition, noise is added to some of the resulting transformed points. Figure 13.7*a* shows the mapping from model A to the observed point pattern. Figure 13.7*b* shows that the best match error is 19.2.

13.6 CONCLUSIONS

A new approach to point pattern recognition has been introduced and discussed. The robustness and fast convergence of the algorithm have been demonstrated through experimental results. To find the "best" match be-

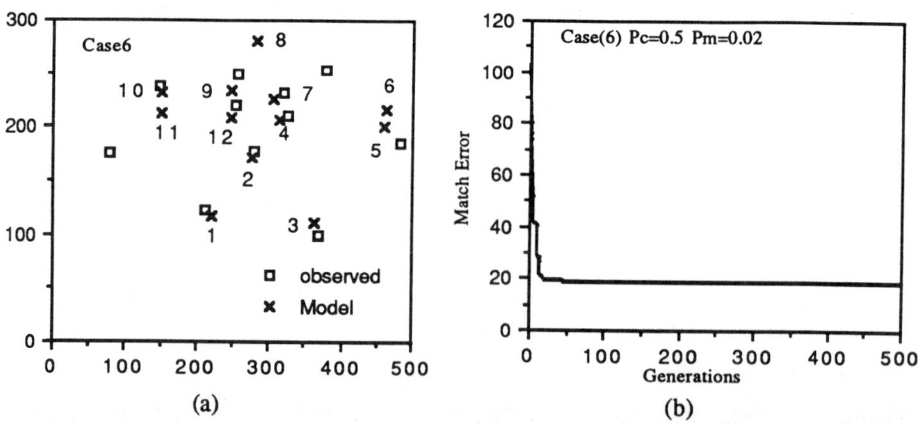

Figure 13.7 *Experiment case 6:* (a) *Mapping model A to the observed pattern;* (b) *the convergence plot.*

tween a set of m model points and a set of n observed points, the algorithm only needs to evaluate NG search nodes, where N is the population size and G is the number of generations at which the algorithm converges or stops. In the experimental results, it usually takes less than 200 generations, in some cases less than 10 generations, to converge, compared with a total of

$$\sum_{i=0}^{m} \binom{n}{m-i}\binom{m}{i}(m-i)! \qquad \text{for } n \geq m \quad \text{where } \binom{n}{k} = \frac{n!}{(n-k)!(k!)}$$

$$\sum_{i=0}^{n} \binom{m}{m-n+i}\binom{n}{n-i}(n-i)! \qquad \text{for } m > n$$

search nodes to be evaluated using exhaustive search.

There is no unique way of setting the probabilities of the reordering (crossover), mutation, and inversion operations. In general, the probability of crossover is large, while those of mutation and inversion are very small. The mutation and inversion operators, however, allow the algorithm to evaluate other nodes that are globally "far" from the current node evaluation; that is, they allow the algorithm to escape from local minima. Though only results for 2D point patterns and the similarity transformation have been presented, the proposed algorithm can be applied to n-dimensional point patterns and any transformation.

REFERENCES

[1] N. Ansari and E. J. Delp, Partial shape recognition: A landmark-based approach, *IEEE Trans. on Pattern Analysis and Machine Intelligence,* 12(5), 470–483 (May 1990).

[2] N. Ansari and E. J. Delp, Recognizing planar objects in 3-D space, *Proc. SPIE Automated Inspection and High-Speed Vision Architectures III,* Vol. 1197, 127–138 (November 5–10, 1987).

[3] S. Ranade and A. Rosenfeld, Point pattern matching by relaxation, *Pattern Recognition,* 12, 269–275 (1980).

[4] B. Bhanu and J. C. Ming, Recognition of occluded object: A cluster-structure algorithm, *Pattern Recognition,* 20(2), 199–211 (1987).

[5] W. E. L. Grimson, On recognition of curved objects, *IEEE Trans. on Pattern Analysis and Machine Intelligence,* PAMI-11(6), 632–643 (June 1989).

[6] Y. Lamdan, J. T. Schwartz, and H. J. Wolfson, Object recognition by affine invariant matching, *Proc. IEEE Conf. Computer Vision and Pattern Recognition,* 335–344 (June 5–9, 1988).

[7] M. C. Ibison and L. Zapalowski, On the use of relaxation labelling in the correspondence problem, *Pattern Recognition Lett.,* 4(2), 103–109 (April 1986).

[8] J. K. Aggarwal and N. Nandhakumar, ON the computation of motion from sequences of images—A review, *Proc. IEEE,* 76, 917–935 (1988).

[9] D. E. Goldberg, *Genetic Algorithms in Search, Optimization & Machine Learning,* Addison Wesley, Reading, Mass. 1989.

CHAPTER 14

Artificial Embryology: The Genetic Programming of an Artificial Embryo

HUGO DE GARIS

14.1 INTRODUCTION

This chapter introduces the concept of genetic programming in a more general way than in earlier publications [3–6]. Genetic programming (GP) is the application of the genetic algorithm (GA) to the creation of systems that are too complex in their dynamics or interactions to be prespecified or analyzed in detail. Such systems can be built (evolved), but (probably) not understood. This chapter shows how the GP approach can be applied to the evolution of artificial embryos in two- and three-dimensional cellular automata. The idea that one can build something successfully without having a full understanding of how the building takes place is one of the fundamental ideas behind GP. Section 14.2 presents arguments relating to future computing technologies which suggest that there will be a need for a GP-type approach to future system design. Section 14.3 describes what GP is, including a presentation of its principal tool, the GA. Section 14.4 introduces the embryo algorithm, which is used to evolve shapes, and some early results in 2D. Section 14.5 presents results of evolving shapes in 2D and 3D on a connection machine at Boston University. Section 14.6 makes some remarks on the preceding sections and suggests how truly arbitrary (nonconvex) shapes might be grown without ad hoc interventions.

Dynamic, Genetic, and Chaotic Programming, By Branko Součsignificant and the IRIS Group.
ISBN 0-471-55717-X

14.2 FUTURE COMPUTING TECHNOLOGIES

One interest of the author is studying the characteristics of future computing technologies and then thinking about the conceptual problems they will create. A brief summary of five of these technologies will be given followed by a discussion of some of the problems and challenges they will pose. These five technologies are wafer-scale integration (WSI), optical computing, molecular electronics, nanotechnology, and quantum computing. The common feature of these technologies is that they will allow computers to be built with an enormous number of components. Several of them will allow an Avogadro number of components. Quantum computing could even produce 10^{30} components.

Wafer-scale integration is the art of putting one huge integrated circuit on a single silicon wafer or slice. The state of the art at the time of writing is a surface area of several inches square. Estimates are that by the middle of the 1990s, it will be possible with ultralarge scale integration (ULSI) (i.e., submicron linewidths), to put roughly 10 million artificial neurons on a WSI wafer [7]. *Optical computing* offers the possibility of computing entirely optically, using optical nonlinear effects to perform light amplification (thus mimicking the transistor) [8]. Three-dimensional optical holographic memories offer the possibility of storing bits at a far higher density than is possible today with silicon techniques. *Molecular electronics* (ME) is the rapidly developing field that recognizes there are limits to the downscaling of microelectronics, which when met will introduce quantum effects that will interfere with the conventional action of the transistor. The alternative offered by molecular electronics is to explore the possibility that molecules can perform computation [9]. Reading ME papers gives one the impression of studying organic chemistry. If ME succeeds, computers based on such devices will obviously contain an Avogadro number of components. *Nanotechnology* [10,11] is even more ambitious than ME. Its goal is nothing short of "mechanical chemistry"—building molecular scale assemblers or robots that can build molecular structures an atom at a time. These assemblers will be able to build virtually any substance and will revolutionize twenty-first-century technology and economics. Assemblers will be capable of building copies of themselves and hence create the exponential numbers needed to build macroscale substances. We know that "nanotech" is possible, because Nature has already done it with its molecular biological (ribosome) assemblers and their DNA coded instructions to build a huge variety of substances. Finally, for the last few years theoretical physicists have been studying the possibility of *quantum computing*—using quantum level entities to perform computation in a characteristic quantum mechanical way [12]. To those who are not familiar with these future technologies, the idea of building devices with an Avogadro number of components probably sounds a bit like science fiction. Nevertheless, such ideas are taken seriously by those who study them. See especially [10].

All these wonderful technologies, most of which humanity will possess within a human generation, pose at least two major issues as far as genetic programming is concerned. They are the need for self-assembly, and the need for evolutionary techniques to be applied to, what is called here, the "complexity problem." When one is considering technologies with an Avogadro number of components, it will obviously be impossible to hand-craft them all and put them together into an integrated whole. They will somehow have to build themselves the way biological creatures do. Hence, some form of artificial embryology becomes essential. When one is confronted with the challenge of building an "Avogadro" machine—one with an Avogadro number of components—one has at least two choices in terms of how complex the machine is to be. One can construct it with a huge number of identical copies of a limited number of component designs that are simple enough for human beings to understand how they are built. Such a device is called a "homogeneous Avogadro machine." Alternatively, the machine may consist of a huge number of complex modules interconnected in complex ways, making analysis of its structure and dynamics virtually impossible. Such a device is called a "heterogeneous Avogadro machine." At first sight it seems that the second possibility would not be possible or interesting, because what is the point of attempting to build such a machine whose functioning would be totally mysterious?

These future technologies will allow the possibility of both approaches. What is interesting is that it may still be worthwhile to build such hypercomplex systems, even though we do not know how they function. Their dynamics or interactions will be so massively complicated that their analysis will be well beyond what the human brain can cope with in theoretical terms. Traditionally speaking, to build something, engineers first make blueprints of their devices. This implies they understand (more or less) how their planned devices will function. In other words, what is buildable and what is (more or less) understandable are often (but not always) identical. An alternative is the empirical hit-or-miss approach, which uses trial and error (e.g., drug testing, which takes numerous possible drugs and tests whether they work; those that do are usually marketed).

However, if one is to allow hypercomplex systems to self-assemble using some form of artificial embryology, how can one be sure that the system that has self-assembled has done so into something that is functional or useful in some sense? What does useful mean in this context? As will become clear in this chapter, using GP applied to the "growth" of artificial embryos is both self-assembling and satisfies demands that the self-assembled system is useful—in other words, it performs well according to some performance criterion. Genetic programming is similar to the trial-and-error approach. Essentially it is a form of simulated or artificial evolution. It is a way of building hypercomplex systems such as (simulated) artificial nervous systems and (as described here), artificial embryos. Genetic programming allows one to "extend the barrier of the buildable" by placing a tool in one's hands that enables one to create useful devices that function, but nevertheless are (usually) too complex to be analyzed. The application of GP to the construction of artificial nervous systems has already been described by de Garis [6]. This chapter extends the discussion of this earlier work by showing how the same principles can be used to build artificial embryos. In other words, GP can be used as a first step to creating self-assembling systems of great complexity yet with a desired functionality.

Before describing how this is done, we give this chapter a reasonable level of self-containment by briefly describing the basic principles of GP.

14.3 GENETIC PROGRAMMING

Genetic programming is "applied evolution"—a form of artificial or simulated evolution called the *genetic algorithm* [1,2] is used to build or evolve hypercomplex systems. This chapter gives a clear example of this process when it is applied to growing artificial desired shapes in two and three dimensions. To understand GP, one needs to understand what the GA is. This section describes its essential features.

The GA, as mentioned, is a form of artificial evolution. But evolution of what? A few key concepts need to be introduced to enable an understanding of how the GA can be employed to evolve such things as shapes. Probably the most important idea is that of a linear mapping of the structure of the system one is dealing with into a string of symbols, usually a binary string. For example, imagine you were trying to find the numerical values of 100 parameters used to specify some complicated nonlinear control process. You could convert these values into binary form and concatenate the results into a long binary string. Alternatively, you could do the reverse and take an "arbitrary" binary string (of suitable length) and extract (or map) the 100 numerical values from it.

Imagine forming a population of 50 of these binary strings, simply by using a random number generator to decide the binary value at each bit position. Each of these bit strings (of appropriate length to agree with the numerical representation chosen) will specify the values of the 100 parameters. Imagine now that you have a means of measuring the quality or performance level (or "fitness," in Darwinian terms) of your (control) process. The next step in the discussion is to actually measure the performance levels of each process as specified by its corresponding bit string. These bit strings are called *chromosomes* by GA specialists, for reasons that will soon become apparent. Let us now reproduce these chromosomes in proportion to their fitnesses; that is, chromosomes with high scores relative to the other members of the population will reproduce themselves more.

If we now assume that the initial population of chromosomes is to be replaced by their offspring, and that the population size is fixed, then we will inevitably have a competition for survival of the chromosomes among themselves into the next generation. Poor-fitness chromosomes may not even survive. We have a Darwinian "survival of the fittest" situation. To increase the closeness of the analogy between biological chromosomes and our bi-

0101010101010 10101010101 010101010101
1111000011110 00011110000 111100001111

0101010101010 00011110000 010101010101
1111000011110 10101010101 111100001111

Figure 14.1 *Crossover of chromosomal pairs.*

nary chromosomes, let us introduce what the GA specialists call *genetic operators,* such as mutation and crossover; and apply them with appropriate probabilities to the offspring.

Mutation in this case is simply flipping a bit, with a given (usually very small) probability. Crossover is (usually) taking two chromosomes, cutting them both at (the same) (one or two) positions along the length of the bit string, and exchanging the two portions thus cut out, as shown in Figure 14.1. If, by chance, the application of one or more of these genetic operators causes the fitness (a scalar) of the resulting chromosome to be slightly superior to the average fitness of the other members of the population, it will have more offspring in the following generation. Over many generations, the average fitness of the population increases. This increase in fitness is due to favorable mutations and the possible combination of more than one favorable mutation into a single offspring due to the effect of crossover. Crossover is synonymous with sex. Biological evolution hit on the efficacy of sex very early in its history. With crossover, two separate favorable mutations, one in each of two parents, can be combined in the same chromosome of the offspring, thus accelerating significantly the adaptation rate (which is vital for species survival when environments change rapidly).

To understand some of the details mentioned in later sections, we introduce some further GA concepts. One concerns the techniques used to select the number of offspring for each member of the current generation. One of the simplest techniques is called *roulette wheel,* which slices up a pie (or roulette wheel) with as many sectors as there are members of the population (assumed fixed over the whole evolution). The angle subtended by the sector (slice of pie) is proportional to the fitness value. High-fitness chromosomes will have slices of pie with large sector angles. To select the next generation (before the genetic operators are applied), one simply "spins" the roulette wheel a number of times equal to the number of chromosomes in the population. If the roulette "ball" lands in a given sector (as simulated with a random number generator), the corresponding chromosome is selected. Since the probability of landing in a given sector is proportional to its angle (and hence fitness), the fitter chromosomes are more likely to survive into the next generation, hence the Darwinian survival of the fittest, and hence the very title of the algorithm, the genetic algorithm.

Another concept is called *scaling,* which is used to linearly transform the fitness scores before selection of the next generation. This is often done for two reasons. One is to avoid premature convergence. Imagine that one chromosome had a fitness value well above the others in the early generations. It would quickly squeeze out the other members of the population if the fitness scores were not transformed. So choose a scaling such that the largest (scaled) fitness is some small factor (e.g., 2) times the average (scaled) fitness. Similarly, if there were no scaling, towards the end of the evolution the average (unscaled) fitness value would approach the largest (unscaled) fitness, because the GA is hitting against the natural (local) optimal behavior of the system being evolved. If the fitness scores differ by too little, no real selection pressure remains, and the search for superior chromosomes becomes increasingly random. To continue the selective pressure, the increasingly small differences between the unscaled average fitness and the largest fitness are magnified by using the same linear scaling employed to prevent premature convergence. This technique is very useful.

There are many forms of crossover in the GA literature. One fairly simple form is as follows. Randomly pair off the chromosomes selected for the next generation and apply crossover to each pair with a user-specified probability (i.e., the "crossprob" value, usually about 0.6). If so-called two-point crossover is to be applied, each chromosome is cut at two random positions (as in Fig. 14.1) and the inner portions of the two chromosomes are swapped.

Another form of crossover is called *uniform crossover,* which works as follows. Randomly pair off the chromosomes in the population. Apply uniform crossover to these pairs (with a user-specified probability, typically about 60%), by creating an offspring pair to replace the parent pair in the next generation. To do this, for each bit position in the chromosome select one of the two parents (with a user-specified probability, typically 50%) and put the selected parent's bit in the corresponding bit position of offspring 1. In offspring 2 put the bit of the parent not selected. Empirical studies have shown that uniform crossover often works well with small populations of chromosomes and for simpler problems [13].

A fairly typical cycle of the GA algorithm is shown in Figure 14.2, where

```
       INITIALIZATION

LOOP:  POPQUAL
       SCALING
       SELECTION
       CROSSOVER
       MUTATION
       ELITE
```

Figure 14.2 *Typical cycle of the genetic algorithm.*

Initialization usually means the creation of random binary strings. Popqual translates the binary strings into the structures whose performances are to be measured, and measures the fitnesses of these performances. Often the chromosome with the highest fitness is saved at this point, to be inserted directly into the next generation once the genetic operators have been applied. Scaling linearly scales the fitness values before selection occurs. Selection is using a technique such as roulette wheel to select the next generation from the present generation of chromosomes. Crossover swaps over portions (or bits, in the case of uniform crossover) of chromosome pairs. Mutation flips the bits of each chromosome with a low probability (typically 0.001 or so) per bit. Elite simply inserts the best chromosome met so far (as stored in the Popqual phase) directly into the next generation. This can be useful, because the stochastic nature of the GA can sometimes eliminate high fitness chromosomes. The elitist strategy prevents this.

This sketch of the GA is far from complete. However, it contains the essence of the subject. For a more detailed analysis, particularly a mathematical justification as to why crossover works so well, see [1] and, especially, [2]. The GA is a flourishing research domain in its own right, characterized by a mix of empirical exploration and mathematical analysis.

Now that the essential principles of the GA have been presented, we describe how the GA can be used to evolve shapes (embryos).

14.4 GENETIC PROGRAMMING (GP) OF 2D SHAPES

Earlier publications [3–6] defined GP as a programming methodology that used the GA to evolve neural network modules. However, the ideas of this section show that the GP approach is quite general. For example, it can be applied to the evolution of artificial embryos.

This section is concerned with how one might create a new specialty called *artificial embryology*. Later, as this subject develops, it is possible that techniques similar to those proposed here, may be used to "grow" (neuro) electronic circuits and to test their functional properties. Such a possibility will be important, as explained in Section 14.2, and is discussed further in Section 14.6. As a first step toward building something that both self-assembles and can have its fitness measured, will be the growth of arbitrary 2D and later 3D shapes. The basic idea is to begin with a small number of "cells" that reproduce until some final shape is formed. The reproduction is obviously the self-assembly, and the fitness can be some function of the final shape. These ideas will now be described in greater detail. We begin by describing an algorithm to grow (evolve) arbitrary 2D shapes. The following section will do the same for 3D shapes (embryos).

The principal idea used in the experiments described in this chapter (when evolving 2D or 3D shapes) was to use the GA to evolve the "neighborhood interaction rules" of cellular automata (CA). Remember that the state of a

CA cell in the next iteration of some cyclical CA algorithm depends on the states of the neighboring cells in the present iteration (e.g., the famous game of Life). Cells in a 2D (square grid) matrix may remain intact, reproduce, or die. Rules (which apply to all cells) are provided for these behaviors. Imagine a grid, partially filled with a contiguous colony of cells (i.e., the colony has no holes) and that a particular cell is to reproduce. Where will this cell put its offspring if there is no (immediate) space for it in the colony? Let us assume that the parent cell pushes all the cells in a given column or row of the grid in a given direction (N, E, W, or S) and that the internal state of the parent cell decides in which direction. We assume that there is a finite number of reproductive iterations of the colony of cells. Hence, with such rules, there will be a final shape whose fitness can be measured.

By introducing a large number of degrees of freedom for the GA to play with, one can imagine that a huge variety of possible final shapes can be made. The aim of the exercise then is to grow a final shape as similar as possible to some predefined form, such as a diamond, a heart, or irregular shapes such as amoebas. One can define the fitness to be simply how closely the final shape resembles the desired shape. Expressed mathematically, this could be as trivial as

$$\text{Fitness} = \frac{\#\text{in} - 0.5 * \#\text{out}}{\#\text{des}}$$

where #in = number of filled cells inside the desired shape
#out = number of filled cells outside the desired shape
#des = number of cells inside the desired shape

If one can grow one shape, one can grow many. If one can grow a body shape (e.g., an ellipsoid), why not limbs, a head, then fingers and toes? It would be nice if new shapes could be grown from the surface cells of old shapes in a time-sequential manner. The GA chromosome that codes all this growth could become "differentiable"; that is, portions of the chromosome could become active and grow a certain kind of shape. Some of the cells in these shapes could transfer "markers," which if present in a cell with an appropriate state, could switch on a new portion of the chromosome (which was previously inactive) and become the germ cell for a new shape. It was thought that using these ideas it would be possible to grow an embryo in a 3D grid.

The previous paragraphs give a quick overview of the essential ideas for evolving shapes. The next few paragraphs provide more detail. The algorithm implemented was as follows. Look at Figure 14.3, which shows an array of contiguous cells. Each cell contains four numbers, *cellular NEWS numbers* (CNNs), from which one derives the NEWS product, which is the product of these four numbers. The N number (for example) of a cell is its position in the column of cells from the top, N(orth). A cell with N = 5 would have four cells above it. If its W number was 5, it would have four

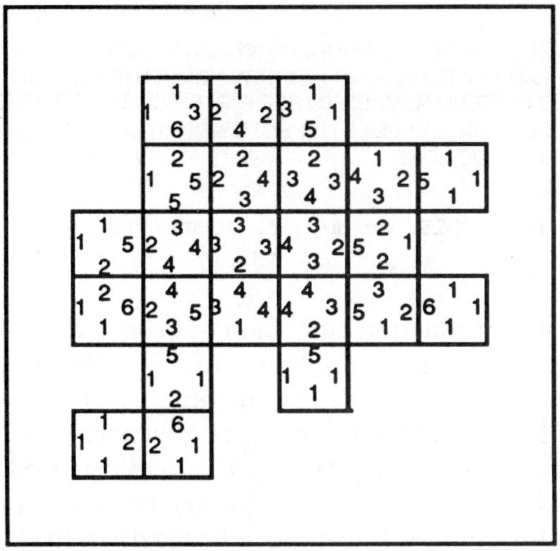

Figure 14.3 *An array of cells and their NEWS numbers.*

cells to the left of it, and so forth. These NEWS numbers tell the cell something about its position relative to other cells in the "colony."

Consider now the rankings of these NEWS numbers rather than their absolute values. If all four numbers of a cell are different, there are 4! = 24 ways these four rankings (1 2 3 4) can be placed around the four NEWS positions. If two (or twice two) of these numbers are the same, there are 42 ways their rankings can be positioned. If three are the same, there are eight ways. If four are the same, there is only one way. Hence, there are 75 ways altogether. We can use these 75 possibilities and define them to be the states of the cells. Each cell will have one of these 75 states. For each of these 75 different positioned rankings, there are corresponding bits in the chromosome (used to control the growth of the colony), which specify whether a cell with a given ranking pattern (and hence state) will reproduce and/or die.

Figure 14.4 shows the various fields of the bit string chromosome used to

NI = NUMBER OF ITERATIONS
RI = WHICH ITERATIONS CAN REPRODUCE
DI = WHICH ITERATIONS CAN DIE
REPRO? = WHICH RANKING PATTERNS CAN REPRODUCE
DEATH? = WHICH RANKING PATTERNS CAN DIE
R DIRNS = REPRODUCTION DIRECTION FOR EACH RANKING PATTERN
D DIRNS = DEATH DIRECTION FOR EACH RANKING PATTERN

Figure 14.4 *Format of the embryo chromosome.*

EMBRYO LOOP:

* CALCULATE CELLULAR NEWS NUMBERS (CNNs) OF EACH CELL
* FROM CNNs CALCULATE RANKING PATTERN NUMBER (RPN) OF EACH CELL
* USE RANKING PATTERN NUMBER TO SEE IF EACH CELL REPRODUCES OR DIES
* FIND REPRODUCTION AND DEATH DIRECTIONS FOR SELECTED CELLS
* PERFORM REPRODUCTIONS
* PERFORM DEATHS

Figure 14.5 *Primary loop of embryo algorithm.*

evolve the rules of reproduction and death of cells in the colony. We discuss these systematically from left to right. Here, NI is the number of iterations that the colony is to evolve over (i.e., the number of loops in the algorithm shown in Fig. 14.5). The maximum number of generations (Gmax) is a user-given system parameter and determines the number of bit positions in this field. The RI field is used to specify whether reproduction can occur in a given iteration of the embryo algorithm. The length of the RI (and DI) field is usually several times Gmax bits long. The *i*th bit in the RI field is set if reproduction is allowed in the *i*th loop. The *j*th bit in the DI field is set if death is allowed in the *j*th loop. It is possible that in a given iteration both reproduction and death occur, or neither, or one or the other. It was thought that these four possibilities would give the embryo algorithm more flexibility.

The REPRO? and DEATH? fields both consist of 75 bits. The 75 ranking patterns are ordered from 1 to 75. For a cell to reproduce, not only must reproduction be allowed for that iteration, but it also has to satisfy the condition that if its ranking pattern number is R, then the Rth bit in the REPRO? field has to be set to 1 (i.e., cells with ranking pattern R are to reproduce, so long as reproduction is allowed for the iteration concerned). A similar story occurs for the DEATH? field (i.e., cells with ranking pattern D are to die, so long as death is allowed for the iteration concerned). These two

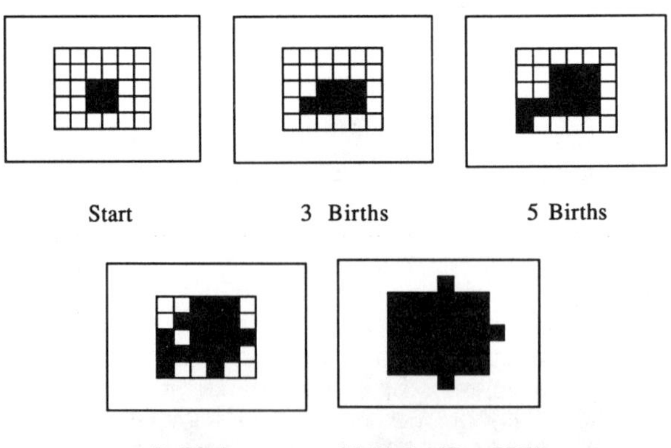

Figure 14.6 *Rectangular target shape.*

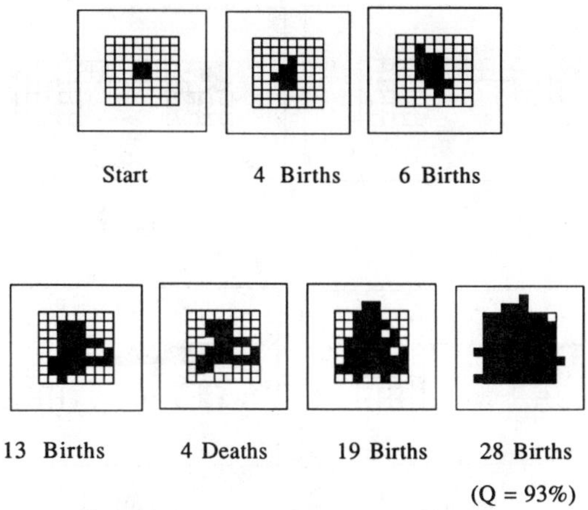

Figure 14.7 *Square target shape.*

fields allow reproduction and death to counteract each other in their influence on the shape of the colony.

If a cell can reproduce, it has to create a space for the offspring cell. Since a cell colony is (mostly) contiguous, a space is created by pushing all the cells lying to the (N, E, W, S) of the parent in one of four directions (N, E, W, S) by one square on the grid. The fields R DIRNS and D DIRNS both contain 75 pairs of bits. If a cell with ranking pattern R is to reproduce, then the direction (one of N, E, W, S) is specified by the Rth pair of bits in the R DIRNS field. A similar story holds for a cell with ranking pattern R that is to die, using the D DIRNS field. When a cell dies, all the cells to (one of the) N, E, W, S of it move one square to fill the vacancy.

Since the final shape of the colony depends on the order in which cells reproduce and die, this order has to be specified. In each iteration of the

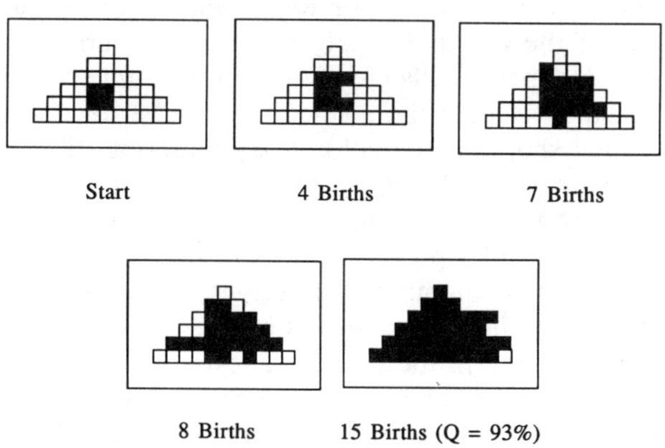

Figure 14.8 *Triangular target shape.*

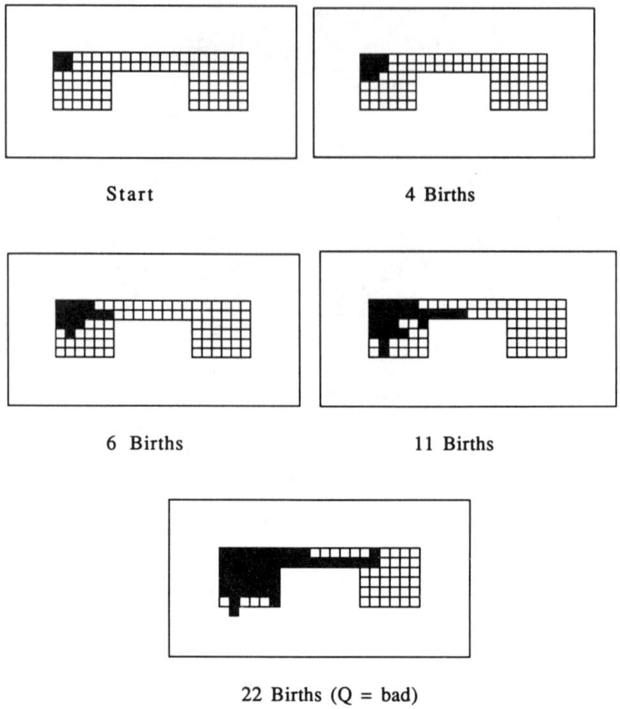

Figure 14.9 *Arch target shape* (*nonconvex*).

algorithm, all the reproductions occur first, then the deaths. At the beginning of each iteration, after the NEWS numbers of all the cells have been found, and before there are any cell modifications, each cell records its NEWS numbers, its NEWS product, and whether it is to reproduce and/or die. The cells reproduce in decreasing order of their NEWS product. If NEWS products are sometimes equal for two or more cells, then the average of the NEWS products of the cell and its eight nearest neighbors can be used in decreasing order. Offspring cells cannot die in the same round. Figure 14.5 summarizes the embryo algorithm. Since the number of iterations is finite, there will be a final shape of the colony. By mutating (flipping) bits in the chromosome and using (uniform) crossover, it is intended that the final shapes will evolve to being very close to the desired shapes.

Figures 14.6 through 14.9 present results of the 2D embryo algorithm as performed on a MAC II computer. The target shapes are indicated by the grid lines. Each frame shows the results at the end of each iteration. The quality or fitness is shown in the figures. These initial experiments showed that the basic idea of being able to grow shapes was feasible, at least for convex shapes such as the rectangle, square, and triangle. The algorithm failed, however, for nonconvex shapes, such as the arch shown in Figure 14.9. In the next section we describe more ambitious experiments performed on a larger scale and in both two and three dimensions.

14.5 2D AND 3D SHAPES ON THE CONNECTION MACHINE

After the encouraging results of the previous experiments on a MAC II, it was considered interesting to see whether more ambitious shapes could be grown in 2D and 3D on a substantial computer such as a connection machine (a massively parallel machine with up to 65,000 little processors all executing the same instruction simultaneously but each with its own data—a "data parallel" machine). This section presents some of the initial results.

If one observes Figures 14.6, 14.7, and 14.8, it is clear that any deaths that occurred seemed to have played a rather minor role, if any at all. To simplify matters, it was decided that deaths could be eliminated from the algorithm without undue loss. It was also decided that only edge or surface cells would reproduce, thus avoiding the need to displace whole rows or columns of cells to make room for offspring cells. Having decided that only edge (in 2D) or surface (in 3D) cells will reproduce allows one to simplify the definition of the state of a cell.

The state of a cell in the new algorithm was defined from the positions of its neighborless sides. For example, for a 2D cell (a square), only four states are possible if three sides are neighborless (i.e., equivalently, there are only four ways of positioning the neighbored side). There were 14 such states ($^4C_1 + {^4C_2} + {^4C_3} = 4 + 6 + 4 = 14$), as shown in Figure 14.10. Neighborless sides are indicated with a 0, neighbored sides with a 1. Any 2D edge cell must be in one of these 14 states. It is assumed that cells always have at least one neighbor; that is, there are no island cells. With these simplifications, the number of possible states for the 2D cells was reduced from 75 to 14. At first sight it appears as though the second algorithm is less flexible because there is less scope for the GA to play with. That this need not be so is explained next.

The foregoing assumptions thus allow the "embryo" chromosome of Figure 14.4 to be simplified as shown in Figure 14.11. Since there are no deaths, the fields DI, DEATH? and D DIRNS can be dropped. With no DI field, it makes no sense to have an RI field. Instead we have reproduction allowed for every iteration. All that remains, therefore, are the NI, REPRO?, and R DIRNS fields. The REPRO? and R DIRNS fields are redefined as follows. Since there are now 14 states, 14 bits are needed in the REPRO? field to specify which edge cells will reproduce. The R DIRNS field also happens to be 14 bits long. This figure was derived from the following considerations. If an edge cell has only one neighborless side, then it can only reproduce in that

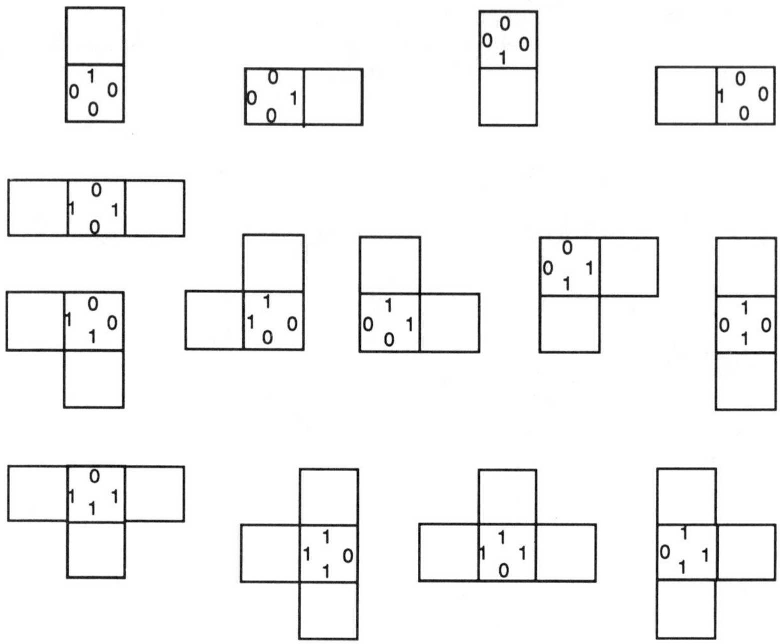

Figure 14.10 *The 14 neighborless patterns for 2D cells.*

direction, so no information is needed to specify the choice of direction. For a cell with two neighborless sides, 1 bit is needed to specify the choice. There are six states with two neighborless sides; hence, 6 bits are needed for those states. For a cell with three neighborless sides, 2 bits are needed to make the choice of direction of reproduction. However, 2 bits can specify four choices, but only three are needed. In practice, if the fourth choice is specified (i.e., a forbidden direction (toward a neighbored side) is chosen), then the reproduction is simply ignored. There are four states with three neighborless sides; hence, 8 bits are needed for them. The total length of the R DIRNS field is thus 6 + 8 = 14 bits. The total length of the REPRO? and R DIRNS fields is only 28 bits, a very short chromosome.

This economy suggested the possibility that one might have a REPRO? and R DIRNS field pair for each iteration. The *i*th iteration would thus take its reproduction instructions from the *i*th pair of fields in the chromosome. This independence of instructions for each iteration allows several possibilities. One is that intermediate target shapes become possible. A specific shape S1 can be evolved in the first I1 iterations. The resulting chromosome can then be frozen and used as an initial component in a longer chromosome that codes for I2 (>I1) iterations, which expands shape S1 into S2. The same process can be continued from S2 to S3, and so on. Another obvious possi-

NI = NUMBER OF ITERATIONS
REPRO1? = WHICH STATES CAN REPRODUCE IN ITERATION 1
R DIRNS1 = REPRODUCTION DIRECTIONS IN ITERATION 1
REPRO2? = WHICH STATES CAN REPRODUCE IN ITERATION 2
R DIRNS2 = REPRODUCTION DIRECTIONS IN ITERATION 2

Figure 14.11 *Format of the simplified embryo chromosome.*

bility is that, with a larger chromosome, more information is specified; hence, a greater range of possible shapes should be evolvable.

Figures 14.12, 14.13, and 14.14 show the results of using the "simplified" embryo algorithm to evolve the convex shapes of a circle, ellipse, and rectangle. As usual, (in the case of 2D shapes) there were four seeder cells in the form of a square, placed inside the target shape to initiate the reproduction. The fitness definition was unchanged. The fitness qualities were 99% for the circle and 96% for the ellipse and rectangle. Figure 14.15 shows a failed attempt at evolving a triangle, showing that sometimes an evolution can get stuck in an intermediate shape that it cannot get out of. For example,

Figure 14.12 *Circular target shape (c.m.).*

Figure 14.13 *Elliptical target shape (c.m.).*

Figure 14.14 *Rectangular target shape (c.m.).*

Figure 14.15 *Triangular target shape (c.m.).*

consider the sawtooth NW-SE edges at the upper right and lower left of the figure. Once such a sawtooth pattern emerges, the evolution only repeats it. Figure 14.16 shows a more successful attempt at triangle evolution where only the mutation rate was changed. However in this case, there were not enough prespecified iterations in the chromosome to cover the target shape. (The number of iterations was usually set at a maximum of 32 or 64). The triangular pattern was evolving well enough, but ran out of steam. Its fitness value was 92%. Figure 14.17 shows the result of an attempt to evolve a nonconvex shape in the form of the letter L. At the bottom and left of the figure, one can see the evolution was successful, but that it failed (again) to "turn corners." A "webbed-foot" phenomenon occurred, filling the space contained between the three corners of the L. The evolution of nonconvex shapes thus remains a challenge requiring additional effort.

We turn now to the 3D case. For 3D cells (cubes), with six faces (east, north, west, south, up, and down), there were 62 states ($^6C_1$ + $^6C_2$ + $^6C_3$ +

Figure 14.16 *Triangular target shape (c.m.).*

Figure 14.17 *L target shape (c.m.).*

$^6C_4 + {}^6C_5) = (6 + 15 + 20 + 15 + 6) = 62$. Thus the REPRO? field for the 3D case contained 62 bits. The length of the R DIRNS field was derived from the following considerations. If there is only one neighborless face, there is only one direction of reproduction; hence, no information is needed to specify any choice. If there are two neighborless faces, 1 bit is needed per state, and there are $^6C_2 = 15$ such states; hence, 15 bits are needed. If there are three neighborless faces, 2 bits are needed per state and there are $^6C_3 = 20$ such states; hence, 40 bits are needed. If the chromosome specified the fourth possible reproduction direction, it was ignored. If there are four neighborless faces, again 2 bits are needed per state, and there are $^6C_4 = 15$ such states; hence, 30 bits are needed. If there are 5 neighborless faces, 3 bits are needed per state, and there are $^6C_5 = 6$ such states. Three of the eight possible "directions" specifiable by the chromosome were simply ignored. The total length of the R DIRNS field was thus $(1 * 15 + 2 * 20 + 2 * 15 + 3 * 6) = (15 + 40 + 30 + 18) = 103$ bits. If there were a maximum of 64 iterations possible as specified by the NI field, this meant that the chromosome had a total length of $6 + 64 * 103 = 6598$, which is rather a large chromosome. For the 3D case, eight seeder cells (in the form of a cube) were placed inside the target shape to initiate reproduction.

The first experiments show that it is possible to evolve a sort of tadpole shape, where one shape was grown out of another. It was reasoned that if this could be done once, it could be done several times. For example, one could grow an ellipsoid body, and then from it grow a head and four limbs, thus creating an embryo shape. At least the tadpole shape showed that the principle of growing one shape out of another was successful.

For the 3D embryo, the target shape was a sphere (the head), which was grown first, and then its cells were frozen (i.e., they could no longer reproduce). Figures 14.18 and 14.19 show its embryological development at 300 cells (halfway) and 600 cells. Contiguous and overlapping slightly with the sphere target shape was an ellipsoid target shape, which was used to grow a "limb bud" or beginnings of a tail (using a completely separate bit string chromosome), thus producing a sort of tadpole shape. Those surface cells that were common to both target shapes (the "neck") were activated artifi-

Figure 14.18 *Spherical target shape* (*c.m.*) 300 cells.

cially and allowed to reproduce into the second target shape. See Figures 14.20 and 14.21 for two different viewing angles of the tadpole shape. With more time it would have been possible to grow limbs this way out of a body shape and produce a human-baby-like embryo. Unfortunately this work was not continued due to the lack of a $1 million connection machine at the author's home university. Evolving 3D shapes containing many thousands of cells on a MAC II was not considered worthwhile for reasons of execution speed.

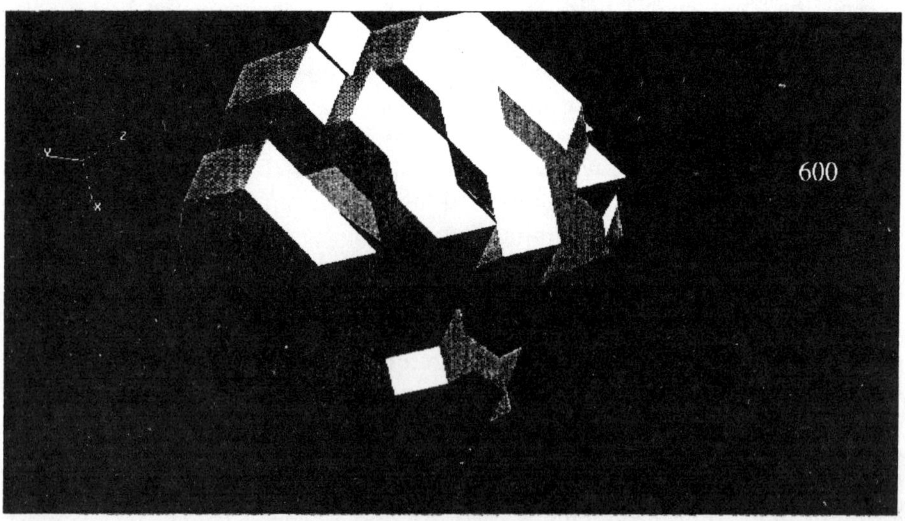

Figure 14.19 *Spherical target shape* (*c.m.*) 600 cells.

Figure 14.20 *Tadpole target shape* (*c.m.*) view 1.

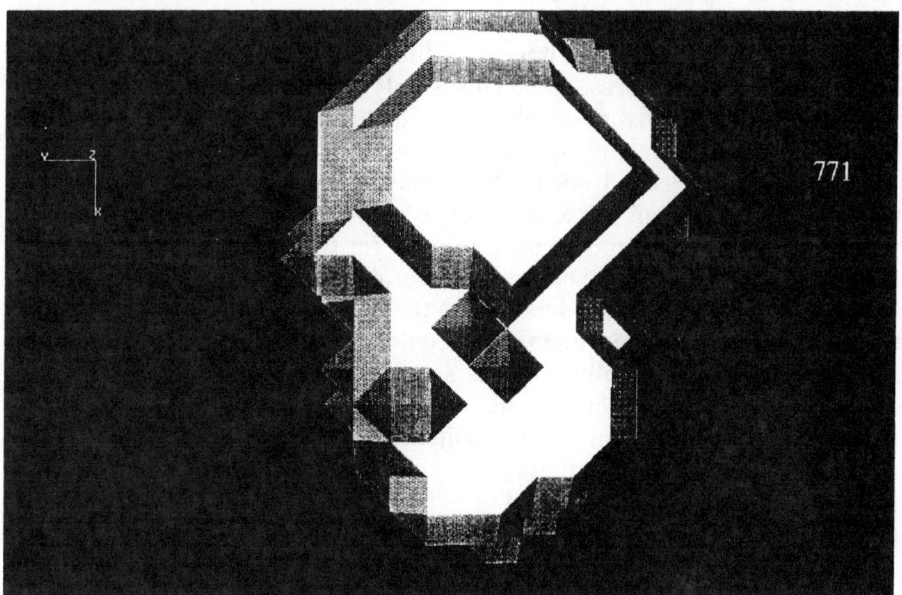

Figure 14.21 *Tadpole target shape* (*c.m.*) view 2.

14.6 REMARKS AND FUTURE IDEAS

The foregoing experiments show that a lot of work still needs to be done to be able to grow truly arbitrary shapes. The two algorithms presented show that nonconvex shapes remain a problem. The growth of the 3D embryo shape still has certain ad hoc elements to it. For example, to get the tail to grow, it was first necessary to freeze the cells of the head and then to unfreeze those cells at the neck that could grow into the tail. It would be nice if whole embryos could be grown in "one hit," so to speak, without such arbitrary intervention. A tentative suggestion as to how this might be done is as follows. Imagine one wanted to grow the L shape. This means that cells must somehow be capable of turning corners. One way of doing this might be to use a "growth substance," assumed to be emitted by some cells at a certain moment (i.e., at a given iteration). This substance could diffuse to its neighbors, allowing them to reproduce. Those cells not within range of such a growth substance cannot reproduce. Hence, if the growth substance source cell were near the bottom of the vertical portion of the L, the cells in the upper portion would not reproduce. Only those cells near the bottom could turn. The GA could be used to decide which cells emit the growth substance and when.

To summarize, the following main ideas have been presented. Future computing technologies will allow the construction of devices with so many components that they will have to self-assemble in an embryological way if they are to be built at all. Genetic programming techniques will be needed to measure the quality of performance of these self-assembled systems. Hence, it looks as though GP has an important future. Initial steps at growing artificial shapes have been presented. This is only a modest beginning toward the creation of a speciality that will deal with the creation and study of self-assembling and self-testing systems.

Much progress needs to be made in this new field. For example, consider the possibility of using GP techniques to grow electronic neurocircuits. Bit string chromosomes could be used to code for the strengths of connections (weights) between artificial neurons in neural networks. The time-dependent output of these neural nets depends on the values of the weights. Using GP techniques to evolve the weights, one could evolve a neural net that delivers an output that successfully controls some process. This could all be done directly in hardware, using WSI as the enabling technology. The WSI wafer could have a population of slave circuits, each of which is sent a different bit string chromosome and a fitness definition. The slave uses the chromosome to build its neurocircuit and then tests and measures its fitness. Results are reported back to a master circuit, which then determines the next generation of chromosomes. Such a piece of hardware is called a *Darwin machine*. It is merely an example of the kind of thing proposed here that self-assembles and self-tests.

ACKNOWLEDGMENTS

The author would like to express his gratitude to the following people at Boston University: Professor Richard Brower (of BU's Center for Computational Science) for giving the author permission to work on BU's connection machine; to Robert Putnam (Thinking Machines Corporation's application engineer for BU) for tolerating the author's constant pestering with technical questions to accelerate the learning curve; Tim Hall and Laura Giannitrapani (of BU's Graphics Lab), who made the video and stills.

REFERENCES

[1] D. E. Goldberg, *Genetic Algorithms in Search, Optimization, and Machine Learning,* Addison-Wesley, Reading, Mass., 1989.

[2] J. H. Holland, *Adaptation in Natural and Artificial Systems,* University of Michigan Press, Ann Arbor, 1975.

[3] H. de Garis, Genetic programming: Modular neural evolution for Darwin machines, *Proc. Internat. Joint Conf. on Neural Networks* (January 1990).

[4] H. de Garis, Genetic programming: Building nanobrains with genetically programmed neural network modules, *Proc. Internat. Joint Conf. on Neural Networks* (June 1990).

[5] H. de Garis, Genetic programming: Building artificial nervous systems using genetically programmed neural network modules, *Proc. 7th Internat. Conf. on Machine Learning* (1990).

[6] H. de Garis, "Genetic Programming," in B. Souček, Ed., *Neural and Intelligent Systems Integration,* Wiley Interscience, New York, 1991.

[7] M. Rudnick and D. Hammerstrom, An interconnect structure for wafer scale neurocomputers, in *Proceedings of the 1988 Connectionist Models Summer School,* D. Touretzky, G. Hinton, and T. Sejnowski, Eds., Morgan Kaufmann, San Mateo, Calif. (1989).

[8] D. Feitelson, *Optical Computing: A Survey for Computer Scientists,* MIT Press, Cambridge, Mass., 1988.

[9] M. A. Reed, "Quantum Semiconductor Devices," in *Molecular Electronic Devices,* F. L. Carter, R. E. Siatkowski, and H. Wohltjen, Eds., North Holland, New York, 1988.

[10] K. E. Drexler, *Engines of Creation: The Coming Era of Nanotechnology,* Doubleday, New York, 1986.

[11] C. Schneiker, "Nano technology with Feynman machines: Scanning tunneling engineering and artificial life," in *Artificial Life: The Synthesis and Simulation of Living Systems,* C. G. Langton, Ed., Addison Wesley, Reading, Mass., 1989.

[12] R. P. Feynman, Quantum mechanical computers, *Optics News,* 11–20 (February 1985).

[13] W. Spears and V. Anand, "The Use of Crossover in Genetic Programming," NRL Tech. Rep., AI Center, Naval Research Labs, Washington D.C. (1990).

CHAPTER 15

Structure Evolution in Neural Systems

REINHARD LOHMANN

15.1 INTRODUCTION

The success of neural networks in information processing tasks depends mostly on well-designed structures of the systems. Structures have to be defined before learning algorithms are applied. Although, in practice, determination of structures takes most of the effort in adjusting a neural system to particular tasks, there are still no effective rules or systematical approaches to determine structures in neural systems.

While a neural system is already a biological approach to solving information processing problems evolution strategy according to Rechenberg [1,2], a computer model of biological evolution, seems to suggest itself as a method for developing and optimizing structures of such systems. Extension of the evolution strategy to a system of several populations that are temporarily isolated and contain different competing structures provides for a method of systematical development of structures in neural systems.

The algorithm for structure evolution has been established for the purpose of developing a small part of a visual system, a local filter, that is expected to count coherent areas in any binary picture. This example is used to study the algorithm of structure evolution in an application and give evidence of structure evolution working efficiently. Efficiency, as it turns out, depends to some extent on overcoming the problem of "overlearning" that occurs in simulations. This problem, however, can be solved easily within the new algorithm.

Dynamic, Genetic, and Chaotic Programming, By Branko Souček and the IRIS Group.
ISBN 0-471-55717-X

15.2 DESIGN OF NEURAL SYSTEMS

15.2.1 Motivation

The performance of technical systems for information processing is intuitively accepted as a comparison with corresponding biological or human capabilities. The difficulties to set up appropriate technical models and computer simulations, however, are still rather great because we are still far from understanding biological systems in sufficient detail. Often, one can give only a vague description of biological capabilities. A vivid demonstration is human perception, which can, for example, easily distinguish between the two leaves in Figure 15.1. But it is not clear what the features are that enable us to distinguish between the leaves. Also, the common features of the two patterns that emerge, if we pay attention to the triangle in addition, are not evident. Taking the picture as a whole, the number of coherent areas may be an important feature.

Although there is no exact description of these features, we get the idea that in one way or another they are important for perception. Therefore, the intent of using neural systems for solving information processing tasks is to avoid the need of knowing and understanding all details in corresponding biological procedures and neural circuitry. The question remains, what has to be done to establish systematically neural systems of optimal performance with respect to only vaguely and incompletely described tasks? First experience shows that evolution strategy may be an answer.

15.2.2 Priorities among System Structure and Learning Algorithm

Usually an application of a neural system begins with the user's choice of a network structure, including the type of neurons, their input, and transition functions as well as the whole structure with its number of neurons and their

Figure 15.1 *Two leaves and a triangle.*

linkages. This choice is governed by the affiliated learning algorithms, which means that the existence of a more or less powerful learning algorithm is a prerequisite that restricts the choice of the network structure; a learning algorithm usually does not fit any structure. If the learning procedure fails, the user will change the network structure or try to improve the learning procedure. If, on the other hand, the learning procedure is comparatively successful, there is still no evidence that the choice of structure has been the best possible.

The dilemma seems to be that it has not always been completely clear that the performance of a neural system depends in the first place on the right structure of the system and in the second place on effective learning algorithms that are necessary to adjust the parameters contained by the structure. So a reasonable treatment of neural systems should include as a first priority algorithms to improve structures. It is comforting to know that a learning algorithm for parameters, or weights as they are commonly called, is at hand in any case, at least the evolution strategy that is a rather universal optimization method.

15.2.3 Design and Optimization of Neural Systems

It turns out that application of neural systems has to be considered as an optimization problem concerning the structure and the parameters of the system. Optimization requires at least that one is able to say whether one system is better or worse than the other. In usual terms the performance of an information processing systems is calculated as the distance between a target output T and the system output P when the system is stimulated by the corresponding input S. For N different stimuli the mean square of all distances could be an appropriate quality function Q, where

$$Q = \frac{1}{N} \sum_{i=1}^{N} (T_i - P_i)^2 \tag{15.1}$$

Other quality functions can be considered and taken as a measure for the performance of a system. In Eq. (15.2) the mean square function is replaced by a more general function G, which is meant to indicate that a larger scale of functions is allowed:

$$Q = G(T_i, P_i) \qquad i = 1, 2, \ldots, N \tag{15.2}$$

Target outputs T_i are constants depending on the stimuli S_i, and the system output P_i can be written as a function F that describes the neural system and whose value also depends on the stimuli S_i:

$$Q = G(T(S_i), F(S_i)) \qquad i = 1, 2, \ldots, N \tag{15.3}$$

The quality function, on the one hand, depends on the selection of inputs S_i and the determination of respective target outputs T_i; thus far, we have a more or less accurate mathematical description of the information processing task, and the quality might change if the set of stimuli S_i is changed. On the other hand, the quality function is influenced by the function F that describes somehow the properties of the neural system. In general, it makes no difference whether F is an analytical function. Perhaps neural systems have been introduced to solving problems of information processing only to explore a larger scale of functions beyond simple analytical ones. In fact, the concept of a function here is reduced to a representation in which the function is separated into a structure C of the neural system and a set of variables or weights W belonging to the structure. The structure C defines the meaning of the weights W when the system output P due to a stimulus S is calculated.

From this point of view the quality function of a neural system mainly depends on three terms: the set of stimuli S including their target outputs T, the structure C, and a set of weights W. Beyond that a fourth term has to be mentioned, the type of function G:

$$Q = G(S, C, W) \tag{15.4}$$

Obviously the objective here is minimization of the quality Q. This demands an algorithm that is at least capable of changing the structure C as well as the weights W at the same time, possibly on different time scales. Due to the treatment of incomplete task descriptions the algorithm should include mechanisms to alter the set of stimuli as well. It is not sufficient to find only the best set of variables W of a neural system, the aim, for example, in the error back-propagation algorithm; more important is to alter the structure C of the system until it allows the quality function Q to converge to a lower minimum.

It makes no significant difference whether one looks at a neural system structure in its graphical representation with a number of units, their connections, and the transition functions of units or at the mathematical equivalent where the structure is some sort of grammar that gives the instructions to calculate a signal from the set of variables and the stimulus. If these instructions do not fit the task, even the most sophisticated efforts to adjust the weights in Eq. (15.4) will be in vain.

Systematic design of a neural system consequently means solving the minimization problem in Eq. (15.4); every other approach seems to be only estimation or belief. The appropriate algorithm for this optimization problem is the evolution strategy.

15.2.4 Evolution Strategy

Evolution is the optimization method of biological systems, and evolution strategy [2,3] is its computational model. The strategy takes into account the most important terms of biological evolution: first, inheritance and then mutation of the object variables, sometimes including recombination, followed by selection, where μ parents for the next generation are chosen from λ offspring. The criterion for selection is a quality function Q.

In the most common case the object is represented by a number N of real numbers, the variables, and mutation is carried out by adding to each variable a randomly chosen number from a normal distribution. This random number is multiplied by the step size S before being added to the variable. The step size S is inherited and mutated as an additional variable assigned to the object. Thus, the selection guarantees that those step sizes dominate in the population that furnishes the best success with respect to the quality function. This part of the algorithm is called the *mutative step size control*, and it is essential for the whole algorithm because it provides for the step size to adapt to the local complexity of the problem to which the evolution strategy is applied. Formal descriptions of evolution strategies have been introduced by Schwefel [3,4]

$$(\mu/\rho +, \lambda) - \mathrm{ES} \tag{15.5}$$

Here μ and λ are the numbers of parents and offspring in a population, and ρ denotes how many parents are possibly recombined in the mutation procedure. The + or , in the strategy refers to different selection rules; in a +-strategy both parents and offspring take part in the competition, while in a ,-strategy parents are chosen from offspring of the last generation only.

The only necessary requirement for evolution strategy being applicable is strong causality of the problem. *Strong causality* means that small alterations of the object result in a small change of its quality, while bigger alterations cause comparatively larger shifts of the quality. If strong causality is violated, adaptive step size control no longer works, which means the loss of the most important part of the algorithm.

As far as it is described here, evolution strategy is suitable for optimization of usual parameters in a system like the set of weights W, for example, in Eq. (15.4). We therefore call it *parameter evolution*.

15.2.5 Structure Evolution

Obviously the variation of structures in neural systems works on a level that differs from that of parameter evolution. Variation of a structure could, for example, change the number of parameters or alter the interpretation of a parameter.

Extension of the evolution strategy to an algorithm with several populations that are temporarily isolated provides for a second level on which mutation and selection of structures can take place. Each structure is assigned to its own population, where, during a certain isolation time τ, parameter evolution is carried out. For μ' parent structures and λ' offspring, corresponding to the same number of populations, the following formulation has been proposed [5,6], recombination being neglected:

$$[\mu' \overset{+}{,} \lambda' \underbrace{(\mu \overset{+}{,} \lambda)^{\tau}_{V1,S1}}_{\text{parameter evolution}}]_{V2,S2} - \text{ES} \tag{15.6}$$

$$\underbrace{\hphantom{[\mu' \overset{+}{,} \lambda'(\mu \overset{+}{,} \lambda)^{\tau}_{V1,S1}]_{V2,S2}}}_{\text{structure evolution}}$$

Both levels of this evolution algorithm are equipped with separate variation and selection mechanisms, V1 and S1 for the parameter evolution and V2 and S2 for the structure or population level. Variation procedure V1 is the same as that explained for the usual evolution strategy. Variation procedure V2, assigned to the brackets, has to be specified with respect to the structure of the application, its restrictions, and, most important, V2 must comply with strong causality. The terms S1 and S2 refer to the selection criteria, the quality functions, which may be different on the two levels as well.

The user of this algorithm for structure evolution may now be disappointed that he or she cannot lean back and wait until a system has organized itself. Much heuristic work remains to be done, especially defining the stock of structures and an appropriate set of variation mechanisms that comply with the demand of strong causality.

15.3 APPLICATION

Evolution methods have been proposed for the development of information processing systems, especially in the field of vision, for a long time [7,8]. But not much success has been reported.

The algorithm for structure evolution (Eq. (15.6)) is not only the result of theoretical reasoning, but it has been developed to solve a problem in the field of vision [6,9].

15.3.1 The Task

In this example the objective is to design a system that extracts the number of coherent areas as a feature from any binary picture. Figure 15.2 shows 12 such pictures. The number of coherent areas N_c is written above each picture.

The choice of these 12 stimuli S_i and the corresponding target signals T_i is a first description of the task. This description is incomplete and by no means can we call it representative of the task that aims at counting coherent areas in any binary picture whose number is infinite. The quality function,

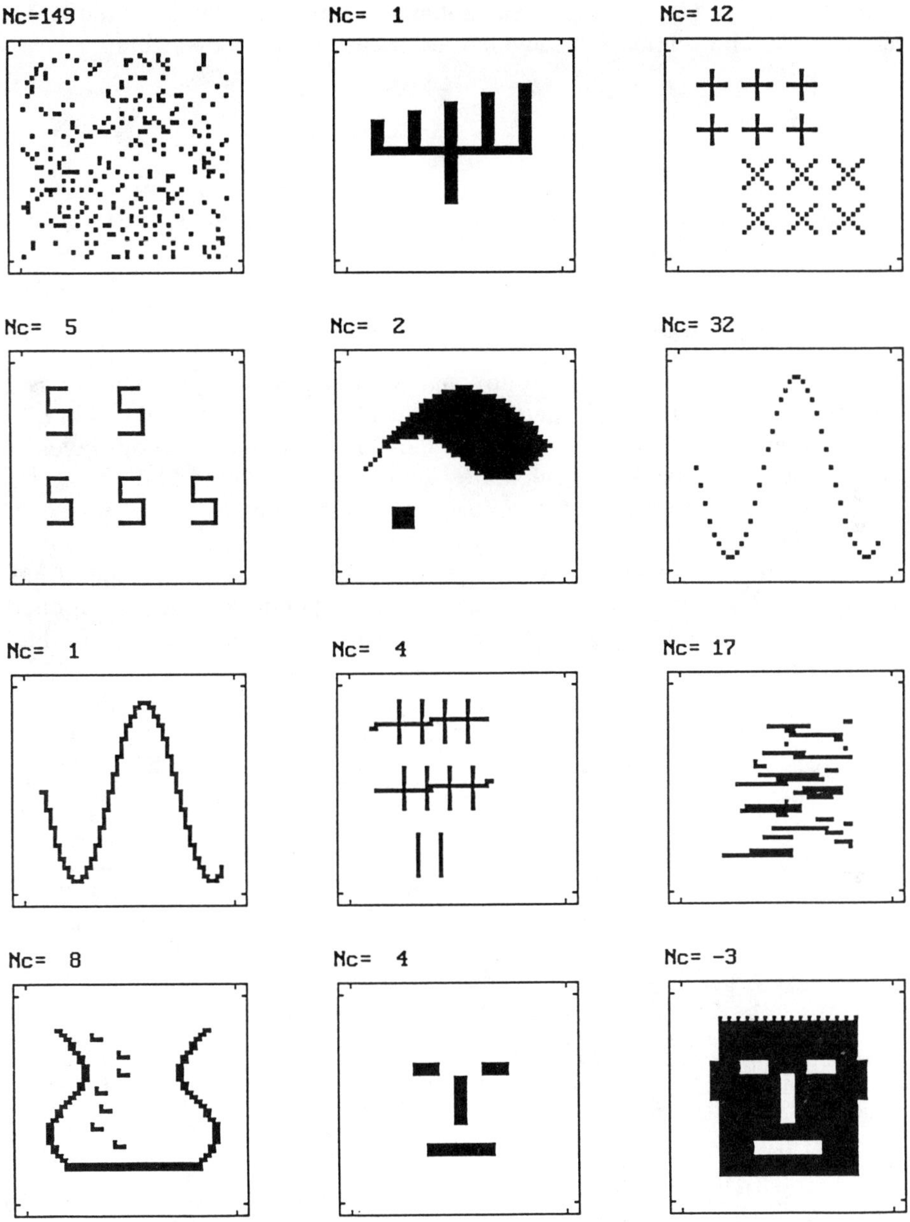

Figure 15.2 *Set of 12 binary pictures with the correct numbers of coherent areas* Nc.

according to Eq. (15.1), is the mean square of differences between the target numbers N_c and numbers N_m, which are measured by the system:

$$Q = \frac{1}{12} \sum_{i=1}^{12} (N_{c_i} - N_{m_i})^2 \tag{15.7}$$

The objective is to develop the structure of a local filter as part of a visual system. The system is already designed in most of its parts.

15.3.2 Visual System

The visual system used in the following experiments has been built up as a rough model of the retina. It mainly consists of a layer of receptors (R in Fig. 15.3) that are directly connected to the elements of a homogeneous layer of local filters (L). A local filter calculates, on the basis of the excitation pattern in its local neighborhood of receptors, a contribution to a certain global feature. The layer of filters is homogeneous because the same operation is carried out at every point of the picture. But local results of these operations may be different from each other because they depend on the locally applied pattern. All local results are added and the sum is called the corresponding global feature (G):

$$F_{\text{global}} = \Sigma F_{\text{local}} \tag{15.8}$$

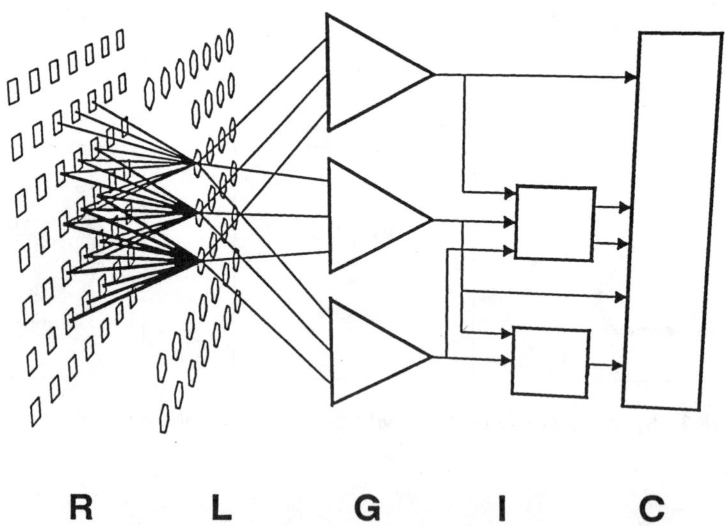

Figure 15.3 *Design of a visual system: R = layer of receptors; L = layer of local filters; G = global features; I = invariant features; C = classification.*

The advantage of this construction is that feature extraction, which involves the most calculations in a visual system, can be distributed to the parallel structure of the filter layer if appropriate hardware is available and used.

Different layers of filters calculate different global features (G), and the idea is to use such filters that support features to become invariant when position, rotation, and largeness of patterns change. Usually, global features are not invariant, but two or more global features sometimes can be combined to build an invariant feature (I). A set of invariant features is then some sort of reduced information about the picture that works as the basis for classification (C).

In the case examined here there is only one global feature, the number of coherent areas, and it is expected to be immediately invariant. That means that the measured number of coherent areas N_m in Eq. (15.7) is identical to F_{global} in Eq. (15.8). Still unknown is the function F_{local} in Eq. (15.8), which will be developed by evolution techniques.

15.3.3 Local Filters in the Retina

A brief look at Figure 15.4 shows the biological circuitry in the retina. Information from one receptor is propagated through rather complicated layers of different cells (e.g., horizontal, bipolar, and amacrine) until it

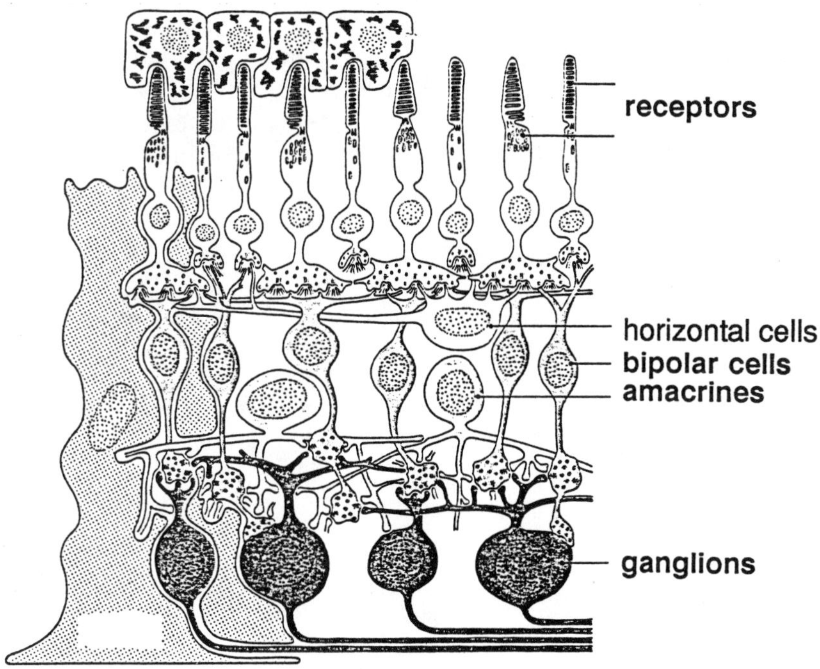

Figure 15.4 *The retina.*

reaches the ganglion cells within a certain area around that receptor; hence, information diverges. The purpose of the circuitry is not very well understood. In fact there is no experimental method to investigate the circuitry in detail. Only rather nonspecific statements can be made—for example that information from receptors in a certain area, the receptive field, converges to a ganglion. The extension of the receptive field can be introduced to the model of a local filter, and also some qualitative properties of the circuitry (i.e., the existence of excitatory and inhibitory synapses). It is now easy to imagine that the level of excitation in a ganglion cell depends on the activation pattern in the receptive field. For example, a ganglion might be only activated if two specific receptors are on and three others are off. A simple logic like this can easily be implemented by superimposing inhibitory and excitatory elements and by demanding coincidence of activations in intermediate cells.

15.3.4 Stock of Structures

In the parameter evolution it is clear that the stock of possible values for the parameters are the real numbers. The main problem in structure evolution is the definition of a stock of possible structures and of the variation procedures that change these structures and are consistent with strong causality.

The first step of the definition restricts the local neighborhood of receptors involved in the computation of the local filter to a 3×3 matrix. This might be a poor simulation of a receptive field, but in this case it turned out to be sufficient. The receptor matrix is represented by the numbers a_1 to a_9 (see Fig. 15.5), which can take the value 1 or 0.

The local filter function is composed as the sum of different binary products. Each product is weighted by a real number r. One element E_j of the sum is, for example

$$E_j = a_5 \times a_4 \times a_7 \times r_j \tag{15.9}$$

With the restriction that combinations of matrix elements are different in all products, the local filter value is

$$F_{\text{local}} = \sum_{j=1}^{L} E_j \tag{15.10}$$

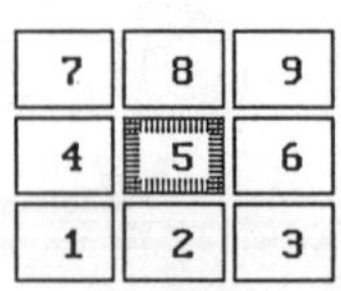

Figure 15.5 *Local matrix of receptors.*

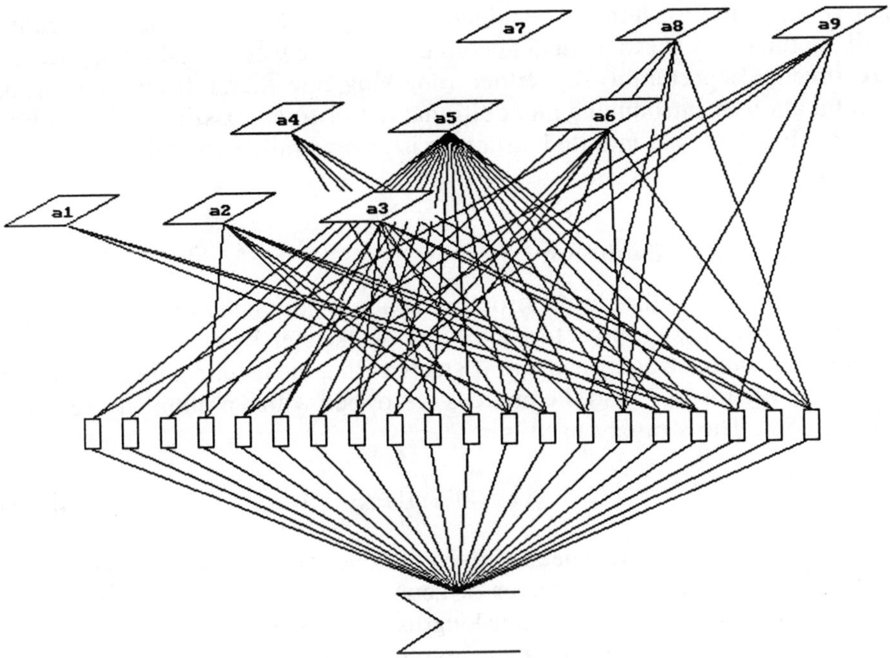

Figure 15.6 *Graphical representation of a local filter.*

The number L of different binary products is here called the filter length, and a filter structure of length L contains L real numbers, the parameters or variables assigned to the structure. The structure itself is described by the number L, the number of factors in each product including the indices of the receptor matrix elements to which the factors refer. A graphical representation of a structure is given in Figure 15.6, with the local receptor matrix at the top, followed by a layer of units that are plotted as squares and are meant to perform binary multiplication; the operator for execution of the weighted sum at the bottom completes the filter.

15.3.5 Variation Procedures for Structures

Variation procedures to be defined here refer to V2 in the description of structure evolution given by Eq. (15.6). The formulation of the stock of structures has already been governed by the need to make variations of structures easy and fairly consistent with strong causality. Removing one of the products, preferably one with a small absolute value of the real coefficient r assigned to it, will not change the value of the quality function very much. So this procedure complies with the demand for strong causality. In a similar way a new product with a combination of matrix elements that does not yet exist in the filter can be added to the list of products if the respective real coefficient is set to a small absolute value. New combinations of factors are invented, preferably by either removing one factor from an existing combination or introducing an additional factor to an existing product. Following these rules, a mutated structure is always rather similar to its parent structure.

15.3.6 Structure Evolution

Local search in a rather large structure space is guaranteed by the variation procedures discussed. Structure evolution walks step by step along a narrow pathway through structure space. It starts with a most simple filter, which is plotted in Figure 15.7, and the process is stopped with a preliminary result in Figure 15.6. The strategy used is

$$[12 + 2(5, 25)^{\tau}_{V1,S1}]_{V2,S2} - \text{ES} \tag{15.11}$$

The isolation time τ has been chosen to cover about 50 generations in the parameter evolution. The number of generations in each of the 14 populations actually depends on the filter lengths, because smaller filters need less time for one cycle in the parameter evolution. Originally the idea of using

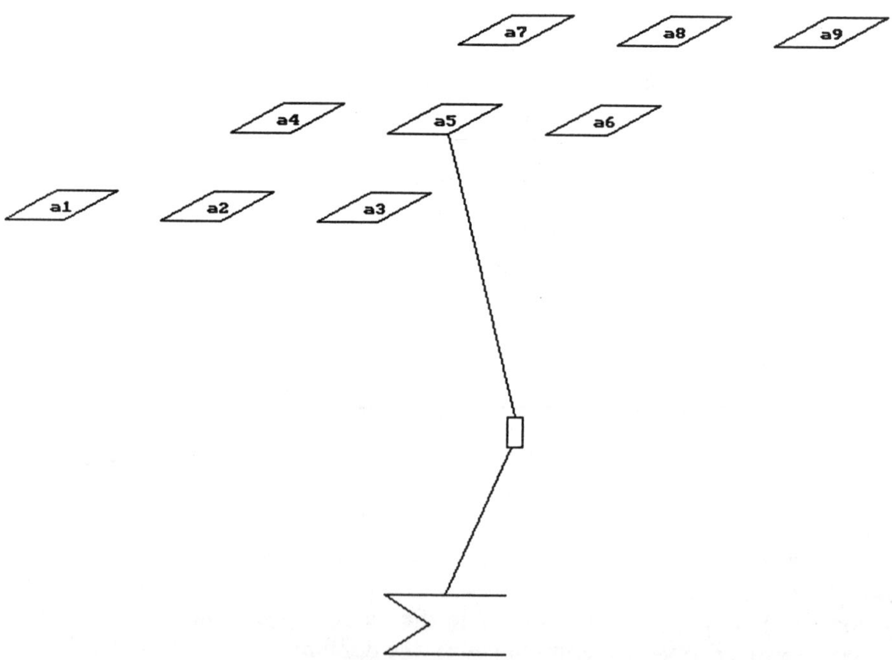

Figure 15.7 *Start configuration of the filter. Compare with the result in Figure 15.6.*

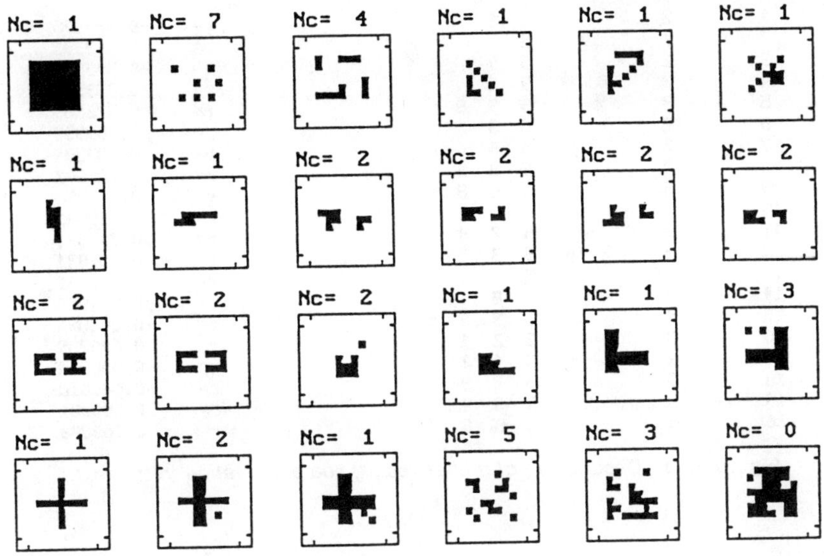

Figure 15.8 *Twenty-four small pictures used in selection mechanism* S_1.

time, instead of the number of generations, as a measure of isolation time has been to take velocities of convergence as a criterion in the competition between different populations.

Note that again there are different selection rules S1 and S2 indicated according to the two levels of the strategy. The meaning of S1 and S2 is that on the level of parameter evolution a quality function is used that is calculated from 24 pictures in Figure 15.8, while S2, assigned to the structure level, refers to the 12 pictures in Figure 15.2. The reasons for two or even more different quality functions being used in the selection mechanisms involved in the algorithm of structure evolution will be explained in the last section.

15.3.7 Results

One of the filters that have been developed by structure evolution is given in the table in Figure 15.9. Each line in the table describes one of the 20 elements of the filter whose sum is the local contribution to the global feature. First there is the number of the line, followed by the number of binary factors of the product. The description continues with the indices of matrix elements involved in the product and is completed by the real number at the end of the line, which is the weight of this element.

The filter is expected to work on any binary picture and to calculate the number of coherent areas as precisely as possible. Therefore, the filter is tested on a set of 12 pictures (Fig. 15.10) that have never occurred in struc-

1	2	5	6			r=	-0.999979
2	1	5				r=	0.999993
3	2	5	9			r=	-0.999981
4	2	5	2			r=	-0.999985
5	3	5	9	8		r=	0.972680
6	2	5	3			r=	-0.999992
7	3	5	9	6		r=	0.987304
8	3	5	3	6		r=	0.786602
9	3	5	6	8		r=	0.379996
10	3	5	3	2		r=	0.619971
11	3	5	2	4		r=	0.213371
12	4	5	3	2	6	r=	-0.997531
13	3	5	1	4		r=	0.027261
14	3	5	8	4		r=	0.011915
15	4	5	9	8	6	r=	-0.002066
16	3	5	2	1		r=	0.000739
17	4	5	4	2	1	r=	-0.000313
18	3	5	2	9		r=	0.000012
19	3	5	3	4		r=	0.000001
20	4	5	6	8	3	r=	0.000000

Figure 15.9 *Description of a filter result; see explanation in the text.*

ture evolution. The comparison of correct numbers of coherent areas N_c and the measured numbers N_m written on top of each picture indicates that the result leaves precious little to be desired.

In addition to a good result, it is important to consider whether the algorithm has worked efficiently. A measure for effectiveness of structure optimization is the ratio between the number of structures that have been tested to some extent during the process and the number of all possible states. An estimation says that not more than 10^6 different structures occurred in the whole process. The number of all possible structures of the stock is about 10^{35}, estimated for filter lengths smaller than $L = 20$. This is an experimental proof that local search in structure space has actually taken place. In this regard, structures occurring in the process are usually subject to parameter evolution only for a few generations until the structure is replaced by a mutant of a better structure including its partly optimized parameters. That means that parameter evolution also performs local search, which is embedded in that of structure evolution.

15.4 INCOMPLETE TASK DESCRIPTION

It has been pointed out that the task of counting coherent areas in any binary picture can necessarily be described only incompletely because a quality function can only involve a limited set of pictures. Therefore, measures have to be taken to provide the neural system being developed as an abstract solution of the incompletely described task. In terms of cognitive science, a solution of an incomplete task is never more than a hypothesis. In structure evolution, one could say, an intermediate solution for a filter within one

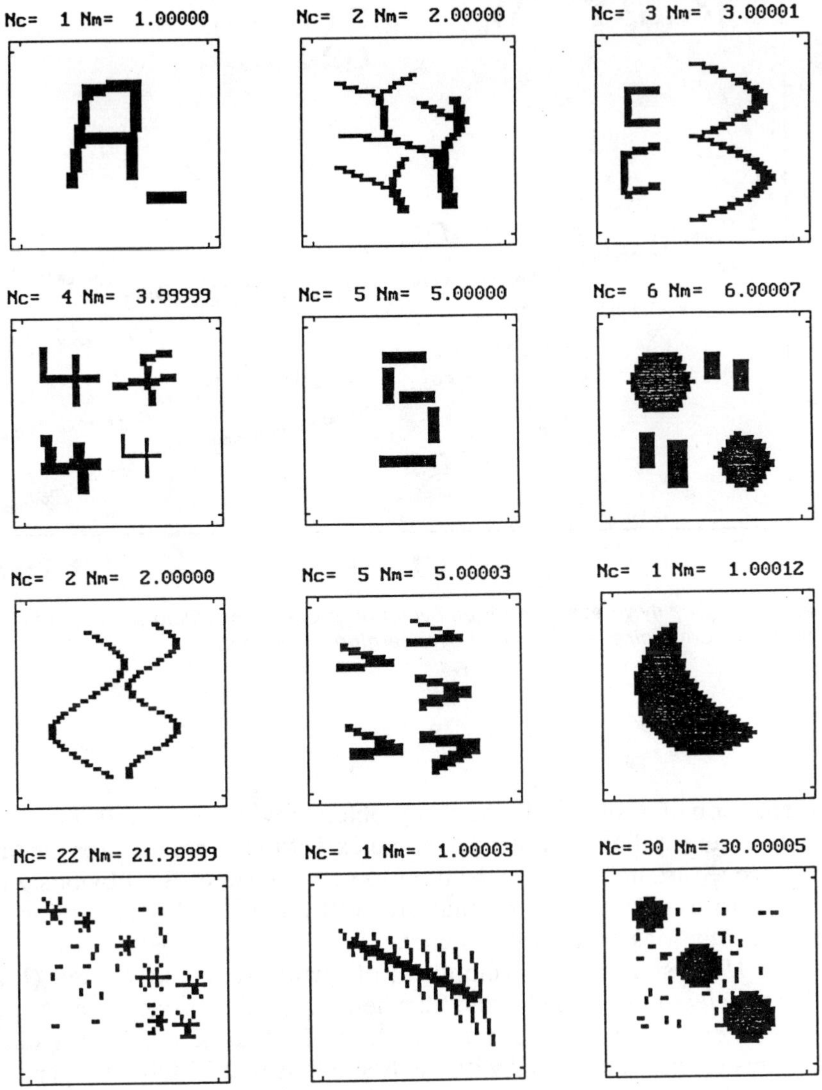

Figure 15.10 *Results of the filter described in Figure 15.9 on a set of 12 pictures that never occurred in the process of structure evolution.*

population is a hypothesis supported and proven only by selection criterion S1. The probability that it approaches a general solution of the task increases if an additional and different selection criterion S2 is fulfilled [10]. In other words, evolution strategy in Eq. (15.11), with selection criteria S1 and S2 being implemented, is some sort of translation of the demand that a filter should not only be good with respect to S1 but also with respect to S2.

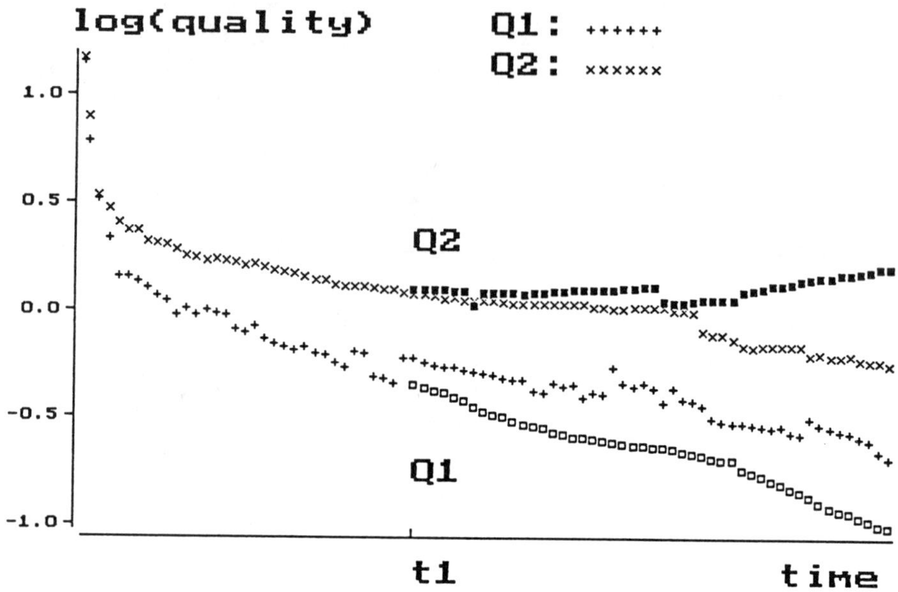

Figure 15.11 *Quality versus time for an evolution process according to Eq. (15.11). See explanations concerning avoidance of overlearning in the text.*

Generalization of a solution for such a problem obviously depends on S1 and S2 being different, but both being to some extent representative for the task.

This procedure may seem to be a bit too complicated. But obviously it is necessary to avoid phenomena that are well known as "overlearning" in other investigations on neural systems.

Figure 15.11 shows the development of quality functions Q_1 and Q_2 according to selection criteria S1 and S2 when Eq. (15.11) is executed. At time t_1 a second evolution process branches from the first one. The only difference in this process compared with the first one is that S2 has been replaced by S1. Qualities Q_1 and Q_2 for the branching process have been registered and plotted in Figure 15.11 as squares. One can observe that Q_2 of the second process stagnates and even becomes worse while Q_1 converges more rapidly to a minimum than Q_1 does in the original experiment. For the second process the offset between the quality of the "learning set" Q_1 and that of the "test set" Q_2 rises, while in the original experiment the corresponding offset keeps the same size during time.

Neither separating a quality function into two functions nor implementing structure evolution according to Eq. (15.11) takes much effort. This treatment of incompletely described tasks, therefore, seems to be a comparatively effective solution of the overlearning problem.

15.5 CONCLUSION

The chapter considered the problem of systematic development and design of neural systems, first in general terms of evolution techniques and then by explaining the approach in more detail with an example. Evolution strategy, proposed as a solution, had to be extended to an algorithm with many temporarily isolated populations. This new algorithm for structure evolution performs a most effective local search in a structure space that is nearly infinitely large. In addition, structure evolution treats successfully the problem of vaguely or incompletely described tasks. This problem is characteristic for many neural system applications. Although the algorithm has not yet been optimized, results in a particular application are promising. A local filter as part of a visual system has been developed. The filter counts very precisely the number of coherent areas in any binary picture. Structure evolution therefore seems to be an appropriate approach for systematically developing and designing neural systems.

REFERENCES

[1] I. Rechenberg, "Cybernatic Solution Path of an Experimental Problem," Library Translation 1122, Royal Aircraft Establishment, Farnborough (1965).

[2] I. Rechenberg, *Evolutionsstrategie—Optimierung technischer Systeme nach Prinzipien der biologischen Evolution,* Frommann-Holzboog, Stuttgart, 1973.

[3] H.-P. Schwefel, *Numerische Optimierung von Computer-Modellen mittels der Evolutionsstrategie,* Birkhäuser, Basel und Stuttgart, 1977.

[4] H.-P. Schwefel, *Numerical Optimization of Computer Models,* John Wiley & Sons, Chichester, 1981.

[5] I. Rechenberg, "Evolutionsstrategie—Optimierung nach Prinzipien der biologischen Evolution," in J. Albertz, Ed., *Evolution und Evolutionsstrategien in Biologie, Technik und Gesellschaft,* Band 9 der Schriftenreihe Freie Akademie, Hofheim, 1989, pp. 25–72.

[6] R. Lohmann, "Selforganization by Evolution Strategy," in H.-M Voigt, H. Mühlenbein, and H.-P. Schwefel, Eds., *Evolution and Optimization '89,* Akademie-Verlag, Berlin, 1990, pp. 61–68.

[7] H. J. Bremermann, "What Mathematics Can and Cannot Do for Pattern Recognition," in O.-J. Grüsser and R. Klinke, Eds., *Zeichenerkennung durch biologische und technische Systeme,* Springer, Berlin, 1973, pp. 31–45.

[8] S. Watanabe, *Pattern Recognition, Human and Mechanical,* Wiley & Sons, New York, 1985.

[9] R. Lohmann, "Bionische Verfahren zur Entwicklung visueller Systeme," dissertation, TU Berlin, D 83, Berlin (1991).

[10] F. Klix, "Der Informationsbegriff und die Bedingungsanalyse kognitiver Leistungen," in *Die Psychologie des 20. Jahrhunderts—Piaget und seine Folgen,* Kindler Verlag, Zürich, 1978.

CHAPTER 16

Evolution Strategies for Circuit Partitioning

MARTIN HULIN

16.1 INTRODUCTION

Partitioning of networks is necessary in several stages of the design process for electrical systems. There are three tasks where partitioning plays an important role:

1. *Decomposition of an Electrical System into Physical Components* A design specified on register transfer level or functional level shall be implemented with a certain technology, such as VLSI gate arrays. If the whole system does not fit on a single chip, it has to be partitioned into smaller parts. The objective is to minimize the number of chips and the number of interconnections between chips.
2. *Placement of Components of a Circuit on a Printed Circuit Board or on a Chip by Recursive Bipartitioning* [1] The objective of one bipartitioning step is to minimize the number of interconnections between the two parts. This helps to reduce the total wire length for routing.
3. *Simulation of Large Circuits with Parallel Computers* The electrical system has to be partitioned into as many parts as processing elements are available. The objective is to attain a similar load on all processing elements and to minimize events on interconnections between parts.

The problem of circuit partitioning is equivalent to the mathematical model of hypergraph partitioning [2,3]. Hyafil and Rivest have shown that graph

Dynamic, Genetic, and Chaotic Programming, By Branko Souček and the IRIS Group.
ISBN 0-471-55717-X

partitioning is np-complete [4]. This induces that all partitioning methods with polynomial time demand with respect to the size of the circuit do not guarantee to find the optimal partitioning for all circuits and constraints. The solutions of different partitioning methods approximate the optimum differently well for various partitioning problems and circuit types.

Evolution strategies (genetic algorithms) have shown to obtain good results for many difficult np-complete problems [5]. In this chapter they are shown to be appropriate for the partitioning task, too. After a list of notations used in this chapter (Section 16.2), a brief description of the principles of evolution strategies for optimization of artificial systems follows in Section 16.3. In Section 16.4 a simple genetic algorithm (GA) for the partitioning task is introduced. It uses a simple, straightforward coding.

Reasons are given why this simple coding is not the best choice for structured circuits described on functional or register transfer level. In Section 16.5 a sophisticated two-step coding is explained that makes the structure of a circuit utilizable for the GA. The genetic operators are adapted to this coding. The two-step coding is enhanced in Section 16.6 to allow multiple instances of components.

Results for some differently structured test circuits are used to compare both GAs and other partitioning methods. It is shown that simulated annealing (SA) is a special case of GAs with population size 1 and a sophisticated selection scheme.

16.2 NOTATIONS

A circuit is given by the set C_{compl} of complex components (like adders, multipliers, registers, etc.) which are themselves composed of atomic components (like 1-bit full adders, flip-flops, AND gates, etc.) and a set V of nets that connect the components.

$C_{\text{compl}} = \{c_1, \ldots, c_n\}$ = set of complex components.

$(c_{i1}, \ldots, c_{i,b_i})$ = atomic components of the complex component c_i with width b_i.

$C = \{c_{11}, \ldots, c_{n,b_n}\}$ = set of atomic components of the circuit.

$V = \{v_1, \ldots, v_u\}$ = set of nets or busses where each net is a nonempty subset of C_{compl}.

$b = \max_{1 \le i \le n}(b_i)$ = maximal width of the complex components

$\theta = \{T_1, \ldots, T_r\}$ = a partition of K into r circuit parts, a collection of disjoint nonempty subsets T_i of K such that their union is K.

Θ = set of all possible partitions θ of K

$S(c)$ = size of a component c.

$P(T \subset K)$ = number of pins (external connections) of a circuit part T.

$\overline{S} \in \mathbb{N}$ = limit for the size of a circuit part.

$\overline{P} \in \mathbb{N}$ = limit for the pins of a circuit part.

16.3 OPTIMIZATION WITH EVOLUTION STRATEGIES

Living organisms in nature are well adapted to their environment. Darwin states that this is due to an evolution: Slightly different organisms are produced by sexual recombination and mutation of genes. Only the fittest survive because resources are limited (selection).

The principles of evolution in biology can be used for optimization of artificial (technical, mathematical, economical) systems [5,6,7]. The goal is to find a set of system parameters that optimizes the system. The parameters are coded and the codes of several instances of the system form a population. A new instance (child) is created by combining the codes of two randomly selected instances (parents). Genetic operators like crossing over and mutation are used for this combination. This new solution of the problem is rated according to the quality function and included into the population. To limit the size of the population selection is used. Good instances are selected and remain in the population the worst instances are eliminated. There are different strategies for the selection. Their purpose is to increase the average quality of the population.

Using this principles a GA for optimization can be defined easily (Algorithm 1, Fig. 16.1). The fundamental algorithm simplifies the processes of multiplication and heredity in biology. It does not consider the existence of generations, the complicated mechanisms choosing a mate, the existence of groups and herds. See Goldberg [5] for a detailed discussion of alternatives of the fundamental algorithm.

Algorithm 1: Fundamental genetic algorithm.

```
Initialize Population: Create instances of the technical system at
                       random.

LOOP
   Mating:          Choose two instances - I1 and I2 - from the population
                    at random.

   Recombination:   Use genetic operators to create a new instance I3 by
                    combining and changing the parameter values of I1 and
                    I2.

   Rating:          Rate I3 according to the quality function and insert it
                    into the population.

   Selection:       If a selection condition is true (e.g. a maximal
                    population size is exceded), select certain instances
                    (normally the best) and eliminate the rest from the
                    population.

   Termination:     STOP, if a termination criterion is met.
ENDLOOP
```

The fundamental algorithm has to be tailored to the actual optimization problem: The coding of the parameters, the genetic operators for recombination, the quality function, the selection strategy and the population size

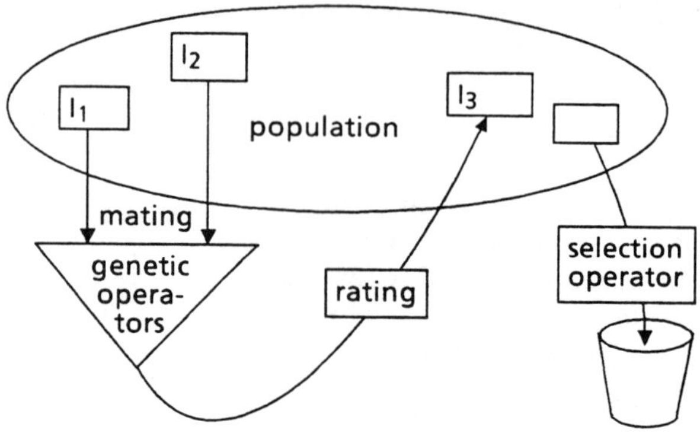

Figure 16.1 *Genetic algorithm for optimization.*

have to be defined. This is described for the partitioning task in the next section.

16.4 SIMPLE GA FOR PARTITIONING OF CIRCUITS; STRAIGHTFORWARD CODING

16.4.1 Coding

The coding of the parameters of a partition is done quite straightforward. A circuit is composed of atomic components, which are never split up in the partitioning process, a 32-bit adder consists of 32 one-bit full adders at register transfer level, while on gate level it consists of atoms like AND gates, OR gates, and inverters.

A partition is coded as an k-tuple $g = (g_1, \ldots, g_k)$, where k is the number of atomic components. $g_i = j$ means that component i is assigned to circuit part j (Fig. 16.2).

16.4.2 Recombination

Because of the simple coding of the partitions the recombination is also very simple. *Crossing over* is used to mix the parameter values of two partitions θ_1 and θ_2 and create a new one: The first parameter values up to a randomly selected index (crossing boundary) are taken from θ_1 the remaining ones from θ_2 (Fig. 16.3).

The *mutation operator* chooses some locations in the string of θ_3 at random and the assignment is changed with low probability. Changes at different loci are independent with the same probability. Thus mutations at many

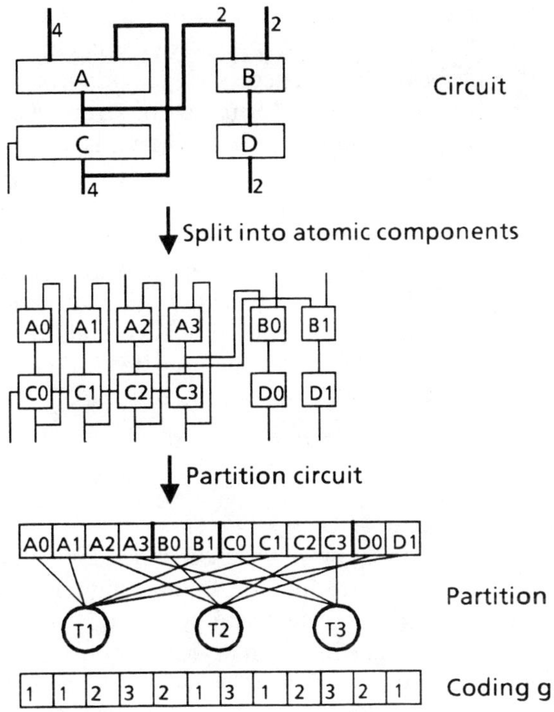

Figure 16.2 *Small example circuit and coding of a partition.*

loci of the genome (sum of genes, heredity) are less probable than mutations at few loci.

It is difficult to determine the appropriate mutation rate. If it is too high, information dissolves; if it is too low, new regions of the search space are not reached [18]. Rechenberg suggests a self adapting mutation rate [6]: The mutation rate is added as a parameter to the genome, it is altered by the

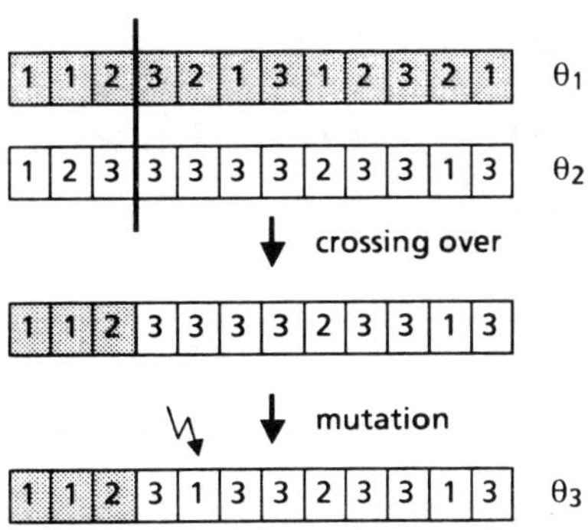

Figure 16.3 *Recombination using crossing over and mutation.*

genetic operators itself, and can evolve to its optimal value for the current situation. This method is used for both GAs of this chapter.

The order of components in the gene string is important for the efficiency of crossing over. The assignment information of strongly connected components should be arranged closely together. Then it is seldom cut by crossing over. Since the problem to find the best-suited permutation of components is almost as difficult as the partitioning problem the GA searches for a good permutation itself using reordering operators like *inversion* or *translocation*. Translocation cuts a substring out of the gene string and positions it at another location. Inversion cuts a substring out of the gene string and positions it at the same location in reverse order. To code the order of components an additional vector g^O is necessary. See [5] for a detailed description of inversion and translocation.

16.4.3 Rating

A predefined cost function $\Phi: \Theta \rightarrow \mathbb{R}$ which assigns a real number to every partition is evaluated for the new solution. Φ depends on the actual partitioning task as described in the introduction. In this chapter the cost function for the first task, decomposition of electrical systems, is chosen.

The difficulty is to rate partitions that violate constraints like size or pin limit. For GAs it is not practicable to assign the same worst possible cost value to all unfeasible partitions. If the space of feasible solutions is small in comparison to the whole search space and not connected, the probability is low to have a feasible partition in the initial population. Selection cannot work and the GA degenerates to random search. After finding a feasible solution eventually, the population is quickly filled up with partitions in the neighborhood of this solution. It is unprobable that the population leaves this part of the search space, even if it contains only solutions of poor quality. The hurdle to other parts of the solution space is too high.

For genetic algorithms the method of penalty functions is appropriate. The cost function Φ consists of two parts: the cost of a partition Φ^* (number of circuit parts, number of cut nets) and a penalty Z if constraints are violated (space or pin restriction). The two components of the cost function have to be combined in the right manner. The penalty function Z must not move the optimum θ_{opt}; that is, for all partitions θ with $Z(\theta) > 0$ the equation $\Phi(\theta) > \Phi(\theta_{\text{opt}}) = \Phi^*(\theta_{\text{opt}})$ must hold.

Experience has shown that a quadratic penalty function is appropriate: Small violations are penalized by low values. If the violations become more serious, the penalty quickly rises to very high values, and those partitions are eliminated soon by selection.

$$\Phi(\theta) = a_1 \frac{r - \lceil S(C)/\overline{S} \rceil + 1}{\lceil S(C)/\overline{S} \rceil + 1} + a_2 \frac{\Sigma_{T \in \theta} P(T)}{\overline{P}} + a_3 Z(\theta) + a_4 Z(\theta)^2$$

where

$$Z(\theta) = \sum_{T\in\theta} Z_P(T) + \sum_{T\in\theta} Z_S(T)$$

where

$$Z_P(T) = \begin{cases} 0 & \text{if } P(T) \le \overline{P} \\ \dfrac{P(T) - \overline{P}}{\overline{P}} & \text{else} \end{cases}$$

and

$$Z_S(T) = \begin{cases} 0 & \text{if } S(T) \le \overline{S} \\ \dfrac{S(T) - \overline{S}}{\overline{S}} & \text{else} \end{cases}$$

The constants $a_1, \ldots, a_4$ are the weights of the parts of the cost function:

- a_1: number of circuit parts r, measured in proportion to the minimal number of necessary circuit parts $\lceil S(C)/\overline{S} \rceil + 1$ due to the size limit,
- a_2: number of cut signals, measured as the number of pins of the circuit parts in proportion to the pin limit $\overline{P}$,
- a_3: violation of constraints Z, linear,
- a_4: violation of constraints Z, quadratic.

The violation of constraints Z is composed of Z_P, the violation of the pin limit, and Z_S, the violation of the size limit.

The values of the constants depend on the actual partitioning problem and the priorities of the user of the partitioning system: Is reduction of circuit parts more important than a small number of cut signals? Is a slight violation of constraints tolerable?

For all test cases the following values were chosen: $a_1 = 1$, $a_2 = 1$, $a_3 = 5$, $a_4 = 25 = a_3^2$. For a bipartitioning task $a_1 = 0$ and $Z_P = 0$ was chosen since the number of circuit parts is fixed at 2.

Size violation and size, pin violation and number of cut nets, and the number of circuit parts are measured in proportion to the size limit $\overline{S}$, the pin limit $\overline{P}$, and the minimal number of circuit parts, respectively, to be independent of measuring units.

Other constraints like electrical constraints, certain test signals that have to be cut anyway, or critical nets that must not be cut can be included into Z easily.

16.4.4 Selection

As indicated in Section 16.2 there are different strategies for selection. A simple possibility is to define two values, N_{max} and N_{min}. If the population size grows above N_{max} the population is reduced to the N_{min} best partitions, the worst partitions are eliminated. The maximum population size is important for the efficiency of the GA. A small population improves faster in the beginning of the optimization process because bad partitions are eliminated more often. In contrast a big population often improves to better solutions later because the genetic potential of the population—the subspace of the search space spanned by the population—is larger.

The proposed GAs use the largest possible population that fits into the memory of the computer. To improve the performance good partitions are selected for mating with higher probability than bad ones.

16.4.5 Termination

The proposed genetic algorithm is an endless loop. It is difficult to determine when to terminate. If the optimal quality value is not known one never knows whether the optimal partition is reached. Four possible termination criteria have been considered for both GAs:

1. *Time Limit* Terminate, if a time limit is exceeded.
2. *Quality Limit* Terminate, if a partition falls below a predefined cost value.
3. *Estimation of the Probability of Finding a Better Solution* Every time a new partition is produced using genetic operators and given the actual population of solutions there is a certain probability p_b that the new solution is better than all other members of the population. The idea is to terminate the algorithm when this probability falls below a predefined limit ε because then a better solution can only be expected with excessive use of computation time. To use this termination criterion, the probability p_b has to be estimated from the observed optimization process (i.e., the number t of partitions produced since the last improvement). The estimated value for p_b is the relative frequency of observed improvements: $1/(t + 1)$. This estimation is admissible, if p_b remains rather constant.

   The estimation of p_b may be wrong due to a statistical error: p_b is much higher and more improvements can be expected soon. The question is: How large must t be such that $p_b < \varepsilon$ with a confidence of $1 - \alpha$? This question is the same as: What is the probability of accepting the hypotheses $p_b < \varepsilon$ though $p_b \geq \varepsilon$? This error probability p_{error} is maximal, when $p_b = \varepsilon$. If p_b is constant, a binomial distribution can be assumed for the event "*t partitions produced, no improvement*" and its complement "*t partitions produced, at least one improvement.*"

Then

$$p_{\text{error}} \leq (1 - \varepsilon)^t < \alpha \Leftrightarrow t > \frac{\ln \alpha}{\ln (1 - \varepsilon)}$$

Example Optimization shall be terminated, when p_b falls below 1/20,000 with a confidence of 95% ($\alpha = 0.05$). Then

$$t > \frac{\ln 0.05}{\ln(19{,}999/20{,}000)} \approx 59{,}913$$

The GA is terminated after 59,914 partitions are produced without improvement.

4. *Loss Minimization* Termination of the optimization process results in a loss, if the optimum is not yet found. To go on with the optimization process results in a loss because computation costs have to be paid. The sum of both loss components should be minimized. The latter can be simply computed, the first loss component has to be estimated since the optimum is not known.

   The author has developed a new method [8] to estimate the cost distribution of solutions reachable with a GA using Bayes' formula. The a posteriori distribution of generation k is interpreted as a priori distribution of the next generation $k + 1$. With this distribution it is possible to estimate the best cost value and the number of generations that are necessary to find it and thus to calculate the first loss component.

   The GA is terminated in generation k, if the estimated loss in all following generations is greater than the actual loss. Since the formula for the loss is easy to compute and the estimated cost distribution by the Bayesian method showed to be very accurate this termination criterion is very well suited for GAs.

The fourth method is used for both GAs presented in this chapter. Nothing can be proved about the quality of the solution using this termination criterion. Without termination the optimum would eventually be reached [9] but this is true for random search and exhaustive search as well.

16.4.6 Limitations of the Simple GA

The simple GA for partitioning has been tested with a couple of circuits of different complexity and structure. It produced good results for circuits where no regular structure was detectable. However, it could not find the optimal solution for complex circuits with regular structures (Table 16.1).

The linear string defining a partition contains no information about the

TABLE 16.1 ***Comparison of Different Partitioning Methods n.o.p. = number of produced partitions × 1000***

	circuit 1		circuit 2		circuit 3		circuit 4	
	n.o.p.	pins	n.o.p.	pins	n.o.p.	pins	n.o.p.	pins
Fiduccia & Matth.	12	38	60	87	90	90	100	2358
SA	3	28	20	211	90	172	2700	1648
CHIPEX	0.25	28	3	87	1	82	1000	3224
simple GA	4	70	14	57	130	126	2300	1368
sophist. GA	1.9	28	5	57	25	82	-	-
soph. GA + copies of comp.	2.7	12	6	57	17	30	-	-

connectivity. Adjacent strongly connected components may be separated by crossing over.

Rearrangement of the atomic components in the string of genes is possible with genetic operators like translocation or inversion but does not solve the problem for many adjacent components. It is impossible to conserve the connectivity structure when the circuit is projected to a one-dimensional string. A completely different representation of a partition is necessary.

16.5 SOPHISTICATED GA FOR PARTITIONING OF CIRCUITS WITH TWO-STEP CODING

The steps of Algorithm 1 are used for the sophisticated GA as well.

16.5.1 Coding

When a design expert does circuit partitioning, he or she does not assign atomic components to circuit parts but uses slicing operators like horizontal or vertical slicing. Horizontal slicing means to pick a group of complex components and assigning them to a circuit part. Vertical slicing means slicing along a data path; that is, selected complex components of the same width that are connected by buses are cut at the same bit boundary. Corresponding parts of these components are then assigned to the same circuit part. The signals of the data path are not cut. On the other hand, internal signals of the complex components like the carry signal of an adder are cut by vertical slicing.

For the sophisticated GA a two-step coding is used that supports a combination of horizontal and vertical slicing. The (complex) components are assigned to groups. This can be interpreted as horizontal slicing. A group is

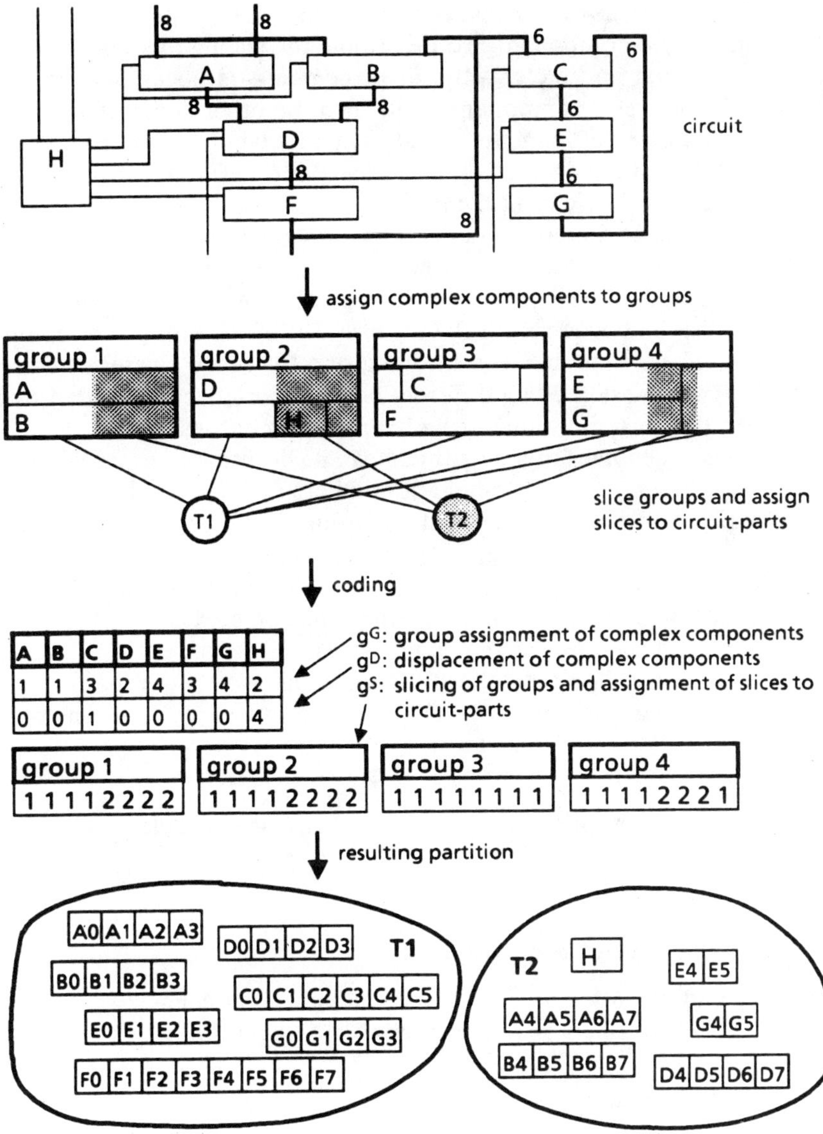

Figure 16.4 *Two-step coding of a small example circuit.*

assumed to be built of bit slices. Each group is sliced vertically, that is, each bit position of a group is assigned to a circuit part. The result are two chromosomes: The first represents the assignment of complex components to groups, the second the slicing of the groups and the assignment of the slices to the circuit parts (Fig. 16.4). The slicing of the groups is transmitted to the slicing of the assigned components. The width of the groups is the width of the widest component. To determine the slicing of smaller components an additional parameter—the displacement—is necessary. It determines the position of a component relative to the other components in this group. Nonsliceable components are alotted as a whole to the part defined by the first bit position in their group. The three parts of the information define a partition of the circuit clearly.

The assignment of the components to groups is not done statically before partitioning; it evolves. During evolution strongly connected components tend to be assigned to the same group. The number of groups is fixed for one partitioning task and grows with the square root of the number of complex components. There must be at least one group for every cluster of components that should be sliced in a different way. Experience shows that this is fulfilled with the aforementioned rule for most circuit designs.

The coding g (genome) of a partition θ can be described formally by three vectors $g = (g^G, g^D, g^S)$: g^G is a field of numbers $(g_1^G, \ldots, g_n^G)$ and defines an assignment of complex components to groups $g^G\colon C_{\text{compl}} \to \{1, \ldots, m\}$, where $m := \lceil \sqrt{n} \rceil$ is the maximal number of groups; $g^D = (g_1^D, \ldots, g_n^D)$ is the displacement of the complex components in their group, where $g_i^D + n_i \leq b$, where b is the maximal width of the complex components; $g^S = (g_1^S, \ldots, g_m^S)$ determines the slicing of the groups, where $g_i^S = (g_{i1}^S, \ldots, g_{ib}^S)$, $g_{ij}^S \in \{1, \ldots, r\}$ and r is the maximal number of circuit parts.

A coding $g = (g^G, g^D, g^S)$ can be translated into a partition unambiguously:

$$g_i^G = x \wedge g_{x,g_i^D+j}^S = l \Rightarrow c_{ij} \in T_l \qquad \text{if } c_i \text{ is sliceable}$$

$$g_i^G = x \wedge g_{x,g_i^D+1}^S = l \Rightarrow c_i \in T_l \qquad \text{if } c_i \text{ is not sliceable}$$

16.5.2 Initialization of the Population

Create $N_{\min}$ codings $g = (g^G, g^D, g^S)$ at random. This defines $N_{\min}$ random partitions. They are rated and form the initial population.

16.5.3 Recombination

Central units to express the partitioning information are the groups. One group represents a subset of complex components that are assigned to it and slicing information that defines the slicing of all these complex components. *Crossing over* works on the groups rather than to combine g^G, g^S, and g^D independently. A difficulty arises if the group assignments of the components differ in θ_1 and θ_2. Then a conflict may occur. This is illustrated best by the simple example of Figure 16.5.

There is a conflict for B. The group assignment for group 1 is copied from θ_1;

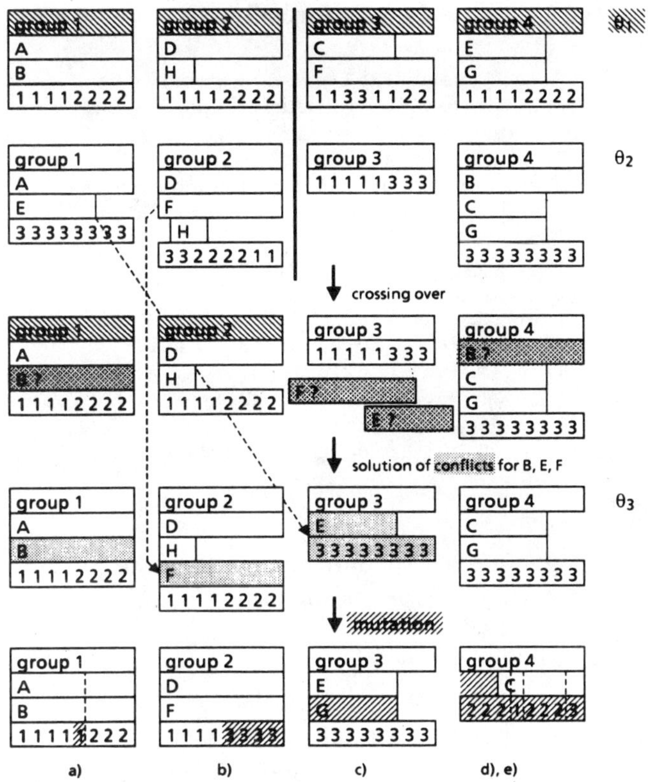

Figure 16.5 *Recombination of the sophisticated GA.*

hence, B is assigned to group 1. The group assignment for group 4 is copied from θ_2; hence, B is assigned to group 4. On the other hand, the components E and F are assigned to no group at all.

The crossing over operator has to be modified to solve this conflict: If a component is assigned to two groups the assignment of θ_1 is taken, if a component is not assigned to any group one of the following strategies is applied with equal chance:

The assignment of θ_2 is taken. This strategy causes a concentration of the components to few groups. In the example, F is assigned to group 2.

A new group is created, if there exists a free group, the slicing information is copied from the group of the component according θ_2, and the component is assigned to this new group. This strategy leads to a distribution of the components to several groups. In the example this is done for component E.

Algorithm 2 describes crossing over formally.

```
1) Choose a crossing boundary x ∈ {1, . . . m-1}
2) Copy the slicing information of the groups:
   FOR i := 1 TO x DO θ3.gS[i] := 1.gS[i]
   FOR i := x+1 TO m DO θ3.gS[i] := θ2.gS[i]
3) Copy the group assignment of the complex components
   FOR i := 1 TO n DO
     IF θ1.gG[i] ≤ x
      THEN θ3.gG[i] := θ1.gG[i]; θ3.gD[i] := θ1.gD[i]
   ELSIF θ2.gG[i] > x
     THEN θ3.gG[i] := θ2.gG[i]; θ3.gD[i] := θ2.gD[i]
   ELSE (* component assigned to no group at all *)
     IF random(0,1)=0 AND there exists an empty group j in θ3
     THEN θ3.gG[i] := j; θ3.gD[i] := θ2.gD[i];
          θ3.gS[j] := θ2.gS[θ2.gG[i]]
     ELSE θ3.gG[i] := θ2.gG[i]; θ3.gD[i] := θ2.gD[i].
```

16.5.4 Mutation

The operation of mutation is very difficult due to the special two step coding of partitions. There are five types of mutation (Fig. 16.5):

a. Move slicing boundary by few bits.
b. Change the assignment of a slice to the circuit parts.
c. Change the group assignment of a component.
d. Change the displacement of a component.
e. Totally new slicing of a group.

16.5.6 Characteristics of This Genetic Algorithm

For circuits with a regular structure it is of advantage to partition clusters of components in the same way. With two-step coding the connectivity structure of a circuit can be expressed by the group assignment of complex components. This group assignment is not fixed at the beginning of the optimization, but evolves since good group assignments are advantageous and more often selected. Tightly coupled components gather in one group, they are sliced and assigned to circuit parts in the same way. They are transmitted during reproduction as a whole because crossing over does not split a group. Good partial solutions are preserved. They are combined with other good partial solutions to result in better global solutions.

16.6 ENHANCEMENT OF THE SOPHISTICATED GA: COPIES OF COMPONENTS POSSIBLE

Design experts often change the circuit slightly during partitioning. Some components, especially control components, often have only few input sig-

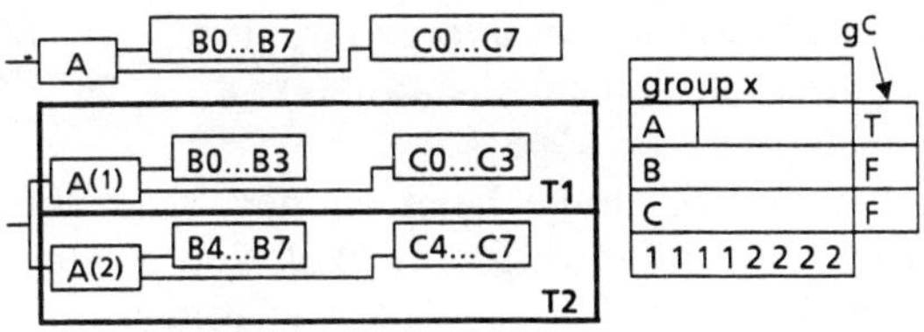

Figure 16.6 *Partition with component* A *copied.*

nals but many output signals (e.g., control signals like write strobes for registers). If the output signals are all cut, for example, are connected to components on different circuit parts, and if the space limit is not exceeded, such components are copied and one instance is assigned to each of the circuit parts. Then the input signals are cut but not the output signals. This does not only reduce the number of cut signals but additionally reduces the skew on the output signals. For pure vertical slicing multiple instantiation of components leads to similar or identical circuit parts. This is important, if electronic systems are partitioned into chips. Identical chips lead to fewer chip types and reduce the fabrication cost of a system considerably.

The possibility to change the circuit by multiple instantiation of components can be easily added to the sophisticated GA. The coding of a partition is extended by an additional vector $g^C = (g_1^C, \ldots, g_n^C)$, $g_i^C \in$ {TRUE, FALSE} = {T, F}, where g_i^C = TRUE means that component i is copied to all slices of the group it is assigned to:

$$g_i^G = x \wedge g_i^C \wedge \exists\, y\colon g_{xy}^S = j \Rightarrow c_i^{(j)} \text{ is instance } (j) \text{ of } c_i,\ c_i^{(j)} \in T_j$$

Crossing over treats g^C like g^G or g^D; g^C can be altered by mutation. As an example, see Figure 16.6.

16.7 RESULTS IN COMPARISON TO OTHER PARTITIONING METHODS

To test the genetic algorithms for their quality and their efficiency, four test circuits have been developed:

Circuit 1: register transfer description of a small circuit with regular structure (12 complex components = 273 atomic components, 547 signal nets);

Circuit 2: register transfer description of a complex circuit with components of different width that are staggered and displaced against another (66 complex components = 860 atomic components, 1050 signal nets);

Circuit 3: mixed description on register transfer level and functional level of a well-structured circuit (150 complex components = 1170 atomic components, 1850 signal nets);

Circuit 4: gate level description of a large circuit with no obvious structure (5000 atomic components, 6000 signal nets).

Many partitioning problems have been defined using these four circuits. They have been used to judge different evolution strategies and compare them with other partitioning methods and algorithms:

- Bipartitioning with the algorithm of Fiduccia and Mattheyses [10],
- Simulated annealing (SA),
- Expert system CHIPEX [11].

Table 16.1 shows the results (number of produced partitions, total number of pins as criterion to be minimized) for a bipartitioning task. Bipartitioning was used to allow a comparison with the algorithm of Fiduccia and Mattheyses. The other partitioning methods can also be used for partitioning in more than two parts. For the algorithm of Fiduccia and Mattheyses the multistart method was used with 20 different random initial partitions.

To produce one new partition the algorithm of Fiduccia and Mattheyses needs only 1% of the time a GA or SA needs since the cost value of a new partition is an update of the cost value of the former partition, whereas a GA or SA has to do a completely new rating. The expert system CHIPEX needs about four times to produce one partial partition in comparison to GAs depending on the size of the knowledge base. The algorithm of Fiduccia and Matheyses is by far the fastest. The algorithm for SA uses the simple coding scheme of Section 16.4 and therefore has to be compared to the simple GA.

Circuit 3 has been constructed in a way such that the optimal solution for a bipartitioning task is known. Without copies of components the optimal value are 41 cut nets or 82 pins. The expert system and the sophisticated GA could find the optimum of this circuit with a regular connectivity structure. If multiple instances of components are allowed, far better results can be achieved.

16.8 ANALYSIS OF SCHEMA DISTRIBUTIONS

The results in the last section show that the special GA with the sophisticated coding is much better suited for the partitioning of circuits with a regular structure than the simple GA. In this section schema distributions are defined and used to prove that theoretically.

We assume that the GA processes bit strings of length l. A schema is defined as the set of all bit strings with a fixed value on certain given positions. It is normally described as a similarity template where the unfixed bit positions are marked by a wild card symbol $*$. For example, the schema $\{000, 001, 010, 011\}$ ($l = 3$) is described by 0**. The number of fixed positions is the order of a schema.

With the cost function Φ we can define the *cost distribution of a schema H* or simply *schema distribution:* $D_H: \mathbb{R} \rightarrow [0, 1]$. $D_H(x)$ is the fraction of elements of schema H with a cost value lower or equal to x or formally:

$$D_H(x) = \frac{|\{h \in H: \Phi(h) \leq x\}|}{|H|}$$

Since every schema is a finite set, it has at least one element with a minimal cost value $\min_H$ and at least one element with a maximal cost value $\max_H$. It is evident that $D_H(x) = 0$ for $x < \min_H$ and $D_H(x) = 1$ for $x \geq \max_H$. Although D_H is a step function, for large l it looks like a continuous function. Like every distribution function D_H grows monotonically. Figure 16.7 shows a typical schema distribution.

Schema distributions can be used to judge whether a problem is deceptive for GAs and in which degree. To look for deceptive schemata we compare competing short, low-order schemata that are defined on the same positions. Figures 16.8, 16.9, and 16.10 show three principal cases. Assume that schema H contains the minimum, while schema K does not. The interesting part of schema distributions is the interval from about $min + (min + av)/3$ to av, where min is the minimal cost value we are searching for and av is the average cost of all solutions. This is true because the average cost value of the population falls below av after the first three to five generations as De Jong has shown [12]. On the other hand, experience shows that the population has already concentrated to a small area of the search space when the cost average of the population is within 30% to 40% of the minimum [13]. Then an analysis of schema distributions is no more relevant because the population has concentrated on a relatively small area of the search space; the members of the population are very similar. In this situation only a very small and specific subset of a schema is likely to be produced by genetic operators and this subset will not represent the cost distribution of the whole schema.

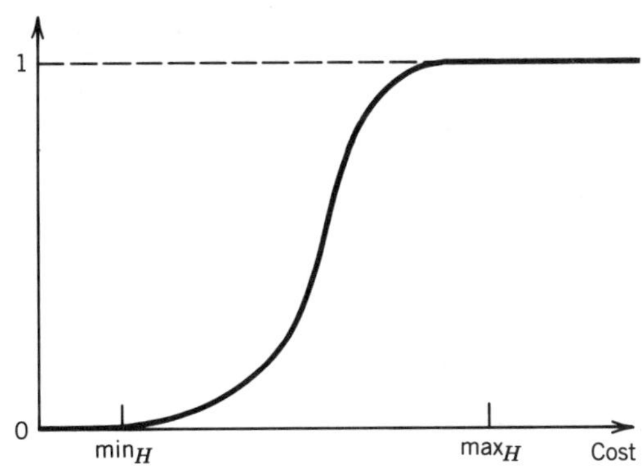

Figure 16.7 *A schema distribution.*

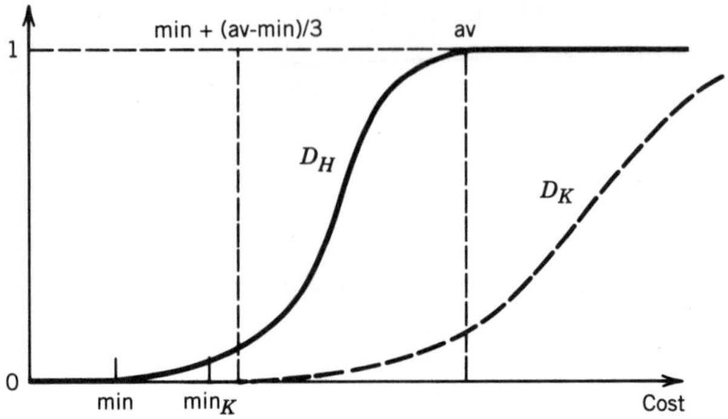

Figure 16.8 *Nondeceptive schema distributions.*

Figure 16.8 shows the nondeceptive case where a GA will work well. Samples of schema H will have above average cost values with high probability while most of the samples of schema K will have definitely worse cost values and be eliminated by selection. The number of samples of schema H in the population will increase the number of samples of schema K will decrease.

Figure 16.9 shows a deceptive case. Only few elements of H are very good or good, most are rather bad. Schema K contains no optimal or near-optimal elements but a large fraction of good elements. Thus during evolution the number of elements of K will increase in the population the number of elements of H will decrease. Schema H may become extinct.

Case 3 (Fig. 16.10) is different. The average of schema H is better than that of schema K, thus indicating no deception. But the analysis of schema distributions shows another result. In the interesting interval schema H and

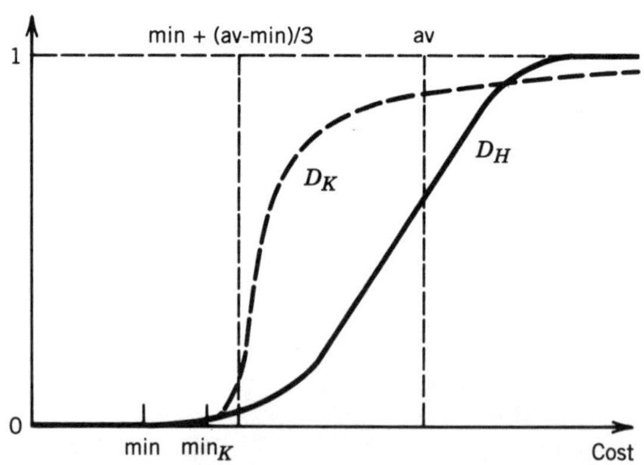

Figure 16.9 *Deceptive schemata distributions.*

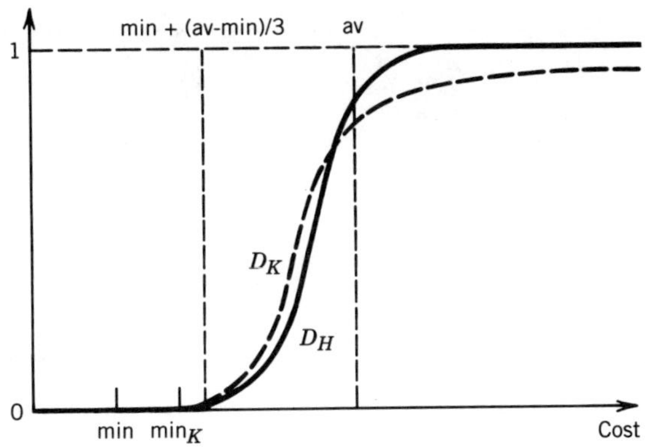

Figure 16.10 *Almost deceptive schema distributions.*

schema K have very similar distributions, schema K is even slightly better. If there are only few samples of H and K in the population, statistical sampling errors will determine whether H or K will win. If a problem has many competing low-order schemata where the schema distributions follow case 3, the problem is deceptive. It is unprobable that all schemata containing the optimum will win.

Figure 16.11 shows a very regular circuit that is built with four complex components like a matrix. The optimal partitioning is a vertical slicing in two 4-bit slices. Schema H contains this optimum whereas schema K does not. In Figure 16.12 the schema distributions are plotted both for simple coding and special coding.

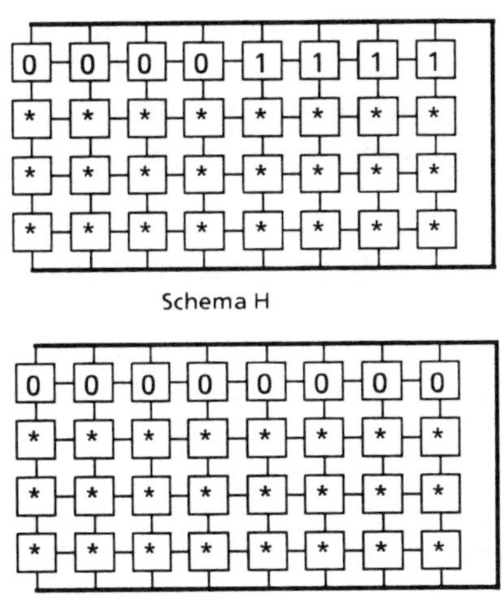

Figure 16.11 *Matrix circuit with two schemata.*

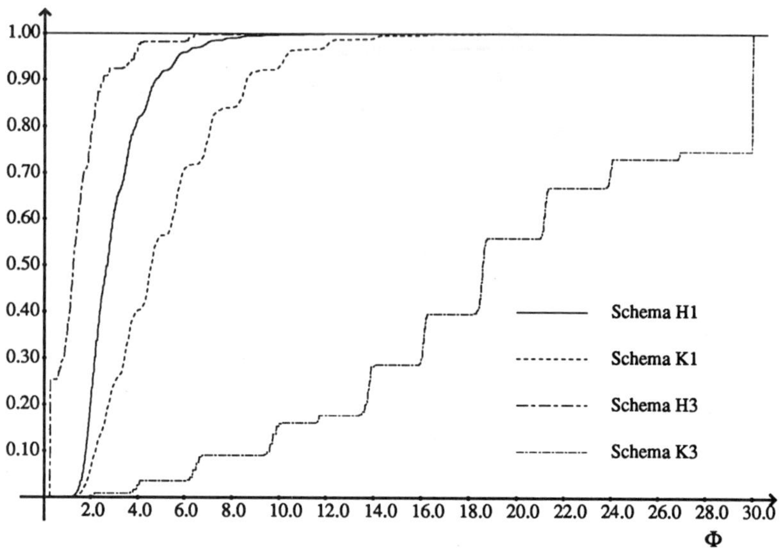

Figure 16.12 *Schema distributions of* H1 *and* K1 *for the simple coding and* H3 *and* K3 *for the sophisticated coding.*

The schema distributions of H and K are very similar for simple coding; this is like case 3. For special coding we detect case 1 without deception.

The qualitative results shown in Figure 16.12 can be quantified. The author has developed a formula for calculating an average over the comparisons of relevant schema distributions, the so called suitability value [8, 14]. For the sophisticated coding the suitability value is much higher than for simple coding. The difference of both values will be lower for larger, less regular circuits than the matrix circuit but the result clearly favors the special two-step coding for circuits with a regular structure.

16.9 COMPARISON WITH OTHER PARTITIONING METHODS

Evolution strategies do not construct one or more partitions by assigning component after component to a part as the algorithms of Breuer [2] or the expert system CHIPEX [11] but start with complete partitions. These are improved by creating and selecting better partitions. The expert system produced only good results for circuits with a regular structure as human experts do. The advantage of GAs is their generality: They are capable to solve new partitioning tasks with new types of circuits or different constraints, whereas the knowledge bases of expert systems often have to be adapted to new problems.

The evolution strategy is a stochastic optimization method and random choice is an important part of the method. This distinguishes evolution strategies from other iterative partitioning methods as the algorithm of Fiduccia and Mattheyses [10].

On the other hand, evolution strategy is not random search at all. Selection eliminates bad partitions, advances the mating of good partitions, and again selects the best partitions of their offspring. The evolution strategy degenerates the random search only if there is no sufficiently dense sequence of partitions with monotonously increasing quality. Then the precondition for evolution strategies does not hold: The possible offspring of good solutions contains better ones.

The great advantage of evolution strategies is the horizontal information transmission [15]. This means that information is exchanged between two different partitions rather than changing one partition step by step. The advantage is that good partial solutions are combined to better total solutions (building block hypotheses).

Horizontal information transmission distinguishes evolution strategies from other stochastic optimization techniques, such as simulated annealing (SA). Simulated annealing can be viewed as a special GA with population size one and a sophisticated selection operator. This can easily be seen by comparing the algorithm of SA with Algorithm 1. Simulated annealing consists of the same steps as a GA. They have to be interpreted in the following way:

Initialization Population size $N := 1$: create only one random partition. Additionally a control parameter t (temperature) is initialized.

Mating Mating is not applicable because there is only one partition in the population. It is used for further steps.

Recombination Recombination of parameter values is not possible since there is only one solution at focus. Create a new solution by small random changes of the parameter values (mutation).

Rating Rate the new solution according to the quality function and add it to the population, $N := 2$.

Selection After the creation of a new solution the population consists of two partitions θ_{old} and θ_{new}. One of them is selected, the other eliminated ($N := 1$). The decision which instance is selected is characteristic for simulated annealing and depends on the cost values of both partitions and the control parameter t:

IF $\Phi(\theta_{new}) < \Phi(\theta_{old})$
THEN select θ_{new}
ELSE $z :=$ random (0, 1);
  IF $z < \exp(-(\Phi(\theta_{new}) - \Phi(\theta_{old}))/t)$
  THEN select θ_{new}
  ELSE select θ_{old}
Decrease t according to a cooling scheme

The selection operator that allows the survival of the worse partition with a probability according to the actual "temperature" gives the possibility to leave local optima. Theoretically the global optimum is always reached, if the cooling is slow enough [16]. But the results of SA are worse even for a very slow cooling scheme with more partitions produced than by the GA.

Youssef Saab and Vasant Rao presented an evolution-based partitioning system at the 26th DAC [17] with good results. The difference in the evolution strategy proposed at the conference is that the population consists of only one partition. Hence, horizontal information transmission is not possible. A new partition is created by a sophisticated concept of component migration depending on calculated component gains rather than by random combination of partitions and random change of assignments. Random operators like crossing over or mutation are not used. A similarity to evolution in Nature is hardly detectable. This method is not a GA as defined in [5, 6, 7].

None of the mentioned partitioning methods offers the possibility of copying components like the presented sophisticated GA. For many circuit partitioning problems this possibility reduces the minimal number of cut signal nets considerably.

16.10 SUMMARY

Evolution strategies can be used for complex optimization problems like partitioning of circuits. A simple straightforward algorithm showed promising results. Therefore a more sophisticated algorithm was developed that produced very good results. This algorithm uses two-step coding to conserve the connectivity structure of circuits and support the advantages of genetic algorithms. The possibility to copy components again improves the quality of the solutions.

Advantages of GA for Partitioning

- Simple algorithm that can easily be structured into modules.
- Easy to parallelize with little communication overhead.
- Few restrictions for the quality function.
- The population with different partitions covers a large subspace of the search space. This helps to avoid getting stuck in local optima.
- Recombination leads to horizontal information transmission: good partial solutions are combined to better total solutions.
- Copies of components are possible.
- Good quality of the solutions.

Disadvantages of GAs

- Large storage demand for big populations.
- Long run time.

- Due to random choices different solutions are possible for different runs of the program (Table 16.2).

TABLE 16.2 Different Runs of the Sophisticated GA for Circuit 3

N.O.P.	23,900	27,350	25,100	24,750	26,000	24,900
Pins	82	84	82	82	82	82

REFERENCES

[1] U. Lauther, A min-cut placement algorithm for general cell assemblies based on a graph representation, *Proc. 16th Design Automation Conf.*, 1–10 (1979).

[2] M. A. Breuer, *Design Automation of Digital Systems*, chap. 4, Prentice Hall, New York, 1972.

[3] D. G. Schweikert and B. W. Kernighan, A proper model for the partitioning of electrical circuits, *Proc. Design Automation Workshop*, 56–62 (June 1972).

[4] L. R. Hyafil and L. Rivest, "Graph Partitioning and Constructing Optimal Decision Trees are Polynomial Complete Problems," Rapport de Recherche nr. 33, IRIA laboria, Le Chesnay, 1973.

[5] D. E. Goldberg, *Genetic Algorithms in Search, Optimization, and Machine Learning*, Addison-Wesley, Reading, Mass., 1989.

[6] I. Rechenberg, *Evolutionsstrategie, Optimierung technischer Systeme nach Prinzipien der biologischen Evolution*, problemata frommann—holzboog, Stuttgart, 1973.

[7] J. H. Holland, *Adaption in Natural and Artificial Systems*, University of Michigan Press, Ann Arbor, 1975.

[8] M. Hulin, "Evolutionsstrategien für die Schaltungspartitionierung," Siemens AG Internal Rep. (1992).

[9] C. de Groot, D. Würtz, and K. H. Hoffmann, Optimizing complex problems by nature's algorithms: Simulated annealing and evolution strategy—A comparative study, *Proc. PPSN Workshop*, Springer Verlag, 445–454 (1990).

[10] C. M. Fiduccia and R. M. Mattheyses, A linear-time heuristic for improving network partitions, *Proc. 19th Design Automation Conf.*, 175–181 (1982).

[11] J. Heistermann, M. Hulin, P. Istavrinos, and N. K. Gupta, Partitionierung digitaler Schaltungen auf vorgegebene physikalische Einheiten, *Informatik Forschung und Entwicklung*, 3 (1988).

[12] K. De Jong and W. M. Spears, An analysis of the interacting roles of population size and crossover in genetic algorithms, *Proc. PPSN Workshop*, Springer Verlag, 38–47 (1990).

[13] D. E. Goldberg and P. Segrest, Finite Markov chain analysis of genetic algorithms, *Proc. 2nd Internat. Conf. on Genetic Algorithms*, Lawrence Erlbaum, Hillsdale, N.J. (1987).

[14] M. Hulin, Analysis of schema distributions, *Proc. 4th Internat. Conf. on Genetic Algorithms (ICGA)*, Morgan Kaufmann Publishers, 204–209 (1991).

[15] E. Jantsch, *Die Selbstorganisation des Universums,* Carl Hanser Verlag, München, 1979.

[16] P. J. M. van Laarhoven, *Theoretical and Computational Aspects of Simulated Annealing,* CWI Tract, Amsterdam (1988).

[17] Y. Saab and V. Rao, An evolution-based approach to partitioning ASIC systems, *Proc. 26th Design Automation Conf.,* 767–770 (1988).

[18] M. Eigen, *Laufen zum Leben,* Piper Verlag, München, (1987).

PART III

The Software of Chaos with Applications

CHAPTER 17

Continuous Chaos and Logical Chaos

VITO LEONARDO PLANTAMURA
BRANKO SOUČEK
IVANKA ŠTAJNER

17.1 INTRODUCTION

Chaos is a seemingly random process generated in some nonlinear dynamical systems that are extremely sensitive to the changes of initial conditions. Chaos is fully deterministic and based on fixed rules that involve no elements of chance. This fact implies that the behavior of many phenomena that were considered random can be explained in terms of simple deterministic laws.

Chaos is best visualized in a state-space—an abstract space whose coordinates are the degrees of freedom of system's motion. The coordinates vary with the context: For example, for a mechanical system they might be position and velocity; for a biological model they might be stimulus and response. A single point in the state-space corresponds to the entire state of a dynamical system in a certain moment of time. In the state-space chaotic behavior is presented in the form of orbits and basins of attraction.

Until now, chaos research has been focused on continuous processes. In this chapter we extend the research to the domain of logical processes. The chapter examines chaotic features of processes generated through logical mapping, including pseudorandom numbers, cyclic codes, and marker passing systems.

Similarities and differences between continuous chaos (CC) and logical chaos (LC) are examined. Both processes are generated by nonlinear dynamical systems. A dynamical system consists of the state, which describes

Dynamic, Genetic, and Chaotic Programming, By Branko Souček and the IRIS Group.
ISBN 0-471-55717-X

the system and conditions, and the dynamics, which specifies the rules of how the state evolves with time.

The CC and LC processes are pseudorandom; CC and LC depend strongly on initial conditions. In CC processes *basins of attraction*—smaller regions of lower dimension in the state-space that attract nearby orbits, called *strange attractors*—exhibit the features of stretching and folding. In LC processes the basins of attraction have a form of clusters that are dispersed over the state-space. The CC processes are nonperiodic. The LC processes examined here are periodic, but the period might be very long. In this case a fraction of the LC processes can be considered nonperiodic.

The first part of this chapter introduces chaos. Simple dynamical systems that generate chaos are presented. In particular, Lorenz equations are studied in detail, using programs in the C language. The results obtained clearly show the basic features of CC processes. A logistic equation was examined, following the work of May, Yorke, Hoppensteadt, and Mandelbrot, to simulate and show the features of bifurcation and fractals.

The second part of the chapter introduces logical chaos. The C software package has been developed to simulate logical mappers. Practical applications are discussed. It is shown that in some nuclear and neurological experiments, LC could be used for data preprocessing. This could lead to the compression of the experimental data field by 100 to 1000 times. As a result the size and the cost of the real-time data acquisition system could be reduced by one or two orders of magnitude. The LC mapping, as a base for pseudoassociative system design, is presented.

17.2 THE LORENZ EQUATIONS

In 1963, E. N. Lorenz [1] described a three-parameter family of three-dimensional ordinary differential equations. The solutions of these equations, using numerical integration on a computer, were extremely complicated. These nonlinear equations, known as the Lorenz equations, are very interesting and have been much studied. They are

$$
\begin{aligned}
\frac{dx}{dt} &= \sigma(y - x) \\
\frac{dy}{dt} &= rx - y - xz \\
\frac{dz}{dt} &= xy - bz
\end{aligned}
\tag{17.1}
$$

where σ, r, and b are three real positive parameters. In this chapter we study this system with $\sigma = 10$, $r = 28$, and $b = \frac{8}{3}$:

$$\frac{dx}{dt} = 10(y - x)$$
$$\frac{dy}{dt} = 28x - y - xz \tag{17.2}$$
$$\frac{dz}{dt} = xy - \tfrac{3}{8}z$$

System (17.1) is deterministic, and there are no terms taking noise or chance into account.

The first program in the C language shown in Figure 17.1 computes the solution system (17.2) by numerical integration using the Runge-Kutta (4,4) method. Input data are initial conditions, integration step, and number of integration steps to complete. The output is a graphical presentation of the solution to Cauchy's problem, given by system (17.2) and initial conditions.

```
#include <graphics.h>
#include <stdlib.h>
#include <stdio.h>
#include <conio.h>
#include <dos.h>
#include <fontl.h>
#include <io.h>

void init(void);
void printviewport(void);

/* Printer commands */
#define LSPC (char)'A'
#define BITS (char) 8
#define GRPH (char)'*'
#define MODE (char) 6
#define ESC (char)0x1b

void printviewport (void) /* prints current screen */
{
   struct viewporttype typ;
   register unsigned i,j,k, width, length, mask;
   char 0;
   static char buff[730];
   int pxcnt, bufflen, prnfd;

   if ((prnfd = open ("LPT1", O_WRONLY|O_BINARY))>=0)
     {
     /* Init printer vert. spacing */
     getviewsettings ( & typ );        /* current viewport*/
     buff[0] = ESC;  buff[1] = LSPC;  buff[2] = BITS;
```

Figure 17.1

```
   buff[3] = "\r'; buff[4] = "\n';
   write(prnfd, buff, 5);

   /* Init graphic sequence */
   width = typ.right - typ.left + 1;
   if ( width > 720 ) width = 720;
   length = typ.bottom - typ.top + 1;
   buff[1] = GRPH;    buff[2] = MODE;
   buff[3] = width; buff[4] = width >> 8;
   bufflen = width + 7;
   buff[bufflen-2] = '\r';    buff[bufflen-1] = '\n';

   for (k=0; k<length; k+=BITS) { /* printer rows */
      pxcnt = 5;
      for (i=0; i<width; i++) {   /* data */
       for   (c=0,j=0,mask=(0x01<<(BITS-1));
        (j<BITS)&&((k+j)<length);j++,mask>>=1)
        if(getpixel(i, k+j) != BLACK) o |=mask;
      buff[pxont++] = o;
     }
     write (prnfd, buff, bufflen);
  }
 }
}
void Init(void) /* Initializes graphics */
{
int gdriver=CGA, gmode=CGAC2, errorcode;

initgraph (&gdriver,&gmode,"");
errorcode=graphresult();
if(errorcode != grOk)
  ( printf ("Graphios error: %s'\n",
            grapherrormsg(errorcode));
                         getch();
                         exit(1);
                 }
}
main()
  {int i,j,k,number_of_steps, again;
  double xinit, yinit, zinit, x, y, z, x1, x2, x3, x4, y1, y2, y3, y4,
              z1,z2,z3,z4,h;
  printf(" Input initial conditions x, y and z \n");
  scanf("%If %If %If", &xinit, &yinit, &zinit);
  printf(" Input the step of numerical integration \");
  soanf("%If", &h);
more: printf(" Input number of steps \n");
  scanf("%Id",&number_of_steps);
  Init();
  printf(" \n %g, %g, %g \n",xinit,yinit,zinit);
  printf(" %g \n",h);
  printf(" %d",number_of_steps);
```

Figure 17.1 *(Continued)*

```
/* numerical integration by Runge-Kutta (4,4) method */
     i=0; x=xinit; y=yinit; z=zinit;
     while(i<number_of_steps)
        {x1=10*(y-x)*h;
            y1=(x*(28-z)-y)*h;
        z1=(x*y-8./3*z)*h;
        x2=10*(y+.5*y1-x-.5*x1)*h;
        y2=((x+.5*x1)*(28-z-.5*z1)-y-.5*y1)*h;
        z2=((x+.5*x1)*(y+.5*y1)-8./3*(z+.5*z1))*h;
        x3=10*(y+.5*y2-x-.5*x2)*h;
        y3=((x+.5*x2)*(28-z-.5*z2)-y-.5*y2)*h;
        z3=((x+.5*x2)*(y+.5*y2)-8./3*(z+.5*z2))*h;
        x4=10*(y+y3-x-x3)*h;
        y4=((x+x3)*(28-z-z3)-y-y3)*h;
        z4=((x+x3)*(y+y3)-8./3*(z+z3))*h;
        x=x+(x1+2*(x2+x3)+x4)/6;
        y=y+(y1+2*(y2+y3)+y4)/6;
        z=z+(z1+2*(z2+z3)+z4)/6;
        j=(x+19)*8;k=z*4;
        putpixel(j,k,1);
        ++i;};

   rectangle(0,199,319,0);
 /* if p is pressed on the keyboard program prints current screen */
     if(getch()=='p') printviewport();
     getch();
     closegraph();
     printf(" Do you want to run the program again for the other",
        "number of steps? \n", "Input  1 for YES or 0 for NO");
     scanf("%d",&again);if(again) goto more;
}
```

Figure 17.1 *(Continued)*

The program's outputs are Figures 17.2 and 17.3, where projections of the approximate solutions on the $[-19,21] \times [0,50]$ part of the xz plane are shown. The x axis is horizontal, with x increasing to the right, and the z axis is vertical, with z increases downward. Numbers in the first row represent x, y, and z coordinates of the initial point (initial conditions), in the second row the integration step is printed, and in third row gives the number of completed steps of integration.

Self-intersection of trajectories in both figures is result of projection of the trajectories in the space on the plane. There are no crossings in the space. (If there were one, the trajectory would repeat itself from that point on because of the uniqueness of the solution of Cauchy's problem.)

We have extracted basic features of the approximate trajectories computed by numerical integration and have obtained results similar to Sparrow's [2]:

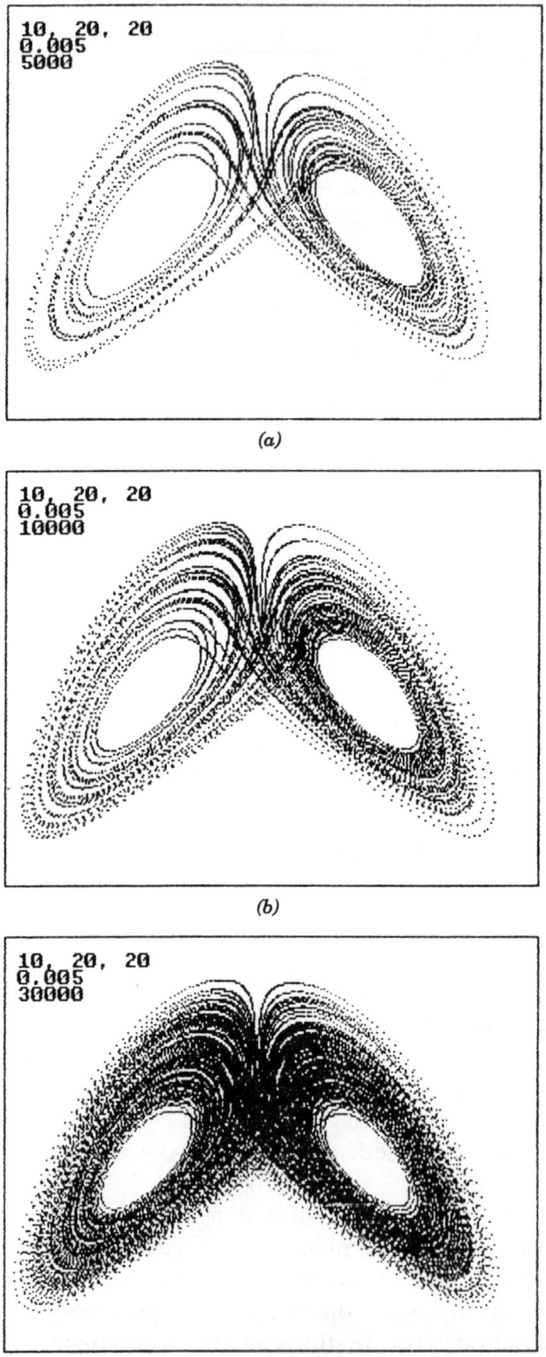

Figure 17.2 *Projection of the solution of the Lorenz equations on the xz plane. As the number of completed integration steps is increased, the trajectory continues winding around in nonperiodic loops.*

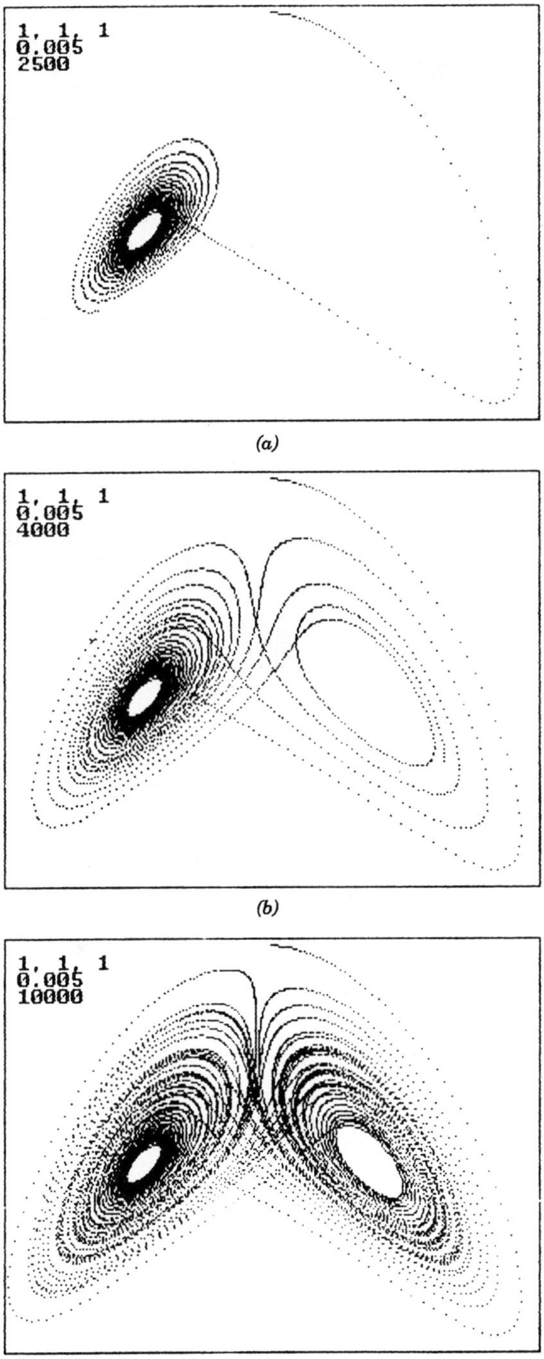

(c)

Figure 17.3 *The trajectory starting at a very different initial point, though looping at the beginning on only one side, soon becomes similar to the one shown in Figure 17.2.*

1. Trajectories are nonperiodic.
2. The form of the trajectories shown in Figure 17.2 and 17.3 is not a transient phenomenon. If numerical integration is continued for a provisionally long time, trajectories form loops first on one side then on the other. They never settle down to a nonchaotical attractor (stationary point, periodical loop, or torus).
3. If the transient section at the beginning of the trajectory is disregarded, the general form of trajectory does not depend either on the choice of the initial conditions or on the choice of the method of numerical integration. Similarly, the changes in the integration step have no influence on the general form.

17.3 PROGRAM TO GENERATE CHAOS

The program in Figure 17.4 is also in the C language. It computes the solution of Cauchy's problem given by system (17.2) and initial conditions (10,20,30), using numerical integration by the explicit Runge-Kutta (4,4) method. By the same method the program also computes the solutions of 500 other Cauchy problems. These problems are given by system (17.2) and initial points taken in small increments, equidistant from the little interval containing the point (10,20,30). This interval is so small that in the graphics resolution we used it cannot be distinguished from that point.

Input data are integration step (which is 0.005 in all examples presented here) and the number of integration steps to complete. Program output (Figs. 17.5–17.8) is a graphical presentation of the projection of the trajectory, starting in (10,20,30), on part of the xz plane ($X \in [-19,21]$, $z \in [0,50]$, x increases to the right, and z downward) as light points. The upper left corner has the number of integration steps completed. Projections of the final points (after the same number of integration steps completed) of the 500 other trajectories are shown as dark points. In Figures 17.7 and 17.8 just dark points are shown to avoid confusion.

```
#include <graphics.h>
#include <stdlib.h>
#include <stdio.h>
#include <oonio.h>
#include <dos.h>

void Init(void)/*Initializes graphics*/
{
int gdriver=CGA, gmode=CGAC2, errorcode;

initgraph (&gdriver,&gmode,"");
errorcode=graphresult();
```

Figure 17.4

```
if (errorcode != grOk)
   ( printf ("Graphics error:%s\n",
            grapherrormsg(errorcode));
                        getch();
                        exit(1);
                  }
}

main()
  {int i,j,k,iz /*number of steps in initial conditions*/,
     number_of_steps /* of numerical integration */;

  double xinit=10, yinit=20, zinit=30 /*first initial conditions */,
       x,y,z,x1,x2,x3,x4,y1,y2,y3,y4,
       z1,z2,z3,z4,h /*step of numerical integration*/,
       init_cond_step=0.0001;

  printf("Input the step of numerical integration \n");
  scanf("%If", &h);
  printf("Input the number of steps for numerical integration \n");
  scanf("%i",&number_of_steps);
  Init();
  printf("\n %i", number_of_steps);

/* plots in lighter points the trajectory starting in the first
initial conditions */
     i=0;x=xinit;y=yinit;z=zinit;
     while(i<number_of_steps)
       {x1=10*(y-x)*h;
       y1=(x*(28-z)-y)*h;
       z1=(x*y-8./3*z)*h;
       x2=10*(y+.5*y1-x-.5*x1)*h;
       y2=((x+.5*x1)*(28-z-.5*z1)-y-.5*y1)*h;
       z2=((x+.5*x1)*(y+.5*y1)- 8./3*(z+.5*z1))*h;
       x3=10*(y+.5*y2-x-.5*x2)*h;
       y3=((x+.5*x2)*(28-z-.5*z2)-y-.5*y2)*h;
       z3=((x+.5*x2)*(y+.5*y2)-8./3*(z+.5*z2))*h;
       x4=10*(y+y3-x-x3)*h;
       y4=((x+x3)*(28-z-z3)-y-y3)*h;
       z4=((x+x3)*(y+y3)-8./3*(z+z3))*h;
       x=x+(x1+2*)(x2+x3)+x4)/6;
       y=y+(y1+2*(y2+y3)+y4)/6;
       z=z+(z1+2*(z2+z3)+z4)/6;
       j=(x+19)*8;k=z*4;

      putpixel(j,k,3);i++;}

/* plots in darker points the final state of the same system
starting with a little different initial conditions */

    iz=1;
    while(iz<501){z=zinit+iz*init_cond_step;
```

Figure 17.4 *(Continued)*

```
    x=xinit-iz*init_cond_step;y=yinit-iz*init_cond_step;++iz;i=0;
    while(i<number_of_steps)
            {x1=10*(y-x)*h;
            y1=(x*(28-z)-y)*h;
            z1=(x*y-8./3*z)*h;
            x2=10*(y+.5*y1-x-.5*x1)*h;
            y2=((x+.5*x1)*(28-z-.5*z1)-y-.5*y1)*h;
            z2=((x+.5*x1)*(y+.5*y1)-8./3*(z+.5*z1))*h;
            x3=10*(y+.5*y2-x-.5*x2)*h;
            y3=((x+.5*x2)*(28-z-.5*z2)-y-.5*y2)*h;
            z3=((x+.5*x2)*(y+.5*y2)-8./3*(z+.5*z2))*h;
            x4=10*(y+y3-x-x3)*h;
            y4=((x+x3)*(28-z-z3)-y-y3)*h;
            z4=((x+x3)*(y+y3)-8./3*(z+z3))*h;
            x=x+(x1+2*(x2+x3)+x4)/6;
            y=y+(y1+2*(y2+y3)+y4)/6;
            z=z+(z1+2*(z2+z3)+z4)/6;++i;};
            j=(x+19)*8;k=z*4;
            putpixel(j,k,2);}
    rectangle(0,199,319,0);
    getch( );
    closegraph( );
}
```

Figure 17.4 *(Continued)*

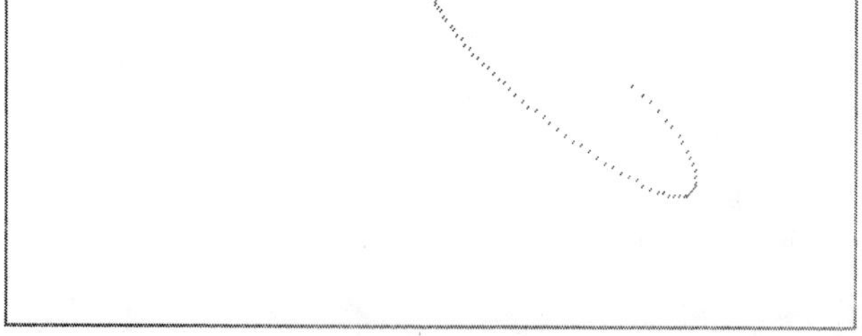

Figure 17.5 *In the first 180 steps, the initially small interval has stretched about 20 times. That kind of behavior is considered predictable.*

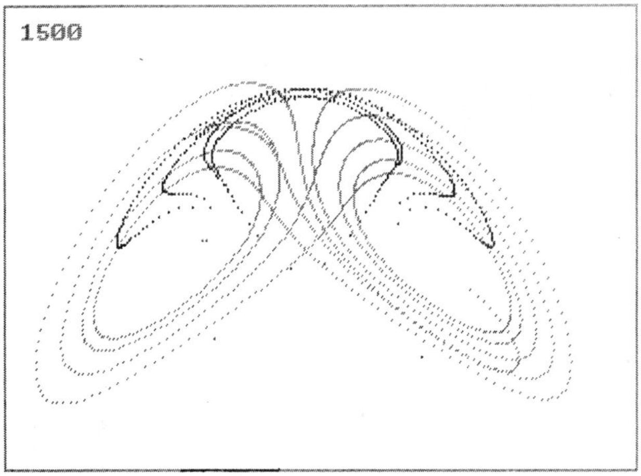

Figure 17.6 *After 1500 steps, trajectories with very close initial points finish at very different parts of the attractor. We can also see stretching and folding of the state-space.*

17.4 STRANGE ATTRACTORS AND THEIR FEATURES

In the case of nonchaotical attractors, stationary points, bounded loops, or tori, trajectories whose initial points differ slightly stay close to one another as they evolve with time. Small errors stay bound, and we say that such a system has predictable behavior.

Lorenz was the first to find the other type of attractor, a strange or chaotic

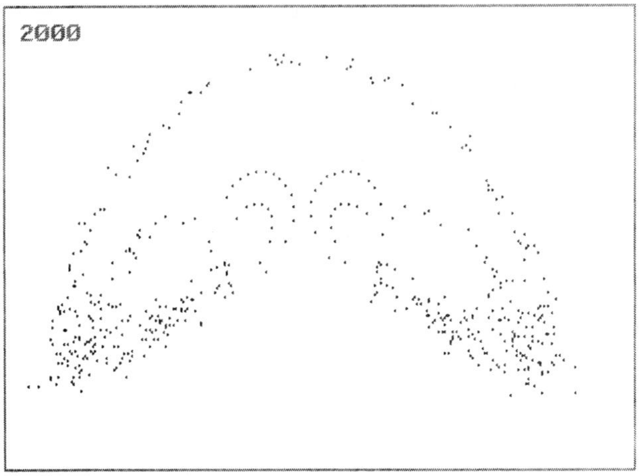

Figure 17.7 *The initial interval has stretched and folded onto itself many times and has covered many parts of the attractor, but some structure is still visible.*

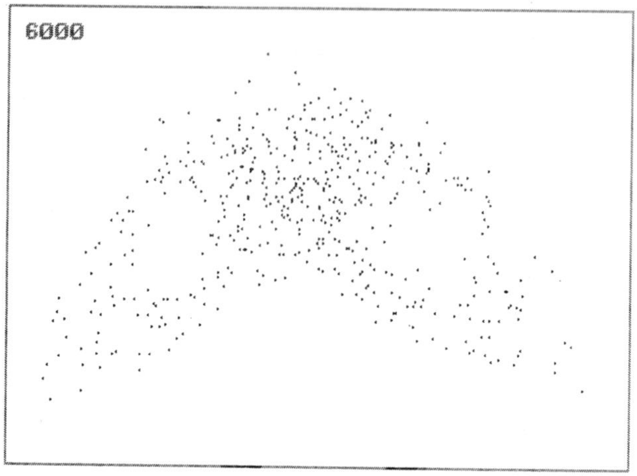

Figure 17.8 *After 6000 steps the points have spread all over the attractor. The final state can be anywhere on the attractor, and therefore prediction has become impossible.*

attractor. On a strange attractor a stretching and folding operation of the state-space is happening. Locally, trajectories diverge exponentially—that is, the state-space is stretched. But since the size of a chaotic attractor is finite, two trajectories cannot diverge exponentially forever, so the attractor has to fold onto itself. While stretching amplifies small uncertainties, folding systematically erases macroscopic information given by the initial conditions.

We can clearly see this stretching and folding operation in Figure 17.6. A small interval of the initial conditions is stretched and folded four times after only 1500 steps of integration. As this operation continues, the final points of the trajectories cover very different parts of the attractor and form a structure in which a process of genesis is still visible (Fig. 17.7). After only 6000 steps (Fig. 17.8), the final points are spread all over the attractor, and any prediction about the system's behavior is impossible.

Obviously the exact form of a trajectory on the Lorenz attractor is extremely sensitive to small changes in the initial conditions. Similarly, it depends crucially on the choice of the integrating routine. Consequently, it is possible to predict development of the trajectory only for a very short time interval.

17.5 BIFURCATION

Nonlinear system of chaos exhibit several unexpected features including bifurcation which was first observed by May [3], who studied the logistic equation of population growth

$$x_{next} = rx(1 - x)$$

By trying different values for the parameter *r*, May found that he could dramatically change the system's character. Yorke [4] proved that in any one-dimensional system, if a regular cycle of period three ever appears, then the same system will also display regular cycles of every other length, as well as completely chaotic cycles. The program presented in Figure 17.9 shows experiments with the logistic equation.

The results of this program are shown in Figure 17.10*a*, *b* and *c*. The horizontal axis represents parameter *r* (increasing from left to right) and vertical axis represents *x* (increasing upwards). The value of *x* is calculated by iteration using logistic equation. The initial value of *x*, x_{init} is 0.4. Results of first 50 iterations in Figure 17.10a and *b* or 200 in Figure 17.10*c* are not shown in the figures so the system will focus on the important values.

While *r* is small, *x* obtained from the logistic equation settles to one fixed value. As *r* increases, *x* alternates between two values, then 4, 8, and so on. After the critical value of parameter *r*, there is no repetition of values of *x* and we cannot easily predict subsequent values of *x*, as we can if *r* is smaller than the critical value. Now we have a case of chaos. But if *r* is increased, intervals of order appear again. We can see them clearly on Fig. 17.10*b* in the form of the white strips.

```
#include <graphics.h>
#include <stdlib.h>
#include <stdio.h>
#include <conio.h>
#include <dos.h>
#include <fcntl.h>
#include <io.h>

void Init(void);
void printviewport(void);

#define LSPC (char)'A' /* Printer commands */
#define BITS (char) 8
#define GRPH (char)'*'
#define MODE (char) 6
#define ESC  (char)0x1b

void printviewport (void) /* subroutine which prints current screen */
{
  struct viewporttype typ;
  register unsigned i,j,k, width, length, mask;
  char c;
  static char buff [730];
  int pxcnt, bufflen, prnfd;
```

Figure 17.9

```
  if ((prnfd = open ("LPT1", O_WRONGLY | O_BINARY)) >=0 )
   {
    /* Init printer vert. spacing */
    getviewsettings ( &typ );     /* current viewport */
    buff[0] = ESC;     buff[1] = LSPC;   buff[2] = BITS;
    buff[3] ='\r';  buff[4] = '\n';
    write(prnfd, buff, 5);

    /* Init graphic sequence */
    width  = typ.right - typ.left + 1;
    if ( width > 720 ) width = 720;
    length = typ.bottom - typ.top + 1;
    buff[1] = GRPH;     buff[2] = MODE;
    buff[3] = width;    buff[4] = width >> 8;
    bufflen = width + 7;
    buff[bufflen-2] = '\r';     buff[bufflen-1] = '\n';

    for (k=0; k<length; k+=BITS (          /* printer rows */
     { pxcnt = 5;
       for (i=0; i<width; i++) { /* data */
       for (c=0,j=0,mask=(0x01<<(BITS-1)); (j<BITS)&&((k+j)<length);
            j++,mask>>=1)
       if(getpixel(i, k+j) !=BLACK) c |= mask;
       buff[pxcnt++] = c;
        }
    write (prnfd, buff, bufflen);
    }
  }
}

void Init(void) /* subroutine which initializes graphics */
{
int gdriver=VGA, gmode=VGAHI, errorcode;

initgraph (&gdriver,&gmode,"");
errorcode=graphresult();
if (errorcode != grOk)
{ printf ("Graphics error: %s\n", grapherrormsg(errorcode));
  getch(); exit(1); }
}

main()
    {int i,j,k;
    double r=0, rstep=.01 ,xinit=.4, x;

    Init();
    i=0;
    while(i<400)
       { x=xinit; k=1;
         while(k<51){ x=r*x*(1-x); ++k;}
         k=1;
```

Figure 17.9 (*Continued*)

```
        while(k<201){x=r*x*(1-x);
                    putpixel(i,200-200*x,63);
                          ++k;}
        ++i, r += rstep;}

    rectangle(0,200,400,0);
    /* if p is pressed on the keyboard, program prints current
screen */
    if (getch()=='p') printviewport();
    getch(); closegraph();
}
```
■

Figure 17.9 (*Continued*)

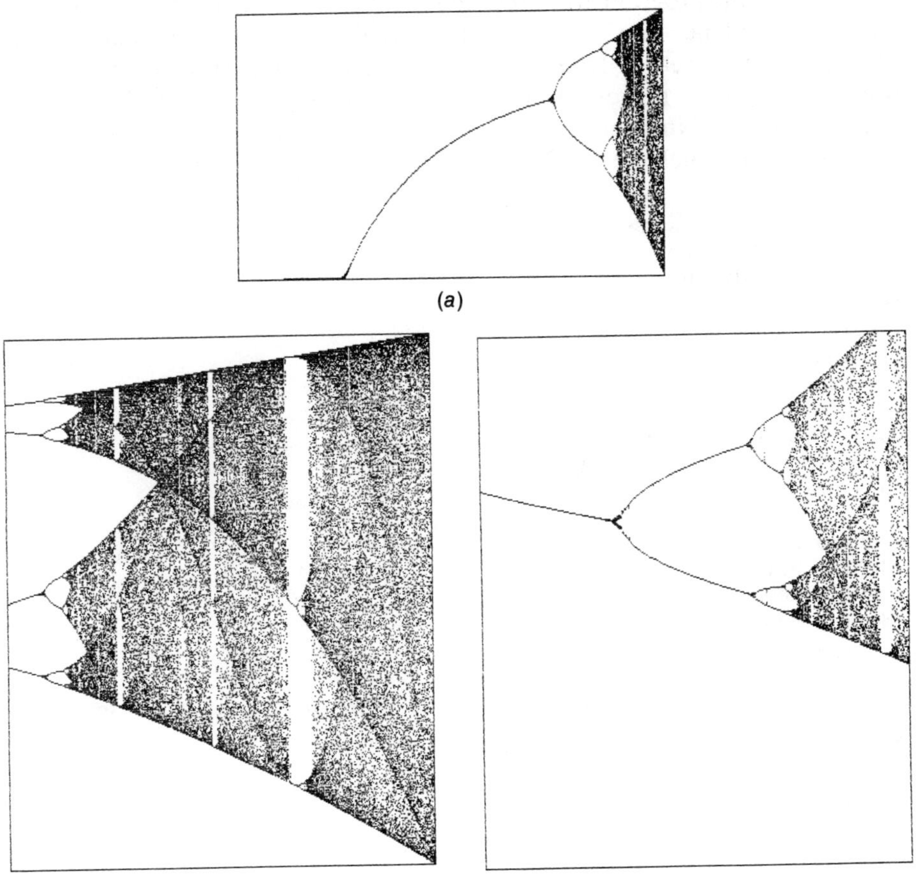

(*a*)

(*b*) (*c*)

Figure 17.10 (a) *Bifurcation diagram with values of* r *changing from 0 to 4;* x *between 0 and 1 are shown.* (b) *Enlarged part of* (a) *with values* r ∈ *[3.5,4]*, x ∈ *[0,1]*. (c) *Enlarged hill from the center of the white strip on Figure 17.10*b *is very similar to the whole diagram shown on Figure 17.10*a.

17.6 FRACTALS

Fractals deal with regularities and irregularities over different scales. The word *fractal* was coined by Mandelbrot [5]. Mandelbrot moved beyond dimensions 0, 1, 2, 3, . . . to the seemingly impossible: fractional dimensions which are a measure of roughness or irregularity in an object. A simple fractal experiment could be performed by using Mandelbrot set

$$z \rightarrow z^2 + c$$

The program loop, producing the numbers and shapes in the complex plane, based on the Mandelbrot set is presented in Figure 17.11.

Results of the program are shown in Figure 17.12, which illustrates parts of the complex plane. The horizontal axis is real and the vertical is imaginary. The real part increases from left to right, and imaginary increases downwards. Black dots represent complex numbers which are elements of the Mandelbrot set. Numbers in the first and the second row are ends of the intervals from which Re z and Im z respectively, are taken.

```
#include <graphics.h>
#include <stdlib.h>
#include <stdio.h>
#include <conio.h>
#include <dos.h>
#include <fontl.h>
#include <io.h>

void Init(void);
int colour(double x,double y);
void printviewport(void);

#define LSPC (char)'A' /*Printer commands*/
#define BITS (char)8
#define GRPH (char)"*"
#define MODE (char)6
#define ESC (char)0x1b

void printviewport (void) /*subroutine which prints current screen*/
{
 struct viewporttype typ;
 register unsigned i,j,k, width, length, mask;
 char c;
 static char buff[730];
 int pxcnt, bufflen,prnfd;

 if((prnfd = open("LPT1",O_WRONLY|O_BINARY))>=0)
 {
 /*Init printer vert. spacing*/
```

Figure 17.11

```
getviewsettings ( &typ );                /*current viewport*/
buff[0] = ESC; buff[1] = LSPC; buff[2] = BITS;
buff[3] = '\'; buff[4] = '\n';
write(prnfd,buff,5);

/*Init graphic sequence*/
width = typ.right - typ.left + 1;
if ( width > 720 ) width = 720;
length = typ.bottom - typ.top + 1;
buff[1] = GRPH; buff[2] = MODE;
buff[3] = width; buff[4] = width >> 8;
bufflen = width + 7;
buff[bufflen-2] = '\r'; buff[bufflen-1] = '\n';

for (k=0; k<length;k+=BITS) /*printer rows*/
 (pxcnt = 5;
  for (i=0; i<width; i++) /*data*/
  for (c=0,j=0,mask=(0x01<<(BITS-1)); (j<BITS)&&((k+j)<length);
     if(getpixel(i,k+j) (=BLACK) o|=mask;
     buff[pxcnt++] = c;
          }
  write(prnfd,buff,bufflen);
  }
 }
}

void Init(void) /*subroutine which initializes graphics*/
{
int gdriver=CGA, gmode=CGAC2, errorcode;

initgraph (&gdriver,&gmode,"");
errorcode=graphresult();
if(errorcode !=grOk)
(printf("Graphics error: %s\n", grapherrormsg(errorcode));
 getch(); exit(1);}
}

int colour(double x,double y)/*subroutine which computes the answer
 to the question: Is complex number c=(x,y) an element of the
 Mandelbrot set or not? For every complex number c a series of
 complex numbers z(n) is defined: z(0)=0, z(n+1)=z(n)*z(n)+c. If lim
 z(n)=0, c is an element of the set, and if series z(n) unbounded, c
 is not an element of the set.*/

 {double f,f1,g,g1; int i;

 i=1,f=x;g=y;
 while(i<=500&&f*f+g*g<=4)
   {f1=f*f-g*g+x;
    g1=2*f*g+y;
    if(f1==f && g1==g) i=500;
    f=f1;g=g1;++i;};
```

Figure 17.11 *(Continued)*

```
if (i==501) return 3; /*(x,y) is an element of the Mandelbrot set
*/
          else return 0; /*(x,y) is not an element of the Mandelbrot
set*/
}

main()
 {int i,j,b;
  double xfirst,xlast,yfirst,ylast,xstep,ystep,x,y;

  printf("input the first and the last value of x\n");
  scanf("%lf%lf",&xfirst, &xlast);
  printf("input the first and the last value of y\n");
  scanf("%lf%lf, &yfirst, &ylast);
  xstep = (xlast - xfirst)/320; ystep = (ylast - yfirst)/190;
  Init(); printf("%g,%g,%g,%g",xfirst,xlast,yfirst,ylast);
  while(i<320) (j=10;y=yfirst;
                 while(j<200) (b=colour(x,y): if(b) putpixel(i,j,b);
                             ++j,y+=ystep;}
                 ++i,x+=xstep;}

  rectangle(0,199,319,10);
  /* if p is pressed on the keyboard, program prints current
screen*/
  if (getch()=='p')printviewport();
  getch(); closegraph();
}
```

Figure 17.11 *(Continued)*

17.7 SHIFT-REGISTER GENERATION OF PSEUDORANDOM NUMBERS

Many computer applications in the laboratory require random numbers or random binary waveforms. Although there are a number of ways in which one can generate pseudorandom binary sequences for various coded waveforms, all sequences of interest can be practically generated by a particular technique involving shift-register implementation.

A linear shift-register generator (LSRG) consists of a basic shift register to which modulo 2 adders have been added. The modulo 2 adder, or exclusive OR gates, will produce the output 1 if either of two inputs, A or B, is in the state 1, but not if both inputs are in the state 1. The truth table for modulo 2 adder is

B \ A	0	1
0	0	1
1	1	0

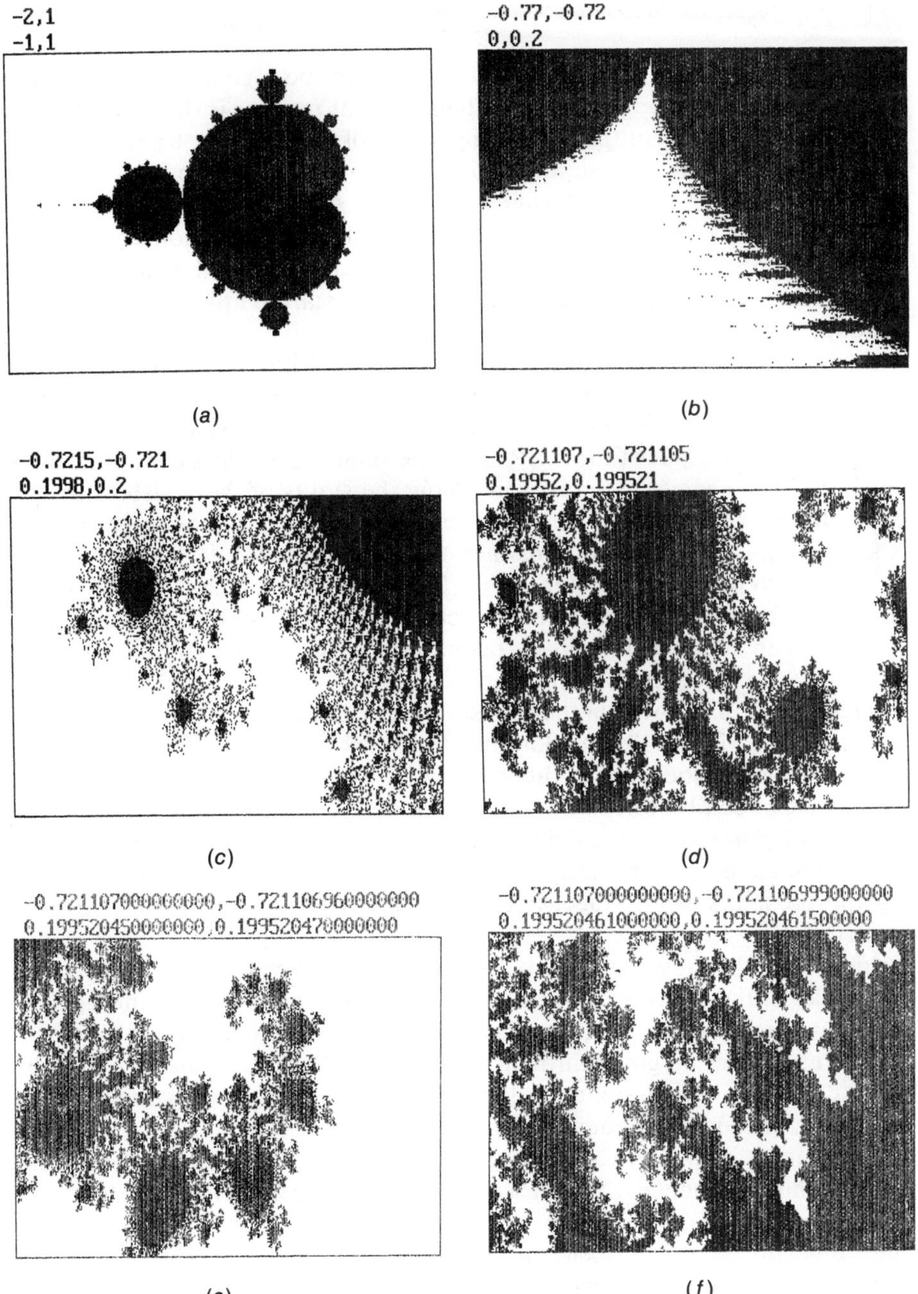

Figure 17.12 (a) *The part of the complex plane. Re z* $\in [-2,1]$, *Im z* $\in [-1,1]$. *Black points represent complex numbers which are elements of Mandelbrot set.* (b) *The part of Mandelbrot set where a heart-like shape and central "circle" meet, enlarged and stretched 10 times horizontally.* (c, d) *When magnified, parts of Figure 17.12*b *reveal the very delicate, lace-like structure of the object.* (e) *The same spiral pattern from the center of Figure 17.12*c *can be found on a smaller scale when a part of Figure 17.12*d *is enlarged.* (f) *The line which separates the set from its complement is so curved that its dimension is more than 1, but less than 2.*

These adders are connected to various stages of the register so that a single or multiple closed loop is formed. When the shift register is then pulsed in its normal manner, the output from any stage of the register forms a binary sequence. In a general case, the digital sequence depends both on the feedback connections and on the initial loading. A shift register generator is shown in Fig. 17.13. If the shift register is loaded with any nonzero number (1000, for example) and is pulsed in a normal manner, it will produce a periodic binary sequence. The sequence can be started at any point and will produce the same cycle.

At the beginning, the shift register is loaded with 1000. The XOR gate takes bits 1 and 4, which have values of 1 and 0 respectively and produces the output 1. After the first shift, the original number is shifted to the right one place. The output of the XOR, 1, at the same time enters the leftmost bit position. In the same way, one can follow the status of the register through other shifting cycles (Fig. 17.13*a*). After 16 cycles, the content of the register is again 1000, and the same sequence will be repeated.

The length of a shift register in Fig. 17.13 is $n = 4$. It is determined by the last stage (fourth) from which the feedback is taken. The shift register in Fig. 17.13*a* has an additional feedback taken from bit 1. This bit is three stages to the left of the right-end bit 4 position.

Figure 17.13*b* shows another possible feedback that is a "reverse" of the one shown in Fig. 17.13; an additional feedback is taken from bit 3. This bit is three stages to the right of the left-end bit 0 position (the output from the adder we can call bit 0). Owing to the symmetry, the sequence produced by the second generator is the delayed exact reverse of the sequence produced by the first generator (indicated by arrows in Figure 17.13). In general, moving the feedback from stage m to the stage n-m will result in a reverse sequence.

Figure 17.13*c* shows another possible four-stage generator. If this generator has an initial content 1000, it will cycle with a period going through six different numbers only. If this generator has an initial contents 1111, it will cycle with the period going through another six different numbers. And if the generator has an initial contents 1011, it will cycle with a very short period going only through a sequence of three numbers.

The output sequences can be grouped into two types: maximum and nonmaximum sequences. For a given number of stages (n) in a register there exists a maximum possible period for any output sequence before this sequence begins to repeat itself, and its length is $2^n - 1$.

The feedback connection determines whether the output sequence will be maximal or nonmaximal. Recently, publication of the most extensive tables to date makes available all feedback connections for a maximum sequence up to degree 17. (See, e.g., [6,7,8].)

Some maximum-length shift-register feedbacks are shown in Table 17.1. Each binary maximum-length shift-register sequence generated by modulo 2 feedback has significant pseudorandom properties which often justify substitution of such sequences for true random sequences [7].

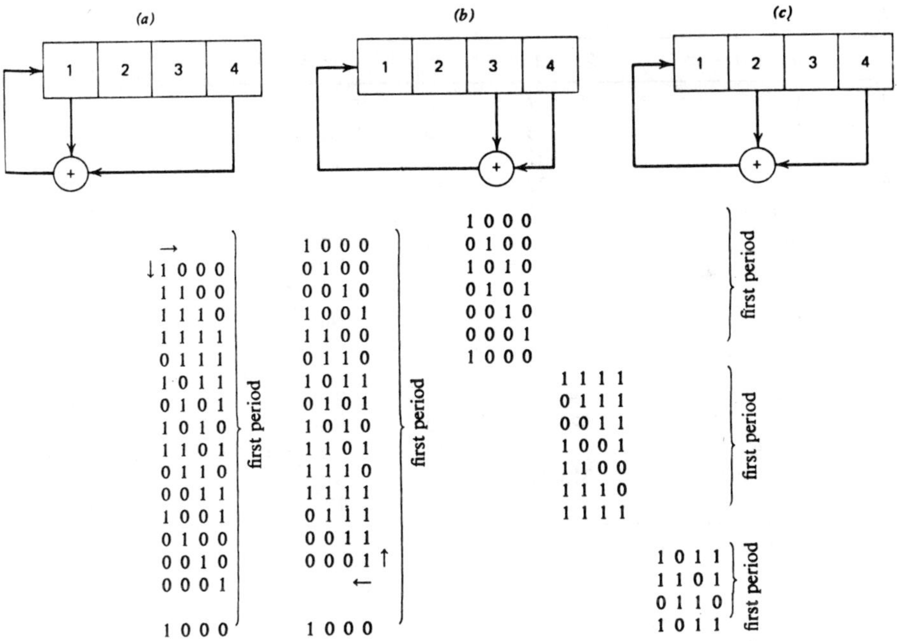

Figure 17.13 *Shift-register generation of pseudorandom numbers.*

In each period of maximum-length sequence, the shift register assumes every possible state (binary number in the register) except for the all-zero state. In each period $2^n - 1$ bits, the number of 1's is, therefore, 2^{n-1} and exceeds the number of 0's by exactly one.

Figure 17.13 shows the dependence of the shift-register pseudorandom sequence on the initial state. For the maximum-length configurations, different initial shift-register states produce identical but delayed sequences. For nonmaximal configuration, different states will belong to different sequences.

Specifically, an n-bit register with modulo 2 feedback can generate $\sigma(p)/n$ different maximum length sequences, where $\sigma(n)$ (Euler's number) is the number of positive integers less than n and relatively prime to n [9]). Generation of some of these sequences requires two or more modulo 2 adders. Table 17.1 lists only simple configuration with a single modulo 2 adder [7]. One can find more extensive tables in the literature.

17.8 PSEUDORANDOM TRANSFORMATION

Each signal describing an event can be expressed as a digital number that we call a descriptor. Any descriptor D may be presented as a polynomial

TABLE 17.1

n	m or $n - m$	$2^n - 1$	n	m or $n - m$	$2^n - 1$
3	1	7	18	7	262,143
4	1	15	19	None	—
5	2	31	20	3	1,048,575
6	1	63	21	2	2,097,151
7	1 or 3	127	22	1	4,194,303
8	None	—	23	5 or 9	8,388,607
9	4	511	24	None	—
10	3	1,023	25	3 or 7	33,554,431
11	2	2,047	26	None	—
12	None	—	27	None	—
13	None	—	28	3, 9, or 13	268,435,455
14	None	—	29	2	536,870,911
15	1, 4, or 7	32,767	30	None	—
16	None	—	31	3, 6, 7, or 13	2,147,483,647
17	3, 5, or 6	131,071	32	None	—
			33	13	8,589,934,591

$$D(x) = a_d x^d + a_{d-1} x^{d-1} + \cdots + a_2 x^2 + a_1 x + a_0$$

where $a_0, a_1, \ldots, a_d$ are elements of the Galois field GF(2) and can be either 0 or 1. For example, the descriptor $D_5 = 000 \cdots 0101$, whose decimal equivalent is 5, will have coefficients

$$a_0 = a_2 = 1 \qquad a_1 = a_3 = a_4 = \cdots = a_d = 0$$

By multiplying the polynomial $D(x)$ of degree d by the polynomial $S(x)$ of the degree s, one obtains the polynomial $M(x)$ of degree $d + s$. If all the coefficients $b_0, b_1, \ldots, b_{s-2}, b_{s-1}$ of the polynomial $S(x)$ are equal to zero, and only $b_s = 1$, the polynomial $M(x)$ will be

$$M(x) = c_d x^{s+d} + \cdots + c_2 x^{s+2} + c_1 x^{s+1} + c_0 x^s$$

where $c_0, c_1, \ldots, c_d$ are also elements of a field GF(2) and can be either 0 or 1.

The polynomial $M(x)$ is in fact the descriptor D, shifted to the left for s places. By dividing the polynomial $M(x)$ by the polynomial $T(x)$, where $s \geq t$,

$$M(x) = Q(x)T(x) + R(x)$$

The remainder $R(x)$ will be of a degree less than t. Experimentations with different spectra and different polynomials $T(x)$ have shown that the remainder $R(x)$ might be used as a descriptor address on the list. Two adjacent descriptors in the physical field of any size will give two remainders far away from each other for almost any possible polynomials of degree t. The descriptor may come from any point of the physical field, and its remainder will always present one of 2^t different memory addresses. If the original descriptor $D(x)$ has a degree less than t, after dividing it by $T(x)$ its remainder would be $R(x) = D(x)$. On such descriptors the transformation would not produce the randomizing effect. That is one reason why all descriptors that have a degree less than t have to be first multiplied by $S(x)$. All descriptors have to be multiplied by the same polynomial because of the increase of the physical field and the distance between adjacent descriptors.

One example of transformation is presented in Figure 17.14. In this example the descriptor $D(x)$ corresponds to decimal 7, and $T(x)$ is of the fourth degree. The first four shifts present the multiplication by $S(x)$, and the shifts from the fourth to the seventh present division by the polynomial $T(x)$ with the action through appropriate feedbacks (determined by the polynomial $T(x)$). The remainder $R(x)$ which is a polynomial of a degree less than or equal to $t - 1$ represents the t-tuple of the address of the descriptor $D(x)$. In this example $R(x)$ presents the address 1101, which corresponds to the decimal number 13. The total number of different addresses is $2^t = 2^4 = 16$.

The number of different addresses depends on the degree of the polynomial t. The polynomials useful for transformation must have $a_t = a_0 = 1$. Hence there are 2^{t-1} different polynomials of the degree t. In the example shown, one can have $2^{t-1} = 2^3 = 8$ different polynomials:

$$T_0(x) = x^4 + 0 + 0 + 0 + 1$$

$$\vdots$$

$$T_4(x) = x^4 + x^3 + 0 + 0 + 1$$

$$\vdots$$

$$T_7(x) = x^4 + x^3 + x^2 + x + 1$$

17.9 PROPERTIES OF PSEUDORANDOM TRANSFORMATION THROUGH THE DIVISION OF POLYNOMIALS

The properties of transformation have been thoroughly investigated by Souček et al. [10,11] through the simulation by a digital computer. Figure 17.15 shows the field of addresses produced by descriptors 0–256 (field of descriptors (16 × 16))^3. Figure 17.15 shows the position of descriptors that

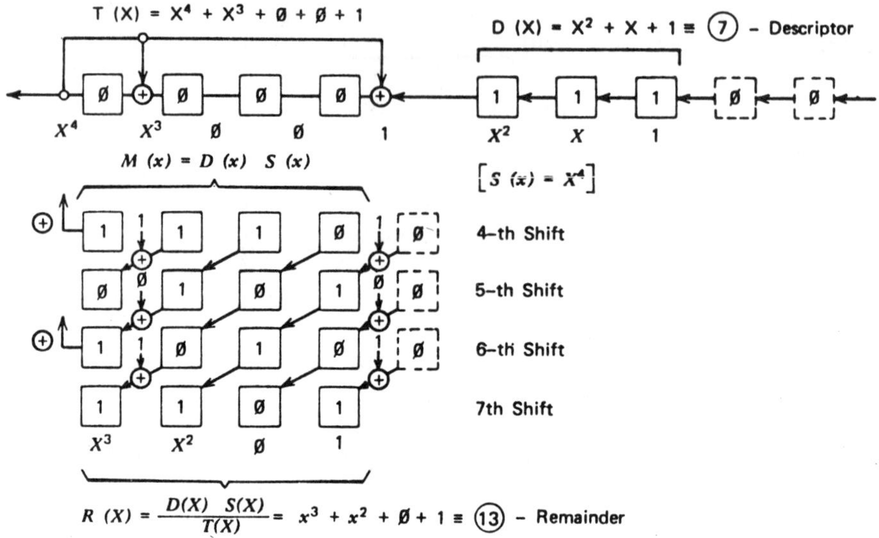

Figure 17.14 *Pseudorandom digital transformation.*

are producing the same address A (or L). Those descriptors are congruent modulo $T(x)$, and they form the same residue class [12].

There are 2^t different residue classes. The descriptors that belong to the same residue class are pseudorandomly distributed between 0 and 256. Their pattern presents the spectrum for which the method would not work, but which is improbable for experimental data.

Changing the structure of the polynomial by changing the coefficients $a_{t-1}, a_{t-2}, \ldots, a_1$, the number of possible different addresses will not change; it is always 2^t. However some structures might produce the pattern resembling the shape of spectra. To avoid even this little probable case, the selection of polynomials has been done. Through computer simulation one can obtain the polynomials of the degree t having the maximum period 2^t by using a circuit for counting in a Galois field code. Such a circuit is shown in Figure 17.14 and consists in this example of a four-stage shift register with a proper feedback through exclusive OR gates (denoted by + sign). For the best feedback a four-stage shift register can have a maximum period of 16, producing 16 different addresses, which are elements of the Galois field GF(2^4).

In general, the Galois field of 2^t elements GF(2^t) may be formed as the field of polynomials over GF(2) modulo $a_t x^t + a_{t-1}x^{t-1} + \cdots + a_1 x + a_0$. This field corresponds to the 2^t different addresses.

The polynomial $T(x)$, giving the maximum period with a circuit for count-

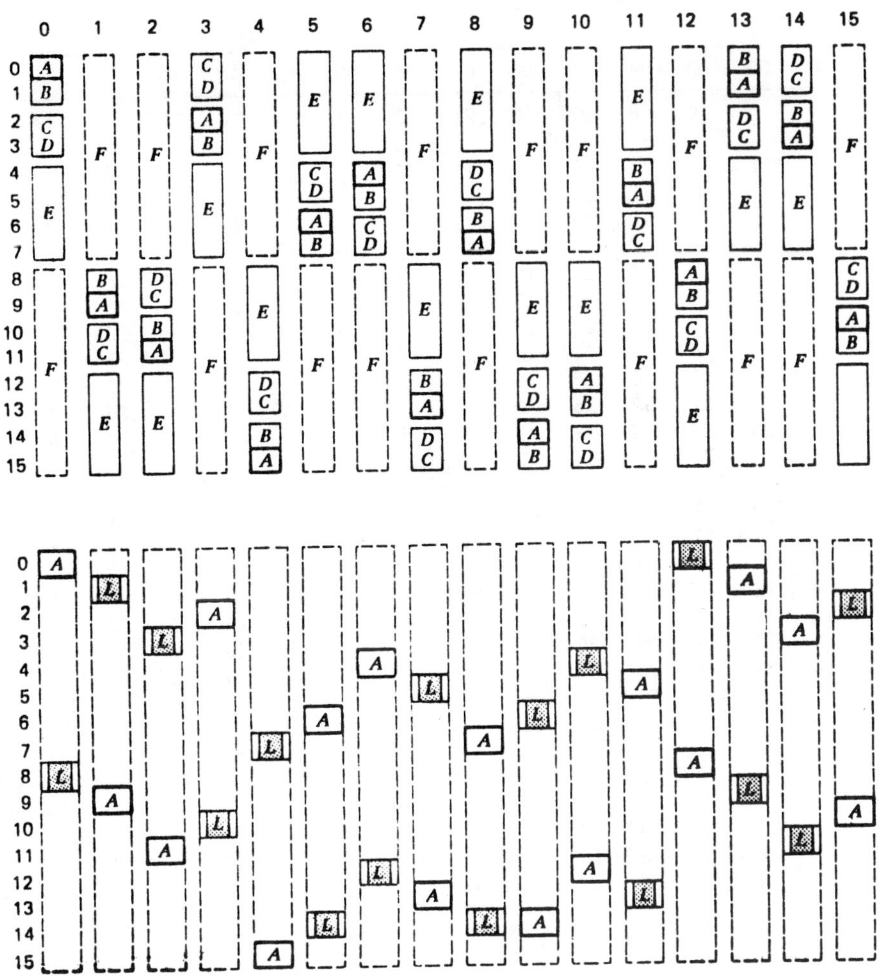

Figure 17.15 *Position of the descriptors producing the same address* A *(or* L*).*

ing in a Galois field code, produces a pseudorandom pattern. Hence, descriptors corresponding to the same residue class are distributed pseudorandomly on the number line.

Table 17.2 shows the pattern of 1024 addresses generated through division from the descriptor field 32 × 32. The polynomial has the form $T(x) = x^5 + x^4 + 0 + x^2 + x + 1$. In the first column is a "first-degree pattern" produced by descriptors 0–31. There are $2^t = 32$ different first degree patterns, forming the "second-degree pattern," covering the whole Table 17.2. The R denotes a few descriptors belonging to the same residue class, producing addresses 0 and 27, which correspond to those classes.

TABLE 17.2

00	01	02	03	04	05	06	07	08	09	10	11	12	13	14	15
0	7	14	9	28	27	18	21	3	4	13	10	31	24	17	22
	R					R									
27	28	21	18	7	0	9	14	24	31	22	17	4	3	10	13
13	10	3	4	17	22	31	24	14	0	0	7	18	21	28	27
22	17	24	31	10	13	4	3	21	18	27	28	9	14	7	0
26	29	20	19	6	1	8	15	25	30	23	16	5	2	11	12
1	6	15	8	29	26	19	20	2	5	12	11	30	25	16	23
23	16	25	30	11	12	5	2	20	19	26	29	8	15	6	1
12	11	2	5	16	23	30	25	15	8	1	6	19	20	29	26
15	8	1	6	19	20	29	26	12	11	2	5	16	23	30	25
20	19	26	29	8	15	6	1	23	16	25	30	11	12	5	2
2	5	12	11	30	25	16	23	1	6	15	8	29	26	19	20
25	30	23	16	5	2	11	12	26	29	20	19	6	1	8	15
21	18	27	28	9	14	7	0	22	17	24	31	10	13	4	3
			R					R							
14	9	0	7	18	21	28	27	13	10	3	4	17	22	31	24
24	31	22	17	4	3	10	13	27	28	21	18	7	0	9	14
									R						
3	4	13	10	31	24	17	22	0	7	14	9	28	27	18	21
30	25	16	23	2	5	12	11	29	26	19	20	1	6	15	8
5	2	11	12	25	30	23	16	6	1	8	15	26	29	20	19
19	20	29	26	15	8	1	6	16	23	30	25	12	11	2	5
8	15	6	1	20	19	26	29	11	12	5	2	23	16	25	30
4	3	10	13	24	31	22	17	7	0	9	14	27	28	21	18
31	24	17	22	3	4	13	10	28	27	18	21	0	7	14	9
9	14	7	0	21	18	27	28	10	13	4	3	22	17	24	31
				R			R								
18	21	28	27	14	9	0	7	17	22	31	24	13	10	3	4
17	22	31	24	13	10	3	4	18	21	28	27	14	9	0	7
10	13	4	3	22	17	24	31	9	14	7	0	21	18	27	28
28	27	18	21	0	7	14	9	31	24	17	22	3	4	13	10
		R			R										
7	0	9	14	27	28	21	18	4	3	10	13	24	31	22	17
11	12	5	2	23	16	25	30	8	15	6	1	20	19	26	29
16	23	30	25	12	11	2	5	19	20	29	26	15	8	1	6
6	1	8	15	26	29	20	19	5	2	11	12	25	30	23	16
29	26	19	20	1	6	15	8	30	25	16	23	2	5	12	11

17.10 ASSOCIATIVE AND TRANSFORMATION MODE ANALYZERS

Souček, Bonačić, and Čuljat [11] have investigated different randomizing transformations, and have found that the most suitable for nuclear spectroscopy is the transformation based on the division of polynomials. The transformation can be realized as a part of a computer data taking interrupt routine, or as a hardware box between analog-to-digital converters and a computer.

By passing through a transformation box, each descriptor produces a pseudorandom address into which it is stored. It would be ideal if any distri-

TABLE 17.2 *(Continued)*

16	17	18	19	20	21	22	23	24	25	26	27	28	29	30	31
6	1	8	15	26	29	20	19	5	2	11	12	25	30	23	16
29	26	19	20	1	6	15	8	30	25	16	23	2	5	12	11
11	12	5	2	23	16	25	30	8	15	6	1	20	19	26	29
16	23	30	25	12	11	2	5	19	20	29	26	15	8	1	6
28	27	18	21	0	7	14	9	31	24	17	22	3	4	13	10
7	0	9	14	27	28	21	18	4	3	10	13	24	31	22	17
17	22	31	24	13	10	3	4	18	21	28	27	14	9	0	7
10	13	4	3	22	17	24	31	9	14	7	0	21	18	27	28
9	14	7	0	21	18	27	28	10	13	4	3	22	17	24	31
18	21	28	27	14	9	0	7	17	22	31	24	13	10	3	4
4	3	10	13	24	31	22	17	7	0	9	14	27	28	21	18
31	24	17	22	3	4	13	10	28	27	18	21	0	7	14	9
19	20	29	26	15	8	1	6	16	23	30	25	12	11	2	5
8	15	6	1	20	19	26	29	11	12	5	2	23	16	25	30
30	25	16	23	2	5	12	11	29	26	19	20	1	6	15	8
5	2	11	12	25	30	23	16	6	1	8	15	26	29	20	19
24	31	22	17	4	3	10	13	27	28	21	18	7	0	9	14
3	4	13	10	31	24	17	22	0	7	14	9	28	27	18	21
21	18	27	28	9	14	7	0	22	17	24	31	10	13	4	3
14	9	0	7	18	21	28	27	13	10	3	4	17	22	31	24
2	5	12	11	30	25	16	23	1	6	15	8	29	26	19	20
25	30	23	16	5	2	11	12	26	29	20	19	6	1	8	15
15	8	1	6	19	20	29	26	12	11	2	5	16	23	30	25
20	19	26	29	8	15	6	1	23	16	25	30	11	12	5	2
23	16	25	30	11	12	5	2	20	19	26	29	8	15	6	1
12	11	2	5	16	23	30	25	15	8	1	6	19	20	29	26
26	29	20	19	6	1	8	15	25	30	23	16	5	2	11	12
1	6	15	8	29	26	19	20	2	5	12	11	30	25	16	23
13	10	3	4	17	22	31	24	14	9	0	7	18	21	28	27
22	17	24	31	10	13	4	3	21	18	27	28	9	14	7	0
0	7	14	9	28	27	18	21	3	4	13	10	31	24	17	22
27	28	21	18	7	0	9	14	24	31	22	17	4	3	10	13

bution of descriptors (spectral shape) would produce a uniform distribution of address throughout the memory. For practical spectra there is, however, the possibility, of two or more descriptors being transformed to the same address. Because of that, the transformation is used only to generate the address on the list at which to start searching. This method makes almost-direct addressing possible, as in conventional analyzers, and high utilization of the memory space, as in associative systems.

The transformation mode analyzer is specially suitable for spectra such as

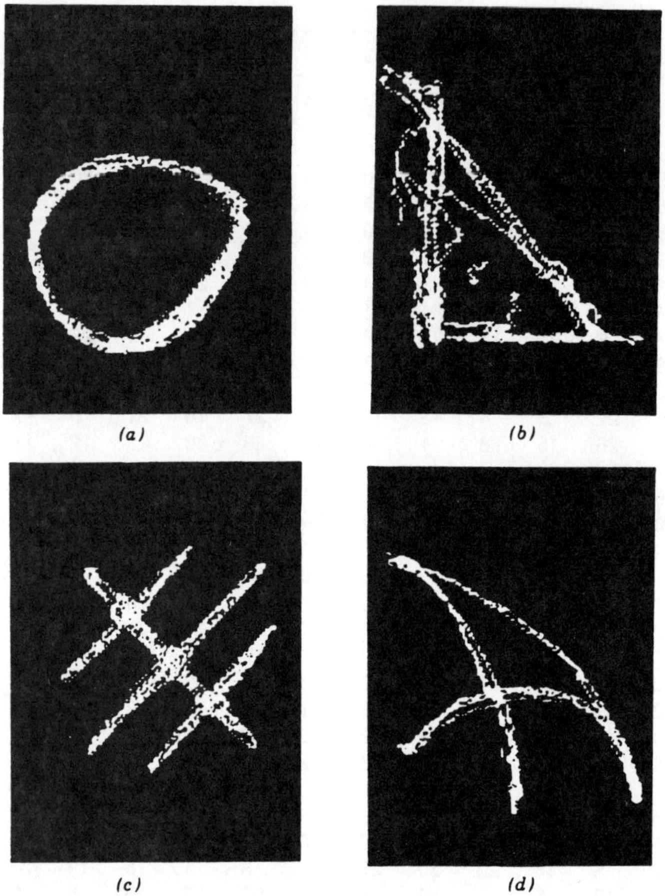

Figure 17.16 *Spectra with a great range but limited number of descriptors;* (a) D + P – P + P + N, *21.1 MeV, 34°, –34°;* (b) *van de Graaff experiment* $^6Li + {}^3He$ – P + P + N, *3 MeV, 37.5°, –37.5°;* (c) *biological spectra;* (d) *two-parameter spectrum* $^3He(^3He,2p)^4He$.

in Figure 17.16. Those spectra are simulated by a CRT-light pen system, according to the known results of the following experiments:

1. $D + P \rightarrow P + P + N$ 21,1 MeV, 34°, −34°.
2. Van de Graaff experiment: ^{6}Li + ^{3}He → $P + \alpha + \alpha$, 3 MeV, 37.5°, −37.5°.
3. Biological spectra.
4. Two-parameter spectrum ^{3}He(^{3}He,2p)^{4}He.

Each of those spectra contains 1024 descriptors in the 128 × 128 field. The descriptors have been fed through the programmed transformation box in the computer, always producing practically uniform distribution of 1024 different addresses.

17.11 CONCLUSIONS

Some nonlinear dynamic systems generate seemingly random, but actually deterministic, processes. Such a process is called chaos. The recent discovery of chaos opens a new dimension in science and technology. Many phenomena believed to be random can be now analyzed as a deterministic chaos. The outcome of the chaotic process very strongly depends on a small change in the initial conditions. Through amplification of a small fluctuation or noise, chaos provides natural system with access to novelty and variability. Biological evolution, cognitive processes, associations, thinking, and free will could use chaotic mechanisms. In this way, seemingly random changes are generated. Yet the changes are under control of the chaotic mechanism, and after the transition, the process converges into the basins of attraction.

Continuous chaos generators transform samples over nonlinear continuous functions. Logical chaos generators deal with individual bits or fits within the sample or word. They map the word, using logical operations. In the case of fuzzy logic, the fuzzy unit or fit, expressed on a scale of 0 to 1, is used in the same way as a bit (0 or 1) in normal, crisp logic.

Babloyantz and Destexe [13,14] look for chaos in brain functions. They analyze typical episodes of electrical activity of the human brain, as recorded from an electroencephalogram (EEG), together with the corresponding phase portraits. This is a new approach in brain and mind research.

Koza, in Chapter 10, shows how genetic programming could be used to find the function that fits a given sample of data. In the case of chaos, often the functions of interest are recursive in the sense that the sequence of values of the function over time depends on one or more initial condition values. Koza [15] takes the example of the logistic function $x(t) = 4x(t-1)(1-x(t-1))$ over the unit interval [0,1], with $x(0) = 0.26$. The object was to discover the function for time steps 1, 2, . . . , 50. The terminal PREV (see Chapter 10) allows access to the value of the function at a previous time step.

In one run, the best individual in the sixth generation was

```
(*PREV(*2.0(*2.0(-1.0 PREV))))
```

Grabec, in Chapter 18, describes the process of learning chaotic dynamics in neural networks. This chapter shows how logical chaos could be used as a base for intelligent system design. A pseudoassociative adaptive real-time data acquisition system is discussed.

The features of continuous and of logical chaos are summarized as follows:

Continuous Chaos

- Seemingly random deterministic process,
- Nonperiodic,
- Transforms samples over nonlinear continuous functions,
- Strongly depends on initial conditions,
- Strongly amplifies noise,
- Orbits converge into strange attractors,
- Exhibits the features of bifurcation and fractals,
- Exhibits the features of stretching and folding of strange attractors.

Logical Chaos

- Pseudorandom deterministic sequence,
- Periodic, a fraction of the process could be considered nonperiodic,
- Maps the bits of the word, using logical operations,
- Strongly depends on initial conditions,
- Noise immune,
- Basins of attraction dispersed over the state-space.

REFERENCES

[1] E. N. Lorenz, Deterministic non-periodic flows, *J. Atmos. Sci.* **20,** 130–141 (1963).

[2] C. Sparrow, *The Lorenz Equations: Bifurcations, Chaos, and Strange Attractors,* Springer-Verlag, New York, 1982.

[3] R. May, Simple mathematical models with very complicated dynamics, *Nature* 261, 259–467 (1976).

[4] J. Yorke and T. Y. Li, Period three implies chaos, *Amer. Math. Monthly,* 82, 985–992 (1975).

[5] B. Mandelbrot, *The Fractal Geometry of Nature,* Freeman, New York, 1977.

[6] W. W. Peterson, *Error-Correcting Codes,* MIT Press, Cambridge, Mass., 1961.

[7] G. Korn, *Random-Process Simulation and Measurement,* McGraw-Hill, New York, 1966.

[8] R. M. Holford, *IEEE Trans. Nucl. Sci.,* NS16, 386 (1969).

[9] S. W. Golomb, "Sequences with Randomness Properties," Internal Rep., Glen L. Martin, Baltimore, Md. (1955).

[10] B. Souček, V. Bonačić, K. Čuljat, I. Radnic, Computer System for Pseudo-random Transformation of Nuclear Data, *Proc. Internat. Conf. on Nucl. Electr.,* Paris (1968).

[11] B. Souček, V. Bonačić, and K. Čuljat, Million Channel Pulse Height Analyzer through Pseudo-random Digital Transformation, *Nucl. Instr. Meth.* 66, 202 (1968).

[12] V. Bonačić, B. Souček, and K. Čuljat, Pseudo-random Digital Transformation, *Nucl. Instr. Meth.* 66, 213 (1968).

[13] A. Babloyantz, "Chaotic Dynamics in Brain Activity," in E. Baser, Ed., *Chaos in Brain Function,* Springer Verlag, 1990.

[14] A. Babloyantz and A. Destexhe, Chaos in neural networks, *IEEE Conf. on Neural Networks,* Vol. IV, 31, 39 (1987).

[15] J. R. Koza, "Genetic Programming," Rep. No. STAN-CS-90-1314, Stanford University (1990).

CHAPTER 18

Prediction of Chaotic Dynamical Phenomena by a Neural Network

IGOR GRABEC

18.1 INTRODUCTION

The aim of the chapter is to show how one can develop information processing systems capable of modeling chaotic dynamical phenomena on the basis of measurements and to predict the time dependence of corresponding chaotic observables. For this purpose some theoretical methods for the description of chaotic phenomena are presented in the first part of the chapter. From them instructions about the basic processing steps needed to predict dynamical phenomena are obtained. A corresponding system is then described, which includes a neural networklike memory, a predictor, two shift registers, and a comparator. An internal empirical model of the phenomenon observed is formed in the memory. It is represented by a set of memorized prototype transitions between successive states of the input time-dependent signal, which can also change chaotically. The adaptation of prototypes corresponds to a self-organization process that maximally preserves information obtained by measurements. In the predictor the forthcoming signal is estimated from the prototypes. The system operation is demonstrated on a chaotic signal generated by various chaotic generators. By minimizing the prediction error determined by the comparator, we can select a proper embedding dimension of the corresponding chaotic attractor, while the maximal Lyapunov coefficient can be estimated from the discrepancy between the predicted and the input signal.

Dynamic, Genetic, and Chaotic Programming, By Branko Souček and the IRIS Group.
ISBN 0-471-55717-X

The evolution of natural and technical sciences over the past centuries has been closely related to experimental study and modeling of natural phenomena. From this evolution the fundamental concept of physical exploration has emerged, which announces that the primary source of information about Nature can only be measurements, while the properties of natural phenomena can be described by relations between measured observables. The most significant feature of the physical description of natural phenomena is that an unknown property can be quantitatively predicted from another one if the relation between the corresponding variables is known. For analytical investigations it is most appropriate if the relations between variables are expressed mathematically as abstract models or physical laws, but for applications several other models, for example mechanical or electrical, can be even more convenient. The development of information processing systems in recent decades has made feasible automatic measurements and simple representation of existing mathematical models by electronic systems. However, future prospects of scientific evolution lie in the development of intelligent systems that could form models of natural phenomena automatically by themselves, and eventually be able to formulate them as physical laws in terms of abstract relations [1,2]. At present this goal is approached from two apparently opposite directions. The first one stems from artificial intelligence and is based on simulation of scientific exploration by applying sophisticated methods of mathematical logic [3,4]. In contrast, the second approach follows natural evolution and tries to construct from very primitive elements, called artificial neurons, more complex networks that could operate like modelers of natural phenomena due to adaptation to influences from the surroundings [5,6,7]. From an analytical point of view the former approach might seem more advanced and attractive, but from an application point of view the latter appears to be simpler and more convenient for empirical modeling and control in various areas of the technical world. In this chapter we follow the second approach and apply a system with a neural network structure for modeling dynamic phenomena [8].

Among various problems related to automatic modeling the prediction of chaotic dynamic phenomena is the most embarrassing [9,10]. The main reason for this is the inherent instability of chaotic phenomena, which causes irregular variability of the appertaining physical observables [11]. Moreover, chaotic phenomena are often observed in complex systems that cannot be simply modeled by analytical methods. As a typical example from engineering technology we can mention a drilling manufacturing process that includes intricate tool and machine geometry, the physically cumbersome deformation of cut material and tool friction, complicated dynamic properties, and so on [12]. As there are many important processes of this kind in engineering, technology, economics, biology, and medicine [11–17], it is challenging to look for a complement to analytical modeling and prediction. For this purpose we apply here empirical modeling stemming from nonparametric regression [1,2].

Although chaotic phenomena exhibit apparently stochastic variability, it is a common feature that they usually also exhibit some degree of order, or structure, that makes incomplete prediction feasible [11]. Our main task is to show how this can be done entirely on an empirical basis without applying any prior information about the system model. We try to extract instruction for the solution of this problem from the fundamentals of the deterministic chaos description presented in the next section. This leads us to the development of a neural-network-like information processing system. It is capable of building a model of chaotic phenomenon by a self-organized adaptation to the input signal and of using it further to predict the same signal. The system structure and operation are described in Section 18.3, which is followed by the presentation of experimental results.

18.2 FUNDAMENTALS OF THE DETERMINISTIC CHAOS DESCRIPTION

18.2.1 Instability of Chaotic Systems

We consider a discrete dynamical system, the state of which can be described by a set of physical variables $\mathbf{X} = \{x_1, \ldots, x_D\}$ representing a point in a D-dimensional phase space. The system dynamics is described by a physical law, relating the velocity of a point in the phase space with its state vector $\mathbf{X}$ and the set of system parameters $\mathbf{p} = \{p_1, p_2, \ldots\}$ [11,16]:

$$\frac{d\mathbf{X}}{dt} = \mathbf{F}(\mathbf{X};\mathbf{p}) \tag{18.1}$$

We further assume that the system is autonomous; the dynamics is thus completely determined by its structure, and therefore the function $\mathbf{F}$ does not depend explicitly on time. By the dynamical law (18.1) and an initial state $\mathbf{X}(0) = \mathbf{X}_0$, a trajectory $\mathbf{X}(t; \mathbf{X}_0)$ is uniquely determined in the phase space. In many cases of practical interest the motion develops in a limited part of the phase space, so the condition $|\mathbf{X}| \leq L$ is fulfilled, where L denotes trajectory span.

Let us consider two trajectories $\mathbf{X}_1$ and $\mathbf{X}_2$ originating from two nearby initial points, and let us analyze positions for a sequence of times $(t_1, t_2, \ldots)$ as indicated in Figure 18.1. With respect to the behavior of distances $d_{12}(t_i) = |\mathbf{X}_1(t_i) - \mathbf{X}_2(t_i)|$, the dynamical systems can be divided into two groups. The first group includes examples where the distance on average increases with increasing time exponentially or more quickly, while the second group includes other examples [11,16]. In the first case the trajectories diverge, in the second they converge. Representative systems from both groups are various self-excitable oscillators in unstable equilibrium and a damped pendulum, respectively. Let us further assume that the initial state

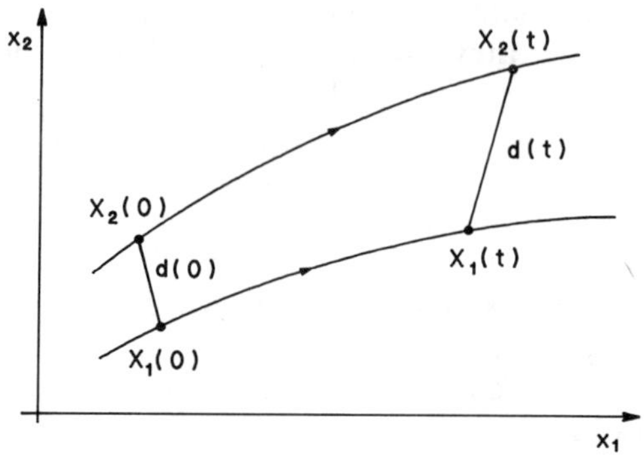

Figure 18.1 *Example of trajectories in the two-dimensional phase space.*

is not determined precisely. In this case we just specify a confining region where the system state can exist. This region changes with increasing time as determined by the flow of trajectories. For a system of the first group the width of the confining region spreads exponentially or more quickly with time and reaches the trajectory span in a finite time interval. This means that after this time, the system state can take place anywhere in the region of all possible states. It is thus practically undetermined, although the corresponding dynamical law is deterministically described. Such a system is called unstable [11,15,16]. The accuracy of the experimental determination of the system state is generally limited. Due to experimental errors, an initial state cannot be exactly described or reproduced. If the experiments on the same unstable system are repeated, then essentially different states can be observed after finite time intervals although the initial states differ less than experimental errors. Due to the divergence of trajectories the behavior of an unstable system is thus unpredictable for long prediction times. If the trajectories diverge everywhere in the phase space, then experimentally unobservable influences can generally lead to unpredictable or chaotic behavior [11,15,16].

Instability, and with it the possibility of chaos development, can be quantitatively characterized by the rate of trajectory divergence in the phase space. Let us select a point $\mathbf{X}_0$ in a phase space and a swarm of possible initial states distributed on a hypersphere of radius d_0 around it, as shown in Figure 18.2. By following the trajectories from the initial points, we obtain a new set of points that, after a short time, is distributed on an approximately ellipsoidal surface. By its principal axes d_k the spectrum of characteristic or Lyapunov exponents is defined by [18;16, p. 277]

$$\lambda_k = \lim_{d_0 \to \infty} \lim_{t \to \infty} \frac{1}{t} \ln \left[\frac{d_k(t)}{d_0} \right] \tag{18.2}$$

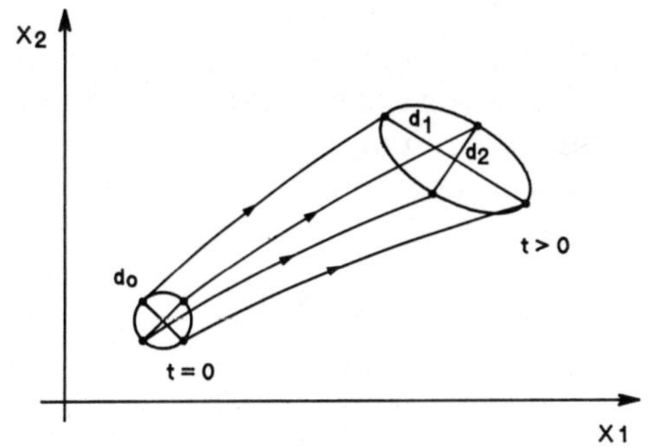

Figure 18.2 *The flow in the phase space changes the form of a confining region of a swarm of representative system states.*

It is convenient to represent the spectrum in a decreasing order ($\lambda_{max}, \ldots, \lambda_{min}$). These exponents characterize the divergence of trajectories originating from the vicinity of the point $\mathbf{X}_0$ in the phase space and generally depend on the position of the selected point. In order to characterize a global property, average values are usually applied. A necessary condition for chaotic behavior is that at least one Lyapunov exponent be positive, which describes an unstable dynamical system [11,15,16].

Observation of distances between simultaneously selected points on trajectories offers an additional possibility of quantitatively characterizing dynamical systems by specifying changes in the differentially small volume element of the phase space. Let us thus now imagine a swarm of points inside a small D-dimensional cube of side Δx_{io} and volume $\Delta V_0 = \Pi_{i=1}^{D} \Delta x_{io}$ that covers them. Following the flow of points in the phase space in a time interval t, this volume becomes

$$\Delta V'(t) = \sum_{i=1}^{D} \frac{\partial x_i'}{\partial x_i} \Delta V_0 \tag{18.3}$$

The average rate of change of the volume element is then defined by [16, p. 382]

$$\Lambda = \lim_{t \to \infty} \frac{1}{t} \ln \left| \frac{\Delta V'(t)}{\Delta V_0} \right| \tag{18.4}$$

The system is conservative if $\Lambda = 0$, and nonconservative or dissipative if $\Lambda < 0$. It has been shown elsewhere [11;16, p. 383] that the average rate of divergence is equal to the sum of Lyapunov exponents:

$$\Lambda = \sum_{k=1}^{N} \lambda_k \tag{18.5}$$

Many technically important systems are dissipative, so we further limit our treatment to this class [14–17]. The chaotic behavior of a dissipative system can be observed if at least one of the Lyapunov exponents is positive, but at the same time their sum must be negative due to a dissipative property. This indicates that a one-dimensional system cannot be chaotic. Moreover, it has been found by Poincaré and Bendixon [19] that chaos is not possible in a two-dimensional system, so continuous chaotic flows can develop only in three- or higher-dimensional dissipative systems. However, the dynamics described by discrete maps can exhibit chaotic behavior at lower dimensions as well [11]. It is apparently paradoxical that unpredictable irregular behavior can appear in systems described by deterministic natural law (18.1); to emphasize this property, the phenomenon is called *deterministic chaos* [11].

When following the flow of trajectories originating from a widespread set of initial points, one can often observe that they asymptotically tend to some specifically formed region called the attractor. Well-known examples in three-dimensional space are a point attractor or a focus for a case of damped oscillations, a cycle for a case of undamped oscillations, and a torus for a case of multidimensional cyclical motion [11,15,16]. The corresponding spectra of Lyapunov coefficients can be described by the sign-schemes $(-, -, -)$, $(0, -, -)$, $(0, 0, -)$. For dissipative chaotic systems the attractor exhibits rather strange properties. Due to system instability the trajectories must diverge in the phase space, but at the same time differentially small volumes must contract on average. This can happen simultaneously if at least one extension of the volume element increases while others decrease at such a high rate that the volume element also decreases. An example of the corresponding spectrum of Lyapunov exponents is represented by the scheme $(+, 0, -)$. Due to the divergence of trajectories one could expect that the motion cannot be limited. But the divergence is just an average local property [16]. The typical span of a strange attractor can still be limited if its geometrical form is stretched and folded over on itself. This stretching and folding is reminiscent of a baker kneading dough and leads to an infinitely leaved structure of strange attractors [11,16]. The structure of leaves in a sense preserves some general properties of motion in a phase space, and therefore chaotic motion appears qualitatively self-similar and to some extent ordered and also partially predictable [20]. Another argument for a kind of predictability is that the applicable physical laws can be deterministically described by function (18.1). We can therefore conclude that the main goal of modeling an observed chaotic phenomenon should not be an exact reproduction of the trajectories, which are, in any case, unstable, but, as far as possible, a correct description of the function $\mathbf{F}(\mathbf{x}, \mathbf{p})$, which we henceforth call a *chaos generator*. Due to the instability of trajectories we can also expect that predicted and really observed trajectories should generally diverge, as approximately described by the maximal Lyapunov exponent [8]. Therefore the correctness of the model can be estimated from the agreement between true and predicted trajectories only in short time intervals.

The simplest example of a dynamical system with diverging trajectories is described by a system of linear differential equations with positive coefficients:

$$\frac{dx_k}{dt} = \lambda_k x_k \tag{18.6}$$

If $_k$ indicates the principal axis corresponding to the Lyapunov exponent λ_k, then such a description can be applied to characterize the local divergence of trajectories around a selected point in a phase space. Trajectories described by the solution $x_k(t) = x_k(0)\exp(\lambda_k t)$ diverge, but they are not confined to a limited part of the phase space. Confinement can be obtained only by including nonlinear terms in Eq. (18.6). From this simple example we can conclude that the nonlinearity of the model is inevitable when treating chaotic phenomena in dissipative systems [11,15,16]. However, the solution of a nonlinear dynamic problem cannot be generally determined by analytical methods, therefore numerical methods must be used. This is also the reason why many properties of deterministic chaos have been discovered only recently by numerical experimentation on computers. A similar conclusion also holds for modeling chaotic systems on the basis of experimental observation, where the irregularity and complexity of experimental data usually require computer-controlled information processing [8].

18.2.2 Characterization of Strange Attractors

A strange attractor is determined by the set of all possible asymptotic trajectories taking place in a limited part of the phase space. Due to the contraction of volume elements caused by the dynamics of dissipative systems, the dimension of the corresponding geometrical structure must be less than the dimension of the phase space. Determination of a proper parameter, whether from the dynamical law or from the records of trajectories, is thus a fundamental task in characterizing strange attractors [11]. A qualitative estimation of attractor dimension can be obtained by observing the set of points where trajectories pierce an arbitrarily selected hypersurface in the phase space. This set, called the *Poincaré section,* is a general aid for characterizing dynamical phenomena [16]. Let us imagine a three-dimensional phase space cut by a simple plane, as shown in Figure 18.3. If the flow develops on a limit cycle or torus, then a typical Poincaré section is a point or a closed loop, respectively.

A strange attractor in a three-dimensional space cannot entirely lie on a two-dimensional surface because in this case chaos is not possible; neither can it fill the phase space because the system is dissipative. Therefore, its structure must be nonhomogeneous, and the Poincaré section can show an isolated point, lines, and continuously distributed points in two dimensions. This indicates that the dimensionality of a strange attractor can describe only its average property [11]. The value of a corresponding parameter can there-

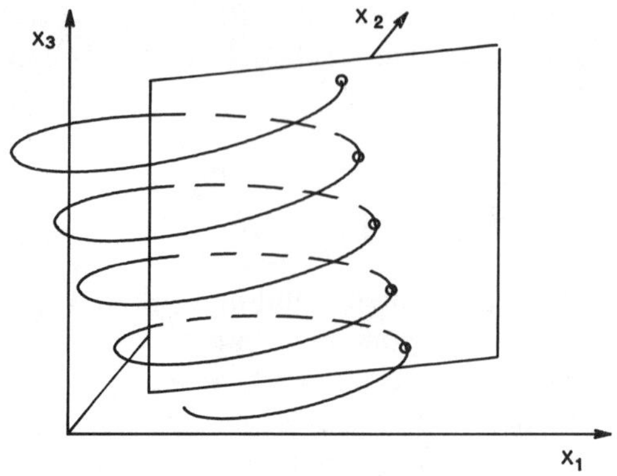

Figure 18.3 *An example of a Poincaré section.*

fore be uneven, and for a three-dimensional phase space should lie between 2 and 3. Very often a proper selection of the cross section reveals a rather simple Poincaré section [15]. By estimating the relation between successive positions $\mathbf{X}_n$ of a trajectory piercing on the plain a transition from a continuous flow description to a discrete map is obtained. The application of the corresponding map

$$\mathbf{X}_{n+1} = \mathbf{f}(\mathbf{X}_n) \tag{18.7}$$

then reduces the dimensionality of the problem and often essentially simplifies the analysis of the dynamic behavior of chaotic systems [11,16]. Very frequently approximately quadratic dependence between successive values of properly selected representative variable can be expressed by the logistic map [11]

$$X_{n+1} = aX_n(1 - X_n) \tag{18.8}$$

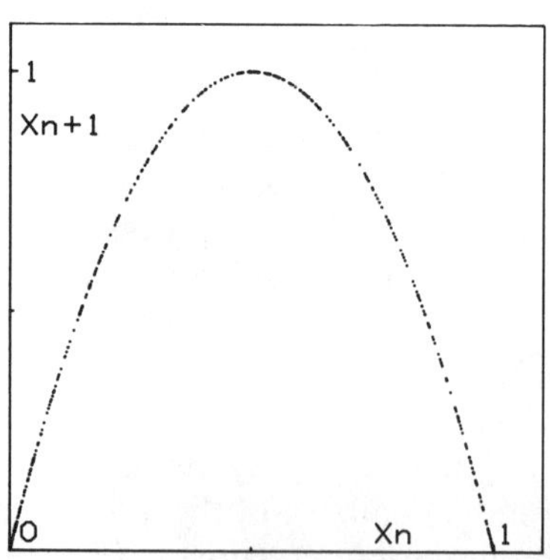

Figure 18.4 *The return map for logistic chaos generator:* $X_{n+1} = 4X_n(1 - X_n)$.

The generic properties of this discrete map have been extensively investigated and can be successfully applied in describing various chaotic phenomena [21]. The map therefore serves as a basic example for demonstrating deterministic chaos. Relations like (18.8) are usually graphically represented as a return map, as shown in Figure 18.4 [15].

A quantitative parameter for the description of attractor dimensionality can be described in the following way [11]. Let us cover the attractor by a net of D-dimensional cube cells of side s, and let us represent a trajectory by a sequence of sample points $\{\mathbf{X}(t_k);\ t_k = kT,\ k = 1, 2, \ldots, D\}$. The distribution of the attractor over the phase space is then described by the probability that a trajectory point takes place in a selected cell:

$$P_i = \lim_{N\to\infty} \frac{N_i}{N} \qquad i = 1, 2, \ldots, M \tag{18.9}$$

Here N_i is the number of sample points in the cell with index i and M is the number of cells applied to cover the attractor. To describe the unhomogeneous attractor structure quantitatively, we define a set of dimensions by the expression

$$D_n = \lim_{s\to 0} \frac{1}{n-1} \frac{\ln\left(\sum_{i=1}^{M} P_i^n\right)}{\ln s} \tag{18.10}$$

For $n = 0$ we get the Hausdorff dimension

$$D_0 = -\lim_{s\to 0} \frac{\ln M}{\ln s} \tag{18.11}$$

The number of cells needed to cover the attractor generally grows with decreasing side length s. Equation (18.11) shows that we can expect for small s a scaling relation

$$M = s^{-D_0} \qquad \text{for } s \to 0 \tag{18.12}$$

Simple geometrical structures like the focus, cycle, or torus are characterized by even values 0, 1, 2 of the Hausdorff dimension, respectively. However, there are many geometrical objects with uneven or fractal dimension and various strange attractors pertain to this group too [22].

For $n = 1$ the dimension is determined by L'Hôpital's rule as the limit for $n \to 1$:

$$D_1 = -\lim_{s\to 0} \frac{S(s)}{\ln s} \tag{18.13}$$

The quantity $S(s)$ is defined by

$$S(s) = -\sum_{i=1}^{M(s)} P_i \ln P_i \tag{18.14}$$

and denotes the entropy of information [17]. It quantitatively describes the information needed to specify the position of an average point of a trajectory in the network of cells if the distribution of probabilities is given by P_i. Therefore, D_1 is called the *information dimension*. For a homogeneous attractor $P_i = 1/M(s)$, $S(s) = \ln M(s)$, and $D_1 = D_0$. Both dimensions coincide in this case, but with the transition to an unhomogeneous structure the entropy of information can only decrease; therefore, more generally, $D_1 \leq D_0$. The similar relation $D_m \leq D_n$ is also valid for higher indexes $m > n$. Equality holds for homogeneous attractors; therefore, attractor nonhomogeneity can be characterized by comparing various dimensions.

Generally, the values of dimensions D_0 and D_1 must be determined numerically. The corresponding limit process $s \to 0$ requires tedious repetition of computations. Less involved is the estimation of D_2, which can be simplified by the following reasoning [11,23].

$$D_2 = \lim_{s \to 0} \frac{\ln \left(\sum_{i=1}^{M} P_i^2 \right)}{\ln s} \tag{18.15}$$

Here P_i^2 denotes the probability that two independently selected points on the attractor take place in the ith cell. The sum $\Sigma_{i=1}^{M} P_i^2$ then corresponds to the probability that two points anywhere on the attractor pertain to the same cell. This value is approximately equal to the probability that the distance between two arbitrary selected points of the attractor is less than s or

$$C(s) = \sum_{i=1}^{M} P_i^2 = \lim_{N \to \infty} \frac{1}{N^2} [\text{number of pairs } ij \text{ with } |\mathbf{X}_i - \mathbf{X}_j| < s] \tag{18.16}$$

This quantity is called the correlation integral and describes the number of correlated pairs of points inside a hypersphere of radius s in the phase space. If the points are homogeneously distributed on a line, surface, and so on, inside a sphere then D_2 scales like s, s^2, and so on. The correlation exponent obtained from the scaling relation $C(s) = s^{D_2}$ as

$$D_2 = \lim_{s \to 0} \frac{\ln C(s)}{\ln s} \tag{18.17}$$

can be simply evaluated. Due to its relation with the correlation integral C, the exponent D_2 is called the *correlation dimension*. It is most widely applied for estimating the dimensionality of strange attractors [23].

Dimensions D_n characterize the statical properties of attractors. The partition of the phase space into cells is also applicable for describing the dynamic properties of the motion on an attractor. For this purpose we first define the joint probability $P_{i_0,i_1,\ldots,i_n}$ that the points $(\mathbf{X}(t_k); k = 1, \ldots, N)$ take place in cells with indexes $i_0, i_1, \ldots, i_n$. Similar to Eq. (18.14) the entropy of joint information is defined by [11,16]

$$K_n = - \sum_{i_0,i_1,\ldots,i_n} P_{i_0,i_1,\ldots,i_n} \ln P_{i_0,i_1,\ldots,i_n} \tag{18.18}$$

The difference $\Delta K_n = K_{n+1} - K_n$ describes how much information must be obtained in order to specify the state in the $(n + 1)$st cell provided the sequence of states is in the cells with indexes $i_0, i_1, \ldots, i_n$; ΔK_n measures the loss of information or the increase of uncertainty due to dynamical change in the system in the time interval $(nT, (n + 1)T)$. Still more than the loss of information, it is interesting to estimate the average rate of its change, defined by the Kolmogorov entropy

$$K = \lim_{T\to 0} \lim_{s\to 0} \lim_{N\to 0} \frac{1}{NT} \sum_{n=0}^{N-1} K_n \tag{18.19}$$

This entropy is 0, greater than 0, and ∞ for deterministic, chaotic, and random motion, respectively [11].

Chaotic behavior is a consequence of the divergence of trajectories, which can be described by positive Lyapunov exponents. It was shown elsewhere [24,25] that the sum of positive Lyapunov exponents averaged over the attractor is equal to the Kolmogorov entropy. A proper quantity for an average characterization of chaotic motion on the attractor is thus the Kolmogorov entropy, which is demonstrated by the following example. Let us assume that a strange attractor is limited to a region of typical span L, and let r denote a typical width of region where an inexactly determined initial state of the system takes place in the phase space. Due to the divergence of trajectories, the system state can move in a characteristic time T_m from the initial region to any point of the complete span. This time can be estimated from the relation

$$L \approx r \exp(KT_m) \qquad \text{or} \qquad T_m \approx \frac{1}{K} \ln \frac{L}{r} \tag{18.20}$$

in which K denotes an estimated average rate of divergence of trajectories, described by the sum of positive Lyapunov exponents or the Kolmogorov entropy. Its inverse value thus predominantly determines a typical time interval in which the behavior of the system can be predicted. Equation (18.20) shows that the uncertainty of the initial state position this time influences only logarithmically or unessentially. Due to the involved numerical treatment, the Kolmogorov entropy is only exceptionally determined in spite of its importance for characterizing the dynamical properties of chaotic phenomena.

18.2.3 Experimental Characterization of Chaotic Phenomena

In a system described by a continuous flow, chaos can appear if the phase space is at least three-dimensional. It is generally difficult to follow fluctuations of various variables simultaneously. Therefore most frequently just one variable, say x, is selected for a representative observation or recording. From the form of corresponding records, obtained by an oscilloscope or similar device, one can qualitatively estimate if the behavior of the system is stationary, periodic, or chaotic [15,25]. However, it is difficult to distinguish between quasi-periodic and chaotic motion. Quasi-periodic motion is composed of many cyclical motions of incommensurable frequencies and is often apparently chaotic. A quantitative method is thus needed to make a distinction. For this purpose the covariance function

$$R(t) = \lim_{T\to\infty} \frac{1}{T} \int_0^\infty (x(t') - m)(x(t + t') - m)\, dt' \tag{18.21}$$

is applicable [11,15]. Here m denotes the average value

$$m = \lim_{T\to\infty} \frac{1}{T} \int_0^\infty x(t')\, dt' \tag{18.22}$$

Often the origin of x is chosen so that $m = 0$, and the covariance function coincides with the correlation function. For periodic or quasi-periodic phenomena the covariance function oscillates between certain limits, while for a chaotic motion it converges to 0 with increasing t. The last property is a consequence of the fact that the system trajectories diverge so that the values of variable x at two separated moments become, on average, ever less correlated with increasing time laps t. Intuitively it can be expected that a typical correlation time corresponds approximately to a time interval in which the behavior of the system could be predicted [11,26]. Its Fourier transform, by which the spectral density is determined, also represents equivalent information to the covariance function. For a quasi-periodic signal the spectral density differs from 0 only at discrete values of frequency. Contrary to this a chaotic phenomenon is characterized by a continuous type of spectral distribution [11,25]. Both types of motion are therefore usually most simply distinguished by observation of spectral density, which is easily measured. More difficult, however, is the determination of other static and dynamic parameters of strange attractors. For this purpose we can either simultaneously measure various time-dependent variables or try to reconstruct the properties of the strange attractor from observation of just one representative variable. The first possibility is experimentally more demanding, so we present here the arguments for the second approach [11,25,27].

From the evolution law (18.1) it follows that the system state at some time $t + T$ is uniquely related with the state at a previous time t. If the representative variable $x(t)$ is applied to form time-shifted components

$$\begin{aligned} x_1(t) &= x(t) \\ x_2(t) &= x(t - T) \\ &\;.\;.\;. \\ x_n(t) &= x(t - (n - 1)T) \end{aligned} \tag{18.23}$$

then it can be expected that the properties of dynamics are transferred to the time dependence of the vector, composed of components

$$\mathbf{X} = (x_1, \ldots, x_n) = (x(t), x(t - T), \ldots, x(t - (n - 1)T)) \tag{18.25}$$

This conclusion further suggests that chaotic properties could also be estimated from the observation of the attractor of the time-dependent vector **X**. A more rigorous analysis of this approach has shown [27] that under relatively mild restrictions the vector composed of $n = 2D + 1$ shifted variables can indeed be applied to represent a smooth embedding of flow with the same metric properties as the original strange attractor in D-dimensional space. In experimental work the dimensionality of strange attractors is therefore most often estimated from just one representative variable by using the correlation exponent [23,25].

However, a further problem is due to be mentioned here. From the observation of just one characteristic variable it is possible to estimate the fractal dimension of the attractor, but the dimension of the phase space needed for a complete representation of the phenomenon cannot be easily determined. In the existing literature on chaotic phenomena it is usually mentioned [11,25,28] that this dimension can be estimated by repeating the calculation of the correlation exponent with an ever greater number N_d of shifted components. A proper dimension of the phase space is then estimated from the formula $N_d = 2N + 1$ when the correlation exponent D_2 reaches approximately its limiting value. This further indicates how many variables are at least needed to model the phenomenon observed. Later we propose a complementary way of estimating the proper dimensions of embedding and of the phase space from the minimum of the prediction error. Besides this problem, there usually also appears the question of how to choose a proper time shift. An acceptable answer can be found in the recent literature [29].

18.3 EMPIRICAL MODELING OF CHAOTIC PHENOMENA

Let us consider a chaotic phenomenon about which a representative observable $x(t)$ is experimentally conveyed by a corresponding sensor. By shifting this signal $2D$ times the embedding space for presenting the chaotic attractor is formed in which the point is described by the representative vector [8,30,31]

$$\mathbf{X}(t) = \{x(t), x(t - T), \ldots, x(t - 2DT)\} \tag{18.26}$$

However, when treating an unknown phenomenon the dimension D of the pertinent phase space is not known and must be determined from the observations. The law describing the flow in the embedding space is then described by

$$\frac{d\mathbf{X}}{dt} = \boldsymbol{\Phi}(\mathbf{X}) \tag{18.27a}$$

For simplicity we further assume that the phenomenon is observed at discrete time moments, described by a nondimensional parameter $t = 1, 2, \ldots$. The dynamical law is then transformed into a corresponding mapping

$$\mathbf{X}(t + 1) = \boldsymbol{\Psi}(\mathbf{X}(t)) \tag{18.27b}$$

If this law is expressed by the components of the representative state vector

$$\{x(t + 1), x(t), \ldots, x(t + 1) - 2D)\} = \boldsymbol{\Psi}\{x(t), \ldots, x(t - 2D)\} \tag{18.28}$$

it becomes obvious that the complete mapping includes shifting of $2D - 1$ components with respect to the discrete time t and the mapping of the state vector $\mathbf{X}(t) = \{x(t), \ldots, x(t - 2D)\}$ onto only one component $x(t + 1)$:

$$x(t + 1) = \boldsymbol{\Psi}\{x(t), \ldots, x(t - 2D)\} \tag{18.29}$$

If the function Ψ is known, then the signal value at $t + 1$ can be predicted from the past values of x. By the predicted value and shifted values of x the vector $\mathbf{X}(t + 1)$ can be formed and the next value $x(t + 2)$ again predicted, and so on. The signal can be shifted in any experimental modeler by the same unit, but the prediction of the signal must be done by a specific function Ψ. Our goal is to build a general modeler by which this mapping can be constructed from the measured signal $x(t)$. For this purpose the modeler must be able to store information presented by the input signal $x(t)$ and to recall it at the prediction of the same signal [1,2,30–33]. A generally applicable modeler must therefore include a memory capable of forming an internal representation of the signal generator Ψ by adaptive operation. Additionally, it must also include a device where the forthcoming signal can be presented in fictitious time. According to these properties, the modeler can be treated as an adaptive system, or network of units, with input $x(t)$ and parallel outputs $\{x(t+1), x(t+2), \ldots, x(t+\tau)\}$. The index of the output channel τ in this case corresponds to the fictitious time.

A modeler of this kind has already been implemented as a recurrent neural network [7]. It consists of a network of artificial neurons interconnected with delay elements. For the neurons adaptable nonlinear responses to input signals are characteristic. The mapping (18.29) is learned from the input signals by adaptive changes of synaptic weights representing input connections to neurons. Problems related to learning nonlinear mappings by adapting synaptic weights have been intensively studied and have led to an acceptable paradigm known as *back propagation* [6,7,34]. This method leads to the improvement of network performance through changing the synaptic weights of neurons by following gradient descent of the mapping error backward from the output to the input. However, the properties of the artificial neurons as well as the network architecture are selected ad hoc, and it is not quite clear how to optimize them. To avoid this arbitrariness, we follow a more physically motivated approach and try to find arguments for constructing modelers from more fundamental principles of the physical description of natural phenomena [1,2,35,36,37]. With this aim we first briefly present some basic concepts of the statistical description of the empirical data.

The natural law given by the mapping (18.29) is empirically represented by the distribution of points

$$\{x(t+1), x(t), \ldots, x(t-2D); t = 1, 2, \ldots, \infty\} \tag{18.30}$$

in the embedding space of $M = 2D + 2 = n_{\text{bed}} + 1$ dimensions. The modeling of function Ψ is statistically equivalent to a multidimensional regression. Contrary to various approaches based on the parametric description of regression functions [9,10,38], we propose here nonparametric treatment because it least restricts the generality of the modeler. We assume that the set of experimental points does not determine a function but an empirical joint probability distribution $P\{x(t+1), x(t), \ldots, x(t-2D)\}$ in the M-dimensional state-space. By it the conditional probability distribution $P\{x(t+1)|x(t), \ldots, x(t-2D)\}$ is determined, in which the vector $\{x(t+1), x(t), \ldots, x(t-D)\}$ plays the role of a condition. The function Ψ of the mapping (18.29) corresponds to an optimal statistical estimator determined by the conditional probability distribution [2,31,32,33]. The problem is then to estimate the probability distribution function from experimental data. For this purpose we apply the maximum entropy principle, which leads us to a modeler resembling the structure of a neural network [35,38]. A complete treatment has been exhaustively described elsewhere, so only its most important results are briefly presented here [35,36,37].

18.3.1 Optimal Storing of Information in a Self-Organizing System

Let us first describe how an empirical probability distribution function can be optimally memorized in a set of discrete memory units. Let $\mathbf{X}$ represent an M-dimensional continuous random variable to which the set of N samples $\{\mathbf{x}_1, \ldots, \mathbf{x}_N\}$ corresponds. The hypothetical probability distribution function of this variable can be empirically estimated by the density function [35,36]

$$f_e(\mathbf{x}) = \frac{1}{N} \sum_{n=1}^{N} \delta(\mathbf{x} - \mathbf{x}_n) \tag{18.31}$$

Due to difficulties related to the memorization of functions of multidimensional variables in discrete systems, we employ a set of K prototypes $\{\mathbf{q}_1, \ldots, \mathbf{q}_K\}$ which should represent the typical points in the sample space of variable $\mathbf{X}$. By them the probability density function is estimated as

$$f_r(\mathbf{x}) = \frac{1}{K} \sum_{k=1}^{K} \delta(\mathbf{x} - \mathbf{q}_k) \tag{18.32}$$

By this step a discrete random variable $\mathbf{Q}$ of a uniform probability distribution $\{P(\mathbf{q}_i) = 1/K : i = 1, \ldots, K\}$ is introduced. It corresponds to a mapping of a continuous to a discrete random variable $\mathbf{X} \mapsto \mathbf{Q}$, which generally causes reduction of information. The reduction is minimal when the distribution of $\mathbf{Q}$ corresponds to the maximal entropy of information, that is, when its distribution is uniform. By assuming a uniform probability distribution of Q, we include the maximum entropy principle in determining an optimal mapping [35,36].

By comparing Eqs. (18.31) and (18.32), one can establish that for $N = K$ it is reasonable to choose $\mathbf{q}_k = \mathbf{x}_k$ while an adaptation process must be applied for $N > K$. With this aim we first replace the singular delta function in Eqs. (18.31) and (18.32) by the smooth Gaussian window function

$$w(\mathbf{x},\mathbf{s}) = \exp\left[\frac{-(\mathbf{x} - \mathbf{s})^2}{2\sigma^2}\right] \tag{18.33}$$

The minimization of the discrepancy between the smooth version of distributions Eqs. (20.31) and (18.32) then leads to self-organized, adaptive changes of prototypes described by the iteration [35]

$$\Delta q_{lm}^{(i+1)} \doteq B_{lm} - \sum_{k \neq l}^{K} \sum_{i \neq m}^{M} C_{lmki}\, \Delta q_{ki} \qquad l = 1, \ldots, K \quad m = 1, \ldots, M \tag{18.34}$$

which starts with $\Delta \mathbf{q}_l^{(1)} = \mathbf{B}_l$. The coefficients are determined by the expressions:

$$C_{lmki} = \left[\delta_{mi} - \frac{(q_{lm} - q_{km})(q_{li} - q_{ki})}{2\sigma^2}\right] \exp\left[\frac{-(\mathbf{q}_l - \mathbf{q}_k)^2}{4\sigma^2}\right] \tag{18.35}$$

$$B_{lm} = \frac{K}{N+1}\left\{(x_{N+1,m} - q_{lm}) \exp\left[\frac{-(\mathbf{x}_{N+1} - \mathbf{q}_l)^2}{4\sigma^2}\right] - \frac{1}{K}\sum_{k=1}^{K} (q_{km} - q_{lm}) \exp\left[\frac{-(\mathbf{q}_k - \mathbf{q}_l)^2}{4\sigma^2}\right]\right\} \tag{18.36}$$

The parameter σ should approximately correspond to the estimated distance between representative prototypes in multidimensional space. If L^M denotes the cube covering the embedded attractor, then it is convenient to choose $\sigma = L/K^{1/M}$.

The prototypes can be treated as stored contents of memory cells or parameters of artificial neurons. As indicated by the foregoing algorithm, their adaptation to input signals is influenced by the interaction between neurons. It is determined by modified bell-shaped functions describing mutual excitation (positive value) or inhibition (negative value). A simplified version of formula (18.34) corresponds to the well-known self-organization rule of Kohonen [39,40].

18.3.2 Optimal Prediction

Let us now show how the prototypes can be applied in the prediction of a dynamic signal. [1,2,30–33] For this purpose we split the vector $\mathbf{x}$ into two truncated vectors

$$\mathbf{x} = \mathbf{p} \oplus \mathbf{r} = (x_1, \ldots, x_t, x_{t+1}, \ldots, x_M) \tag{18.37}$$

with

$$\mathbf{p} = (x_1, \ldots, x_t; \#) \qquad \text{and} \qquad \mathbf{r} = (\#; x_{t+1}, \ldots, x_M) \tag{18.38}$$

Here # denotes the missing part. Let us further assume that partial information about the phenomenon is conveyed by the vector $\mathbf{p}$ and we want to estimate the remaining components of the complementary vector $\mathbf{r}$ from it as shown in Figure 18.5. The optimal estimator $\hat{\mathbf{r}} = \hat{\mathbf{r}}(\mathbf{p})$, which minimizes the mean square error

$$D = \int [\mathbf{r} - \hat{\mathbf{r}}(\mathbf{p})]^2 f(\mathbf{x})\, d^M x \tag{18.39}$$

corresponds to the conditional average

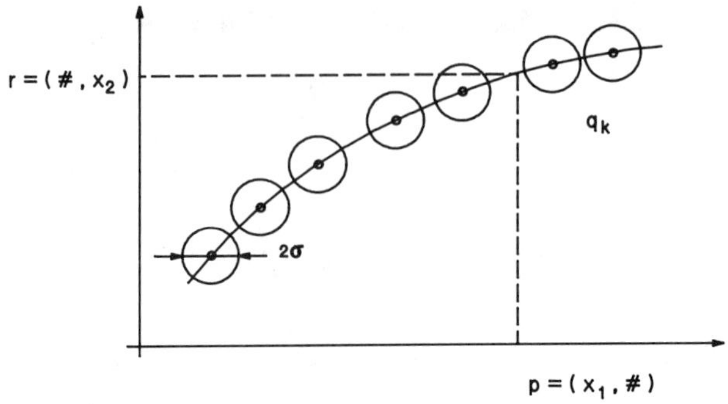

Figure 18.5 *Estimation of one component from another one by using prototypes.*

$$\hat{\mathbf{r}}_o = \int \mathbf{r} f(\mathbf{r}|\mathbf{p})\, dx_{t+1} \cdots dx_M \tag{18.40}$$

If the conditional probability density is expressed by prototypes

$$f(\mathbf{r}|\mathbf{p}) = \sum_k w(\mathbf{r} - \mathbf{r}_k) w(\mathbf{p} - \mathbf{p}_k) \Big/ \sum_n w(\mathbf{p} - \mathbf{p}_n) \tag{18.41}$$

the conditional average becomes a linear superposition of truncated prototype vectors

$$\hat{\mathbf{r}}_o = \sum_k A_k \mathbf{r}_k \tag{18.42}$$

The coefficients

$$A_k = w(\mathbf{p} - \mathbf{p}_k) \Big/ \sum_n w(\mathbf{p} - \mathbf{p}_n) \tag{18.43}$$

are strongly nonlinear functions, representing the measure of similarity between vector **p** and prototypes $\mathbf{p}_k$. The completed data vector

$$\mathbf{y} = \mathbf{p} \oplus \hat{\mathbf{r}}_o(\mathbf{p}) \tag{18.44}$$

represents the response of the predictor to excitation by the truncated signal **p.**

18.4 NUMERICAL EXPERIMENTS

In accordance with the foregoing presentation, the modeler of chaotic dynamical phenomena must be able to perform the following operations [8,30–33]:

- Sample and shift the input signal;
- Form from shifted components the latched vector **X;**
- Adapt prototypes by self-organization to the input vector;
- Repeat prediction of the forthcoming signal by conditional average estimation;
- Present predicted values on parallel outputs.

Its experimental scheme, shown in Figure 18.6, consists of two shift registers, a memory, and a conditional average estimator. The signal $x(t)$ is fed from the chaos generator to the shift register, where a sample of the state vector **X** is formed by latching M successive data values. The sample is then transferred to the simulated neural network representing the self-organizing memory and to the predictor composed of a shift register and the conditional average estimator. Numerical experiments were done with 30 prototypes, formed by self-organization in the simulated neural network. The parameters of prototypes are transferred to the conditional average estimator taking place in the predictor. There the components of the state vector **X** are first shifted to obtain a truncated vector

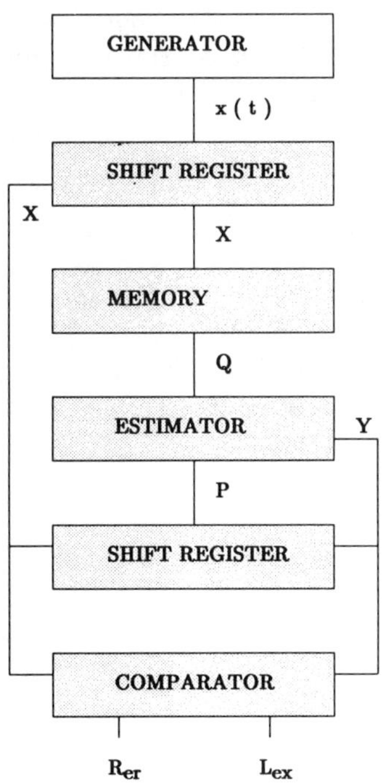

Figure 18.6 *Scheme of the system applicable for empirical modeling and prediction of chaotic time series.*

$$\mathbf{p} = (\#, x(t), x(t-1), \ldots, x(t+1-M)) \tag{18.45}$$

The missing component corresponds to the forthcoming value $x(t + 1)$ of the signal. It is predicted by the conditional average estimation and concatenated to the output vector

$$\mathbf{y} = (x(t+1), x(t), x(t-1), \ldots, x(t+1-M)) \tag{18.46}$$

This vector is then iteratively fed back to the predictor input in order to obtain a prediction of the forthcoming time series. The predicted terms of the series can be simultaneously presented on parallel outputs.

The agreement between the true input signal and the predicted one can be assessed from a comparison of short signal sections in the comparator. The predictor performance is described by the relative prediction error defined with respect to the variance of the input signal Var(x):

$$R_{\text{er}}(s) = \frac{1}{\text{Var}(x)N} \sum_{t=1}^{N} (y(t+s) - x(t+s))^2 \tag{18.47}$$

Parameter s denotes the number of prediction steps. The prediction error for a chaotic signal increases approximately exponentially with the number of steps. The reason for this is mainly the instability of chaotic trajectories as well as the accumulation of errors caused by approximate modeling. We conjecture that the characteristic exponent of the prediction error defined by the formula

$$L_{\text{ex}} = \frac{1}{s} \ln \left(\frac{R_{\text{er}}(s+1)}{R_{\text{er}}(1)} \right) \tag{18.48}$$

should be approximately two times greater than the largest Lyapunov exponent λ of the input signal. For the purpose of visually estimating the predictor performance we also apply the return map of true and predicted signals. Here we describe the prediction of the chaotic signals generated by

I. the logistic map $\quad x_{n+1} = 3.8x_n(1 - x_n) \quad$ (18.49)

II. the Hénon map $\quad x_{n+2} = 1 + 0.3x_n - 1.4x_{n+1}^2 \quad$ (18.50)

III. the Lorenz system

$$\begin{aligned} \dot{x} &= 20(y - x) \\ \dot{y} &= (28 - z)x - y \\ \dot{z} &= -8z + xy \end{aligned} \tag{18.51}$$

In the last example the value $dt = 0.015$ was selected for numerical treatment, while sample values were taken $10dt$ apart.

The initial conditions were arbitrarily selected, and the initial 500 sample values of the calculated signals, representing the transition from initial con-

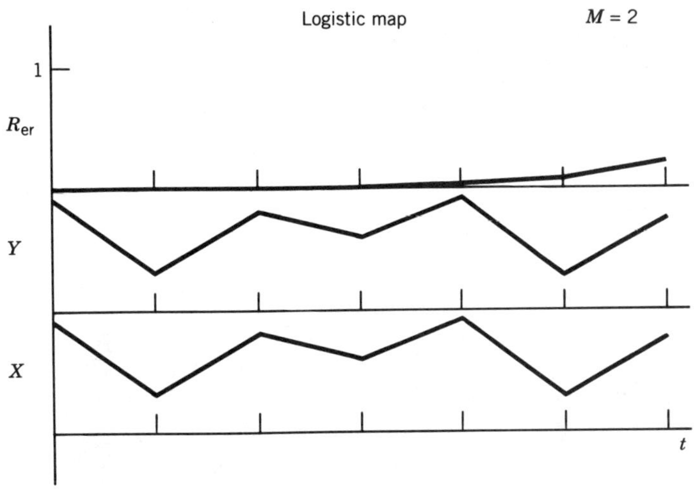

Figure 18.7 *Records of the signal* X *generated by a logistic map, predicted signal* Y, *and relative error* R_{er} *for* M = 2.

ditions to the chaotic attractor, were discarded in all cases. The self-organization of prototypes was then carried out using 500 sample values.

Most simple for demonstrating predictor performance is the first example, where the two-dimensional return map is sufficient for a complete graphical presentation of the chaos generator. An example of the numerical results obtained with $M = 2$ is shown in Figure 18.7. The bottom record represents the true signal from the chaos generator, while the middle record shows the signal predicted from the first value. With the increasing number of prediction steps, from left to right, the discrepancy between both signals becomes evident. The average error, estimated from 500 of prediction trials, is shown as a function of the number of prediction steps in the upper record of the same figure. The average relative error for the first step of prediction is $R_{er}(1) = 0.003$, which indicates a good modeling of chaos. This error then increases with the number of prediction steps in an approximately exponential manner. The exponent estimated from the numerical experiment is approximately $L_{ex} \approx 1$. For the same logistic map the Lyapunov exponent is approximately $\lambda \approx 0.45$ [15] so that conjecture $L_{exp} \approx 2\lambda$ is confirmed. Presumably the higher estimated value is a consequence of the approximate modeling of the logistic map by only 30 prototypes. For the purpose of visually demonstrating the predictor performance, the return maps of the signal, repeatedly predicted by five steps, and of the original chaotic signal are shown in Figure 18.8 by two dotted curves. The good overlapping of both maps indicates the applicability of the system for modeling simple chaos generators. Apart from both return maps it is also instructive to present graphically the positions of prototypes as shown in Figure 18.9. Each circle

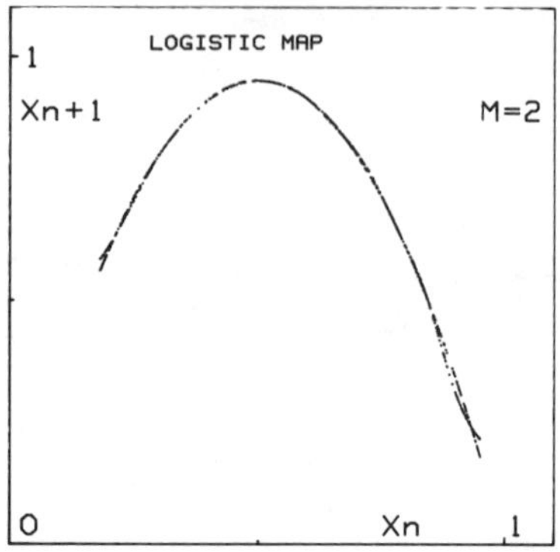

Figure 18.8 *Return maps of original and predicted logistic signals for* M = 2.

indicates by its center the position of the prototype and by its radius the range σ of the Gaussian window used in smoothing the delta functions and in estimating the conditional average. As the self-organization is derived from the assumption that an equal probability $1/K$ should correspond to each prototype, the prototypes are more densely distributed in that region of the attractor, or in our case of the return map, where the occurrence of the system state is greater. The distribution of the prototypes thus also indicates the probability distribution.

An individual prototype represents a typical transition between successive states; the example shown presents a transition between two of them. The set of prototypes therefore represents various typical transitions occurring in the chaotic time series. Figure 18.10 shows the transitions $x_n \rightarrow x_{n+1}$ by the line starting at the first value and finishing at the second one. Successive lines are displaced by the same amount in the vertical direction.

The same procedure as described before has been repeated for several

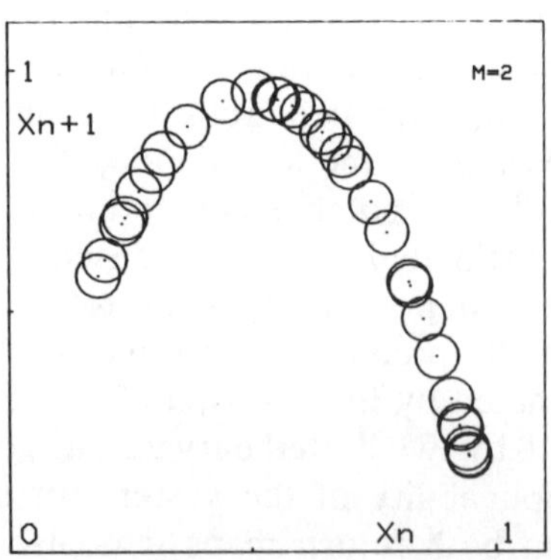

Figure 18.9 *Position of prototypes in the return map.*

Figure 18.10 *Transitions between successive states represented by prototypes. The graphs of particular prototypes are shifted in the vertical direction for the same displacement.*

prototype dimensions M. The results obtained with $M = 3$ are shown in Figures 18.11 and 18.12. It is characteristic that the prediction error increases with the dimension in this case. For the simulation of the applied chaotic signal the two-dimensional state-space is therefore the most appropriate.

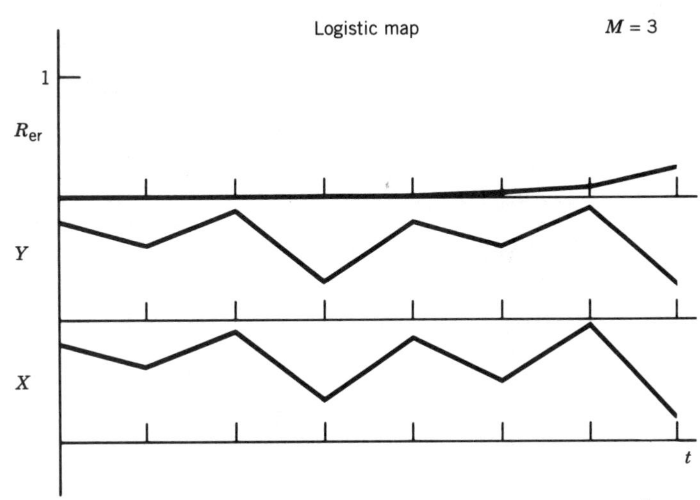

Figure 18.11 *Records of the signal X generated by a logistic map, predicted signal Y, and relative error R_{er} for M = 3.*

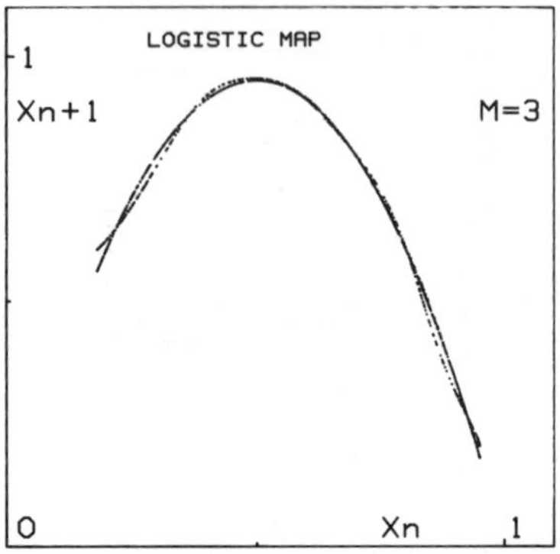

Figure 18.12 *Return maps of original and predicted logistic signals for* M = 3.

The complete numerical experiment was repeated with the Hénon chaos generator, which requires three-dimensional state-space. The representative records and the corresponding return maps are shown in Figures 18.13 and 18.14. For the applied map $2\lambda \approx 0.4$ while $L_{ex} \approx 0.47$. A good overlapping of the original and predicted return map is again obtained. The relative prediction error estimated from 500 steps is $R_{er}(1) = 0.045$. Its greater value with respect to the previous example is mainly caused by a minor discrepancy between return maps in the middle of the graph. This discrepancy can be diminished by increasing the number of prototypes. The system states occupy this part of the return map with relatively low frequency. The minimal prediction error in the case of the Hénon generator was obtained at $M = 3$.

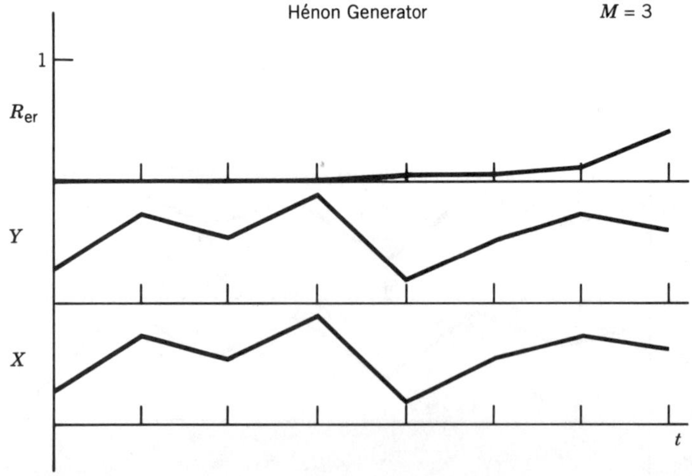

Figure 18.13 *Records of the signal* X *generated by the Hénon map, predicted signal* Y, *and relative error* R_{er} *for* M = 3.

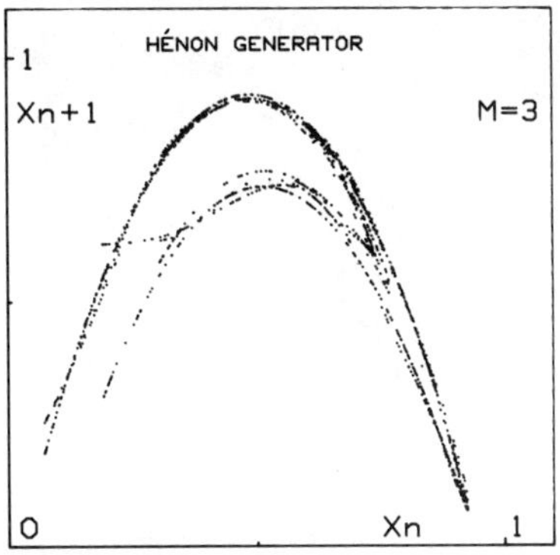

Figure 18.14 *Return maps of original and predicted signals of the Hénon map for* M = 3.

The agreement between the dimensionality of the chaos generator and the dimension M, where the minimal prediction error is obtained, suggests that a proper dimension of the space for presenting chaos generator could be found by searching for the minimum of the prediction error. Presumably the estimated value corresponds to the embedding dimension plus one. In order to confirm this presumption, the same information processing system was applied to the prediction of chaotic signals generated by the Lorenz equations, as shown in Figures 18.15 and 18.16. For the parameters selected, the best prediction was obtained at $M = 7$, which indicates that the corresponding chaotic attractor is low-dimensional (the embedding dimension is approximately $n_{\text{bed}} = 6$) [23]. The estimated value of the optimal dimension M

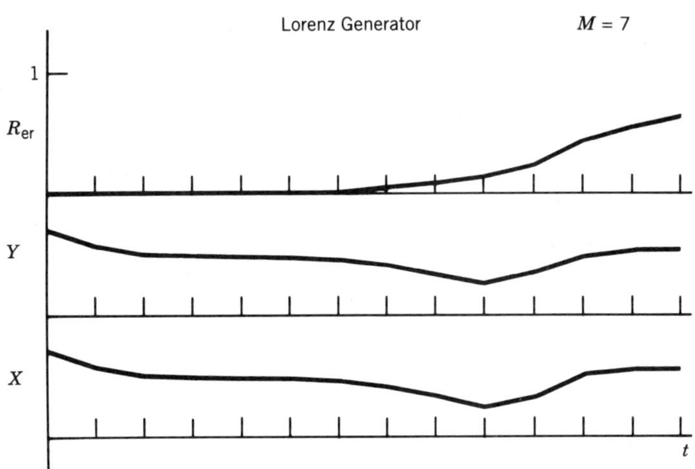

Figure 18.15 *Records of signal* X *generated by the Lorenz equations, predicted signal* Y, *and relative error* R_{er} *for* M = 7.

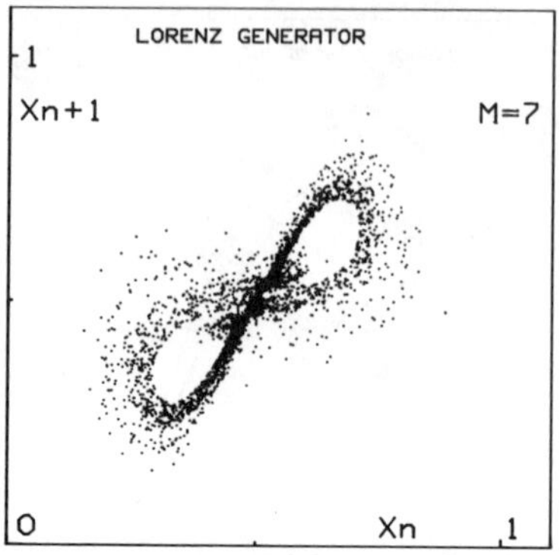

Figure 18.16 *Return maps of original and predicted signals of the Lorenz generator for* M = 7.

indeed corresponds to $M \doteq n_{\text{bed}} + 1$, which is in agreement with the fact that empirical distribution representing the mapping (18.30) includes one component more than the vector **X** used to describe the embedding of the attractor.

The divergence of the trajectories, caused by the instability of the chaotic systems, causes long-term predictions not to be accurate. Figures 18.17 to 18.19 show true and long-term predicted signals for all the examples. Although the signals start from the same initial values, the difference between them appears obvious after several steps of prediction. But in spite of the divergence, both signals exhibit similar properties, which is due to the chaos generator being well modeled.

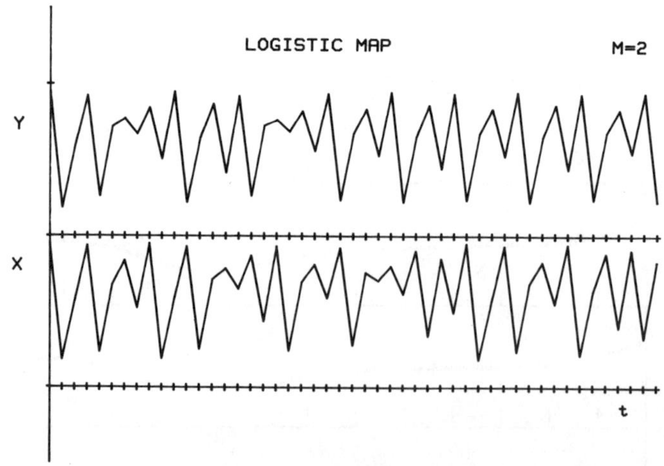

Figure 18.17 *Original,* X, *and long-term predicted chaotic signal* Y *from a logistic generator.*

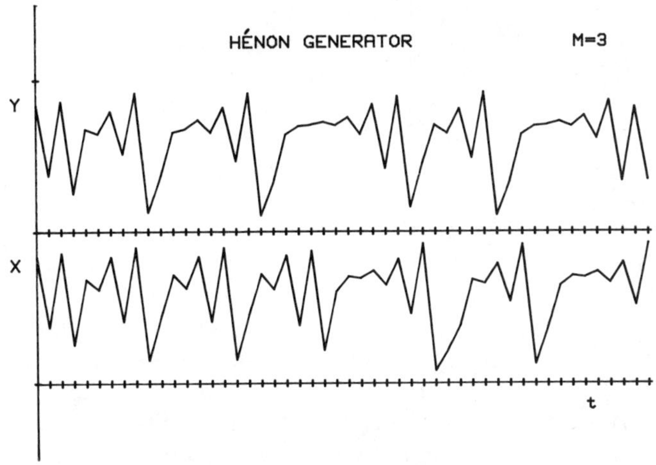

Figure 18.18 *Original,* X, *and long-term predicted chaotic signal* Y *from the Hénon generator.*

Similar properties as presented here have also been observed in predictions of acoustic signals generated by friction between elastic objects and noise in instrumentation. Prediction of regular signals representing movements on attractors of limited extensions has also been successful. Additionally, a similar model has been applied for multidimensional modeling of elastodynamic phenomena like acoustic emission generated by impacts or scattering of ultrasound on inclusions in solid materials [1,2,35,36,37].

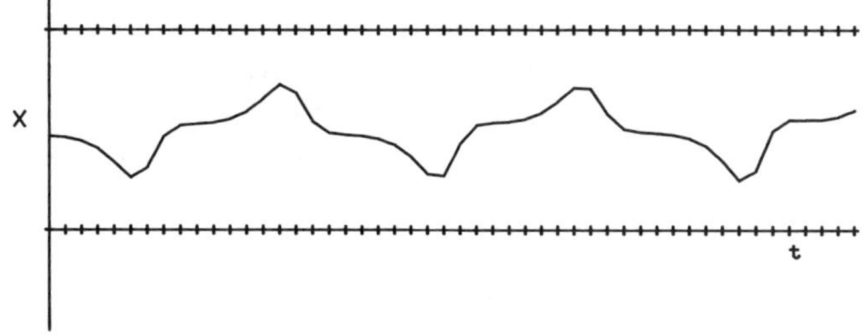

Figure 18.19 *Original,* X, *and long-term predicted chaotic signal* Y *from the Lorenz generator.*

18.5 CONCLUSIONS

In the current literature on artificial neural networks two distinct trends are present [39,40]. In the first one the properties of neurons and the architecture of their network are specified on the grounds of some biologically motivated suggestions, and then the performance of the network is studied. In the second one some task, often of a technical nature, is first specified, and then an attempt to find a proper network of artificial neurons is made by varying its architecture. The aim of this chapter is to link the latter trend with the field of physical description of natural phenomena. It is instructive that in our treatment the properties of neurons and their interactions emerge from the very fundamental principles of optimal information processing and need not be specified ad hoc in advance. This shows that the second trend of neural network research could be treated as part of a much broader scientific discipline of empirical description of natural phenomena from which some fundamental suggestions for further developments of neural networks can be obtained [2].

The numerical experiments presented indicate that the developed information processing system with incorporated self-organizing neural-network-like memory, shift registers and predictor, based on an estimator of the conditional average, is applicable for modeling and predicting dynamical phenomena, and especially chaotic generators. A proper embedding dimension of the corresponding chaotic attractor can be estimated, at least in the applied examples, by searching for the minimum of prediction error. From the characteristic exponent of the divergence between the input and the predicted signal, the largest Lyapunov exponent can be further estimated. These new results suggest that the modeler could also be applied to obtain another statistical and dynamic parameters of chaotic attractors which requires further research.

The accuracy of the modeling depends on the number of applied prototypes. In our approach this number is taken as a parameter determined by the construction of the system. How this number could be optimized on the grounds of some fundamental principles is still not exactly known, although some preliminary studies show that a properly defined entropy of empirical information could be applied for this purpose [38]. Another open problem is how to incorporate a priori information or symmetries into a modeler or predictor and how to treat multicomponent chaotic phenomena. In the field of elastodynamics various attempts stemming from linear optimal multicomponent deconvolution have already led to a neural-network-like structure capable of time-invariant operation and prediction [41]; but the general method of solving these problems is still not known.

The developed system can be treated as an adaptive empirical modeler of natural phenomena. Its prototypes corresponds to typical transitions occurring in the observed chaotic time series. The model is therefore adapted only to a specific example. An interesting problem is then how the collected knowledge could be generalized and finally presented in terms of abstract natural laws [38]. Ad hoc replacement of prototypes by various abstract functions only replaces nonparametric treatment by parametric; but it does not solve the problem because the question of how the functions can be automatically defined appears. For this purpose further levels of neural networks should be applied, but the fundamental physical principles for their development, which could lead to hierarchical scientific reasoning, are still not formulated.

REFERENCES

[1] I. Grabec, "Empirical modeling of natural phenomena by a self-organizing system," *Proc. Neural Network Conf. 90,* Vol. 2, 529–532 (1990).

[2] I. Grabec and W. Sachse, Automatic modeling of physical phenomena: Application to ultrasonic data, *J. Appl. Phys.* **69,** 6233–6244 (1991).

[3] I. Bratko, S. Muggleton, and A. Varšek, Learning qualitative models of dynamic systems, *Proc. ILP-91,* 270–224 (1991).

[4] J. de Kleer and J. S. Brown, A qualitative physics based on confluences, *Artificial Intelligence* 28, 127–162 (1986).

[5] I. Grabec and W. Sachse, Experimental characterization of ultrasonic phenomena by a learning system, *J. Appl. Phys.,* **66,** 3993–4000 (1989).

[6] J. A. Anderson and E. Rosenfeld, Eds., *Neurocomputing, Foundations of Research,* I, II, MIT Press, Cambridge, Mass., 1988.

[7] R. Hecht-Nielsen, *Neurocomputing,* Addison-Wesley, Reading, Mass., 1990.

[8] I. Grabec, "Prediction of a Chaotic Time Series by a Self-Organizing Neural Network," poster, Dynamic Days, Düsseldorf (1990).

[9] J. D. Farmer and J. J. Sidorowich, "Predicting Chaotic Time Series," Rep. No LA-UR-87-1502, Los Alamos Natl. Lab., and *Phys. Rev. Lett,* **59,** 845–848 (1987).

[10] A. Lapedes and R. Farber, "Nonlinear Signal Processing Using Neural Networks: Prediction and System Modelling," Rep. No LA-UR-1987-2662, Los Alamos Natl. Lab.,

[11] H. G. Schuster, *Deterministic Chaos,* Physik-Verlag, New York, 1989.

[12] E. Govekar, I. Grabec, and J. Peklenik, Monitoring of a drilling process by a neural network, *Proc. 21st CIRP Seminar on Manufacturing Systems,* Vol. 2 (1989).

[13] I. Grabec, Chaotic dynamics of the cutting process, *Internat. J. Mach. Tools Manufact.,* **28,** 19–32 (1988).

[14] I. Grabec, "Sources of Chaos in Mechanical Machines, IMACS 1989," in W. F. Ames, Ed., *Numerical and Applied Mathematics,* J. C. Baltzer AG, Sci. Pub. Co. Basel, 309–314 (1989).

[15] F. C. Moon, *Chaotic Vibrations, An Introduction for Applied Scientists and Engineers,* J. Wiley & Sons, New York, 1987.

[16] A. J. Lichtenberg and M. A. Lieberman, *Regular and Stochastic Motion,* Springer Verlag, New York, 1983.

[17] H. Haken, *Synergetics,* Springer Verlag, Berlin, 1983.

[18] V. I. Oseledec, "A multiplicative ergodic theorem: Lyapunov characteristic numbers for dynamical systems," *Trans. Moscow Math. Soc.,* **19,** 197 (1968).

[19] M. W. Hirsch and S. Smale, *Differential Equations, Dynamic Systems and Linear Algebra,* Academic Press, New York, 1965.

[20] H. Haken, Ed., *Evolution of Order and Chaos,* Springer Verlag, Berlin, 1982.

[21] M. Feingenbaum, *Dynamical Systems and Chaos,* Springer Verlag, Berlin, 1983.

[22] B. B. Mandelbrot, *The Fractal Geometry of Nature,* Freeman, San Francisco, Calif., 1982.

[23] P. Grassberger and I. Procaccia, Characterization of strange attractors, *Phys. Rev. Lett.,* **50,** 346–349 (1983).

[24] Ya. B. Pesin, "Characteristic Lyapunov exponents and smooth ergodic theory," *Usp. Math. Nauk,* **32,** 55 (1977).

[25] J. P. Eckmann and D. Ruelle, "Ergodic theory of chaos and strange attractors," *Rev. Mod. Phys.,* **57,** 617 (1985).

[26] H. Atmanspacher and H. Scheingraber, A fundamental link between system theory and statistical mechanics, *Found. Phys.,* **17,** 939 (1987).

[27] F. Takens, Detecting strange attractors in fluid turbulence, in D. A. Rand and L. S. Young, Eds., *Lecture Notes in Mathematics,* vol. **898,** Springer Verlag, Berlin, 1981, 366–381.

[28] G. Nicolis, Dissipative systems, *Rep. Prog. Phys,* **49,** 873–949 (1986).

[29] W. Liebert and H. G. Schuster, Proper choice of the time delay for the analysis of chaotic time series, *Phys. Lett.,* **142,** 107–111 (1989).

[30] I. Grabec, Prediction of dynamical phenomena by a neural network, *MELECON '91,* Vol. 1, 18–23 (1991).

[31] I. Grabec, Modeling of chaos by a self-organizing neural network, *Internat. Conf. on Artificial Neurol Networks '91,* Vol 1, 151–156 (1991).

[32] I. Grabec, Modeling of natural phenomena by a self-organizing neural network, *Proc. ECPD,* Vol. 1, 142–150 (1990).

[33] I. Grabec and W. Sachse, Automatic modeling of ultrasonic phenomena, *Progr. in Acoustic Emission V, Jap. Soc. NDI,* 196–202 (1990).

[34] D. E. Rumelhart, J. McClelland, and The PDP Group, Eds., *Parallel Distributed Processing,* MIT Press, Cambridge, Mass., 1986.

[35] I. Grabec, Self-organization based on the second maximum entropy principle, *1st IEE Internat. Conf. on Artificial Neural Networks,* 313, 12–16 (1989).

[36] I. Grabec, Self-organization of neurons described by the maximum entropy principle, *Biol. Cybernetics,* **63,** 403 (1990).

[37] I. Grabec, "Automatic modeling of acoustic emission phenomena by neural networks." Chapter 7 herein.

[38] J. P. Crutchfild and B. S. McNamara, Equations of motion from data series, *Complex Systems,* **1,** 417–452 (1987).

[39] T. Kohonen, *Self-Organization and Associative Memory,* Springer Verlag, Berlin, 1988, 119.

[40] Review articles, *Neural Networks,* **1**(1) (1988).

[41] K. Zgonc and I. Grabec, A multidimensional optimal deconvolution applied to hetero-associative recall of AE signals, *Proc. ECPD,* Vol 1, 206–212 (1990).

CHAPTER 19

Dynamic versus Genetic versus Chaotic Programming

BORUT MARIČIĆ

19.1 INTRODUCTION

This chapter approaches the problem of neural network design as being composed of two levels: evolution of network connectivity and the adaptation of connection weights. While the first level implies network architecture optimization, the second implies adaptation of connection weights. Ideally, a network design tools should support both levels. While conventional tools effectively support weights adaptation level, the network designer searches the space of possible network configurations in an essentially random fashion. During the last few years the problem of neural network design, especially in the context of error back-propagation (BP) model and its variations, has been approached in a new way by several groups of researchers. This approach strives at automation of both levels of network design, based on optimization techniques known as genetic algorithms (GA).

Section 19.2 presents an overview of recent research in application of GA optimization techniques to neural network design. It is assumed that reader is familiar with basics of both artificial neural network principles and genetic algorithms.

In Section 19.3 the approach is illustrated with several experiments in which connection weights are evolved in small networks. It is shown how a supervised learning procedure could be replaced by GA. Results confirm, however, that GA are encountering difficulties when applied to neural network design problem, what has been already suggested by several authors.

Dynamic, Genetic, and Chaotic Programming, By Branko Souček and the IRIS Group.
ISBN 0-471-55717-X

Nevertheless, in Section 19.4 the approach is successfully applied to the problem of pole-balancing controller synthesis, a situation requiring an unsupervised learning procedure. It is shown how weights of a network may be evolved, in order to obtain a dynamic system controller. The controller consists of a fully interconnected recurrent network, whose connection weights are being evolved using GA.

Section 19.5 suggests that the behavior of some of the systems evolved in this way may possess some chaotic characteristics.

19.2 GENETIC ALGORITHMS IN ARTIFICIAL NEURAL NETWORK DESIGN: AN OVERVIEW

Suppose a set of objects is defined, each being described by a set of numerical attributes. We want to construct a system that would, based on a given set of attribute values (an input vector), form an output vector characterizing the class of objects described by the input vector. This is clearly a classification problem, a paradigm that may (among other ways) be approached using neural network models. A well-known error back-propagation model [1], or any of its variations, could be applied. Such a network is of a feedforward type, consisting of processing units grouped in sets (layers). Units are linked by connections of varying conductivities (weights). The basic model prohibits connections among units of the same layer, as well as those leading to units of a previous layer. Each unit's output is defined by a sigmoid function of weighted sum of its inputs and its threshold. The model differentiates between the training mode and normal operation mode. During the iterative training procedure, descriptions of training set objects are applied to network inputs, while generated output vectors are compared with the required ones. Based on this difference, weights and threshold values are modified, using error back propagation, in such a way as to decrease the error. The procedure is effectively minimizing the error, gradient descending in the weight space.

The space being searched, that is, the error surface on which a minimum is to be found, depends on network configuration and the application. Under *configuration* a connectivity pattern is assumed. For a fixed application, some network configurations do not guarantee a satisfactory solution, while others may lead to slower or faster convergence. The training process also depends on the initial weights; as with all gradient procedures the process suffers from local minima problem.

Whereas for simple problems, such as the XOR problem, it could be shown that using some network configurations the error would never drop below a certain level, the correlation between the network configuration and the learning talent is generally unknown. We are thus approaching this question: Which configuration would enable the formation of weights corresponding to a satisfactory network operation? Moreover, if the network is to be realized in hardware using currently obtainable technology [2,3], the following question may also be raised: What is the minimal network (in terms of processing units and/or number of connections) to solve a given problem with an acceptable error?

There are only a few inconclusive texts discussing the dependence of decision boundaries on network configurations [4–7]. In addition, in multidimensional problem spaces it is difficult or even impossible to visualize the shape of decision regions needed to give us a hint on network configuration that would suffice. In practice, a configuration is selected and trained using the error back-propagation algorithm (or any of its variations). Based on the training results, another configuration is selected for a try, or it is determined to bring the process to an end.

The task of a network adaptation to a given problem, then, may be seen as consisting of two levels (at least when we speak of networks whose weights are adapted using error back propagation). The first level implies configuration (i.e., connectivity) adaptation, while the second implies weights adaptation. Ideally, a network design tool should effectively support both levels.

19.2.1 Conventional versus Recent Approaches

Neural network simulators were recently grouped into two generations [8]. The first consists of systems developed primarily for modeling biological aspects of neural networks, while the second comprises more general systems. Probably the most widely known and available ones of the second group are Rochester Connectionist Simulator [9,10], P3 [11], MIRRORS/II [12,13], and the software package accompanying [14]. While these originated in university environments, a dozen commercial systems are also available.*

The process used, and supported by these tools, is that of a design-evaluate-modify cycle. During the design a network structure (i.e., connectivity) is being defined, along with activation and training functions selection. Evaluation is based on simulation results obtained during network training and testing on a set of examples. Finally, the initial design is being modified in view of the results obtained, and the cycle is repeated.

While using such a system, neural network designer searches the space of possible network configurations in an essentially random fashion. If, however, the network configuration could be described by a set of parameters and some configuration quality function established, a set of parameter values associated with high-quality configuration could be searched for, using some adequate optimization method. First suggestions toward this approach appeared in 1987 and 1988 [15–18]. All are based on analogy with biological evolution, implying the existence of a set of different network configurations (population); a method of configuration quality estimation (fitness); a way of concise configuration representation (genotype), as well as the operator for

* See, for example, *AI Expert,* December 1989 issue, for a list of vendors.

genotype modification (such as crossover and mutation). While Dress [16] is oriented toward the development of a simulated "synthetic insect" and, as well as Bergman [17], considers essentially a nonregressive random walk search, Todd [18] discusses various problem aspects in detail, based on his acquaintance with GA theory.

For the chapter to be reasonably self-contained, the basic sketch of GA's *reproductive plan* is shown in Figure 19.1. The key steps here are the parent selection and the formation of new genotypes. Parents are selected based on their fitness—the "better" ones have greater chances to be selected. New genotypes are formed by genetic operators, most important of which are crossover and mutation. The crossover operator builds a new genotype consisting partly of one and partly of the other parent's bits. In this way an offspring is formed having characteristics of both already "well-adapted" parents. The mutation operator changes genotype bits in a random manner with a low probability, sustaining in this way population's diversity. The basic notion in the analysis of GA's characteristics is that of a *schema,* which is considered "a similarity template describing a subset of strings with similarities at certain string positions" [19]. Detailed analysis of interactions between the reproductive plan and genetic operators reveals that short, low-order above-average schemata receive exponentially increasing number of trials. These highly fit schemata, known as *building blocks,* hold implicit "knowledge" GA acquires about basic elements that could be used in construction of highly fit objects.

Theoretical foundations of GA suggest that the best way objects being optimized are *represented* is with finite-length binary strings (genotypes). However, their successful application to optimization problems depends on the way in which the search space is mapped onto the representation space. Generally, it is helpful if mutually close genotype bits represent object characteristics that are also close, that is, in a logical or structural relation (this is not strictly necessary, though, since genetic operators that reposition genotype bits may be used).

Finally, a *fitness function* should be constructed in such a way as to mirror the quality of optimized objects in accordance with the optimization purpose being defined in advance.

```
Create initial population of genotypes and structures to be optimized;
Evaluate structures in the population;
repeat
 | Select genotypes, forming the new population;
 | Form new genotypes, recombining the old ones;
 | Evaluate structures created according to new genotypes;
until terminating condition is satisfied.
```

Figure 19.1 *Reproductive plan of a genetic algorithm.*

For a gentle introduction to GA their theory and applications, see Goldberg [19], and Davidor and Schwefel [20]. Descriptions of early applications of GA to design of physical systems may be found in Rechenberg [21]. For extensive treatment of mathematical foundations see Holland [22] and De Jong [23], while current research and applications are covered in a series of conference proceedings, for example, Schaffer [24]. Application of GA to function optimization is discussed in [25,26,27]. The remaining part of this section is an overview of research efforts to apply GA to the neural network optimization problem. As will be seen, it is not only network configuration that may be optimized.

19.2.2 Connectivity Space

By connectivity space a set of network configurations to be searched is assumed. The problem is being approached in essentially two ways: the first one could be termed *network building* [18,28–34], while the second is known as *network pruning* [36,37]. Both depend on genetic operators for network genotypes construction. The difference lies in the definition of search space and network evaluation procedure. The network building approach requires full error back-propagation training procedure to be carried out for each network evaluation. For larger networks and training sets this tends to be time-consuming. Moreover, since the training is susceptible to local minima, it should be repeated in order to gain a better impression of network learning ability. Network pruning defines some "largest" network at the beginning of a search, supposedly being sufficient for solving a given problem. It is trained just once. The reproductive plan and genetic operators form its variations by removing some connections. Each new network's initial weights correspond to those of the largest network, so its weights should just be refreshed. The main drawback of the approach is the choice of initial network, since for nontrivial problems there is no theory to rely on. While the building approach defines the largest possible network implicitly by the search space characteristics (being evaluated only when, and if, corresponding genotype is explicitly created), the success of network pruning depends heavily on the training of the initially chosen largest network.

Representation. The basic approach being set aside, authors differ mostly in the choice of network/genotype mapping. The way in which a bit string (genotype) mirrors the network structure (phenotype) not only defines the set of possible networks but may have subtle effects on the quality of GA workings. As Miller et al. notice [34], representations may be graded from weak to strong ones. Strong ones tend to define each particular network connection, and therefore the appropriate network construction procedure may be straightforward. Conversely, weak representations describe connectivity using more abstract terms (such as sets of connections, connectivity projections, and density, etc.), so fairly complex construction procedures are needed. In the biological world, the representations are apparently much closer to the weak ones.

Harp et al. [29] use weak representation in which network genotypes need not even be the same length. Each one consists of several segments describing network unit sets that are defined in terms of size, unit organization, and projections (i.e., sets of units being connected with). The relationships between different sets may be expressed in absolute or relative terms, thus sustaining functional modules if these develop during the course of optimization.

Miller et al. [34] use strong representation. A network of n units may be represented by a connectivity matrix of the order $n(n + 1)$ defining connections as well as unit thresholds. A genotype is formed by concatenation of such matrix rows.

Somewhere in between are Schaffer et al. [33] and Maričić and Nikolov [32], whose representations define a number of hidden layers and their sizes, assuming full connectivity from the ith to the $(i + 1)^{\text{st}}$ layer. Maričić and Nikolov [32], and apparently Schaffer et al. [33], are not able to describe networks having connections between other than adjoining layers. This appears to be a substantial limitation, since networks having direct connections from input to output layers reportedly have better learning capabilities [34,37,38].

Whitley and Bogart [37] are using network pruning, where a simple representation suffices: Each genotype bit corresponds to a particular weight in the initial (largest) network.

Fitness Evaluation. Although this line of research has been motivated by network size optimization, this need not be the only evaluation criterion. If a network adapted to frequent relearning of similar training sets is needed, learning speed is critical. A simple comparison of learning abilities could be based on the error observed after a fixed number of training epochs [32,34]. However, a learning curve may oscillate because of inadequately chosen BP algorithm parameters. Therefore, the integral of a learning curve [28] is a more appropriate indicator in such cases. If a network is to be used in a noisy environment, its ability to generalize is of primary interest. In such cases fitness should be evaluated by testing the network on examples not used during training [33]. Finally, all of these aspects could be united in a weighted sum. By changing the coefficient values, the designer may then emphasize elements significant for an application [29].

In network pruning [37], network quality is based on the error observed after a fixed number of training epochs, but networks with more connections pruned are given more training epochs to utilize.

Reproductive Plan. In addition to variants of the basic GA used, the crossover operator is frequently adapted to the representation employed. For representations allowing variable genotype size and structure a crossover operator has been developed capable of detecting homologue segments of two genotypes (by exploiting special intersegment markers) and swapping them [28]. The operator of Miller et al. [34] approaches the network processing unit as being a basic network building block, combining in this way units of different networks. Each unit description consists of its incoming connections and threshold variability information. Whitley and Bogart [37] use the reproductive plan GENITOR [39,40], which contrasts others mainly by allocating reproductive trials to individuals based on their rank in the population (being determined from individuals fitness) and by preventing offspring from replacing their parents. The system of Maričić and Nikolov [32] facilitates the choice among few reproductive plans in order to enable their comparison.

Results. Experiments are at present confined to small non-real-world problems. Almost all available texts on the subject describe design of networks for XOR problem, whereas some report investigations regarding digit recognition [28], minimum interesting coding problem [33], extended XOR [34], or a 2-bit adder [37]. Algorithms used usually tend to derive messy asymmetric networks that have better characteristics than those designed manually by humans. It has been noticed independently [34,37,38] that networks having direct connections from input to output layers may have better learning capabilities than those lacking them. In some cases [28] the characteristics of the problem being solved were discovered, of which the authors had no previous knowledge. Since various fitness functions are used, it is not possible to compare results of the experiments, even in cases when the same problem is being solved. However, the processing time frequently appears to be a limiting factor [28,34]. This might reasonably be expected, considering the error back propagation as a training method, and may be circumvented in several ways. The first alternative is the network pruning approach. The results of more systematic comparisons between the two approaches have to be waited for, however. The second alternative is the use of architectures that would enable training of several networks in parallel. Such an approach, based on a network of several Apollo workstations, Symbolics computers, and a VAX is mentioned in [30,31]. The authors expect a speedup in execution of a few orders of magnitude. Finally, perhaps, a back propagation could be substituted by some faster training procedure.

19.2.3 Weights Space

In the preceding section the application of GA to the first level of network adaptation has been considered. Here their application to the second level, the adaptation of weights, is discussed. It is the area in which back propagation is predominantly used. Its deficiencies—lengthy training when large training sets are used, problems with networks with multiple hidden layers [6], susceptibility to local minima—are well known and even more stressed when automation of network configuration design is considered. It comes as no surprise then, that GA were considered as back-propagation replacement. In spite of its apparent mismatch with the biological world, there is no reason to hesitate to investigate this possibility. Genetic algorithms are implying unsupervised learning procedure that does not require output vectors to be available during learning. Hence, the same algorithms might be used when supervised and unsupervised learning are required. However, before we review recent research, a word of caution is in order.

Already in their early texts some authors mention difficulties that may arise when the crossover operator is applied to problems such as this one [15,18]. In Figure 19.2*a* two typical XOR problem networks are shown (according to Rumelhart and McClelland [1]). They are structurally and functionally the same, except that internal roles of hidden units have been exchanged (by appropriately swapping the weight values around them). Suppose that during the GA weights optimization two networks of a similar kind evolved. Their genotypes represent their weight values (thresholds being ignored here, although they are also coded). The crossover operator may combine them in such a way as to create a genotype corresponding to dysfunctional network shown in Figure 19.2*b*. Generally, when several hidden units are connected with the rest of the network in the same way, they may undertake internal functions in several ways, leaving the global network functionality unchanged. Whitley et al. [38] discuss this as a "structural/functional mapping," while Montana and Davis [41] term it "the roles of hidden units." For a trivial network with a single hidden layer of n units, all being connected in the same manner, there may be up to $n!$ such mappings. This problem may be perceived in still another way: The weight values in a successful network are strongly coupled—it is an epistatic problem. Therefore, useful building blocks of the network need not be small, but, on the contrary, long (even noncontiguous) bit strings may exist in the genotype, that must not be split but manipulated as a whole. Standard GA are success-

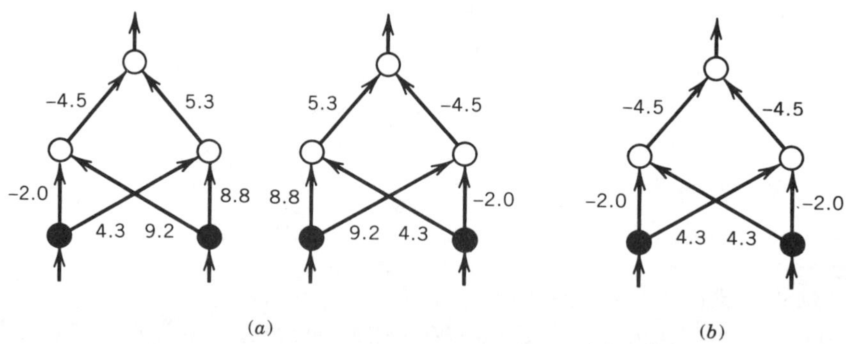

Figure 19.2 *Structural/functional mapping problem:* (a) *two functionally equivalent networks;* (b) *their potential dysfunctional offspring.*

ful as optimization procedures because of the manner in which they construct a good solution combining smȧll building blocks. If a good solution may not be constructed using such blocks, problems with GA might be expected.

There are few research groups trying to use GA instead of back propagation. Whitley and his collaborators were motivated by the possibility of testing their GENITOR reproductive plan on more complex problems than widely used De Jong's test-suite functions [23]. They represent the network of fixed connectivity (i.e., a set of weight and threshold values) using genotype consisting of concatenated 8-bit binary encoded values. Each network is being evaluated via total sum of squares error determined using a set of training patterns (in the sense of back propagation, of course). Based on this error, networks are ranked, in order to define selection probabilities according to their rank. Two-point recombination operator is used. Experiments concentrate mostly on networks for solving XOR, 4-2-4-encoder, or 2-bit adder problems. In the early papers [42,43] the need for larger populations in order to sustain population diversity has been observed. This implied prolonged training times. To sustain population diversity while keeping population smaller, an adaptive mutation operator has been developed, in which mutation probabilities are defined proportionally to the similarity of the parents being combined. When applied to fully connected 2-bit adder networks, the procedure encounters the problem of epistatic [36]. In most recent papers [38,44] the application of distributed GA GENITOR II is described. The algorithm maintains several isolated populations evolving autonomously, swapping from time to time genotypes among them. It is shown that in this way somewhat better results are obtained. However, contradictory requirements are being encountered, since too frequent swapping leads to a conventional single population algorithm behavior, while, according to the authors, too infrequent swapping leads to incompatible solutions being evolved in isolated populations, whose combination induces dysfunctional networks. Whitley reports that in spite of every effort taken, training time compares badly with back propagation.

Montana and Davis [41] have used a fundamentally different approach. Their research has been motivated by complex real-world underwater acoustic signal recognition problem in a noisy environment. They represent weight and threshold values of a fixed connectivity network using genotype consisting of a set of real values (i.e., no binary encoding is used). Network quality is estimated via total sum of squares error. Several knowledge-augmented mutation and crossover operators are introduced in the classical GA. In contrast to the conventional approach, where operators manipulate genotypes without any additional knowledge of the problem domain, these operators are aware of the network node concept, in connection with which strength and functionality notions are established. Experiments have been designed in order to investigate, among other things, the influence of problem-domain knowledge on mutation and crossover operators, as well as to compare the method with back propagation. It is shown that better results are achieved when the mutation operator acts simultaneously on each connection of a certain node. Rather high mutation rates have been employed. A special crossover operator, designed to "homologize two networks structurally and functionally" before recombination, showed no advantage over the classical crossover. This implies that structural/functional mapping presented no problem. A hybrid training system is also recommended, which would use GA in the first training phase and back propagation afterwards. In this way a robustness of GA could be used to approach a good minimum, while back propagation would than rapidly improve the solution. While it has been shown that this particular problem was handled better with GA than with pure back propagation, it should be noted that back propagation depends on few learning constants, whose inappropriately chosen values may lead to training oscillations. Whitley et al. [38] notice that, taking into account relatively small populations and higher mutation rates, usual search mechanisms of GA are presumably replaced here by stochastic hill climbing.

In addition to these two research groups, Caudell and Dolan [45] used GA to train the networks on generalized XOR problem. Binary-coded genotypes, classical GA and single-point crossover have been used. However, there has been no report on structural/functional mapping problem, neither was GA compared to back propagation.

19.2.4 Modular Programming

Recently a still different line of research has been reported in [46–49]. Though essentially being a weights space optimization method, it requires a separate treatment. The approach is motivated by the problem of constructing a neural network to control a dynamic system (for which the required outputs might not be known), such as a pair of walking stick legs or a simple lizard creature. In this respect it is similar to early attempts of Dress [16] in evolving a simple artificial insect behavior. The approach of de Garis rests, however, on a two-level modularization process. The first level might be termed *structural modularization,* by which a subdivision in a set of cooperative networks is assumed. These are typically seen as detector, control logic, and effector subnetworks [50]. With each subnetwork (i.e., module), the genetic programmer associates certain behavioral characteristics, size, and configuration (currently fully self-interconnected networks are considered). The module weights are then evolved using GA. However, with a network quality function a second level of modularization is associated. It may be termed *functional modularization*. It assumes the evolution of modules capable of performing progressively more complicated subtasks of the final task they are being trained for. This means a module is evolved to solve a simplified version of the final task at the beginning, and it is only then that evolution starts with a more complex task being learned. The GA employed does not use the crossover operator. It has been reported that by far the best evolution speeds are obtained using solely mutation [50]. This is in good accord with previously mentioned Whitley's observations [38] on epistatic problems such as 2-bit fully connected adder network.

The approach described is advantageous for the same reasons any GA applied to weights space optimization is: It may be used in the cases when required output vectors are unknown, thus effectively transforming the supervised learning process to a form of unsupervised one (if by supervision the availability of input-output vector pairs is assumed). Moreover, transfer functions of network processing units need not be semilinear any more—a requirement being posed by the theory supporting BP algorithm. However, there are potential pitfalls as well, the primary one being the necessity of problem modularization. One may imagine problems difficult to modularize. Furthermore, employing GA without crossover is essentially a nonregressive random search. While this may work well for some problems and relatively small networks, it need not scale up well.

19.2.5 Growth-Rules Space

While not employing GA, Mjolsness and his colleagues describe an interesting approach in a series of reports [51,52,53]. They are motivated by problems for which large networks are required, while it is expected that these may be constructed repetitively using a smaller network structure. Such is a continuous code problem, in which a network of N input nodes equally spaced on the unit interval, and $A = 2 \log N$ output nodes is to map input to output in such a way that two unary inputs that are geometrically close to one another produce two outputs that are close in the Hamming metric. The construction of such a network is viewed as an optimization, not of the network itself but of the growth rules for its construction. While the underlying mathematics is somewhat involved, the approach is intuitively simple. A parametrized recursion relation may define a search space consisting of families of network connection matrices of increasing size. A search is being conducted (via simulated annealing [54]) using a finite number of small tasks. The resultant recursion relation with optimized and fixed parameters is used to construct a connection matrix for a larger task but involving no further learning.

19.3 EXAMPLES OF WEIGHTS SPACE SEARCH

In this section some of the issues regarding weights space search are illustrated on a few simple problems. These are XOR, 4-2-4 encoder, and 2-bit adder. Respective networks (named 221, 424, and 443) as well as input-output training (testing) vector pairs are shown on Figure 19.3. In order to be able to compare learning curves among different problems and training algorithms, a function for evaluating network fitness should be defined. BP is a

221 Network (9-dimensional search space)

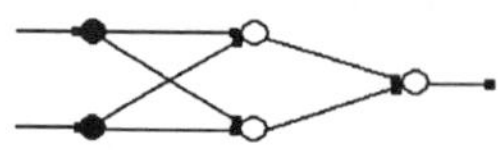

Input:	Output:
0 0	0
0 1	1
1 0	1
1 1	0

424 Network (22-dimensional search space)

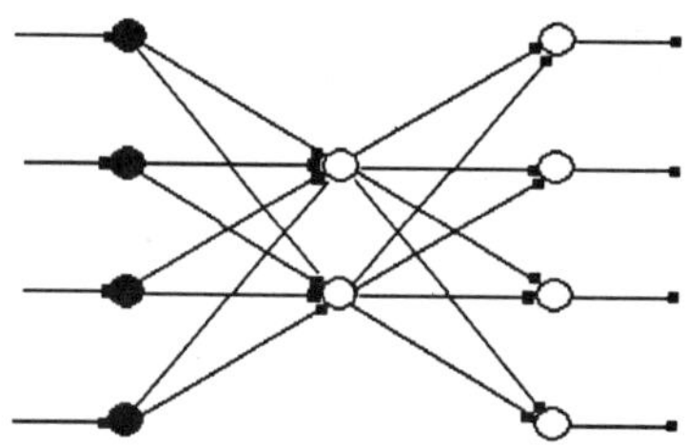

Input:	Output:
0 0 0 1	0 0 0 1
0 0 1 0	0 0 1 0
0 1 0 0	0 1 0 0
1 0 0 0	1 0 0 0

443 Network (35-dimensional search space)

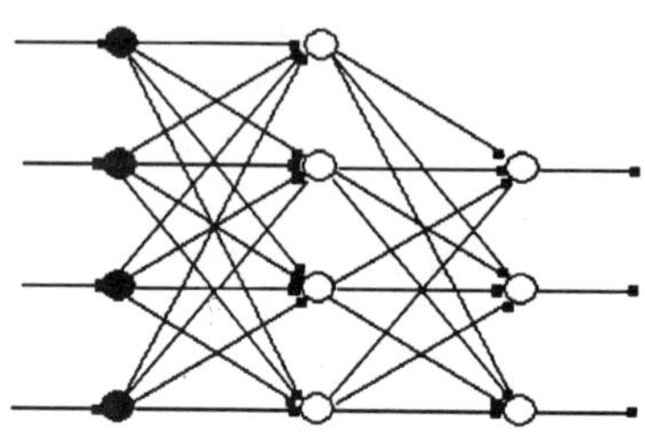

Input:	Output:
0 0 0 0	0 0 0
0 0 0 1	0 0 1
0 0 1 0	0 1 0
0 0 1 1	0 1 1
0 1 0 0	0 0 1
0 1 0 1	0 1 0
0 1 1 0	0 1 1
0 1 1 1	1 0 0
1 0 0 C	0 1 0
1 0 0 1	0 1 1
1 0 1 0	1 0 0
1 0 1 1	1 0 1
1 1 0 0	0 1 1
1 1 0 1	1 0 0
1 1 1 0	1 0 1
1 1 1 1	1 1 1

Figure 19.3 *Networks and input-output vector pairs for solving XOR function, 4-2-4 encoder, and 2-bit adder problems (top to bottom).*

steepest-descent algorithm searching for minimum total sum of squares error e_{tss} in the space of connection weights. It starts with a single network, initialized to random weights, and works toward minimum e_{tss} in a well-known forward-backward cycles (that constitute an epoch when repeated over the complete training set). The GA is a stochastic search procedure searching for a weights set associated with higher fitness values. Fitness f is defined in terms of e_{tss}.

$$f = \begin{cases} 1 - \dfrac{e_{tss}}{e_{max}} & \text{for } e_{tss} \le e_{max} \\ 0 \quad e_{max} & \text{otherwise} \end{cases}$$

where $e_{max} = 0.36ot$
o = number of processing elements in output network layer
t = number of training input-output vector pairs

The definition of e_{max} is such that condition $e_{tss} > e_{max}$ is true only in rare cases at the training outset. In order to appreciate this fitness definition, refer to Figure 19.4, where BP learning curves for all three problems are

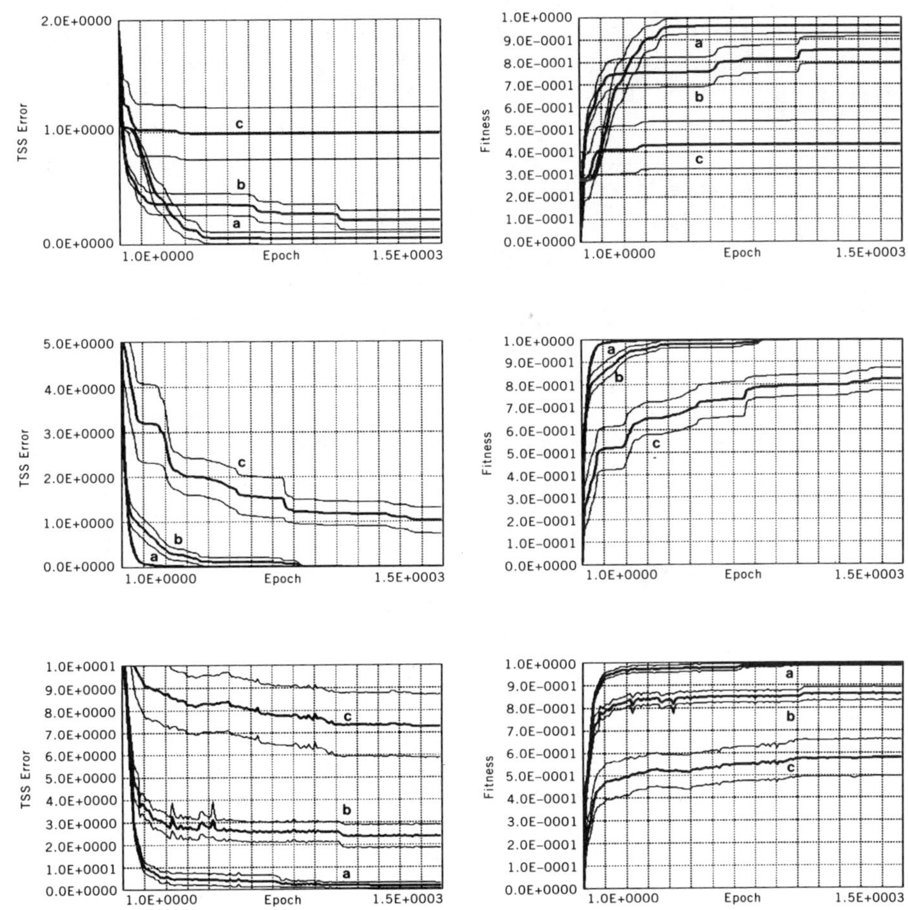

Figure 19.4 *Back-propagation learning curves for XOR, 4-2-4 encoder, and 2-bit adder problems (top to bottom). Standard error margins are indicated, based on 10 runs. Left column shows curves in terms of* e_{tss}, *right in terms of fitness* f. (a) *initial weights from [−0.5, 0.5],* (b) *initial weights from [−5, 5],* (c) *initial weights from [−10, 10].*

shown in terms of e_{tss} and fitness f. Each diagram shows three curves, depending on the initial weight values interval. Results are averaged over ten runs, with standard error margins indicated. Since BP relies on a few parameters, they were set to fairly standard values; that is, learning rate was 0.5 and learning momentum was 0.9. These could perhaps be better tuned (especially for a 2-bit adder problem, for which learning curve oscillations are noticeable), although this was not found necessary for the present discussion. Figure 19.4 reveals that success of BP on problems discussed depends heavily on initial weight values. When chosen uniformly among those close to zero, results are positive. This is a known fact [1], therefore usually taken care of.

For comparing the progress of BP and GA it is necessary to estimate their time complexity. Each GA network fitness evaluation consists of only forward passes of analogous forward-backward BP epoch. If it is supposed that time used for fitness evaluations is much larger than one used for GA housekeeping and genotypes decoding, it follows that $2n$ GA network evaluations correspond to n BP epochs. In most of experiments presented the total number of fitness evaluations performed (which equals the number of generations times the population size) is 3000.

Two variants of GA shall be used in experiments described in this and the following sections: standard GA and elitist GA. They differ in that elitist GA does not allow the best-entity-so-far to vanish. If there is no better entity in the current generation, than the best-entity-so-far replaces the worst-of-current-generation one. Figure 19.5 presents results of experiments comparing the efficiency of random search versus two GA variants. Parameters being common to both GA alternatives are given in Figure 19.6*a*. It is interesting to note the remarkable success of pure random search on XOR problem, indicating its relative simplicity. Elitist GA is approaching the top fitness seemingly more consistently than BP on the same problem. The difference is not significant, however. Unfortunately, a rapid degradation in performance of both standard and elitist GA on 4-2-4 encoder and 2-bit adder problems is obvious. This may simply be the result of a larger chromosome length used with these problems. Namely, a 221 network is evolved using 54-bit chromosomes, while for 424 and 443 networks 132- and 210-bit chromosomes are used, respectively.

In Figure 19.7, the influence of varying crossover and mutation probability changes on an elitist GA evolving a 221 network is illustrated. Although the values of $p_m = 0.003$, 0.3, and 0.6 were also investigated, their influence was found to be insignificant; in all these cases the corresponding results were worse than the one for $p_m = 0.033$. Other GA parameters used are shown on Figure 19.6*b*.

Finally, Figure 19.8 reveals that changing the chromosome length has no significant influence on an elitist GA evolving a 221 network. Detailed GA parameters used are shown on the same figure. These results suggest that epistatic nature of the problem has more detrimental impact on the GA performance than do larger chromosome lengths.

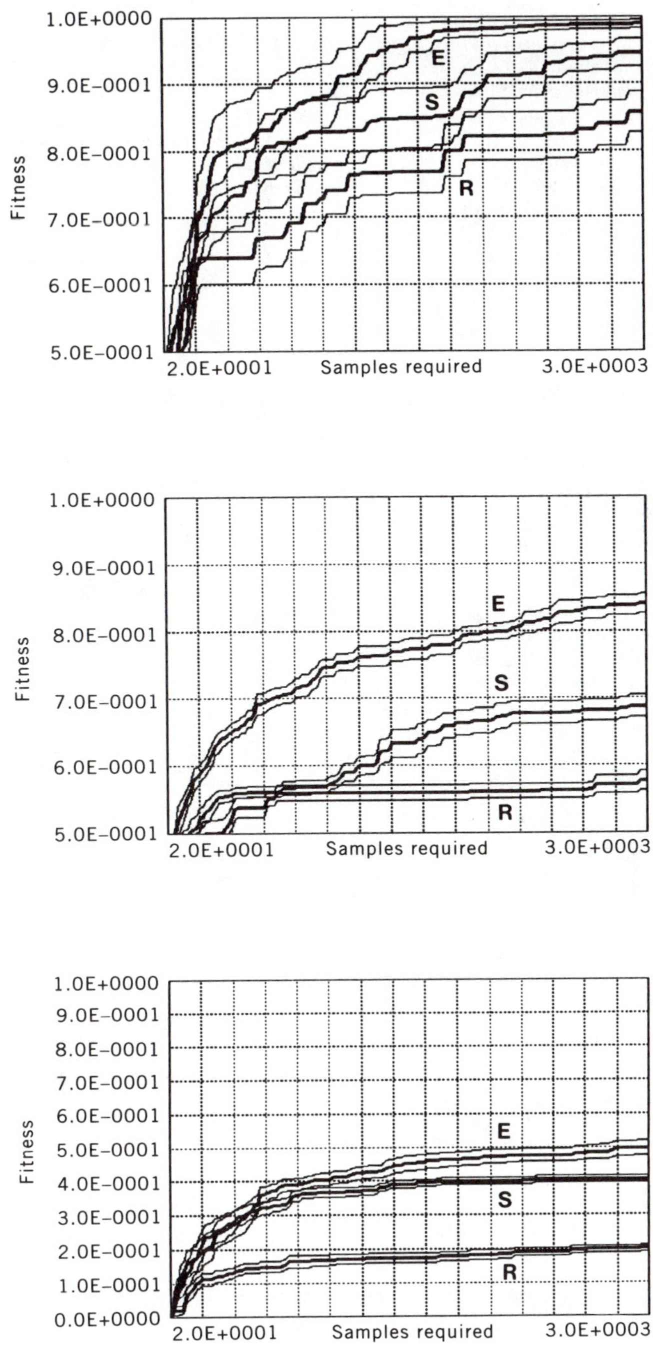

Figure 19.5 *The best-entity-so-far for XOR problem (top), 4-2-4 encoder problem (center), and 2-bit adder problem (bottom): R = random search, S = standard GA, E = elitist GA. Standard error margins are indicated, based on 10 runs.*

Number of generations:	150
Generation size:	20
Total number of samples:	3000
Crossover probability p_c:	0.6
Mutation probability p_m:	0.0333
Selection type:	Stochastic sampling with replacement ('roulette wheel')
Scaling factor:	Scaling not used
Chromosome bits per weight/threshold:	6
Weight/threshold value interval:	-10.0 ... 10.0
Weight/threshold initial value interval:	-10.0 ... 10.0
Weight/threshold resolution:	0.3175

a)

GA variant:	Elitist
Number of generations:	150
Generation size:	20
Total number of samples:	3000
Selection type:	Remainder stochastic sampling without replacement
Scaling factor:	2.0
Chromosome bits per weight/threshold:	6
Weight/threshold value interval:	-10.0 ... 10.0
Weight/threshold initial value interval:	-10.0 ... 10.0
Weight/threshold resolution:	0.3175

b)

Figure 19.6 (a) *GA parameters used to obtain results shown in Figure 19.5* (b) *GA parameters used to obtain results shown on Figure 19.7.*

These experiments illustrated what is believed to be the most likely performance of a fairly standard GAs when applied to neural networks design problem. Although they seem to be skepticism provoking, in the following section we try to use this approach in developing a pole-balancing controller based on a recurrent neural network.

19.4 THE POLE-BALANCING PROBLEM REVISITED

The pole-balancing system is defined in Figure 19.9, in accordance with [55]. Cart-pole system, described by four state variables (cart position x, cart velocity $\dot{x}$, pole angle θ, and pole angular velocity $\dot{\theta}$), is controlled by a "bang-bang" force of fixed magnitude F that may take one of two possible directions. Nonlinear differential equations describing the system are

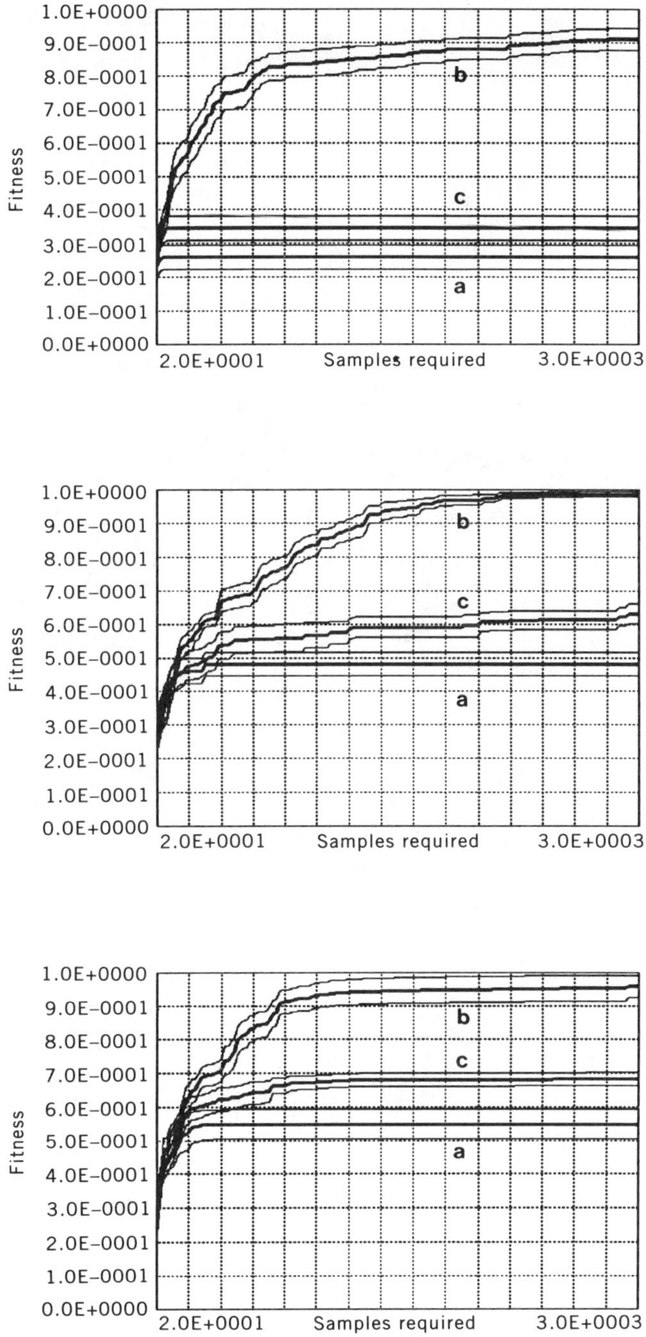

Figure 19.7 *The best-entity-so-far for XOR problem, when* p_c *and* p_m *are varied: (top)* $p_c = 0.0$*, (center)* $p_c = 0.6$*, (bottom)* $p_c = 1.0$. (a) $p_m = 0.0$, (b) $p_m = 0.0333$, (c) $p_m = 1.0$. *Standard error margins are indicated, based on 10 runs.*

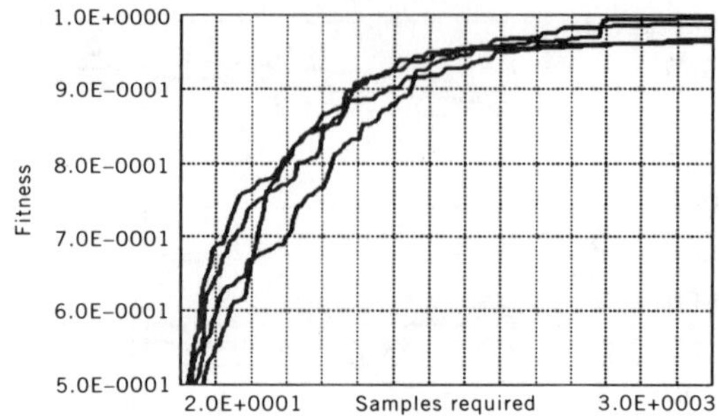

a)

GA variant:	Elitist
Number of generations:	150
Generation size:	20
Total number of samples:	3000
Selection type:	Remainder stochastic sampling without replacement
Scaling factor:	2.0
Weight/threshold value interval:	-10.0 ... 10.0
Weight/threshold initial value interval:	-10.0 ... 10.0

b)

Figure 19.8 (a) *The best-entity-so-far for XOR problem for 4, 6, 8, and 16 chromosome bits per network weight/threshold value. Averaged over 10 runs.* (b) *GA parameters used to obtain these results.*

$$\dot{\theta}_t = \frac{g \sin \theta_t + \dfrac{-F_t - m_p l \dot{\theta}_t^2 \sin \theta_t}{m_c + m_p} \cos \theta_t}{l\left[\dfrac{4}{3} - \dfrac{m_p \cos^2 \theta_t}{m_c + m_p}\right]}$$

$$\ddot{x}_t = \frac{F_t + m_p l[\dot{\theta}_t^2 \sin \theta_t - \ddot{\theta}_t \cos \theta_t]}{m_c + m_p}$$

In experiments to be described, the pole-balancing system is simulated by approximating solutions of these equations, using the fourth-order Runge-Kutta method with a constant time step of 0.02 s. At each sampling time step, values of all state variables are made available to the controller, which should determine force direction to be applied to the cart during the next

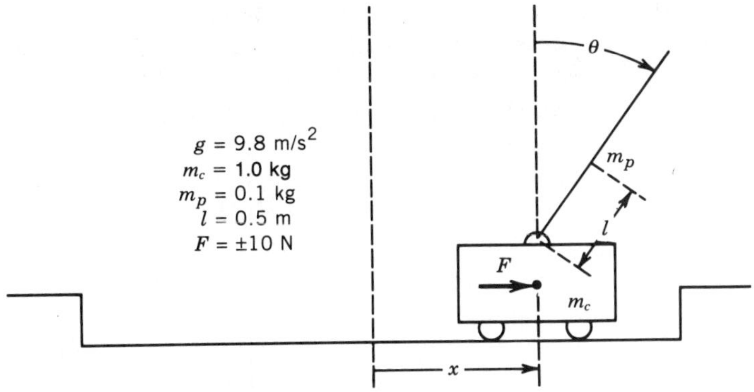

Figure 19.9 *The pole-balancing system.*

time step. Several control objectives may be defined for this system. According to the most usual one, the controller should keep the system inside a specified state-space region for as long as possible. The failure signal is triggered by leaving this region. On the other hand, it is also possible to search for the time-optimal control strategy [56,57] in which the system is required to come to rest in a minimal time, with the pole balanced.

The problem has been approached by a multitude of techniques, ranging from classical control theory, quantitative modeling, artificial neural networks (NN) [55,58], and genetic algorithms [56]. Overviews of the most of these may be found in [35,59]. Here we mention only those using an NN or GA approach. Barto et al. [55] adopt the objective of keeping the system inside a specified state-space region for as long as possible. The failure signal, emitted when leaving this region, gives no hint for improving the controller, since it is not obvious when a decision leading to failure has been made. Under these conditions, the neural network to be used as a controller cannot be trained using supervised learning techniques. Thus, a sort of reinforcement learning is employed—"learning with a critic." It uses two adaptive devices: While the *associative search element* (ASE) specifies control actions, an *adaptive critic element* (ACE) predicts consequences of each action. The learning rule of ASE takes into account ACE's predictions. Such a system is, in principle, able to control a time-varying system. Koza [56,57] genetically evolves LISP code that should act as a time-optimal controller.

The interest in the pole-balancing problem also stems from the fact that its nature is similar to that of a two-legged walking. Recently, de Garis [48,49; video presentation at 46] has described an approach to a two-legged walking problem that has been classified as a modular programming in Section 19.2.4. De Garis names it *genetic programming,* although it is not related in any way with the issues presented by Koza. A 12-node fully connected recurrent neural network is used as a four-joint two-legged walking system controller. Eight input network nodes receive samples of joints' angles and angular velocities, while four output nodes generate angular acceleration control signals. Network connection weights are evolved via GA. It has been mentioned in [48] that no crossover operator was used in the experiments performed (i.e., crossover probability $p_c = 0$), since its influence has been found detrimental. This has lead to some remarks [60] about the possible nature of the search space and the search itself. While it is questionable if GA without crossover should be regarded a proper GA, its operation has a form of a stochastic hill-climbing search. A more recent report by de Garis [49] mentions a usual value of $p_c = 0.6$ in the same experiments. This has lead us to conduct a series of experiments, which were to explore the influence of crossover probabilities, when GA is applied to a pole-balancing problem.

19.4.1 Methodology

The complete system for genetically evolving pole-balancing network controllers is shown in Figure 19.10. While network size and connectivity are fixed, connection weights should be modified in order for a network to learn its task. The analog of the learning rule is realized using a GA, which breeds appropriate network weight values. In this context, structure to be optimized is a network of fixed connectivity and variable connection weight values; evaluation of the network implies its testing in order to acquire some numeric measure of its fitness for the control task; network genotype represents suitably encoded network weight values; and finally, formation of new genotypes implies using genetic operators (such as crossover and mutation) on selected genotypes, thus forming new ones.

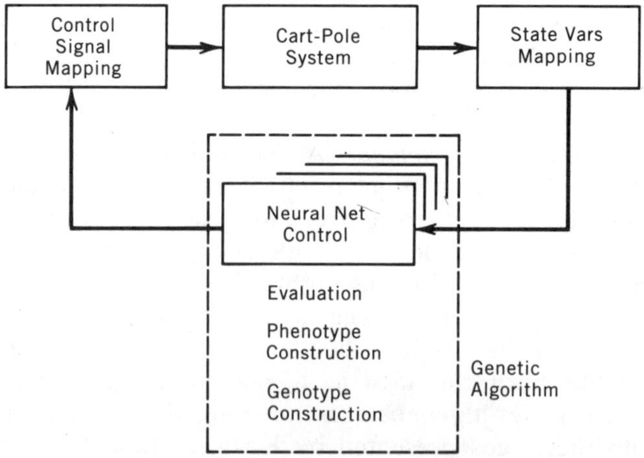

Figure 19.10 *Genetically programmed pole-balancing controller.*

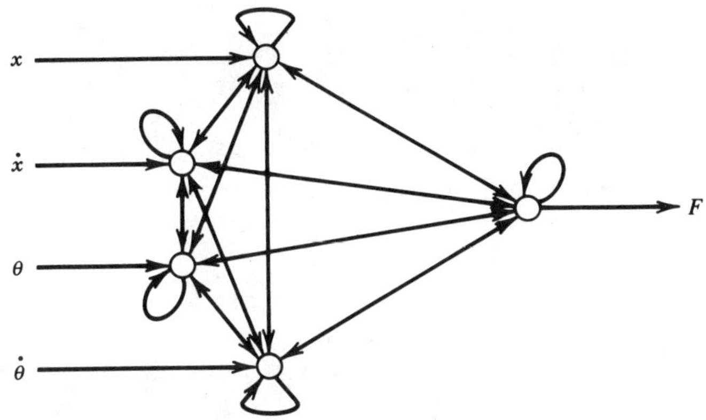

Figure 19.11 *Connectivity of a recurrent network used as a controller.*

In this section the architecture of a network whose weights should be evolved, a way network input signals are normalized and output signal is used to drive a controlling force, as well as several possible definitions of network fitness function are described.

The Network. Neural network consists of five fully self-interconnected processing elements (PEs), as shown in Figure 19.11. Four of them act as input elements, receiving normalized cart-pole state variable values. The fifth PE's output is used to determine the direction (and possibly magnitude) of the control force F during the next time step. Output o_i of the ith PE is defined by

$$o_i = \frac{2}{1 + e^{-\text{net}_i}} - 1$$

where net_i is a weighted sum of all the incoming signals to the ith PE (plus the network input signal, where appropriate). Processing elements calculate their outputs synchronously. After each presentation of network input values, they are allowed some settling time before network output signal is made available to the controlled system. In all our experiments settling time was set to 10 PEs synchronous processing steps.

Network Input and Output Signals. Controlled system state variables are mapped on the interval [−1.0, 1.0] in order to correspond to the PE's input-output signals. Two mapping systems were used in our experiments. These systems are defined in Figure 19.12.

When following the approach discussed, it is not necessary to employ a controlling force of a fixed magnitude (i.e., of a bang-bang nature). It seems

State variable	Mapping A 'from' interval	Mapping B 'from' interval	'to' interval
Hor. position [m]	-2.40 ... 2.40	-1.00 ... 1.00	-1.0 ... 1.0
Hor. velocity [m/s]	-4.80 ... 4.80	-2.00 ... 2.00	-1.0 ... 1.0
Angle [rad]	-1.57 ... 1.57	-1.57 ... 1.57	-1.0 ... 1.0
Ang. velocity [rad/s]	-3.14 ... 3.14	-3.14 ... 3.14	-1.0 ... 1.0

Figure 19.12 *Two mapping systems of network input signals.*

interesting to explore the possibility of evolving a controller that will use a force of varying magnitude. Therefore, in some experiments the sign of network's output signal determines the force direction, while in others its value (suitably mapped) determines the force's magnitude as well.

The Fitness Function. In his application of GP to this problem, Koza [57] defines the fitness function in terms of time required to bring the system at rest, with the pole balanced. To establish the final fitness value for a controller, fitness is averaged over 10 initial condition cases with random initial system states.

In our preliminary experiments [61] fitness was based on the time during which the system, initialized to a random state, stays inside a predefined region. Since maximum simulated time had to be imposed, it was associated with a maximum fitness of 1.0. The fitness measure, as defined, is a noisy one, since a network evaluation is based on a random initial controlled system state. For experiments presented in this chapter two fitness functions were defined. The first one, f_A, is similar to the one just mentioned, except that the initial system state is now fixed for all evaluations, and maximal simulated time is set to 20 s. There is only one simulation (i.e., one initial state) per fitness evaluation. With fitness function, f_A, network input signal mapping system **A** is used. Details of initial state regions are given in Figure 19.13.

For evaluation of optimal control systems, several error measures are suggested, such as

$$e_{\text{abs}} = \int_t |y - y_r| \qquad e_{\text{sq}} = \int_t (y - y_t)^2 \qquad e_{\text{ita}} = \int_t |y - y_r| t$$

where y is the controlled value and y_r is the required value.

Fitness type	Initial state: Hor. pos.	Hor. vel.	Angle	Ang. vel.	Allowed range: Hor. pos.	Angle	Evaluat. duration
f_A	-0.20	0.00	-0.10	0.00	-2.4 ... 2.4	-0.20 .. 0.20	20
f_B	0.00	0.00	-0.10	0.00	-0.5 ... 0.5	-1.57 .. 1.57	6

Figure 19.13 *Elements of two different fitness function definitions.*

Our second fitness function, f_B, is based on e_{ita} (integrated time-absolute error). However, when considering pole-balancing problem, two aspects should be taken care of (both of them are usually included in a definition of allowed state region): balancing the pole and avoiding limitless horizontal skidding. Taking this into account, f_B is defined as follows. The fitness value is based on a single simulation starting from a predefined state, and lasting for a predefined simulated time (refer to Fig. 19.13 for details). If the system reaches a forbidden state, its variables are forced to their border values, and simulation continues in order to correctly compute e_{ita}, which is based on the pole angle. A precomputed maximal value of e_{ita} is associated with $f_B = 0.0$, while $e_{ita=0.0}$ corresponds to $f_B = 1.0$. With fitness function f_B, network input signal mapping system **B** is used.

19.4.2 Experimental Results and Discussion

Here attempts toward evolving controllers employing either constant magnitude or varying magnitude force are described. All four combinations of two fitness functions and two force types have been tried. These are enumerated on Figure 19.14*a*, using the same positional arrangement as will be used for presentation of results. Each *fitness function–force type* combination was approached using random search, standard GA, and elitist GA. Genetic algorithm variants did not differ with respect to their parameters, which are presented in Figure 19.14*b*. The definition of elitist GA was given in Section 19.3. Results are reproduced in three figures: Figure 19.15 presents best-fitness-so-far, Figure 19.16 average-of-generation, and Figure 19.17 off-line GA performance measure. The off-line performance is an average of all best-of-generation values up to and including the current one. It illustrates the quality of GA's approach toward the best entities, while disregarding collective migration of the whole populations toward better fitness values.

The major difference among these results arises from a problem definition. It is obvious that a fixed-force-magnitude problem is an easy one. A simple random search quickly stumbles across a good solution, usually after several tens of samples. Figure 19.15 even indicates that random search is superior, although not significantly, to GA on this problem. It is no problem then for GA (especially an elitist one) to improve the average population fitness, what is noticeable in Figure 19.16. Good off-line performance of a random search confirms that good solutions are common for this problem definition.

A varying-force-magnitude problem is not so easy. The advantage of using GA over random search is clear. Elitist GA has a particular advantage when fitness is defined using e_{ita}. Off-line performance indicates, however, that neither GA versions are capable of rapidly advancing towards good solutions. In addition, the average-of-generation data of Figure 19.16 suggests that for the varying force magnitude problem genetic algorithms are

Constant force magnitude Fitness f_A	Varying force magnitude Fitness f_A
Constant force magnitude Fitness f_B	Varying force magnitude Fitness f_B

Force definitions: Constant magnitude $F = \pm 10$ N
Varying magnitude $-20 \text{ N} \leq F \leq 20$ N

a)

GA variant:	Elitist
Number of generations:	40
Generation size:	20
Total number of samples:	800
Crossover probability p_c:	0.6
Mutation probability p_m:	0.0333
Selection type:	Stochastic sampling with replacement ('roulette wheel')
Scaling factor:	2.0
Search space dimensionality:	25
Chromosome bits per weight/threshold:	6
Total chromosome length:	150
Weight/threshold value interval:	-1.0 ... 1.0
Weight/threshold initial value interval:	-1.0 ... 1.0
Weight/threshold resolution:	0.03175

b)

Figure 19.14 *Additional data on pole-balancing experiments.* (a) *Four combinations of force and fitness types.* (b) *GA parameters used.*

almost completely unable to upgrade generation averages by recombining good solutions in a constructive way.

These findings confirm that results of applying GAs to the evolution of recurrent network weights should be analyzed carefully. It is obviously possible to generate trivial search spaces on which random search would do fine. Why this is so is at present unknown to author.

19.5 CHAOS?

Fitness functions used in experiments described were based on a single (and always the same) initial cart-pole state. Therefore, it is necessary to see how large the space of possible initial states is for which the controller is able to stabilize the system.

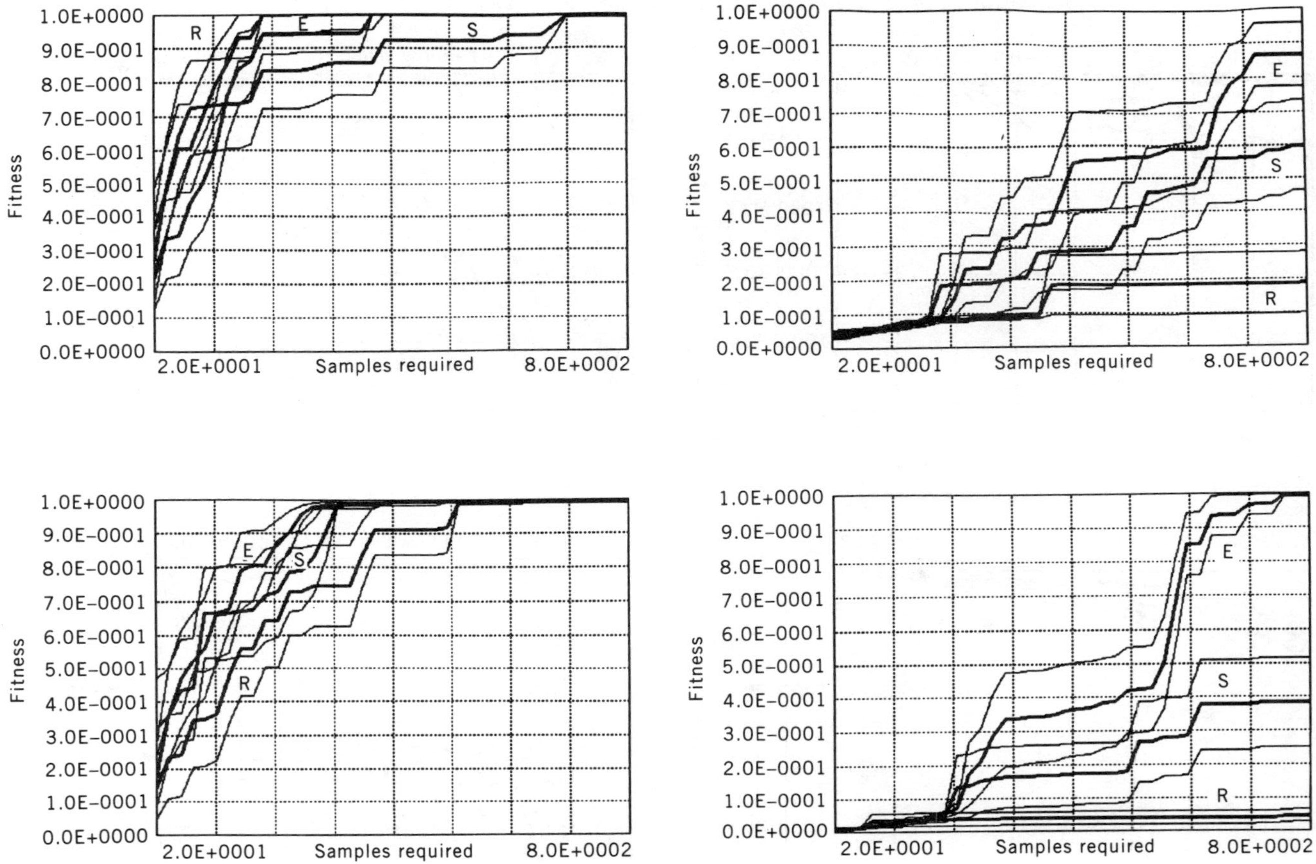

Figure 19.15 *The best-entity-so-far curves for four variations of the pole-balancing problem (see Figure 19.14 for explanation): R = random search, S = standard GA, E = elitist GA. Standard error margins are indicated, based on 10 runs.*

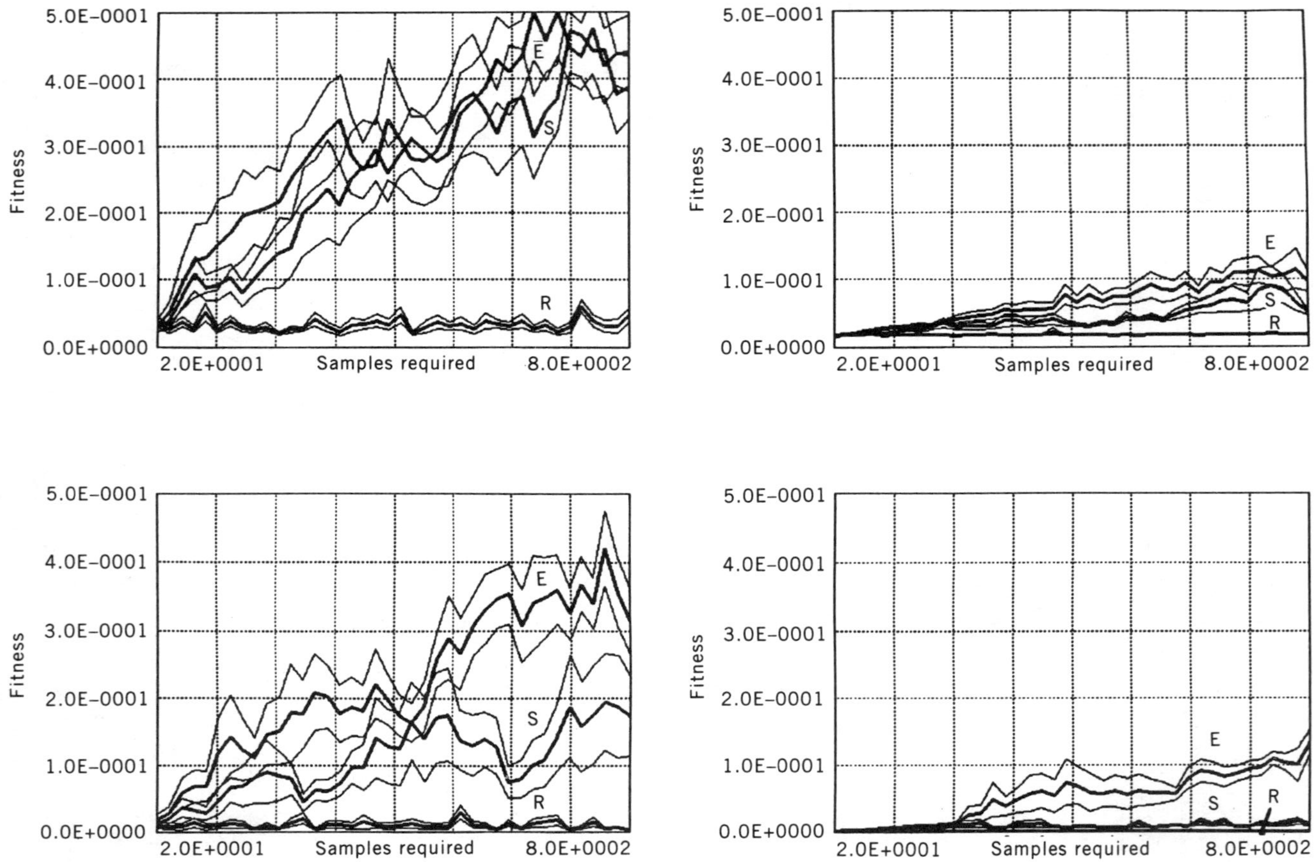

Figure 19.16 *The generation average curves for four variations of the pole-balancing problem (see Fig. 19.14 for explanation): R = random search, S = standard GA, E = elitist GA. Standard error margins are indicated, based on 10 runs.*

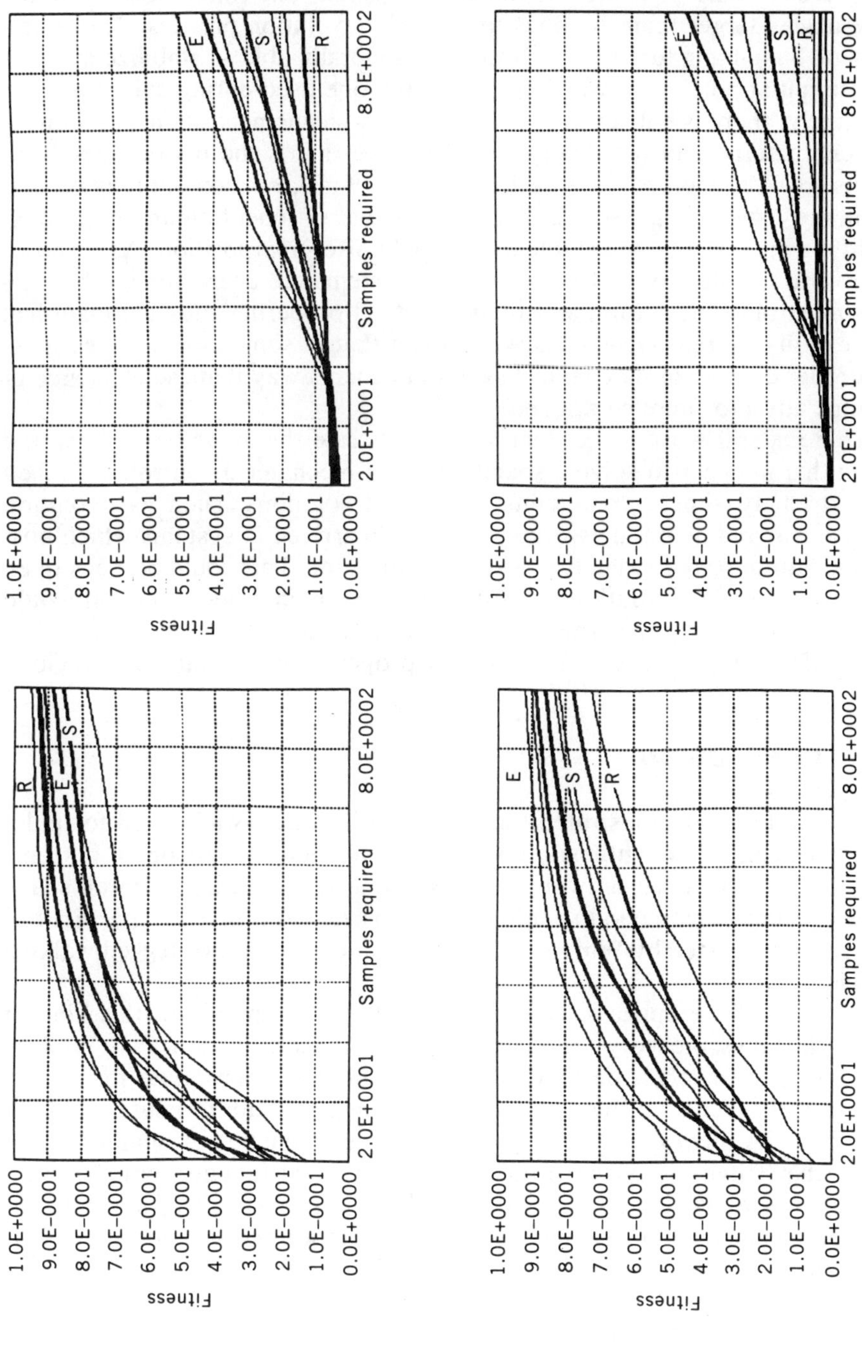

Figure 19.17 *Off-line performance curves for four variations of the pole-balancing problem (see Fig. 19.14 for explanation): R = random search, S = standard GA, E = elitist GA. Standard error margins are indicated, based on 10 runs.*

It has been observed that controllers which employ a varying driving force are extremely sensitive to initial system state and cannot tolerate initial pole angles larger than the ones used in the evolution process. Those employing bang-bang force were, however, generally able to stabilize systems whose initial pole angle was larger than the one used during evolution.

Finally, there is still another aspect of pole-balancing systems, and this is the characteristic of a "steady-state" regime that is the period after transients are over and system is oscillating near ($\theta = 0, x = \text{cons}$). Many natural oscillatory systems possess an intriguing blend of repetition and unpredictability, which is not explainable by a trivial noise superposition. As is shown in several chapters of this volume, such systems are characterized by possessing strange attractors, and their chaotical properties may be quantified by several different measures. We suspect that in some cases, the evolved controller drives our mechanical system in such a way that the existence of strange attractor may be noticed.

There is still work to be done to demonstrate this hypothesis. It would mean that in order to solve a specific task of mechanical control, we relied on extremely simple emulations of natural solutions, such as evolution mechanism and neural network systems, and arrived at systems which possess a natural property such as a strange attractor. This could perhaps open the possibility for evolution of controllers for which fitness function would not be defined only in terms of duration of successful stabilization or the speed of gaining stability, but also on the properties of a steady-state regime.

19.6 CONCLUSION

Although it was demonstrated that GA may be successfully used for pole-balancing controller synthesis, a number of questions remain open. It seems that it is the particular network type used that is generating a search space relatively dense with good solutions of the particular problem. This fact has been also suggested by Whitley [60] in the context of the two-legged walking problem.

Because of the epistatic nature of objects being optimized, this kind of problem brings the very foundations of a GA research to a test. While a possible answer might be that GAs are simply not appropriate for such a problem, it is felt that the issue could be beneficial both to neural network research, GA theory, and theoretical biology and genetics. A number of GA researchers investigate the problem of multimodal function optimization. While some explore distributed GA implying the existence of several subpopulations instead of a single one [44,62], or notions of distance and neighborhood among population members placed on ring or planar grids [63,64], others compare various schemes of not so spaciously defined subpopulations, along with restrictive mating policies [65]. The laws of restricted breeding and species formation seem to be of fundamental importance in both approaches.

Constraints on recombination of different natural species chromosomes may be viewed as evolutionary shortcuts avoiding experiments known in advance to yield poor results (the knowledge in advance being somehow based on extensive failures encountered in the past). This seems a good strategy approach to epistatic problems. Genetic algorithm models currently incorporate similar features usually by means of globally defined parameters. Although adequate in a lot of situations, these models impose the problem of global parameter tuning. Much more appealing would be the model of GA independent of such global parameters, the one controlled by information distributed in the very genotypes of objects being optimized.

It is appropriate to view the rules of biological evolution as a result of evolutionary process itself [21]. Findings in genetics indicate that a great part of chromosome length in higher species does not contain information necessary to build a system. It may be speculated that information controlling the very process of evolution is stored there, describing the current state of the algorithm in a distributed manner. Perhaps the mechanics of species formation, that is mechanism disabling recombination between excessively different chromosomes, is encoded there, being itself modified.

There has been little research along these lines in the GA community [19,66,67], and it is believed that from the exchange of ideas between genetics and GA research a synergistic effect might be expected, contributing to neural network learning algorithms research as well.

ACKNOWLEDGMENTS

The author acknowledges the help and constant encouragement of Professor Branko Souček of Faculty of Mathematics at the University of Zagreb, who made numerous valuable suggestions.

REFERENCES

[1] D. E. Rumelhart and J. L. McClelland, *Parallel Distributed Processing—Explorations in the Microstructure of Cognition, Volume 1: Foundations,* MIT Press, Cambridge, Mass., 1989.

[2] J. Yestrebsky, P. Basehore, and J. Reed, ''Neural Bit-Slice Computing Element,'' Micro Devices Tech. Rep. (December 1989).

[3] R. C. Johnson, Neural microchips debut, *PC AI,* 38–41 (January/February, 1990).

[4] R. P. Lippmann, An inroduction to computing with neural nets, *IEEE ASSP Mag.*, 4–22 (April 1987).

[5] W. Y. Huang, and R. P. Lippmann, (1987). Comparisons between neural net and conventional classifiers, *Proc. IEEE 1st Internat. Conf. on Neural Networks,* IV-485–IV–493 (1987).

[6] H. C. Lui, Decision boundary formation from the back-propagation algorithm, *Proc. Internat. Symp. on Computer Architecture and Digital Signal Processing* (1989).

[7] H. C. Lui, Analysis of decision contour of neural network with sigmoidal nonlinearity. *Proc. Internat. Joint Conf. on Neural Networks (IJCNN-90),* Washington, D.C., I-655–I-659 (1990).

[8] C. L. D'Autrechy, J. A. Reggia, G. G. Sutton, III, and S. M. Goodall, A general-purpose simulation environment for developing connectionist models, *Simulation,* 51(1), 5–19 (1988).

[9] J. A. Feldman, M. A. Fanty, and N. H. Goddard, Computing with structured neural networks, *Computer,* 21(3) 91–103 (March 1988).

[10] N. G. Goddard, K. J. Lynne, T. Mintz, and L. Bukys, "Rochester Connectionist Simulator," Tech. Rep. 233 (revised), Computer Science, University of Rochester, (1989).

[11] D. Zipser and D. Rabin, (1986). "P3: A Parallel Network Simulating Program," in D. E. Rumelhart and J. L. McClelland, *Parallel Distributed Processing—Explorations in the Microstructure of Cognition, Volume 1: Foundations,* MIT Press, Cambridge, Mass., 1986.

[12] C. L. D'Autrechy, J. A. Reggia, G. G. Sutton, III, and S. M. Goodall, Maryland MIRRORS/II: A connectionist model simulator, M.D. *Computing,* 7(1), 12–24 (1990).

[13] C. L. D'Autrechy, J. A. Reggia, G. G. Sutton, III, S. M. Goodall, M. A. Tagamets, and P. M. Marsland "Mirrors/II Reference Manual," Computer Science Tech. Rep. UMIACS-TR-88-41, CS-TR-2043, University of Maryland, (1988).

[14] J. L. McClelland, and D. E. Rumelhart, *Explorations in Parallel Distributed Processing—A Handbook of Models, Programs and Exercises,* MIT Press, Cambridge, Mass., 1988.

[15] A. Bergman and M. Kerszberg, Breeding intelligent automata, *Proc. IEEE 1st Internat. Conf. on Neural Networks.* II-63–II-70 (1987).

[16] W. B. Dress, Darwinian optimization of synthetic neural systems, *Proc. IEEE Internat. Conf. on Neural Networks,* III-769–III-775 (1987).

[17] A. Bergman, Variation and selection: An evolutionary model of learning in neural networks, *1st Annual INNS Meeting,* Book of Abstracts, 75 (1988).

[18] P. M. Todd, "Evolutionary Methods for Connectionist Architectures," unpublished manuscript, Psychology Depart., Stanford University (1988).

[19] D. E. Goldberg, *Genetic Algorithms in Search, Optimization, and Machine Learning,* Addison-Wesley, Reading, Mass., 1989.

[20] Y. Davidor and H.-P. Schwefel, "An Introduction to Adaptive Optimization Algorithms Based on Principles of Natural Evolution," Chapter 9 herein.

[21] I. Rechenberg, "Artificial Evolution and Artificial Intelligence," in R. Forsyth, Ed., *Machine Learning—Principles and Techniques,* Chapman and Hall, London, 1989.

[22] J. H. Holland, *Adaptation in Natural and Artificial Systems,* University of Michigan Press, Ann Arbor, 1975.

[23] K. A. De Jong, "Analysis of the Behavior of a Class of Genetic Adaptive Systems," Ph.D. theses, Dept. of CC Sciences, University of Michigan, Ann Arbor MI (1975).

[24] J. D. Schaffer, Ed., *Proc. 3rd Internat. Conf. on Genetic Algorithms.* (1989).

[25] K. A. De Jong, Adaptive system design: A genetic approach, *IEEE Trans. on Systems, Man, and Cybernetics,* SMC-10(9) 566–574 (1980).

[26] A. D. Bethke, "Genetic Algorithms as Function Optimizers," Ph.D. theses, Dept. of CC Sciences, University of Michigan, Ann Arbor (1980).

[27] D. H. Ackley, "An Empirical Study of Bit Vector Function Optimization," in L. Davis, Ed., *Genetic Algorithms and Simulated Annealing,* Pitman, London, 1987.

[28] S. A. Harp, T. Samad, and A. Guha, Towards the Genetic Synthesis of Neural Networks. Proc. 3rd Internat. Conf. on Genetic Algorithms, 360–369 (1989).

[29] S. A. Harp, T. Samad, and A. Guha, "The Genetic Synthesis of Neural Networks," Tech. Rep. CSDD-89-I4852-2, Corporate Systems Development Divison, Honeywell, Golden Valley, Minn. (1989).

[30] S. A. Harp, T. Samad, and A. Guha, (1990). "Designing Application-Specific Neural Networks Using the Genetic Algorithm," In D. S. Touretsky, ed. *Advances in Neural Information Processing* Systems 2, Morgan Kaufman, San Mateo, Ca.

[31] S. A. Harp, T. Samad, and A. Guha, "Genetic Synthesis of Neural Networks Architecture," in L. Davis, Ed., *The Genetic Algorithms Handbook,* Van Nostrand Reinhold, New York, 1990.

[32] B. Maričić and Z. Nikolov, GENNET—System for computer aided neural network design using genetic algorithms, *Proc. Internat. Joint Conf. on Neural Networks (IJCNN-90),* Washington, D.C., I-102–I-105 (1990).

[33] J. D. Schaffer, R. A. Caruana, and L. J. Eshelman, Using genetic search to exploit the emergent behavior of neural networks, *Physica-D* (1990).

[34] G. F. Miller, P. M. Todd, and S. U. Hegde, Designing neural networks using genetic algorithms, *Proc. 3rd Internat. Conf. on Genetic Algorithms,* 379–384 (1989).

[35] V. Gullapalli, "Dynamic Systems Control via Associative Reinforcement Learning," Chapter 2 herein.

[36] D. Whitley and T. Starkweather, Optimizing small neural networks using a distributed genetic algorithm, *Proc. Internat. Joint Conf. on Neural Networks (IJCNN-90-WASH DC),* I-206–I-209 (1990).

[37] D. Whitley and C. Bogart, The evolution of connectivity: Pruning neural networks using genetic algorithms, *Proc. Internat. Joint Conf. on Neural Networks (IJCNN-90-WASH DC),* I-134–I-137 (1990).

[38] D. Whitley, T. Starkweather, and C. Bogart, Genetic algorithms and neural networks: Optimizing connections and connectivity, *Parallel Computing* (1990).

[39] D. Whitley and J. Kauth, GENITOR: A different genetic algorithm, *Proc. 1988 Rocky Mountain Conf. on Artificial Intelligence* (1988).

[40] D. Whitley and J. Kauth, "Sampling Long Schemata in Genetic Algorithms," Tech. Rep. CS-88-105, Dept. of Computer Science, Colorado State University, (1988).

[41] D. J. Montana and L. Davis, Training feedforward neural networks using genetic algorithms, *Proc. Internat. Joint Conf. on Artificial Intelligence* (1989).

[42] D. Whitley, The GENITOR algorithm and selection pressure: Why rank-based allocation of reproductive trials is best, *Proc. 3rd Internat. Conf. on Genetic Algorithms,* pp. 116–121 (1989).

[43] D. Whitley and T. Hanson, Optimizing neural networks using faster, more accurate genetic search, *Proc. 3rd Internat. Conf. on Genetic Algorithms,* 391–396 (1989).

[44] D. Whitley and T. Starkweather, (1990b). GENITOR II: A distributed genetic algorithm, *J. Experimental and Theoretical Artificial Intelligence* (1990).

[45] T. P. Caudell and C. P. Dolan, Parametric connectivity: Training of constrained networks using genetic algorithms, *Proc. 3rd Internat. Conf. on Genetic Algorithms,* 370–374 (1989).

[46] H. de Garis, Genetic programming: Modular neural evolution for Darwin machines, *Proc. Internat. Joint Conf. on Neural networks (IJCNN-90),* Washington, D.C., I-194–I-197 (1990).

[47] H. de Garis, "Genetic Programming: Building Nanobrains with Genetically Programmed Neural Network Modules," Report, CADEPS Artificial Intelligence Research Unit, Universite Libre de Bruxelles, (February 1990).

[48] H. de Garis, Genetic programming: Building artificial nervous systems using genetically programmed neural network modules, *Proc. 7th Internat. Conf. on Machine Learning* (1990).

[49] H. de Garis, "Genetic Programming: Building Artificial Nervous Systems with Genetically Programmed Neural Network Modules," in B. Souček and IRIS Group, *Neural and Intelligent Systems Integrated Reasoning Information Systems,* John Wiley, New York, 1991.

[50] H. de Garis, pers. comm. (May 1990).

[51] E. Mjolsness, D. H. Sharp, and B. K. Alpert, "Scaling, Machine Learning, and Genetic Neural Nets," Tech. Rep. LA-UR-88-142, Los Alamos National Lab. (1988).

[52] E. Mjolsness, D. H. Sharp, and B. K. Alpert, Recursively generated neural networks, *Proc. IEEE 1st Internat. Conf. on Neural Networks,* III-165–III-171 (1987).

[53] E. Mjolsness and D. H. Sharp, "A Preliminary Analysis of Recursively Generated Networks," Research Rep. YALEU/DCS/RR-476, Dept. of Computer Science, Yale University, (1986).

[54] D. H. Ackley, G. E. Hinton, and T. J. Sejnowski, A learning algorithm for Boltzmann machines, *Cognitive Sci.,* 9(1), 147–169 (1985).

[55] A. G. Barto, R. S. Sutton, and C. W. Anderson, Neuronlike adaptive elements that can solve difficult learning control problems, *IEEE Trans. on Systems, Man, and Cybernetics,* SMC-13, 834–846 (1983).

[56] J. R. Koza, "Genetic Programming: A Paradigm for Genetically Breeding Populations of Computer Programs to Solve Problems," Tech. Rep. STAN-CS-90-1314, Dept. of CS, Stanford University, Stanford, Calif. (1990).

[57] J. R. Koza, "Genetic Programming: A Paradigm for Genetically Breeding Populations of Computer Programs to Solve Problems," Chapter 10 herein.

[58] C. W. Anderson, "Learning and Problem Solving with Multilayer Connectionist Systems," Ph.D. theses, University of Massachusetts, (1986).

[59] T. Urbančić and I. Bratko, "Controlling Inverted Pendulum: A Case Study in Automatic Knowledge Acquisition for Dynamic System Control," Chapter 3 herein.

[60] D. Whitley, The author responds (In response to H. de Garis, Genetic neural networks can be dynamic too, you know!), *Neural Network Rev.,* 4(1), 50–53 (1990).

[61] B. Maričić, Genetically programmed neural network for solving pole-balancing problem, *Internat. Conf. on Artificial Neural Networks (ICANN-91) (1991).*

[62] R. Tanase, Distributed genetic algorithms, *Proc. 3rd Internat. Conf. on Genetic Algorithms,* 434–439 (1989).

[63] B. Manderick and P. Spiessens, Fine-grained parallel genetic algorithms, *Proc. 3rd Internat. Conf. on Genetic Algorithms,* 428–433 (1989).

[64] H. Muhlenbein, Parallel genetic algorithms, population genetics and combinatorial optimization, *Proc. 3rd Internat. Conf. on Genetic Algorithms,* 416–421 (1989).

[65] K. Deb and D. E. Goldberg, An investigation of niche and species formation in genetic function optimziation, *Proc. 3rd Internat. Conf. Genetic Algorithms,* Fairfax, Va., 42–50 (1989).

[66] L. B. Booker, "Intelligent Behavior as an Adaptation to the Task Environment," Ph.D. theses, Dept of CC Sciences, University of Michigan, Ann Arbor (1982).

[67] L. B. Booker, Improving the performance of genetic algorithms in classifier systems, *Proc. Internat. Conf. on Genetic Algorithms and Their Applications,* 80–92 (1985).

CHAPTER 20

Parallel Scheduling of Random and Chaotic Processes

CHARLES SCHELBERG

20.1 INTRODUCTION

With the advent of fast and deterministic parallel processors comes the opportunity of implementing dynamic scheduling algorithms and other applications where a real-time response is necessary. These can take the form of direct control of processes and simulating the reaction of an on-line processes to different stimuli. The applications are varied and many.

Before we can go into any details as to how to accomplish this, we must first stop and step back to see where we came from in our basic problem-solving thinking. It goes all the way back to the Age of Enlightenment, which started in the eighteenth century. There is where the classical theories of understanding our physical universe started. Observations and experiments proved the hypotheses. From this the modern age of physics was derived. That is, the notion of synchronization and an orderly approach to solutions were inspired: Simplify until the problem is within some bounds, so we could study it in detail. We are taught that when we study basic physical phenomena we first pick an area where it is fairly easy to study, then extrapolate the results to the end of the envelope. For the past 300 years that seemed to be true. When we got into trouble, we would dismiss it as an aberration or something that wasn't in a steady state. We were great at saying "Wait until it stabilizes and we can figure out what will come next." Well we now are coming around to see that that type of reasoning is not true. We will have to

Dynamic, Genetic, and Chaotic Programming, By Branko Souček and the IRIS Group.
ISBN 0-471-55717-X

take everything into account, and that doesn't fit into the classical models that we all knew and loved.

An example of this new way of thinking is what happened when Copernicus said in order for us to understand the motions of the heavenly bodies we have to picture ourselves standing on the sun to observe the motion of the planets. It was radically different then, but it allowed people to think of the basic problem in a fundamentally different light. The combination of parallel processing and chaos now gives us the ability of approaching the solution to a problem in a completely different manner.

Another example of this is the falling bodies discussions. All bodies fall at the same rate, regardless of their mass. If we go to the moon and hold a feather and a golf ball at the same height, then release them, both will fall to the ground at the same rate and hit the ground at the same time. Now that's fine if we were on the moon, which has no atmosphere. If we try the very same experiment on the earth, we all know what will happen, the golf ball will hit first while the feather slips back and forth until it finally hits the ground. The reason is simple, the feather is being acted upon by the atmosphere, where the air resistance is not great enough to act on the golf ball. So the physicist says the atmosphere is interfering with the experiment. But what if I had a leaf and a feather and performed the same experiment here on the earth. The results of the experiment will be very difficult (if not impossible) to predict. Why? Because we have to take into account all of the aerodynamic conditions of the feather and the leaf, and that is extremely complex. And, that is where chaos comes in. Using classical equations it is next to impossible to predict the path of the objects. Chaos theory will not allow us to precisely predict the path nor the time the two objects will stay in flight. Chaos theory will give us an idea as to when the two objects will strike the ground and what type of flight path they will take. The basic premise is that chaos will help us understand the envelope of motions the objects will take. It will not tell us the intimate details that we want to know as to exactly what path they will take and exactly when they will touch the ground. That is the basic premise of chaos. It will give us a range in which things will happen, but it will not give us the exact, precise, numerical, answer we might be looking for. So we must get rid of the notion of trying to precisely predict exactly when and where something will occur. All we can predict is the range in which something will happen.

20.2 SCHEDULING OF TAXICABS

With that in mind, let's look at another example: the scheduling of taxicabs in a large city. But first let's step into our imaginary helicopter and hover over a major city and, with perfect vision, watch all of the taxicabs move around the city. We can see every taxicab in the city. We notice that during the morning hours the cabs seem to congregate around the hotels, airports, and train stations. During the day they disperse randomly and then congregate again around the business districts and department stores around lunchtime. Then, around 5:00 p.m. they congregate around the business districts, airports, and train stations. We wonder why this phonomania occurs and come down to talk to several of the cab drivers to see just who is in charge here. Who is controlling the placement of these taxicabs? After many interviews we find, to our horror, there is no central, control point that is controlling all of the cabs. As a matter of fact there is no central control point at all. There is a dispatcher, but that is only a mechanism to announce that a person needs a cab. The dispatcher does not assign a specific cab to a person in need of a cab. The dispatcher calls out that a fare needs a cab at a certain location, and the cabs in the area bid on the fare. The closest cab gets the fare. There is no one with overall control of the placement of the cabs. But, we have noticed, over days, that there is a very definite pattern. Why? What causes this to happen? So, we ask more questions of the cabbies. After an exhaustive questioning period, we discover there are two basic rules that all taxis respond to.

1. If there is a queue of cabs of over five, then go to another place where the probability of picking up a fare is better.
2. When the dispatcher calls for a bid on a fare, always bid on it. The distance to the prospective fare will determine who wins the bid.

And that's it. There are no other rules the cabbies go by. They are not thinking of any grand and global traffic patterns or anything like that. They only have their self-preservation in mind, they are driven by the profit motive and these two simple rules.

With that, the observed pattern arises. The individual cabs have rules, that they always abide by, and because of their interaction they make the overall system have a pattern or life of its own. Can the perceived system guarantee that if we were a prospective fare and standing in the airport at 8:00 A.M. we would get a cab? Probably we would. If we were standing in the airport at midnight, would we get a cab? Probably not; we would have to call the dispatcher. Notice the word *probably*. We can't say for sure, but it would be a good guess that there wouldn't be a cab at the airport at midnight. The point is, we could predict the cab placement within some range but we couldn't predict it exactly. That's the point of chaos.

Another observation about the taxicab system is that it is not brittle. That is, it works no matter how many cabs are available. At any given moment not all of the taxicabs that are registered in the city are available for work. Either by design, working on a different shift, or not by design, the cab broke down. Because of this, the system is said to be *self-healing*.

Now, what would it take to simulate this taxicab problem on a computer? If we were to use the classical approach to solving the problem, we would have to know exactly when and where each customer (or fare) would place demands on the model. We would have to know how many cabs were available and figure in some amount of cabs that were in the shop for repairs. We would also need to know something of the demands that would be placed on the system so that we could plan ahead for peak demands for cabs. That's on the system analysis side. What would we need on the computer implementation side? We would need routines to simulate the taxicabs themselves, the dispatcher, the customers or fares, and a map of the city. Further we would need data on the relationships between the time of day and the number of requests for fares, where are the busy spots, when are they busy? The list goes on and on. Pretty soon we would get to wondering if the problem can be solved at all. We get into these dilemmas when we are thinking of how to organize from the top down. That is the type of organizational structuring that has been taught to all of us in the computer field.

Chaos, randomness, and parallelism show us a different way of looking at and solving the problem. Look at it from the bottom up. What would happen if we gave the simulation of each cab a unique "personality" or "soul"? In other words, program the "object" or taxicab so it had a set of "rules" to live by and it reacted to its local environment. Let those objects loose on a simulated city map with fares hailing cabs and the dispatcher requesting bids and see what happens.

Lets not get bogged down here on implementation; let's do a thought experiment. We have a computer that has the ability of executing the language of our dreams, and it runs infinitely fast. Let's also assume that the city map contains enough information about the city in order to navigate our way around the city. Each taxicab will be simulated by a unique piece of computer code that is autonomous. That is, it will follow the rules that were previously mentioned. It will also have to be ruled by the traffic laws of the city, it cannot crash through buildings or other cars to get to the destination, it must obey the speed limits, it must drive on the right, cannot drive on sidewalks, and must go in the pointed direction while on one-way streets, and any other mundane rules of the road.

Further, the objects have one very important trait: They can remember where and when they made a profit. They will remember the place and time and how much they made in profit for each fare, and they will use that knowledge each time they are asked to respond to the dispatcher's request. They will use that knowledge to find the places where it has been profitable in the past to queue up and wait for a fare.

It is this set of rules, executed by the individual cabs that will give the system of taxicabs its ability to adapt to the various conditions that are met each day.

Enough said. Now let's examine some code. The language that the code will be written in is Paracell, and it is modeled after English. The different objects (cabs, dispatcher, and fares) will be written in Paracell and loaded into the various virtual processor cells of the parallel inference machine (PIM). It is not the intent of the author to teach the reader the Paracell

```
If dispatcher is requesting a cab and flag is up

     then set Dispatcher list (my position)'s my current position
              to current position.


If dispatcher is requesting me and flag is up

                                        /* We're dispatched to a fare! */
     then set flag to down and
          set destination to dispatched destination,
          set dispatcher acknowledge to on.
```

Figure 20.1 *Respond to the dispatcher.*

language, but you will see as we go through the exercise the intent of the statements.

The code in Figure 20.1 will handle the dispatcher's request for a bid on a fare and the subsequent winning of the fare. Lets look in detail on just how it does it.

The first rule will respond to the dispatcher's request for any cab that is idle. *Dispatcher* and *flag* are variables, where *dispatcher* is a global variable and is set by the dispatcher when it wants the cabs to respond. *Flag* is a local variable and gives the status of the cab. If the *flag* is up, the cab is not carrying a fare or idle. If the *flag* is down, the cab is carrying a fare or is not available. The variable *my current position* is an entry to an array that is assigned to the dispatcher. Each cab has a unique array position. When the dispatcher requests the cabs to respond to a request for bid, the cabs that are available place their current position into the array. The dispatcher then scans the array and finds the closest cab to the fare.

When the dispatcher decides which cab is to respond to the fare it will place the cab's number into *dispatcher*. That will match the constant called *requesting me*. *Dispatched destination* is a global variable that is set by the dispatcher, and *destination* is a local variable that gives the destination of the cab. The cab acknowledges the dispatcher that the cab is responding by setting *dispatcher acknowledge*. The dispatcher will turn it off. Once that is set the cab will move through the city, using the city map to guide it, to the *destination*. The routing code will not be shown here, since it is not the purpose of this exercise. The routing routine will handle the pickup of the fare and will set the time stamp for the pickup. The cab will then go to the fare's requested destination. When the fare arrives at the destination the next set of code will be executed.

Figure 20.2 is the code that handles the event of the fare arriving at the destination. The router announces when the cab has arrived at the requested

```
If arrived at destination

     Then set flag to up and  /* The passenger has been delivered
                                  to the destination. */

     If elapsed time * time rate is greater than elapsed distance
          * distance rate

                    /* Calculate the fare, whichever is greater */

          Then set collection of fares (index)'s collected fare to
                    initial fare + elapsed time * time rate

          Else set collection of fares (index)'s collected fare to
                    initial fare + elapsed distance * distance
                    rate,

          set collection of fares (index)'s collected tip to tip,
          set collection of fares (index)'s pickup point to this
               fares pickup point,
          set collection of fares (index)'s destination to this
               fares destination,
          set collection of fares (index)'s arrival time to time
               of day,

          increment index,      /* Get ready for the next entry */

          set idle timer to 0.      /* Start the idle timer */
```

Figure 20.2 *Fare arrived at destination.*

destination by setting the local variable called *arrived at destination*. The first thing that has to be done is to set the taxicab's *flag* up, it is available for another fare. The tip is collected along with the calculated fare. Note the fare calculation: how much time was spent getting to the destination, or how much distance was traveled to get there—whichever is greater.

The *collected fare* is then placed into the *collection of fares* array along with other facts about the fare. One piece of data in the array is the amount of money collected for each trip. This will become the bases for all decisions when the cab is idle and looking for a place to queue up.

After the fare leaves the cab, the cab will stay in that spot, for a limited time, waiting to see if a fare hails the cab.

When the waiting time has been exceeded and the cab is still idle, it's time to move on to where it picked up the best-paying fare this hour. This decision is made in the code shown in Figure 20.3. The first order of business is to find the pickup point that had the highest fare this hour. This is done with the *collect* command. There is a master time of day clock that sets the global variable *this hour*. All of the fares this hour are collected and placed into a new array called *best fares this hour*. In that array are all of the fares this

```
If flag is up and not in queue and idle timer is greater than 5

   /* We've been sitting here too long.  It's time to move on. */

     Then Collect this hour in collection of fares into fares this
               hour,
          Find largest fare in fares this hour and
          Place fare into best fare this hour and
          Place pickup point into closest queue point,
          Wait for location of queue point,
          Set destination to location of queue point.

               /* Off we go to the best pickup point this hour. */
```

Figure 20.3 *When to move on.*

hour. The code then requests a queue point that is closest to the pickup point that was associated with the largest fare this hour. Please note that the cab will go to the new destination with its *flag* up. If it gets hailed on the way, it will be able to respond to the new fare immediately.

Figure 20.4 shows the code that handles the event of arriving at a queue point. The first thing to check is how many cabs are in the queue. If there are more than six, then it will not enter the queue but look for some other place to queue up. The number 6 is quite arbitrary and can be replaced by a rule that is governed by the time of day. But for this example let's us use 6. If there is room in the queue for the cab, then it will enter the queue and stay there until a fare comes along. Please note in this example there is no time limit when sitting in a queue. When refining the code, it would be wise to place more code here to watch the time of day clock. When a new hour was entered, the cab should determine if a new queue point should be moved to. The next paragraph discusses that code.

If the cab finds the queue is not to its liking, then it will find the next lowest fare for this hour. First it will collect all of the fares that were collected this hour. From that collection it will find the next lower fare from the one that got it there. If it finds the pickup point was this queue point, then it will enter this queue since it is already there. If the pickup point is not this queue point, then off it goes to the pickup point that gave it that fare. Again it will keep its *flag* up while it is traveling just in case it is hailed by a fare on the street or win a bid from the dispatcher.

And that's it for one cab. Please note that it was done in four computing cells. Each cell is an independent entity, and between the four of them they make up the code that governs a taxicab. Also note that there is no overall scheme of things with regard to a system of cabs. The pattern of pickup and delivery of fares is completely determined by the load that will be placed by the fares needing a cab. As the demands for cabs changes during the day, so

```
If flag is up and not in queue and destination is a queue point and
    have arrived

    Then If number in this queue is less than 6
              Then set in queue to on,
                   increment number in this queue

          /* There is no time limit while staying in the queue */

              Else Collect this hour in collection of fares to
                        Fares this hour,

              /* The queue is full, find a queue point that offers
                   the next best choice in fares */

                   Find lesser of best fare this hour in Fares
                        this hour and
                   Place pickup into closest queue point,
                   Wait for location of queue point,
                   If location of queue point is current position
                        Then set in queue to on,
                             increment number in this queue

  /* Can't get any better than where we are now, so stay here. */

                        Else Set destination to location of queue
                                  point.

         /* Off we go to the next best pickup point this hour. */
```

Figure 20.4 *Check if other cabs are queued near this location.*

will the response of the cabs. The cabbies will remember where the more profitable fares were picked up, and they will tend to congregate around those points in the city.

To repeat, there is no overall plan to place the cabs at pickup points. That is determined by the individual cabs, and all the cabs will make the pattern of cab placement emerge by themselves.

What computer resource will it take to implement this code? First, how many cabs are to be simulated? Lets say 1000 cabs; that means at a minimum 4000 cells plus, say, 100 more for overhead and the dispatcher. That's 4100 computing cells. If we were to run this simulation on a von Neumann machine, the code would fit but the execution time of the simulation would be of some concern since the simulation is to run in real time.

In order to watch the simulation of the cabs move the fares around the city second by second, we need a machine that can deliver real time responses to very large computing tasks. Such machines are now becoming available with new parallel architectures. When we take the taxicab simulation and disperse the 4100 code cells over 4100 computing cells all running in parallel, the simulation will run in real time. Now city planners and taxicab operators can watch the simulation and predict the effects of adding, say, a convention center to the city. They can see ahead of time just what the effect on the city's taxicab service will be.

It is this kind of simulation that is becoming available now due to the change in thinking on how to solve a problem. No longer are we confined to think of the grand scheme or top-down view. When we approach some problems from the bottom up and let the individual units take on a life of their own, within bounds and rules of behavior, a pattern of behavior for the entire body will appear. As a thought experiment, the reader might want to consider how to program a school of fish or a flock of birds. Those groupings have no leader and no grand scheme. It is the individual members following certain simple rules that make the group respond the way it does.

20.3 SCHEDULING TASKS IN A PLANT

Now let's move to another problem, how to schedule parts through a manufacturing plant. People have been working on this one for years and have many varied and expensive solutions for it. But all of them are brought to their knees when an event occurs that was not planned for. The truck that was supposed to deliver the raw material on Monday broke down and didn't arrive until Wednesday. The lathe that was to turn the threads on the shaft broke, or the operator is out sick. The list goes on and on. To counter these events, contingency plans are put in place. But no matter how well these plans are, there is always something that will occur that is unexpected and not covered by the contingency plans.

So let's look at the problem in a different light. First as we saw in the taxicab example, if a single taxicab breaks it has almost no effect on the overall pattern of cabs. The system is self-healing, it would be nice to have something like that in the manufacturing plant simulation. Well let's see what we can do. Again, let's stand on the sun and see what's going on. In other words, lets look at the problem in a completely different manner.

We present the following machine shop. It's a general job shop, it can do a myriad of jobs—milling, turning, heat treating, welding, broaching—you name it, they can do it, including the assembly of the parts into a finished product. They're expensive, but they can do any type of machining and assembly operations that are needed to do the job. They have a unique quoting system: they can tell *about* when the job will be ready (providing they have the materials), but they can't tell *exactly* when the job will be ready. They have done good work in the past, and you have never questioned their funny quoting style. One day you get curious and sneak into the shop to see for yourself just how they schedule the jobs with each machine. To your horror, you find no schedule at all. Each machine with its human operator works on only those jobs that are in the job card rack with very little regard as to when the job has to get done. Each operator is paid by the piece and will grab jobs on the rack that he is set up for. If he has to change the setup of the machine, he will only do it if there are no jobs in the queue that do not call for his present setup. You discover that the operators select jobs from the queue using the following rules:

1. If I'm idle I will look for the highest priority job that I am presently set up to do (regardless of the number of pieces to make).
2. If I'm idle I will look for the highest priority job that my machine can do (regardless of the number of pieces to make).

And that's it. The operators don't care about the overall coordination of jobs; they only want to work on jobs they are presently set up to do or their machine can do. That is, an operator on a milling machine will not bid on a job that must be turned on a lathe, and vice versa. The sequence of the jobs is governed by the shop foreman. He will put out a job for bid only when a unique operation is to be performed on the part. If, for example, the following sequence of machining has to be done on a part:

1. Take raw stock and cut it to the prescribed length using a cutoff saw,
2. Rough bore prescribed holes on a milling machine,
3. Heat-treat.

The foreman will put job 1 out for bids first. When that job is done, the foreman will put job 2 out for bids. When that's done, he will put job 3 out for bids. When this part is complete, it will move into the assembly area where it will take its place in the assembly process.

Because there is no preplanning, the entire system is dynamic, it is self-adapting to failures in the system. What happens when there is no raw stock to start a job? Nothing, the job is not queued up. The individual machines don't see it, no one has preplanned anything so there is no failure in the plan, because there was no plan to begin with.

This also applies to machines that break; they do that at the most inopportune time. Because there is no preplanned schedule, there is no schedule to revise. The system will produce what it can with the material at hand. But no one is running around redoing the preplanned schedule, because there is none. The system is self-adapting or self-healing; it all depends on how you want to look at it.

Now let's look at the code that performs this shop management: first, the job rack. The job rack is like any rack of cards. In it are the jobs that are in the shop, their priority, job description, and who is working on them. The cards are not removed from the rack, the contents of the cards are changed as the job is worked on by the various operators in the shop. This way everyone in the shop knows the status of each job in the shop. Figure 20.5

```
Job cards is a structure containing

     Priority an integer;            /* The job's priority */
     Machine type an integer;        /* What machine can do the job
                                        */
     Queued time stamp a time;       /* When the job was put in the
                                        rack */
     Bid for job an integer;         /* The winning bidder's number
                                        */
     Job status an integer;
     Machine that has the job an integer;
     Part descripter an integer;    /*  Index  to  further  details
                                        about the part */
     Disbursed time stamp a time;   /* Time the job was taken */
     Number of parts to be made an integer;
     Returned time stamp a time;    /* Time the job was returned */
     Number of parts completed an integer.

Job rack is an array of 100 job cards.
```

Figure 20.5 *Job cards and rack definitions.*

shows the card and rack definitions. *Priority* contains the job's priority. The author prefers to have the priority numbers in inverse order. That is, a priority of 0 is the highest priority, drop everything, the job must be done now. When a positive-going priority number scheme is used, the highest priority number has to be defined and that can be changed easily. When the inverse numbering system is used, it's hard to get by zero, and everyone knows the heat is on as the number approaches zero. *Machine type* is the machine that is to do the job. *Queued time stamp* is the time when the job was placed in the job rack (or job queue). The shop foreman uses this piece of information to see if the job is aging in the queue. If the job is waiting too long, the foreman will increase its priority. *Bid for job* is used by the machines when they are bidding for the job. The identification of the machine that won the job will be here. *Job status* is just that, it shows what is happening with this job. When the foreman places the job in the rack, it will have the status of *available*. *Machine that has the job* is the identification number of the machine currently working on this job. *Part descriptor* is a pointer to more information about the part. The NC part program, fixturing data, tooling data, stock considerations, special machining or assembly instruction, and so on. *Disbursed time stamp* is the time the job was taken by a machine. *Number of parts to be made* is just that. *Returned time stamp* is the time when the completed job was returned to the job rack. *Number of parts completed* is just that. Notice that the *number of parts completed* can be different from the *number of parts to be made*. The reason why will have to be ascertained by the shop foreman.

```
/* Look for jobs
    Scan the job rack
    Find the highest priority job that this machine is setup for.
    If none, find the highest priority job this machine can do.
    If a job is found then bid on the job. */

If my status is idle

    Then (
        Loop using index from 1 through 100
        Initially
            Set highest priority found to lowest priority;
            Set bid this job to 0;
        Do
            If Job rack (index)'s machine type is my machine
                type and job rack (index)'s priority is less
                than highest priority found and job rack
                (index)'s job status is available and job rack
                (index)'s part descripter is my present part
                descripter

                Then set highest priority found to job rack
                        (index)'s priority,
                    set bid this job to index.
                  /* Remember where we saw the job we want. */

        If bid this job is 0

            Then Loop using index from 1 through 100
                Do
                    If Job rack (index)'s machine type is my
                        machine type and job rack (index)'s
                        priority is less than highest
                        priority found and job rack (index)'s
                        job status is available

                        Then set highest priority found to
                                job rack (index)'s
                                priority,
                            set bid this job to index.
                          /* Remember where we saw the job
                            we want. */
        )
    If bid this job is not 0

            /* There's a job in the rack, let's bid on it. */
        Then Set job rack (bid this job)'s bid for job to my
                name;
            Set my status to bidding.
```

Figure 20.6 *Find a job.*

The *job rack* is an array of 100 *job cards*. The number 100 is quite arbitrary. It is the number of jobs that can fit in the rack without overflowing when the shop gets busy.

Each machine in the shop has the code shown in Figures 20.6 to 20.9. The code in each figure is loaded into an independent, parallel processor and is

```
/* Check if high bidder
     If yes then take the job
          Time stamp the job taken by this machine */

If my status is bidding

     Then If job rack (bid this job)'s bid for job is my name

                                        /* Won the bid for the job */
               Then Set my status to starting a job;
                    Set job rack (bid this job)'s machine that has
                         the job to my name;
                    Set job rack (bid this job)'s job status to
                         taken;
                    Set job rack (bid this job)'s disbursed time
                         stamp to now

                                        /* Lost the bid for the job */
               Else Set my status to idle.
```

Figure 20.7 *Was the job won?*

allowed to run independently of the rest of the processors in the system. Figure 20.6 is the most complex code because it is the bidding code. It looks through the job rack for a job to bid on. *My status* is a local variable that contains the status of the individual machine. When the machine is idle, start looking through the job rack for a job to bid on. First initialize two local variables, *highest priority found* and *bid this job,* then look through the job rack using the rule stated in the first *if.* Note the indexing into the array (the

```
/* Run the job */

If my status is starting a job

     Then Set part count to zero;

          /* Transfer all of the necessary data to the machine to
               start the job.  When the job starts:  */

          Set my status to running a job.


If my status is running a job

     Then /* Wait for the job to get done, then: */

          Set my status to done the job.
```

Figure 20.8 *Start then run the job.*

```
/* Return the completed job
     With the number of completed parts
     Time stamp the job returned */

If my status is done the job

     Then Set job rack (bid this job)'s returned time stamp to now;
          Set job rack (bid this job)'s number of parts completed
              to part count;
          Set my status to idle;
          Set job rack (bid this job)'s job status to done.
```

Figure 20.9 *Job complete.*

job rack). As the highest priority job is found, it is set into the local variable *bid this job* and *highest priority found*. When the search through the *job rack* is complete, if a job was not found then search through the *job rack* again, looking for the highest priority job that this machine can do. When these two searches are done, if a job was found then bid on it. The awarding of the bid is simply that the last machine to bid on this job, wins the bid.

Figure 20.7 is the code that looks to see if this machine has won the bid for the job. Using the local variable *bid this job* as the index into the *job rack,* it looks to see if it was the winner of the bidding. If it is, then claim the job for itself and start to fetch further information about the job out of the rack. If this machine did not win the bid for the job, then its status is set to idle. This will force the code in Figure 20.6 to look through the *job rack* again until it finds a job.

Figure 20.8 is the code that handles the actual start and running of the job. The code that transfers the data with the machine is not shown here since it is not the intent of this example to get bogged down in those details. It is shown that when the data is sent down to the machine, *my status* is set to *running a job*. When the machine has completed the job, it will send a signal that will end the wait loop, and the code will set *my status* to *done the job.* When that event occurs, the code in Figure 20.9 is allowed to run. The first thing that occurs is to time-stamp the return of the job to the rack. The global variable *now* is the current date and time. The *number of parts completed* is sent from the machine. Finally, housekeeping is done so the shop knows this job is done, and this machine is now idle.

Please note again, there is no overall planning on who gets a job and when. The jobs are taken by priority order and conditioned with the present setup of the machine. Those are the only criteria for getting things done in this shop.

Since the tracking of the jobs in the shop is done in this program, the owner of the shop has a powerful planning tool at his disposal. He can now start playing the "what-if" games. He can put into the computer another shop floor machine and run the jobs through that model and see what the response of the shop would be. That is, he could see if he spent, say, $100,000 on a new machine what would be the effect of it on the throughput of the shop. If it turns out to be insignificant, he might not buy the machine because the projected payback is too long. He has a tool that will allow him to model his shop so he can make informed business decisions as to what to buy to make more profit. This will allow him to not predict exactly when a job will get done, but only predict with more certainty by what time the job will be completed. By keeping a data base of the details of the throughtput of the shop, he can run historical data through the model with different modeled machines and see what the throughput would be. This is called *predictive modeling*. The key here is the user can predict what the response of the system will be based on real, historical data. This is an extremely powerful tool.

20.4 CONCLUSION

Parallel processors have opened up a new way of thinking of how to solve problems. Parallel simulation programs for taxis and for factory floor scheduling present examples of powerful new tools. A real breakthrough is expected through the mixture of three techniques: parallel processing, random process simulation, and the theory of chaos.

INDEX

D

F

G

J

K

L

O

P

T